VASICEK AND BEYOND

Approaches to Building and Applying Interest Rate Models

VASICEK AND BEYOND

Approaches to Building and Applying Interest Rate Models

Edited by Lane Hughston

Published by Risk Publications
104-112 Marylebone Lane
London W1M 5FU
Tel +44 (0)171 487 5326; fax +44 (0)171 486 0879

ISBN 1 899332 55 3 – Softback
ISBN 1 899332 50 2 – Hardback

Designer: Judith Charlton
In-house Editor: Conrad Gardner
Production Editor: Miles Smith-Morris

ABOUT THE SPONSORS

EURO BROKERS, FOUNDED in 1970, is recognised as one of the world's leading independent brokers. The company provides financial services in a broad range of areas including money markets, securities, derivatives and commodities. Operating from offices in New York, London, Tokyo, Hong Kong, Sydney, Toronto and Greenwich, Connecticut, Euro Brokers employs over 750 professionals who serve a wide range of international banks, multinational corporations, investment dealers, governments and a growing list of investors. These extensive operations, supported by state-of-the-art computerised installation and global telecommunications, facilitate a volume in excess of $30 billion in daily transactions, executed with over 3,000 counterparties worldwide.

Euro Brokers International Ltd
133 Houndsditch
London EC3A 7AJ

FOREWORD

The aim of this book is to provide the reader with all the essential approaches to interest rate modelling in a freshly edited publication. Because interest rate derivatives have developed so significantly and become widespread, Risk Publications felt that this was an opportune time to collate a representative sample of the most influential work of the past 20 years. The editor's commentary will help to equip the reader with an overview of interest rate dynamics sufficiently comprehensive to embrace the entire theoretical development from the earliest single-factor valuation approaches to the modern state-of-the-art whole yield curve methodologies.

Reflecting the historical advance in interest rate modelling, the collection is divided into three sections: Option Pricing Fundamentals, Dynamic Arbitrage Models and the Heath-Jarrow-Morton Family. We hope that this division gives some sense of the logical and chronological development of the model families, and the continuing progress in this area.

We also hope that *Vasicek and Beyond*, produced by Risk Publications in association with Euro Brokers, will prove to be a valuable and useful tool for researchers in both financial houses and academic institutions.

Cindy Buggins
Managing Director, Euro Brokers
December 1996

CONTENTS

III. THE HEATH-JARROW-MORTON FAMILY

AUTHORS

Kaushik Amin is the head of the Mortgage Swaps desk at Lehman Brothers in New York. Prior to this he was in the finance faculty at the University of Michigan, where he taught courses on derivative securities and managerial finance. Kaushik Amin obtained his PhD from Cornell University in 1989. His main professional interests include the pricing, hedging, trading and use of derivative securities. He has published over a dozen articles in most of the leading finance journals.

Simon Babbs is head of Quantitative Research at the First National Bank of Chicago, London, and is responsible for fixed income and equity derivatives models, which involves product development, client risk analysis, and marketing. The main focus of his research is interest rate derivatives. Since gaining a first in Mathematics at Oxford, he has worked at the Bank of England and various other banks in London. He acquired a PhD in Finance in 1990.

Alain Bensoussan is president of the CNES (French Space Research Centre) and has been a full-time professor at the University of Paris Dauphine since 1969. He graduated from the Ecole Polytechnique in 1962 and obtained his PhD in Mathematics in 1969. Between 1984 and 1986 Professor Bensoussan was president of the Institut National de Recherche en Informatique et Automatique (INRIA) and was responsible for creating a scientific forum for the interchange of information between 14 European countries and helped create the Lyapunov Institute in Moscow. His research interests include the filtering and control of stochastic distributed systems, optimal stopping, and variational and quasi-variational inequalities. Professor Bensoussan has written 13 books and over 300 articles.

Fischer Black was Professor of Finance at the University of Chicago's Graduate School of Business from 1971 and, in 1975, joined the MIT's Sloan School of Management. In 1984 he joined Goldman Sachs, where he later became a partner. He will be best remembered for developing the Black–Scholes option pricing formula with Myron Scholes. He died in August 1995, at the age of 57.

Alan Brace worked in industry, university and government before entering finance in 1988. He started as a quantitative analyst in a trading team at ANZ before joining Citibank, where he concentrated on interest rate modelling for several years. At present he teaches at the University of New South Wales and consults through Financial Mathematics Modelling and Analysis.

Michael Brennan is the Irwin Professor and Goldyne Hearsh Professor of Banking and Finance at the University of California, Los Angeles and Professor of Finance at the London Business School. His research interests focus on asset pricing, corporate finance, the pricing and role of derivative securities, market microstructure and the role of information in capital markets. He has published extensively in all of these areas. Professor Brennan is currently working on several issues, including the problem of asset allocation *vis à vis* time-varying opportunity sets, the role of convertible securities in corporate finance, and corporate hedging strategies. He is a former president of the American Finance Association and is currently President of the Society for Financial Studies and the Western Finance Association. He has served as editor of the *Journal of Finance* and was the founding editor of the *Review of Financial Studies.* In 1995 he was awarded the INQUIRE Europe prize for his work on hedging strategies.

John C. Cox is the Nomura Professor of Finance in the Sloan School of Management at MIT. He received his PhD from the Wharton School at the University of Pennsylvania. He has published a number of articles in finance and economics journals and is co-author of the book *Options Markets.* His research interests include derivatives markets, the term structure of interest rates, dynamic investment strategies and optimal security design.

Emanuel Derman was born in South Africa. He obtained his PhD in Theoretical Particle Physics from Columbia University, and then undertook research at various universities and at AT&T Bell Laboratories. He is co-author of the widely used Black–Derman–Toy yield curve model and, with Iraj Kani, *The Implied Tree Model for the Volatility Smile*. He is head of the Quantitative Strategies Group in the equities division at Goldman Sachs.

Darrell Duffie is a professor of finance in the Graduate School of Business at Stanford University, and has writen articles in economics, finance, and applied mathematics for various journals, as well as several books, including *Dynamic Asset Pricing Theory*. Professor Duffie received his PhD in 1984 and has remained on the faculty at Stanford University. His current research interests are in the design and valuation of financial securities, the modelling of credit risk and interest rates, and risk management.

Bjorn Flesaker is a managing director in the Financial Analytics & Structured Transactions Group at Bear Stearns, where he is responsible for derivatives research and modelling. Previously he managed the Global Fixed Income Derivatives Quantitative Group at UBS and the fixed income trading research group at Merrill Lynch. In 1990 he earned a PhD in Finance from the University of California at Berkeley, after which he spent two years as an assistant professor of finance at the University of Illinois at Urbana-Champaign. He has published papers and lectured on a variety of topics in mathematical finance, with particular focus on term structure modelling and derivatives pricing.

Dariusz Gatarek is an associate professor in Systems Research at the Polish Academy of Sciences, Warsaw and has been a visiting lecturer at many universities in Europe and Australia. He has an MSc in Applied Mathematics from Warsaw University of Technology and a PhD and DSc in Control Engineering from the Academy of Sciences in 1984 and 1993 respectively. At present, he is researching the pricing of swap and interest rate derivatives and, with Alan Brace and Marek Musiela, a contributor on the BGM interest rate dynamics approach.

Hélyette Geman is a professor of finance at the University of Paris IX Dauphine and ESSEC Graduate Business School. She is a graduate from Ecole Normale Supérieure and holds a PhD in Theoretical Physics, as well as PhDs in Mathematics and Finance. Previously a director with Caisse des Dépôts et Consignations, in charge of research and development, she is currently a scientific expert for major financial institutions and insurance companies in Europe. Professor Geman has published extensively in the field of interest rate modelling, exotic option pricing and insurance derivatives. Her Merrill Lynch research award focuses on the use of Bessel processes in the exact pricing of Asian options and interest rate derivatives in the Cox–Ingersoll–Ross framework. Professor Geman is editor of the *European Finance Review*, associate editor of *Mathematical Finance* and the *Geneva Papers on Insurance*.

David Heath studied mathematics and economics at the University of Illinois, receiving his PhD in 1969. He taught mathematics at the University of Minnesota from 1969 to 1975 and then joined Cornell University, where he is now Merrill Lynch Professor of Financial Engineering.
He has worked with many large financial institutions and is currently a director of Lehman Brothers Financial Products. With Robert Jarrow, he founded the Financial Engineering option in the Business and Engineering Masters course at Cornell in 1995.

Thomas S. Y. Ho was a professor of finance at Stern School of Business from 1978 to 1990 and is a leading pioneer in the field of fixed-income research. He received his PhD in 1978 from the University of Pennsylvania. Thomas Ho founded the Global Advanced Technology Corporation in 1987, which provides software, research and consultancy services to the fixed income market. He was research analyst at the US government bond trading desk, Yamaichi Securities, in 1988. He has published articles in the *Journal of Finance* and the *Journal of Fixed Income*, and is editor of the publications, *Fixed Income Management: Issues and Solutions, Fixed Income Investment: Research*, and *Frontiers in Fixed Income*.

Lane Hughston is a director in the Fixed Income Division at Merrill Lynch in London and is responsible for the development of pricing models for interest rate, foreign exchange, commodity, and credit related derivative products. Dr Hughston obtained his DPhil in mathematics from Oxford University, which he attended as a Rhodes scholar, and where, as a fellow of Lincoln College, he served on the faculty for a number of years. Before joining Merrill Lynch he worked at Robert Fleming, where he specialised in Japanese equity derivatives. Dr Hughston is the author of numerous publications and is a regular speaker at academic and finance conferences. He holds the title of visiting professor in the Mathematics department at King's College, London.

John Hull is a professor of finance at the University of Toronto and a principal of A–J Financial Systems. He was, with

Alan White, a winner of the Nikko-LOR research competition for the research that led to the Hull–White interest rate model. He has acted as consultant to over 30 major financial institutions throughout the world. He has written two books on derivatives, *Options, Futures, and Other Derivatives,* and *Introduction to Futures and Options Markets.*

Jonathan E. Ingersoll is the Adrian C. Israel Professor of International Trade and Finance at Yale University's School of Management. He was a member of the Founding Committee of the Society for Financial Studies and served as editor of the *Review of Financial Studies.* He is currently an associate editor of the *Review of Derivatives Research.* Professor Ingersoll is a specialist in the valuation of options and derivative securities and is the author of numerous articles in this area, including the paper: *Theory of Financial Decision Making.* Professor Ingersoll received his SB in Physics from MIT in 1971 and his SM and PhD from the Sloan School of Management, MIT, in 1973 and 1976 respectively.

Farshid Jamshidian is managing director of New Products and Strategic Trading at Sakura Global Capital, where he develops models and trading systems for the valuation and risk management of complex financial products. He also runs a book of exotic swap derivatives. Prior to this Dr Jamshidian was executive director of Technical Trading at Fuji International Finance from 1991 to 1994, where he engaged in arbitrage trading of international equities. He was director of Financial Strategies Group at Merrill Lynch in New York from 1986 to 1991, where he headed a research and development team. Jamshidian holds a PhD in Mathematics from Harvard University and an MSc in Computer Science from Stanford University. He has published extensively on interest rate models and option pricing theory.

Robert Jarrow is the Ronald P. and Susan E. Lynch Professor of Investment Management at the Johnson Graduate School of Management, Cornell University. He is also managing director and director of research at the Kamakura Corporation. He is a graduate of Duke University, Dartmouth College and MIT. Professor Jarrow is known for his pioneering work on the Heath–Jarrow–Morton model for pricing interest rate derivatives. His current research includes the pricing of exotic interest rate options and other derivative securities, as well as investment management theory. His publications include *Option Pricing, Finance Theory, Modelling Fixed Income Securities and Interest Rate Options,* and *Derivative Securities,* and he has written over 50 articles in leading financial and economic journals. Professor Jarrow is currently co-editor of *Mathematical Finance* and an associate editor of the *Review of Financial Studies,* the *Journal of Financial and Quantitative Analysis,* and the *Review of Derivatives Research.*

Piotr Karasinski is an independent consultant specialising in the pricing and risk management of derivative products. He is a graduate of Warsaw University, where he obtained his MSc in Physics, and in 1987 obtained his PhD in Theoretical Physics from Yale University. He was vice president in the Quantitative Strategies Group at Goldman Sachs, where he worked on many special-situations projects which involved options, warrants, convertibles and securities with unusual features. He was also a director and manager of Research and Development at Deutsche Bank. Most recently he was managing director in Derivatives Research at Chemical Bank in London and New York. He has been responsible for the development of a number of derivative pricing models and, with Fischer Black, the author of the important Black–Karasinski Model.

Nicole El Karoui is a professor at the University of Paris VI and the Ecole Polytechnique. She is an expert on stochastic control and in the probabilistic aspects of mathematical finance. Professor El Karoui is responsible for the co-ordination and formulation of courses at the Laboratory of Probabilities, University of Paris VI.

Sang-Bin Lee is currently Professor of Finance at Hanyang University in Seoul, Korea. Professor Lee received his MA in Economics from Cornell University and a PhD in Finance from New York University. He has published articles in a number of professional journals, including the *Journal of Finance, Journal of Portfolio Management, Research in Finance, Review of Futures Market* and *Journal of Futures Markets.* Professor Lee has contributed chapters to the *Handbook of International Financial Markets* and *Interest Rate Risk Management.* In addition, he has been the editor of the *Korean Journal of Financial Management.* Professor Lee's research is mainly in the pricing of derivative securities and bond portfolio management.

Andrew Morton is a senior vice president and head of the Fixed Income Derivatives Research Group at Lehman Brothers. His group produces valuation models for derivatives and other taxable fixed income instruments. Before joining Lehmans he spent four years as an assistant professor at the University of Illinois at Chicago and one year as a visiting assistant professor at the

University of Michigan. He has an undergraduate degree in mathematics from the University of Waterloo and a PhD in Operations Research from Cornell University.

Marek Musiela has held a number of academic appointments at Polish, French and Australian universities. He is head of the Financial Mathematics Group at the University of New South Wales in Sydney. In recent years he has concentrated his research and teaching activities on mathematical finance, with a particular emphasis on term structure modelling and the pricing of exotic options. His publications include numerous articles on stochastic calculus, interest rate models. and derivatives. His forthcoming book, co-authored with Marek Rutkowski, is entitled *Arbitrage Pricing*. He is an associate editor of *Finance and Stochastics* and a consultant to banks and software companies.

Jean-Charles Rochet, a former student of the Ecole Normale Supérieure in Paris, obtained his PhD at Paris Dauphine and taught at ENSAE and Ecole Polytechnique. He is now a professor at Toulouse University and research director in the Institut d'Economie Industrielle. He has worked on contract theory, the micro-economics of banking, insurance theory and mathematical finance. He has published over 50 articles in academic journals and has written: *Microeconomics of Insurance* (with Dominique Henriet), *Mathematical Methods of Finance* (with Gabrielle Demange) and *Microeconomics of Banking* (with Xavier Freixas), to be published by MIT Press in 1997.

Chris Rogers is Professor of Probability at the University of Bath and has an MA and PhD degree from the University of Cambridge. He is the author of more than 80 publications, including the well known two-volume, *Diffusions, Markov Processes, and Martingales* (with David Williams). Many of his papers cover topics on mathematical finance and focus on areas such as the term structure of interest rates, complete models of stochastic volatility (with David Hobson), portfolio turnpike theorems (with Phil Dybvig and Kerry Black), and improved binomial pricing (with Emily Stapleton). Professor Rogers is an associate editor of several journals, including *Mathematical Finance*, and was the principal organiser of the 1995 Programme on Financial Mathematics, held at the Isaac Newton Institute in Cambridge.

Stephen A. Ross is the Sterling Professor of Economics and Finance at Yale University and was previously a professor of economics and finance at the Wharton School at the University of Pennsylvania. Professor Ross is the author of more than 75 articles in economics and finance and is the co-author of an introductory textbook in finance. He received his BSc with honours from CalTech in 1965, where he majored in physics, and his PhD in Economics from Harvard in 1970. He is probably best known for inventing the arbitrage pricing theory, the theory of agency, and as the co-discoverer of risk neutral pricing and the binomial model for pricing derivatives. Models developed by him and his co-authors, including term structure models and option pricing models, are now standards for pricing in major securities trading firms. He has been the recipient of numerous prizes, awards and honourary degrees, including the Graham and Dodd Award for Financial Writing, the Pomerance Prize for Excellence and the 1996 IAFE Financial Engineer of the Year Award. He is a fellow of the Econometric Society and a member of the American Academy of Arts and Sciences. He is also Chairman of Roll and Ross Asset Management Corporation

Mark Rubinstein is the Paul Stephens Professor of Applied Investment Analysis at the University of California at Berkeley. As co-author of *Options Markets* he is best known for his work on the Cox–Ross–Rubinstein binomial option pricing approach, and more recently for a series of articles on exotic options published in *Risk* magazine. Professor Rubinstein is the winner of ten prizes for papers in financial economics, was named "Businessman of the Year" by Fortune Magazine for 1987, and "Financial Engineer of the Year" for 1995. He is also an associate editor of eight academic and business finance journals. During 1993 he was president of the American Finance Association where he presented his new approach to option pricing and hedging entitled *Implied Binomial Trees*.

Myron S. Scholes is a principal, co-founder and limited partner at Long-Term Capital Management, an investment management firm based in Greenwich, Connecticut. This firm specialises in the development and application of sophisticated financial technology to investment. Professor Scholes has been the Frank E. Buck Professor of Finance at the Stanford University of Business since 1983 and a senior research fellow at the Hoover Institute since 1987. He received his PhD in 1969 from the University of Chicago, where he was on the Finance faculty from 1973 to 1983. From 1969 to 1974, he taught at MIT's Sloan School of Management. He was made a managing director at Salomon Brothers in 1991 and, as co-head of its Fixed Income Derivatives Sales and Trading Department, was instrumental in building Salomon Swapco and expanding its derivative sales and trading group. Professor Scholes also served on Salomon's risk management committee. He left Salomon in 1993. Professor Scholes is widely known for his seminal work on options pricing, capital markets, financial services and the effects of global tax policies on decision making. He is a co-originator of the famous Black–Scholes options pricing model, which is used to trade derivative instruments around the world.

Eduardo S. Schwartz is the California Professor of Real Estate and Professor of Finance, Anderson Graduate School of Management at the University of California, Los Angeles. His wide-ranging research has focused on different dimensions in asset and securities pricing. Topics in recent years range from interest rate volatility to asset allocation issues to evaluating natural resource investments. His collected works include more than 60 articles in finance and economic journals, two monographs and a large number of monograph chapters, conference proceedings and special reports. He is the winner of a number of awards for both teaching excellence and for the quality of his published work. He is associate editor of at least a dozen journals, including the *Journal of Finance*, the *Journal of Financial Economics* and the *Journal of Financial and Quantitative Analysis*. He is a former president of the Western Finance Association. He has also been a consultant to governmental agencies, banks, investment banks and industrial corporations.

William W. Toy is a vice president in the Equity Derivatives Department at Goldman Sachs and is involved in the structuring and development of customised derivatives instruments. His previous responsibilities were in the area of derivatives research, and he is a co-developer of the Black–Derman–Toy interest rate model. Dr Toy holds a PhD in Experimental Particle Physics from MIT. Prior to joining Goldman Sachs he was employed at Bell Laboratories in the area of microwave communications.

Oldrich A. Vasicek works in the field of mathematical finance, particularly in the development of probabilistic models of financial instruments and markets. He is co-founder and a director of KMV Corporation in San Francisco, and a consultant to Gifford Fong. His prior experience includes eight years as a vice president in the Management Science Department of Wells Fargo Bank. He was a professor at the Graduate School of Management at the University of Rochester, and for two years a visiting professor at the University of California at Berkeley. He is a native of the Czech republic and holds a PhD in Probability Theory from the Charles University in Prague. He is author of many articles in financial and mathematical journals and has received several honours, including the Graham and Dodd Award and the Award of the Institute for Quantitative Research in Finance.

Alan White is a professor of finance in the Faculty of Management at the University of Toronto and a principal of A–J Financial Systems Inc. His research is principally in the area of derivative securities: their pricing and use by financial institutions for risk management. Recently this research has focused on the pricing and hedging of credit risk. Other current research examines modelling the term structure of interest rates in a way that is consistent with observed market data, and the valuation of path-dependent securities such as indexed amortising interest rate swaps.

Omar Zane is a research officer in the School of Mathematical Sciences at the University of Bath. He received his PhD in Mathematics from the University of Kansas in 1995 and his *Laurea in Matematica* from the University of Padua in 1988. He has written a number of research articles on a variety of topics, including parameter estimation, stochastic control, investment and consumption optimisation, and interest rate modelling.

Introduction

Vasicek and Beyond

Lane Hughston
Merrill Lynch International, London

The theory and application of interest rate modelling is one of the most important and fascinating areas of modern finance. Interest rate dynamics is a relatively new discipline that has grown up over the last twenty-five years more or less hand in hand with the theory of option pricing. This development has coincided with a great expansion in the range and volume of interest rate related derivatives being traded in the international financial markets. Such products now constitute a significant element in the world economy; investment banks and other financial institutions, as well as corporate and government treasury offices, thus require ever more accurate, objective, and scientific control of the pricing, hedging, and general risk management of the resulting positions. It is appropriate, then, that the opportunity has arisen to gather together in one volume a number of the key papers that have contributed to the development of the modern theory of interest rate dynamics.

It would be out of place here to attempt a comprehensive survey, history, or critique of the developments that have taken place in the theory of interest rate models over the last twenty-five years. For the most part, the papers that follow in this volume speak for themselves, and do not really need an introduction. In any case a number of fine reviews and books have been written recently covering various aspects of this area. These include, for example, Berger (1992), Duffie and Kan (1994), Rogers (1994), Ho (1995), Rebonato (1996*a,b*), Smithson and Song (1996), Strickland (1996), de Munnik (1996), Hull (1996), Jarrow and Turnbull (1996), Musiela and Rutkowski (1996), and Duffie (1996*a*). See also Duffie (1996*b*) in Chapter 17 of this volume, where the reader will find a masterly survey of interest rate models admitting a Markovian state-space representation.

Our purpose, instead, will be to set the stage for the rest of this collection by placing the theory of interest rates in the context of the general theory of dynamic asset pricing. Emphasis will be placed on certain key concepts and developments - particularly the no-arbitrage assumption and the change of measure argument, and the reasoning behind the extraordinary interplay between interest rate modelling and derivatives pricing. Some brief remarks will also be made to indicate some of the new directions in which the subject is currently moving.

The most widely accepted paradigm for modelling asset price movements is based on the idea that asset prices can be represented by stochastic processes. The theory of asset pricing is thus essentially probabilistic in character, and the relevant mathematical tools derive from modern probability theory. See, for example, Dothan (1990), Baxter and Rennie (1996), and Lamberton and Lapeyre (1996). Setting up the entire mathematical theory here, with all the relevant probabilistic apparatus carefully laid out, is beyond the scope of the present discussion - partly because it is too complicated for a brief exposition, but also because the foundations are still in the process of being developed, and it would be a mistake to insist too firmly at this stage on any one given framework.

For example, it is very convenient to price assets in continuous time, with the additional assumption that the assets themselves can take on a continuum of values. It is natural, then, to assume that the underlying source of randomness in the economy can be modelled by Brownian motion, which feeds into the asset price processes via a system of stochastic differential equations. Almost (but not quite) all the interest rate models we consider here make an assumption more or less to this effect - but is it *entirely* reasonable?

Clearly not entirely, since prices by their very nature have to be rational numbers - "I'll give you so many of these for so many of those" is the way of trade. Yet the utility of continuum models is so great that one is almost tempted to believe in an underlying reality of continuous prices that nevertheless can only be expressed as rational prices. Discrete-time models are generally viewed as approximations to continuous-time models, rather than realistic models in their own right, but it would be a mistake to underestimate the substantial impact that discrete models such as those of Cox, Ross and Rubinstein (1979), and later Ho and Lee (1986) - both reprinted in this volume - have had on subsequent developments in the subject.

Indeed, it may be that the right criterion for judging the generality and appropriateness of a continuous pricing model is that it should admit a completely natural analogue in a discrete setting - this is also relevant for implementation. Even if we accept the principle of continuous-time stochastic models much freedom remains, and it has to be said that one of the important open problems in mathematical finance is to settle on the most appropriate way of incorporating asset price jumps into the theory (see, eg, Jarrow and Madan 1992). This is closely related to the valuation of risky debt, credit-linked derivatives, and emerging markets products.

Dynamic asset pricing

The standard continuous dynamical model for an asset price is obtained by assuming that the stochastic process S_t for the price of the asset at time t is an Itô process, characterised by a stochastic equation of the following form:

$$\frac{dS_t}{S_t} = \mu_t dt + \sigma_t dW_t \qquad (1)$$

This can be interpreted as saying that the infinitesimal price movement dS_t at time t, expressed as a percentage of the price, is given by the sum of a drift, $\mu_t dt$, and a fluctuation, $\sigma_t dW_t$, with magnitude σ_t. In general the process μ_t, called the drift rate, and the process σ_t, called the volatility, can depend in an essentially arbitrary way on the history of the Wiener process (Brownian motion) W_t from the present (time 0) up to time t. In that sense we say that the random processes for the price, the drift and the volatility are all "adapted" to the Brownian motion.

Simplifying assumptions are often imposed on the drift and volatility, for example by making them constant, or deterministically time-dependent, or functions of W_t (ie, functions of the value of the Wiener process at time t), or functions of S_t. It is important to bear in mind, however, that the general framework of asset pricing does not require such simplifying assumptions despite their usefulness in the formulation of specific models. Indeed, the theory is in some respects most transparent when formulated in general terms, and it often pays to delay the specialisation process until a reasonably late stage in model development.

If the drift and volatility processes in the stochastic equation (1) are specified exogenously, then the solution for the price process can be represented as follows:

$$S_t = S_0 \exp\left[\int_{s=0}^{t} \mu_s \, ds\right] \exp\left[\int_{s=0}^{t} \sigma_s \, dW_s - \tfrac{1}{2}\int_{s=0}^{t} \sigma_s^2 \, ds\right] \qquad (2)$$

Thus the asset price process can be represented as a product $S_t = S_0 A_t Z_t$ of three terms: the initial value S_0, a finite variation process A_t defined by

$$A_t = \exp\left[\int_{s=0}^{t} \mu_s \, ds\right] \tag{3}$$

satisfying $dA_t = \mu_t A_t dt$, and a positive martingale Z_t defined by

$$Z_t = \exp\left[\int_{s=0}^{t} \sigma_s \, dW_s - \tfrac{1}{2}\int_{s=0}^{t} \sigma_s^2 \, ds\right] \tag{4}$$

satisfying $dZ_t = \sigma_t Z_t dW_t$. A process of the form (4) is called an "exponential martingale", and we shall have a bit more to say about such processes shortly. The fact that $dZ_t = \sigma_t Z_t dW_t$ follows from Itô's lemma, one of the most useful tools in stochastic calculus.

Itô's lemma says that if X_t is an Itô process, satisfying $dX_t = \alpha_t dt + \beta_t dW_t$, and if F is a function of one variable with continuous first and second derivatives F' and F'', and if the process F_t is defined by $F_t = F(X_t)$, then

$$dF_t = \left(\alpha_t F_t' + \tfrac{1}{2}\beta_t^2 F_t''\right) dt + F_t' \beta_t dW_t \tag{5}$$

Thus Itô's lemma tells us that if X_t is an Itô process, then so is $F_t = F(X_t)$. Then the fact that Z_t as given by (4) satisfies $dZ_t = \sigma_t Z_t dW_t$ follows directly if we set $Z_t = \exp(X_t)$ and apply Itô's lemma.

It turns out to be useful to express the asset drift rate μ_t in the form $\mu_t = r_t + \lambda_t \sigma_t$, where r_t is the short rate. The significance of r_t, more specifically, is that it represents the random value at time t of the instantaneous (eg, "overnight") rate of return offered on a risk-free deposit (risk-free in the sense that the return is absolutely guaranteed). Then λ_t, the so-called market premium of risk, represents the additional rate of return, above the short rate, offered by the given asset, per unit of volatility.

The fact that the product $\lambda_t \sigma_t$ is usually taken to be positive represents the economic idea that in an efficient market we normally expect a rate of return for a given risky investment that is, on average, greater than the rate of return offered on a less risky investment.

There is a subtlety here inasmuch as these considerations only apply strictly to non-dividend-paying assets. The point is that, for example, if a company pays a large dividend, then the share price might be expected to drop, but under the circumstances it would hardly be right to say that the investment was offering a negative rate of return. In this case the appropriate non-dividend-paying asset might be represented by a combination of shares together with a deposit account containing the relevant dividends together with accumulated interest. Similar remarks apply in the case of foreign currency investments.

Another, slightly less tangible aspect of the same phenomenon develops in the case of commodities, and material assets in general, where we have the notion of the convenience yield. This concept quantifies the abstract benefits associated with actual possession, to be set off against storage costs, insurance costs, and so on. Likewise, an investment in insurance may have on average an apparent negative rate of return, unless one takes into account the intangible positive benefit associated with "peace of mind".

Note that in the special case when μ_t, σ_t, r_t and λ_t are constant, formula (2) for the asset price process reduces to

$$S_t = S_0 \exp\left[(r + \lambda\sigma)t + \sigma W_t - \tfrac{1}{2}\sigma^2 t\right] \tag{6}$$

which is the so-called "geometric Brownian motion" model for price movements. The simplifying assumptions here are strong; nevertheless the resulting model is useful in a variety of situations, and indeed forms the dynamical basis of the original basic option pricing model of Black and Scholes (1973).

Martingales and Brownian motion

To proceed further it will be helpful if we briefly review some of the ideas of the theory of continuous stochastic processes – particularly the concept of a martingale, a central notion in modern finance theory. The reason why we are interested in martingales in finance is on account of an important set of results (due to Harrison and Kreps, 1979, and Harrison and Pliska, 1981, and later refined by a number of authors, in particular Bensoussan, 1984, and Delbaen and Schachermayer, 1994) relating martingales and ratios of asset prices under changes of probability measure. We shall look at these results in more detail shortly.

The idea of a martingale is that it gives a mathematical embodiment to the notion of a fair game of chance. We want to consider processes that satisfy a condition of the form $M_s = E_s[M_t]$, where E_s is the conditional expectation given information up to time s. This says that the expected value of the process at time t, given information up to time s, is equal to the value of the process at time s.

First we consider continuous stochastic processes taking values in the real numbers. The basic process in this case is the so-called Wiener process W_t, otherwise known as Brownian motion. The Wiener process is of great significance in finance inasmuch as it acts as the primary mechanism whereby the source of randomness or noise is modelled in the movements of asset prices.

The intention here is not to present a rigorous account of the properties of Brownian motion but rather simply to touch briefly on the main points for the benefit of readers less acquainted with this process, supplying in an informal way some of the information implicit in the finance literature and used frequently in a number of the articles in this volume.

The Wiener process can be characterised as follows. On a probability space (set of events) with a given filtration (sense of information flow in time) and measure (assignment of probabilities) we consider a random process W_t such that:

(1) W_t is almost surely continuous, with $W_0 = 0$;
(2) W_t $(t \geq 0)$ has independent increments, ie, for successive times p, q, r and s the random variables $W_q - W_p$ and $W_s - W_r$ are independent; and
(3) for any $0 \leq s \leq t$ the probability that $W_t - W_s \leq x$ for some given real value of x is given by

$$P\left[W_t - W_s \leq x\right] = \frac{1}{\sqrt{2\pi(t-s)}} \int_{-\infty}^{x} \exp\left[\frac{-\eta^2}{2(t-s)}\right] d\eta$$

These properties are sufficient to characterise the Wiener process. For the mean and variance of $W_t - W_s$ we then find by familiar arguments that $E[W_t - W_s] = 0$ and that $E[(W_t - W_s)^2] = t - s$.

We say that a process is adapted to the filtration generated by a Wiener process if its random value at time t can be characterised by the knowledge of the history of the Wiener process up to that time. Suppose we fix a time interval $[0, T]$ and consider processes for which $t \in [0, T]$. If β_t is an adapted process over this interval, then the stochastic integral

$$M_t = \int_0^t \beta_s \, dW_s \tag{7}$$

exists if the process β_t is square-integrable in the sense that for all $t \in [0, T]$ we have

$$P\left[\int_0^t \beta_s^2 \, ds < \infty\right] = 1 \tag{8}$$

ie, the integral of the square of β_t exists with probability one. If β_t satisfies the stronger condition that the expectation of the integral of its square exists, so

$$E\left[\int_0^t \beta_s^2 \, ds\right] < \infty \tag{9}$$

then the process M_t defined by (7) is a martingale, ie, it satisfies the measurability condition $E[|M_t|] < \infty$ and the martingale condition $M_s = E_s M_t$, where E_s denotes the expectation conditional on knowledge of events up to time s.

In particular, we have $E[M_t] = 0$. The variance of M_t also exists (ie, M_t is a square-integrable martingale) and is given by the relation

$$E[M_t^2] = E\left[\int_0^t \beta_s^2 \, ds\right] \tag{10}$$

This relation is known as the Itô isometry. Conversely (by a theorem of Kunita and Watanabe, 1967), any square-integrable martingale over the interval $0 \leq t \leq T$ based on the Wiener filtration is necessarily of the form (7) plus a constant, for some adapted process β_t satisfying (9).

Some examples of continuous martingales based on Brownian motion include: (*a*) the constant process; (*b*) the Wiener process itself; (*c*) $W_t^2 - t$; (*d*) $W_t^3 - 3tW_t$; and (*e*) $W_t^4 - 6tW_t^2 + 3t^2$.

To see that the process $W_t^2 - t$ is a martingale we note, by use of the independent increments property, that

$$\begin{aligned} E_s\left[W_t^2 - t\right] &= E_s\left[\left(W_s + \left(W_t - W_s\right)\right)^2 - t\right] \\ &= E_s\left[W_s^2\right] + E_s\left[\left(W_t - W_s\right)^2\right] - t \\ &= W_s^2 - s \end{aligned}$$

More generally, for any constant ξ the process $Z_t = \exp[\xi W_t - \frac{1}{2}\xi^2 t]$ is a martingale. In particular, if we define the polynomials $H^n(x, y)$ by

$$\exp[\xi x - \tfrac{1}{2}\xi^2 y] = \sum_0^\infty (n!)^{-1} \xi^n H^n(x,y) \tag{11}$$

then for each value of n the process $H^n(W_t, t)$ is a martingale, and the examples mentioned above correspond to the first five values of n. The polynomials $H^n(x, y)$ are given by $H^n(x, y) = (y/2)^{n/2} h_n[x/(2y)^{1/2}]$, where $h_n[u]$ are the standard Hermite polynomials. If ξ is complex, we deduce for example that $\exp(\frac{1}{2}t)\cos(W_t)$ is a martingale. The correction term $\exp(\frac{1}{2}t)$ is due to the fact that the expectation of the process $\cos(W_t)$ tends to zero exponentially even though it starts at one.

Another way of generating martingales is by taking expectations; thus, if Z_T is a random variable based on the filtration of a Brownian motion over the interval $[0, T]$ such that $E[|Z_T|] < \infty$, then $M_t = E_t[Z_T]$ is a martingale over that interval by virtue of the "tower" property $E_s E_t = E_s$ for $s < t$. For example, if $Z_T = W_T^2$, then $M_t = T + (W_t^2 - t)$.

If M_t is a square-integrable martingale starting at the origin, then there is a unique increasing process Q_t, called the quadratic variation of M_t, such that $M_t^2 - Q_t$ is a (zero-initialised) martingale. If the martingale is given by the representation (7), then the quadratic variation is given by

$$Q_t = \int_0^t \beta_s^2 \, ds \tag{12}$$

For example, the quadratic variation of W_t is $Q_t = t$. We note also that if M_t is a martingale, Q_t is its quadratic variation, and $E[\exp\frac{1}{2}Q_t] < \infty$, then $H^n(M_t, Q_t)$ is a martingale for each value of n.

So is the process $Z_t = \exp(M_t - \frac{1}{2}Q_t)$, which is called the exponential martingale associated with M_t. We have already met the concept of exponential martingales in our general solution (2) of the asset price equation (1). For further discussion in this spirit see, for example, Dothan (1990) or Karatzas and Shreve (1991). Armed with these technical details we now return to our main line of argument.

No arbitrage, existence of the market risk premium

When we generalise the basic price process model for a single asset to the case of many assets, some new features emerge that are important in the theory of derivatives pricing and are also of significance in the theory of interest rates. These features arise in connection with the so-called "no-arbitrage" and "market completeness" conditions. The no-arbitrage argument forms the heart of the reasoning that led Black and Scholes to their original option pricing formula. The same argument also plays, in a slightly different way, a central role in Vasicek's (1977) pioneering work on interest rates.

Let us assume that we have a system of several assets with prices S_t^i at time t, where $i = 1, \ldots, m$. Here we consider the case of a discrete family of assets, but later when we examine the case of interest rates more explicitly we consider the situation where we have a continuous one-parameter family of assets (ie, the one-parameter family of discount bonds, parameterised by maturity date). The price processes for the m assets are determined by the following system of stochastic equations:

$$\frac{dS_t^i}{S_t^i} = \mu_t^i dt + \sum_{\alpha=1}^{n} \sigma_t^{i\alpha} dW_t^\alpha \tag{13}$$

In this case we have a set of n independent Wiener processes labelled W_t^α ($\alpha = 1, \ldots, n$). Generally we require that m should be greater than or equal to n, in other words that there should be at least as many distinct assets as there are sources of randomness. Otherwise the markets may be "incomplete" in the sense that there may be more sources of randomness than there are independent means of hedging away the given sources of uncertainty. Of course, it may be that some markets really are incomplete, so this is an assumption that needs to be considered with care. We shall return to the issue of market completeness shortly, since there is still more to say on this matter.

In (13) we have for each asset a set of n distinct volatility processes labelled $\sigma_t^{i\alpha}$. Thus, at time t the magnitude in the price fluctuation of asset number i due to the source of randomness number α is given by $\sigma_t^{i\alpha}$, which we call the volatility matrix associated with the given set of assets. This is an m-by-n rectangular matrix process, the exogenous specification of which, along with the drift rate processes μ_t^i, determines the asset price processes S_t^i once initial prices have been given. In fact, following the example of formula (2), we find that

$$S_t^i = S_0^i \exp\left[\int_{s=0}^{t} \mu_s^i \, ds\right] \exp\left[\int_{s=0}^{t} \sigma_s^i \, dW_s - \frac{1}{2}\int_{s=0}^{t} \sigma_s^{i2} \, ds\right] \tag{14}$$

is the general solution of (13), subject to the given initial condition. This observation is the starting point for the illuminating treatment of the options pricing problem in the case of multiple assets given in the paper by Bensoussan (1984), which is reprinted in this volume. Here, and occasionally elsewhere, for convenience we suppress the Wiener process indices, and there is an implied summation. For example, we write

$$\sigma_s^i \, dW_s \text{ for } \sum_{\alpha=1}^{n} \sigma_s^{i\alpha} dW_s^\alpha \text{ and } \sigma_s^{i2} \text{ for } \sum_{\alpha=1}^{n} \sigma_s^{i\alpha}\sigma_s^{i\alpha}$$

For each value of i we are thus to think of σ_s^i as representing a "vector" volatility process with n components, one for each independent Brownian motion. The context will usually make it clear what the implied summation runs over.

Now we turn to the matter of no arbitrage. This is a rather intricate issue, which, if pursued in detail, would take us away from the main point. Nevertheless we can present a line of argument that gets the key ideas across and captures the essence of the modern point of view. In accordance with our earlier discussion in the case of a single asset, we shall assume that a risk-free investment over a short period of time (eg, overnight) offering a definite rate of return necessarily pays a rate of return given by an exogenously specified short-rate process r_t adapted to the information flow of the multi-dimensional Brownian motion. The idea, then, is that if any portfolio of assets with price processes S_t^i and portfolio weightings θ^i offers, instantaneously, at time t, a definite rate of return, then that rate of return also has to be the short rate. If the portfolio offers a definite rate of return at time t, that means in particular that

$$\sum_i \theta^i S_t^i \sigma_s^{i\alpha} = 0 \tag{15}$$

at that time, ie, the fluctuating term vanishes. For any choice of θ^i satisfying this condition we therefore require that

$$\sum_i \theta^i S_t^i \mu_t^i = r_t \sum_i \theta^i S_t^i \tag{16}$$

which is the condition that the rate of return on the portfolio at that time is given by the short rate. This implies a condition on the structure of the drift rate, namely, that it should be of the form

$$\mu_t^i = r_t + \sum_{\alpha=1}^{n} \lambda_t^\alpha \sigma_t^{i\alpha} \tag{17}$$

for some vector process λ_t^α that is independent of the value of i. This is the market premium of risk vector, which has the economic interpretation of being the extra rate of return, above the risk-free rate, per unit of volatility in factor number α. The no-arbitrage condition thus tells us that the entire family of assets shares a common market risk premium process, given by the vector λ_t^α.

Market completeness, uniqueness of the market risk premium

Once we have deduced the existence of a market risk premium process we can insert (17) into (13) to obtain the following more succinct expression for the asset price dynamics:

$$\frac{dS_t^i}{S_t^i} = r_t \, dt + \sum_{\alpha=1}^{n} \sigma_t^{i\alpha} (dW_t^\alpha + \lambda_t^\alpha dt) \tag{18}$$

The fact that we are able to combine the market risk premium in this way with the Wiener process may at first seem rather arbitrary, but this turns out to be related to one of the key mathematical concepts of modern finance, namely the "change of measure" operation, which will be described shortly.

First, however, we return briefly to the issue of market completeness. This is mathematically expressed by the requirement that the m-by-n rectangular matrix $\sigma_t^{i\alpha}$ should be of maximal rank, which must be n, since by assumption m is not less than n. The interpretation of this condition is essentially to say that any fluctuation in the Brownian motion is necessarily picked up by the assets in the form of some price fluctuation. More precisely, we say that $\sigma_t^{i\alpha}$ has maximal rank if for any non-vanishing vector ξ^α we have

$$\sum_\alpha \xi^\alpha \sigma_t^{i\alpha} \neq 0 \tag{19}$$

If (19) holds for all ξ^α, then any fluctuation dW_t^α results in a non-trivial fluctuation dS_t^i in at least one of the given assets, thereby "expressing" the underlying noise source.

Then the symmetric matrix

$$\rho^{\alpha\beta} = \sum_i \sigma_t^{i\alpha} \sigma_t^{i\beta} \tag{20}$$

is non-singular, and hence possesses an inverse $\rho^{-1}_{\alpha\beta}$ such that

$$\sum_\beta \rho^{\alpha\beta} \rho^{-1}_{\beta\gamma} = \delta^\alpha_\gamma \tag{21}$$

With these expressions at our disposal we can now solve for the market risk premium vector in (17) to obtain

$$\lambda_t^\alpha = \sum_\beta \sum_i \rho^{-1}_{\alpha\beta} \sigma_t^{i\beta} (\mu_t^i - r_t) \tag{22}$$

Thus it becomes apparent that the condition of market completeness ensures that the market risk premium vector is unique and can be determined from the exogenously specified drift rate, short rate and volatility processes by (22). It follows that the no-arbitrage and market completeness conditions together are necessary and sufficient to ensure the existence of a unique market risk premium vector λ_t^α such that the basic asset price dynamics are given by (18).

Change of measure, risk neutrality

Now we are in a position to apply the change of measure technique and value derivatives. First we need to introduce the idea of the money market account process B_t. This process represents the value at time t of a bank account, initialised with one unit of currency at time zero, that accumulates interest at the short rate. Thus for B_t we have

$$B_t = \exp \int_0^t r_s \, ds \tag{23}$$

The asset is locally risk-free in the sense that B_t is an increasing process with no fluctuating term, ie, we have $dB_t = r_t B_t dt$. The key idea that needs to be appreciated to understand the modern literature on derivatives pricing - and interest rate modelling in particular - is that if we form the system of ratios given by S_t^i/B_t, then, under the no-arbitrage and market completeness conditions, there exists a unique "change of probability measure" such that these ratios are all martingales. This is the famous observation of Harrison and Kreps (1979) and Harrison and Pliska (1981). To get a feeling for what is involved here one can proceed as follows. First we note that the ratio process satisfies the following stochastic equation:

$$\frac{d(S_t^i/B_t)}{S_t^i/B_t} = \sum_{\alpha=1}^n \sigma_t^{i\alpha} (dW_t^\alpha + \lambda_t^\alpha dt) \tag{24}$$

In other words, the term in the drift involving the short rate drops out. Now suppose we form the following exponential martingale from the market risk premium vector:

$$\rho_t = \exp\left[-\int_{s=0}^t \lambda_s \, dW_s - \frac{1}{2} \int_{s=0}^t \lambda_s^2 \, ds \right] \tag{25}$$

From Itô's lemma we have

$$d\rho_t = -\rho_t \sum_\alpha \lambda_t^\alpha dW_t^\alpha \tag{26}$$

We shall be interested in the stochastic differential of the product $\rho_t S_t^i/B_t$, for which we obtain

$$\frac{d(\rho_t S_t^i / B_t)}{\rho_t S_t^i / B_t} = \frac{d(S_t^i / B_t)}{S_t^i / B_t} + \frac{d\rho_t}{\rho_t} + \frac{d\rho_t \, d(S_t^i / B_t)}{\rho_t S_t^i / B_t} \tag{27}$$

by the Itô product rule $d(XY) = Y dX + X dY + dX dY$. Then, by use of (24) and (26) and the basic formula $dW_t^\alpha dW_t^\beta = \delta^{\alpha\beta} dt$ for independent Brownian motions, we obtain

$$\frac{d(\rho_t S_t^i / B_t)}{\rho_t S_t^i / B_t} = \sum_{\alpha=1}^{n} (\sigma_t^{i\alpha} - \lambda_t^\alpha) dW_t^\alpha \tag{28}$$

Thus we see that $\rho_t S_t^i / B_t$ is a martingale, since the stochastic derivative only contains a fluctuating term, and as a consequence we have

$$\frac{\rho_s S_s^i}{B_s} = E_s \left[\frac{\rho_t S_t^i}{B_t} \right] \tag{29}$$

Since ρ_t is an exponential martingale, it follows that $\rho_s = E_s[\rho_t]$, so (29) can be rewritten in the form

$$\frac{S_s^i}{B_s} = \frac{E_s \left[\rho_t \frac{S_t^i}{B_t} \right]}{E_s [\rho_t]} \tag{30}$$

For any random variable, X, adapted to the Brownian motion up to time t we can use the "density martingale" ρ_t to define a new expectation operator, $\hat{E}$, according to the following prescription:

$$\hat{E}_s [X] = \frac{E_s [\rho_t X]}{E_s [\rho_t]} \tag{31}$$

Here, for convenience, we have given the definition of the new expectation conditionally, based on information up to time s. The move from one expectation operator to another is called a "change of measure" by probabilists because in the special case when X is the indicator function for an event A we have $E[X] = P(A)$, the probability of the event A, and $\hat{E}[X] = \hat{P}(A)$, the probability of the same event "in the new measure". A further investigation then shows that the process $\hat{W}_t^\alpha$, defined by

$$\hat{W}_t^\alpha = W_t^\alpha + \int_0^t \lambda_s^\alpha \, ds \tag{32}$$

satisfies the axioms of Brownian motion with respect to the new measure $\hat{E}$. Since $d\hat{W}_t^\alpha = dW_t^\alpha + \lambda_t^\alpha dt$, it follows that with respect to the Brownian motion in the new measure the asset price dynamics can be written as follows:

$$\frac{dS_t^i}{S_t^i} = r_t \, dt + \sum_{\alpha=1}^{n} \sigma_t^{i\alpha} d\hat{W}_t^\alpha \tag{33}$$

It should be apparent that in the new measure all of the assets have the same drift, namely the short rate. For this reason the new measure is called the "risk-neutral" measure, since in this measure the same rate of return is offered on all assets, regardless of their riskiness. The risk-neutral measure is characterised by the property that in a complete market with no arbitrage it is the unique measure with respect to which the ratio of any asset price to the money market account is a martingale. This can be put another way, namely that if we choose the money market account to be the "numeraire", that is, the asset in terms of which all other assets prices are expressed, then the risk-neutral measure is the unique probability measure (agreeing with the original measure on events with probability zero) with respect to which the value processes of all assets, with this choice of numeraire, are martingales.

Valuation of derivatives

Let us turn now more explicitly to the valuation of derivatives. Suppose we have a complete market consisting of a number of traded assets, and suppose also that among them are some derivatives. In a fairly abstract way we can define a derivative as a contract that entitles the owner to a cashflow C_T at time T, where C_T is a random variable adapted to the flow of market information up to time T. In practice we take C_T to be a contractually specified function of the various basic (underlying) asset prices at one or more times between the present and time T. In the case of a simple call option, for example, there is a single risky asset with price S_t, and the relevant cashflow at time T is given by $C_T = \max[S_T - K, 0]$, where K is the strike price and $\max[X, Y]$ denotes the maximum of X and Y. Options are "exotic" to the extent that C_T exhibits some complicated or novel feature.

There is a great deal of significant discussion in the literature and, indeed, on trading floors about various derivative "structures". The particular structure of a derivative contract is typically formulated by an investment bank or other financial institution in the course of discussions with its clients. This interface forms the bread and butter of the derivatives business and is a central element in the client relationship. By a structure we mean a choice of the random variable C_T. Some structures are simpler than others; some structures are easier to price than others; and some structures are easier to hedge than others.

Let us therefore as a matter of notation write C_t for the value of the derivative at time t that has the payoff structure C_T at time T. Since the derivative is itself an asset, it follows from the arguments presented in the previous section that in the risk-neutral measure the ratio of C_t to the money market account B_t must be a martingale; that is to say:

$$\left[\frac{C_s}{B_s}\right] = \hat{E}_s\left[\frac{C_t}{B_t}\right] \tag{34}$$

But, as a special case of this relation obtained by setting $s = 0$ and $t = T$, we deduce that

$$C_0 = \hat{E}\left[\frac{C_T}{B_T}\right] \tag{35}$$

This is the main valuation formula for derivatives, which shows that the present value of a derivative is obtained by taking the expectation, in the risk-neutral measure, of the ratio of the payoff structure to the money market account.

It can be instructive to review how (35) leads to the famous Black–Scholes formula. Suppose we refer back to formula (6) for the asset price process in the case of a simple geometric Brownian motion model. This is essentially the situation studied in the original article by Black and Scholes, reprinted in this volume. In this case, after we transform to the risk-neutral measure, we have

$$S_t = S_0 \exp\left[rt + \sigma\hat{W}_t - \tfrac{1}{2}\sigma^2 t\right] \tag{36}$$

where the process $\hat{W}_t = W_t + \lambda t$ is a $\hat{P}$-Brownian motion - that is to say, a Brownian motion with respect to the risk-neutral measure.

Now we substitute the price process (36), valued at time T, into the payoff structure $C_T = \max[S_T - K, 0]$ and the result into the valuation formula (35).

A straightforward probabilistic calculation, making use only of the fact that in the measure $\hat{P}$ the random variable $\hat{W}_T$ is normally distributed with mean zero and variance T, leads us immediately to the well known Black–Scholes options pricing formula

$$C_0 = S_0 N\left[\frac{\ln[S_0 e^{rT}/K] + \frac{1}{2}\sigma^2 T}{\sigma\sqrt{T}}\right] - e^{-rT} K N\left[\frac{\ln[S_0 e^{rT}/K] - \frac{1}{2}\sigma^2 T}{\sigma\sqrt{T}}\right] \tag{37}$$

where $N(x)$ is the standard $N(0, 1)$ normal distribution function, given by

$$N(x) = \frac{1}{\sqrt{2\pi}} \int_{-\infty}^{x} \exp(-\tfrac{1}{2}\xi^2)\, d\xi \tag{38}$$

It is important to note that the market premium of risk parameter λ does not enter into the formula (37), which allows us therefore to be able to value options without necessarily taking a view on the market. This is the marvellous feature of the Black–Scholes methodology that makes it so useful in practical applications. The arguments just presented are from a more or less modern perspective, and it is interesting to compare this line of thought to the original ingenious arguments used by Black and Scholes.

When we go to the world of interest rates much of the structure outlined above survives, but instead of a finite set of assets we have an entire one-parameter family of assets. These are the discount bonds, and the relevant parameter is the maturity date. The special twist that arises in connection with interest rates is that the short rate is no longer exogenously specified, but rather is defined as the rate of return on an instantaneously maturing discount bond. Interest rate models are therefore more self-contained than other asset-pricing models, and this is one of the reasons they are so basic in finance.

Another aspect of the relationship of interest rates and derivatives worth mentioning is that the discount bonds themselves can be viewed as a species of derivative. In this case the payoff structure at time T is simply the maturity value of the bond, namely one unit of the relevant currency. The point is that the theory of interest rates is also, in essence, a theory of interest rate derivatives, wherein the basic assets themselves, the discount bonds, can be viewed as derivatives. This helps to explain why the theory of interest rates has more or less kept pace with the theory of derivative pricing over the last twenty-five years and why the two areas have interacted so fruitfully with one another.

Discount bond dynamics

There are a number of ways of approaching the problem of interest rate dynamics, but perhaps the most straightforward from a modern perspective is to regard discount bonds (that is, zero-coupon bonds) as primary assets and impose on them the conditions of no arbitrage and market completeness, along with other appropriate constraints, such as the condition that interest rates must always be positive. There is an element of abstraction that comes in here, since the discount bonds under consideration will be "ideal bonds", ie, default-free, and available in a complete continuum of maturities. Actual interest rate products are complicated by a great variety of incidental features - market spreads, transaction costs, liquidity issues, market segmentation, credit quality, tax considerations, inflation, and so on - but it is useful to take the view that there is an abstract underlying system of pure discount bonds that drives all the real products. Nevertheless, just because a rose smells better than a cabbage doesn't mean it makes better soup; the importance of "real" instruments needs to be borne in mind at all stages.

We shall write P_{ab} for the value at time a of a discount bond that matures at time b to deliver one unit of the relevant currency. Thus, the initial discount function is given by P_{0b}, and we have the maturity condition $P_{aa} = 1$ for all a. For a given fixed value of b we can regard P_{ab} as a random process in the a variable over the range $0 \le a \le b$. The idea of the discount bond process is that from the point of view of the present (time 0) the process P_{ab} is given by the random value at time a of a contract that guarantees delivery of one unit of currency at time b.

This is a helpful way of thinking about discount bonds since it generalises readily to other assets; in other words, for any choice of asset A (a foreign currency, a commodity, a company share, etc.) we can define an associated one-parameter family of A-bonds, where an A-bond is a contract that delivers one unit of the asset A at the specified maturity date b. The conventional discount bonds arise in the case that the asset in question is the domestic currency.

Thus we have a one-parameter family of assets with prices given by P_{ab}, and we assume that the entire market is driven by an n-dimensional family of independent Wiener processes W_t^{α}, where $\alpha = 1, \ldots, n$. The relevant bond dynamics are then given by the following stochastic equations:

$$\frac{dP_{ab}}{P_{ab}} = \mu_{ab}\, da + \Omega_{ab}\, dW_a \tag{39}$$

Here μ_{ab} is the drift process for the b-maturity bond and Ω_{ab} is the corresponding local vector volatility process which satisfies $\Omega_{aa} = 0$. In the term $\Omega_{ab} dW_a$ there is an implied summation over the suppressed "vector" indices on Ω_{ab} and W_a.

Note that, as a matter of notation, we use the symbol Ω_{ab} for the discount bond volatility rather than σ_{ab}, which is reserved for the instantaneous forward rate volatility.

Calculation of the interest rate risk premium

So far we have simply assumed that the discount bond prices are given by a general family of Itô processes. Now we impose the no-arbitrage condition. By analogy with the argument presented in the case of a finite number of assets, this can be seen to ensure the existence of a market risk premium vector, λ_a^{α} $(\alpha = 1, \ldots, n)$ such that the drift process μ_{ab} is given by

$$\mu_{ab} = r_a + \sum_{\alpha=1}^{n} \lambda_a^{\alpha}\, \Omega_{ab}^{\alpha} \tag{40}$$

which, suppressing vector indices, we write as $\mu_{ab} = r_a + \lambda_a \Omega_{ab}$. Here r_a is the short rate, which is defined as the rate of return on an instantaneously maturing discount bond. Since a discount bond has a definite value at maturity, the volatility necessarily vanishes for such a bond, and thus we have $\Omega_{aa} = 0$ and $r_a = \mu_{aa}$. By insertion of (40) into (39) we then get

$$\frac{dP_{ab}}{P_{ab}} = r_a\, da + \Omega_{ab}\,(dW_a + \lambda_a\, da) \tag{41}$$

for the general discount bond dynamics under the no-arbitrage assumption. For market completeness we want the volatility process Ω_{ab}^{α} to be of maximal rank at each time a. It suffices, for example, to require that the matrix

$$\rho^{\alpha\beta} = \int_a^{\infty} \Omega_{ab}^{\alpha}\, \Omega_{ab}^{\beta}\, db \tag{42}$$

is invertible, in which case the unique market premium of interest rate risk is given by the vector process

$$\lambda_a^{\alpha} = \sum_{\beta} \int_{b=a}^{\infty} \rho_{\alpha\beta}^{-1}\, \Omega_{ab}^{\beta}\, (\mu_{ab} - r_a) \tag{43}$$

by analogy with (20) and (30), provided that the relevant integrals exists.

Explicit representations of bond price processes

The stochastic equation (41) for the bond price process involves the bond volatility, the market risk premium and the short rate. Now we shall show that the short rate can be eliminated from the solution of (41) to give a representation of the bond price processes in which the only exogenously specified variables are the volatility process and the market risk premium. Following the analogy of the multiple asset case (14), we find that the solution of stochastic equation (41) can be expressed in the form

$$P_{ab} = P_{0b}\, B_a \exp\left[\int_{s=0}^{a} \Omega_{sb}\,(dW_s + \lambda_s\, ds) - \tfrac{1}{2}\int_{s=0}^{a} \Omega_{sb}^2\, ds\right] \tag{44}$$

where B_a is the money market account process, defined as in formula (23). Note that the market risk premium is combined suggestively with the Brownian motion so as to indicate a change of measure.

This we shall come to shortly. First, however, we observe that the maturity condition $P_{aa} = 1$ allows us to solve for the money market process in (44). For if we set $a = b$, we immediately get

$$B_a = (P_{0a})^{-1} \exp\left[-\int_{s=0}^{a} \Omega_{sa} (dW_s + \lambda_s ds) + \tfrac{1}{2} \int_{s=0}^{a} \Omega_{sa}^2 ds \right] \tag{45}$$

Finally, inserting (45) into (44) we obtain the following formula for the discount bond price processes:

$$P_{ab} = \tilde{P}_{ab} \frac{\exp\left[\int_{s=0}^{a} \Omega_{sb} (dW_s + \lambda_s ds) - \tfrac{1}{2} \int_{s=0}^{a} \Omega_{sb}^2 ds \right]}{\exp\left[\int_{s=0}^{a} \Omega_{sa} (dW_s + \lambda_s ds) - \tfrac{1}{2} \int_{s=0}^{a} \Omega_{sa}^2 ds \right]} \tag{46}$$

where $\tilde{P}_{ab} = P_{0b}/P_{0a}$ is the forward value of a b-maturity discount bond – that is to say, the value we would negotiate today for receipt at time a of a b-maturity discount bond. Formula (46) is an explicit representation of the bond price process in terms of the two exogenously specified variables, ie, the volatility and the market risk premium. The short rate has been eliminated.

On the other hand, we can recover a formula for the short rate process by differentiating (45) and using $dB_a = r_a B_a da$. A calculation then gives

$$r_a = -\partial_a \ln P_{0a} + \int_{s=0}^{a} \sigma_{sa} \Omega_{sa} ds - \int_{s=0}^{a} \sigma_{sa} (dW_s + \lambda_s ds) \tag{47}$$

where ∂_a denotes differentiation with respect to a and $\sigma_{sa} = \partial_a \Omega_{sa}$ is the instantaneous forward rate volatility. Indeed, if we define the instantaneous forward rates f_{ab} by $f_{ab} = -\partial_b \ln P_{ab}$, it follows from (46) that these rates are given explicitly by the relation

$$f_{ab} = -\partial_b \ln P_{0b} + \int_{s=0}^{a} \sigma_{sb} \Omega_{sb} ds - \int_{s=0}^{a} \sigma_{sb} (dW_s + \lambda_s ds) \tag{48}$$

and that the short rate is given by $r_a = f_{aa}$. Heath, Jarrow and Morton (1992) in their famous article take the instantaneous forward rates as their starting point and impose no-arbitrage and market completeness conditions to obtain an expression of the form (48). Here we have to some extent inverted the order of exposition, starting first with consideration of the bond price processes, which in many respects improves the flow of the argument.

Valuation of interest rate derivatives

Once we have explicit representations of the bond price processes and the money market account in terms of the volatility structure and the market risk premium, the valuation of interest rate derivatives proceeds more or less along the same lines as already indicated in the case of a finite collection of assets. First we define the risk-neutral measure $\hat{P}$ by introducing a density martingale based on the market risk premium as in (25) and defining a new expectation operator as in (31). Our treatment of the finite asset number case was designed to make it clear that these features carry over more or less intact into the world of interest rates. Then we introduce the n-dimensional Brownian motion $\hat{W}_t^\alpha$ with respect to the risk-neutral measure according to formula (32). In terms of these variables we have the following formula for the discount bond prices:

$$P_{ab} = \tilde{P}_{ab} \frac{\exp\left[\int_{s=0}^{a} \Omega_{sb}\, d\hat{W}_s - \frac{1}{2}\int_{s=0}^{a} \Omega_{sb}^2\, ds\right]}{\exp\left[\int_{s=0}^{a} \Omega_{sa}\, d\hat{W}_s - \frac{1}{2}\int_{s=0}^{a} \Omega_{sa}^2\, ds\right]} \tag{49}$$

For the money market account we have:

$$B_a = (P_{0a})^{-1} \exp\left[-\int_{s=0}^{a} \Omega_{sa}\, d\hat{W}_s + \frac{1}{2}\int_{s=0}^{a} \Omega_{sa}^2\, ds\right] \tag{50}$$

For the instantaneous forward rates we have:

$$f_{ab} = -\partial_b \ln P_{0b} + \int_{s=0}^{a} \sigma_{sb}\, \Omega_{sb}\, ds - \int_{s=0}^{a} \sigma_{sb}\, d\hat{W}_s \tag{51}$$

And for the short rate process we have:

$$r_a = -\partial_a \ln P_{0a} + \int_{s=0}^{a} \sigma_{sa}\, \Omega_{sa}\, ds - \int_{s=0}^{a} \sigma_{sa}\, d\hat{W}_s \tag{52}$$

Note that in the risk-neutral measure the market risk premium drops out in all these formulae.

Now suppose that C_T is the payoff structure of an interest rate derivative. Even if there are various intermediate payments (as with swap-like structures, caps, etc.), we can formally think of all such payments as simply being "postponed" until some time T, appropriately future-valued to that time. Thus, for the sake of argument, it suffices only to consider derivatives with a single terminal payment C_T, which is to be thought of as a random variable based on interest rate information available up to that time.

In practice, C_T will depend on the values of one or more discount bonds at one or more times between the present and the terminal date. The payoff structures of interest rate derivatives often depend on various rates specified in the contract (swap rates, Libor rates, etc.), rather than on discount bonds directly, but these rates can always be expressed in terms of discount bonds. Then for the valuation of derivatives we have the martingale relation

$$\left[\frac{C_a}{B_a}\right] = \hat{E}_a\left[\frac{C_b}{B_b}\right] \tag{53}$$

and the fundamental pricing formula

$$C_0 = \hat{E}\left[\frac{C_T}{B_T}\right] \tag{54}$$

In particular, it is worth noting that if the payoff of a derivative at time b is simply a unit of currency, then its value at time a must be the discount bond price P_{ab}. Thus it follows from (53) that for the discount bond we can write

$$\frac{P_{ab}}{B_a} = \hat{E}_a\left[\frac{1}{B_b}\right] \tag{55}$$

which, by use of the definition (23) for the money market account, says

$$P_{ab} = \hat{E}_a\left[\exp\left(-\int_a^b r_s\, ds\right)\right] \tag{56}$$

This is a very useful formula for the discount bond process, and for some purposes it can be regarded as a natural starting point for interest rate derivatives pricing.

Vasicek's model and subsequent developments

It is interesting to write down equation (56) in the original "natural" measure. By use of (25) and (31) we find

$$P_{ab} = E_a\left[\exp\left(-\int_a^b \lambda_s \, dW_s - \frac{1}{2}\int_a^b \lambda_s^2 \, ds\right)\exp\left(\int_a^b r_s \, ds\right)\right] \tag{57}$$

This formula appears in the pioneering article of Vasicek (1977), reprinted in this volume, in the section of his paper called "Stochastic representation of the bond price".

In fact, his result is derived in the special case of a short rate model, in which it is assumed (*a*) that there is a single source of noise, (*b*) that r_t follows a diffusion process and (*c*) that the bond price can be expressed as a function of r_t and t. He deduces the existence of a market premium of risk process by bond arbitrage arguments, along the same lines as we have discussed here, then derives a partial differential equation that has to be satisfied by the bond price. Finally he shows that the solution of the bond pricing equation is given by (57) above. It is an astonishing piece of work that still has a modern feel to it and anticipates in subtle ways many elements of what is to come in later developments in interest rate modelling and, indeed, derivatives pricing in general. Although his paper is entitled "An equilibrium characterisation of the term structure", no assumptions about equilibrium are actually made in the general arguments that make up the bulk of the exposition. Instead, he says at the outset that the development of his model is based on an arbitrage argument similar to that of Black and Scholes for option pricing. The equilibrium concept is introduced only at the end, almost as an afterthought, as "A special case". There he makes some strong simplifying assumptions and derives the famous constant-parameter model that now bears his name.

It is also interesting to note that Vasicek's paper, for all its accomplishments, does not actually address the problem of interest rate derivative valuation. His formulas include the market risk premium explicitly, and his theory is concerned exclusively with the valuation of bonds. And yet in formula (57) we are hovering on the brink of the change of measure argument – all the necessary ingredients are in place, but this last step is not taken. Ten years have to pass before we come to the work of Heath, Jarrow and Morton (not published until 1992), who succeed in putting together the pieces of the puzzle and build a general arbitrage-free model for discount bond dynamics and contingent claims valuation.

In the intervening years much of the work that was carried out continued more or less in the spirit of Vasicek's "special case", and a host of new interest rate models were constructed. Many of the key articles are reproduced in this volume. These include the well-known models of Brennan and Schwartz (1977), Cox, Ingersoll, and Ross (1985), Jamshidian (1987, 1989, 1991), Hull and White (1990), Black, Derman and Toy (1991) and Black and Karasinski (1991). In a lengthier volume we might have hoped to have incorporated a number of other articles as well, including some of the seminal work of Merton and papers such as those by Dothan (1978), Richard (1978), Courtadon (1982), Ball and Torous (1983), Jamshidian 1990, Beaglehole and Tenney (1991), Constantinides (1992), Babbs and Webber (1995), and Ritchken and Sankarasubramanian (1995).

If Vasicek's paper pays only a brief visit to the concept of equilibrium pricing, the influential work of Cox, Ingersoll, and Ross (1985) stands out in sharp contrast in its attempt to formulate a theory of interest rate dynamics within the foundations of equilibrium economics. In the course of doing so the paper takes potshots against arbitrage models and is rather casual in its approach to derivatives valuation. A close reading of the article suggests that the authors may have derived their famous model first and only later attempted to justify it by means of economic arguments.

Whatever the current status of the underlying equilibrium assumptions, the model itself remains of great interest for both theoretical and practical reasons, and important new work continues to be done on it (see, for example, Jamshidian, 1995, and Maghsoodi, 1996).

There is another respect in which the Cox–Ingersoll–Ross paper is of considerable historical interest, and this is that the authors study in some detail the question of what additional features arise when the drift term in the short rate process is given an essentially arbitrary time dependence, and they point out that the information contained in the term structure can be used to obtain the drift "without having to place prior restrictions on its functional form".

The point was not really taken up, and it was only some years later that Ho and Lee (1986) proposed in their celebrated paper, reprinted in this volume, a discrete-time model that allows for an essentially arbitrary specification of the initial yield. This development caught the wave of the rapidly growing interest rate derivative markets. Practitioners needed to calibrate models accurately to current market data – in particular, to the current yield curve. As a consequence a number of advances were made in quick succession, in some cases more or less simultaneously at separate institutions.

The so-called "extended Vasicek"-type models that were then developed, with time-dependent parameters allowing for flexible initial yield curve and volatility specification, have been especially influential on account of their analytical tractability and ease of implementation (Jamshidian, 1987; Hull and White, 1990). Lognormal short rate models, such as those of Black, Derman and Toy (1991) and Black and Karasinski (1991), though slightly awkward on account of their lack of analytical tractability, have enjoyed considerable success in trading rooms. The article by Duffie included in this volume presents a sophisticated and up-to-date overview of such state variable models.

Perhaps the most striking and influential advance in interest rate modelling over the last decade is represented by the work of Heath, Jarrow and Morton (1992). Their scheme, also pursued by Babbs (1990, 1996), is more aptly termed a framework than a model, since it amounts to a general theory for interest rate dynamics and the valuation of interest rate derivatives, allowing for an arbitrary initial yield curve specification and a very general volatility structure in a multi-factor setting. Interestingly, although the Heath–Jarrow–Morton (HJM) argument is based around consideration of the dynamics of the instantaneous forward rates, for which the relevant stochastic equation is

$$df_{ab} = \sigma_{ab}\,\Omega_{ab}\,da - \sigma_{ab}\,(dW_a + \lambda_a\,ds) \qquad (58)$$

it has emerged that it is not strictly necessary to start from this vantage point to obtain a consistent arbitrage-free theory. It suffices to start with the consideration of general discount bond dynamics, more or less as indicated earlier in this discussion. The resulting framework is essentially the same, though there remain numerous interesting questions, both practical and technical, relating to the specific assumptions that need to be made about the nature of the processes involved here. For further discussion along these lines see, for example, Rogers (1994), Hughston (1994), Carverhill (1995), Baxter (1997), Musiela and Rutkowski (1996), Hughston (1996), and Flesaker and Hughston (1997*a*,*b*).

The additional ingredient that Heath, Jarrow and Morton brought into play in their formulation of the interest rate dynamics problem, and which was missing in Vasicek's original arbitrage dynamics, is the change of measure argument. The body of technique associated with the change of measure idea represents perhaps the single most important conceptual development in mathematical economics of the last two decades. It is important to realise that under the no-arbitrage and market-completeness assumptions there is considerable flexibility in the choice of numeraire; the use of the money market account as numeraire, leading to the so-called risk-neutral measure, is only one such choice, albeit a convenient and natural one for many purposes. The use of a discount bond of fixed maturity as numeraire, for example, can be extremely useful both for theoretical considerations as well as for practical applications (see, for example, the article by Geman, El Karoui and Rochet, 1995, reprinted in the present volume, and references cited therein) and frequently finds its way into implementations.

The change of measure idea also plays a key role in the theoretical discussions and model constructions advanced recently by Brace, Gatarek and Musiela (1996), included in this collection. This work has attracted a good deal of attention on account of the way that it clarifies, and to some extent, justifies the use of the simple Black-style lognormal rate models in trading situations. Further details of their ingenious methods can be found in Musiela and Rutkowski (1996).

Another application of the change of measure technique can be found in this volume in the so-called "positive interest" approach advocated by Flesaker and Hughston (1996*a*), who give a general characterisation of the sub-class of HJM-type models for which interest rates are positive. In this approach interest rate models are specified in a natural way in terms of a one-parameter family of positive martingales.

Risky business

One of the most attractive features of the general interest rate framework is the readiness with respect to which other risky assets can be incorporated, particularly foreign currencies. Amin and Jarrow (1991, 1992) pioneered the approach to this problem in two significant papers, the second of which is reproduced in this volume. The basic interest rate model is extended to an international setting, where we now have a set of currencies and a system of interest rates associated with each currency.

A further development in this line is pursued in another paper by Flesaker and Hughston (1996*b*) in this volume, where they construct a general framework for interest rates and foreign exchange that builds in interest rate positivity for each currency in a natural way and brings out the inherent symmetries in the foreign exchange markets.

Once again the change of measure argument comes into play, as it does also in the empirical study, presented here, by Rogers and Zane (1996) who within the context of an equilibrium framework build on the work of Constantinides (1992), J. Saã-Requejo (1993), Rogers (1995), and others.

The essential idea of the Amin–Jarrow approach is to choose one of the currencies as the domestic currency and then to use the money market account in that currency as numeraire. The foreign discount bonds are viewed as risky assets, to be valued in the domestic currency. In the risk-neutral measure associated with the given choice of the domestic money market account as numeraire, the ratio of the value in domestic currency of a foreign discount bond to the value of the domestic money market account is a martingale. It follows that the domestic currency value of a foreign discount bond can be expressed as the product of its initial value, times the domestic money market account process, times an exponential martingale.

At maturity, the domestic value of a foreign discount bond is equal to the exchange rate at that time. Thus the exchange rate processes do not need to be introduced as separate ingredients. Dividing the domestic value processes for the foreign bonds by the exchange rate, we obtain processes for the foreign bonds as denominated in foreign currency. With this set-up one is then in a position to value international interest rate and foreign exchange derivatives. For this purpose a risk-neutral measure with respect to one of the currencies has been singled out, but the choice here is to some extent arbitrary and can be adjusted to suit the particular derivative structure that is being valued. The answer is, of course, independent of the choice of numeraire. An alternative, though essentially equivalent, formulation for the dynamics of interest rates and foreign exchange, based entirely on the "natural" measure, is described in Hughston (1996).

The Amin–Jarrow approach, although naturally adapted to the foreign exchange markets, is also applicable to other risky assets, such as stocks, commodities and risky debt. The last of these is significant both for the sake of modelling default risk and its consequences, as well as the valuation of credit derivatives and other credit-linked structures. See, for example, Lando (1994*a*,*b*), Jarrow, Lando and Turnbull (1994), Jarrow and Madan (1992), Jarrow and Turnbull (1995*a*,*b*), Flesaker, Hughston, Schreiber and Sprung (1994), Duffie, Schroder and Skiadas (1994), and Duffie and Singleton (1995).

Despite all the great advances that have been made in interest rate modelling over the last two decades, it has to be said that there is still no definitive model for interest rate dynamics. In practice many different models are used, and no one model has yet emerged as being clearly superior to the rest. I think most practitioners agree on this point. As a consequence there remains a great deal of work to be done, both at theoretical and practical levels. Although sophisticated general schemes are now available, such as the HJM framework, the process of model specialisation is much trickier. In particular, the issue of calibration looms large, and what seems to be lacking is a good mathematical characterisation of the factors that would determine just to what extent such a model should be calibrated. These considerations already apply in ideal circumstances, ie, where we ignore the effects of credit risk, liquidity factors, inflation and transaction costs. Once the latter are brought into play, we also have to bear in mind the possible implications of market incompleteness and unhedgeable stochastic volatility (see, eg, Lyons, 1995). In any case, there is certainly plenty of opportunity for exciting and potentially rewarding new research in these areas.

Bibliography

Amin, K. I., and R. Jarrow, 1991, "Pricing Foreign Currency Options under Stochastic Interest Rates", *Journal of International Money and Finance* 10, pp. 310-329.

Amin, K. I., and R. Jarrow, 1992, "Pricing Options and Risky Assets in a Stochastic Interest Rate Economy", *Mathematical Finance*, 2 (4), pp. 217-237; reprinted as Chapter 15 of the present volume.

Babbs, S., 1990, "The Term Structure of Interest Rates: Stochastic Processes and Contingent Claims", Ph.D. thesis, University of London.

Babbs, S., 1996, "A Family of Itô Process Models for the Term Structure of Interest Rates", Chapter 16 of the present volume.

Babbs, S., and N. Webber, 1995, "A Theory of the Term Structure with an Official Short Rate" (preprint).

Ball, C. A., and W. N. Torous, 1983, "Bond Price Dynamics and Options", *Journal of Financial and Quantitative Analysis* 18, pp. 517-31.

Baxter, M. W., 1997, "General Interest Rate Models and the Universality of HJM" in *Mathematics of Derivative Securities*, M. Dempster and S. Pliska, eds (Cambridge University Press).

Baxter, M. W., and A. Rennie, 1996, *Financial Calculus* (Cambridge University Press).

Beaglehole, D. R., and M. S. Tenney, 1991, "General Solutions to some Interest Rate Contingent Claim Pricing Equations", *Journal of Fixed Income* 1 (2).

Bensoussan, A., 1984, "On the Theory of Option Pricing", *Acta Applicandae Mathematicae* 2, pp. 139-158; reprinted as Chapter 3 of the present volume.

Berger, E., 1992, "Modelling Interest Rates: Fundamental Issues", *Bloomberg*, Nov. 1992, pp. 44-47.

Black, F., E. Derman and W. Toy, 1990, "A One-Factor Model of Interest Rates and its Application to Treasury Bond Options", *Financial Analysts Journal*, Jan.-Feb. 1990, pp. 33-39; reprinted as Chapter 10 of the present volume.

Black, F., and P. Karasinski, 1991, "Bond and Option Pricing when Short Rates are Lognormal", *Financial Analysts Journal*, July-Aug. 1991, pp. 52-59; reprinted as Chapter 11 of the present volume.

Black, F., and M. Scholes, 1973, "The Pricing of Options and Corporate Liabilities", *J. Political Economy* 81, pp. 637-654; reprinted as Chapter 1 of the present volume.

Brace, A., D. Gatarek and M. Musiela, 1996, "The Market Model of Interest Rate Dynamics", Chapter 19 of the present volume.

Brennan, M. J., and E. S. Schwartz, 1979, "A Continuous Time Approach to the Pricing of Bonds", *Journal of Banking and Finance* 3, 133-155; reprinted as Chapter 5 of the present volume.

Brown, R. H., and S. M. Schaefer, 1994, "The Term Structure of Interest Rates and the Cox, Ingersoll and Ross Model", *Journal of Financial Economics*, 35, pp. 3-42.

Carverhill, A., 1995, "A Simplified Exposition of the Heath, Jarrow, and Morton Model", *Stochastics and Stochastics Reports* 53, pp. 227-240.

Constantinides, G. M., 1992, "A Theory of the Nominal Term Structure of Interest Rates", *Review of Financial Studies* 5, pp. 531-552.

Courtadon, G., 1982, "The Pricing of Options on Default-Free Bonds", *Journal of Financial and Quantitative Analysis* 17, pp. 75-101.

Cox, J. C., J. E. Ingersoll, and S. A. Ross, 1985, "A Theory of the Term Structure of Interest Rates", *Econometrica* 53 (2), pp. 385–407; reprinted as Chapter 6 of the present volume.

Cox, J. C., S. A. Ross and M. Rubinstein, 1979, "Option Pricing: A Simplified Approach", *Journal of Financial Economics* 7, pp. 229–263; reprinted as Chapter 2 of the present volume.

Delbaen, F., and W. Schachermayer, 1994, "A General Version of the Fundamental Theorem of Asset Pricing, " *Mathematical Annals* 300, pp. 463–520.

de Munnik, J. F. J., 1996, *The Valuation of Interest Rate Derivative Securities* (Routledge).

Dothan, L. U., 1978, "On the Term Structure of Interest Rates", *Journal of Financial Economics* 6, pp. 59–69.

Dothan, L. U., 1990, *Prices in Financial Markets* (Oxford University Press).

Duffie, D., 1996*a*, *Dynamic Asset Pricing Theory*, Second edition (Princeton University Press).

Duffie, D., 1996*b*, "State-Space Models of the Term Structure of Interest Rates", Chapter 17 of the present volume.

Duffie, D., and R. Kan, 1994, "Multi-factor Term Structure Models", *Phil. Trans. Roy. Soc. Lond.* 347, pp. 577–586.

Duffie, D., M. Schroder and C. Skiadas, 1994, "Recursive Valuation of Defaultable Securities and the Timing of Resolution of Uncertainty" (working paper, Stanford and Northwestern Universities).

Duffie, D., and K. Singleton, 1995, "Econometric Modelling of the Term Structures of Defaultable Bonds" (working paper, Stanford University).

El Karoui N., H. Geman and J. C. Rochet, 1995, "Changes of Numeraire, Changes of Probability Measure and Option Pricing", *Journal of Applied Probability* 32, pp. 443–458; reprinted as Chapter 18 of the present volume.

Flesaker, B., L. P. Hughston, B. L. Schreiber and L. Sprung, 1994, "Taking All the Credit", *RISK* 7, (9) pp. 104–108. Reprinted in *Yearbook of Fixed Income Investing 1995*, J. D. Finnerty and M. S. Fridson, eds (Irwin Professional Publishing, 1996).

Flesaker, B., and L. P. Hughston, 1996*a*, "Positive Interest", *RISK* 9, 46–49; reprinted as Chapter 21 of the present volume.

Flesaker, B., and L. P. Hughston, 1996*b*, "Positive Interest: Foreign Exchange", Chapter 22 of the present volume.

Flesaker, B., and L. P. Hughston, 1997*a*, "Dynamic Models of Yield Curve Evolution", in *Mathematics of Derivative Securities*, M. Dempster and S. Pliska, eds (Cambridge University Press).

Flesaker, B., and L. P. Hughston, 1997*b*, "Exotic Interest Rate Options", in *Exotic Options: The State of the Art*, L. Clewlow and C. Strickland, eds (Chapman and Hall).

Harrison, J. M., and D. Kreps, 1979, "Martingales and Arbitrage in Multiperiod Securities Markets", *Journal of Economic Theory* 20, pp. 381–408.

Harrison, J. M., and S. R. Pliska, 1981, "Martingales and Stochastic Integrals in the Theory of Continuous Trading", *Stochastic Processes and their Applications*, 11, pp. 215–260.

Heath, D., R. Jarrow and A. Morton, 1992, "Bond Pricing and the Term Structure of Interest Rates: A New Methodology for Contingent Claims Valuation", *Econometrica* 60, pp. 77–105; reprinted as Chapter 14 of the present volume.

Ho, T. S. Y., 1995, "Evolution of Interest Rate Models: A Comparison", *Journal of Derivatives* 2 (4), pp. 9–20.

Ho, T. S. Y., and S. B. Lee, 1986, "Term Structure Movements and Pricing Interest Rate Contingent Claims", *Journal of Finance*, 41 (5), pp. 1011–1029; reprinted as Chapter 13 of the present volume.

Hughston, L. P., 1994, "Financial Observables", *International Derivative Review*, December 1994, pp. 11–14.

Hughston, L. P., 1996, "International Models for Interest Rates and Foreign Exchange" (working paper, Merrill Lynch).

Hull, J. C., 1996, *Options, Futures, and Other Derivatives,* Third edition (Prentice Hall).

Hull, J. C., and A. White, 1990, "Pricing Interest Rate Derivative Securities", *Review of Financial Studies*, 3 (4), pp. 573–592; reprinted as Chapter 9 of the present volume.

Jamshidian, F., 1987, "Pricing of Contingent Claims in the One Factor Term Structure Model" (working paper, Merrill Lynch); reprinted as Chapter 7 of the present volume.

Jamshidian, F., 1989, "An Exact Bond Option Formula", *Journal of Finance* 44, pp. 205-209; reprinted as Chapter 8 of the present volume.

Jamshidian, F., 1990, "The Preference-Free Determination of Bond and Option Prices from the Spot Rate", *Advances in Futures and Options Research*, 4, pp. 51-67.

Jamshidian, F., 1991, "Bond and Option Evaluation in the Gaussian Interest Rate Model", *Research in Finance* 9, pp. 131-170; reprinted as Chapter 12 of the present volume.

Jamshidian, F., 1995, "A Simple Class of Square-Root Interest Rate Models", *Applied Mathematical Finance* 2, pp. 61-72.

Jarrow, R., D. Lando and S. Turnbull, 1994, "A Markov Model for the Term Structure of Credit Risk Spreads" (working paper, Cornell University and Queen's University, Ontario).

Jarrow, R., and D. Madan, 1992, "Option Pricing Using the Term Structure of Interest Rates to Hedge Systematic Discontinuities in Asset Returns" (working paper, Cornell University and University of Maryland).

Jarrow, R., and S. Turnbull, 1995*a*, "Pricing Credit Risk, The Forex Analogy", in *Derivative Credit Risk* (*RISK* Publications), pp. 72-78.

Jarrow, R., and S. Turnbull, 1995*b*, "Pricing Derivatives on Financial Securities Subject to Credit Risk", *Journal of Finance*, 50 (1), pp. 53-85.

Karatzas, I., and S. Shreve, 1991, *Brownian Motion and Stochastic Calculus*, Second edition (Springer Verlag).

Kunita, H., and S. Watanabe, 1967, "On Square Integrable Martingales", *Nagoya Mathematics Journal* 30, pp. 209-245.

Lamberton, D., and B. Lapeyre, 1996, *Introduction to Stochastic Calculus in Applied Finance*, N. Rabeau and F. Mantion, translators (Chapman and Hall).

Lando, D., 1994*a*, *Three Essays on Contingent Claims Pricing*, Ph.D. thesis, Department of Statistics, Cornell University.

Lando, D., 1994*b*, "On Cox Processes and Credit Risky Bonds" (preprint, University of Copenhagen).

Lyons, T. J., 1995, "Uncertain Volatility and the Risk-Free Synthesis of Derivatives", *Applied Mathematical Finance* 2, pp. 117-133.

Maghsoodi, Y., 1996, "Solution of the Extended CIR Term Structure and Bond Option Valuation", *Mathematical Finance* 6 (1), pp. 89-109.

Musiela, M., and M. Rutkowski, 1996, *Arbitrage Pricing of Derivative Securities. Theory and Applications* (forthcoming).

Rebonato, R., 1996, "Interest Rate Option Models: A Critical Survey", in *The Handbook of Risk Management and Analysis,* C. Alexander, ed. (Wiley).

Rebonato, R., 1996, "Interest-Rate Option Models" (Wiley).

Richard, S., 1978, "An Arbitrage Model of the Term Structure of Interest Rates", *Journal of Financial Economics* 6, pp. 33-57.

Ritchken, P., and L. Sankarasubramanian, 1995, "Volatility Structure of Forward Rates and the Dynamics of the Term Structure", *Mathematical Finance* 5, pp. 55-72.

Rogers, L. C. G., 1994, "Which Model of the Term Structure of Interest Rates Should One Use?" *Mathematical Finance*, IMA volume 65, pp. 63-116 (Springer-Verlag).

Rogers, L. C. G., 1995, "The Potential Approach to the Term Structure of Interest Rates and Foreign Exchange Rates" (preprint, Bath University).

Rogers, L. C. G., and O. Zane, 1996, "Fitting Potential Models to Interest Rate and Foreign Exchange Data", Chapter 20 of the present volume.

Saã-Requejo, J., 1993, "The Dynamics and the Term Structure of Risk Premia in Foreign Exchange Markets" (preprint).

Smithson, C., and S. Song, 1996, "Extended Family I", *RISK* 10, pp. 19-21, and "Extended Family II", *RISK* 11, pp. 52-53.

Strickland, C., 1996, "A Comparison of Diffusion Models of the Term Structure" *European Journal of Finance* 2, pp. 103-123.

Vasicek, O. A., 1977, "An Equilibrium Characterisation of the Term Structure", *Journal of Financial Economics* 5, pp. 177-188; reprinted as Chapter 4 of the present volume.

I

OPTION PRICING FUNDAMENTALS

1

The Pricing of Options and Corporate Liabilities*

Fischer Black† and Myron Scholes
Long-Term Capital Management

If options are correctly priced in the market, it should not be possible to make definite profits by creating portfolios of long and short positions in options and their underlying stocks. Using this principle, a theoretical valuation formula for options is derived. Since almost all corporate liabilities can be viewed as combinations of options, the formula and the analysis that led to it are also applicable to corporate liabilities such as common stock, corporate bonds and warrants. In particular, the formula can be used to derive the discount that should be applied to a corporate bond due to the possibility of default.

An option is a security giving the right to buy or sell an asset, subject to certain conditions, within a specified period of time. An "American option" is one that can be exercised at any time up to the date the option expires. A "European option" is one that can be exercised only on a specified future date. The price that is paid for the asset when the option is exercised is called the "exercise price" or "striking price". The last day on which the option may be exercised is called the "expiration date" or "maturity date".

The simplest kind of option is one that gives the right to buy a single share of common stock. Throughout most of the paper, we will be discussing this kind of option, which is often referred to as a "call option".

In general, it seems clear that the higher the price of the stock, the greater the value of the option. When the stock price is much greater than the exercise price, the option is almost sure to be exercised. The current value of the option will thus be approximately equal to the price of the stock minus the price of a pure discount bond that matures on the same date as the option, with a face value equal to the striking price of the option.

On the other hand, if the price of the stock is much less than the exercise price, the option is almost sure to expire without being exercised, so its value will be near zero.

If the expiration date of the option is very far in the future, then the price of a bond that pays the exercise price on the maturity date will be very low, and the value of the option will be approximately equal to the price of the stock.

On the other hand, if the expiration date is very near, the value of the option will be approximately equal to the stock price minus the exercise price, or zero if the stock

This paper was first published in the Journal of Political Economy, *Vol. 81 (1973). It is reprinted with the permission of The University of Chicago Press. The inspiration for this work was provided by Jack L. Treynor (1961a, 1961b). We are grateful for extensive comments on earlier drafts by Eugene F. Fama, Robert C. Merton and Merton H. Miller. This work was supported in part by the Ford Foundation.*
†Fischer Black died in August 1995. Fischer Black, January 11, 1938–August 30, 1995.

price is less than the exercise price. Normally, the value of an option declines as its maturity date approaches, if the value of the stock does not change.

These general properties of the relation between the option value and the stock price are often illustrated in a diagram like Figure 1. Line *A* represents the maximum value of the option, since it cannot be worth more than the stock. Line *B* represents the minimum value of the option, since its value cannot be negative and cannot be less than the stock price minus the exercise price. Lines T_1, T_2, and T_3 represent the value of the option for successively shorter maturities.

Normally, the curve representing the value of an option will be concave upward. Since it also lies below the 45° line, *A*, we can see that the option will be more volatile than the stock. A given percentage change in the stock price, holding maturity constant, will result in a larger percentage change in the option value. The relative volatility of the option is not constant, however. It depends on both the stock price and maturity.

Most of the previous work on the valuation of options has been expressed in terms of warrants. For example, Sprenkle (1961), Ayres (1963), Boness (1964), Samuelson (1965), Baumol, Burton, and Quandt (1966), and Chen (1970) all produced valuation formulas of the same general form. Their formulas, however, were not complete, since they all involved one or more arbitrary parameters.

For example, Sprenkle's formula for the value of an option can be written as follows:

$$kxN(b_1) - k^*cN(b_2)$$

$$b_1 = \frac{\ln\frac{kx}{c} + \frac{1}{2}v^2(t^* - t)}{v\sqrt{t^* - t}}$$

$$b_2 = \frac{\ln\frac{kx}{c} - \frac{1}{2}v^2(t^* - t)}{v\sqrt{t^* - t}}$$

In this expression, x is the stock price, c is the exercise price, t^* is the maturity date, t is the current date, v^2 is the variance rate of the return on the stock,[1] $\ln$ is the natural logarithm, and $N(b)$ is the cumulative normal density function. But k and k^* are unknown parameters. Sprenkle (1961) defines k as the ratio of the expected value of the stock price at the time the warrant matures to the current stock price, and k^* as a discount factor that depends on the risk of the stock. He tries to estimate the values of k and k^* empirically, but finds that he is unable to do so.

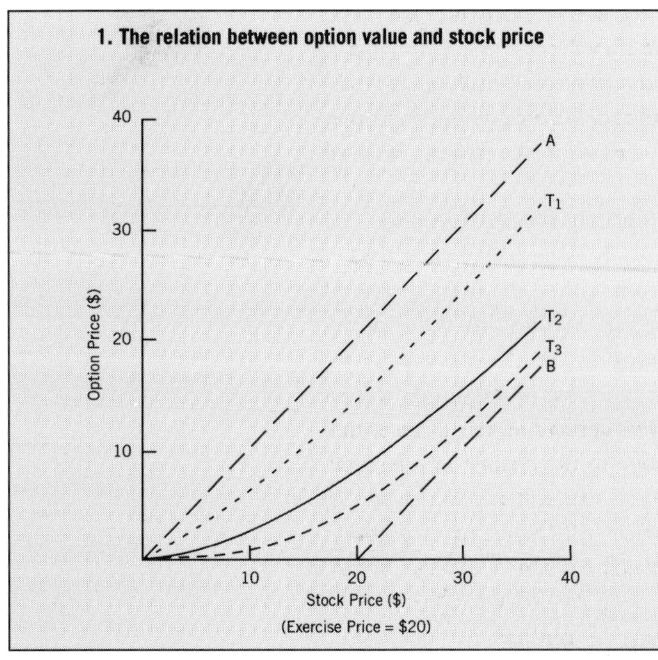

More typically, Samuelson (1965) has unknown parameters α and β, where α is the rate of expected return on the stock, and β is the rate of expected return on the warrant or the discount rate to be applied to the warrant.[2] He assumes that the distribution of possible values of the stock when the warrant matures is lognormal and takes the expected value of this distribution, cutting it off at the exercise price. He then discounts this expected value to the present at the rate β. Unfortunately, there seems to be no model of the pricing of securities under conditions of capital market equilibrium that would make this an appropriate procedure for determining the value of the warrant.

In a subsequent paper, Samuelson and Merton (1969) recognise the fact that discounting the expected value of the distribution of possible values of the warrant when it is exercised is not an appropriate procedure. They advance the theory by treating the option price as a function of the stock price. They also recognise that the discount rates are determined in part by the requirement that investors be willing to hold all of the outstanding amounts of both the stock and the option. But they do not make use of the fact that investors must hold other assets as well, so that the risk of an option or stock that affects its discount rate is only that part of the risk that cannot be diversified away. Their final formula depends on the shape of the utility function that they assume for the typical investor.

One of the concepts that we use in developing our model is expressed by Thorp and Kassouf (1967). They obtain an empirical valuation formula for warrants by fitting a curve to actual warrant prices. Then they use this formula to calculate the ratio of shares of stock to options needed to create a hedged position by going long in one security and short in the other. What they fail to pursue is the fact that in equilibrium, the expected return on such a hedged position must be equal to the return on a riskless asset. What we show below is that this equilibrium condition can be used to derive a theoretical valuation formula.

The valuation formula

In deriving our formula for the value of an option in terms of the price of the stock, we will assume "ideal conditions" in the market for the stock and for the option:

a) The short-term interest rate is known and is constant through time.
b) The stock price follows a random walk in continuous time with a variance rate proportional to the square of the stock price. Thus the distribution of possible stock prices at the end of any finite interval is lognormal. The variance rate of the return on the stock is constant.
c) The stock pays no dividends or other distributions.
d) The option is "European", that is, it can only be exercised at maturity.
e) There are no transaction costs in buying or selling the stock or the option.
f) It is possible to borrow any fraction of the price of a security to buy it or to hold it, at the short-term interest rate.
g) There are no penalties to short selling. A seller who does not own a security will simply accept the price of the security from a buyer, and will agree to settle with the buyer on some future date by paying him an amount equal to the price of the security on that date.

Under these assumptions, the value of the option will depend only on the price of the stock and time and on variables that are taken to be known constants. Thus, it is possible to create a hedged position, consisting of a long position in the stock and a short position in the option, whose value will not depend on the price of the stock, but will depend only on time and the values of known constants. Writing $w(x,t)$ for the value of the option as a function of the stock price x and time t, the number of options that must be sold short against one share of stock long is:

$$\frac{1}{w_1(x,t)} \qquad (1)$$

In expression (1), the subscript refers to the partial derivative of $w(x,t)$ with respect to its first argument.

To see that the value of such a hedged position does not depend on the price of the stock, note that the ratio of the change in the option value to the change in the stock price, when the change in the stock price is small, is $w_1(x,t)$. To a first approximation, if the stock price changes by an amount Δx, the option price will change by an amount $w_1(x,t)\Delta x$, and the number of options given by expression (1) will change by an amount Δx. Thus, the change in the value of a long position in the stock will be approximately offset by the change in value of a short position in $1/w_1$ options.

As the variables x and t change, the number of options to be sold short to create a hedged position with one share of stock changes. If the hedge is maintained continuously, then the approximations mentioned above become exact, and the return on the hedged position is completely independent of the change in the value of the stock. In fact, the return on the hedged position becomes certain.[3]

To illustrate the formation of the hedged position, let us refer to the solid line (T_2) in Figure 1 and assume that the price of the stock starts at \$15.00, so that the value of the option starts at \$5.00. Assume also that the slope of the line at that point is $\frac{1}{2}$. This means that the hedged position is created by buying one share of stock and selling two options short. One share of stock costs \$15.00, and the sale of two options brings in \$10.00, so the equity in this position is \$5.00.

If the hedged position is not changed as the price of the stock changes, then there is some uncertainty in the value of the equity at the end of a finite interval. Suppose that two options go from \$10.00 to \$15.75 when the stock goes from \$15.00 to \$20.00, and that they go from \$10.00 to \$5.75 when the stock goes from \$15.00 to \$10.00. Thus, the equity goes from \$5.00 to \$4.25 when the stock changes by \$5.00 in either direction. This is a \$0.75 decline in the equity for a \$5.00 change in the stock in either direction.[4]

In addition, the curve shifts (say from T_2 to T_3 in Figure 1) as the maturity of the options changes. The resulting decline in value of the options means an increase in the equity in the hedged position and tends to offset the possible losses due to a large change in the stock price.

Note that the decline in the equity value due to a large change in the stock price is small. The ratio of the decline in the equity value to the magnitude of the change in the stock price becomes smaller as the magnitude of the change in the stock price becomes smaller. Note also that the direction of the change in the equity value is independent of the direction of the change in the stock price. This means that under our assumption that the stock price follows a continuous random walk and that the return has a constant variance rate, the covariance between the return on the equity and the return on the stock will be zero. If the stock price and the value of the "market portfolio" follow a joint continuous random walk with constant covariance rate, it means that the covariance between the return on the equity and the return on the market will be zero.

Thus the risk in the hedged position is zero if the short position in the option is adjusted continuously. If the position is not adjusted continuously, the risk is small, and consists entirely of risk that can be diversified away by forming a portfolio of a large number of such hedged positions.

In general, since the hedged position contains one share of stock long and $1/w_1$ options short, the value of the equity in the position is:

$$x - \frac{w}{w_1} \tag{2}$$

The change in the value of the equity in a short interval Δt is:

$$\Delta x - \frac{\Delta w}{w_1} \tag{3}$$

Assuming that the short position is changed continuously, we can use stochastic calculus[5] to expand Δw, which is $w(x+\Delta x, t+\Delta t) - w(x,t)$, as follows:

$$\Delta w = w_1 \Delta x + \tfrac{1}{2} w_{11} v^2 x^2 \Delta t + w_2 \Delta t \tag{4}$$

In equation (4), the subscripts on w refer to partial derivatives, and v^2 is the variance rate of the return on the stock.[6] Substituting from equation (4) into expression (3), we find that the change in the value of the equity in the hedged position is:

$$-\left(\tfrac{1}{2} w_{11} v^2 x^2 + w_2\right) \frac{\Delta t}{w_1} \tag{5}$$

Since the return on the equity in the hedged position is certain, the return must be equal to $r\Delta t$. Even if the hedged position is not changed continuously, its risk is small and entirely risk that can be diversified away, so the expected return on the hedged position must be at the short-term interest rate.[7] If this were not true, speculators would try to profit by borrowing large amounts of money to create such hedged positions, and would in the process force the returns down to the short-term interest rate.

Thus the change in the equity (5) must equal the value of the equity (2) times $r\Delta t$.

$$-\left(\tfrac{1}{2}w_{11}v^2x^2 + w_2\right)\frac{\Delta t}{w_1} = \left(x - \frac{w}{w_1}\right)r\Delta t \tag{6}$$

Dropping the Δt from both sides, and rearranging, we have a differential equation for the value of the option.

$$w_2 = rw - rxw_1 - \tfrac{1}{2}v^2x^2w_{11} \tag{7}$$

Writing t^* for the maturity date of the option and c for the exercise price, we know that:

$$\begin{aligned} w(x, t^*) &= x - c \qquad x \geq c \\ &= 0 \qquad x < c \end{aligned} \tag{8}$$

There is only one formula $w(x,t)$ that satisfies the differential equation (7) subject to the boundary condition (8). This formula must be the option valuation formula.

To solve this differential equation, we make the following substitution:

$$\begin{aligned} w(x,t) = e^{r(t-t^*)}y &\left\{\left(\frac{2}{v^2}\right)\left(r - \tfrac{1}{2}v^2\right)\left[\ln\frac{x}{c} - \left(r - \tfrac{1}{2}v^2\right)(t-t^*)\right] - \right. \\ &\left. \left(\frac{2}{v^2}\right)\left(r - \tfrac{1}{2}v^2\right)^2(t-t^*)\right\} \end{aligned} \tag{9}$$

With this substitution, the differential equation becomes:

$$y_2 = y_{11} \tag{10}$$

and the boundary condition becomes:

$$\begin{aligned} y(u,0) &= 0 && u < 0 \\ &= c\left[e^{u\left(\frac{1}{2}v^2\right)/\left(r-\frac{1}{2}v^2\right)} - 1\right] && u \geq 0 \end{aligned} \tag{11}$$

The differential equation (10) is the heat-transfer equation of physics, and its solution is given by Churchill (1963, p. 155). In our notation, the solution is:

$$y(u,s) = \frac{1}{\sqrt{2\pi}}\int_{\frac{-u}{\sqrt{2s}}}^{\infty} c\left[e^{\left(u+q\sqrt{2s}\right)\left(\frac{1}{2}v^2\right)/\left(r-\frac{1}{2}v^2\right)} - 1\right]e^{\frac{-q^2}{2}}\,dq \tag{12}$$

Substituting from equation (12) into equation (9), and simplifying, we find:

$$\begin{aligned} w(x,t) &= xN(d_1) - ce^{r(t-t^*)}N(d_2) \\ d_1 &= \frac{\ln\frac{x}{c} + \left(r + \frac{1}{2}v^2\right)(t^* - t)}{v\sqrt{t^* - t}} \\ d_2 &= \frac{\ln\frac{x}{c} + \left(r - \frac{1}{2}v^2\right)(t^* - t)}{v\sqrt{t^* - t}} \end{aligned} \tag{13}$$

In equation (13), $N(d)$ is the cumulative normal density function.

Note that the expected return on the stock does not appear in equation (13). The option value as a function of the stock price is independent of the expected return on the stock. The expected return on the option, however, will depend on the expected return on the stock. The faster the stock price rises, the faster the option price will rise through the functional relationship (13).

Note that the maturity $(t^* - t)$ appears in the formula only multiplied by the interest rate r or the variance rate v^2. Thus, an increase in maturity has the same effect on the value of the option as an equal percentage increase in both r and v^2.

Merton (1973) has shown that the option value as given by equation (13) increases continuously as any one of t^*, r, or v^2 increases. In each case, it approaches a maximum value equal to the stock price.

The partial derivative w_1 of the valuation formula is of interest, because it determines the ratio of shares of stock to options in the hedged position as in expression (1). Taking the partial derivative of equation (13), and simplifying, we find that:

$$w_1(x, t) = N(d_1) \tag{14}$$

In equation (14), d_1 is as defined in equation (13).

From equations (13) and (14), it is clear that xw_1/w is always greater than one. This shows that the option is always more volatile than the stock.

An alternative derivation

It is also possible to derive the differential equation (7) using the "capital-asset pricing model". This derivation is given because it gives more understanding of the way in which one can discount the value of an option to the present, using a discount rate that depends on both time and the price of the stock.

The capital-asset pricing model describes the relation between risk and expected return for a capital asset under conditions of market equilibrium.[8] The expected return on an asset gives the discount that must be applied to the end-of-period value of the asset to give its present value. Thus, the capital-asset pricing model gives a general method for discounting under uncertainty.

The capital-asset pricing model says that the expected return on an asset is a linear function of its β, which is defined as the covariance of the return on the asset with the return on the market, divided by the variance of the return on the market. From equation (4) we see that the covariance of the return on the option $\Delta w/w$ with the return on the market is equal to xw_1/w times the covariance of the return on the stock $\Delta x/x$ with the return on the market. Thus, we have the following relation between the option's β and the stock's β:

$$\beta_w = \left(\frac{xw_1}{w}\right)\beta_x \tag{15}$$

The expression xw_1/w may also be interpreted as the "elasticity" of the option price with respect to the stock price. It is the ratio of the percentage change in the option price to the percentage change in the stock price, for small percentage changes, holding maturity constant.

To apply the capital-asset pricing model to an option and the underlying stock, let us first define a as the rate of expected return on the market minus the interest rate.[9] Then the expected returns on the option and the stock are:

$$E\left(\frac{\Delta x}{x}\right) = r\Delta t + a\beta_x \Delta t \tag{16}$$

$$E\left(\frac{\Delta w}{w}\right) = r\Delta t + a\beta_w \Delta t \tag{17}$$

Multiplying equation (17) by w, and substituting for β_w from equation (15), we find:

$$E(\Delta w) = rw\Delta t + axw_1 \beta_x \Delta t \tag{18}$$

Using stochastic calculus,[10] we can expand Δw, which is $w(x + \Delta x, t + \Delta t) - w(x, t)$, as follows:

$$\Delta w = w_1 \Delta x + \tfrac{1}{2} w_{11} v^2 x^2 \Delta t + w_2 \Delta t \tag{19}$$

Taking the expected value of equation (19), and substituting for $E\Delta(x)$ from equation (16), we have:

$$E(\Delta w) = rxw_1 \Delta t + axw_1 \beta_x \Delta t + \tfrac{1}{2} v^2 x^2 w_{11} \Delta t + w_2 \Delta t \tag{20}$$

Combining equations (18) and (20), we find that the terms involving a and β_x cancel, giving:

$$w_2 = rw - rxw_1 - \tfrac{1}{2} v^2 x^2 w_{11} \tag{21}$$

Equation (21) is the same as equation (7).

More complicated options

The valuation formula (13) was derived under the assumption that the option can only be exercised at time t*. Merton (1973) has shown, however, that the value of the option is always greater than the value it would have if it were exercised immediately $(x - c)$. Thus, a rational investor will not exercise a call option before maturity, and the value of an American call option is the same as the value of a European call option.

There is a simple modification of the formula that will make it applicable to European put options (options to sell) as well as call options (options to buy). Writing $u(x, t)$ for the value of a put option, we see that the differential equation remains unchanged.

$$u_2 = ru - rxu_1 - \tfrac{1}{2} v^2 x^2 u_{11} \tag{22}$$

The boundary condition, however, becomes:

$$\begin{aligned} u(x, t^*) &= 0 & x \geq c \\ &= c - x & x < c \end{aligned} \tag{23}$$

To get the solution to this equation with the new boundary condition, we can simply note that the difference between the value of a call and the value of a put on the same stock, if both can be exercised only at maturity, must obey the same differential equation, but with the following boundary condition:

$$w(x, t^*) - u(x, t^*) = x - c \tag{24}$$

The solution to the differential equation with this boundary condition is:

$$w(x, t) - u(x, t) = x - ce^{r(t - t^*)} \tag{25}$$

Thus the value of the European put option is:

$$u(x, t) = w(x, t) - x + ce^{r(t - t^*)} \tag{26}$$

Putting in the value of $w(x,t)$ from (13), and noting that $1 - N(d)$ is equal to $N(-d)$, we have:

$$u(x,t) = -xN(-d_1) + ce^{-rt^*}N(-d_2) \tag{27}$$

In equation (27), d_1 and d_2 are defined as in equation (13).

Equation (25) also gives us a relation between the value of a European call and the value of a European put.[11] We see that if an investor were to call buy a call and sell a put, his returns would be exactly the same as if he bought the stock on margin, borrowing $ce^{r(t-t^*)}$ towards the price of the stock.

Merton (1973) has also shown that the value of an American put option will be greater than the value of a European put option. This is true because it is sometimes advantageous to exercise a put option before maturity, if it is possible to do so. For example, suppose the stock price falls almost to zero and that the probability that the price will exceed the exercise price before the option expires is negligible. Then it will pay to exercise the option immediately, so that the exercise price will be received sooner rather than later. The investor thus gains the interest on the exercise price for the period up to the time he would otherwise have exercised it. So far, no one has been able to obtain a formula for the value of an American put option [see Brennan and Schwartz (1977)].

If we relax the assumption that the stock pays no dividend, we begin to get into some complicated problems. First of all, under certain conditions it will pay to exercise an American call option before maturity. Merton (1973) has shown that this can be true only just before the stock's ex-dividend date. Also, it is not clear what adjustment might be made in the terms of the option to protect the option holder against a loss due to a large dividend on the stock and to ensure that the value of the option will be the same as if the stock paid no dividend. Currently, the exercise price of a call option is generally reduced by the amount of any dividend paid on the stock. We can see that this is not adequate protection by imagining that the stock is that of a holding company and that it pays out all of its assets in the form of a dividend to its shareholders. This will reduce the price of the stock and the value of the option to zero, no matter what adjustment is made in the exercise price of the option. In fact, this example shows that there may not be any adjustment in the terms of the option that will give adequate protection against a large dividend. In this case, the option value is going to be zero after the distribution, no matter what its terms are. Merton (1973) was the first to point out that the current adjustment for dividends is not adequate.

Warrant valuation

A warrant is an option that is a liability of a corporation. The holder of a warrant has the right to buy the corporation's stock (or other assets) on specified terms. The analysis of warrants is often much more complicated than the analysis of simple options, because:

a) The life of a warrant is typically measured in years, rather than months. Over a period of years, the variance rate of the return on the stock may be expected to change substantially.

b) The exercise price of the warrant is usually not adjusted at all for dividends. The possibility that dividends will be paid requires a modification of the valuation formula.

c) The exercise price of a warrant sometimes changes on specified dates. It may pay to exercise a warrant just before its exercise price changes. This too requires a modification of the valuation formula.

d) If the company is involved in a merger, the adjustment that is made in the terms of the warrant may change its value.

e) Sometimes the exercise price can be paid using bonds of the corporation at face value, even though they may at the time be selling at a discount. This complicates the analysis and means that early exercise may sometimes be desirable.

f) The exercise of a large number of warrants may sometimes result in a significant increase in the number of common shares outstanding.

In some cases, these complications can be treated as insignificant, and equation (13) can be used as an approximation to give an estimate of the warrant value. In other cases, some simple modifications of equation (13) will improve the approximation. Suppose, for example, that there are warrants outstanding, which, if exercised, would double the number of shares of the company's common stock. Let us define the "equity" of the company as the sum of the value of all of its warrants and the value of all of its common stock. If the warrants are exercised at maturity, the equity of the company will increase by the aggregate amount of money paid in by the warrant holders when they exercise. The warrant holders will then own half of the new equity of the company, which is equal to the old equity plus the exercise money.

Thus, at maturity, the warrant holders will either receive nothing, or half of the new equity, minus the exercise money. Thus, they will receive nothing or half of the difference between the old equity and half the exercise money. We can look at the warrants as options to buy shares in the equity rather than shares of common stock, at half the stated exercise price rather than at the full exercise price. The value of a share in the equity is defined as the sum of the value of the warrants and the value of the common stock, divided by twice the number of outstanding shares of common stock. If we take this point of view, then we will take v^2 in equation (13) to be the variance rate of the return on the company's equity, rather than the variance rate of the return on the company's common stock.

A similar modification in the parameters of equation (13) can be made if the number of shares of stock outstanding after exercise of the warrants will be other than twice the number of shares outstanding before exercise of the warrants.

Common stock and bond valuation

It is not generally realised that corporate liabilities other than warrants may be viewed as options. Consider, for example, a company that has common stock and bonds outstanding and whose only asset is shares of common stock of a second company. Suppose that the bonds are "pure discount bonds" with no coupon, giving the holder the right to a fixed sum of money, if the corporation can pay it, with a maturity of 10 years. Suppose that the bonds contain no restrictions on the company except a restriction that the company cannot pay any dividends until after the bonds are paid off. Finally, suppose that the company plans to sell all the stock it holds at the end of 10 years, pay off the bond holders if possible, and pay any remaining money to the stockholders as a liquidating dividend.

Under these conditions, it is clear that the stockholders have the equivalent of an option on their company's assets. In effect, the bond holders own the company's assets, but they have given options to the stockholders to buy the assets back. The value of the common stock at the end of 10 years will be the value of the company's assets minus the face value of the bonds, or zero, whichever is greater.

Thus, the value of the common stock will be $w(x, t)$, as given by equation (13), where we take v^2 to be the variance rate of the return on the shares held by the company, c to be the total face value of the outstanding bonds, and x to be the total value of the shares held by the company. The value of the bonds will simply be $x - w(x, t)$.

By subtracting the value of the bonds given by this formula from the value they would have if there were no default risk, we can figure the discount that should be applied to the bonds due to the existence of default risk.

Suppose, more generally, that the corporation holds business assets rather than financial assets. Suppose that at the end of the 10-year period, it will recapitalise by selling an entirely new class of common stock, using the proceeds to pay off the bond holders, and paying any money that is left to the old stockholders to retire their stock. In the absence of taxes, it is clear that the value of the corporation can be taken to be the sum of the total value of the debt and the total value of the common stock.[12] The amount of debt outstanding will not affect the total value of the corporation, but will affect the division of that value between the bonds and the stock. The formula for $w(x, t)$ will again describe the total value of the common stock, where x is taken to be the sum of the value of the bonds and the value of the stock. The formula for $x - w(x, t)$ will again describe the total value of the bonds. It can be shown that, as the face value c of the bonds increases, the market value $x - w(x, t)$ increases by a smaller percentage. An increase in the corporation's debt, keeping the total value of the corporation constant, will increase the probability of default and will thus reduce the market value of one of the corporation's bonds. If the company changes its capital structure by issuing more bonds and using the proceeds to retire common stock, it will hurt the existing bond holders, and help the existing stockholders. The bond price will fall, and the stock price will rise. In this sense, changes in the capital structure of a firm may affect the price of its common stock.[13] The price changes will occur when the change in the capital structure becomes certain, not when the actual change takes place.

Because of this possibility, the bond indenture may prohibit the sale of additional debt of the same or higher priority in the event that the firm is recapitalised. If the corporation issues new bonds that are subordinated to the existing bonds and uses the proceeds to retire common stock, the price of the existing bonds and the common stock price will be unaffected. Similarly, if the company issues new common stock and uses the proceeds to retire completely the most junior outstanding issue of bonds, neither the common stock price nor the price of any other issue of bonds will be affected.

The corporation's dividend policy will also affect the division of its total value between the bonds and the stock.[14] To take an extreme example, suppose again that the corporation's only assets are the shares of another company, and suppose that it sells all these shares and uses the proceeds to pay a dividend to its common stockholders. Then the value of the firm will go to zero, and the value of the bonds will go to zero. The common stockholders will have "stolen" the company out from under the bond holders. Even for dividends of modest size, a higher dividend always favours the stockholders at the expense of the bond holders. A liberalisation of dividend policy will increase the common stock price and decrease the bond price.[15] Because of this possibility, bond indentures contain restrictions on dividend policy, and the common stockholders have an incentive to pay themselves the largest dividend allowed by the terms of the bond indenture. However, it should be noted that the size of the effect of changing dividend policy will normally be very small.

If the company has coupon bonds rather than pure discount bonds outstanding, then we can view the common stock as a "compound option". The common stock is an option on an option on … an option on the firm. After making the last interest payment, the stockholders have an option to buy the company from the bond holders for the face value of the bonds. Call this "option 1". After making the next-to-the-last interest payment, but before making the last interest payment, the stockholders have an option to buy option 1 by making the last interest payment. Call this "option 2". Before making the next-to-the-last interest payment, the stockholders have an option to buy option 2 by making that interest payment. This is "option 3". The value of the stockholders' claim at any point in time is equal to the value of option $n + 1$, where n is the number of interest payments remaining in the life of the bond.

If payments to a sinking fund are required along with interest payments, then a similar analysis can be made. In this case, there is no "balloon payment" at the end of the life of the bond. The sinking fund will have a final value equal to the face value of the bond. Option 1 gives the stockholders the right to buy the company from the bond holders by making the last sinking fund and interest payment. Option 2 gives the stockholders the right to buy option 1 by making the next-to-the-last sinking fund and interest payment. And the value of the stockholders' claim at any point in time is equal to the value of option n, where n is the number of sinking fund and interest payments remaining in the life of the bond. It is clear that the value of a bond for which sinking fund payments are required is greater than the value of a bond for which they are not required.

If the company has callable bonds, then the stockholders have more than one option. They can buy the next option by making the next interest or sinking fund and interest payment, or they can exercise their option to retire the bonds before maturity at prices specified by the terms of the call feature. Under our assumption of a constant short-term interest rate, the bonds would never sell above face value, and the usual kind of call option would never be exercised. Under more general assumptions, however, the call feature would have value to the stockholders and would have to be taken into account in deciding how the value of the company is divided between the stockholders and the bond holders.

Similarly, if the bonds are convertible, we simply add another option to the package. It is an option that the bond holders have to buy part of the company from the stockholders.

Unfortunately, these more complicated options cannot be handled by using the valuation formula (13). The valuation formula assumes that the variance rate of the return on the optioned asset is constant. But the variance of the return on an option is certainly not constant: it depends on the price of the stock and the maturity of the option. Thus the formula cannot be used, even as an approximation, to give the value of an option on an option. It is possible, however, that an analysis in the same spirit as the one that led to equation (13) would allow at least a numerical solution to the valuation of certain more complicated options.

Empirical tests

We have done empirical tests of the valuation formula on a large body of call-option data (Black and Scholes 1972). These tests indicate that the actual prices at which options are bought and sold deviate in certain systematic ways from the values predicted by the formula. Option buyers pay prices that are consistently higher than those predicted by the formula. Option writers, however, receive prices that are at about the level predicted by the formula. There are large transaction costs in the option market, all of which are effectively paid by option buyers.

Also, the difference between the price paid by option buyers and the value given by the formula is greater for options on low-risk stocks than for options on high-risk stocks. The market appears to underestimate the effect of differences in variance rate on the value of an option. Given the magnitude of the transaction costs in this market, however, this systemic misestimation of value does not imply profit opportunities for a speculator in the option market.

1 *The variance rate of the return on a security is the limit, as the size of the interval of measurement goes to zero, of the variance of the return over that interval divided by the length of the interval.*

2 *The rate of expected return on a security is the limit, as the size of the interval of measurement goes to zero, of the expected return over that interval divided by the length of the interval.*

3 *This was pointed out to us by Robert Merton.*

4 *These figures are purely for illustrative purposes. They correspond roughly to the way Figure 1 was drawn, but not to an option on any actual security.*

5 *For an exposition of stochastic calculus, see McKean (1969).*

6 *See footnote 1.*

7 *For a thorough discussion of the relation between risk and expected return, see Fama and Miller (1972) or Sharpe (1970). To see that the risk in the hedged position can be diversified away, note that if we don't adjust the hedge continuously, expression (5) becomes:*

$$\frac{-\left(\frac{1}{2} w_{11} \Delta x^2 + w_2 \Delta t\right)}{w_1} \qquad (5')$$

Writing Δm for the change in the value of the market portfolio between t and $t + \Delta t$, the "market risk" in the hedged position is proportional to the covariance between the change in the value of the hedged *portfolio, as given by expression (5′), and* $\Delta m : -\frac{1}{2}\Delta w_{11} \text{cov}(\Delta x^2, \Delta m)$. *But if* Δx *and* Δm *follow a joint distribution for small intervals* Δt, *this covariance will be zero. Since there is no market risk in the hedged position, all of the risk due to the fact that the hedge is not continuously adjusted must be risk that can be diversified away.*

8 *The model was developed by Treynor (1961b), Sharpe (1964), Lintner (1965), and Mossin (1966). It is summarised by Sharpe (1970), and Fama and Miller (1972). The model was originally stated as a single-period model. Extending it to a multi-period model is, in general, difficult. Fama (1970), however, has shown that if we make an assumption that implies that the short-term interest rate is constant through time, then the model must apply to each successive period in time. His proof also goes through under somewhat more general assumptions.*

9 *See footnote 2.*

10 *For an exposition of stochastic calculus, see McKean (1969).*

11 *The relation between the value of a call option and the value of a put option was first noted by Stoll (1969). He does not realise, however, that his analysis applies only to European options.*

12 *The fact that the total value of a corporation is not affected by its capital structure, in the absence of taxes and other imperfections, was first shown by Modigliani and Miller (1958).*

13 *For a discussion of this point, see Fama and Miller (1972, pp. 151–52).*

14 *Miller and Modigliani (1961) show that the total value of a firm, in the absence of taxes and other imperfections, is not affected by its dividend policy. They also note that the price of the common stock and the value of the bonds will not be affected by a change in dividend policy if the funds for a higher dividend are raised by issuing common stock or if the money released by a lower dividend is used to repurchase common stock.*

15 *This is true assuming that the liberalisation of dividend policy is not accompanied by a change in the company's current and planned financial structure. Since the issue of common stock or junior debt will hurt the common shareholders (holding dividend policy constant), they will normally try to liberalise dividend policy without issuing new securities. They may be able to do this by selling some of the firm's financial assets, such as ownership claims on other firms. Or they may be able to do it by adding to the company's short-term bank debt, which is normally senior to its long-term debt. Finally, the company may be able to finance a higher dividend by selling off a division. Assuming that it receives a fair price for the division, and that there were no economies of combination, this need not involve any loss to the firm as a whole. If the firm issues new common stock or junior debt in exactly the amounts needed to finance the liberalisation of dividend policy, then the common stock and bond prices will be affected. If the liberalisation of dividend policy is associated with a decision to issue more common stock or junior debt than is needed to pay the higher dividends, the common stock price will fall and the bond price will rise. But these actions are unlikely, since they are not in the stockholders' best interests.*

Bibliography

Ayres, H. F., 1963, "Risk Aversion in the Warrants Market", *Industrial Management Review* 4, Fall 1963, pp. 497–505.

Baumol, W. J., G. M. Burton and R. E. Quandt, 1966, "The Valuation of Convertible Securities", *Quarterly Journal of Economics* 80, February 1966, pp. 48–59.

Black, F., and M. Scholes, 1972, "The Valuation of Option Contracts and a Test of Market Efficiency", *Journal of Finance* May 1972, pp. 399–417.

Boness, A. J., 1964, "Elements of a Theory of Stock-Option Values", *Journal of Political Economy* 72, April 1964, pp. 163–75.

Brennan, M. J., and E. S. Schwartz, 1977, "The Valuation of American Put Options", *Journal of Finance* 32, pp. 449–62.

Chen, A. H. Y., 1970, "A Model of Warrant Pricing in a Dynamic Market", *Journal of Finance* December 1970, pp. 1041–60.

Churchill, R. V., 1963, *Fourier Series and Boundary Value Problems*, 2nd ed. New York: McGraw-Hill.

Cootner, Paul A., 1967, *The Random Character of Stock Market Prices*, Cambridge, Mass.: M.I.T. Press.

Fama, E. F., 1970, "Multiperiod Consumption-Investment Decisions", *A.E.R.* 60, March 1970, pp. 163–74.

Fama, E. F., and M. H. Miller, 1972, *The Theory of Finance*, New York: Holt, Rinehart & Winston.

Lintner, J., 1965, "The Valuation of Risk Assets and the Selection of Risky Investments in Stock Portfolios and Capital Budgets", *Review of Economics and Statistics* 47, February 1965, pp. 768–83.

McKean, H. P., Jr., *Stochastic Integrals*, New York: Academic Press, 1969.

Merton, R. C., 1973, "Theory of Rational Option Pricing", *Bell Journal of Economic and Management Science* 4, pp. 141–83.

Miller, M. H., and F. Modigliani, "Dividend Policy, Growth, and the Valuation of Shares", *Journal of Business* 34, October 1961, pp. 411–33.

Modigliani, F., and M. H. Miller, 1958, "The Cost of Capital, Corporation Finance, and the Theory of Investment", *A.E.R.* 48, June 1958, pp. 261–97.

Mossin, J., 1966, "Equilibrium in a Capital Asset Market", *Econometrica* 34, October 1966, pp. 768–83.

Samuelson, P. A., 1965, "Rational Theory of Warrant Pricing", *Industrial Management Review* 6, Spring 1965, pp. 13–31. Reprinted in Cootner (1967), pp. 506–32.

Samuelson, P. A., and R. C. Merton, 1969, "A Complete Model of Warrant Pricing that Maximizes Utility", *Industrial Management Review* 10, Winter 1969, pp. 17–46.

Sharpe, W. F., 1964, "Capital Asset Prices: A Theory of Market Equilibrium Under Conditions of Risk", *Journal of Finance* 19, September 1964, pp. 425–42.

Sharpe, W. F., 1970, *Portfolio Theory and Capital Markets*, New York: McGraw-Hill.

Sprenkle, C., 1961, "Warrant Prices as Indications of Expectation", *Yale Economic Essays* 1, 1961, pp. 179–232. Reprinted in Cootner (1967), pp. 412–74.

Stoll, H. R, 1969, "The Relationship Between Put and Call Option Prices", *Journal of Finance* 24, December 1969, pp. 802–24.

Thorp, E. O., and S. T. Kassouf, 1967, *Beat the Market*, New York: Random House.

Treynor, J. L., 1961*a*, "Implications for the Theory of Finance", Unpublished memorandum.

Treynor, J. L., 1961*b*, "Toward a Theory of Market Value of Risky Assets", Unpublished memorandum.

2

Option Pricing: A Simplified Approach*

John C. Cox, Stephen A. Ross and Mark Rubinstein
Massachusetts Institute of Technology; Yale University; University of California at Berkeley

This paper presents a simple discrete-time model for valuing options. The fundamental economic principles of option pricing by arbitrage methods are particularly clear in this setting. Its development requires only elementary mathematics, yet it contains as a special limiting case the celebrated Black–Scholes model, which has previously been derived only by much more difficult methods. The basic model readily lends itself to generalisation in many ways. Moreover, by its very construction, it gives rise to a simple and efficient numerical procedure for valuing options for which premature exercise may be optimal.

An option is a security which gives its owner the right to trade in a fixed number of shares of a specified common stock at a fixed price at any time on or before a given date. The act of making this transaction is referred to as exercising the option. The fixed price is termed the striking price, and the given date, the expiration date. A call option gives the right to buy the shares; a put option gives the right to sell the shares.

Options have been traded for centuries, but they remained relatively obscure financial instruments until the introduction of a listed options exchange in 1973. Since then, options trading has enjoyed an expansion unprecedented in the American securities markets.

Option pricing theory has a long and illustrious history, but it also underwent a revolutionary change in 1973. At that time, Fischer Black and Myron Scholes presented the first completely satisfactory equilibrium option pricing model. In the same year, Robert Merton extended their model in several important ways. These path-breaking articles have formed the basis for many subsequent academic studies.

As these studies have shown, option pricing theory is relevant to almost every area of finance. For example, virtually all corporate securities can be interpreted as portfolios of puts and calls on the assets of the firm.[1] Indeed, the theory applies to a very general class of economic problems – the valuation of contracts where the outcome to each party depends on a quantifiable uncertain future event.

Unfortunately, the mathematical tools employed in the Black–Scholes and Merton articles are quite advanced and have tended to obscure the underlying economics.

**This paper was first published in the* Journal of Financial Economics, *Vol. 7 (1979). It is reprinted with the permission of JAI Press Inc.*
Our best thanks go to William Sharpe, who first suggested to us the advantages of the discrete-time approach to option pricing developed here. We are also grateful to our students over the past several years. Their favourable reactions to this way of presenting things encouraged us to write this article. We have received support from the National Science Foundation under Grants Nos. SOC-77-18087 and SOC-77-22301.

However, thanks to a suggestion by William Sharpe, it is possible to derive the same results using only elementary mathematics.[2]

In this article we will present a simple discrete-time option pricing formula. The fundamental economic principles of option valuation by arbitrage methods are particularly clear in this setting. The following two sections illustrate and develop this model for a call option on a stock which pays no dividends. The fourth section shows exactly how the model can be used to lock in pure arbitrage profits if the market price of an option differs from the value given by the model. In the fifth section, we will show that our approach includes the Black–Scholes model as a special limiting case. By taking the limits in a different way, we will also obtain the Cox–Ross (1975) jump process model as another special case.

Other more general option pricing problems often seem immune to reduction to a simple formula. Instead, numerical procedures must be employed to value these more complex options. Michael Brennan and Eduardo Schwartz (1977) have provided many interesting results along these lines. However, their techniques are rather complicated and are not directly related to the economic structure of the problem. Our formulation, by its very construction, leads to an alternative numerical procedure which is both simpler, and for many purposes, computationally more efficient.

The sixth section introduces these numerical procedures and extends the model to include puts and calls on stocks which pay dividends. The final section concludes the paper by showing how the model can be generalised in other important ways and discussing its essential role in valuation by arbitrage methods.

The basic idea

Suppose the current price of a stock is $S = \$50$, and at the end of a period of time, its price must be either $S^* = \$25$ or $S^* = \$100$. A call on the stock is available with a striking price of $K = \$50$, expiring at the end of the period.[3] It is also possible to borrow and lend at a 25% rate of interest. The one piece of information left unfurnished is the current value of the call, C. However, if riskless profitable arbitrage is not possible, we can deduce from the given information *alone* what the value of the call *must* be!

Consider forming the following levered hedge:

(1) Write three calls at C each,
(2) buy two shares at $50 each, and
(3) borrow $40 at 25%, to be paid back at the end of the period.

Table 1 gives the return from this hedge for each possible level of the stock price at expiration. Regardless of the outcome, the hedge exactly breaks even on the expiration date. Therefore, to prevent profitable riskless arbitrage, its current cost must be zero; that is,

$$3C - 100 + 40 = 0$$

The current value of the call must then be $C = \$20$.

If the call were not priced at $20, a sure profit would be possible. In particular, if $C = \$25$, the above hedge would yield a current cash inflow of $15 and would experience

Table 1. Arbitrage table illustrating the formation of a riskless hedge

	Present date	Expiration date $S^* = \$25$	$S^* = \$100$
Write 3 calls	3C	—	−150
Buy 2 shares	−100	50	200
Borrow	40	−50	−50
Total		—	—

no further gain or loss in the future. On the other hand, if $C = \$15$, then the same thing could be accomplished by buying three calls, selling short two shares and lending \$40.

Table 1 can be interpreted as demonstrating that *an appropriately levered position in stock will replicate the future returns of a call*. That is, if we buy shares and borrow against them in the right proportion, we can, in effect, duplicate a pure position in calls. In view of this, it should seem less surprising that all we needed to determine the *exact* value of the call was its *striking price*, *underlying price*, *range of movement in the underlying stock price* and *the rate of interest*. What may seem more incredible is what we do not need to know: among other things, *we do not need to know the probability that the stock price will rise or fall*. Bulls and bears must agree on the value of the call, relative to its underlying stock price!

This example is very simple, but it shows several essential features of option pricing. And we will soon see that it is not as unrealistic as it seems.

The binomial option pricing formula

In this section, we will develop the framework illustrated in the example into a complete valuation method. We begin by assuming that the stock price follows a multiplicative binomial process over discrete periods. The rate of return on the stock over each period can have two possible values: $u - 1$ with probability q, or $d - 1$ with probability $1 - q$. Thus, if the current stock price is S, the stock price at the end of the period will be either uS or dS. We can represent this movement with the following diagram:

$$S \begin{cases} uS & \text{with probability } q \\ dS & \text{with probability } 1 - q \end{cases}$$

We also assume that the interest rate is constant. Individuals may borrow or lend as much as they wish at this rate. To focus on the basic issues, we will continue to assume that there are no taxes, transaction costs, or margin requirements. Hence, individuals are allowed to sell short any security and receive full use of the proceeds.[4]

Letting r denote one plus the riskless interest rate over one period, we require $u > r > d$. If these inequalities did not hold, there would be profitable riskless arbitrage opportunities involving only the stock and riskless borrowing and lending.[5]

To see how to value a call on this stock, we start with the simplest situation: the expiration date is just one period away. Let C be the current value of the call, C_u be its value at the end of the period if the stock price goes to uS, and C_d be its value at the end of the period if the stock price goes to dS. Since there is now only one period remaining in the life of the call, we know that the terms of its contract and a rational exercise policy imply that $C_u = \max[0, uS - K]$ and $C_d = \max[0, dS - K]$. Therefore,

$$C \begin{cases} C_u = \max[0, uS - K] & \text{with probability } q \\ C_d = \max[0, dS - K] & \text{with probability } 1 - q \end{cases}$$

Suppose we form a portfolio containing Δ shares of stock and the dollar amount B in riskless bonds.[6] This will cost $\Delta S + B$. At the end of the period, the value of this portfolio will be

$$\Delta S + B \begin{cases} \Delta uS + rB & \text{with probability } q \\ \Delta dS + rB & \text{with probability } 1 - q \end{cases}$$

Since we can select Δ and B in any way we wish, suppose we choose them to equate the end-of-period values of the portfolio and the call for each possible outcome. This requires that

$$\Delta uS + rB = C_u$$

$$\Delta dS + rB = C_d$$

Solving these equations, we find

$$\Delta = \frac{C_u - C_d}{(u-d)S}, \qquad B = \frac{uC_d - dC_u}{(u-d)r} \tag{1}$$

With Δ and B chosen in this way, we will call this the hedging portfolio.

If there are to be no riskless arbitrage opportunities, the current value of the call, C, cannot be less than the current value of the hedging portfolio, $\Delta S + B$. If it were, we could make a riskless profit with no net investment by buying the call and selling the portfolio. It is tempting to say that it also cannot be worth more, since then we would have a riskless arbitrage opportunity by reversing our procedure and selling the call and buying the portfolio. But this overlooks the fact that the person who bought the call we sold has the right to exercise it immediately.

Suppose that $\Delta S + B < S - K$. If we try to make an arbitrage profit by selling calls for more than $\Delta S + B$, but less than $S - K$, then we will soon find that we are the source of arbitrage profits rather than their recipient. Anyone could make an arbitrage profit by buying our calls and exercising them immediately.

We might hope that we will be spared this embarrassment because everyone will somehow find it advantageous to hold the calls for one more period as an investment rather than take a quick profit by exercising them immediately. But each person will reason in the following way. If I do not exercise now, I will receive the same payoff as a portfolio with ΔS in stock and B in bonds. If I do exercise now, I can take the proceeds, $S - K$, buy this same portfolio and some extra bonds as well, and have a higher payoff in every possible circumstance. Consequently, no one would be willing to hold the calls for one more period.

Summing up all of this, we conclude that if there are to be no riskless arbitrage opportunities, it must be true that

$$\begin{aligned} C &= \Delta S + B \\ &= \frac{C_u - C_d}{u-d} + \frac{uC_d - dC_u}{(u-d)r} \\ &= \frac{\left(\frac{r-d}{u-d}\right)C_u + \left(\frac{u-r}{u-d}\right)C_d}{r} \end{aligned} \tag{2}$$

if this value is greater than $S - K$, and if not, $C = S - K$.[7]

Equation (2) can be simplified by defining

$$p \equiv \frac{r-d}{u-d} \quad \text{and} \quad 1-p \equiv \frac{u-r}{u-d}$$

so that we can write

$$C = \frac{pC_u + (1-p)C_d}{r} \tag{3}$$

It is easy to see that in the present case, with no dividends, this will always be greater than $S - K$ as long as the interest rate is positive. To avoid spending time on the unimportant situations where the interest rate is less than or equal to zero, we will now assume that r is always greater than one. Hence, (3) is the exact formula for the value of a call one period prior to expiration in terms of S, K, u, d and r.

To confirm this, note that if $uS \leqq K$, then $S < K$ and $C = 0$, so $C > S - K$. Also, if $dS \geqq K$, then $C = S - (K/r) > S - K$. The remaining possibility is $uS > K > dS$. In this case, $C = p(uS - K)/r$. This is greater than $S - K$ if $(1-p)dS > (p-r)K$, which is certainly true as long as $r > 1$.

This formula has a number of notable features. First, the probability q does not appear in the formula. This means, surprisingly, that even if different investors have different subjective probabilities about an upward or downward movement in the stock, they could still agree on the relationship of C to S, u, d and r.

Second, the value of the call does not depend on investors' attitudes toward risk. In constructing the formula, the only assumption we made about an individual's behaviour was that he prefers more wealth to less wealth and therefore has an incentive to take advantage of profitable riskless arbitrage opportunities. We would obtain the same formula whether investors are risk-averse or risk-preferring.

Third, the only random variable on which the call value depends is the stock price itself. In particular, it does not depend on the random prices of other securities or portfolios, such as the market portfolio containing all securities in the economy. If another pricing formula involving other variables was submitted as giving equilibrium market prices, we could immediately show that it was incorrect by using our formula to make riskless arbitrage profits while trading at those prices.

It is easier to understand these features if it is remembered that the formula is only a relative pricing relationship giving C in terms of S, u, d and r. Investors' attitudes toward risk and the characteristics of other assets may indeed influence call values indirectly, through their effect on these variables, but they will not be separate determinants of call value.

Finally, observe that $p \equiv (r-d)/(u-d)$ is always greater than zero and less than one, so it has the properties of a probability. In fact, p is the value q would have in equilibrium if investors were risk-neutral. To see this, note that the expected rate of return on the stock would then be the riskless interest rate, so

$$q(uS) + (1-q)(dS) = rS$$

and

$$q = \frac{r-d}{u-d} = p$$

Hence, the value of the call can be interpreted as the expectation of its discounted future value in a risk-neutral world. In light of our earlier observations, this is not surprising. Since the formula does not involve q or any measure of attitudes toward risk, then it must be the same for any set of preferences, including risk neutrality.

It is important to note that this does not imply that the equilibrium expected rate of return on the call is the riskless interest rate. Indeed, our argument has shown that, in equilibrium, holding the call over the period is exactly equivalent to holding the hedging portfolio. Consequently, the risk and expected rate of return of the call must be the same as that of the hedging portfolio. It can be shown that $\Delta \geqq 0$ and $B \leqq 0$, so the hedging portfolio is equivalent to a particular levered long position in the stock. In equilibrium, the same is true for the call. Of course, if the call is currently mispriced, its risk and expected return over the period will differ from that of the hedging portfolio.

Now we can consider the next simplest situation: a call with two periods remaining before its expiration date. In keeping with the binomial process, the stock can take on three possible values after two periods,

$$S \begin{array}{l} \nearrow uS \begin{array}{l} \nearrow u^2S \\ \searrow duS \end{array} \\ \searrow dS \begin{array}{l} \nearrow duS \\ \searrow d^2S \end{array} \end{array}$$

similarly, for the call,

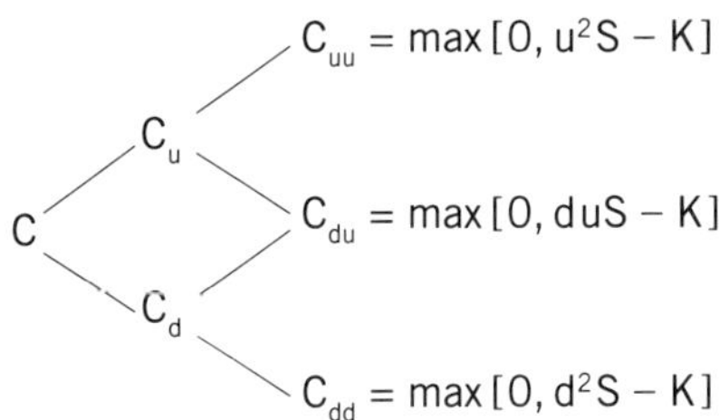

C_{uu} stands for the value of a call two periods from the current time if the stock price moves upward each period; C_{du} and C_{dd} have analogous definitions.

At the end of the current period there will be one period left in the life of the call and we will be faced with a problem identical to the one we just solved. Thus, from our previous analysis, we know that when there are two periods left,

$$C_u = \frac{pC_{uu} + (1-p)C_{ud}}{r}$$

and

$$C_d = \frac{pC_{du} + (1-p)C_{dd}}{r} \tag{4}$$

Again we can select a portfolio with ΔS in stock and B in bonds whose end-of-period value will be C_u if the stock price goes to uS and C_d if the stock price goes to dS. Indeed, the functional form of Δ and B remains unchanged. To get the new values of Δ and B, we simply use equation (1) with the new values of C_u and C_d.

Can we now say, as before, that an opportunity for profitable riskless arbitrage will be available if the current price of the call is not equal to the new value of this portfolio or $S - K$, whichever is greater? Yes, but there is an important difference. With one period to go, we could plan to lock in a riskless profit by selling an overpriced call and using part of the proceeds to buy the hedging portfolio. At the end of the period, we knew that the market price of the call must be equal to the value of the portfolio, so the entire position could be safely liquidated at that point. But this was true only because the end of the period was the expiration date. Now we have no such guarantee. At the end of the current period, when there is still one period left, the market price of the call could still be in disequilibrium and be greater than the value of the hedging portfolio. If we closed out the position then, selling the portfolio and repurchasing the call, we could suffer a loss which would more than offset our original profit. However, we could always avoid this loss by maintaining the portfolio for one more period. The value of the portfolio at the end of the current period will always be exactly sufficient to purchase the portfolio we would want to hold over the last period. In effect, we would have to readjust the proportions in the hedging portfolio, but we would not have to put up any more money.

Consequently, we conclude that even with two periods to go, there is a strategy we could follow which would guarantee riskless profits with no net investment if the current market price of a call differs from the maximum of $\Delta S + B$ and $S - K$. Hence, the larger of these is the current value of the call.

Since Δ and B have the same functional form in each period, the current value of the call in terms of C_u and C_d will again be $C = [pC_u + (1 - p)C_d]/r$ if this is greater than $S - K$, and $C = S - K$ otherwise. By substituting from equation (4) into the former expression, and noting that $C_{du} = C_{ud}$, we obtain

$$C = \frac{p^2 C_{uu} + 2p(1-p)C_{ud} + (1-p)^2 C_{dd}}{r^2}$$

$$= \frac{p^2 \max[0, u^2S - K] + 2p(1-p)\max[0, duS - K] + (1-p)^2 \max[0, d^2S - K]}{r^2} \tag{5}$$

A little algebra shows that this is always greater than $S - K$ if, as assumed, r is always greater than one, so this expression gives the exact value of the call.[8]

All of the observations made about formula (3) also apply to formula (5), except that the number of periods remaining until expiration, n, now emerges clearly as an additional determinant of the call value. For formula (5), $n = 2$. That is, the full list of variables determining C is S, K, n, u, d and r.

We now have a recursive procedure for finding the value of a call with any number of periods to go. By starting at the expiration date and working backwards, we can write down the general valuation formula for any n:

$$C = \frac{\sum_{j=0}^{n}\left(\frac{n!}{j!(n-j)!}\right) p^j (1-p)^{n-j} \max[0, u^j d^{n-j} S - K]}{r^n} \qquad (6)$$

This gives us the complete formula, but with a little additional effort we can express it in a more convenient way.

Let a stand for the minimum number of upward moves which the stock must make over the next n periods for the call to finish in-the-money. Thus a will be the smallest non-negative integer such that $u^a d^{n-a} S > K$. By taking the natural logarithm of both sides of this inequality, we could write a as the smallest non-negative integer greater than $\log(K/Sd^n)/\log(u/d)$.

For all $j < a$,

$$\max[0, u^j d^{n-j} S - K] = 0$$

and for all $j \geqq a$

$$\max[0, u^j d^{n-j} S - K] = u^j d^{n-j} S - K$$

Therefore,

$$C = \frac{\sum_{j=a}^{n}\left(\frac{n!}{j!(n-j)!}\right) p^j (1-p)^{n-j} [u^j d^{n-j} S - K]}{r^n}$$

Of course, if $a > n$, the call will finish out-of-the-money even if the stock moves upward every period, so its current value must be zero.

By breaking up C into two terms, we can write

$$C = S\left[\sum_{j=a}^{n}\left(\frac{n!}{j!(n-j)!}\right) p^j (1-p)^{n-j} \left(\frac{u^j d^{n-j}}{r^n}\right)\right]$$
$$- Kr^{-n}\left[\sum_{j=a}^{n}\left(\frac{n!}{j!(n-j)!}\right) p^j (1-p)^{n-j}\right]$$

Now, the latter bracketed expression is the complementary binomial distribution function $\Phi[a; n, p]$. The first bracketed expression can also be interpreted as a complementary binomial distribution function $\Phi[a; n, p']$, where

$$p' \equiv \left(\frac{u}{r}\right) p \quad \text{and} \quad 1 - p' \equiv \left(\frac{d}{r}\right)(1-p)$$

p' is a probability, since $0 < p' < 1$. To see this, note that $p < (r/u)$ and

$$p^j (1-p)^{n-j} \left(\frac{u^j d^{n-j}}{r^n}\right) = \left[\left(\frac{u}{r}\right) p\right]^j \left[\frac{d}{r}(1-p)\right]^{n-j} = p'^j (1-p')^{n-j}$$

In summary:

Binomial Option Pricing Formula

$$C = S\Phi[a; n, p'] - Kr^{-n}\Phi[a; n, p]$$

where $p \equiv \frac{r-d}{u-d}$ and $p' \equiv \left(\frac{u}{r}\right)p$

a ≡ the smallest non-negative integer greater than $\dfrac{\log\left(\frac{K}{Sd^n}\right)}{\log\left(\frac{u}{d}\right)}$

If $a > n$, $C = 0$

It is now clear that all of the comments we made about the one period valuation formula are valid for any number of periods. In particular, the value of a call should be the expectation, in a risk-neutral world, of the discounted value of the payoff it will receive. In fact, that is exactly what equation (6) says. Why, then, should we waste time with the recursive procedure when we can write down the answer in one direct step? The reason is that while this one-step approach is always technically correct, it is really useful only if we know in advance the circumstances in which a rational individual would prefer to exercise the call before the expiration date. If we do not know this, we have no way to compute the required expectation. In the present example, a call on a stock paying no dividends, it happens that we can determine this information from other sources: the call should never be exercised before the expiration date. As we will see in the fifth section, with puts or with calls on stocks which pay dividends, we will not be so lucky. Finding the optimal exercise strategy will be an integral part of the valuation problem. The full recursive procedure will then be necessary.

For some readers, an alternative "complete markets" interpretation of our binomial approach may be instructive. Suppose that π_u and π_d represent the state-contingent discount rates to states u and d, respectively. Therefore, π_u would be the current price of one dollar received at the end of the period, if and only if state u occurs. Each security - a riskless bond, the stock and the option - must all have returns discounted to the present by π_u and π_d if no riskless arbitrage opportunities are available. Therefore,

$$1 = \pi_u r + \pi_d r$$

$$S = \pi_u(uS) + \pi_d(dS)$$

$$C = \pi_u C_u + \pi_d C_d$$

The first two equations, for the bond and the stock, imply

$$\pi_u = \left(\frac{r-d}{u-d}\right)\frac{1}{r} \quad \text{and} \quad \pi_d = \left(\frac{u-r}{u-d}\right)\frac{1}{r}$$

Substituting these equalities for the state-contingent prices in the last equation for the option yields equation (3).

It is important to realise that we are not assuming that the riskless bond and the stock and the option are the only three securities in the economy, or that other securities must follow a binomial process. Rather, however these securities are priced in relation to others in equilibrium, among themselves they must conform to the above relationships.

From either the hedging or complete markets approaches, it should be clear that three-state or trinomial stock price movements will not lead to an option pricing formula based solely on arbitrage considerations. Suppose, for example, that over each period the stock price could move to uS or dS or remain the same at S. A choice of Δ and B which would equate the returns in two states could not in the third. That is, the riskless arbitrage position could not be taken. Under the complete markets interpretation, with three equations in now three unknown state-contingent prices, we would lack the redundant equation necessary to price one security in terms of the other two.

Riskless trading strategies

The following numerical example illustrates how we could use the formula if the current *market price* M ever diverged from its *formula value* C. If $M > C$, we would hedge, and if $M < C$, "reverse hedge", to try and lock in the profit. Suppose the values of the underlying variables are

$$S = 80, \quad n = 3, \quad K = 80, \quad u = 1.5, \quad d = 0.5, \quad r = 1.1$$

In this case, $p = (r - d)/(u - d) = 0.6$. The relevant values of the discount factor are

$$r^{-1} = 0.909, \quad r^{-2} = 0.826, \quad r^{-3} = 0.751$$

The paths the stock price may follow and their corresponding probabilities (using probability p) are:

when $n = 3$, with $S = 80$,

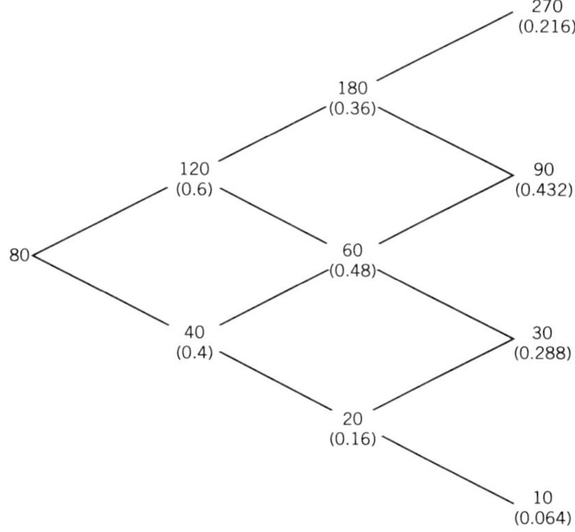

when $n = 2$, if $S = 120$,

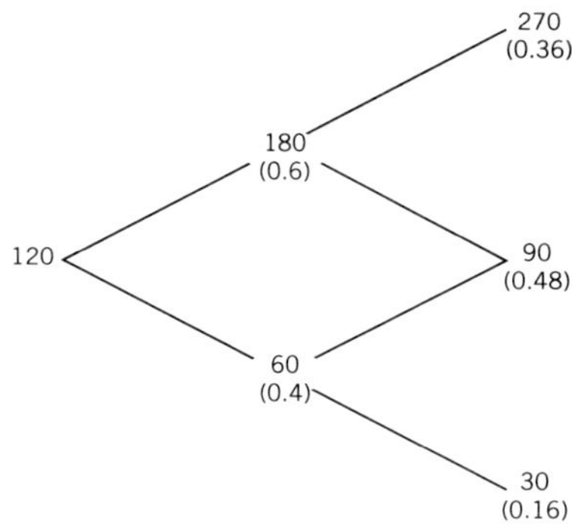

when n = 2, if S = 40,

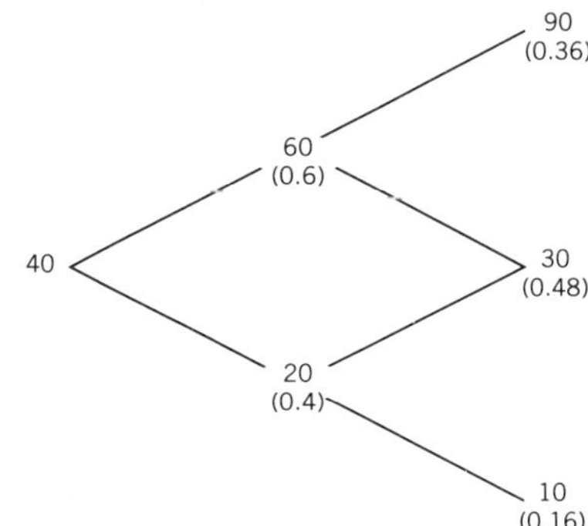

Using the formula, the current value of the call would be

$$C = 0.751[0.064(0) + 0.288(0) + 0.432(90 - 80) + 0.216(270 - 80)]$$
$$= 34.065$$

Recall that to form a riskless hedge, for each call we sell, we buy and subsequently keep adjusted a portfolio with ΔS in stock and B in bonds, where $\Delta = (C_u - C_d)/(u - d)S$. The following tree diagram gives the paths the call value may follow and the corresponding values of Δ:

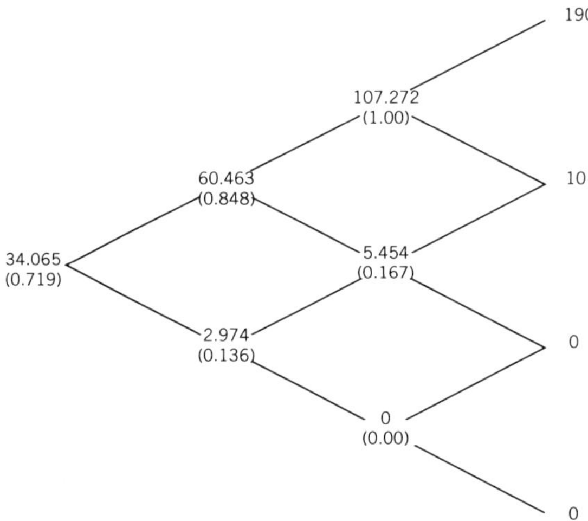

With this preliminary analysis, we are prepared to use the formula to take advantage of mispricing in the market. Suppose that when n = 3, the market price of the call is 36. Our formula tells us that the call should be worth 34.065. The option is overpriced, so we could plan to sell it and assure ourselves of a profit equal to the mispricing differential. Here are the steps you could take for a typical path the stock might follow.

Step 1 (n = 3): Sell the call for 36. Take 34.065 of this and invest it in a portfolio containing $\Delta = 0.719$ shares of stock by borrowing 0.719(80) - 34.065 = 23.455. Take the remainder, 36 - 34.065 = 1.935, and put it in the bank.

Step 2 (n = 2): Suppose the stock goes to 120 so that the new Δ is 0.848. Buy 0.848 - 0.719 = 0.129 more shares of stock at 120 per share for a total expenditure of 15.480. Borrow to pay the bill. With an interest rate of 0.1, you already owe 23.455(1.1) = 25.801. Thus, your total current indebtedness is 25.801 + 15.480 = 41.281.

Step 3 (n = 1): Suppose the stock price now goes to 60. The new Δ is 0.167. Sell 0.848 - 0.167 = 0.681 shares at 60 per share, taking in 0.681(60) = 40.860. Use this to pay back part of your borrowing. Since you now owe 41.281(1.1) = 45.409, the repayment will reduce this to 45.409 - 40.860 = 4.549.

Step *4d* (n = 0): Suppose the stock price now goes to 30. The call you sold has expired worthless. You own 0.167 shares of stock selling at 30 per share, for a total value of 0.167(30) = 5. Sell the stock and repay the 4.549(1.1) = 5 that you now owe on the borrowing. Go back to the bank and withdraw your original deposit, which has now grown to $1.935(1.1)^3 = 2.575$.

Step *4u* (n = 0): Suppose, instead, the stock price goes to 90. The call you sold is in the money at the expiration date. Buy back the call, or buy one share of stock and let it be exercised, incurring a loss of 90 - 80 = 10 either way. Borrow to cover this, bringing your current indebtedness to 5 + 10 = 15. You own 0.167 shares of stock selling at 90 per share, for a total value of 0.167(90) = 15. Sell the stock and repay the borrowing. Go back to the bank and withdraw your original deposit, which has now grown to $1.935(1.1)^3 = 2.575$.

In summary, if we were correct in our original analysis about stock price movements (which did not involve the unenviable task of predicting whether the stock price would go up to down), and if we faithfully adjust our portfolio as prescribed by the formula, then we can be assured of walking away in the clear at the expiration date, while still keeping the original differential and the interest it has accumulated. It is true that closing out the position before the expiration date, which involves buying back the option at its then current market price, might produce a loss which would more than offset our profit, but this loss could always be avoided by waiting until the expiration date. Moreover, if the market price comes into line with the formula value before the expiration date, we can close out the position then with no loss and be rid of the concern of keeping the portfolio adjusted.

It still might seem that we are depending on rational behaviour by the person who bought the call we sold. If instead he behaves foolishly and exercises at the wrong time, could he make things worse for us as well as for himself? Fortunately, the answer is no. Mistakes on his part can only mean greater profits for us. Let us suppose that he exercises too soon. In that circumstance, the hedging portfolio will always be worth more than S – K, so we could close out the position then with an extra profit.

Suppose, instead, that he fails to exercise when it would be optimal to do so. Again there is no problem. Since exercise is now optimal, our hedging portfolio will be worth S – K.[9] If he had exercised, this would be exactly sufficient to meet the obligation and close out the position. Since he did not, the call will be held at least one more period, so we calculate the new values of C_u and C_d and revise our hedging portfolio accordingly. But now the amount required for the portfolio, $\Delta S + B$, is less than the amount we have available, S – K. We can withdraw these extra profits now and still maintain the hedging portfolio. The longer the holder of the call goes on making mistakes, the better off we will be.

Consequently, we can be confident that things will eventually work out right no matter what the other party does. The return on our total position, when evaluated at prevailing market prices at intermediate times, may be negative. But over a period ending no later than the expiration date, it will be positive.

In conducting the hedging operation, the essential thing was to maintain the proper proportional relationship: for each call we are short, we hold Δ shares of stock and the dollar amount B in bonds in the hedging portfolio. To emphasise this, we will refer to the number of shares held for each call as the hedge ratio. In our example, we kept the number of calls constant and made adjustments by buying or selling stock and bonds. As a result, our profit was independent of the market price of the call between the time we initiated the hedge and the expiration date. If things got worse before they got better, it did not matter to us.

Instead, we could have made the adjustments by keeping the number of shares of stock constant and buying or selling calls and bonds. However, this could be dangerous.

Suppose that after initiating the position, we needed to increase the hedge ratio to maintain the proper proportions. This can be achieved in two ways:

a) buy more stock, or
b) buy back some of the calls.

If we adjust through the stock, there is no problem. If we insist on adjusting through the calls, not only is the hedge no longer riskless, but it could even end up losing money! This can happen if the call has become even more overpriced. We would then be closing out part of our position in calls at a loss. To remain hedged, the number of calls we would need to buy back depends on their value, not their price. Therefore, since we are uncertain about their price, we then become uncertain about the return from the hedge. Worse yet, if the call price gets high enough, the loss on the closed portion of our position could throw the hedge operation into an overall loss.

To see how this could happen, let us rerun the hedging operation, where we adjust the hedge ratio by buying and selling calls.

Step 1 ($n = 3$): Same as before.

Step 2 ($n = 2$): Suppose the stock goes to 120, so that the new $\Delta = 0.848$. The call price has gone further out of line and is now selling for 75. Since its value is 60.463, it is now overpriced by 14.537. With 0.719 shares, you must buy back 1 - 0.848 = 0.152 calls to produce a hedge ratio of 0.848 = 0.719/0.848. This costs 75(0.152) = 11.40. Borrow to pay the bill. With the interest rate of 0.1, you already owe 23.455(1.1) = 25.801. Thus, your total current indebtedness is 25.801 + 11.40 = 37.201.

Step 3 ($n = 1$): Suppose the stock goes to 60 and the call is selling for 5.454. Since the call is now fairly valued, no further excess profits can be made by continuing to hold the position. Therefore, liquidate by selling your 0.719 shares for 0.719(60) = 43.14 and close out the call position by buying back 0.848 calls for 0.848(5.454) = 4.625. This nets 43.14 - 4.625 = 38.515. Use this to pay back part of your borrowing. Since you now owe 37.20(1.1) = 40.921, after repayment you owe 2.406. Go back to the bank and withdraw your original deposit, which has now grown to $1.935(1.1)^2$ = 2.341. Unfortunately, after using this to repay your remaining borrowing, you still owe 0.065.

Since we adjusted our position at Step 2 by buying overpriced calls, our profit is reduced. Indeed, since the calls were considerably overpriced, we actually lost money despite apparent profitability of the position at Step 1. We can draw the following adjustment rule from our experiment: *To adjust a hedged position, never buy an overpriced option or sell an underpriced option*. As a corollary, whenever we can adjust a hedged position by buying more of an underpriced option or selling more of an overpriced option, our profit will be enhanced if we do so. For example, at Step 3 in the original hedging illustration, had the call still been overpriced, it would have been better to adjust the position by selling more calls rather than selling stock. In summary, by choosing the right side of the position to adjust at intermediate dates, *at a minimum* we can be assured of earning the original differential and its accumulated interest, and we may earn considerably more.

Limiting cases

In reading the previous sections, there is a natural tendency to associate with each period some particular length of calendar time, perhaps a day. With this in mind, you may have had two objections. In the first place, prices a day from now may take on many more than just two possible values. Furthermore, the market is not open for trading only once a day, but, instead, trading takes place almost continuously.

These objections are certainly valid. Fortunately, our option pricing approach has the flexibility to meet them. Although it might have been natural to think of a period as one day, there was nothing that forced us to do so. We could have taken it to be a much shorter interval - say an hour, or even a minute. By doing so, we have met both objections simultaneously. Trading would take place far more frequently, and the stock price could take on hundreds of values by the end of the day.

However, if we do this, we have to make some other adjustments to keep the probability small that the stock price will change by a large amount over a minute. We do not want the stock to have the same percentage up and down moves for one minute as it did before for one day. But again there is no need for us to have to use the same values. We could, for example, think of the price as making only a very small percentage change over each minute.

To make this more precise, suppose that h represents the elapsed time between successive stock price changes. That is, if t is the fixed length of calendar time to expiration and n is the number of periods of length h prior to expiration, then

$$h \equiv \frac{t}{n}$$

As trading takes place more and more frequently, h gets closer and closer to zero. We must then adjust the interval-dependent variables r, u and d in such a way that we obtain empirically realistic results as h becomes smaller, or, equivalently, as $n \to \infty$.

When we were thinking of the periods as having a fixed length, r represented both the interest rate over a fixed length of calendar time and the interest rate over one period. Now we need to make a distinction between these two meanings. We will let r continue to mean one plus the interest rate over a fixed length of calendar time. When we have occasion to refer to one plus the interest rate over a period (trading interval) of length h, we will use the symbol $\hat{r}$.

Clearly, the size of $\hat{r}$ depends on the number of subintervals, n, into which t is divided. Over the n periods until expiration, the total return is $\hat{r}^n$, where $n = t/h$. Now not only do we want $\hat{r}$ to depend on n, but we want it to depend on n in a particular way - so that as n changes the total return $\hat{r}^n$ over the fixed time t remains the same. This is because the interest rate obtainable over some fixed length of calendar time should have nothing to do with how we choose to think of the length of the time interval h.

If r (without the "hat") denotes one plus the rate of interest over a *fixed* unit of calendar time, then over elapsed time t, r^t is the total return.[10] Observe that this measure of total return does not depend on n. As we have argued, we want to choose the dependence of $\hat{r}$ on n, so that

$$\hat{r}^n = r^t$$

for any choice of n. Therefore, $\hat{r} = r^{t/n}$. This last equation shows how $\hat{r}$ must depend on n for the total return over elapsed time t to be independent of n.

We also need to define u and d in terms of n. At this point, there are two significantly different paths we can take. Depending on the definitions we choose, as $n \to \infty$ (or, equivalently, as $h \to 0$), we can have either a continuous or a jump stochastic process. In the first situation, very small random changes in the stock price will be occurring in each very small time interval. The stock price will fluctuate incessantly, but its path can be drawn without lifting pen from paper. In contrast, in the second case, the stock price will usually move in a smooth deterministic way, but will occasionally experience sudden discontinuous changes. Both can be derived from our binomial process simply by choosing how u and d depend on n. We examine in detail only the continuous process which leads to the option pricing formula originally derived by Fischer Black and Myron Scholes. Subsequently, we indicate how to develop the jump process formula originally derived by John Cox and Stephen Ross.

Recall that we supposed that over each period the stock price would experience a one plus rate of return of u with probability q and d with probability $1 - q$. It will be easier and clearer to work, instead, with the natural logarithm of the one plus rate of return, $\log u$ or $\log d$. This gives the continuously compounded rate of return on the stock over each period. It is a random variable which in each period will be equal to $\log u$ with probability q and $\log d$ with probability $1 - q$.

Consider a typical sequence of five moves, say u, d, u, u, d. Then the final stock price will be $S^* = uduudS$; $S^*/S = u^3d^2$, and $\log(S^*/S) = 3\log u + 2\log d$. More generally, over n periods,

$$\log\left(\frac{S^*}{S}\right) = j\log u + (n-j)\log d = j\log\left(\frac{u}{d}\right) + n\log d$$

where j is the (random) number of upward moves occurring during the n periods to expiration. Therefore, the expected value of $\log(S^*/S)$ is

$$E\left[\log\left(\frac{S^*}{S}\right)\right] = \log\left(\frac{u}{d}\right)\cdot E(j) + n\log d$$

and its variance is

$$\operatorname{var}\left[\log\left(\frac{S^*}{S}\right)\right] = \left[\log\left(\frac{u}{d}\right)\right]^2 \cdot \operatorname{var}(j)$$

Each of the n possible upward moves has probability q. Thus, $E(j) = nq$. Also, since the variance each period is $q(1-q)^2 + (1-q)(0-q)^2 = q(1-q)$, then $\operatorname{var}(j) = nq(1-q)$. Combining all of this, we have

$$E\left[\log\left(\frac{S^*}{S}\right)\right] = \left[q\log\left(\frac{u}{d}\right) + \log d\right]n \equiv \hat{\mu}n$$

$$\operatorname{var}\left[\log\left(\frac{S^*}{S}\right)\right] = q(1-q)\left[\log\left(\frac{u}{d}\right)\right]^2 n \equiv \hat{\sigma}^2 n$$

Let us go back to our discussion. We were considering dividing up our original longer time period (a day) into many shorter periods (a minute or even less). Our procedure calls for, over fixed length of calendar time t, making n larger and larger. Now if we held everything else constant while we let n become large, we would be faced with the problem we talked about earlier. In fact, we would certainly not reach a reasonable conclusion if either $\hat{\mu}n$ or $\hat{\sigma}^2 n$ went to zero or infinity as n became large. Since t is a fixed length of time, in searching for a realistic result, we must make the appropriate adjustments in u, d and q. In doing that, we would at least want the mean and variance of the continuously compounded rate of return of the assumed stock price movement to coincide with that of the actual stock price as $n \to \infty$. Suppose we label the actual empirical values of $\hat{\mu}n$ and $\hat{\sigma}^2 n$ as μt and $\sigma^2 t$, respectively. Then we would want to choose u, d and q so that

$$\left.\begin{aligned} &\left[q\log\left(\frac{u}{d}\right) + \log d\right]n \to \mu t \\ &q(1-q)\left[\log\left(\frac{u}{d}\right)\right]^2 n \to \sigma^2 t \end{aligned}\right\} \quad \text{as } n \to \infty$$

A little algebra shows we can accomplish this by letting

$$u = e^{\sigma\sqrt{t/n}}, \quad d = e^{-\sigma\sqrt{t/n}}, \quad q = \tfrac{1}{2} + \tfrac{1}{2}\left(\tfrac{\mu}{\sigma}\right)\sqrt{\tfrac{t}{n}}$$

In this case, for any n,

$$\hat{\mu}n = \mu t \quad \text{and} \quad \hat{\sigma}^2 n = \left[\sigma^2 - \mu^2\left(\tfrac{t}{n}\right)\right]t$$

Clearly, as $n \to \infty$, $\hat{\sigma}^2 n \to \sigma^2 t$, while $\hat{\mu} n = \mu t$ for all values of n.

Alternatively, we could have chosen u, d and q so that the mean and variance of the future stock price for the discrete binomial process approach the prespecified mean and variance of the actual stock price as $n \to \infty$. However, just as we would expect, the same values will accomplish this as well. Since this would not change our conclusions, and it is computationally more convenient to work with the continuously compounded rates of return, we will proceed in that way.

This satisfies our initial requirement that the limiting means and variances coincide, but we still need to verify that we are arriving at a sensible limiting probability distribution of the continuously compounded rate of return. The mean and variance only describe certain aspects of that distribution.

For our model, the random continuously compounded rate of return over a period of length t is the sum of n independent random variables, each of which can take the value $\log u$ with probability q and $\log d$ with probability $1 - q$. We wish to know about the distribution of this sum as n becomes large and q, u and d are chosen in the way described. We need to remember that as we change n, we are not simply adding one more random variable to the previous sum, but instead are changing the probabilities and possible outcomes for every member of the sum. At this point, we can rely on a form of the central limit theorem which, when applied to our problem, says that, as $n \to \infty$, if

$$\frac{q\left|\log u - \hat{\mu}\right|^3 + (1-q)\left|\log d - \hat{\mu}\right|^3}{\hat{\sigma}^3 \sqrt{n}} \to 0$$

then

$$\text{Prob}\left[\left(\frac{\log\left(S^*/S\right) - \hat{\mu} n}{\hat{\sigma}\sqrt{n}}\right) \leq z\right] \to N(z)$$

where $N(z)$ is the standard normal distribution function. Putting this into words, as the number of periods into which the fixed length of time to expiration is divided approaches infinity, the probability that the standardised continuously compounded rate of return of the stock through the expiration date is not greater than the number z approaches the probability under a standard normal distribution.

The initial condition says roughly that higher-order properties of the distribution, such as how it is skewed, become less and less important, relative to its standard deviation, as $n \to \infty$. We can verify that the condition is satisfied by making the appropriate substitutions and finding

$$\frac{q\left|\log u - \hat{\mu}\right|^3 + (1-q)\left|\log d - \hat{\mu}\right|^3}{\hat{\sigma}^3 \sqrt{n}} = \frac{(1-q)^2 + q^2}{\sqrt{nq(1-q)}}$$

which goes to zero as $n \to \infty$ since

$$q = \tfrac{1}{2} + \tfrac{1}{2}\left(\tfrac{\mu}{\sigma}\right)\sqrt{\tfrac{t}{n}}$$

Thus, the multiplicative binomial model for stock prices includes the lognormal distribution as a limiting case.

Black and Scholes began directly with continuous trading and the assumption of a lognormal distribution for stock prices. Their approach relied on some quite advanced mathematics. However, since our approach contains continuous trading and the lognormal distribution as a limiting case, the two resultant formulas should then coincide. We will see shortly that this is indeed true, and we will have the advantage of using a much simpler method. It is important to remember, however, that the economic arguments we used to link the option value and the stock price are exactly the same as those advanced by Black and Scholes (1973) and Merton (1973, 1977).

The formula derived by Black and Scholes, rewritten in terms of our notation, is

Black–Scholes Option Pricing Formula

$$C = SN(x) - Kr^{-t}N\left(x - \sigma\sqrt{t}\right)$$

where

$$x \equiv \frac{\log\left(\frac{S}{Kr^{-t}}\right)}{\sigma\sqrt{t}} + \frac{1}{2}\sigma\sqrt{t}$$

We now wish to confirm that our binomial formula converges to the Black-Scholes formula when t is divided into more and more subintervals and $\hat{r}$, u, d and q are chosen in the way we described - that is, in a way such that the multiplicative binomial probability distribution of stock prices goes to the lognormal distribution.

For easy reference, let us recall our binomial option pricing formula:

$$C = S\Phi[a; n, p'] - K\hat{r}^{-n}[a; n, p]$$

The similarities are readily apparent. $\hat{r}^{-n}$ is, of course, always equal to r^{-t}. Therefore, to show the two formulas converge, we need only show that as $n \to \infty$,

$$\Phi[a; n, p'] \to N(x) \quad \text{and} \quad \Phi[a; n, p] \to N(x - \sigma\sqrt{t})$$

We will consider only $\Phi[a; n, p]$, since the argument is exactly the same for $\Phi[a; n, p']$.

The complementary binomial distribution function $\Phi[a; n, p]$ is the probability that the sum of n random variables, each of which can take on the value 1 with probability p and 0 with probability $1 - p$, will be greater than or equal to a. We know that the random value of this sum, j, has mean np and standard deviation $\sqrt{np(1-p)}$. Therefore,

$$1 - \Phi[a; n, p] = \text{Prob}[j \leq a - 1]$$

$$= \text{Prob}\left[\frac{j - np}{\sqrt{np(1-p)}} \leq \frac{a - 1 - np}{\sqrt{np(1-p)}}\right]$$

Now we can make an analogy with our earlier discussion. If we consider a stock which in each period will move to uS with probability p and dS with probability $1 - p$, then $\log(S^*/S) = j\log(u/d) + n\log d$. The mean and variance of the continuously compounded rate of return of this stock are

$$\hat{\mu}_p = p\log\left(\frac{u}{d}\right) + \log d \quad \text{and} \quad \hat{\sigma}_p^2 = p(1-p)\left[\log\left(\frac{u}{d}\right)\right]^2$$

Using these equalities, we find that

$$\frac{j - np}{\sqrt{np(1-p)}} = \frac{\log\left(S^*/S\right) - \hat{\mu}_p n}{\hat{\sigma}_p\sqrt{n}}$$

Recall from the binomial formula that

$$a - 1 = \frac{\log\left(K/Sd^n\right)}{\log\left(u/d\right)} - \varepsilon$$

$$= \frac{\left[\log\left(K/S\right) - n\log d\right]}{\log\left(u/d\right)} - \varepsilon$$

where ε is a number between zero and one. Using this and the definitions of $\hat{\mu}_p$ and $\hat{\sigma}_p^2$, with a little algebra, we have

$$\frac{a-1-np}{\sqrt{np(1-p)}}=\frac{\log(K/S)-\hat{\mu}_p n-\varepsilon\log(u/d)}{\hat{\sigma}_p\sqrt{n}}$$

Putting these results together,

$$1-\Phi[a;n,p]=\text{Prob}\left[\frac{\log(S^*/S)-\hat{\mu}_p n}{\hat{\sigma}_p\sqrt{n}}\leq\frac{\log(K/S)-\hat{\mu}_p n-\varepsilon\log(u/d)}{\hat{\sigma}_p\sqrt{n}}\right]$$

We are now in a position to apply the central limit theorem. First, we must check if the initial condition,

$$\frac{p\left|\log u-\hat{\mu}_p\right|^3+(1-p)\left|\log d-\hat{\mu}_p\right|^3}{\hat{\sigma}_p\sqrt{n}}=\frac{(1-p)^2+p^2}{\sqrt{np(1-p)}}\to 0$$

as $n\to\infty$, is satisfied. By first recalling that $p\equiv(\hat{r}-d)/(u-d)$, and then $\hat{r}=r^{t/n}$, $u=e^{\sigma\sqrt{(t/n)}}$, and $d=e^{-\sigma\sqrt{(t/n)}}$, it is possible to show that as $n\to\infty$,

$$p\to\tfrac{1}{2}+\tfrac{1}{2}\left(\frac{\log r-\frac{1}{2}\sigma^2}{\sigma}\right)\sqrt{\frac{t}{n}}$$

As a result, the initial condition holds, and we are justified in applying the central limit theorem.

To do so, we need only evaluate $\hat{\mu}_p n$, $\hat{\sigma}_p^2 n$ and $\log(u/d)$ as $n\to\infty$.[11] Examination of our discussion for parameterising q shows that as $n\to\infty$,

$$\hat{\mu}_p n\to\left(\log r-\tfrac{1}{2}\sigma^2\right)t \quad\text{and}\quad \hat{\sigma}_p\sqrt{n}\to\sigma\sqrt{t}$$

Furthermore, $\log(u/d)\to 0$ as $n\to\infty$.

For this application of the central limit theorem, then, since

$$\frac{\log(K/S)-\hat{\mu}_p n-\varepsilon\log(u/d)}{\hat{\sigma}_p\sqrt{n}}\to z=\frac{\log(K/S)-\left(\log r-\frac{1}{2}\sigma^2\right)t}{\sigma\sqrt{t}}$$

we have

$$1-\Phi[a;n,p]\to N(z)=N\left[\frac{\log\left(Kr^{-t}/S\right)}{\sigma\sqrt{t}}+\tfrac{1}{2}\sigma\sqrt{t}\right]$$

The final step in the argument is to use the symmetry property of the standard normal distribution that $1-N(z)=N(-z)$. Therefore, as $n\to\infty$,

$$\Phi[a;n,p]\to N(-z)=N\left[\frac{\log\left(S/Kr^{-t}\right)}{\sigma\sqrt{t}}-\tfrac{1}{2}\sigma\sqrt{t}\right]=N(x-\sigma\sqrt{t})$$

Since a similar argument holds for $\Phi[a;n,p']$, this completes our demonstration that the binomial option pricing formula contains the Black-Scholes formula as a limiting case.[12, 13]

As we have remarked, the seeds of both the Black-Scholes formula and a continuous-time jump process formula are both contained within the binomial formulation. At which end point we arrive depends on how we take limits. Suppose, in place of our former correspondence for u, d and q, we instead set

$$u=u,\quad d=e^{\zeta(t/n)},\quad q=\lambda(t/n)$$

This correspondence captures the essence of a pure jump process in which each successive stock price is almost always close to the previous price ($S \rightarrow dS$), but occasionally, with low but continuing probability, significantly different ($S \rightarrow uS$). Observe that, as $n \rightarrow \infty$, the probability of a change by d becomes larger and larger, while the probability of a change by u approaches zero.

With these specifications, the initial condition of the central limit theorem we used is no longer satisfied, and it can be shown the stock price movements converge to a log-Poisson rather than a lognormal distribution as $n \rightarrow \infty$. Let us define

$$\Psi[x; y] \equiv \sum_{i=x}^{\infty} \frac{e^{-y} y^i}{i!}$$

as the complementary Poisson distribution function. The limiting option pricing formula for the above specification of u, d and q is then

Jump Process Option Pricing Formula

$$C = S\Psi[x; y] - Kr^{-t}\Psi[x; y/u]$$

where $y \equiv \frac{(\log r - \zeta)ut}{u-1}$

and $x \equiv$ the smallest non-negative integer greater than $\frac{\log\left(\frac{K}{S}\right) - \zeta t}{\log u}$

A very similar formula holds if we let $u = e^{\zeta(t/n)}$, $d = d$, and $1 - q = \lambda(t/n)$.

Dividends and put pricing

So far we have been assuming that the stock pays no dividends. It is easy to do away with this restriction. We will illustrate this with a specific dividend policy: the stock maintains a constant yield, δ, on each ex-dividend date. Suppose there is one period remaining before expiration and the current stock price is S. If the end of the period is an ex-dividend date, then an individual who owned the stock during the period will receive at that time a dividend of either δuS or δdS. Hence, the stock price at the end of the period will be either $u(1 - \delta)^v S$ or $d(1 - \delta)^v S$, where $v = 1$ if the end of the period is an ex-dividend date and $v = 0$ otherwise. Both δ and v are assumed to be known with certainty.

When the call expires, its contract and a rational exercise policy imply that its value must be either

$$C_u = \max[0, u(1 - \delta)^v S - K]$$

or

$$C_d = \max[0, d(1 - \delta)^v S - K]$$

Therefore,

$$C \begin{cases} C_u = \max[0, u(1 - \delta)^v S - K] \\ C_d = \max[0, d(1 - \delta)^v S - K] \end{cases}$$

Now we can proceed exactly as before. Again we can select a portfolio of Δ shares of stock and the dollar amount B in bonds which will have the same end-of-period value as the call.[14] By retracing our previous steps, we can show that

$$C = \frac{pC_u + (1-p)C_d}{\hat{r}}$$

if this is greater than $S - K$, and $C = S - K$ otherwise. Here, once again, $p = (\hat{r} - d)/(u - d)$ and $\Delta = (C_u - C_d)/(u - d)S$.

Thus far the only change is that $(1 - \delta)^v S$ has replaced S in the values for C_u and C_d. Now we come to the major difference: early exercise may be optimal. To see this, suppose that $v = 1$ and $d(1 - \delta)S > K$. Since $u > d$, then, also, $u(1 - \delta)S > K$. In this case, $C_u = u(1 - \delta)S - K$ and $C_d = d(1 - \delta)S - K$. Therefore, since $(u/\hat{r})p + (d/\hat{r})(1 - p) = 1$, $[pC_u + (1 - p)C_d]/\hat{r} = (1 - \delta)S - (K/\hat{r})$. For sufficiently high stock prices, this can obviously be less than $S - K$. Hence, there are definitely some circumstances in which no one would be willing to hold the call for one more period.

In fact, there will always be a critical stock price, $\hat{S}$, such that if $S > \hat{S}$, the call should be exercised immediately. $\hat{S}$ is the stock price at which $[pC_u + (1 - p)C_d]/\hat{r} = S - K$.[15] That is, it is the lowest stock price at which the value of the hedging portfolio exactly equals $S - K$. This means $\hat{S}$ will, other things equal, be lower the higher the dividend yield, the lower the interest rate, and the lower the striking price.

We can extend the analysis to an arbitrary number of periods in the same way as before. There is only one additional difference, a minor modification in the hedging operation. Now the funds in the hedging portfolio will be increased by any dividends received, or decreased by the restitution required for dividends paid while the stock is held short.

Although the possibility of optimal exercise before the expiration date causes no conceptual difficulties, it does seem to prohibit a simple closed-form solution for the value of a call with many periods to go. However, our analysis suggests a sequential numerical procedure which will allow us to calculate the continuous-time value to any desired degree of accuracy.

Let C be the current value of a call with n periods remaining. Define

$$\bar{v}(n,i) \equiv \sum_{k=1}^{n-i} v_k$$

so that $\bar{v}(n, i)$ is the number of ex-dividend dates occurring during the next $n - i$ periods. Let $C(n, i, j)$ be the value of the call $n - i$ periods from now, given that the current stock price S has changed to $u^j d^{n-i-j}(1 - \delta)^{\bar{v}(n,i)}S$, where $j = 0, 1, 2, \ldots, n - i$.

With this notation, we are prepared to solve for the current value of the call by working backward in time from the expiration date. At expiration, $i = 0$, so that

$$C(n,0,j) = \max[0, u^j d^{n-j}(1-\delta)^{\bar{v}(n,0)} S - K] \quad \text{for } j = 0,1,\ldots,n$$

One period before the expiration date, $i = 1$ so that

$$C(n,1,j) = \max\left[u^j d^{n-1-j}(1-\delta)^{\bar{v}(n,1)} S - K, \quad \frac{pC(n,0,j+1) + (1-p)C(n,0,j)}{\hat{r}}\right]$$

$$\text{for } j = 0,1,\ldots,n-1$$

More generally, i periods before expiration

$$C(n,i,j) =$$

$$\max\left[u^j d^{n-i-j}(1-\delta)^{\bar{v}(n,i)} S - K, \quad \frac{pC(n,i-1,j+1) + (1-p)C(n,i-1,j)}{\hat{r}}\right]$$

$$\text{for } j = 0,1,\ldots,n-i$$

Observe that each prior step provides the inputs needed to evaluate the right-hand arguments of each succeeding step. The number of calculations decreases as we move backward in time. Finally, with n periods before expiration, since $i = n$,

$$C = C(n,n,0) = \max\left[S - K, \quad \frac{pC(n,n-1,1) + (1-p)C(n,n-1,0)}{\hat{r}}\right]$$

and the hedge ratio is

$$\Delta = \frac{C(n, n-1, 1) - C(n, n-1, 0)}{(u-d)S}$$

We could easily expand the analysis to include dividend policies in which the amount paid on any ex-dividend date depends on the stock price at that time in a more general way.[16] However, this will cause some minor complications. In our present example with a constant dividend yield, the possible stock prices $n - i$ periods from now are completely determined by the total number of upward moves (and ex-dividend dates) occurring during that interval. With other types of dividend policies, the enumeration will be more complicated, since then the terminal stock price will be affected by the timing of the upward moves as well as their total number. But the basic principle remains the same. We go to the expiration date and calculate the call value for all of the possible prices that the stock could have then. Using this information, we step back one period and calculate the call values for all possible stock prices at that time, and so forth.

We will now illustrate the use of the binomial numerical procedure in approximating continuous-time call values. In order to have an exact continuous-time formula to use for comparison, we will consider the case with no dividends. Suppose that we are given the inputs required for the Black-Scholes option pricing formula: S, K, t, σ and r. To convert this information into the inputs d, u and $\hat{r}$ required for the binomial numerical procedure, we use the relationships:

$$d = \frac{1}{u}, \quad u = e^{\sigma\sqrt{t/n}}, \quad \hat{r} = r^{t/n}$$

Table 2 gives us a feeling for how rapidly option values approximated by the binomial method approach the corresponding limiting Black-Scholes values given by $n = \infty$. At $n = 5$, the values differ by at most \$0.25, and at $n = 20$, they differ by at most \$0.07. Although not shown, at $n = 50$, the greatest difference is less than \$0.03, and at $n = 150$, the values are identical to the penny.

To derive a method for valuing puts, we again use the binomial formulation. Although it has been convenient to express the argument in terms of a particular security, a call, this is not essential in any way. The same basic analysis can be applied to puts.

Letting P denote the current price of a put, with one period remaining before expiration, we have

$$P \begin{cases} P_u = \max[0, K - u(1-\delta)^v S] \\ P_d = \max[0, K - d(1-\delta)^v S] \end{cases}$$

Table 2. Binomial approximation of continuous-time call values for (1) January, (2) April and (3) July options; S = 40 and r = 1.05[a]

			n = 5			n = 20			n = ∞	
σ	K	(1)	(2)	(3)	(1)	(2)	(3)	(1)	(2)	(3)
	35	5.14	5.77	6.45	5.15	5.77	6.39	5.15	5.76	6.40
0.2	40	1.05	2.26	3.12	0.99	2.14	2.97	1.00	2.17	3.00
	45	0.02	0.54	1.15	0.02	0.51	1.11	0.02	0.51	1.10
	35	5.21	6.30	7.15	5.22	6.26	7.19	5.22	6.25	7.17
0.3	40	1.53	3.21	4.36	1.44	3.04	4.14	1.46	3.07	4.19
	45	0.11	1.28	2.12	0.15	1.28	2.23	0.16	1.25	2.24
	35	5.40	6.87	7.92	5.39	6.91	8.05	5.39	6.89	8.09
0.4	40	2.01	4.16	5.61	1.90	3.93	5.31	1.92	3.98	5.37
	45	0.46	1.99	3.30	0.42	2.09	3.42	0.42	2.10	3.43

[a] The January options have one month to expiration, the Aprils, four months, and the Julys, seven months; r and σ are expressed in annual terms.

Once again, we can choose a portfolio with ΔS in stock and B in bonds which will have the same end-of-period values as the put. By a series of steps which are formally equivalent to the ones we followed in the second section, we can show that

$$P = \frac{pP_u + (1-p)P_d}{\hat{r}}$$

if this is greater than $K - S$, and $P = K - S$ otherwise. As before, $p = (\hat{r} - d)/(u - d)$ and $\Delta = (P_u - P_d)/(u - d)S$. Note that for puts, since $P_u \leqq P_d$, then $\Delta \leqq 0$. This means that if we sell an overvalued put, the hedging portfolio which we buy will involve a short position in the stock.

We might hope that with puts we will be spared the complications caused by optimal exercise before the expiration date. Unfortunately, this is not the case. In fact, the situation is even worse in this regard. Now there are always some possible circumstances in which no one would be willing to hold the put for one more period. To see this, suppose $K > u(1 - \delta)^v S$. Since $u > d$, then, also, $K > d(1 - \delta)^v S$. In this case, $P_u = K - u(1 - \delta)^v S$ and $P_d = K - d(1 - \delta)^v S$. Therefore, since $(u/\hat{r})p + (d/\hat{r})(1 - p) = 1$,

$$\frac{pP_u + (1-p)P_d}{\hat{r}} = \left(\frac{K}{\hat{r}}\right) - (1-\delta)^v S$$

If there are no dividends (that is, $v = 0$), then this is certainly less than $K - S$. Even with $v = 1$, it will be less for a sufficiently low stock price.

Thus, there will now be a critical stock price, $\hat{S}$, such that if $S < \hat{S}$, the put should be exercised immediately. By analogy with our discussion for the call, we can see that this is the stock price at which $[pP_u + (1 - p)P_d]/\hat{r} = K - S$. Other things equal, $\hat{S}$ will be higher the lower the dividend yield, the higher the interest rate, and the higher the striking price. Optimal early exercise thus becomes more likely if the put is deep-in-the-money and the interest rate is high. The effect of dividends yet to be paid diminishes the advantages of immediate exercise, since the put buyer will be reluctant to sacrifice the forced declines in the stock price on future ex-dividend dates.

This argument can be extended in the same way as before to value puts with any number of periods to go. However, the chance for optimal exercise before the expiration date once again seems to preclude the possibility of expressing this value in a simple form. But our analysis also indicates that, with slight modification, we can value puts with the same numerical techniques we use for calls. Reversing the difference between the stock price and the striking price at each stage is the only change.[17]

The diagram below shows the stock prices, put values and values of Δ obtained in this way for the example given in the third section. The values used there were $S = 80$, $K = 80$, $n = 3$, $u = 1.5$, and $\hat{r} = 1.1$. To include dividends as well, we assume that a cash dividend of five percent ($\delta = 0.05$) will be paid at the end of the last period before the expiration date. Thus, $(1 - \delta)^{\bar{v}(n,0)} = 0.95$, $(1 - \delta)^{\bar{v}(n,1)} = 0.95$, and $(1 - \delta)^{\bar{v}(n,2)} = 1.0$. Put values in italics indicate that immediate exercise is optimal.

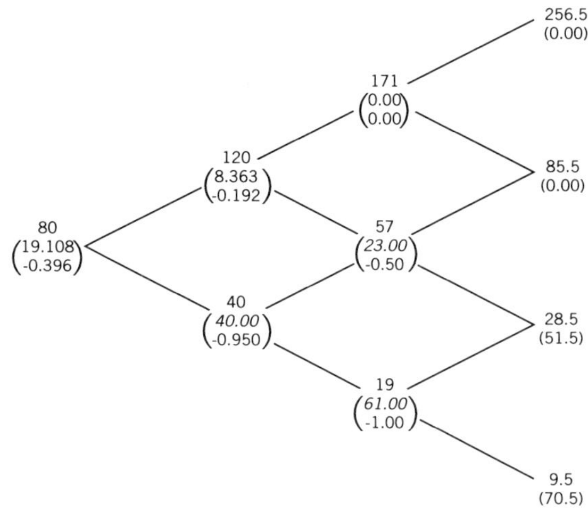

Conclusion

It should now be clear that whenever stock price movements conform to a discrete binomial process, or to a limiting form of such a process, options can be priced solely on the basis of arbitrage considerations. Indeed, we could have significantly complicated the simple binomial process while still retaining this property.

The probabilities of an upward or downward move did not enter into the valuation formula. Hence, we would obtain the same result if q depended on the current or past stock prices or on other random variables. In addition, u and d could have been deterministic functions of time. More significantly, the size of the percentage changes in the stock price over each period could have depended on the stock price at the beginning of each period or on previous stock prices.[18] However, if the size of the changes were to depend on any other random variable, not itself perfectly correlated with the stock price, then our argument will no longer hold. If any arbitrage result is then still possible, it will require the use of additional assets in the hedging portfolio.

We could also incorporate certain types of imperfections into the binomial option pricing approach, such as differential borrowing and lending rates and margin requirements. These can be shown to produce upper and lower bounds on option prices, outside of which riskless profitable arbitrage would be possible.

Since all existing preference-free option pricing results can be derived as limiting forms of a discrete two-state process, we might suspect that two-state stock price movements, with the qualifications mentioned above, must be in some sense necessary, as well as sufficient, to derive option pricing formulas based solely on arbitrage considerations. To price an option by arbitrage methods, there must exist a portfolio of other assets which exactly replicates in every state of nature the payoff received by an optimally exercised option. Our basic proposition is the following. Suppose, as we have, that markets are perfect, that changes in the interest rate are never random, and that changes in the stock price are always random. In a discrete time model, a necessary and sufficient condition for options of all maturities and striking prices to be priced by arbitrage using only the stock and bonds in the portfolio is that in each period,

a) the stock price can change from its beginning-of-period value to only two-ex-dividend values at the end of the period, and
b) the dividends and the size of each of the two possible changes are presently known functions depending at most on: (i) current and past stock prices, (ii) current and past values of random variables whose changes in each period are perfectly correlated with the change in the stock period, and (iii) calendar time.

The sufficiency of the condition can be established by a straightforward application of the methods we have presented. Its necessity is implied by the discussion at the end of the second section.[19, 20, 21]

This rounds out the principal conclusion of this paper: the simple two-state process is really the essential ingredient of option pricing by arbitrage methods. This is surprising, perhaps, given the mathematical complexities of some of the current models in this field. But it is reassuring to find such simple economic arguments at the heart of this powerful theory.

1 *To take an elementary case, consider a firm with a single liability of a homogeneous class of pure discount bonds. The stockholders then have a "call" on the assets of the firm which they can choose to exercise at the maturity date of the debt by paying its principal to the bondholders. In turn, the bonds can be interpreted as a portfolio containing a default-free loan with the same face value as the bonds and a short position in a put on the assets of the firm.*

2 *Sharpe (1978) has partially developed this approach to option pricing in his excellent new book,* Investments. *Rendleman and Bartter (1978) have recently independently discovered a similar formulation of the option pricing problem.*

3 *To keep matters simple, assume for now that the stock will pay no cash dividends during the life of the call. We also ignore transaction costs, margin requirements and taxes.*

4 *Of course, restitution is required for payouts made to securities held short.*

5 *We will ignore the uninteresting special case where* q *is zero or one and* u = d = r.

6 *Buying bonds is the same as lending; selling them is the same as borrowing.*

7 *In some applications of the theory to other areas, it is useful to consider options which can be exercised only on the expiration date. These are usually termed European options. Those which can be exercised at any earlier time as well, such as we have been examining here, are then referred to as American options. Our discussion could be easily modified to include European calls. Since immediate exercise is then precluded, their values would always be given by (2), even if this is less than* S – K.

8 *In the current situation, with no dividends, we can show by a simple direct argument that if there are no arbitrage opportunities, then the call value must always be greater than* S – K *before the expiration date. Suppose that the call is selling for* S – K. *Then there would be an easy arbitrage strategy which would require no initial investment and would always have a positive return. All we would have to do is buy the call, short the stock and invest* K *dollars in bonds. See Merton (1973). In the general case, with dividends, such an argument is no longer valid, and we must use the procedure of checking every period.*

9 *If we were reverse hedging by buying an undervalued call and selling the hedging portfolio, then we would ourselves want to exercise at this point. Since we will receive* S – K *from exercising, this will be exactly enough money to buy back the hedging portfolio.*

10 *The scale of this unit (perhaps a day, or a year) is unimportant as long as* r *and* t *are expressed in the same scale.*

11 *A surprising feature of this evaluation is that although* $p \neq q$ *and thus* $\hat{\mu}_p \neq \hat{\mu}$, *and* $\hat{\sigma}_p \neq \hat{\sigma}$, *nonetheless* $\hat{\sigma}_p\sqrt{n}$ *and* $\hat{\sigma}\sqrt{n}$ *have the same limiting value as* $n \to \infty$. *By contrast, since* $\mu \neq \log r - (\tfrac{1}{2}\sigma^2)$, $\hat{\mu}_p n$ *and* $\hat{\mu} n$ *do not. This results from the way we needed to specify* u *and* d *to obtain convergence to a lognormal distribution. Rewriting this as* $\sigma\sqrt{t} = (\log u)\sqrt{n}$, *it is clear that the limiting value* σ *of the standard deviation does not depend on* p *or* q, *and hence must be the same for either. However, at any point before the limit, since*

$$\hat{\sigma}^2 n = \left(\sigma^2 - \mu^2 \frac{t}{n}\right)t \quad \text{and} \quad \hat{\sigma}_p^2 n = \left[\sigma^2 - \left(\log r - \tfrac{1}{2}\sigma^2\right)^2 \frac{t}{n}\right]t$$

$\hat{\sigma}$ *and* $\hat{\sigma}_p$ *will generally have different values.*

The fact that $\hat{\mu}_p n \to (\log r - \tfrac{1}{2}\sigma^2)t$ *can also be derived from the property of the lognormal distribution that*

$$\log E[S^*/S] = \mu_p t + \tfrac{1}{2}\sigma^2$$

where E *and* μ_p *are measured with respect to probability* p. *Since* $p = (\hat{r} - d)/(u - d)$, *it follows that* $\hat{r} = pu + (1 - p)d$. *For independently distributed random variables, the expectation of a product equals the product of their expectations. Therefore,*

$$E[S^*/S] = [pu + (1 - p)d]^n = \hat{r}^n = r^t$$

Substituting r^t *for* $E[S^*/S]$ *in the previous equation, we have*

$$\mu_p = \log r - \tfrac{1}{2}\sigma^2 t$$

12 *The only difference is that, as* $n \to \infty$, $p' \to \tfrac{1}{2} + \tfrac{1}{2}[(\log r + \tfrac{1}{2}\sigma^2)/\sigma]\sqrt{(t/n)}$. *Further, it can be shown that as* $n \to \infty$, $\Delta \to N(x)$. *Therefore, for the Black-Scholes model,* $\Delta S = SN(x)$ *and* $B = -Kr^{-t}N(x - \sigma\sqrt{t})$.

13 *In our original development, we obtained the following equation (somewhat rewritten) relating the call prices in successive periods:*

$$\left(\frac{\hat{r} - d}{u - d}\right)C_u + \left(\frac{u - \hat{r}}{u - d}\right)C_d - \hat{r}C = 0$$

By their more difficult methods, Black and Scholes obtained directly a partial differential equation analogous to our discrete-time difference equation. Their equation is

$$\tfrac{1}{2}\sigma^2 S^2 \frac{\partial^2 C}{\partial S^2} + (\log r)S\frac{\partial C}{\partial S} - \frac{\partial C}{\partial t} - (\log r)C = 0$$

The value of the call, C, *was then derived by solving this equation subject to the boundary condition* $C^* = \max[0, S^* - K]$.

Based on our previous analysis, we would now suspect that, as $n \to \infty$, *our difference equation would approach the Black-Scholes partial differential equation. This can be confirmed by substituting our definitions of* $\hat{r}$, u, d *in terms of* n *in the way described earlier, expanding* C_u, C_d *in a Taylor series around*

$(e^{\sigma\sqrt{h}}S, t - h)$ *and* $(e^{-\sigma\sqrt{h}}S, t - h)$, *respectively, and then expanding* $e^{\sigma\sqrt{h}}$, $e^{-\sigma\sqrt{h}}$, *and* r^h *in a Taylor series, substituting these in the equation and collecting terms. If we then divide by* h *and let* $h \rightarrow 0$, *all terms of higher order than* h *go to zero. This yields the Black-Scholes equation.*

14 *Remember that if we are long the portfolio we will receive the dividend at the end of the period; if we are short, we will have to make restitution for the dividend.*

15 *Actually solving for* $\hat{S}$ *explicitly is straightforward but rather tedious, so we will omit it.*

16 *We could also allow the amount to depend on previous stock prices.*

17 *Michael Parkinson (1977) has suggested a similar numerical procedure based on a trinomial process, where the stock price can either increase, decrease, or remain unchanged. In fact, given the theoretical basis for the binomial numerical procedure provided, the numerical method can be generalised to permit* $k + 1 \leqq n$ *jumps to new stock prices in each period. We can consider exercise only every* k *periods, using the binomial formula to leap across intermediate periods. In effect, this means permitting* $k + 1$ *possible new stock prices before exercise is again considered. That is, instead of considering exercise* n *times, we would only consider it about* n/k *times. For fixed* t *and* k, *as* $n \rightarrow \infty$, *option values will approach their continuous-time values.*

This alternative procedure is interesting since it may enhance computer efficiency. At one extreme, for calls on stocks which do not pay dividends, setting $k + 1 = n$ *gives the most efficient results. However, when the effect of potential early exercise is important and greater accuracy is required, the most efficient results are achieved by setting* $k = 1$, *as in our description above.*

18 *Of course, different option pricing formulas would result from these more complex stochastic processes. See Cox and Ross (1976) and Geske (1979). Nonetheless, all option pricing formulas in these papers can be derived as limiting forms of a properly specified discrete two-state process.*

19 *Note that option values need not depend on the present stock price alone. In some cases, formal dependence on the entire series of past values of the stock price and other variables can be summarised in a small number of state variables.*

20 *In some circumstances, it will be possible to value options by arbitrage when this condition does not hold by using additional assets in the hedging portfolio. The value of the option will then in general depend on the values of these other assets, although in certain cases only parameters describing their movement will be required.*

21 *Merton's (1976) model, with both continuous and jump components, is a good example of a stock price process for which no exact option pricing formula is obtainable purely from arbitrage considerations. To obtain an exact formula, it is necessary to impose restrictions on the stochastic movements of other securities, as Merton did, or on investor preferences. For example, Rubinstein (1976) has been able to derive the Black-Scholes option pricing formula, under circumstances that do not admit arbitrage, by suitably restricting investor preferences. Additional problems arise when interest rates are stochastic, although Merton (1973) has shown that some arbitrage results may still be obtained.*

Bibliography

Black, F. and M. Scholes, 1973, "The Pricing of Options and Corporate Liabilities", *Journal of Political Economy* 3, pp. 637–654; reprinted as Chapter 1 of the present volume.

Brennan, M. J. and E. S. Schwartz, 1977, "The Valuation of American Put Options", *Journal of Finance* 32, pp. 449–462.

Cox, J. C. and S. A. Ross, 1975, "The Pricing of Options for Jump Processes", Rodney L. White Center Working Paper no. 2-75, University of Pennsylvania.

Cox, J. C. and S. A. Ross, 1976, "The Valuation of Options for Alternative Stochastic Processes", *Journal of Financial Economics* 3, pp. 145–166.

Geske, R., 1979, "The Valuation of Compound Options", *Journal of Financial Economics* 7, pp. 63–81.

Harrison, J. M. and D. M. Kreps, 1979, "Martingales and Arbitrage in Multiperiod Securities Markets", *Journal of Economic Theory* 20, pp. 381–408.

Merton, R. C., 1973, "The Theory of Rational Option Pricing", *Bell Journal of Economics and Management Science* 4, pp. 141–183.

Merton, R. C., 1976, "Option Pricing when Underlying Stock Returns are Discontinuous", *Journal of Financial Economics* 3, pp. 125–144.

Merton, R. C., 1977, "On the Pricing of Contingent Claims and the Modigliani-Miller Theorem", *Journal of Financial Economics* 5, pp. 241-250.

Parkinson, M., 1977, "Option pricing: The American put", *Journal of Business* 50, pp. 21-36.

Rendleman, R. J., and B. J. Bartter, 1978, "Two-state Option Pricing", unpublished paper, Graduate School of Management, Northwestern University.

Rubinstein, M., 1976, "The Valuation of Uncertain Income Streams and the Pricing of Options", *Bell Journal of Economics* 7, pp. 407-425.

Sharpe, W. F., 1978, *Investments* (Prentice-Hall, Englewood Cliffs, NJ).

3

On the Theory of Option Pricing*

Alain Bensoussan
CNES, Paris

The objective of this article is to provide an axiomatic framework in order to define the concept of value function for risky operations for which there is no market. There is a market for assets, whose prices are characterised as stochastic processes. The method consists of constructing a portfolio of these assets which will mimic the risks involved in the operation. We follow the terminology of the theory of options, although the set-up goes beyond that particular problem.

Since the celebrated work of Black and Scholes (1973), there has been an extensive interest in the finance literature to present a rigorous theory of option pricing. The basic idea of Merton (1973) is to introduce a *hedging* portfolio consisting of the option itself, shares on the risky asset and a short position in bonds (non-risky asset). Then choosing a strategy which eliminates risks and possibilities of arbitrage, supposing that the prices of the risky asset and of the bond evolve according to diffusions and relying on Itô's calculus, he derives a valuation equation for options similar to that of Black and Scholes (they had obtained it by more formal arguments).

Although very appealing, the theory of Merton poses some questions. The main assumption is that the value of the option at any time is a *deterministic* function of the price of the risky asset and of the bond (if its price is not deterministic). Moreover, he assumes that it is a sufficiently regular function to apply Itô's calculus (this point has been clarified by Gabay (1982) relying on mathematical results for partial differential equations).

It is clear that the valuation equation itself depends strongly on the mathematical model for the prices of assets and on Itô's calculus, but the fact that it is possible to give a value to the option should depend only on the economic considerations, such as absence of risks and no arbitrage opportunities.

This is apparent in the discrete-time model of Cox, Ross and Rubinstein (1979) generalised in Harrison and Pliska (1982). To back this argument, Harrison and Pliska have developed a theory of continuous trading which uses the theory of martingales and representation theorems of martingales. The main advantage of this theory is to show that the pricing of options is possible under general assumptions for asset prices. Moreover, they point out that what is important for pricing options is the fact that for some probability the discount prices of assets behave like martingales. This implies the existence of a price. The Markovian property assumed in Black and Scholes (1973) and Merton (1973) is not basic.

**This paper was first published in the* Acta Applicandae Mathematicae, *2 (1984)*, pp. 139–158. *It is reprinted with the permission of Kluwer Academic International, Dordrecht, The Netherlands.*

Let us briefly discuss the ideas in Harrison and Pliska (1981). It is assumed that there exists a probability for which the discounted prices of the risky assets (not just one in this model) become martingales. The authors then define the concept of *trading strategy* which corresponds to a portfolio made of the bond and the risky assets (not the option) with the possibility of continuous adjustment. The value of the portfolio at any time is called the *value process of the trading strategy*. Trading strategies are requested to be *self-financing*. This concept can be defined in a mathematically rigorous way, while keeping all its economic meaning. Harrison and Pliska (1982) call *admissible* a trading strategy to which corresponds a value process which is a *positive martingale*. The main role of this definition is to prove the following property. Call *attainable contingent claims* all positive random variables which equal the value process at T (the horizon) of some admissible strategy. Then there is a *unique price* attached to attainable contingent claims. This, of course, prevents the possibility of arbitrage and permits the building of a hedging portfolio for the option. The authors of Harrison and Pliska (1981) claim that their market model is *complete* when every (integrable) claim is attainable.

The drawback is that all these concepts are defined on mathematical (rather than economic) considerations (namely the existence of value processes which are martingales). What characterises exactly complete markets from the economic viewpoint? Here Harrison and Pliska (1981) pay the price of their great generality. Indeed, they do not find a characterisation which has the same economic meaning as the one in the discrete time and finite probability space case. In the finite theory they argue that completeness of the market is a matter of dimension, that is at each time t, given the information available, the various cases which can occur at $t + 1$, because of randomness, should equal the total number of securities (risky assets plus bond). In other words, the size of the portfolio should match the number of random cases one step ahead of time. Apparently there is no analogue of that fundamental property in continuous trading.

The first purpose of this paper is to show that, in fact, something similar exists. Completeness of the market amounts to building portfolios containing sufficiently many assets to match the *number of independent exogenous sources of uncertainties*. We analyse this statement when the exogenous sources of uncertainties are a finite number of Wiener processes. But it will become apparent that more general independent martingales will do.

We prove that there exists one, and only one, portfolio with self-financing strategy, involving no risk and no possibility of arbitrage, which hedges against any given contingent claim. A unique price is then obtained for any contingent claim. Note that, although the underlying sources of uncertainty are Wiener processes, we do not assume that asset prices behave like diffusion processes (although they are Itô's processes). Moreover, we do not assume any Markovian property. The completeness of the market, adequately defined mathematically in the spirit of the above discussion, is the unique source of the pricing theory.

Harrison and Pliska have also considered a diffusion model as an example of a complete market along the lines of their general definitions. But our presentation has the advantage of making the economic content more apparent. We give a set of properties with economic meaning, which should be satisfied by a value function of a contingent claim (the price being the value at present time). The problem then amounts to showing that this set of properties characterises one, and only one, value function.

The second contribution of this article, and the main one, is to give a rigorous theory of the valuation of "American" contingent claims. We represent the claims which can be made at any time before maturity in this way. Again we present a set of properties, with the economic meaning to be satisfied by a value function of an "American" claim. We show that this set characterises one and only one function. This problem has not been considered in Harrison and Pliska (1981), and probably their setting is not adequate to solve it.

Setting of the model

NOTATION AND ASSUMPTIONS

Let (Ω, A, P) be a probability space, in which a filtration F^t and an **N**-dimensional standardised F^t Wiener process $w(t)$ are given. In fact, we shall assume for some results that

$$F^t = \sigma(w(s), s \leq t) \tag{1}$$

We consider **N** risky assets, whose prices $S_k(t)$, $k = 1, \ldots, N$ behave like Itô processes as follows:

$$dS_k(t) = S_k(t)\,(\alpha_k(t)\,dt + \beta_k(t) \cdot dw(t)) \tag{2}$$

where $S_k(0)$ is deterministic and positive.

In (2) we assume that

$$\alpha_k(t) \text{ and } \beta_k(t) \tag{3}$$

are processes with values in **R** and $\mathbf{R}^N$, respectively, which are adapted to F_t and bounded by a deterministic constant on $[0, T]$.

Note that the solution of (2) is given by

$$S_k(t) = S_k(0)\exp\left(\int_0^t \left[\alpha_k(s) - \tfrac{1}{2}|\beta_k(s)|^2\right]ds + \int_0^t \beta_k(s)\cdot dw(s)\right) \tag{4}$$

and a.s. $S_k(t) > 0\ \forall\, t$.

Besides the risky assets, there is a "non-risky" asset called the "bond", whose price $S_0(t)$ evolves according to the equation

$$\frac{dS_0(t)}{dt} = S_0(t)\alpha_0(t)\,dt \qquad S_0(0) = 1 \tag{5}$$

where

$$\alpha_0(t) \text{ is adapted to } F^t \text{ and bounded to } [0, T] \text{ by a deterministic constant} \tag{6}$$

The solution of (5) is given by

$$S_0(t) = \exp\int_0^t \alpha_0(s)\,ds \tag{7}$$

We do not need to assume that α_0 is deterministic, nor ≥ 0, so the bond is not completely riskless. However, there is no term in dw like all other risky assets.

We define the *discount factor*:

$$r(t) = \frac{1}{S_0(t)} = \exp - \int_0^t \alpha_0(s)\,ds \tag{8}$$

and we have

$$\frac{dr}{dt} = -r(t)\alpha_0(t) \qquad r(0) = 1 \tag{9}$$

We assume that the risky asset k yields a dividend given by $z_k(t)\,S_k(t)$ per unit of time at t, where

$$z_k(t) \text{ is a scalar process which is adapted and bounded on } [0, T] \tag{10}$$

THE PROBLEM

The problem is to define a "value" for the following claim: a fixed payout $f(t)$ per unit of time up to T and a payout at maturity T, equal to $h(T)$, where

$$f \text{ is an adapted process}, \quad f(t) \geq 0 \tag{11}$$

$h(T)$ is a positive random variable which is F^T measurable.

For technical reasons we shall assume that

$$Eh(T)^s < \infty, \quad E\int_0^T f(t)^s dt < \infty, \quad s > 2 \tag{12}$$

Hedging portfolio

TRADING STRATEGIES

Let $\upsilon_0(t), \ldots, \upsilon_N(t)$ be stochastic processes satisfying

$$\upsilon_0(t), \upsilon_k(t), \quad k = 1, \ldots, \mathbf{N} \tag{13}$$

are adapted processes such that

$$\text{a.s.} \int_0^T |\upsilon_0(t)|^2 dt, \quad \int_0^T |\upsilon_k(t)|^2 dt < \infty$$

We term υ_0, υ_k a *trading strategy*.[1]

A portfolio corresponding to a trading strategy has a value defined by the stochastic process

$$u(t) = \upsilon_0(t)S_0(t) + \sum_{k=1}^{N} \upsilon_k(t)S_k(t) \tag{14}$$

We shall say that the portfolio is a ***hedging portfolio*** against the claim defined in 1.2 whenever $u(t)$ has an Itô differential given by

$$du(t) = -f(t)dt + \upsilon_0(t)dS_0(t) + \sum_k \upsilon_k(t)dS_k(t) + \sum_k \upsilon_k(t)z_k(t)S_k(t)dt$$
$$u(T) = h(T) \tag{15}$$

The justification is economically clear. For $u(t)$ to be a correct valuation of the claim at time t, we need to consider that the potential (stochastic) gains on a small interval Δt, namely $\Delta u(t) + f(t)\Delta t$ correspond exactly to the gains due to the possession of the portfolio, which are

$$\upsilon_0(t)\Delta S_0(t) + \sum_k \upsilon_k(t)\Delta S_k(t) + \sum_k \upsilon_k(t)z_k(t)S_k(t)\Delta t$$

Thus on any small interval Δt the risks are identical and no arbitrage opportunities exist.

The mathematical abstraction enters only at the stage of replacing the variations on small intervals by differentials and interpreting them in the sense of Itô differentials, therefore the valuation problem is equivalent to the existence of an Itô process $u(t)$ satisfying the conditions (14), (15) in which $\upsilon_0, \upsilon_1, \ldots, \upsilon_N$ form a trading strategy to be chosen conveniently. Such a process is called a ***valuation*** of the claim (11). This claim will be termed "European" in comparison with the "American claims" considered in the third section.

DISCOUNTED VALUES AND DISCOUNTED ASSET PRICES
We have the following:

LEMMA 2.1: *The following formulas hold:*

$$dr(t)u(t) =$$

$$-r(t)f(t)dt+r(t)\sum_{k=1}^{n}\upsilon_k(t)S_k(t)\,(\beta_k(t)\cdot dw+(\alpha_k(t)+z_k(t)-\alpha_0(t))dt) \quad (16)$$

$$dr(t)\,S_k(t) = -r(t)\,z_k(t)\,S_k(t)\,dt + r(t)\,S_k(t)\,(\beta_k(t)\cdot dw + (\alpha_k(t) + z_k(t) - \alpha_0(t))\,dt) \quad (17)$$

PROOF: We replace in (15) $\upsilon_0(t)$ by its expression taken from (14), then use (9) and (15) to get (16). Now (17) is clearly derived from (9) and (2).

COMPLETE MARKETS
We shall say that the market model is *complete* when the following assumption holds:

$$\beta(t)\,\beta^*(t) \geq \delta I, \quad \delta > 0 \quad (18)$$

where $\beta(t)$ denotes the matrix whose rows are $\beta_k(t)$. This is a compatibility condition between the number of risky assets and the independent sources of noise.

There exists one, and only one, $\theta(t)$ adapted to F_t such that

$$\beta_k(t)\cdot\theta(t) = \alpha_k(t) + z_k(t) - \alpha_0(t) \quad (19)$$

Clearly we have

$$\theta(t) = \beta(t)\,(\beta(t)\,\beta^*(t))^{-1}\,(\alpha(t) + z(t) - \alpha_0(t)) \quad (20)$$

where $\alpha(t) + z(t) - \alpha_0(t)$ is the vector whose components are $\alpha_k(t) + z_k(t) - \alpha_0(t)$.

Introduce the vector $\tilde{w}(t)$, defined by

$$\tilde{w}(t) = w(t) + \int_0^t \theta(s)\,ds \quad (21)$$

Then the relations (16) and (17) yield

$$dr(t)u(t) = -r(t)f(t)dt+r(t)\sum_{k=1}^{N}\upsilon_k(t)S_k(t)\beta_k(t)\cdot d\tilde{w} \quad (22)$$

$$dr(t)\,S_k(t) = -r(t)\,z_k(t)\,S_k(t)\,dt + r(t)\,S_k(t)\,\beta_k(t)\cdot d\tilde{w} \quad (23)$$

On the space Ω, A, consider the probability Q whose Radon-Nikodym derivative with respect to P is given by

$$\left.\frac{dQ}{dP}\right|_{F^T} = \exp\left(-\int_0^T\theta\cdot dw - \frac{1}{2}\int_0^T|\theta^2 ds|\right) = \mu(T) \quad (24)$$

We can then state:

THEOREM 2.1: *Under the assumption of complete market* (18), *there exists one, and only one, valuation function* $u(t)$ *for the claim* (11). *The corresponding hedging portfolio is also uniquely defined. The valuation function is expressed as*

$$u(t) = E^Q\left(h(T)\exp-\int_t^T\alpha_0(s)ds+\int_t^T f(s)\exp-\int_t^s\alpha_0(\sigma)d\sigma\,\Big|\,F^t\right) \quad (25)$$

PROOF: Under the probability Q, $\tilde{w}(t)$ becomes a standardised Wiener process. The formula (25) follows immediately from (22), which proves that the valuation, if it exists, is unique and given by (25).

On the other hand, $u(t)$ defined by (25) is a valuation function. Indeed, we have

$$u(t) = -\int_0^t f(s)\frac{r(s)}{r(t)}\,ds + \frac{1}{r(t)}E^Q\left[X \middle| F^t\right] \tag{26}$$

where

$$X = h(T)\,r(T) + \int_0^T f(x)\,r(s)\,ds \tag{27}$$

and

$$E^Q\left[X \middle| F^t\right] = \frac{E\left[\mu(T)X \middle| F^t\right]}{\mu(t)} \tag{28}$$

where

$$\mu(T) = \exp\left(-\int_0^t \theta\cdot dw - \frac{1}{2}\int_0^t |\theta|^2\,ds\right) \tag{29}$$

Now, $E[\mu(T)X \mid F^t]$ is a square-integrable F^t-martingale. This property follows from the assumption (1.12). Since F^t is generated by $w(t)$, it follows from Kunita and Watanabe (1967) that

$$E[\mu(T)X \mid F^t| = E\mu(T)X + \int_0^t g(s)\cdot dw(s)$$

where $g(t)$ is a uniquely determined F^t-adapted, square-integrable stochastic process.

We deduce from (26):

$$\begin{aligned} r(t)u(t) &= -\int_0^t f(s)r(s)\,ds + \frac{E\mu(T)X + \int_0^t g(s)\cdot dw(s)}{\mu(t)} \\ &= -\int_0^t f(s)r(s)\,ds + \frac{\xi(t)}{\mu(t)} \end{aligned} \tag{30}$$

hence

$$dr(t)u(t) = -f(t)r(t)dt + \frac{1}{\mu}g\cdot dw + \frac{\xi}{\mu}\left[\theta\cdot dw + |\theta|^2\,dt\right] + \frac{g\cdot\theta}{\mu}dt$$

Comparing this expression with (16), we can identify using (19):

$$r(t)\sum_{k=1}^N \upsilon_k(t)S_k(t)\beta_k(t) = \frac{1}{\mu(t)}g(t) + \frac{\xi(t)\theta(t)}{\mu(t)}$$

$$r(t)\sum_{k=1}^N \upsilon_k(t)S_k(t)\beta_k(t)\cdot\theta(t) = \frac{\xi(t)}{\mu(t)}|\theta|^2 + \frac{g(t)\cdot\theta(t)}{\mu(t)} \tag{31}$$

the second relation is redundant and thus can be omitted.

The relation (31) defines $\upsilon_k(t)\,S_k(t)$ in a unique way: consider the vector

$$q(t) = \frac{1}{\mu(t)}\beta\beta^*(t)^{-1}\,[g(t) + \xi(t)\theta(t)] \tag{32}$$

then

$$\upsilon_k(t)\,S_k(t) = q_k(t), \quad k = 1, \ldots, N \tag{33}$$

and since $S_k(t) > 0$, the process $\upsilon_k(t)$ is well defined.

One then defines $\upsilon_0(t)$ by

$$\upsilon_0(t)S_k(t) = u(t) - \sum_{k=1}^{N} \upsilon_k(t)S_k(t) \tag{34}$$

From (34) and (16), which is satisfied, we deduce the first relation (15). The second relation (15) follows from the definition of (25). The proof is now complete.

REMARK 2.1: We deduce from (23) that

$$dS_k(t) = (\alpha_0(t) - z_k(t))\, S_k(t)\, dt + S_k(t)\, \beta_k(t) \cdot d\tilde{w} \tag{35}$$

Therefore, the change of probability induces a modification of the drift of the processes representing the asset prices.

REMARK 2.2: Consider the process

$$Z_k(t) = r(t)\, S_k(t) + \int_0^t r(s)\, z_k(s)\, S_k(s)\, ds \tag{36}$$

which represents the discounted value of the asset k. From (23) it follows that $Z_k(t)$ is a Q, F^t-martingale. We can write

$$r(t)u(t) = u(0) - \int_0^t r(s)f(s)ds + \sum_{k=1}^{N} \int_0^t \upsilon_k(s)dZ_k(s) \tag{37}$$

Valuation of "American claims"

THE PROBLEM

In "American claims" one introduces the possibility of *stopping* the process at any time $\theta \leq T$, where θ is a F^t stopping time. In that case the claim consists of the payout $f(t)$ per unit of time up to θ and the amount $h(\theta)$ at time θ. We assume that

> $h(t)$ is adapted to F^t, positive and bounded by a deterministic constant on $[0, T]$; $h(t)$ is a continuous process (in fact some more regularity will be needed (cf. (79)) (38)

and

> $f(t)$ is bounded by a deterministic constant on $[0, T]$, positive, adapted (39)

VALUATION PROBLEM

A valuation for the "American claim" will be a *continuous adapted bounded* process satisfying the following conditions:

> $u(t)$ can be obtained by a trading strategy, namely

$$u(t) = \upsilon_0(t)S_0(t) + \sum_{k=1}^{N} \upsilon_k(t)S_k(t) \tag{40}$$

where $\upsilon_0, \upsilon_1, \ldots, \upsilon_N$ is a trading strategy as (13).

$$u(t) \geq h(t), \quad \forall t \in [0, T], \quad u(T) = h(T) \tag{41}$$

These conditions mean that the value of the claim is at any time larger or equal to the gain corresponding to the decision of stopping the process at this time. At maturity T, the two quantities are equal as in the case of "European" claims.

We request also that

$$u(t_2)-u(t_1)+\int_{t_1}^{t_2} f(s)ds \le$$

$$\int_{t_1}^{t_2}\left(\upsilon_0(s)dS_0(s)+\sum_k \upsilon_k(s)dS_k(s)+\sum_k \upsilon_k(s)z_k(s)S_k(s)ds\right),\quad \forall t_1 \le t_2 \le T \quad (42)$$

This condition expresses the protective hedge property of the portfolio. Indeed, at any time t_1, all random gains on any future time interval (t_1, t_2) which can be obtained from possessing the portfolio are at least larger than those derived from possessing the claim.

Of course, (42) means that

$$u(t)+\int_0^t f(s)ds -$$

$$\int_0^t\left(\upsilon_0(s)dS_0(s)+\sum_k \upsilon_k(s)dS_k(s)+\sum_k \upsilon_k(s)z_k(s)S_k(s)ds\right) \quad (43)$$

is a continuous non-increasing process. Let

$$\hat{\theta}_t = \inf\{s \ge t \mid u(s)-h(s)=0\} \quad (44)$$

which is an F^s stopping time, since it is the first exit time of the continuous process $u(s)-h(s)$ from the open set $\{x>0\}$. Note that, because of the second condition (41), we have $\hat{\theta}_t \le T$.

We shall also request that

$$u(s\wedge\hat{\theta}_t)-u(t)+\int_t^{s\wedge\hat{\theta}_t} f(\lambda)d\lambda-\int_t^{s\wedge\hat{\theta}_t}\left(\upsilon_0(\lambda)dS_0(\lambda)+\sum_k \upsilon_k(\lambda)dS_k(\lambda)+\right.$$

$$\left.\sum_k \upsilon_k(\lambda)z_k(\lambda)S_k(\lambda)d\lambda\right)=0,\quad \forall s \ge T \quad (45)$$

The reason for (45) is as follows. In the interval $[t, \hat{\theta}_t]$ we have $u(s)-h(s)>0$; therefore, one should not exert the claim before $\hat{\theta}_t$ since the value of the claim is strictly larger than one can get from exerting it. On this interval, the situation is the same as in the case of a "European claim". Therefore, the gains on any interval in $[t, \hat{\theta}_t]$ from the claim coincide with those obtained from the portfolio.

REMARK 3.1: As we shall see, we cannot expect in the case of "American" claims $u(t)$ to be an Itô process. That is why we write (42) and (45), which play a role similar to (15).

REMARK 3.2: The problem of evaluating an "American claim" is thus to find a continuous adapted bounded process $u(t)$ satisfying conditions (40), (41), (42) and (45).

UNIQUENESS OF THE SOLUTION OF THE VALUATION PROBLEM IN THE CASE OF COMPLETE MARKETS

Let us make the assumption (18) of complete markets.

LEMMA 3.1: *Under the assumption of complete markets* (18), (38) *and* (39), *there exists only one possible valuation function for the "American" claim. It is given by*

$$u(t)=\operatorname*{ess\,sup}_{t\le\theta\le T} E^Q\left(h(\theta)\exp-\int_t^\theta \alpha_0(s)ds+\int_t^\theta f(s)\exp-\int_t^s \alpha_0(\sigma)d\sigma \,\middle|\, F^t\right) \quad (46)$$

where θ *is any possible* F^t *stopping time.*

PROOF: Under the probability Q, $\tilde{w}(t)$ is a standardised Wiener process. Therefore, we deduce from (43) that

$$u(t)+\int_0^t [f(s)-\alpha_0(s)u(s)]ds-\int_0^t \sum_k \upsilon_k(s)S_k(s)\beta_k(\beta)\cdot d\tilde{w}=\mu(t) \qquad (47)$$

is a continuous, non-increasing process. Hence

$$d(u-\mu)=(-f+\alpha_0 u)\,dt+\sum_k \upsilon_k S_k \beta_k \cdot d\tilde{w}$$

Therefore,

$$dr(u-\mu)=-r\alpha_0(u-\mu)dt+r(-f+\alpha_0 u)dt+\sum_k r\upsilon_k S_k\beta_k\cdot d\tilde{w}$$

$$=r\alpha_0\mu\,dt-rf\,dt+\sum_k r\upsilon_k S_k\beta_k\cdot d\tilde{w} \qquad (48)$$

Integrating between t_1 and t_2 we obtain

$$r(t_2)u(t_2)-r(t_1)u(t_1)=$$

$$r(t_2)\mu(t_2)-r(t_1)\mu(t_1)+\int_{t_1}^{t_2} r\alpha_0\mu\,ds-\int_{t_1}^{t_2} rf\,ds+\sum_k\int_{t_1}^{t_2} r\upsilon_k S_k\beta_k\cdot d\tilde{w} \qquad (49)$$

but

$$r(t_2)\mu(t_2)-r(t_1)\mu(t_1)+\int_{t_1}^{t_2} r\alpha_0\mu\,ds=\int_{t_1}^{t_2} r(s)d\mu(s) \qquad (50)$$

where the integral to the right-hand side is a Stieltjes integral and is defined almost surely. Note also that it is negative. Therefore, it follows from (49) that

$$r(t_2)u(t_2)-r(t_1)u(t_1)\le-\int_{t_1}^{t_2} rf\,ds+\sum_k\int_{t_1}^{t_2} r\upsilon_k S_k\beta_k\cdot d\tilde{w} \qquad (51)$$

Since (51) holds a.s. Q (or P), we can take $t_1 = t$ and $t_2 = \theta$ any stopping time larger, or equal to, t. Hence

$$r(t)u(t)\ge r(\theta)u(\theta)+\int_t^\theta r(s)f(s)ds-\sum_k\int_t^\theta r(s)\upsilon_k(s)S_k(s)\beta_k\cdot d\tilde{w}$$

$$\ge r(\theta)h(\theta)+\int_t^\theta r(s)f(s)ds-\sum_k\int_t^\theta r(s)\upsilon_k(s)S_k(s)\beta_k(s)\cdot d\tilde{w}(s)$$

Taking the conditional expectation with respect to F^t, we deduce

$$u(t)\ge E^Q\left(h(\theta)\frac{r(\theta)}{r(t)}+\int_t^\theta \frac{r(s)}{r(t)}f(s)ds\,\middle|\,F^t\right) \qquad (52)$$

Next, from (45), we deduce

$$u(s\wedge\hat{\theta}_t)-u(t)+\int_t^{s\wedge\hat{\theta}_t}(f-\alpha_0 u)d\lambda=\int_t^{s\wedge\hat{\theta}_t}\sum_k \upsilon_k S_k\beta_k\cdot d\tilde{w}$$

hence

$$r(s)u(s\wedge\hat{\theta}_t)-r(t)u(t)+\int_t^{s\wedge\hat{\theta}_t} fr\,d\lambda=\int_t^{s\wedge\hat{\theta}_t}\sum_k r\upsilon_k S_k\beta_k\cdot d\tilde{w}$$

Taking $s = \hat{\theta}_t$, we deduce that

$$u(t)=E^Q\left(h(\hat{\theta}_t)\frac{r(\hat{\theta}_t)}{r(t)}+\int_t^{\hat{\theta}_t}\frac{r(s)}{r(t)}f(s)ds\,\middle|\,F^t\right) \qquad (53)$$

By the continuity of the processes involved, it is sufficient that (52) holds for all θ which are rational; then from (52) and (53) the desired result (46) follows.

REMARK 3.3: To proceed we have to prove that $u(t)$ defined by (46) or (53) is a valuation function. This requires some technical steps, in particular to prove that $u(t)$ is a continuous process. We shall rely on the penalisation technique defined in the next paragraph.

THE PENALISED PROBLEM

SETTING OF THE PROBLEM: We shall say that $u_\varepsilon(t)$ is a solution of the penalised problem (for ε fixed) whenever

$u_\varepsilon(t)$ is continuous adapted, bounded by a deterministic constant (54)

$$u_\varepsilon(t) = E^Q\left[h(T)\exp - \int_t^T \alpha_0(s)\,ds + \int_t^T ds\left(f(s) + \frac{1}{\varepsilon}[u_\varepsilon(s) - h(s)]^-\right)\exp - \int_t^s \alpha_0(\sigma)\,d\sigma \,\middle|\, F^t\right] \tag{55}$$

Clearly, (55) is an equation and not an explicit expression for $u_\varepsilon(t)$. We shall use the functional space $L_F^\infty(\Omega, A, Q; C(0, T))$ of processes z with continuous trajectories, adapted to F^t, and such that $\sup_{0\le t\le T}|z(t)| \in L^\infty(\Omega, A, Q)$.

We consider the norm

$$\|z\| = \operatorname{ess\,sup} \sup_{0\le t\le T}|z(t)| \tag{56}$$

SOLUTION OF THE PENALISED PROBLEM: We note that if (54), (55) have a solution, then $u_\varepsilon(t)$ is necessarily an Itô process and can be written

$$r(t)u_\varepsilon(t) = -\int_0^t f_\varepsilon(s)r(s)\,ds + \int_0^t g_\varepsilon(s)\cdot d\tilde{w}(s) + u_\varepsilon(0) \tag{57}$$

where we have set for convenience

$$f_\varepsilon(s) = f(s) + \frac{1}{\varepsilon}[u_\varepsilon(s) - h(s)]^- \tag{58}$$

and where $g_\varepsilon(s)$ is an adequate adapted process.

Note that if $\beta(s)$ is adapted and bounded, (55) is equivalent to

$$u_\varepsilon(t) = E^Q\left[h(T)\exp - \int_t^T \beta(s)\,ds + \int_t^T \left(f(s) + [\beta(s) - \alpha_0(s)]u_\varepsilon(s) + \frac{1}{\varepsilon}[u_\varepsilon(s) - h(s)]^-\right)\exp - \int_t^s \beta(\sigma)\,d\sigma \,\middle|\, F^t\right] \tag{59}$$

In particular, taking $\beta(s) = \alpha_0(s) + 1/\varepsilon$ we get

$$u_\varepsilon(t) = E^Q\left[h(T)\exp - \int_t^T \left(\alpha_0 + \frac{1}{\varepsilon}\right)ds + \int_t^T \left(f(s) + \frac{1}{\varepsilon}u_\varepsilon(x)\vee h(s)\right)\exp - \int_t^s \left(\alpha_0 + \frac{1}{\varepsilon}\right)ds \,\middle|\, F^t\right] \tag{60}$$

LEMMA 3.2: *There exists one, and only one, solution of* (54), (55).

PROOF: Let us consider the map T_ε from $L_F^\infty(\Omega, A, Q; C(0,T))$, which is itself defined by

$$T_\varepsilon z(t) = E^Q\Bigg[h(T)\exp - \int_t^T \left(\alpha_0 + \frac{1}{\varepsilon}\right) ds +$$

$$\int_t^T \left(f(s) + \frac{1}{\varepsilon} z(s) \vee h(s)\right) \exp - \int_t^s \left(\alpha_0 + \frac{1}{\varepsilon}\right) d\sigma \,\Big|\, F^t\Bigg] \tag{61}$$

If $\alpha_0 \geq \bar{\sigma}_0$, a deterministic positive constant, then T_ε is a contraction, since

$$\left\| T_\varepsilon z_1 - T_\varepsilon z_2 \right\| \leq \left\| z_1 - z_2 \right\| \frac{1}{1 + \alpha_0 \varepsilon}$$

Otherwise, T_ε^k is a contraction, for a sufficiently large k (depending on ε). Indeed, we have

$$\left| T_\varepsilon z_1(t) - T_\varepsilon z_2(t) \right| \leq \frac{1}{\varepsilon} \left\| z_1 - z_2 \right\| (T - t) \quad \text{a.s.}$$

hence

$$\left| T_\varepsilon^2 z_1(t) - T_\varepsilon^2 z_2(t) \right| \leq \frac{1}{\varepsilon} \left| E^Q\left(\int_t^T \left| T_\varepsilon z_1(s) - T_\varepsilon z_2(s) \right| ds \,\Big|\, F^t \right) \right|$$

$$\leq \frac{1}{\varepsilon^2} \left\| z_1 - z_2 \right\| \frac{(T-t)^2}{2}$$

More generally

$$\left| T_\varepsilon^k z_1(t) - T_\varepsilon^k z_2(t) \right| \leq \frac{(T-t)^k}{\varepsilon^k k!} \left\| z_1 - z_2 \right\|$$

Therefore,

$$\left\| T_\varepsilon^k z_1 - T_\varepsilon^k z_2 \right\| \leq \frac{T^k}{\varepsilon^k k!} \left\| z_1 - z_2 \right\|$$

which proves that, for a sufficiently large k, T_ε^k is a contraction. This proves the desired result.

LEMMA 3.3: *We have*

$$u_\varepsilon(t) \geq u_{\varepsilon'}(t) \quad \textit{if } \varepsilon \leq \varepsilon' \tag{62}$$

$$u_\varepsilon(t) = E^Q\left[h(\theta_\varepsilon^t) \exp - \int_t^{\theta_\varepsilon^t} \alpha_0 \, ds + \int_t^{\theta_\varepsilon^t} f(s) \exp - \int_t^s \alpha_0 \, d\sigma \,\Big|\, F^t \right] \tag{63}$$

where θ_ε^t *is a* F^s *stopping time with* $\theta_\varepsilon^t \geq t \,\forall t$.

PROOF: We have

$$T_\varepsilon u_\varepsilon(t) = E^Q\Bigg[h(t)\exp - \int_t^T \left(\alpha_0 + \frac{1}{\varepsilon}\right) ds +$$

$$\int_t^T \left(f(s) + \frac{1}{\varepsilon} u_\varepsilon(s) h(s)\right) \exp - \int_t^s \left(\alpha_0 + \frac{1}{\varepsilon}\right) d\sigma \,\Big|\, F^t\Bigg]$$

$$u_{\varepsilon'}(t) = E^Q\Bigg[h(T)\exp - \int_t^T \left(\alpha_0 + \frac{1}{\varepsilon}\right) ds +$$

$$\int_t^T \left(f(s) + \frac{1}{\varepsilon} u_{\varepsilon'}(s) + \frac{1}{\varepsilon'} [u_{\varepsilon'}(s) - h(s)]^-\right) \exp - \int_t^s \left(\alpha_0 + \frac{1}{\varepsilon}\right) d\sigma \,\Big|\, F^t\Bigg]$$

hence

$$T_\varepsilon u_{\varepsilon'}(t) - u_{\varepsilon'}(t) = E^Q\left[\int_t^T \left(\frac{1}{\varepsilon} - \frac{1}{\varepsilon'}\right)[u_{\varepsilon'}(s) - h(s)]^- \exp - \int_t^s \left(\alpha_0 + \frac{1}{\varepsilon}\right) d\sigma \,\middle|\, F^t\right.$$

$$\geq 0 \text{ if } \varepsilon \leq \varepsilon'$$

Since T_ε is monotone in the sense

$$T_\varepsilon z_1 \geq T_\varepsilon z_2 \quad \text{if } z_1(t) \geq z_2(t)\ \forall t$$

we deduce

$$T_\varepsilon^k u_{\varepsilon'}(t) \geq u_{\varepsilon'}(t)\ \forall k$$

Letting k tend to $+\infty$, it follows from the construction of u_ε that (62) holds.

Next, let $\theta_\varepsilon^t = \inf\{s \geq t \mid u_\varepsilon(s) - h(s) \leq 0\}$ which is an F^s stopping time since $u_\varepsilon(s) - h(s)$ is a continuous process. Note that $\theta_\varepsilon^t \leq T$ since $u_\varepsilon(T) = h(T)$.

Now,

$$u_\varepsilon(t) = E^Q\left[\int_t^{\theta_\varepsilon^t} f \exp - \int_t^s \alpha_0 d\sigma + h(T)\exp - \int_t^T \alpha_0 ds + \right.$$

$$\left.\int_{\theta_\varepsilon^t}^T \left(f + \frac{1}{\varepsilon}(u_\varepsilon - h)^-\right) \exp - \int_t^s \alpha_0 d\sigma \,\middle|\, F^t\right]$$

$$= E^Q\left[+\int_t^{\theta_\varepsilon^t} f \exp - \int_t^s \alpha_0 d\sigma + u_\varepsilon(\theta_\varepsilon^t) \exp - \int_t^{\theta_\varepsilon^t} \alpha_0 d\sigma \,\middle|\, F^t\right]$$

and, since $u_\varepsilon(\theta_\varepsilon^t) = h(\theta_\varepsilon^t)$, the result (63) follows.

Suppose now that h is an Itô process, namely that

$$h(t) = h(0) + \int_0^t a(s)\, ds + \int_0^t b(s) \cdot d\tilde{w} \tag{64}$$

where a, b are adapted processes, bounded by a deterministic constant (on $[0, T]$). By redefining a in a convenient way, we can assume, without loss of generality, that

$$h(t) \exp - \int_0^t \alpha_0 ds \text{ is an Itô process} \tag{65}$$

It follows, then, that we can write

$$h(t) = E^Q\left(h(T)\exp - \int_t^T \alpha_0 ds + \int_t^T \phi(s)\exp - \int_t^s \alpha_0 d\sigma \,\middle|\, F^t\right) \tag{66}$$

where ϕ is a bounded, adapted process.

We then state the following:

LEMMA 3.4: *When* (64) *is satisfied, then*

$$u_\varepsilon \to u \text{ in } L_F^\infty(\Omega, A, Q; C(0, T)) \tag{67}$$

PROOF: From Lemma 3.3 it follows that

$$u_\varepsilon(t) \uparrow u(t) \text{ pointwise, as } \varepsilon \downarrow 0 \tag{68}$$

and, using (63), u is bounded, positive and adapted.

Let us set $\tilde{u}_\varepsilon(t) = u_\varepsilon(t) - h(t)$, then from (55) and (66) we have

$$\tilde{u}_\varepsilon(t) = E^Q\left[\int_t^T \left(f - \phi + \frac{1}{\varepsilon}\tilde{u}_\varepsilon^-\right) \exp - \int_t^s \alpha_0 d\sigma \middle| F^t\right]$$

$$= E^Q\left[\int_t^T \left(f - \phi + \frac{1}{\varepsilon}\tilde{u}_\varepsilon + \frac{1}{\varepsilon}\tilde{u}_\varepsilon^-\right) \exp - \int_t^s \left(\alpha_0 + \frac{1}{\varepsilon}\right) d\sigma \middle| F^t\right]$$

$$\geq E^Q\left[\int_t^T (f - \phi) \exp - \int_t^s \left(\alpha_0 + \frac{1}{\varepsilon}\right) d\sigma \middle| F^t\right]$$

$$\geq -\|\phi\|\varepsilon$$

which implies that

$$\frac{\tilde{u}_\varepsilon^-}{\varepsilon} \leq \|\phi\| \tag{69}$$

We have seen in Lemma 3.3 that

$$T_\varepsilon u_{\varepsilon'}(t) - u_{\varepsilon'}(t) = E^Q\left[\int_t^T \left(\frac{1}{\varepsilon} - \frac{1}{\varepsilon'}\right)(u_{\varepsilon'} - h) \exp - \int_t^s \left(\alpha_0 + \frac{1}{\varepsilon}\right) d\sigma \middle| F^t\right]$$

$$\leq \varepsilon'\left(\frac{1}{\varepsilon} - \frac{1}{\varepsilon'}\right)\|\phi\|\varepsilon$$

$$\leq (\varepsilon' - \varepsilon)\|\phi\| \tag{70}$$

Next we have

$$T_\varepsilon^2 u_{\varepsilon'}(t) - h(t) = E^Q\left[\int_t^T \left(f - \phi - \frac{1}{\varepsilon}h + \frac{1}{\varepsilon}T_\varepsilon u_{\varepsilon'} \vee h\right) \exp - \int_t^s \left(\alpha_0 + \frac{1}{\varepsilon}\right) d\sigma \middle| F^t\right]$$

$$= E^Q\left[\int_t^T \left(f - \phi + \frac{1}{\varepsilon}(h - T_\varepsilon u_{\varepsilon'})^-\right) \exp - \int_t^s \left(\alpha_0 + \frac{1}{\varepsilon}\right) d\sigma \middle| F^t\right]$$

But, from (70),

$$T_\varepsilon u_{\varepsilon'} - h \leq u_{\varepsilon'} + (\varepsilon' - \varepsilon)\|\phi\| \leq \tilde{u}_{\varepsilon'} + \varepsilon'\|\phi\|$$

hence

$$(h - T_\varepsilon u_{\varepsilon'})^- \leq \tilde{u}_{\varepsilon'} + \varepsilon'\|\phi\|$$

Therefore,

$$T_\varepsilon^2 u_{\varepsilon'}(t) - h(t) \leq E^Q\left[\int_t^T \left(f - \phi + \frac{\tilde{u}_{\varepsilon'}}{\varepsilon} + \frac{\varepsilon'}{\varepsilon}\|\phi\|\right) \exp - \int_t^s \left(\alpha_0 + \frac{1}{\varepsilon}\right) d\sigma \middle| F^t\right]$$

But, from the expression of $\tilde{u}_{\varepsilon'}$, we have

$$\tilde{u}_{\varepsilon'}(t) = E^Q\left[\int_t^T \left(f - \phi + \frac{1}{\varepsilon}\tilde{u}_{\varepsilon'} + \frac{1}{\varepsilon}\tilde{u}_{\varepsilon'}^-\right) \exp - \int_t^s \left(\alpha_0 + \frac{1}{\varepsilon}\right) d\sigma \middle| F^t\right]$$

$$\geq E^Q\left[\int_t^T \left(f - \phi + \frac{1}{\varepsilon}\tilde{u}_{\varepsilon'}\right) \exp - \int_t^s \left(\alpha_0 + \frac{1}{\varepsilon}\right) d\sigma \middle| F^t\right]$$

Therefore,

$$T_\varepsilon^2 u_{\varepsilon'}(t) - h(t) \leq \tilde{u}_{\varepsilon'}(t) + \varepsilon'\|\phi\|$$

hence,

$$T_\varepsilon^2 u_{\varepsilon'}(t) - u_{\varepsilon'}(t) \le \varepsilon' \|\phi\|$$

More generally, we shall have

$$T_\varepsilon^k u_{\varepsilon'}(t) - u_{\varepsilon'}(t) \le \varepsilon' \|\phi\|$$

hence, letting $k \to \infty$, we deduce that

$$0 \le u_\varepsilon(t) - u_{\varepsilon'}(t) \le \varepsilon' \|\phi\| \tag{71}$$

From the pointwise convergence (68) we get $u(t) - u_{\varepsilon'}(t) \le \varepsilon' \|\phi\|$, which completes the proof of (67).

EXISTENCE OF A SOLUTION OF THE VALUATION PROBLEM FOR THE "AMERICAN CLAIM" IN THE CASE OF COMPLETE MARKETS

We are now in a position to state the following.

LEMMA 3.5: *Assuming* (64), *the process* u *defined by* (67) *is a solution of the valuation problem* (40), (41), (42), (45).

PROOF: We have $u \in L_F^\infty(\Omega, A, Q; C[0,T])$ by construction. From (55) we can write

$$u_\varepsilon(t) = E^Q\left[\int_t^\theta ds\left(f(s) + \frac{1}{\varepsilon}[u_\varepsilon(s) - h(s)]^-\right)\exp - \int_t^s \alpha_0 d\sigma + u_\varepsilon(\theta)\exp - \int_t^\theta \alpha_0 d\sigma \,\Big|\, F^t\right], \quad \forall t \le \theta \le T \tag{72}$$

Multiplying by ε and letting ε tend towards 0, we get

$$E^Q\left(\int_t^\theta [u(s) - h(s)]^- \exp - \int_t^s \alpha_0 d\sigma \,\Big|\, F^t\right) = 0, \quad \forall t \le \theta \le T$$

from which it is easy to deduce that $(u(t) - h(t))^- = 0$; hence, the first part of (41) holds. Since $u_\varepsilon(T) = h(T)$, the second part of (41) is also satisfied.

Now, from (72) we deduce that

$$u_\varepsilon(t) \ge E^Q\left[\int_t^\theta f(s)\left(\exp - \int_t^s \alpha_0 d\sigma\right) ds + u_\varepsilon(\theta)\exp - \int_t^\theta \alpha_0 d\sigma \,\Big|\, F^t\right]$$

As ε tends towards 0, we get

$$u(t) \ge E^Q\left[\int_t^\theta f(s)\left(\exp - \int_t^s \alpha_0 d\sigma\right) ds + u(\theta)\exp - \int_t^\theta \alpha_0 d\sigma \,\Big|\, F^t\right]$$

hence,

$$u(t)\exp - \int_0^t \alpha_0 ds + \int_0^t f(s)\left(\exp - \int_0^s \alpha_0 d\sigma\right) ds \tag{73}$$

is an F^t, Q-continuous supermartingale.

From the Doob-Meyer decomposition theorem (cf. Meyer), there exists a unique non-increasing adapted process $v(t)$ such that

$$u(t)\exp - \int_0^t \alpha_0 ds + \int_0^t f(s)\left(\exp - \int_0^s \alpha_0 d\sigma\right) ds - v(t)$$

is an F^t, Q-martingale.

From the Kunita-Watanabé representation theorem we can assert that

$$u(t)\exp-\int_0^t \alpha_0 ds+\int_0^t f(s)\left(\exp-\int_0^s \alpha_0 d\sigma\right) ds = v(t)+u(0)+\int_0^t \gamma(s)\cdot d\tilde{w} \quad (74)$$

where we have assumed, without loss of generality, that $v(0) = 0$.

It also follows that

$$u(t)+\int_0^t f(s)ds=\int_0^t u\alpha_0 ds+\mu(t)+\int_0^t \frac{\gamma}{r} d\tilde{w}+u(0) \quad (75)$$

where we have set

$$\mu(t)=\int_0^t \frac{dv(s)}{r(s)}$$

which is a *continuous* non-increasing adapted process.

Identifying the expressions (75) and (47), we have

$$\sum_{k=1}^{N} \upsilon_k(s) S_k(s) \beta_k(s) = \frac{\gamma(s)}{r(s)} \quad (76)$$

As in (31), this relation defines a unique portfolio $\upsilon_1(t), \ldots, \upsilon_N(t)$. We define υ_0 as in (34). Therefore, (42) is satisfied.

Define $\hat{\theta}_t$ as in (44). Consider θ_ε^t which has been defined in Lemma 3.3. We have

$$\hat{\theta}_t \geq \theta_\varepsilon^t \quad (77)$$

Indeed, $u(\hat{\theta}_t) = h(\hat{\theta}_t) \geq u_\varepsilon(\hat{\theta}_t)$, which implies (77). The sequence θ_ε^t increases as $\varepsilon \downarrow 0$. From $u_\varepsilon(\theta_\varepsilon^t) = h(\theta_\varepsilon^t)$ and the convergence (67), as well as the continuity of u, h, we see that $u(\bar{\theta}^t) = h(\bar{\theta}^t)$, where $\bar{\theta}^t = \lim \uparrow \theta_\varepsilon^t$. Therefore, $\bar{\theta}^t \geq \hat{\theta}_t$. But from (77) $\bar{\theta}^t \leq \hat{\theta}_t$; hence $\theta_\varepsilon^t \uparrow \hat{\theta}_t$ a.s.

Now, for $s \geq t$, we deduce from (72) that

$$u_\varepsilon(t)=E^Q\left[\int_t^{s\wedge\theta_\varepsilon^t} f(\lambda)\left(\exp-\int_t^\lambda a_0 d\sigma\right) d\lambda+u_\varepsilon(s\wedge\theta_\varepsilon^t)\exp-\int_t^{s\wedge\theta_\varepsilon^t} a_0 d\sigma \,\middle|\, F^t\right]$$

Letting ε tend towards 0, we get

$$u(t)=E^Q\left[\int_t^{s\wedge\hat{\theta}^t} f(\lambda)\left(\exp-\int_t^\lambda a_0 d\sigma\right) d\lambda+u(s\wedge\hat{\theta}^t)\exp-\int_t^{s\wedge\hat{\theta}^t} a_0 d\sigma \,\middle|\, F^t\right] \quad (78)$$

It is easy to check that (78), together with (74), implies

$$v(s\wedge\hat{\theta}^t)=v(t) \quad \forall t\leq s\leqq\hat{\theta}^t$$

hence, also

$$\mu(s\wedge\hat{\theta}^t)=\mu(t) \quad \forall t\leq s\leq\hat{\theta}^t$$

This, together with (45), (76), proves that (45) holds. This completes the proof of the desired results.

In the proof of Lemma 3.4, which has been instrumental in obtaining the existing result, we have some regularity of the process $h(t)$, namely (64). We shall see that it is possible to relax this assumption slightly.

Let us assume that $h(t)$ satisfies

$$\left| E^Q[h(s) - h(t) \mid F^t] \right| \leq C(s-t), \quad t \leq s \tag{79}$$

where C is a deterministic constant.

Note that an Itô process satisfies (79). Indeed, using (64) we get

$$E^Q\left[h(s) - h(t) \mid F^t\right] = E^Q\left(\int_t^s a(\sigma)d\sigma \mid F^t\right)$$

hence (79) since a is bounded by a deterministic constant.

Let us prove the following approximation result:

LEMMA 3.6: *If* (79) *is satisfied, then there exists a sequence* h_n *of Itô processes converging to* h *in* $L_F^\infty(\Omega, A, Q; C[0,T])$.

PROOF: Let us define

$$h_n(t) = E^Q\left(h(T)e^{-n(T-t)} + \int_t^T nh(s)e^{-n(s-t)}\,ds \mid F^t\right) \tag{80}$$

Then

$$h_n(t) - h(t) = E^Q\left([h(T) - h(t)]e^{-n(T-t)} + \int_t^T n[h(s) - h(t)]e^{-n(s-t)}\,ds \mid F^t\right)$$

Using (79), we obtain

$$\left| h_n(t) - h(t) \right| \leq C(T-t)e^{-n(T-t)} + C\int_t^T n(s-t)e^{-n(s-t)}\,ds \leq \frac{C}{n}$$

hence $\|h_n - h\| \leq C/n$. However, $h_n(t)$ is an Itô process. Indeed,

$$\begin{aligned} h_n(t) &= -\int_0^t nh(s)e^{-n(s-t)}ds + E^Q\left(h(T)e^{-n(T-t)} + \int_0^T nh(s)e^{-n(s-t)}\,ds \mid F^t\right) \\ &= -\int_0^t nh(s)e^{-n(s-t)}ds + h_n(0) + \int_0^t g_n \cdot d\tilde{w} \end{aligned}$$

which proves the desired result.

COROLLARY 3.1: *The result of Lemma 3.4 holds when* (79) *holds instead of* (64).

PROOF: Denote by u_ε^n the solution of (55) corresponding to h_n instead of h, then

$$\|u_\varepsilon^n - u_\varepsilon\| \leq \|h_n - h\| \tag{81}$$

Indeed, let us term T_ε^n the map (61) with h_n instead of h. The following property holds:

$$\text{if } \|z_1 - z_2\| \leq \|h_n - h\|, \text{ then } \|T_\varepsilon z_1 - T_\varepsilon z_2\| \leq \|h_n - h\|$$

Iterating, we deduce (81). The uniform estimate (81) is clearly sufficient to derive the desired result.

We can then state the main result of the section:

THEOREM 3.1: *We make the assumption of complete markets* (18), *and* (38), (39), (79). *Then there exists one, and only one, solution of the valuation problem for the "American claim" described in the first two parts of this section. It is given by* (46). *Moreover, the hedging portfolio is uniquely defined.*

REMARK 3.4: If

$$h(t)\exp-\int_0^t \alpha_0 ds + \int_0^t f(s)\left(\exp-\int_0^s \alpha_0 d\sigma\right) ds$$

is Q, F^t-submartingale, then the solution of "American" and "European" claims coincides. This follows easily from the fact that the process (25) satisfies the constraint (41).

1 *From the definition of the Itô integral w.r.t. a Wiener process, it is not necessary to impose predictability (as in Harrison and Pliska (1982)). However, one can modify the processes to get predictable ones without loss of generality.*

Bibliography

Black, F., and M. Scholes, 1973, "The Pricing of Options and Corporate Liabilities", *Journal of Political Economy* 81, pp. 637–59; reprinted as Chapter 1 of the present volume.

Cox, J. C., S. A. Ross and M. Rubinstein, 1979, "Option Pricing: A Simplified Approach", *Journal of Financial Economics* 7, pp. 229–63; reprinted as Chapter 2 of the present volume.

Gabay, D., 1982, "Stochastic Processes in Models of Financial Markets: The Valuation Equation of Finance and its Applications", Preprint.

Harrison, J. L., and S. R. Pliska, 1981, "Martingales and Stochastic Integrals in the Theory of Continuous Trading", *Stochastic Processes Applied* 11, pp. 215–260.

Kunita, H., and S. Watanabe, 1967, "On Square Integrable Martingales", *Nagoya Mathematics Journal* 30, pp. 209–45.

Merton, R. C., 1973, "Theory of Rational Option Pricing", *Bell Journal of Economic and Management Science* 4, pp. 141–83.

Meyer, P. A., "Integrales Stochastiques, Sem. Prob. X", *Lecture Notes in Mathematics,* Vol. 511, Springer-Verlag, New York, pp. 245–400.

II

DYNAMIC ARBITRAGE MODELS

4

An Equilibrium Characterisation of the Term Structure*

Oldrich A. Vasicek
KMV Corporation

The paper derives a general form of the term structure of interest rates. The following assumptions are made: (A.1) The instantaneous (spot) interest rate follows a diffusion process; (A.2) the price of a discount bond depends only on the spot rate over its term; and (A.3) the market is efficient. Under these assumptions, it is shown by means of an arbitrage argument that the expected rate of return on any bond in excess of the spot rate is proportional to its standard deviation. This property is then used to derive a partial differential equation for bond prices. The solution to that equation is given in the form of a stochastic integral representation. An interpretation of the bond pricing formula is provided. The model is illustrated on a specific case.

Although considerable attention has been paid to equilibrium conditions in capital markets and the pricing of capital assets, few results are directly applicable to description of the interest rate structure. The most notable exceptions are the works of Roll (1970, 1971), Merton (1973, 1974), and Long (1974). This paper gives an explicit characterisation of the term structure of interest rates in an efficient market. The development of the model is based on an arbitrage argument similar to that of Black and Scholes (1973) for option pricing. The model is formulated in continuous time, although some implications for discrete interest rate series are also noted.

Notation and assumptions

Consider a market in which investors buy and issue default-free claims on a specified sum of money to be delivered at a given future date. Such claims will be called (discount) bonds. Let $P(t, s)$ denote the price at time t of a discount bond maturing at time s, $t \leqq s$, with unit maturity value,

$$P(s, s) = 1$$

The yield to maturity $R(t, T)$ is the internal rate of return at time t on a bond with maturity date $s = t + T$,

$$R(t,T) = -\frac{1}{T}\log P(t,t+T), \qquad T > 0 \tag{1}$$

**This paper was first published in the* Journal of Financial Economics, *Vol. 5 (1977). It is reprinted with the permission of JAI Press Inc. The author wishes to thank P. Boyle, M. Garman, M. Jensen, and the referees, R. Roll and S. Schaefer, for their helpful comments and suggestions.*

The rates $R(t,T)$ considered as a function of T will be referred to as the term structure at time t.

The forward rate $F(t,s)$ will be defined by the equation

$$R(t,T)=\frac{1}{T}\int_t^{t+T}F(t,\tau)\,d\tau \tag{2}$$

In the form explicit for the forward rate, this equation can be written as

$$F(t,s)=\frac{\partial}{\partial s}[(s-t)R(t,s-t)] \tag{3}$$

The forward rate can be interpreted as the marginal rate of return from committing a bond investment for an additional instant.

Define now the spot rate as the instantaneous borrowing and lending rate,

$$r(t)=R(t,0)=\lim_{T\to 0}R(t,T) \tag{4}$$

A loan of amount W at the spot rate will thus increase in value by the increment

$$dW = Wr(t)\,dt \tag{5}$$

This equation holds with certainty. At any time t, the current value $r(t)$ of the spot rate is the instantaneous rate of increase of the loan value. The subsequent values of the spot rate, however, are not necessarily certain. In fact, it will be assumed that $r(t)$ is a stochastic process, subject to two requirements: First, $r(t)$ is a continuous function of time, that is, it does not change value by an instantaneous jump. Second, it is assumed that $r(t)$ follows a Markov process. Under this assumption, the future development of the spot rate given its present value is independent of the past development that has led to the present level. The following assumption is thus made:

(A.1) The spot rate follows a continuous Markov process.

The Markov property implies that the spot rate process is characterised by a single state variable, namely its current value. The probability distribution of the segment $\{r(\tau), \tau \geqq t\}$ is thus completely determined by the value of $r(t)$.

Processes that are Markov and continuous are called diffusion processes. They can be described (cf. Itô (1961), Gikhman and Skorokhod (1969)) by a stochastic differential equation of the form

$$dr = f(r,t)\,dt + \rho(r,t)\,dz \tag{6}$$

where $z(t)$ is a Wiener process with incremental variance dt. The functions $f(r,t)$, $\rho^2(r,t)$ are the instantaneous drift and variance, respectively, of the process $r(t)$.

It is natural to expect that the price of a discount bond will be determined solely by the spot interest rate over its term or, more accurately, by the current assessment of the development of the spot rate over the term of the bond. No particular form of such relationship is presumed. The second assumption will thus be stated as follows:

(A.2) The price $P(t,s)$ of a discount bond is determined by the assessment, at time t, of the segment $\{r(\tau), t \leqq \tau \leqq s\}$ of the spot rate process over the term of the bond.

It may be noted that the expectation hypothesis, the market segmentation hypothesis and the liquidity preference hypothesis all conform to assumption (A.2), since they all postulate that:

$$R(t,T)=E_t\left(\frac{1}{T}\int_t^{t+T} r(\tau)\,d\tau\right)+\bar{\pi}[t,T,r(t)]$$

with various specifications for the function $\bar{\pi}$.

Finally, it will be assumed that the following is true:

(A.3) The market is efficient; that is, there are no transactions costs, information is available to all investors simultaneously, and every investor acts rationally (prefers more wealth to less, and uses all available information).

Assumption (A.3) implies that investors have homogeneous expectations, and that no profitable riskless arbitrage is possible.

By assumption (A.1) the development of the spot rate process over an interval (t, s), $t \leqq s$, given its values prior to time t, depends only on the current value $r(t)$. Assumption (A.2) then implies that the price $P(t, s)$ is a function of $r(t)$,

$$P(t, s) = P(t, s, r(t)) \tag{7}$$

Thus, the value of the spot rate is the only state variable for the whole term structure. Expectations formed with the knowledge of the whole past development of rates of all maturities, including the present term structure, are equivalent to expectations conditional only on the present value of the spot rate.

Since there exists only one state variable, the instantaneous returns on bonds of different maturities are perfectly correlated. This means that the short bond and just one other bond completely span the whole of the term structure. It should be noted, however, that bond returns over a finite period are not correlated perfectly. Investors unwilling to revise the composition of their portfolio continuously will need a spectrum of maturities to fulfil their investment objectives.

The term structure equation

It follows from equations (6), (7) by the Itô differentiation rule (cf., for instance, Itô (1961), Kushner (1967), Åström (1970)), that the bond price satisfies a stochastic differential equation

$$dP = P\mu(t, s)\,dt - P\sigma(t, s)\,dz \tag{8}$$

where the parameters $\mu(t, s) = \mu(t, s, r(t))$, $\sigma(t, s) = \sigma(t, s, r(t))$ are given by

$$\mu(t,s,r)=\frac{1}{P(t,s,r)}\left(\frac{\partial}{\partial t}+f\frac{\partial}{\partial r}+\tfrac{1}{2}\rho^2\frac{\partial^2}{\partial r^2}\right)P(t,s,r) \tag{9}$$

$$\sigma(t,s,r)=-\frac{1}{P(t,s,r)}\rho\frac{\partial}{\partial r}P(t,s,r) \tag{10}$$

The functions $\mu(t, s, r)$, $\sigma^2(t, s, r)$ are the mean and variance, respectively, of the instantaneous rate of return at time t on a bond with maturity date s, given that the current spot rate is $r(t) = r$.

Now consider an investor who at time t issues an amount W_1 of a bond with maturity date s_1, and simultaneously buys an amount W_2 of a bond maturing at time s_2. The total worth $W = W_2 - W_1$ of the portfolio thus constructed changes over time according to the accumulation equation

$$dW = (W_2\mu(t, s_2) - W_1\mu(t, s_1))\,dt - (W_2\sigma(t, s_2) - W_1\sigma(t, s_1))\,dz \tag{11}$$

(cf. Merton (1971)). This equation follows from equation (8) by application of the Itô rule.

Suppose that the amounts W_1, W_2 are chosen to be proportional to $\sigma(t, s_2)$, $\sigma(t, s_1)$, respectively,

$$W_1 = \frac{W\sigma(t,s_2)}{\sigma(t,s_1) - \sigma(t,s_2)}$$

$$W_2 = \frac{W\sigma(t,s_1)}{\sigma(t,s_1) - \sigma(t,s_2)}$$

Then the second term in equation (11) disappears, and the equation takes the form

$$dW = W\frac{\mu(t,s_2)\sigma(t,s_1) - \mu(t,s_1)\sigma(t,s_2)}{\sigma(t,s_1) - \sigma(t,s_2)}dt \tag{12}$$

The portfolio composed of such amounts of the two bonds is instantaneously riskless, since the stochastic element dz is not present in (12). It should therefore realise the same return as a loan at the spot rate described by equation (5). If not, the portfolio can be bought with funds borrowed at the spot rate, or otherwise sold and the proceeds lent out, to accomplish a riskless arbitrage.

As such arbitrage opportunities are ruled out by Assumption (A.3), comparison of equations (5) and (12) yields

$$\frac{\mu(t, s_2)\sigma(t, s_1) - \mu(t, s_1)\sigma(t, s_2)}{\sigma(t, s_1) - \sigma(t, s_2)} = r(t)$$

or equivalently,

$$\frac{\mu(t,s_1) - r(t)}{\sigma(t,s_1)} = \frac{\mu(t,s_2) - r(t)}{\sigma(t,s_2)} \tag{13}$$

Since equation (13) is valid for arbitrary maturity dates s_1, s_2, it follows that the ratio $(\mu(t, s) - r(t))/\sigma(t, s)$ is independent of s. Let $q(t, r)$ denote the common value of such ratio for a bond of any maturity date, given that the current spot rate is $r(t) = r$,

$$q(t,r) = \frac{\mu(t,s,r) - r}{\sigma(t,s,r)}, \qquad s \geqq t \tag{14}$$

The quantity $q(t, r)$ can be called the market price of risk, as it specifies the increase in expected instantaneous rate of return on a bond per an additional unit of risk.

Equation (14) will now be used to derive an equation for the price of a discount bond. Writing (14) as

$$\mu(t, s, r) - r = q(t, r)\sigma(t, s, r)$$

and substituting for μ, σ from equations (9), (10) yields, after rearrangement,

$$\frac{\partial P}{\partial t} + (f + \rho q)\frac{\partial P}{\partial r} + \tfrac{1}{2}\rho^2\frac{\partial^2 P}{\partial r^2} - rP = 0, \qquad t \leqq s \tag{15}$$

Equation (15) is the basic equation for pricing of discount bonds in a market characterised by Assumptions (A.1), (A.2), (A.3). It will be called the term structure equation.

The term structure equation is a partial differential equation for $P(t, s, r)$. Once the character of the spot rate process $r(t)$ has been described and the market price of risk $q(t, r)$ specified, the bond prices are obtained by solving equation (15) subject to the boundary condition

$$P(s, s, r) = 1 \tag{16}$$

The term structure $R(t, T)$ of interest rates is then readily evaluated from the equation

$$R(t,T) = -\frac{1}{T}\log P(t,t+T,r(t)) \tag{17}$$

Stochastic representation of the bond price

Solutions to partial differential equations of the parabolic or elliptic type, such as equation (15), can be represented in an integral form in terms of an underlying stochastic process (cf. Friedman (1975)). Such representation for the bond price as a solution to the term structure equation (15) and its boundary condition is as follows:

$$P(t,s) = E_t \exp\left(-\int_t^s r(\tau)\,d\tau - \tfrac{1}{2}\int_t^s q^2(\tau,r(\tau))\,d\tau + \int_t^s q(\tau,r(\tau))\,dz(\tau)\right), \quad t \leqq s \qquad (18)$$

To prove (18), define

$$V(u) = \exp\left(-\int_t^u r(\tau)\,d\tau - \tfrac{1}{2}\int_t^u q^2(\tau,r(\tau))\,d\tau + \int_t^u q(\tau,r(\tau))\,dz(\tau)\right)$$

and apply Itô's differential rule to the process $P(u,s)\,V(u)$. Then

$$\begin{aligned} d(PV) &= VdP + PdV + dPdV \\ &= V\left(\frac{\partial P}{\partial t} + f\frac{\partial P}{\partial r} + \tfrac{1}{2}\rho^2\frac{\partial^2 P}{\partial r^2}\right)du + V\frac{\partial P}{\partial r}\rho dz + PV\left(-r - \tfrac{1}{2}q^2\right)du + \\ &\quad PVqdz + \tfrac{1}{2}PVq^2du + V\frac{\partial P}{\partial r}\rho q du \\ &= V\left(\frac{\partial P}{\partial t} + (f+\rho q)\frac{\partial P}{\partial r} + \tfrac{1}{2}\rho^2\frac{\partial^2 P}{\partial r^2} - rP\right)du + PVqdz + V\frac{\partial P}{\partial r}\rho dz \\ &= PVqdz + V\frac{\partial P}{\partial r}\rho dz \end{aligned}$$

by virtue of equation (15). Integrating from t to s and taking expectation yields

$$E_t(P(s,s)\,V(s) - P(t,s)\,V(t)) = 0$$

and equation (18) follows.

In the special case when the expected instantaneous rates of return on bonds of all maturities are the same,

$$\mu(t,s) = r(t), \quad s \geqq t$$

(this corresponds to $q = 0$), the bond price is given by

$$P(t,s) = E_t \exp\left(-\int_t^s r(\tau)\,d\tau\right) \qquad (19)$$

Equation (18) can be given an interpretation in economic terms. Construct a portfolio consisting of the long bond (bond whose maturity approaches infinity) and lending or borrowing at the spot rate, with proportions $\lambda(t)$, $1-\lambda(t)$, respectively, where

$$\lambda(t) = \frac{\mu(t,\infty) - r(t)}{\sigma^2(t,\infty)}$$

The price $Q(t)$ of such portfolio follows the equation

$$dQ = \lambda Q(\mu(t,\infty)\,dt - \sigma(t,\infty)\,dz) + (1-\lambda)\,Qr\,dt$$

This equation can be integrated by evaluating the differential of $\log Q$ and noting that

$\lambda(t)\sigma(t,\infty) = q(t, r(t))$. This yields

$$d(\log Q) = \lambda\mu(t,\infty)dt - \lambda\sigma(t,\infty)dz + (1-\lambda)rdt - \tfrac{1}{2}\lambda^2\sigma^2(t,\infty)dt$$
$$= rdt + \tfrac{1}{2}q^2dt - qdz$$

and consequently

$$\frac{Q(t)}{Q(s)} = \exp\left(-\int_t^s r(\tau)\,d\tau - \frac{1}{2}\int_t^s q^2(\tau,r(\tau))d\tau + \int_t^s q(\tau,r(\tau))dz(\tau)\right)$$

Thus, equation (18) can be written in the form

$$P(t,s) = E_t\frac{Q(t)}{Q(s)}, \quad t \leqq s \tag{20}$$

This means that a bond of any maturity is priced in such a way that the same portion of a certain well-defined combination of the long bond and the riskless asset (the portfolio Q) can be bought now for the amount of the bond price as is expected to be bought at the maturity date for the maturity value.

Equivalently, equation (20) states that the price of any bond measured in units of the value of such portfolio Q follows a martingale,

$$\frac{P(t,s)}{Q(t)} = E_t\frac{P(\tau,s)}{Q(\tau)}, \quad t \leqq \tau \leqq s$$

Thus, if the present bond price is a certain fraction of the value of the portfolio Q, then the future value of the bond is expected to stay the same fraction of the value of that portfolio.

In empirical testing of the model, as well as for applications of the results, it is necessary to know the parameters f, ρ of the spot rate process and the market price of risk q. The former two quantities can be obtained by statistical analysis of the (observable) process $r(t)$. Although the market price of risk can be estimated from the defining equation (14), it is desirable to have a more direct means of observing q empirically. The following equality can be employed:

$$\left.\frac{\partial R}{\partial T}\right|_{T=0} = \tfrac{1}{2}\{f(t,r(t)) + \rho(t,r(t))\cdot q(t,r(t))\} \tag{21}$$

Once the parameters f, ρ are known, q could thus be determined from the slope at the origin of the yield curves. Equation (21) can be proven by taking the second derivative with respect to s of (18) (Itô's differentiation rule is needed), and putting $s = t$. This yields

$$\left.\frac{\partial^2 P}{\partial s^2}\right|_{s=t} = r^2(t) - f(t,r(t)) - \rho(t,r(t))\cdot q(t,r(t)) \tag{22}$$

But from (1),

$$\left.\frac{\partial^2 P}{\partial s^2}\right|_{s=t} = r^2(t) - 2\left.\frac{\partial R}{\partial T}\right|_{T=0} \tag{23}$$

By comparison of (22), (23), equation (21) follows.

A specific case

To illustrate the general model, the term structure of interest rates will now be obtained explicitly in the situation characterised by the following assumptions: First, that the market price of risk $q(t, r)$ is a constant,

$$q(t, r) = q$$

independent of the calendar time and of the level of the spot rate. Second, that the spot rate $r(t)$ follows the so-called Ornstein-Uhlenbeck process,

$$dr = \alpha(\gamma - r)\,dt + \rho\,dz \tag{24}$$

with $\alpha > 0$, corresponding to the choice $f(t, r) = \alpha(\gamma - r)$, $\rho(t, r) = \rho$ in equation (6). This description of the spot rate process has been proposed by Merton (1971).

The Ornstein-Uhlenbeck process with $\alpha > 0$ is sometimes called the elastic random walk. It is a Markov process with normally distributed increments. In contrast to the random walk (the Wiener process), which is an unstable process and after a long time will diverge to infinite values, the Ornstein-Uhlenbeck process possesses a stationary distribution. The instantaneous drift $\alpha(\gamma - r)$ represents a force that keeps pulling the process towards its long-term mean γ with magnitude proportional to the deviation of the process from the mean. The stochastic element, which has a constant instantaneous variance ρ^2, causes the process to fluctuate around the level γ in an erratic, but continuous, fashion. The conditional expectation and variance of the process given the current level are

$$E_t r(s) = \gamma + (r(t) - \gamma)\, e^{-\alpha(s-t)}, \quad t \leqq s \tag{25}$$

$$\mathrm{Var}_t\, r(s) = \frac{\rho^2}{2\alpha}\left(1 - e^{-2\alpha(s-t)}\right), \quad t \leqq s \tag{26}$$

respectively.

It is not claimed that the process given by equation (24) represents the best description of the spot rate behaviour. In the absence of empirical results on the character of the spot rate process, this specification serves only as an example.

Under such assumptions, the solution of the term structure equation (15) subject to (16) (or alternatively, the representation (18)) is

$$P(t,s,r) = \exp\left\{\frac{1}{\alpha}\left(1 - e^{-\alpha(s-t)}\right)\left(R(\infty) - r\right) - (s-t)R(\infty) - \frac{\rho^2}{4\alpha^3}\left(1 - e^{-\alpha(s-t)}\right)^2\right\}, \quad t \leqq s \tag{27}$$

where

$$R(\infty) = \gamma + \frac{\rho q}{\alpha} - \frac{\rho^2}{2\alpha^2} \tag{28}$$

The mean $\mu(t, s)$ and standard deviation $\sigma(t, s)$ of the instantaneous rate of return of a bond maturing at time s is, from equations (9), (10),

$$\mu(t,s) = r(t) + \frac{\rho q}{\alpha}\left(1 - e^{-\alpha(s-t)}\right)$$

$$\sigma(t,s) = \frac{\rho}{\alpha}\left(1 - e^{-\alpha(s-t)}\right)$$

with $t \leqq s$. It is seen that the longer the term of the bond, the higher the variance of the instantaneous rate of return, with the expected return in excess of the spot rate being proportional to the standard deviation. For a very long bond (i.e., $s \to \infty$) the mean and standard deviation approach the limits

$$\mu(\infty) = r(t) + \frac{\rho q}{\alpha} \quad \text{and} \quad \sigma(\infty) = \frac{\rho}{\alpha}$$

The term structure of interest rates is then calculated from equations (17) and (22).

It takes the form

$$R(t,T) = R(\infty) + (r(t) - R(\infty))\frac{1}{\alpha T}\left(1 - e^{-\alpha T}\right) + \frac{\rho^2}{4\alpha^3 T}\left(1 - e^{-\alpha T}\right)^2, \quad T \geq 0 \quad (29)$$

Note that the yield on a very long bond, as $T \to \infty$, is $R(\infty)$, thus explaining the notation (28).

The yield curves given by (29) start at the current level $r(t)$ of the spot rate for $T = 0$, and approach a common asymptote $R(\infty)$ as $T \to \infty$. For values of $r(t)$ smaller or equal to

$$R(\infty) - \frac{\rho^2}{4\alpha^2}$$

the yield curve is monotonically increasing. For values of $r(t)$ larger than that but below

$$R(\infty) + \frac{\rho^2}{2\alpha^2}$$

it is a humped curve. When $r(t)$ is equal to or exceeds this last value, the yield curves are monotonically decreasing.

Equation (29), together with the spot rate process (24), fully characterises the behaviour of interest rates under the specific assumptions of this section. It provides both the relationship, at a given time t, among rates of different maturities, and the behaviour of interest rates, as well as bond prices, over time. The relationship between the rates $R(t, T_1)$, $R(t, T_2)$ of two arbitrary maturities can be determined by eliminating $r(t)$ from equation (29) written for $T = T_1$, $T = T_2$. Moreover, (29) describes the development of the rate $R(t, T)$ of a given maturity over time. Since $r(t)$ is normally distributed by virtue of the properties of the Ornstein-Uhlenbeck process, and $R(t, T)$ is a linear function of $r(t)$, it follows that $R(t, T)$ is also normally distributed. The mean and variance of $R(\tau, T)$ given $R(t, T)$, $t < \tau$, are obtained from (29) by use of (25), (26). The calculations are elementary and will not be done here. It will only be noted that equations (24), (29) imply that the discrete rate series

$$R_n = R(nT, T), \quad n = 0, 1, 2, \ldots,$$

follows a first-order linear normal autoregressive process of the form

$$R_n = c + a(R_{n-1} - c) + \varepsilon_n \quad (30)$$

with independent residuals ε_n (cf. Nelson (1972)). The process (30) is the discrete elastic random walk, fluctuating around its mean c. The parameters c, a, and $s^2 = E\varepsilon_n^2$ could be expressed in terms of γ, α, ρ, q. In particular, the constant a, which characterises the degree to which the next term in the series $\{R_n\}$ is tied to the current value, is given by $a = e^{-\alpha T}$.

Also, equation (29) can be used to ascertain the behaviour of bond prices. The price $P(\tau, s)$ given its current value $P(t, s)$, $t \leq \tau \leq s$, is lognormally distributed, with parameters of the distribution calculated using equations (1), (25), (26), and (29).

The difference between the forward rates and expected spot rates, considered as a function of the term is usually referred to as the liquidity premium (although, as Nelson (1972) argues, a more appropriate name would be the term premium). Using equations (3) and (25), the liquidity premium implied by the term structure (29) is given by

$$\pi(T) = F(t, t+T) - E_t r(t+T)$$
$$= \left(R(\infty) - \gamma + \frac{\rho^2}{2\alpha^2} e^{-\alpha T}\right)\left(1 - e^{-\alpha T}\right), \quad T \geq 0 \quad (31)$$

The liquidity premium (31) is a smooth function of the term T. It is similar in form to the shape of the curves used by McCulloch (1975) in fitting observed estimates of liquidity premia. Its values for $T = 0$ and $T = \infty$ are $\pi(0) = 0$, $\pi(\infty) = R(\infty) - \gamma$, respectively, the latter being the difference between the yield on the very long bond and the long-term mean of the spot rate. If $q \geqq \rho/\alpha$, $\pi(T)$ is a monotonically increasing function of T. For $0 < q < \rho/\alpha$, it has a humped shape, with maximum of $q^2/2$ occurring at

$$T = \frac{1}{\alpha}\log\left(\frac{\rho}{\rho - \alpha q}\right)$$

If the market price of risk $q \leqq 0$, then $\pi(T)$ is a monotonically decreasing function.

Bibliography

Åström, K. J., 1970, *Introduction to Stochastic Control Theory*, Academic Press, New York.

Black, F. and M. Scholes, 1973, "The Pricing of Options and Corporate Liabilities", *Journal of Political Economy* 81, pp. 637–654; reprinted as Chapter 1 of the present volume.

Friedman, A., 1975, *Stochastic Differential Equations and Applications*, Academic Press, New York.

Gikhman, I. I. and A. V. Skorokhod, 1969, *Introduction to the Theory of Random Processes*, W. B. Saunders, Philadelphia, PA.

Itô, K., 1961, *Lectures on Stochastic Processes*, Tata Institute, Bombay.

Kushner, H. J., 1967, *Stochastic Stability and Control*, Academic Press, New York.

Long, J. B., 1974, "Stock Prices, Inflation, and the Term Structure of Interest Rates", *Journal of Financial Economics* 1, pp. 131–170.

McCulloch, J. H., 1975, "An Estimate of the Liquidity Premium", *Journal of Political Economy* 83, pp. 95–119.

Merton, R. C., 1971, "Optimum Consumption and Portfolio Rules in a Continuous-Time Model", *Journal of Economic Theory* 3, pp. 373–413.

Merton, R. C., 1973, "An Intertemporal Capital Asset Pricing model", *Econometrica* 41, pp. 867–887.

Merton, R. C., 1974, "On the Pricing of Corporate Debt: The Risk Structure of Interest Rates", *Journal of Finance* 29, pp. 449–470.

Nelson, C. R., 1972, *The Term Structure of Interest Rates*, Basic Books, New York.

Roll, R., 1970, *The Behavior of Interest Rates: The Application of the Efficient Market Model to U.S. Treasury Bills*, Basic Books, New York.

Roll, R., 1971, "Investment Diversification and Bond Maturity", *Journal of Finance* 26, pp. 51–66.

5

A Continuous Time Approach to the Pricing of Bonds*

Michael J. Brennan and Eduardo S. Schwartz
University of California, Los Angeles

This paper develops an arbitrage model of the term structure of interest rates based on the assumptions that the whole term structure at any point in time may be expressed as a function of the yields on the longest and shortest maturity default-free instruments and that these two yields follow a Gauss-Wiener process. Arbitrage arguments are used to derive a partial differential equation which must be satisfied by the values of all default-free bonds. The joint stochastic process for the two yields is estimated using Canadian data and the model is used to price a sample of Government of Canada bonds.

A theory of the term structure of interest rates is intended to explain the relative pricing of default-free bonds of different maturities. Complete theories of the term structure take as given the exogenous specifications of the economy: tastes, endowments, productive opportunities, and beliefs about possible future states of the world; then the prices of default-free bonds of different maturities are derived from these exogenous specifications.[1] However, most extant theories of the term structure are partial equilibrium in nature and take as given beliefs about future realisations of the spot rate of interest, which are combined with simple assumptions about tastes to derive yields to maturity on discount bonds of different maturities.

The theory of the term structure has been cast traditionally in terms of the relationship between the forward rates which are inherent in the term structure and the corresponding expected future spot rates of interest. Thus the typical version of the pure expectations hypothesis asserts that forward rates are equal to expected future spot rates.[2] In contrast to the pure expectations hypothesis stands the liquidity premium hypothesis which asserts that forward rates always exceed the corresponding expected future spot rates by a liquidity premium, which is required to compensate investors for the greater capital risk inherent in longer-term bonds. The market segmentation hypothesis can be regarded as a modification of the liquidity premium hypothesis to allow for positive or negative liquidity premia on longer-term bonds: this hypothesis recognises that long-term bonds are not necessarily more risky than short-term bonds for investors who have long-term horizons, so that the prices of bonds of different maturities are determined by the preferences of investors with different horizons, with the result that forward rates may bear no systematic relationship to expected future

**This paper was first published in the* Journal of Banking and Finance, *Vol. 3 (1979). It is reprinted with the permission of Elsevier Science - NL, Burgerhartstraat 25, 1055 KV Amsterdam, The Netherlands.*

spot rates. A major limitation of both liquidity premium and market segmentation hypotheses is their lack of specificity: since the relationship of liquidity premium to maturity is not specified, there are as many undetermined parameters in the model as there are bond maturities considered.

More recently it has been recognised that, if assumptions are made about the stochastic evolution of the instantaneous rate of interest in a continuous model, much richer theories of bond pricing can be derived, which constrain the relationship between the risk premia on bonds of different maturities. Thus Merton (1973), Brennan and Schwartz (1977), and Vasicek (1976) have all assumed that the instantaneous spot rate of interest follows a Gauss–Wiener process. Then the arbitrage arguments, which are familiar from the option pricing literature, may be adduced to show that the prices of riskless bonds of all maturities must obey the same partial differential equation which contains only a single utility-dependent function. Since the whole term structure may be derived by solution of this partial differential equation, it follows that the liquidity premia for all maturities must depend upon this single function.

A significant deficiency of this arbitrage model of the term structure is the unrealism of the assumption about the stochastic process for the interest rate. It is assumed that since the instantaneous interest rate follows a Markov process, all that is known about future interest rates is impounded in the current instantaneous interest rate, so that the value of a default-free bond of any maturity may be written as a function of this instantaneous interest rate and time. This implies that, apart from deterministic shifts over time in tastes, the whole term structure of interest rates may be inferred from the current instantaneous interest rate. This is clearly at odds with reality.

In this paper we take a step towards a more realistic approach to the relative pricing of bonds of different maturities by allowing changes in the instantaneous interest rate to depend not only on its current value but also on the long-term rate of interest, so that the long-term rate and the instantaneous rate follow a joint Gauss–Markov process. This expansion of the state space from one rate of interest to two is intended to reflect the assumption, which is the basis of both the pure expectations hypothesis and the liquidity premium hypothesis, that the current long-term rate of interest contains information about future values of the spot rate of interest. It should be clear that the model developed here, viewed simply as a model of the term structure, is less ambitious than the single state variable models referred to above: where they derive the long-term rate of interest, we take it as exogenous and attempt to explain only the intermediate portion of the yield curve in terms of its extremities. On the other hand, we avoid the objectionable implication of the above models that the long rate is a deterministic function of the current instantaneous interest rate. It is anticipated that the major contribution of the model developed here will be for the pricing of interest dependent contingent claims which contain an option element, such as savings bonds, retractable bonds and callable bonds. Then, just as the original Black–Scholes (1973) model determines the price of a call option in terms of the price of the underlying stock, without considering how the price of the underlying stock itself is determined, this model will permit the pricing of interest dependent claims in terms of the two exogenously given interest rates. However, before advancing to the more ambitious task of pricing bonds with an option element, it is useful to evaluate the ability of the model to price straight bonds of different maturities and this is the major objective of this paper: a subsidiary task is the estimation of the utility-dependent function in the partial differential equation.

In two contemporaneous papers Richard (1976) and Cox, Ingersoll and Ross (1977) have also developed models of the term structure which incorporate two state variables. While our model takes these as the instantaneous rate and the long-term rate, their models take the state variables as the instantaneous real rate of interest and the rate of inflation, changes in which are assumed to be independent: from these state variables they are able to derive the long-term rate of interest. The advantage of their models then lies in the endogeneity of the long-term rate of interest, but this is obtained at the cost of introducing two utility-dependent functions into the partial differential equation for bond prices, which considerably complicates the problems of empirical estimation. Our model avoids the need for one of the utility-dependent functions by taking as the second state variable the long-term rate of interest which is inversely proportional to an asset price - the price of the consol bond: the risk associated with this state variable may then be hedged away. Both Richard and Cox, Ingersoll and Ross avoid the estimation problems posed by the two utility-dependent functions in the partial differential equation by making explicit assumptions about the tastes of the representative investor: Richard considers both linear and logarithmic utility functions while Cox, Ingersoll and Ross consider only the logarithmic case. We assume that the utility-dependent functions are constants and estimate their values from the data at hand.

In the following section the partial differential equation which must be satisfied by the value of any default-free discount bond is derived. In the third section the parameters of the assumed stochastic process for interest rates are estimated using data on Canadian interest rates. The fourth section reports the results of using the model to price a sample of Government of Canada bonds.

The pricing equation for discount bonds

Letting r denote the instantaneous rate of interest and ℓ the long-term rate of interest which is taken as the yield on a consol bond which pays coupons continuously, it is assumed that r and ℓ follow a joint stochastic process of the general type

$$
\begin{aligned}
dr &= \beta_1(r, \ell, t)\,dt + \eta_1(r, \ell, t)\,dz_1 \\
d\ell &= \beta_2(r, \ell, t)\,dt + \eta_2(r, \ell, t)\,dz_2
\end{aligned}
\tag{1}
$$

where t denotes calendar time and dz_1 and dz_2 are Wiener processes with $E[dz_1] = E[dz_2] = 0$, $dz_1^2 = dz_2^2 = dt$, $dz_1 dz_2 = \rho dt$. $\beta_1(\cdot)$ and $\beta_2(\cdot)$ are the expected instantaneous rates of change in the instantaneous and long-term rates of interest respectively, where $\eta_1^2(\cdot)$ and $\eta_2^2(\cdot)$ are the instantaneous variance rates of the changes in the two interest rates. ρ is the instantaneous correlation between the unanticipated changes in the two interest rates. Equation system (1) describes a situation in which changes in the instantaneous and long-term rates of interest are partially interdependent: both the expected change and the variance of the change in each interest rate may depend on the value of the other interest rate as well as on its own value. It is reasonable to suppose that the expected change in the instantaneous rate of interest will depend on the long-term rate of interest insofar as the long-term rate carries information about future values of the instantaneous rate further, the expected change in the long rate must also depend on the current instantaneous rate if the expected rate of return on consol bonds is to be related to the rate of return on instantaneously riskless securities. In addition, (1) allows the unanticipated changes in the two interest rates to be correlated. While the degree of correlation is an empirical matter which will be addressed below, one may envisage the instantaneous rate changing as expectations of the instantaneous rate of inflation change, while the long rate responds to changing expectations about the long-run rate of inflation: it seems reasonable to suppose that changes in these expectations will be correlated but not perfectly so.

The price of a default-free discount bond promising $1 at maturity is assumed to be a function of the current values of the interest rates, r and ℓ and time to maturity, τ, which we write as $B(r, \ell, \tau)$. Applying Itô's Lemma, the stochastic process for the price of a discount bond is

$$
\frac{dB}{B} = \mu(r, \ell, \tau)\,dt + s_1(r, \ell, \tau)\,dz_1 + s_2(r, \ell, \tau)\,dz_2 \tag{2}
$$

where

$$
\mu(r, \ell, \tau) = \frac{B_1\beta_1 + B_2\beta_2 + \frac{1}{2}B_{11}\eta_1^2 + \frac{1}{2}B_{22}\eta_2^2 + B_{12}\rho\eta_1\eta_2 - B_3}{B}
$$

$$s_1(r, \ell, \tau) = \frac{B_1 \eta_1}{B}$$

$$s_2(r, \ell, \tau) = \frac{B_2 \eta_2}{B}$$

and $B_1 = \partial B/\partial r$, $B_2 = \partial B/\partial \ell$, $B_3 = \partial B/\partial \tau$ etc.

To derive the equilibrium relationship between expected returns on bonds of different maturities, consider forming a portfolio, P, by investing amounts x_1, x_2, x_3 in bonds of maturity τ_1, τ_2, τ_3, respectively. The rate of return on this portfolio is[3]

$$\begin{aligned}\frac{dP}{P} = &[x_1\mu(\tau_1) + x_2\mu(\tau_2) + x_3\mu(\tau_3)]dt + \\ &[x_1 s_1(\tau_1) + x_2 s_1(\tau_2) + x_3 s_1(\tau_3)]dz_1 + \\ &[x_1 s_2(\tau_1) + x_2 s_2(\tau_2) + x_3 s_2(\tau_3)]dz_2\end{aligned} \tag{3}$$

The rate of return on the portfolio will be non-stochastic if the portfolio proportions are chosen so that the coefficients of dz_1 and dz_2 in (3) are zero. That is, so that

$$\begin{aligned}x_1 s_1(\tau_1) + x_2 s_1(\tau_2) + x_3 s_1(\tau_3) = 0 \\ x_1 s_2(\tau_1) + x_2 s_2(\tau_2) + x_3 s_2(\tau_3) = 0\end{aligned} \tag{4}$$

Then, to avoid the possibility of arbitrage profits, it is necessary that the rate of return on this portfolio be equal to the instantaneous riskless rate of interest, r, so that

$$x_1[\mu(\tau_1) - r] + x_2[\mu(\tau_2) - r] + x_3[\mu(\tau_3) - r] = 0 \tag{5}$$

The zero-risk conditions (4) and the no arbitrage condition (5) constitute a set of three linear homogeneous equations in the three portfolio proportions. They will possess a solution if and only if

$$\mu(\tau) - r = \lambda_1(r, \ell, t)\, s_1(\tau) + \lambda_2(r, \ell, t)\, s_2(\tau) \tag{6}$$

where the functions $\lambda_1(\cdot)$ and $\lambda_2(\cdot)$ are independent of maturity, τ. Equation (6) is an equilibrium relationship which constrains the relative risk premium on bonds of different maturities. It expresses the instantaneous risk premium on a discount bond of any maturity as the sum of two elements: these are proportional to the partial covariances of the bond's rate of return with the unanticipated changes in the instantaneous and long-term rates of interest, $s_1(\cdot)$ and $s_2(\cdot)$ respectively. $\lambda_1(\cdot)$ and $\lambda_2(\cdot)$ may then be regarded as the market prices of instantaneous and long-term interest rate risk and will depend upon the utility functions of market participants. If the expressions for $\mu(\cdot)$, $s_1(\cdot)$ and $s_2(\cdot)$ are substituted in (6), the result will be a partial differential equation for the price of a discount bond, $B(r, \ell, \tau)$, which will contain the two utility-dependent functions $\lambda_1(\cdot)$ and $\lambda_2(\cdot)$.[4] However, by making use of the fact that ℓ is a function of the price of an asset which we assume to be traded, a consol bond, it can be shown[5] that $\lambda_2(\cdot)$ is given by

$$\lambda_2(r, \ell, t) = -\frac{\eta_2}{\ell} + \frac{\beta_2 - \ell^2 + r\ell}{\eta_2} \tag{7}$$

Equation (7) expresses $\lambda_2(\cdot)$ in terms of the two rates of interest and the parameters of the stochastic process for the long-term rate of interest. It therefore enables us to eliminate this utility-dependent function from the partial differential equation for the price of a discount bond, so that substitution in the equilibrium relationship (6) of the expressions for $\mu(\tau)$, $s_1(\tau)$ and $s_2(\tau)$, and use of equation (7) to eliminate $\lambda_2(\cdot)$, permits us to rewrite the equilibrium relationship (6) as the partial differential equation

$$\tfrac{1}{2}B_{11}\eta_1^2 + B_{12}\rho\eta_1\eta_2 + \tfrac{1}{2}B_{22}\eta_2^2 + B_1(\beta_1 - \lambda_1\eta_1) + B_2\left(\frac{\eta_2^2}{\ell^2} + \ell^2 - r\ell\right) - B_3 - Br = 0 \quad (8)$$

Given the stochastic process (1) for the two interest rates r and ℓ, (8) is the basic partial differential equation for the pricing of default-free discount bonds. This equation, together with the boundary condition specifying the payment to be received at maturity, say $B(r, \ell, 0) = 1$, may be solved to yield the prices of discount bonds of all maturities from which the whole term structure of interest rates may be inferred. The term structure at any point in time will depend upon the current values of the state variables r and ℓ, as well as upon the unknown function $\lambda_1(\cdot)$. The prices of regular coupon bonds may be obtained by treating them as portfolios of discount bonds; alternatively, if coupons are paid continuously at the rate c, then c should be added to the left-hand side of the partial differential equation (8). In addition, this equation is valid for all types of default-free interest dependent claims, so that it may be applied for example to the pricing of saving bonds or callable bonds by the introduction of the appropriate boundary conditions defining the payoffs on the claims.

It is interesting to note that the partial differential equation is not only independent of $\lambda_2(\cdot)$, the market price of long-term interest rate risk, it is also independent of $\beta_2(\cdot)$, the drift parameter for the long-term interest rate, so that the solution is independent of the expected rate of return on the consol bond. This result is analogous to the finding within the simple Black–Scholes (1973) model for the pricing of stock options that the function expressing the equilibrium price of the option in terms of the price of the underlying stock is independent of the expected rate of return on the underlying stock. The reason for the two results is the same: there exists an asset for which the partial derivatives of its value with respect to all of the state variables are known: in this case the consol bond, and in the Black–Scholes case the stock. It can be shown that in general the number of unknown utility-dependent parameters left in the partial differential equation will be equal to the number of state variables, excluding time, less the number of assets for which the partial derivatives of the value function are known: in the Black–Scholes case this is zero and in the present case it is one. The time variable is excluded since the pure reward for the passage of time is equal to the interest rate. This proposition is illustrated more formally in the appendix.

The coefficients of the partial differential equation (8) are the utility-dependent function $\lambda_2(\cdot)$ and the parameters of the underlying stochastic process for the two interest rates, (1). Empirical application of the model requires that the parameters of this stochastic process be estimated, and this is taken up in the next section.

Estimation of the stochastic process

THE FORM OF THE STOCHASTIC PROCESS

Estimation of the stochastic process for interest rates (1) presupposes some stronger assumptions about the form of the process than we have made hitherto. The first restriction comes from the requirement that the excess of the expected rate of return on the consol bond over the instantaneous rate of interest be commensurate with the degree of long-term interest rate risk of the consol. This requirement is expressed in equation (7): solving this equation for $\lambda_2(\cdot)$, we find

$$\beta_2(r, \ell, t) = \ell^2 - r\ell + \frac{\eta_2^2}{\ell} + \lambda_2\eta_2 \quad (9)$$

For empirical tractability it is assumed that $\lambda_2(\cdot)$, the market price of long-term interest rate risk, is constant.

The only other *a priori* restrictions which can be imposed on the stochastic process derive from the requirement that dominance by money be avoided, so that neither of the interest rates can be allowed to become negative. This possibility is avoided by assuming that

$$\eta_1(r, \ell, t) = r\sigma_1, \qquad \eta_2(r, \ell, t) = \ell\sigma_2 \tag{10}$$

and requiring that

$$\beta_1(0, \ell, t) \geq 0 \tag{11}$$

Equations (10) and (11) jointly imply that $\beta_2(r, 0, t) \geq 0$. Equation (10) specifies that the standard deviation of the instantaneous change in each interest rate is proportional to its current level.

To reflect the premise that the long-term rate contains information about future values of the instantaneous rate, it is assumed that the instantaneous rate stochastically regresses towards a function of the current long-term rate. This assumption and conditions (10) and (11) are satisfied by taking as the stochastic process for the logarithm of the instantaneous rate

$$d\ln r = \alpha(\ln \ell - \ln p - \ln r)\,dt + \sigma_1 dz_1 \tag{12}$$

which is equivalent to the assumptions that

$$\beta_1(r, \ell, t) = r\left[\alpha \ln\left(\frac{\ell}{pr}\right) + \tfrac{1}{2}\sigma_1^2\right] \tag{13}$$

$$\eta_1(r, \ell, t) = r\sigma_1 \tag{14}$$

The coefficient α represents the speed of adjustment of the logarithm of the instantaneous rate towards its current target value, $\ln(\ell/p)$, and p is a parameter relating the target value of $\ln r$ to the current value of $\ln \ell$.

Finally substituting for $\beta_2(\cdot)$ and $\eta_2(\cdot)$ from (9) and (10) in equation (1), the stochastic process for the long-term rate of interest is

$$d\ell = \ell[\ell - r + \sigma_2^2 + \lambda_2\sigma_2]\,dt + \ell\sigma_2 dz_2 \tag{15}$$

THE LINEARISED FORM OF THE STOCHASTIC PROCESS

Equations (12) and (15) constitute a non-linear system of stochastic differential equations governing the behaviour of the two interest rates. In order to estimate the system it is necessary first to linearise it, and to this end we approximate ℓ and r by linear functions of $\ln \ell$ and $\ln r$. Thus, writing ℓ and r as functions of $\ln \ell$ and $\ln r$ and expanding in Taylor series about the mean sample values, $e^{\overline{\ln \ell}}$ and $e^{\overline{\ln r}}$,

$$\ell - r = e^{\overline{\ln \ell}} - e^{\overline{\ln r}} \approx e^{\overline{\ln \ell}}(1 - \overline{\ln \ell}) - e^{\overline{\ln r}}(1 - \overline{\ln r}) + e^{\overline{\ln \ell}}\ln \ell - e^{\overline{\ln r}}\ln r \tag{16}$$

Then using Itô's Lemma to obtain the stochastic process for $\ln \ell$ from (15), and substituting for $(\ell - r)$ from (16), the linearised stochastic differential equation for the logarithm of the long-term rate may be written as

$$d\ln \ell = (q - k_1 \ln r + k_2 \ln \ell)\,dt + \sigma_2 dz_2 \tag{17}$$

where

$$q = e^{\overline{\ln \ell}}(1 - \overline{\ln \ell}) - e^{\overline{\ln r}}(1 - \overline{\ln r}) + \tfrac{1}{2}\sigma_2^2 + \lambda_2\sigma_2$$

while we may write the stochastic differential equation for the logarithm of the instantaneous rate as

$$d\ln r = \alpha(\ln \ell - \ln r - \ln p)\,dt + \sigma_1 dz_1 \tag{18}$$

This linearised system of stochastic differential equations for the logarithms of the two interest rates is written in matrix notation as

$$dy(t) = Ay(t)\,dt + b\,dt + d\zeta(t) \tag{19}$$

where

$$y(t) = \begin{pmatrix} \ln r(t) \\ \ln \ell(t) \end{pmatrix} \qquad d\xi(t) = \begin{pmatrix} \sigma_1 dz_1(t) \\ \sigma_2 dz_2(t) \end{pmatrix}$$

$$A = \begin{pmatrix} -\alpha & \alpha \\ -k_1 & k_2 \end{pmatrix} \qquad b = \begin{pmatrix} -\alpha \ln p \\ q \end{pmatrix}$$

THE EXACT DISCRETE MODEL

While (19) is a system of linear stochastic differential equations, the data on interest rates which are required to estimate it are available only at discrete intervals. One approach to estimation when there are prior restrictions on the parameters[6] has been proposed by Bergstrom (1966). This involves first substituting finite differences for differentials and averages of beginning and end of period values for the time-dated vector $y(t)$ and then estimating the resulting linear equations by standard simultaneous equations methods. Unfortunately, as Phillips (1972) points out, the undesirable feature of this approach is the specification error which causes the resulting parameter estimates to be asymptotically biased. A more efficient and elegant procedure is to obtain the exact discrete model corresponding to (19) and to estimate the parameters from this model.

The exact discrete model corresponding to (19) is[7]

$$y(t) = e^{A}y(t-1) + A^{-1}[e^{A} - I]\,b + \zeta(t) \tag{20}$$

where

$$\zeta(t) = \int_{t-1}^{t} e^{(t-s)A}\,d\zeta(s)$$

and the variance covariance matrix of errors is

$$E[\zeta(t)\zeta'(t)] = \int_0^t e^{sA}\Sigma e^{sA'} ds \tag{21}$$

where Σ is the instantaneous variance-covariance matrix with elements σ_1^2, σ_2^2, $\rho\sigma_1\sigma_2$.[8]

The matrix e^A is defined by

$$e^{A} \equiv T e^{\Lambda} T^{-1} \tag{22}$$

where

$$e^{\Lambda} = \begin{pmatrix} e^{v_1} & 0 \\ 0 & e^{v_2} \end{pmatrix}$$

and v_1 and v_2 are the characteristic roots of the matrix A, while T is the matrix of characteristic vectors. In this case the characteristic roots are

$$v_1 = \frac{k_2 - \alpha + \sqrt{(k_2 - \alpha)^2 - 4(k_1 - k_2)}}{2}$$

$$v_2 = \frac{k_2 - \alpha - \sqrt{(k_2 - \alpha)^2 - 4(k_1 - k_2)}}{2} \tag{23}$$

and the matrix of characteristic vectors is

$$T \equiv \begin{pmatrix} 1 & 1 \\ k_1/(k_2 - v_1) & k_1/(k_2 - v_2) \end{pmatrix} \tag{24}$$

Inverting A and carrying out the appropriate matrix multiplications in (20), the exact discrete model to be estimated is

$$\begin{aligned} y_1(t) = {} & \frac{1}{v_1 - v_2}\left[e^{v_2}(k_2 - v_2) - e^{v_1}(k_2 - v_1)\right] y_1(t-1) + \\ & \frac{1}{k_1(v_1 - v_2)}\left[(k_2 - v_1)(k_2 - v_2)(e^{v_1} - e^{v_2})\right] y_2(t-1) + \\ & \frac{1}{(k_1 - k_2)(v_1 - v_2)}\left\langle \ln p\left\{k_2\left[e^{v_1}(k_2 - v_1) - e^{v_2}(k_2 - v_2) + v_1 - v_2\right] - \right.\right. \\ & \left.\alpha k_1(e^{v_1} - e^{v_2})\right\} + q\left[\frac{k_2(k_2 - v_1)(k_2 - v_2)(e^{v_1} - e^{v_2})}{\alpha k_1} - \right. \\ & \left.\left. e^{v_1}(k_2 - v_2) + e^{v_2}(k_2 - v_1) + v_1 - v_2\right]\right\rangle + \xi_1(t) \end{aligned} \tag{25}$$

$$\begin{aligned} y_2(t) = {} & \frac{k_1}{v_1 - v_2}(e^{v_2} - e^{v_1}) y_1(t-1) + \frac{1}{v_1 - v_2} \times \\ & \left[e^{v_1}(k_2 - v_2) - e^{v_2}(k_2 - v_1)\right] y_2(t-1) + \frac{1}{(k_1 - k_2)(v_1 - v_2)} \times \\ & \left\langle \ln p\left\{k_1\left[e^{v_1}(k_2 - v_1) - e^{v_2}(k_2 - v_2) + v_1 - v_2\right] - \alpha k_1(e^{v_1} - e^{v_2})\right\} + \right. \\ & q\left[\frac{(k_2 - v_1)(k_2 - v_2)(e^{v_1} - e^{v_2})}{\alpha} - \right. \\ & \left.\left. e^{v_1}(k_2 - v_2) + e^{v_2}(k_2 - v_1) + v_1 - v_2\right]\right\rangle + \xi_1(t) \end{aligned} \tag{26}$$

Summarising the analysis to this point, the system of stochastic differential equations (1) was first specialised by assuming that the standard deviation of the unanticipated instantaneous changes in each interest rate is proportional to the current level of that rate (10); by requiring that the instantaneous expected rate of return on a consol bond be commensurate with its degree of long-term interest rate risk (9), where $\lambda_2(\cdot)$, the market price of long-term interest rate risk, is taken as constant; and by requiring that the logarithm of the instantaneous interest rate stochastically regress towards a target value which depends on the current value of the long-term rate (12). The resulting system of stochastic differential equations (12) and (15), was then linearised to yield the system (19), where $y_1(t)$ and $y_2(t)$ are the logarithms of the instantaneous rate and the long-term rate respectively. Finally, since the equation system is to be estimated using data on r and ℓ at discrete time intervals, the exact discrete model, (25) and (26), corresponding to the linearised form (19) was found.

EMPIRICAL RESULTS

The three coefficients of the equation system (25), (26) to be estimated are α, $\ln p$ and q. In addition we require an estimate of the variance-covariance matrix Σ, since the elements of this matrix appear as coefficients in the partial differential equation (8) for the value of a bond. The estimation was carried out using a non-linear procedure described by Malinvaud (1966) and employed by Phillips (1972) in a similar context. The data for the instantaneous rate of interest were the yields on 30-day Canadian Bankers' Acceptances converted to an equivalent continuously compounded annual rate of interest, while the long-term rate of interest was the continuously compounded equivalent of the average yields to maturity on Government of Canada bonds with maturities in excess of 10 years. Both interest rates series are mid-market closing rates on the last Wednesday of each month from January 1964 to December 1976.[9]

The estimated equation system is

$$d\ln r = \underset{(0.0050)}{0.0701}\,[\ln \ell/r - \underset{(0.0050)}{0.0599}]\,dt + 0.0736\,dz_1$$

$$d\ln \ell = [\underset{(0.0020)}{0.0060} - 0.0051\ln r + 0.0058\ln \ell]\,dt + 0.0250\,dz_2$$

where the standard errors of the estimated coefficient are in parentheses and the coefficients of $-\ln r$ and $\ln \ell$ are the computed values of k_1 and k_2. The estimated correlation between the errors in the two equations, ρ, is 0.3747, and the adjustment coefficient of 0.0701 in the first equation implies that half of the adjustment in the instantaneous rate occurs within 10 months.

In terms of the coefficients of the basic partial differential equation (8) for the pricing of discount bonds, the parameter estimates imply

$$\eta_1 \equiv r\sigma_1 = 0.0736r, \quad \eta_2 \equiv \ell\sigma_2 = 0.0250\ell, \quad \rho = 0.3747$$

$$\beta_1(r,\ell,t) = r\left[\alpha \ln\left(\frac{\ell}{pr}\right) + \tfrac{1}{2}\sigma_1^2\right]$$

$$= r\left\{0.0701\left[\ln\left(\frac{\ell}{r}\right) - 0.0599\right] + \tfrac{1}{2}(0.0736^2)\right\}$$

Bond pricing and the term structure of interest rates

Rewriting the partial differential equation (8) to take account of the specific stochastic process for r and ℓ assumed in the previous section, we have, substituting for $\beta_1(\cdot)$, $\eta_1(\cdot)$ and $\eta_2(\cdot)$,

$$\tfrac{1}{2}B_{11}r^2\sigma_1^2 + B_{12}r\ell\rho\sigma_1\sigma_2 + \tfrac{1}{2}B_{22}\ell^2\sigma_2^2 + B_1 r\left[\alpha\ln\left(\frac{\ell}{pr}\right) + \tfrac{1}{2}\sigma_1^2 - \lambda_1\sigma_1\right] +$$
$$B_2\ell\left[\sigma_2^2 + \ell - r\right] - B_3 - Br = 0 \qquad (27)$$

Then the value of a discount bond promising \$1 at maturity, $\tau = 0$, is given by the solution to equation (27) subject to the boundary condition

$$B(r, \ell, 0) = 1 \qquad (28)$$

Using the values of α, $\ln p$, ρ, σ_1 and σ_2 estimated in the third section, equation (27) with boundary condition (28) was solved[10] for values of λ_1, the market price of instantaneous interest rate risk, of -0.04, 0.0, 0.09. The resulting values of $B(r, \ell, \tau)$ are present value factors: for a given value of λ_1, $B(r, \ell, \tau)$ is the present value of $1 payable with certainty in τ periods when the instantaneous and long-term rates of interest are r and ℓ, respectively.

A sample of 101 Government of Canada bonds was priced using the present value factors computed for each of the three values of λ_1. The bonds were priced on the last Wednesday of each quarter from January 1964 to January 1977 by applying the present value factors appropriate to the prevailing instantaneous and long-term rates of interest to the promised coupon and principal payments for each bond. The sample includes all Government of Canada bonds with maturities less than 10 years for which prices were available in the *Bank of Canada Quarterly Review* and which were neither callable nor exchangeable. The root mean square price prediction error was calculated for each of the three values of λ_1, and quadratic interpolation was used to estimate the value of λ_1, which minimises the root mean square prediction error.[11] This estimated value of λ_1 was 0.0355, and the bonds were then priced for this value of λ_1.

In addition, for each of the four values of λ_1, yields to maturity were calculated based on the predicted bond values each quarter and these predicted yields to maturity were compared with the actual yields to maturity. The comparison of actual and predicted bond values and yields to maturity is reported, for each value of λ_1, in Table 1: in this table all bonds are treated as having a par value of 100. Thus, for the estimated value of $\lambda_1 = 0.0355$, the root mean square prediction error for bond prices is 1.56 and the mean error is -0.17. For the same value of λ_1, the root mean square prediction error for yields to maturity is 0.67% and the mean error is 0.24%. It is to be anticipated that the model will be less successful in predicting yields to maturity than in predicting bond prices, since a small error in the predicted bond price will cause a very large error in the predicted yield to maturity for short-dated bonds.

For both bond prices and yields to maturity, the actual values were regressed on the predicted values and the resulting regression statistics are reported in Table 1 also. For unbiased predictions the intercept term (α) should be zero and the slope coefficient (β) should be equal to unity. The actual slope coefficients for $\lambda_1 = 0.0355$ are 0.93 for bond prices and 0.79 for yields to maturity. While these regression results should be treated with caution since there is no assurance that the errors are either independent or normally distributed, it is encouraging to observe that there is a strong, though certainly not perfect, correspondence between the actual and predicted values.

Tables 2 and 3 report the results of predicting bond values and yields to maturity for the last Wednesday of each January from 1964 to 1977. These results are representative of those obtained for the other quarters for which predictions were made. While there

Table 1. Predicted and actual bond prices and yields to maturity for alternative values of λ_1 (t-ratios in parentheses)

	Values of λ_1			
	-0.04	0.0	0.0355	0.09
Bond prices				
RMSE	1.95	1.65	1.56	1.74
Mean error	-1.05	-0.59	-0.17	0.41
α	13.44	10.01	7.28	4.12
	(21.44)	(15.40)	(10.46)	(5.04)
β	0.87	0.90	0.93	0.95
	(134.04)	(134.44)	(129.57)	(114.23)
R^2	0.93	0.93	0.93	0.91
Yields to maturity				
RMSE (%)	0.81	0.72	0.67	0.64
Mean error (%)	0.52	0.37	0.24	0.06
α (%)	1.12	1.15	1.18	1.25
	(18.40)	(18.24)	(18.23)	(18.40)
β	0.77	0.78	0.79	0.80
	(90.63)	(87.61)	(84.44)	(79.56)
R^2	0.86	0.86	0.85	0.83

Table 2. Predicted and actual bond prices by period for $\lambda_1 = 0.355$ (α, β are the coefficients from the regression of actual values on predicted values)

Year (last Wednesday of January)	Number of observations	RMSE	Mean error (predicted/actual)	α (t-statistic)	β (t-statistic)	R^2	Instantaneous interest rate, %	Long-term interest rate, %
1964	17	1.09	0.61	4.62 (0.43)	0.95 (8.68)	0.82	3.69	5.17
1965	16	1.04	0.39	23.29 (2.91)	0.76 (9.59)	0.86	3.81	4.69
1966	20	2.15	1.63	37.75 (3.24)	0.61 (5.23)	0.59	4.00	5.41
1967	21	0.91	−0.58	9.49 (1.10)	0.91 (10.44)	0.84	5.85	5.60
1968	22	1.64	0.93	−37.57 (−4.60)	1.38 (16.38)	0.93	6.40	6.54
1969	28	0.97	0.46	−14.97 (−3.53)	1.15 (26.39)	0.96	6.60	7.16
1970	31	1.06	0.07	−10.98 (−5.52)	1.11 (53.39)	0.99	8.90	8.31
1971	30	2.01	−1.61	−0.45 (−0.10)	1.02 (22.66)	0.95	6.00	6.67
1972	32	1.36	0.43	−7.84 (−1.67)	1.07 (23.17)	0.95	3.95	6.73
1973	28	0.46	−0.06	−0.22 (−0.13)	1.00 (59.39)	0.99	4.75	7.16
1974	24	1.95	−1.84	2.42 (1.19)	0.99 (46.00)	0.99	8.75	7.75
1975	22	3.37	−2.84	17.04 (3.32)	0.85 (15.86)	0.92	7.00	8.30
1976	22	1.71	−1.44	5.32 (2.02)	0.96 (33.76)	0.98	9.00	9.29
1977	16	0.99	−0.94	3.70 (1.18)	0.97 (30.88)	0.98	8.33	9.09

Table 3. Predicted and actual yields to maturity by period for $\lambda_1 = 0.0355$ (α, β are the coefficients from regression of actual values on predicted values)

Year (last Wednesday of January)	Number of observations	RMSE	Mean error (predicted/actual)	α (t-statistic)	β (t-statistic)	R^2	Instantaneous interest rate, %	Long-term interest rate, %
1964	17	0.21%	−0.16%	−1.56 (−2.86)	1.40 (11.05)	0.88	3.69	5.16
1965	16	0.25	0.01	−5.26 (−6.13)	2.22 (11.15)	0.89	3.81	4.69
1966	20	0.53	−0.50	−1.52 (−2.06)	1.44 (9.02)	0.81	4.00	5.41
1967	21	0.64	0.50	13.93 (10.38)	−1.57 (−6.58)	0.68	5.85	5.60
1968	22	0.39	−0.12	35.38 (5.09)	−4.54 (−4.16)	0.45	6.40	6.54
1969	28	0.24	−0.06	−27.45 (−8.26)	5.05 (10.44)	0.80	6.60	7.16
1970	31	0.79	0.42	16.66 (11.44)	−1.00 (−5.88)	0.54	8.90	8.31
19.71	30	0.85	0.76	−18.70 (−4.40)	3.86 (5.70)	0.53	6.00	6.67
1972	32	0.35	−0.04	−0.66 (−0.95)	1.13 (8.69)	0.71	3.95	6.73
1973	28	0.20	0.05	−0.48 (−1.24)	1.07 (16.64)	0.91	4.75	7.16
1974	24	1.20	1.04	11.04 (14.58)	−0.51 (−5.37)	0.56	8.75	7.75
1975	22	1.11	1.05	2.52 (0.98)	0.53 (1.57)	0.10	7.00	8.30
1976	22	0.75	0.68	6.80 (0.88)	0.17 (0.198)	0.00	9.00	9.29
1977	16	0.52	0.49	7.55 (1.35)	0.04 (0.06)	0.00	8.33	9.09

Table 4. The influence of taxes on bond prices: (bond price – predicted value of principal) = α + β (predicted value of coupons)

	Values of λ_1			
	−0.04	**0.0**	**0.0355**	**0.09**
α	0.62	0.67	0.71	0.78
	(8.03)	(9.11)	(10.04)	(11.28)
β	1.03	0.99	0.96	0.92
	(249.33)	(254.09)	(256.38)	(256.24)
R^2	0.98	0.98	0.98	0.98

is reasonable stability in the relationship between actual and predicted bond values, the relationship between actual and predicted yields to maturity is much more erratic. This reflects the greater difficulty in predicting this variable, referred to above, and also suggests that there are factors which are not encompassed in our model that determine the shape of the term structure.

One factor which has been neglected in the model developed in this paper is the role of income taxes and their differential impact on coupon income and capital gains. To test whether income taxes cause the coupon stream of a bond to be valued less highly than the principal repayment at maturity, the predicted value of the principal payment was subtracted from the actual bond price and the difference was regressed on the predicted value of the coupon stream. If income taxes are important in the pricing of bonds, the resulting regression coefficient should be less than unity, the difference between unity and the estimated regression coefficient measuring the effective tax rate on coupon income. The regression results are reported in Table 4 for the different values of λ_1. The evidence presented in this table suggests that the effect of income taxes is slight: for the estimated value of $\lambda_1 = 0.0355$, the estimated tax rate is only 4%, and even for $\lambda_1 = 0.09$ the estimated tax rate is only 8%.

Conclusion

In this paper we have developed a theory of the term structure of interest rates based on the assumption that the values of all default-free discount bonds may be written as a function of time and two interest rates, the instantaneous rate and the long-term rate, which follow a joint Markov process in continuous time. This assumption permitted us to derive in the second section, a partial differential equation which must be satisfied by the values of all default-free discount bonds. The partial differential equation contains two utility-dependent functions $\lambda_1(\cdot)$ and $\lambda_2(\cdot)$, but $\lambda_2(\cdot)$ was eliminated by making use of the assumption that there exists a traded asset, a consol bond, which corresponds to one of the state variables, the long-term rate of interest.

In the third section, the stochastic process for the two interest rates was specialised and estimated using data on Canadian interest rates. The partial differential equation was then solved using the estimated parameters and selected values for the market price of instantaneous interest rate risk, λ_1, to find the value of λ_1 which minimised the price prediction errors for a sample of Canadian government bonds, and the predictive ability of the model was evaluated: the root mean square prediction error for bond prices was of the order of 1.5%.

It is anticipated that models of this type will have application in the management of bond portfolios and studies of the efficiency of bond markets. Perhaps the most interesting application is to the pricing of bonds which contain an option such as callable bonds and saving bonds. The latter are default-free securities allowing the holder the right of redemption prior to maturity at a predetermined series of redemption prices. While instruments of this type are common in North America and several European countries, including France, Germany, Italy and the United Kingdom, they have received virtually no attention to date from financial economists. Work is currently in progress to apply the model developed in this paper to Canadian savings bonds.

This model should be seen as a first step in the application of a new approach to the term structure of interest rates and the pricing of default-free securities. Further work is required on the specification and estimation of both the stochastic process for the interest rates and the market price of interest rate risk.

Appendix

A.1 THE MARKET PRICE OF LONG-TERM INTEREST RATE RISK, $\lambda_2(r, \ell, t)$

It is shown here that if there exists a consol bond, the utility-dependent market price of long-term interest rate risk may be expressed in terms of the two interest rates and the parameters of the stochastic process for the long-term rate of interest. Let $V(\ell)$ denote the price of a consol bond paying a continuous coupon at the rate of \$1 per period. Then the long-term rate of interest is defined by

$$V(\ell) = \ell^{-1} \tag{29}$$

so that, applying Itô's Lemma, the stochastic process for the price of a consol bond is

$$\frac{dV}{V} = \left(\frac{\eta_2^2}{\ell^2} - \frac{\beta_2}{\ell}\right) dt - \left(\frac{\eta_2}{\ell}\right) dz_2 \tag{30}$$

Then, defining $s_1(\infty)$ and $s_2(\infty)$ as the partial covariances of the consol bond's rate of return with the unanticipated changes in the two interest rates, it follows from equation (30) that $s_1(\infty) = 0$, $s_2(\infty) = -\eta_2/\ell$. Further, defining $\mu(\alpha)$ as the expected instantaneous rate of return on the consol bond including both the expected capital gain which is obtained from (30) and the rate of coupon payment per dollar of principal,

$$\mu(\infty) = \frac{\eta_2^2}{\ell^2} - \frac{\beta_2}{\ell} + \ell \tag{31}$$

Now the expected rate of return on the consol bond must also satisfy the equilibrium risk premium equation (6), so that substituting in this equation for $\mu(\infty)$, $s_1(\infty)$ and $s_2(\infty)$ and solving for $\lambda_2(\cdot)$, we obtain

$$\lambda_2(r, \ell, t) = \frac{\eta_2}{\ell} + \frac{(\beta_2 - \ell^2 + r\ell)}{\eta_2} \tag{32}$$

which is equation (7) of the text.

A.2 ASSET PRICES AND STATE VARIABLES

This section illustrates for equation (6) that the number of utility-dependent functions left in the partial differential equation is equal to the number of state variables, excluding time, less the number of assets for which the partial derivatives of the value functions are known. Substitute in the equilibrium condition (6) the expressions for $\mu(\cdot)$, $s_1(\cdot)$ and $s_2(\cdot)$ to obtain

$$B_1\beta_1 + B_2\beta_2 + \tfrac{1}{2}B_{11}\eta_1^2 + \tfrac{1}{2}B_{22}\eta_2^2 + B_{12}\rho\eta_1\eta_2 - B_3 - rB = \lambda_1 B_1\eta_1 + \lambda_2 B_2\eta_2 \tag{33}$$

Now suppose that there exists an asset with value G, all of whose partial derivatives with respect to the state variables are known. The value of the asset must also satisfy the same partial differential equation.

$$G_1\beta_1 + G_2\beta_2 + \tfrac{1}{2}G_{11}\eta_1^2 + \tfrac{1}{2}G_{22}\eta_2^2 + G_{12}\rho\eta_1\eta_2 - G_3 - rG = \lambda_1 G_1\eta_1 + \lambda_2 G_2\eta_2 \tag{34}$$

Then, to eliminate λ_2 and β_2, equation (34) is multiplied by B_2/G_2 and subtracted from (33) to yield

$$\left(\frac{B_1 - B_2G_1}{G_2}\right)\beta_1 + \frac{1}{2}\left(\frac{B_{11} - B_2G_{11}}{G_2}\right)\eta_1^2 + \frac{1}{2}\left(\frac{B_{22} - B_2G_{22}}{G_2}\right)\eta_2^2 +$$

$$\left(\frac{B_{12} - B_2G_{12}}{G_2}\right)\rho\eta_1\eta_2 - \left(\frac{B_3 - B_2G_3}{G_2}\right) - r\left(\frac{B - B_2G}{G_2}\right) = \lambda_1\left(\frac{B_1 - B_2G_1}{G_2}\right)\eta_1 \quad (35)$$

Since G and all of its partial derivatives are known functions, (35) contains only a single utility-dependent function, $\lambda_1(\cdot)$, and the drift parameter for the corresponding state variable, β_1. If G is the consol bond, then substitution of the appropriate partial derivatives in (35) will yield our partial differential equation (8). It should be clear that if G_1 were not zero, it would have been possible to eliminate λ_1 and β_1 instead of λ_2 and β_2, and that if a second distinct asset exists whose partial derivatives are known it will be possible to eliminate all four parameters.

A.3 SOLUTION OF THE PARTIAL DIFFERENTIAL EQUATION

Since there is no known analytic solution to the differential equation (27) we apply a finite difference solution procedure. This requires that the equation be transformed to take advantage of the natural boundary conditions which occur as the interest rates approach zero and infinity.

To transform the equation, define the new state variables, μ_1 and μ_2, where[12]

$$\mu_1 = 1/(1 + nr), \qquad u_2 = 1/(1 + n\ell)$$

and let $B(r, \ell, \tau) \equiv b(u_1, u_2, \tau)$.

Writing the partial derivatives of $B(\cdot)$ in terms of those of $b(\cdot)$, we have

$$B_1 = -nu_1^2 b_1, \qquad B_2 = -nu_2^2 b_2$$

$$B_{11} = n^2u_1^4 b_{11} + 2n^2u_1^3 b_1, \qquad B_{22} = n^2u_2^4 b_{22} + 2n^2u_2^3 b_2$$

$$B_3 = b_3$$

Substituting for r, ℓ and the derivatives of $B(\cdot)$ in (27), we obtain the transformed equation

$$\tfrac{1}{2}b_{11}u_1^2(1-u_1^2)\sigma_1^2 + b_{12}u_1u_2(1-u_1)(1-u_2)\rho u_1u_2 + \tfrac{1}{2}b_{22}u_2^2(1-u_2^2)\sigma_2^2 +$$

$$b_1u_1(1-u_1)\left[\sigma_1^2\left(\tfrac{1}{2}-u_1\right) - \alpha\left(\frac{\ln u_1(1-u_2)}{pu_2(1-u_1)}\right) + \lambda_1\sigma_1\right] +$$

$$b_2u_2(1-u_2)\left[-\sigma_2^2u_2 - \frac{(1-u_2)/nu_2 + (1-u_1)}{nu_1}\right] - b_3 - \frac{b(1-u_1)}{nu_1} = 0 \quad (36)$$

The solution to this differential equation must satisfy the maturity boundary condition which is defined by assuming that the bond pays \$1 at maturity:

$$b(u_1, u_2, 0) = 1 \quad (37)$$

In addition we have the following natural boundaries obtained by letting u_1, u_2 approach zero and one[13] in the differential equation (36):

(i) For $r = \infty(u_1 = 0)$, $\ell = \infty(u_2 = 0)$.
Multiply (36) by nu_1 and let u_1 and u_2 approach zero to obtain

$$b(0, 0, \tau) = 0 \quad (38)$$

(ii) For $r = \infty (u_1 = 0)$, $\ell \neq \infty$.
Multiply (36) by nu_1 and let u_1 approach zero to obtain the ordinary differential equation

$$b_2(0, u_2, \tau)\, u_2(1 - u_2) - b(0, u_2, \tau) = 0$$

Solving this equation and imposing the requirement that $b(0, u_2, \tau) \leq 1$, we have

$$b(0, u_2, \tau) = 0 \tag{39}$$

(iii) For $\ell = \infty (u_2 = 0)$, $r \neq \infty$.
Divide (36) by $\ln u_2$ and let u_2 approach zero to obtain

$$\alpha u_1(1 - u_1)\, b_1(u_1, 0, \tau) = 0$$

and since $b(0, 0, \tau) = 0$ from (38), this implies that

$$b(u_1, 0, \tau) = 0 \tag{40}$$

The boundary conditions (38)-(40) state that if either interest rate is infinite, the value of the bond is zero.

(iv) For $r = 0\ (u_1 = 1)$, $\ell = 0\ (u_2 = 1)$.
Setting u_1 and u_2 equal to unity in (36),

$$b_3(1, 1, \tau) = 0$$

Combining this with the maturity value boundary, (37), we obtain

$$b(1, 1, \tau) = 1 \tag{41}$$

(v) For $r = 0 (u_1 = 1)$, $\ell \neq 0$.
Taking the limit in (36) as $u_1 \to 1$,

$$\tfrac{1}{2} b_{22} u_2^2 (1-u_2^2)\sigma_2^2 + b_2 u_2 (1-u_2)\left(-\sigma_2^2 u_2 - \frac{(1-u_2)}{nu_2}\right) - b_2 = 0 \tag{42}$$

$b(1, u_2, \tau)$ is obtained as the solution to (42) subject to the boundary conditions (37), (40) and (41).

(vi) For $\ell = 0\ (u_2 = 1)$, $r \neq 0$.
Divide (36) by $\ln(1 - u_2)$ and let $u_2 \to 1$ to obtain

$$\alpha u_1(1 - u_1)\, b_1(u_1, \ell, \tau) = 0 \tag{43}$$

The solution to (43) subject to the boundary (40) is

$$b(u_1, 1, \tau) = 1 \tag{44}$$

The finite difference approximation to (36) is obtained by defining $b(\cdot)$ at discrete intervals.

$$\begin{aligned} b(u_{1i}, u_{2j}, \tau_k) &\equiv b(hi, hj, gk) \\ &\equiv b_{i,j,k}, \quad i, j = 0, \ldots, m, \;\; k = 0, \ldots, K \end{aligned} \tag{45}$$

where h and g are the step sizes for the interest rates and time to maturity, respectively; since u_1 and u_2 are defined on the interval (0, 1), hm = 1. Then writing finite differences in place of partial derivatives, (36) may be approximated by

$$c_1^{i,j} b_{i-1,j-1,k} + c_2^{i,j} b_{i-1,j,k} + c_3^{i,j} b_{i-1,j+1,k} +$$

$$c_4^{i,j} b_{i,j-1,k} + c_5^{i,j} b_{i,j,k} + c_6^{i,j} b_{i,j+1,k} +$$

$$c_7^{i,j} b_{i+1,j-1,k} + c_8^{i,j} b_{i+1,j,k} + c_9^{i,j} b_{i+1,j+1,k}$$

$$= b_{i,j,k-1}, \quad i = 1, \ldots, m-1, \; j = 1, \ldots, m-1 \qquad (46)$$

where $c_1^{i,j}$ etc. are coefficients derived from the parameters of the equation.

(46) is a system of $(m-1)^2$ equations in the $(m+1)^2$ unknowns $b_{i,j,k}$ (i, j = 0, 1, ..., m); the remaining 4m equations are provided by the natural boundary conditions (i)–(vi) above.[14] The augmented system of equations may be solved recursively for the unknowns $b_{i,j,k}$ in terms of $b_{i,j,k-1}$, since the values $b_{i,j,0}$ are given by the maturity boundary condition (37). To take advantage of the structure of the coefficient matrix the equations were solved by the method of successive over-relaxation.[15]

1 *For example, Stiglitz (1970), Rubinstein (1976) and Roll (1970).*

2 *It is now realised that this assumption is incompatible with universal risk neutrality, the assumption on which this version of the pure expectations hypothesis is usually based. See Merton (1973), Brennan and Schwartz (1977), Cox, Ingersoll and Ross (1977).*

3 *The arguments,* r *and* ℓ, *are omitted from the functions* $\mu(\cdot)$, $s_1(\cdot)$ *and* $s_2(\cdot)$ *for the sake of brevity; they are to be understood.*

4 *This would be identical to the partial differential equation obtained by Richard (1976) if the variable* ℓ *is interpreted as the rate of inflation rather than as the long-term rate of interest.*

5 *See Appendix.*

6 k_1 *and* k_2 *are known and the coefficients of the two variables in the first equation are known to be equal in magnitude but of opposite signs.*

7 *See Bergstrom (1966), Phillips (1972), Wymer (1972).*

8 *It can be shown that* $\int_0^t e^{sA} \Sigma e^{sA} ds \approx \Sigma$, *so that the variance-covariance matrix of errors from (20) provides good estimates of* σ_1, σ_2 *and* $\sigma_{12} = \rho\sigma_1\sigma_2$.

9 *Taken from the* Bank of Canada Review, *Cansim Series 2560.33 and 2560.13.*

10 *The solution procedure is described in the Appendix.*

11 *That is, a quadratic curve was fitted to the three pairs of RMSE and* λ_1, *and the RMSE minimising value of* λ_1 *was computed. When the bonds were priced using this value of* λ_1 *the RMSE agreed with the interpolated value. This non-linear estimation procedure leads to a maximum likelihood estimator under the usual assumption of normal, independent, homoscedastic errors. A more efficient estimator which would allow for a generalised error structure was contemplated but ruled out on the basis of computational cost.*

12 *The parameter* n *was chosen so that approximately one half of the range of* u_1 *and* u_2(0, 1) *relates to the relevant range of interest rates, 0–20%, in which solution accuracy is required, ie,* n = 40.

13 *This corresponds to letting the interest rates* r *and* ℓ *approach infinity and zero, respectively.*

14 *Values of* $b(1, u_2, \tau)$ *are obtained by solving the finite difference approximation to (42).*

15 *Westlake (1968).*

Bibliography

Bergstrom, A. R., 1966, "Non-Recursive Models as Discrete Approximations to Systems of Stochastic Differential Equations", *Econometrica* 34, pp. 173-182.

Black, F. and M. J. Scholes, 1973, "The Pricing of Options and Corporate Liabilities", *Journal of Political Economy* 81, pp. 637-659; reprinted as Chapter 1 of the present volume.

Brennan, M. J., and E. S. Schwartz, 1977, "Saving Bonds, Retractable Bonds and Callable Bonds", *Journal of Financial Economics* 5, pp. 67-88.

Cox, J. C., J. E. Ingersoll and S. A. Ross, 1977, "Notes on a Theory of the Term Structure of Interest Rates", Unpublished working paper.

Malinvaud, E., 1966, "Statistical Methods of Econometrics" (North-Holland, Amsterdam).

Merton, R. C., 1973, "The Theory of Rational Option Pricing", *Bell Journal of Economics and Management Science* 4, pp. 141-183.

Phillips, P. C. B., 1972, "The Structural Estimation of a Stochastic Differential Equation System", *Econometrica* 40, pp. 1021-1041.

Richard, S. F., 1976, "An Analytical model of the Term Structure of Interest Rates", Working paper no. 1976-77 (Carnegie-Mellon University, Pittsburgh, PA).

Roll, R., 1970. "The Behavior of Interest Rates" (Basic Books, New York).

Rubinstein, M., 1976, "The Valuation of Uncertain Income Streams and the Pricing of Options", *The Bell Journal of Economics* 7, pp. 407-425.

Stiglitz, J. E., 1970, "A Consumption-Oriented Theory of the Demand for Financial Assets and the Term Structure of Interest Rates", *Review of Economic Studies* pp. 321-352.

Vasicek, O., 1977, "An Equilibrium Characterization of the Term Structure", *Journal of Financial Economics* 5, pp. 177-188; reprinted as Chapter 4 of the present volume.

Westlake, J. R., 1968, "A Handbook of Numerical Matrix Inversion and Solution of Linear Equations" (Wiley, New York).

Wymer, C. R., 1972, "Econometric Estimation of Stochastic Differential Equation Systems", *Econometrica* 40, pp. 565-577.

6

A Theory of the Term Structure of Interest Rates*

John C. Cox, Jonathan E. Ingersoll and Stephen A. Ross
Massachusetts Institute of Technology; Yale University

This paper uses an intertemporal general equilibrium asset pricing model to study the term structure of interest rates. In this model, anticipations, risk aversion, investment alternatives and preferences about the timing of consumption all play a role in determining bond prices. Many of the factors traditionally mentioned as influencing the term structure are thus included in a way which is fully consistent with maximising behaviour and rational expectations. The model leads to specific formulas for bond prices which are well suited for empirical testing.

The term structure of interest rates measures the relationship among the yields of default-free securities that differ only in their term to maturity. The determinants of this relationship have long been a topic of concern for economists. By offering a complete schedule of interest rates across time, the term structure embodies the market's anticipations of future events. An explanation of the term structure gives us a way to extract this information and to predict how changes in the underlying variables will affect the yield curve.

In a world of certainty, equilibrium forward rates must coincide with future spot rates, but when uncertainty about future rates is introduced the analysis becomes much more complex. By and large, previous theories of the term structure have taken the certainty model as their starting point and have proceeded by examining stochastic generalisations of the certainty equilibrium relationships. The literature in the area is voluminous, and a comprehensive survey would warrant a paper in itself. It is common, however, to identify much of the previous work in the area as belonging to one of four strands of thought.

First, there are various versions of the expectations hypothesis. These place predominant emphasis on the expected values of future spot rates or holding-period returns. In its simplest form, the expectations hypothesis postulates that bonds are priced so that the implied forward rates are equal to the expected spot rates. Generally, this approach is characterised by the following propositions: (*a*) the return on holding a long-term bond to maturity is equal to the expected return on repeated investment in a series of the short-term bonds, or (*b*) the expected rate of return over the next holding period is the same for bonds of all maturities.

**This paper was first published in* Econometrica, *Vol. 53 (1985). It is reprinted with the permission of The Econometric Society.*
The paper is an extended version of the second half of an earlier working paper with the same title. We are grateful for the helpful comments and suggestions of many of our colleagues, both at our own institutions and others. This research was partially supported by the Dean Witter Foundation, the Center for Research in Security Prices and the National Science Foundation.

The liquidity preference hypothesis, advanced by Hicks (1946), concurs with the importance of expected future spot rates but places more weight on the effects of the risk preferences of market participants. It asserts that risk aversion will cause forward rates to be systematically greater than expected spot rates, usually by an amount increasing with maturity. This term premium is the increment required to induce investors to hold longer-term ("riskier") securities.

Third, there is the market segmentation hypothesis of Culbertson (1957) and others, which offers a different explanation of term premiums. Here it is asserted that individuals have strong maturity preferences and that bonds of different maturities trade in separate and distinct markets. The demand and supply of bonds of a particular maturity are supposedly little affected by the prices of bonds of neighbouring maturities. Of course, there is now no reason for the term premiums to be positive or to be increasing functions of maturity. Without attempting a detailed critique of this position, it is clear that there is a limit to how far one can go in maintaining that bonds of close maturities will not be close substitutes. The possibility of substitution is an important part of the theory which we develop.

In their preferred habitat theory, Modigliani and Sutch (1966) use some arguments similar to those of the market segmentation theory. However, they recognise its limitations and combine it with aspects of other theories. They intended their approach as a plausible rationale for term premiums which does not restrict them in sign or monotonicity, rather than as a necessary causal explanation.[1]

While the focus of such modern and eclectic analyses of the term structure on explaining and testing the term premiums is desirable, there are two difficulties with this approach. First, we need a better understanding of the determinants of the term premiums. The previous theories are basically only hypotheses which say little more than that forward rates should or need not equal expected spot rates. Second, all of the theories are couched in *ex ante* terms and they must be linked with *ex post* realisations to be testable.

The attempts to deal with these two elements constitute the fourth strand of work on the term structure. Roll (1970, 1971), for example, has built and tested a mean-variance model which treated bonds symmetrically with other assets and used a condition of market efficiency to relate *ex ante* and *ex post* concepts.[2] If rationality requires that *ex post* realisations not differ systematically from *ex ante* views, then statistical tests can be made on *ex ante* propositions by using *ex post* data.

We consider the problem of determining the term structure as being a problem in general equilibrium theory, and our approach contains elements of all of the previous theories. Anticipations of future events are important, as are risk preferences and the characteristics of other investment alternatives. Also, individuals can have specific preferences about the timing of their consumption, and thus have, in that sense, a preferred habitat. Our model thus permits detailed predictions about how changes in a wide range of underlying variables will affect the term structure.

The plan of our paper is as follows. The first section summarises the equilibrium model developed in Cox, Ingersoll, and Ross (1985) and specialises it for studying the term structure. In the second and third sections, we derive and analyse a model which leads to a single-factor description of the term structure and show how this model can be applied to other related securities such as options on bonds. In the fourth section we compare our general equilibrium approach with an alternative approach based purely on arbitrage, and in the fifth section we consider some more general term structure models and show how the market prices of bonds can be used as instrumental variables in empirical tests of the theory. In the final two sections, we present some models which include the effects of random inflation and give some brief concluding comments.

The underlying equilibrium model

In this section, we briefly review and specialise the general equilibrium model of Cox, Ingersoll, and Ross (1985). The model is a complete intertemporal description of a continuous-time competitive economy. We recall that in this economy there is a single good and all values are measured in terms of units of this good. Production opportunities consist of a set of n linear activities. The vector of expected rates of return on these activities is α and the covariance matrix of the rates of return is GG'. The components of α and G are functions of a k-dimensional vector Y which represents the state of the technology and is itself changing randomly over time. The development of Y thus determines the production opportunities that will be available to the economy in the future. The vector of expected changes in Y is μ and the covariance matrix of the changes is SS'.

The economy is composed of identical individuals, each of whom seeks to maximise an objective function of the form

$$E\int_t^{t'} U[C(s), Y(s), s]\,ds \tag{1}$$

where $C(s)$ is the consumption flow at time s, U is a Von Neumann–Morgenstern utility function and t' is the terminal date. In performing this maximisation, each individual chooses his optimal consumption C^*, the optimal proportion a^* of wealth W to be invested in each of the production processes and the optimal proportion b^* of wealth to be invested in each of the contingent claims. These contingent claims are endogenously created securities whose payoffs are functions of W and Y. The remaining wealth to be invested in borrowing or lending at the interest rate r is then determined by the budget constraint. The indirect utility function J is determined by the solution to the maximisation problem.

In equilibrium in this homogeneous society, the interest rate and the expected rates of return on the contingent claims must adjust until all wealth is invested in the physical production processes. This investment can be done either directly by individuals or indirectly by firms. Consequently, the equilibrium value of J is given by the solution to a planning problem with only the physical production processes available. For future reference, we note that the optimality conditions for the proportions invested will then have the form

$$\psi \equiv \alpha W J_W + GG'a^* W^2 J_{WW} + GS'WJ_{WY} - \lambda^* 1 \le 0 \tag{2}$$

and $a^{*\prime}\psi = 0$, where subscripts on J denote partial derivatives, J_{WY} is a $(k \times 1)$ vector whose ith element is J_{WY_i}, 1 is a $(k \times 1)$ unit vector and λ^* is a Lagrangian multiplier. With J explicitly determined, the similar optimality conditions for the problem with contingent claims and borrowing and lending can be combined with the market clearing conditions to give the equilibrium interest rate and expected rates of return on contingent claims.

We now cite two principal results from our previous paper, "An Intertemporal General Equilibrium Model of Asset Prices" (1985), which we will need frequently in this paper. First, the equilibrium interest rate can be written explicitly as

$$\begin{aligned} r(W, Y, t) &= \frac{\lambda^*}{WJ_W} = a^{*\prime}\alpha + a^{*\prime}GG'a^*W\left(\frac{J_{WW}}{J_W}\right) + a^{*\prime}GS'\left(\frac{J_{WY}}{J_W}\right) \\ &= a^{*\prime}\alpha - \left(\frac{-J_{WW}}{J_W}\right)\left(\frac{\operatorname{var} W}{W}\right) - \sum_{i=1}^{k}\left(\frac{-J_{WY_i}}{J_W}\right)\left(\frac{\operatorname{cov} W, Y_i}{W}\right) \end{aligned} \tag{3}$$

where $(\operatorname{cov} W, Y_i)$ is the covariance of the changes in optimally invested wealth with the changes in the state variable Y_i, with $(\operatorname{var} W)$ and $(\operatorname{cov} Y_i, Y_j)$ defined in an analogous way; note that $a^{*\prime}\alpha$ is the expected rate of return on optimally invested wealth. Second, the equilibrium value of any contingent claim, F, must satisfy the following differential equation:

$$\tfrac{1}{2}a^{*\prime}GG'a^{*}W^{2}F_{WW} + a^{*\prime}GS'WF_{WY} +$$

$$\tfrac{1}{2}\mathrm{tr}(SS'F_{YY}) + (a^{*\prime}\alpha W - C^{*})F_{W} + \mu'F_{Y} + F_{t} + \delta - rF = \phi_{W}F_{W} + \phi_{Y}F_{Y} \qquad (4)$$

where $\delta(W, Y, t)$ is the payout flow received by the security and

$$\phi_W = (a^{*\prime}\alpha - r)W$$

$$\phi_Y = \left(\frac{-J_{WW}}{J_W}\right)a^{*\prime}GS'W + \left(\frac{-J_{WY}}{J_W}\right)'SS' \qquad (5)$$

In (4) subscripts on F denote partial derivatives; F_Y and F_{WY} are $(k \times 1)$ vectors and F_{YY} is a $(k \times k)$ matrix. The left-hand side of (4) gives the excess expected return on the security over and above the risk-free return, while the right-hand side gives the risk premium that the security must command in equilibrium. For future reference, we note that (4) can be written in the alternative form:

$$\frac{1}{2}(\mathrm{var}\,W)F_{WW} + \sum_{i=1}^{k}(\mathrm{cov}\,W, Y_i)F_{WY_i} + \frac{1}{2}\sum_{i=1}^{k}\sum_{j=1}^{k}(\mathrm{cov}\,Y_i, Y_j)F_{Y_iY_j} + (rW - C^{*})F_W +$$

$$\sum_{i=1}^{k}\left[\mu_i - \left(\frac{-J_{WW}}{J_W}\right)(\mathrm{cov}\,W, Y_i) - \sum_{j=1}^{k}\left(\frac{-J_{WY_j}}{J_W}\right)(\mathrm{cov}\,Y_i, Y_j)\right]F_{Y_i} + F_t - rF + \delta = 0 \qquad (6)$$

To apply these formulas to the problem of the term structure of interest rates, we specialise the preference structure first to the case of constant relative risk aversion utility functions and then further to the logarithmic utility function. In particular, we let $U[C(s), Y(s), s]$ be independent of the state variable Y and have the form

$$U[C(s), s] = e^{-\rho s}\left(\frac{C(s)^{\gamma} - 1}{\gamma}\right) \qquad (7)$$

where ρ is a constant discount factor.

It is easy to show that in this case the indirect utility function takes the form:[3]

$$J(W, Y, t) = f(Y, t)\,U(W, t) + g(Y, t) \qquad (8)$$

This special form brings about two important simplifications. First, the coefficient of relative risk aversion of the indirect utility function is constant, independent of both wealth and the state variables:

$$\frac{-WJ_{WW}}{J_W} = 1 - \gamma \qquad (9)$$

Second, the elasticity of the marginal utility of wealth with respect to each of the state variables does not depend on wealth, and we have

$$\frac{-J_{WY}}{J_W} = \frac{-f_Y}{f} \qquad (10)$$

Furthermore, it is straightforward to verify that the optimal portfolio proportions a^* will depend on Y but not on W. Consequently, the vector of factor risk premiums, ϕ_Y, reduces to $(1 - \gamma)a^{*\prime}GS' + (f_Y/f)SS'$, which depends only on Y. In addition, it can be seen from (3) that the equilibrium interest rate also depends only on Y.

The logarithmic utility function corresponds to the special case of $\gamma = 0$. For this case, it can be shown that $f(Y, t) = [1 - \exp(-\rho(t' - t))]/\rho$. The state-dependence of the indirect utility function thus enters only through $g(Y, t)$. As a result, ϕ_Y reduces further to $a^{*\prime}GS$. In addition, the particular form of the indirect utility function allows us to solve (2) explicitly for a^* as

$$a^* = (GG')^{-1}\alpha + \left(\frac{1 - 1'(GG')^{-1}\alpha}{1'(GG')^{-1}1}\right)(GG')^{-1}1 \qquad (11)$$

when all production processes are active, with an analogous solution holding when some processes are inactive.

In the remainder of the paper, we will be valuing securities whose contractual terms do not depend explicitly on wealth. Since with constant relative risk aversion neither the interest rate r nor the factor risk premiums ϕ_Y depend on wealth, for such securities the partial derivatives F_W, F_{WW} and F_{WY} are all equal to zero and the corresponding terms drop out of the valuation equation (4).

By combining these specialisations, we find that the valuation equation (4) then reduces to

$$\tfrac{1}{2}\mathrm{tr}(SS'F_{YY}) + [\mu' - a^{*\prime}GS']F_Y + F_t + \delta - rF = 0 \qquad (12)$$

Equation (12) will be the central valuation equation for this paper. We will use it together with various specifications about technological change to examine the implied term structure of interest rates.

A single-factor model of the term structure

In our first model of the term structure of interest rates, we assume that the state of technology can be represented by a single sufficient statistic or state variable. This is our most basic model, and we will examine it in some detail. This will serve to illustrate how a similarly detailed analysis can be conducted for the more complicated models that follow in the fourth and fifth sections of this paper.

We make the following assumptions:

ASSUMPTION 1: *The change in production opportunities over time is described by a single state variable*, Y ($\equiv Y_1$).

ASSUMPTION 2: *The means and variances of the rates of return on the production processes are proportional to* Y.[4] *In this way, neither the means nor the variances will dominate the portfolio decision for large values of* Y. *The state variable* Y *can be thought of as determining the rate of evolution of the capital stock in the following sense. If we compare a situation where* $Y = \bar{Y}$, *a constant, with a situation in which* $Y = 2\bar{Y}$, *then the first situation has the same distribution of rate of return on a fixed investment in any process over a two-year period that the second situation has over a one-year period. We assume that the elements of* α *and* G *are such that the elements of* a^* *given by* (11) *are positive, so that all processes are always active, and that* $1'(GG')^{-1}\alpha$ *is greater than one.*[5]

ASSUMPTION 3: *The development of the state variable* Y *is given by the stochastic differential equation*

$$dY(t) = [\xi Y + \zeta]dt + \upsilon\sqrt{Y}dw(t) \qquad (13)$$

where ξ *and* ζ *are constants, with* $\zeta \geq 0$, *and* υ *is a* $1 \times (n + k)$ *vector, each of whose components is the constant* υ_0.

This structure makes it convenient to introduce the notation $\alpha \equiv \hat{\alpha}Y$, $GG' \equiv \Omega Y$ and $GS' \equiv \Sigma Y$, where the elements of $\hat{\alpha}$, Ω and Σ are constants.

With these assumptions about technological change and our earlier assumptions about preferences, we can use (3) to write the equilibrium interest rate as

$$r(Y) = \left(\frac{1'\Omega^{-1}\hat{\alpha} - 1}{1'\Omega^{-1}1} \right) Y \tag{14}$$

The interest rate thus follows a diffusion process with

$$\text{drift } r = \left(\frac{1'\Omega^{-1}\hat{\alpha} - 1}{1'\Omega^{-1}1} \right) (\xi Y + \zeta) \equiv \kappa(\theta - r)$$

$$\text{var } r = \left(\frac{1'\Omega^{-1}\hat{\alpha} - 1}{1'\Omega^{-1}1} \right)^2 \upsilon\upsilon' Y \equiv \sigma^2 r \tag{15}$$

where κ, θ and σ^2 are constants, with $\kappa\theta \geq 0$ and $\sigma^2 > 0$. It is convenient to define a new one-dimensional Wiener process, $z_1(t)$, such that:

$$\sigma\sqrt{r} dz_1(t) \equiv \upsilon\sqrt{Y} dw(t) \tag{16}$$

This is permissible since each component of $w(t)$ is a Wiener process. The interest rate dynamics can then be expressed as:

$$dr = \kappa(\theta - r)dt + \sigma\sqrt{r} dz_1 \tag{17}$$

For κ, $\theta > 0$, this corresponds to a continuous-time first-order autoregressive process where the randomly moving interest rate is elastically pulled toward a central location or long-term value, θ. The parameter κ determines the speed of adjustment.[6]

An examination of the boundary classification criteria shows that r can reach zero if $\sigma^2 > 2\kappa\theta$. If $2\kappa\theta \geq \sigma^2$, the upward drift is sufficiently large to make the origin inaccessible.[7] In either case, the singularity of the diffusion coefficient at the origin implies that an initially non-negative interest rate can never subsequently become negative.

The interest rate behaviour implied by this structure thus has the following empirically relevant properties: (i) Negative interest rates are precluded. (ii) If the interest rate reaches zero, it can subsequently become positive. (iii) The absolute variance of the interest rate increases when the interest rate itself increases. (iv) There is a steady-state distribution for the interest rate.

The probability density of the interest rate at time s, conditional on its value at the current time, t, is given by:

$$f[r(s), s; r(t), t] = ce^{-u-\upsilon} \left(\frac{\upsilon}{u} \right)^{\frac{q}{2}} I_q\left(2(u\upsilon)^{\frac{1}{2}} \right) \tag{18}$$

where

$$c \equiv \frac{2\kappa}{\sigma^2 \left(1 - e^{-\kappa(s-t)} \right)} \qquad u \equiv cr(t)e^{-\kappa(s-t)}$$

$$\upsilon \equiv cr(s) \qquad q \equiv \frac{2\kappa\theta}{\sigma^2} - 1$$

and $I_q(\cdot)$ is the modified Bessel function of the first kind of order q. The distribution function is the non-central chi-square, $\chi^2[2cr(s); 2q+2, 2u]$, with $2q+2$ degrees of freedom and parameter of non-centrality $2u$ proportional to the current spot rate.[8]

Straightforward calculations give the expected value and variance of $r(s)$ as:

$$E\left[r(s)|r(t)\right] = r(t)e^{-\kappa(s-t)} + \theta\left(1 - e^{-\kappa(s-t)}\right)$$

$$\text{var}\left[r(s)|r(t)\right] = r(t)\left(\frac{\sigma^2}{\kappa}\right)\left(e^{-\kappa(s-t)} - e^{-2\kappa(s-t)}\right) + \theta\left(\frac{\sigma^2}{2\kappa}\right)\left(1 - e^{-\kappa(s-t)}\right)^2 \tag{19}$$

The properties of the distribution of the future interest rates are those expected. As κ approaches infinity, the mean goes to θ and the variance to zero, while as κ approaches zero, the conditional mean goes to the current interest rate and the variance to $\sigma^2 r(t) \times (s - t)$.

If the interest rate does display mean-reversion ($\kappa, \theta > 0$), then as s becomes large its distribution will approach a gamma distribution. The steady-state density function is:

$$f[r(\infty), \infty; r(t), t] = \frac{\omega^{\nu}}{\Gamma(\nu)} r^{\nu-1} e^{-\omega r} \tag{20}$$

where $\omega \equiv 2\kappa/\sigma^2$ and $\nu \equiv 2\kappa\theta/\sigma^2$. The steady state mean and variance are θ and $\sigma^2\theta/2\kappa$, respectively.

Consider now the problem of valuing a default-free discount bond promising to pay one unit at time T.[9] The prices of these bonds for all T will completely determine the term structure. Under our assumptions, the factor risk premium in (12) is

$$\left[\hat{\alpha}'\Omega^{-1}\Sigma + \left(\frac{1 - 1'\Omega^{-1}\hat{\alpha}}{1'\Omega^{-1}1}\right)1'\Omega^{-1}\Sigma\right]Y \equiv \lambda Y \tag{21}$$

By using (15) and (21), we can write the fundamental equation for the price of a discount bond, P, most conveniently as

$$\tfrac{1}{2}\sigma^2 r P_{rr} + \kappa(\theta - r)P_r + P_t - \lambda r P_r - rP = 0 \tag{22}$$

with the boundary condition $P(r, T, T) = 1$. The first three terms in (22) are, from Itô's formula, the expected price change for the bond. Thus, the expected rate of return on the bond is $r + (\lambda r P_r/P)$. The instantaneous return premium on a bond is proportional to its interest elasticity. The factor λr is the covariance of changes in the interest rate with percentage changes in optimally invested wealth (the "market portfolio"). Since $P_r < 0$, positive premiums will arise if this covariance is negative ($\lambda < 0$).

We may note from (22) that bond prices depend on only one random variable, the spot interest rate, which serves as an instrumental variable for the underlying technological uncertainty. While the proposition that current (and future) interest rates play an important and, to a first approximation, predominant role in determining the term structure would meet with general approval, we have seen that this will be precisely true only under special conditions.[10]

By taking the relevant expectation (see Cox, Ingersoll, and Ross (1985)), we obtain the bond prices as:

$$P(r, t, T) = A(t, T)e^{-B(t, T)r}$$

where

$$A(t,T) \equiv \left(\frac{2\gamma e^{[(\kappa+\lambda+\gamma)(T-t)]/2}}{(\gamma+\kappa+\lambda)\left(e^{\gamma(T-t)}-1\right)+2\gamma}\right)^{2\kappa\theta/\sigma^2}$$

$$B(t,T) \equiv \frac{2\left(e^{\gamma(T-t)}-1\right)}{(\gamma+\kappa+\lambda)\left(e^{\gamma(T-t)}-1\right)+2\gamma}$$

$$\gamma \equiv \left[(\kappa+\lambda)^2 + 2\sigma^2\right]^{\frac{1}{2}} \tag{23}$$

The bond price is a decreasing convex function of the interest rate and an increasing (decreasing) function of time (maturity). The parameters of the interest rate process have the following effects. The bond price is a decreasing convex function of the mean interest rate level θ and an increasing concave (decreasing convex) function of the speed of adjustment parameter κ if the interest rate is greater (less) than θ. Both of these results are immediately obvious from their effects on expected future interest rates. Bond prices are an increasing concave function of the "market" risk parameter λ. Intuitively, this is mainly because higher values of λ indicate a greater covariance of the interest rate with wealth. Thus, with large λ it is more likely that bond prices will be higher when wealth is low and, hence, has greater marginal utility. The bond price is an increasing concave function of the interest rate variance σ^2. Here several effects are involved. The most important is that a larger σ^2 value indicates more uncertainty about future real production opportunities and, thus, more uncertainty about future consumption. In such a world, risk-averse investors would value the guaranteed claim in a bond more highly.

The dynamics of bond prices are given by the stochastic differential equation:

$$dP = r[1 - \lambda B(t,T)]P\,dt - B(t,T)P\sigma\sqrt{r}\,dz_1 \tag{24}$$

For this single-state variable model, the returns on bonds are perfectly negatively correlated with changes in the interest rate. The returns are less variable when the interest rate is low. Indeed, they become certain if a zero interest rate is reached, since interest rate changes are then certain. As we would intuitively expect, other things remaining equal, the variability of returns decreases as the bond approaches maturity. In fact, letting t approach T and denoting $T - t$ as Δt, we find that the expected rate of return is $r\Delta t + O(\Delta t^2)$ and the variance of the rate of return is $O(\Delta t^2)$ rather than $O(\Delta t)$, as would be the case for the returns on an investment in the production processes over a small interval. It is in this sense that the return on very short-term bonds becomes certain.

Bonds are commonly quoted in terms of yields rather than prices. For the discount bonds we are now considering, the yield-to-maturity, $R(r,t,T)$, is defined by $\exp[-(T-t)R(r,t,T)] \equiv P(r,t,T)$. Thus, we have:

$$R(r,t,T) = \frac{rB(t,T) - \log A(t,T)}{T-t} \tag{25}$$

As maturity nears, the yield-to-maturity approaches the current interest rate independently of any of the parameters. As we consider longer and longer maturities, the yield approaches a limit which is independent of the current interest rate:

$$R(r,t,\infty) = \frac{2\kappa\theta}{\gamma + \kappa + \lambda} \tag{26}$$

When the spot rate is below this long-term yield, the term structure is uniformly rising. With an interest rate in excess of $\kappa\theta/(\kappa + \lambda)$, the term structure is falling. For intermediate values of the interest rate, the yield curve is humped.

Other comparative statics for the yield curve are easily obtained from those of the bond pricing function. An increase in the current interest rate increases yields for all maturities, but the effect is greater for shorter maturities. Similarly, an increase in the steady state mean θ increases all yields, but here the effect is greater for longer maturities. The yields-to-maturity decrease as σ^2 or λ increases, while the effect of a change in κ may be of either sign depending on the current interest rate.

There has always been considerable concern with unbiased predictions of future interest rates. In the present situation, we could work directly with equation (19), which gives expected values of future interest rates in terms of the current rate and the parameters κ and θ. However, in the rational expectations model we have constructed, all of the information that is currently known about the future movement of interest rates is impounded in current bond prices and the term structure. If the model is correct, then any single parameter can be determined from the term structure and the values of the other parameters.

This approach is particularly important when the model is extended to allow a time-dependent drift term, $\theta(t)$. We can then use information contained in the term structure to obtain $\theta(t)$ and expected future spot rates without having to place prior restrictions on its functional form.

Now, the future expected spot rate given by (19) is altered to:

$$E\left[r(T)\middle|r(t)\right] = r(t)e^{-\kappa(T-t)} + \kappa\int_t^T \theta(s)\, e^{-\kappa(T-s)}\, ds \quad (27)$$

The bond pricing formula (30), in turn, is modified to:

$$P(r,t,T) = \hat{A}(t,T)\, e^{-B(t,T)r} \quad (28)$$

where

$$\hat{A}(t,T) = \exp\left(-\kappa\int_t^T \theta(s)B(s,T)\, ds\right) \quad (29)$$

which reduces to (23) when $\theta(s)$ is constant.

Assuming, for illustration, that the other process parameters are known, we can then use the term structure to determine unbiased forecasts of future interest rates. By (28), $\hat{A}(t,T)$ is an observable function of T, given the term structure and the known form of $B(t,T)$, and standard techniques can be invoked to invert (29) and obtain an expression for $\theta(t)$ in terms of $\hat{A}(t,T)$ and $B(t,T)$. Equation (27) can now be used to obtain predictions of the expected values of future spot rates implicit in the current term structure.

Note that these are not the same values that would be given by the traditional expectations assumption that the expected values of future spot rates are contained in the term structure in the form of implicit forward rates. In a continuous-time model, the forward rate $\hat{r}(T)$ is given by $-P_T/P$. Then, by differentiating (28):

$$\hat{r}(T) = \frac{-P_T(r,t,T)}{P(r,t,T)}$$

$$= rB_T(t,T) + \kappa\int_t^T \theta(s)B_T(s,T)\, ds \quad (30)$$

Comparing (27) and (30), we see they have the same general form. However, the traditional forward rate predictor applies the improper weights $B_T(s,T) \neq e^{-\kappa(T-s)}$, resulting in a biased prediction.

A number of alternative specifications of time-dependence may also be included with only minor changes in the model. One particularly tractable example leads to an interest rate of $\bar{r}(t) + g(t)$, where $\bar{r}(t)$ is given by (17) and $g(t)$ is a function which provides a positive lower bound for the interest rate. The essential point in all such cases is that in the rational expectations model, the current term structure embodies the information required to evaluate the market's probability distribution of the future course of interest rates. Furthermore, the term structure can be inverted to find these expectations.

Other single variable specifications of technological change will in turn imply other stochastic properties for the interest rate. It is easy to verify that, in our model, if α and GG' are proportional to some function $h(Y,t)$, then the interest rate will also be proportional to $h(Y,t)$. By a suitable choice of $h(Y,t)$, $\mu(Y,t)$ and $S(Y,t)$, a wide range of *a priori* properties of interest rate movements can be included within the context of a completely consistent model.

Valuing assets with general interest rate-dependent payoffs

Our valuation framework can easily be applied to other securities whose payoffs depend on interest rates, such as options on bonds and futures on bonds. This flexibility enables the model to make predictions about the pricing patterns that should prevail simultaneously across several financial markets. Consequently, applications to other securities may permit richer and more powerful empirical tests than could be done with the bond market alone.

As an example of valuing other kinds of interest rate securities, consider options on bonds. Denote the value at time t of a call option on a discount bond of maturity date s, with exercise price K and expiration date T as $C(r, t, T; s, K)$.[12] The option price will follow the basic valuation equation with terminal condition:

$$C(r, t, T; s, K) = \max[P(r, T, s) - K, 0] \tag{31}$$

It is understood that $s \geq T \geq t$ and K is restricted to be less than $A(T, s)$, the maximum possible bond price at time T, since otherwise the option would never be exercised and would be worthless. By again taking the relevant expectations, we arrive at the following formula for the option price:

$$C(r,t,T;s,K) = P(r,t,s)\chi^2\left(2r^*[\phi+\psi+B(T,s)]; \frac{4\kappa\theta}{\sigma^2}, \frac{2\phi^2 r\, e^{\gamma(T-t)}}{\phi+\psi+B(T,s)}\right) -$$

$$KP(r,t,T)\chi^2\left(2r^*[\phi+\psi]; \frac{4\kappa\theta}{\sigma^2}, \frac{2\phi^2 r\, e^{\gamma(T-t)}}{\phi+\psi}\right) \tag{32}$$

where

$$\gamma \equiv \left[(\kappa+\lambda)^2 + 2\sigma^2\right]^{\frac{1}{2}} \qquad \phi \equiv \frac{2\gamma}{\sigma^2\left(e^{\gamma(T-t)}-1\right)}$$

$$\psi \equiv \frac{\kappa+\lambda+\gamma}{\sigma^2} \qquad r^* \equiv \frac{\log\left[A(T,s)/K\right]}{B(T,s)}$$

and $\chi^2(\cdot)$ is the previously introduced non-central chi-square distribution function. r^* is the critical interest rate below which exercise will occur; ie, $K = P(r^*, T, s)$.

The call option is an increasing function of maturity (when the expiration date on which the underlying bond matures remains fixed). Call options on stocks are increasing functions of the interest rate, partly because such an increase reduces the present value of the exercise price. However, here an increase in the interest rate will also depress the price of the underlying bond. Numerical analysis indicates that the latter effect is stronger and that the option value is a decreasing convex function of the interest rate. The remaining comparative statics are indeterminate.

A comparison with bond pricing by arbitrage methods

In this section, we briefly compare our methodology to some alternative ways to model bond pricing in continuous time. It is useful to do this now rather than later because the model in the second section provides an ideal standard for comparison.

Our approach begins with a detailed description of the underlying economy. This allows us to specify the following ingredients of bond pricing: (*a*) the variables on which the bond price depends, (*b*) the stochastic properties of the underlying variables which are endogenously determined, and (*c*) the exact form of the factor risk premiums. Merton (1970) shows that if one begins instead by imposing assumptions directly about (*a*) and (*b*), then Itô's formula can be used to state the excess expected return on a bond in the same form as the left-hand side of (4). If the functional form of the right-hand side of (4) were known, one could obtain a bond pricing equation. For example, if one arbitrarily assumed that bond prices depend only on the spot interest rate r, that the interest rate follows the process given by (17) and that the excess expected return on a bond with maturity date T is $\Upsilon(r, t, T)$, then one would obtain

$$\tfrac{1}{2}\sigma^2 r P_{rr} + \kappa(\theta - r)P_r + P_t - rP = \Upsilon(r, t, T) \tag{33}$$

If there is some underlying equilibrium which will support the assumptions (*a*) and (*b*), then there must be some function Υ for which bond prices are given by (33). However, as Merton notes, this derivation in itself provides no way to determine Υ or to relate it to the underlying real variables.

An arbitrage approach to bond pricing was developed in a series of papers by Brennan and Schwartz (1979), Dothan (1978), Garman (1977), Richard (1978), and Vasicek (1977). Arguments similar to those employed in the proof of Theorem 2 of Cox, Ingersoll, and Ross (1985) are used to show that if there are no arbitrage opportunities, Υ must have the form

$$\Upsilon(r, t, T) = \psi(r, t)\, P_r(r, t, T) \tag{34}$$

where ψ is a function depending only on calendar time and not on the maturity date of the bond. This places definite restrictions on the form of the excess expected return; not all functions Υ will satisfy both (33) and (34).

There are some potential problems, however, in going one step further and using the arbitrage approach to determine a complete and specific model of the term structure. The approach itself provides no way of guaranteeing that there is some underlying equilibrium for which assumptions (*a*) and (*b*) are consistent. Setting this problem aside, another difficulty arises from the fact that the arbitrage approach does not imply that every choice of ψ in (34) will lead to bond prices which do not admit arbitrage opportunities. Indeed, closing the model by assuming a specific functional form for ψ can lead to internal inconsistencies.

As an example of the potential problem, consider (33) with Υ as shown in (34). This gives the valuation equation

$$\tfrac{1}{2}\sigma^2 r P_{rr} + \kappa(\theta - r)P_r + P_t - rP = \psi(r, t)P_r \tag{35}$$

which is identical to (22) apart from a specification of the function ψ. We could now close the model by assuming that ψ is linear in the spot rate, $\psi(r, t) = \psi_0 + \lambda r$. The solution to (35) is then

$$P(r, t, T) = [A(t, T)]^{(\kappa\theta - \psi_0)/\kappa\theta} \exp[-rB(t, T)] \tag{36}$$

and the dynamic behaviour of the bond price is given by

$$dP = [r - (\psi_0 + \lambda r)B(t, T)]\, P\, dt - B(t, T)\,\sigma\sqrt{r}\, P\, dz_1 \tag{37}$$

The linear form assumed for the risk premium seems quite reasonable and would appear to be a good choice for empirical work, but it in fact produces a model that is not viable. This is most easily seen when $r = 0$. In this case, the bond's return over the next instant is riskless: nevertheless, it is appreciating in price at the rate $-\psi_0 B(t, T)$, which is different from the prevailing zero rate of interest.[12] We thus have a model that guarantees arbitrage opportunities rather than precluding them. The difficulty, of course, is that there is no underlying equilibrium which would support the assumed premiums.

The equilibrium approach developed here thus has two important advantages over alternative methods of bond pricing in continuous time. First, it automatically ensures that the model can be completely specified without losing internal consistency. Second, it provides a way to predict how changes in the underlying real economic variables will affect the term structure.

Multifactor term structure models and the use of prices as instrumental variables

In the second section, we specialised the general equilibrium framework of Cox, Ingersoll, and Ross (1985) to develop a complete model of bond pricing. We purposely chose a simple specialisation in order to illustrate the detailed information that such a model can produce. In the model, the prices of bonds of all maturities depended on a single random explanatory factor, the spot interest rate. Although the resulting term structure could assume several alternative shapes, it is inherent in a single-factor model that price changes in bonds of all maturities are perfectly correlated. Such a model also implies that bond prices do not depend on the path followed by the spot rate in reaching its current level. For some applications, these properties may be too restrictive. However, more general specifications of technological opportunities will in turn imply more general bond pricing models. The resulting multifactor term structures will have more flexibility than the single-factor model, but they will inevitably also be more cumbersome and more difficult to analyse.

To illustrate the possibilities, we consider two straightforward generalisations of our previous model. Suppose that in our description of technological change in (13) and (15) the central tendency parameter θ is itself allowed to vary randomly according to the equation

$$d\theta = \nu(Y - \theta)\,dt \tag{38}$$

where ν is a positive constant. That is, we let $\theta \equiv Y_2$ and $\mu_2 = \nu(Y_1 - Y_2)$. The value of θ at any time will thus be an exponentially weighted integral of past values of Y. It can then be verified that the interest rate r is again given by (14) and that the bond price P will have the form

$$P(r, \theta, t, T) = \exp[-rf(t, T) - \theta g(t, T)] \tag{39}$$

where f and g are explicitly determinable functions of time. In this case, both the yields-to-maturity of discount bonds and the expected values of future spot rates are linear functions of current and past spot rates.[13]

As a second generalisation, suppose that the production coefficients α and GG' are proportional to the sum of two independent random variables, Y_1 and Y_2, each of which follows an equation of the form (13). Then it can be shown that the spot interest rate r will be proportional to the sum of Y_1 and Y_2 and that bond prices will again have the exponential form

$$P(r, Y_2, t, T) = f(t, T)\exp[-rg(t, T) - Y_2 h(t, T)] \tag{40}$$

where f, g and h are other explicitly determinable functions of time. In this model, price changes in bonds of all maturities are no longer perfectly correlated.

Each of these generalisations gives a two-factor model of the term structure, and the resulting yield curves can assume a wide variety of shapes. Further multifactor generalisations can be constructed along the same lines.

In each of the models considered in this section, one of the explanatory variables is not directly observable. Multifactor generalisations will typically inherit this drawback to an even greater degree. Consequently, it may be very convenient for empirical applications to use some of the endogenously determined prices as instrumental variables to eliminate the variables that cannot be directly observed. In certain instances, it will be possible to do so. Let us choose the spot rate, r, and a vector of long interest rates, ℓ, as instrumental variables. In general, each of these interest rates will be functions of W (unless the common utility function is isoelastic) and all the state variables. If it is possible to invert this system globally and express the latter as twice-differentiable functions of r and ℓ, then r and ℓ can be used as instrumental variables in a manner consistent with the general equilibrium framework.

For the purposes of illustration, suppose that there are two state variables, Y_1 and Y_2, and that utility is isoelastic so that the level of wealth is immaterial. Then, for instrumental variables r and ℓ, a scalar, direct but involved calculation shows that the valuation equation (4) may be rewritten as:

$$\tfrac{1}{2}(\operatorname{var} r)F_{rr} + (\operatorname{cov} r, \ell)F_{r\ell} + \tfrac{1}{2}(\operatorname{var}\ell)F_{\ell\ell} + [\mu_r - \lambda_r(r,\ell)]F_r + [\mu_\ell - \lambda_\ell(r,\ell)]F_\ell - rF + F_t + \delta = 0 \tag{41}$$

The functions λ_r and λ_l serve the role of the factor risk premiums in (5). They are related to the factor risk premiums, ϕ_Y, by:

$$\lambda_r(r,\ell) = \frac{\psi_1(\partial g/\partial\ell) - \psi_2(\partial f/\partial\ell)}{\Delta}$$

$$\lambda_\ell(r,\ell) = \frac{\psi_2(\partial f/\partial r) - \psi_1(\partial g/\partial r)}{\Delta}$$

where

$$Y_1 \equiv f(r,\ell,t), \quad Y_2 \equiv g(r,\ell,t)$$

$$\phi_{Y_1}(Y_1, Y_2, t) \equiv \psi_1(r,\ell,t), \quad \phi_{Y_2}(Y_1, Y_2, t) \equiv \psi_2(r,\ell,t) \tag{42}$$

and

$$\Delta \equiv \frac{\partial f}{\partial r}\frac{\partial g}{\partial\ell} - \frac{\partial f}{\partial\ell}\frac{\partial g}{\partial r}$$

Thus far we have not used the fact that ℓ is an interest rate, and the transformation of (4) to (41) can be performed for an arbitrary instrumental variable if the inversion is possible. The advantage of choosing an interest rate instrument is that the second risk factor premium λ_ℓ and the drift μ_ℓ can be eliminated from (41) as follows.

Let Q denote the value of the particular bond for which ℓ is the continuously compounded yield-to-maturity. Denote the payment flow from the bond, including both coupons and return of principal, by $c(t)$. In general, this flow will be zero most of the time, with impulses representing an infinite flow rate when payments are made. Since by definition $Q \equiv \int_t^T c(s)\exp[-\ell(s-t)\,ds$, we can write:

$$Q \equiv \Lambda_0(\ell), \quad Q_l = \Lambda_1(\ell), \quad Q_{\ell\ell} = \Lambda_2(\ell)$$

$$Q_t = -c(t) + \ell\Lambda_0(\ell) = -\delta + \ell\Lambda_0(\ell)$$

$$Q_r = Q_{rr} = Q_{r\ell} = 0 \tag{43}$$

where

$$\Lambda_n \equiv \int_t^T (t-s)^n\, c(s)\, e^{-\ell(s-t)}\, ds$$

and the integral is to be interpreted in the Stieltjes sense. If (43) is substituted into (41), we then obtain:

$$\mu_\ell - \lambda_\ell(r,\ell) = \frac{(r-\ell)\Lambda_0(\ell) - \tfrac{1}{2}(\operatorname{var}\ell)\Lambda_2(\ell)}{\Lambda_1(\ell)} \tag{44}$$

and the unobservable factor risk premium may be replaced by the observable function in (44). If Q is a consol bond with coupons paid continuously at the rate c, then $\Lambda_0 = c/\ell$, $\Lambda_1 = -c/\ell^2$, $\Lambda_2 = 2c/\ell^3$, and (44) may be written as:[14]

$$\mu_\ell - \lambda_\ell(r,\ell) = \frac{(\operatorname{var}\ell)}{\ell} + \ell(\ell - r) \tag{45}$$

These representations may be a useful starting point for empirical work. However, it is important to remember that they cannot be fully justified without considering the characteristics of the underlying economy. In the next section, we examine some additional multiple state variable models, all of which could be re-expressed in this form.

Uncertain inflation and the pricing of nominal bonds

The model presented here deals with a real economy in which money would serve no purpose. To provide a valid role for money, we would have to introduce additional features which would lead far afield of our original intent. However, for a world in which changes in the money supply have no real effects, we can introduce some aspects of money and inflation in an artificial way by imagining that one of the state variables represents a price level and that some contracts have payoffs whose real value depends on this price level. That is, they are specified in nominal terms. None of this requires any changes in the general theory.

Suppose that we let the price level, p, be the kth state variable. Since we assume that this variable has no effect on the underlying real equilibrium, the functions α, μ, G, S and J will not depend on p. Of course, this would not preclude changes in p from being statistically correlated with changes in real wealth and the other state variables. Under these circumstances, the real value of a claim whose payoff is specified in nominal terms still satisfies equation (4). All that needs to be done is to express the nominal payoff in real terms for the boundary conditions. Alternatively, the valuation equation (4) will also still hold if p is a differentiable function of W, Y and t.[15]

We can illustrate some of these points in the context of the model in the second section. Let us take a second state variable to be the price level, p ($\equiv Y_2$), and consider how to value a contract which will at time T pay with certainty an amount $1/p(T)$. Call this a nominal unit discount bond and denote its value at time t in real terms as $N(r, p, t, T)$. Suppose that the price level p moves according to

$$dp = \mu(p)\,dt + \sigma(p)\,dw_{n+2}(t) \tag{46}$$

and that it is uncorrelated with W and Y_1. Assume also that the coefficients in (45) are such that $E[p^{-1}(s)]$ exists for all finite s.

We would then have the valuation equation for N

$$\tfrac{1}{2}\sigma^2 r N_{rr} + \tfrac{1}{2}\sigma^2(p) N_{pp} + [\kappa\theta - (\kappa + \lambda)r] N_r + \mu(p) N_p + N_t - rN = 0 \tag{47}$$

with terminal condition $N(r, p, T, T) = 1/p(T)$. It can be directly verified that the solution is

$$N(r, p, t, T) = P(r, t, T)\, \underset{p(t),t}{E} \left(\frac{1}{p(T)} \right) \tag{48}$$

where P is the price of a real discount bond given in (23).

In this formulation, the expected inflation rate changes only with the price level. For the commonly assumed case of lognormally distributed prices, however, $\mu(p) = \mu_p p$, $\sigma(p) = \sigma_p p$, and

$$N(r, p, t, T) = e^{-(\mu_p - \sigma_p^2)(T-t)} \frac{P(r, t, T)}{p(t)} \tag{49}$$

so in this case the price of a nominal bond in nominal terms, $\hat{N} \equiv p(t)N$, would be independent of the current price level. With lognormally distributed prices, the expected inflation rate is constant, although of course realised inflation will not be.

As a somewhat more general example, we can separate the expected inflation rate factor from the price level factor and identify it with a third state variable. Again, no change in the general theory is necessary. Label the expected inflation rate as y. We propose two alternative models for the behaviour of the inflation rate:

Model 1

$$dy = \kappa_1 y(\theta_1 - y)\,dt + \sigma_1 y^{3/2}\,dz_3 \tag{50}$$

Model 2

$$dy = \kappa_2(\theta_2 - y)\,dt + \sigma_2 y^{1/2}\,dz_3 \tag{51}$$

with the stochastic differential equation governing the movement of the price level being in each case

$$dp = yp\,dt + \sigma_p p y^{1/2}\,dz_2 \tag{52}$$

with $(\text{cov}\, y, p) \equiv \rho\sigma_1\sigma_p y^2 p$ in Model 1, $(\text{cov}\, y, p) \equiv \rho\sigma_1\sigma_p yp$ in Model 2, and $\sigma_p < 1$. Here, as in (17), we have for convenience defined $z_2(t)$ and $z_3(t)$ as the appropriate linear combinations of $w_{n+2}(t)$ and $w_{n+3}(t)$.

Model 1 may well be the better choice empirically since informal evidence suggests that the relative (percentage) variance of the expected inflation rate increases as its level increases. Model 1 has this property, while Model 2 does not. However, the solution to Model 2 is more tractable, so we will record both for possible empirical use. In both models the expected inflation rate is pulled toward a long-run equilibrium level. Both models also allow for correlation between changes in the inflation rate and changes in the price level, thus allowing for positive or negative extrapolative forces in the movement of the price level.

The valuation equation for the real value of a nominal bond, specialised for our example with Model 1, will then be

$$\tfrac{1}{2}\sigma^2 r N_{rr} + \tfrac{1}{2}\sigma_1^2 y^3 N_{yy} + \rho\sigma_1\sigma_p y^2 p N_{yp} + \tfrac{1}{2}\sigma_p^2 p^2 y N_{pp} + [\kappa\theta - (\kappa+\lambda)r]N_r + \kappa_1 y(\theta_1 - y)N_y + ypN_p + N_t - rN = 0 \tag{53}$$

with $N(r, y, p, T, T) = 1/p(T)$. The solution to equation (53) is

$$N(r, y, p, t, T) = \frac{\Gamma(v-\delta)}{\Gamma(v)}\left(\frac{c(t)}{y}\right)^{\delta} M\left(\delta, v, -\frac{c(t)}{y}\right)\frac{P(r, t, T)}{p(t)}$$

where

$$c(t) \equiv \frac{2\kappa_1\theta_1}{\sigma_1^2\left(e^{\kappa_1\theta_1(T-t)} - 1\right)}$$

$$\delta \equiv \frac{\left[\left(\kappa_1 + \rho\sigma_1\sigma_p + \tfrac{1}{2}\sigma_1^2\right)^2 + 2\left(1-\sigma_p^2\right)\sigma_1^2\right]^{\frac{1}{2}} - \left(\kappa_1 + \rho\sigma_1\sigma_p + \tfrac{1}{2}\sigma_1^2\right)}{\sigma_1^2}$$

$$v \equiv \frac{2\left[(1+\delta)\sigma_1^2 + \kappa_1 + \rho\sigma_1\sigma_p\right]}{\sigma_1^2} \tag{54}$$

$M(\cdot,\cdot,\cdot)$ is the confluent hypergeometric function and $\Gamma(\cdot)$ is the gamma function.[16]

Proceeding in the same way with Model 2, we obtain the valuation equation:

$$\tfrac{1}{2}\sigma^2 r N_{rr} + \tfrac{1}{2}\sigma_2^2 y N_{yy} + \rho\sigma_2\sigma_p yp N_{yp} + \tfrac{1}{2}\sigma_p^2 yp^2 N_{pp} + [\kappa\theta - (\kappa+\lambda)r]N_r + \kappa_2(\theta_2 - y)N_y + ypN_p + N_t - rN = 0 \tag{55}$$

with $N(r, y, p, T, T) = 1/p(T)$. The corresponding valuation formula is:

$$N(r, y, p, t, T) = \left(\frac{2\xi e^{\left[(\kappa_2 + \rho\sigma_2\sigma_p + \xi)(T-t)\right]/2}}{\left(\xi + \kappa_2 + \rho\sigma_2\sigma_p\right)\left(e^{\xi(T-t)} - 1\right) + 2\xi} \right)^{2\kappa_2\theta_2/\sigma_2^2} \times$$

$$\exp\left(\frac{-2\left(e^{\xi(T-t)} - 1\right)(1 - \sigma_p^2)\, y}{(\xi + \kappa_2 + \rho\sigma_2\sigma_p)\left(e^{\xi(T-t)} - 1\right) + 2\xi} \right) \frac{P(r, t, T)}{p(t)} \tag{56}$$

where

$$\xi \equiv [(\kappa_2 + \rho\,\sigma_2\sigma_p)^2 + 2\sigma_2^2(1 - \sigma_p^2)]^{\frac{1}{2}}$$

The term structure of interest rates implied by (54) and (56) can assume a wide variety of shapes, depending on the relative values of the variables and parameters. More complex models incorporating more detailed effects can be built along the same lines.

Throughout our paper, we have used specialisations of the fundamental valuation equation (6). This equation determines the real value of a contingent claim as a function of real wealth and the state variables. For some empirical purposes, it may be convenient to have a corresponding valuation equation in which all values are expressed in nominal terms.

In our setting, this is given by the following proposition. In this proposition, we let nominal wealth be $X \equiv pW$, the indirect utility function in terms of nominal wealth be $V(X, Y, t) \equiv J(X/p, Y, t) \equiv J(W, Y, t)$, and the nominal value of a claim in terms of nominal wealth be $H(X, Y, t) \equiv pF(X/p, Y, t) \equiv pF(W, Y, t)$. As before, we let p be the kth element of Y.

PROPOSITION: *The nominal value of a contingent claim in terms of nominal wealth,* $H(X, Y, t)$, *satisfies the partial differential equation*

$$\frac{1}{2}(\text{var}\, X) H_{XX} + \sum_{i=1}^{k} (\text{cov}\, X, Y_i) H_{XY_i} + \frac{1}{2}\sum_{i=1}^{k}\sum_{j=1}^{k} (\text{cov}\, Y_i, Y_j) H_{Y_iY_j} + (\iota X - pC^*) H_X +$$

$$\sum_{i=1}^{k} \left[\mu_i - \left(\frac{-V_{XX}}{V_X}\right)(\text{cov}\, X, Y_i) - \sum_{j=1}^{k} \left(\frac{-V_{XY_j}}{V_X}\right)(\text{cov}\, Y_i, Y_j) \right] H_{Y_i} +$$

$$H_t + p\delta - \iota H = 0 \tag{57}$$

where the nominal interest rate, ι, *is given by*

$$\iota = \alpha_X - \left(\frac{-V_{XY}}{V_X}\right)\left(\frac{\text{var}\, X}{X}\right) - \sum_{i=1}^{k}\left(\frac{-V_{X_i}}{V_X}\right)\left(\frac{\text{cov}\, X, Y_i}{X}\right) \tag{58}$$

and α_x *is the expected rate of return on nominal wealth,*

$$\alpha_X = a^{*\prime}\alpha + \left(\frac{\mu_p}{p}\right) + \left(\frac{\text{cov}\, p, X}{pX}\right) - \left(\frac{\text{var}\, p}{p^2}\right) \tag{59}$$

PROOF: Itô's multiplication rule implies that

$$(\text{var}\, W) = \frac{1}{p^2}(\text{var}\, X) - \frac{2X}{p^3}(\text{cov}\, X, p) + \frac{X^2}{p^4}(\text{var}\, p)$$

$$(\text{cov}\, W, p) = \frac{1}{p}(\text{cov}\, X, p) - \frac{X}{p^2}(\text{var}\, p)$$

$$(\text{cov}\, W, Y) = \frac{1}{p}(\text{cov}\, X, Y) - \frac{X}{p^2}(\text{cov}\, p, Y)$$

and

$$\alpha_X = a^{*\prime}\alpha + \frac{\mu_p}{p} + \frac{1}{pX}(\operatorname{cov} X, p) - \frac{1}{p^2}(\operatorname{var} p)$$

With

$$J(W, Y, t) \equiv J\left(\frac{X}{p}, Y, t\right) \equiv V(X, Y, t)$$

we have

$$\frac{J_{WW}}{J_W} = p\left(\frac{V_{XX}}{V_X}\right)$$

$$\frac{J_{WY_i}}{J_W} = \frac{V_{XY_i}}{V_X} \quad \text{and}$$

$$\frac{V_{Xp}}{V_X} = -\frac{1}{p} - \frac{X}{p}\left(\frac{V_{XX}}{V_X}\right)$$

Equation (57) follows by writing the derivatives of $F(W, Y, t)$ in terms of those of $H(X, Y, t)$ and substituting all of the above into (6). The nominal interest rate can then be identified as the nominal payout flow necessary to keep the nominal value of a security identically equal to one, which is ι as given in (58). *Q.E.D.*

A comparison of (57) and (58) with (6) and (3) shows that the interest rate equation and the fundamental valuation equation have exactly the same form when all variables are expressed in nominal terms as when all variables are expressed in real terms. By using the arguments given in the proof of the proposition, the nominal interest rate can be expressed in terms of real wealth as

$$\iota = r + \frac{1}{p}\left[\mu_p - \left(\frac{-J_{WW}}{J_W}\right)(\operatorname{cov} W, p) - \sum_{i=1}^{k}\left(\frac{-J_{WY_i}}{J_W}\right)(\operatorname{cov} Y_i, p) - \left(\frac{\operatorname{var} p}{p}\right)\right] \tag{60}$$

where r, the real interest rate, is as given by equation (3). The term (μ_p/p) is the expected rate of inflation. The remaining terms may in general have either sign, so the nominal interest rate may be either greater or less than the sum of the real interest rate and the expected inflation rate.[17]

Concluding comments

In this paper, we have applied a rational asset pricing model to study the term structure of interest rates. In this model, the current prices and stochastic properties of all contingent claims, including bonds, are derived endogenously. Anticipations, risk aversion, investment alternatives and preferences about the timing of consumption all play a role in determining the term structure. The model thus includes the main factors traditionally mentioned in a way which is consistent with maximising behaviour and rational expectations.

By exploring specific examples, we have obtained simple closed-form solutions for bond prices which depend on observable economic variables and can be tested. The combination of equilibrium intertemporal asset pricing principles and appropriate modelling of the underlying stochastic processes provides a powerful tool for deriving consistent and potentially refutable theories. This is the first such exercise along these lines, and the methods developed should have many applications beyond those which we considered here.

In a separate paper (Cox, Ingersoll, and Ross (1981)), we use our approach to examine some aspects of what may be called traditional theories of the term structure. There we show that some forms of the classical expectations hypothesis are consistent with our simple equilibrium model and more complex ones, while other forms in general are not. We also show the relationship between some continuous-time equilibrium models and traditional theories which express expected future spot rates as linear combinations of past spot rates.

1 *We thank Franco Modigliani for mentioning this point.*

2 *Stiglitz (1970) emphasises the portfolio theory aspects involved with bonds of different maturities, as do Dieffenbach (1975), Long (1974), and Rubinstein (1976), who incorporate the characteristics of other assets as well. Modigliani and Shiller (1973) and Sargent (1972) have stressed the importance of rational anticipations.*

3 *This type of separability has been shown in other contexts by Hakansson (1970), Merton (1971) and Samuelson (1969).*

4 *Although our assumptions in this section do not satisfy all of the technical growth restrictions placed on the utility function and the coefficients of the production function in Cox, Ingersoll, and Ross (1985), they do in combination lead to a well-posed problem having an optimal solution with many useful properties. The optimal consumption function is* $C^*(W, Y, t) = [\rho/(1 - \exp(-\rho(t' - t)))]W$ *and the indirect utility function has the form* $J(W, Y, t) = a(t)\log W + b(t)Y + c(t)$, *where* $a(t)$, $b(t)$ *and* $c(t)$ *are explicitly determinable functions of time.*

5 *The condition* $1'(GG')^{-1}\alpha > 1$, *together with (13) and (14), insures that the interest rate will always be nonnegative. If* $1'(GG')^{-1}\alpha < 1$, *the interest rate will always be nonpositive.*

6 *The discrete time equivalent of this model was tested by Wood (1964), although, being concerned only with expectations, he left the error term unspecified.*

7 *See Feller (1951).*

8 *Processes similar to (17) have been extensively studied by Feller. The Laplace transform of (18) is given in Feller (1951). See Johnson and Kotz (1970) for a description of the noncentral chi-square distribution. Oliver (1965) contains properties of the modified Bessel function.*

9 *A number of contractual provisions are sufficient to preclude default risk and make the value of a bond independent of the wealth of its seller. For example, the terms of the bond could specify that the seller must repurchase the bond at the price schedule given by (23) whenever his wealth falls to a designated level.*

10 *In our framework, the most important circumstances sufficient for bond prices to depend only on the spot interest rate are: (i) individuals have constant relative risk aversion, uncertainty in the technology can be described by a single variable and the interest rate is a monotonic function of this variable, or (ii) changes in the technology are non-stochastic and the interest rate is a monotonic function of wealth.*

11 *Since the underlying security, a discount bond, makes no payment during the life of the option, the analysis of Merton (1973) implies that premature exercise is never optimal, and, hence, American and European calls have the same value.*

12 *As stated earlier, the origin is accessible only if* $\sigma^2 > 2\kappa\theta$. *Somewhat more complex arguments can be used to demonstrate that the model is not viable even if the origin is inaccessible.*

13 *Studies which have expressed expected future spot rates as linear combinations of current and past spot rates include Bierwag and Grove (1967), Cagan (1956), De Leeuw (1965), Duesenberry (1958), Malkiel (1966), Meiselman (1962), Modigliani and Shiller (1973), Modigliani and Sutch (1966), Van Horne (1965), and Wood (1964). Cox, Ingersoll, and Ross (1981) examine this issue in a diffusion setting.*

14 *See Brennan and Schwartz (1979) for this representation.*

15 *If one wished to make real money balances an argument in the direct utility function* U, *it would be straightforward to do so in our model. A utility-maximising money supply policy would depend only on the state variables, real wealth and time, so the induced price level would depend only on these variables as well.*

16 *Slater (1965) gives properties of the confluent hypergeometric function.*

17 *For a related discussion, see Fischer (1975).*

Bibliography

Beja, A., 1979, "State Preference and the Riskless Interest Rate: A Markov Model of Capital Markets", *Review of Economic Studies* 46, pp. 435–446.

Bierwag, G. O., and M. A. Grove, 1967, "A Model of the Term Structure of Interest Rates", *Review of Economics and Statistics* 49, pp. 50–62.

Brennan, M. J., and E. S. Schwartz, 1979, "A Continuous Time Approach to the Pricing of Bonds", *Journal of Banking and Finance* 3, pp. 133–155; reprinted as Chapter 5 of the present volume.

Cagan, P., 1956, "The Monetary Dynamics of Hyperinflation", in *Studies in the Quantity Theory of Money*, ed. by M. Friedman, University of Chicago Press.

Cox, J. C., J. E. Ingersoll, Jr., and S. A. Ross, 1981, "A Re-examination of Traditional Hypotheses about the Term Structure of Interest Rates", *Journal of Finance* 36, pp. 769–799.

Cox, J. C., J. E. Ingersoll, Jr., and S. A. Ross, 1985, "An Intertemporal General Equilibrium Model of Asset Prices", *Econometrica* 53, pp. 363–384.

Culbertson, J. M., 1957, "The Term Structure of Interest Rates", *Quarterly Journal of Economics* 71, pp. 485–517.

De Leeuw, F., 1965, "A Model of Financial Behavior", in *The Brookings Quarterly Econometric Model of the United States*, ed. by J. S. Duesenberry et al., Rand McNally.

Dieffenbach, B. C., 1975, "A Quantitative Theory of Risk Premiums on Securities with an Application to the Term Structure of Interest Rates", *Econometrica* 43, pp. 431–454.

Dothan, L. U., 1978, "On the Term Structure of Interest Rates", *Journal of Financial Economics* 6, pp. 59–69.

Duesenberry, J. A., 1958, *Business Cycles and Economic Growth*. McGraw-Hill.

Feller, W., 1951, "Two Singular Diffusion Problems", *Annals of Mathematics* 54, pp. 173–182.

Fischer, S., 1975, "The Demand for Index Bonds", *Journal of Political Economy* 83, pp. 509–534.

Garman, M. B., 1977, "A General Theory of Asset Valuation Under Diffusion Processes", University of California, Berkeley, Institute of Business and Economic Research, Working Paper No. 50.

Hakansson, N. H., 1970, "Optimal Investment and Consumption Strategies under Risk for a Class of Utility Functions", *Econometrica* 38, pp. 587–607.

Hicks, J. R., 1946, *Value and Capital*, 2nd edition. Oxford University Press.

Johnson, N. L., and S. Kotz, 1970, *Distributions in Statistics: Continuous Univariate Distributions - 2*. Boston: Houghton Mifflin Company.

Long, J. B., 1974, "Stock Prices, Inflation, and the Term Structure of Interest Rates", *Journal of Financial Economics* 1, pp. 131–170.

Malkiel, B. G., 1966, *The Term Structure of Interest Rates: Expectations and Behavior Patterns*, Princeton University Press.

Meiselman, D., 1962, *The Term Structure of Interest Rates*, Englewood Cliffs, Prentice Hall.

Merton, R. C., 1970, "A Dynamic General Equilibrium Model of the Asset Market and Its Application to the Pricing of the Capital Structure of the Firm", Massachusetts Institute of Technology, Sloan School of Management, Working Paper No. 497–70.

Merton, R. C., 1971, "Optimum Consumption and Portfolio Rules in a Continuous Time Model", *Journal of Economic Theory* 3, pp. 373–413.

Merton, R. C., 1973, "Theory of Rational Option Pricing", *Bell Journal of Economics and Management Science* 4, pp. 141–183.

Modigliani, F., and R. J. Shiller, 1973, "Inflation, Rational Expectations and the Term Structure of Interest Rates", *Econometrica* 40 N.S., pp. 12–43.

Modigliani, F., and R. Sutch, 1966, "Innovations of Interest Rate Policy", *American Economic Review* 56, pp. 178–197.

Nelson, C. R., 1972, *The Term Structure of Interest Rates*. New York: Basic Books, Inc.

Oliver, F. W. J., 1965, "Bessel Functions of Integer Order", *Handbook of Mathematical Functions*, ed. by M. A. Abramowitz and I. A. Stegun. New York: Dover.

Richard, S. F., 1978, "An Arbitrage Model of the Term Structure of Interest Rates", *Journal of Financial Economics* 6, pp. 33–57.

Roll, R., 1970, *The Behavior of Interest Rates*. New York: Basic Books, Inc.

Roll, R., 1971, "Investment Diversification and Bond Maturity", *Journal of Finance* 26, pp. 51–66.

Rubinstein, M. E., 1976, "The Valuation of Uncertain Income Streams and the Pricing of Options", *Bell Journal of Economics* 7, pp. 407–425.

Samuelson, P. A., 1969, "Lifetime Portfolio Selection by Dynamic Stochastic Programming", *Review of Economics and Statistics* 51, pp. 239–246.

Sargent, T. J., 1972, "Rational Expectations and the Term Structure of Interest Rates", *Journal of Money, Credit, and Banking* 4, pp. 74–97.

Slater, L. J., 1965, "Confluent Hypergeometric Functions", in *Handbook of Mathematical Functions*, ed. by M. Abramowitz and I. A. Stegun. New York: Dover.

Stiglitz, J. E., 1970, "A Consumption-Oriented Theory of Demand for Financial Assets and the Term Structure of Interest Rates", *Review of Economic Studies* 37, pp. 321–351.

Van Horne, J. C., 1965, "Interest-Rate Risk and the Term Structure of Interest Rates", *Journal of Political Economy* 73, pp. 344–351.

Vasicek, O. A., 1977, "An Equilibrium Characterization of the Term Structure", *Journal of Financial Economics* 5, pp. 177–188; reprinted as Chapter 4 of the present volume.

Wood, J. H., 1964, "The Expectations Hypothesis, the Yield Curve and Monetary Policy", *Quarterly Journal of Economics* 78, pp. 457–470.

7

Pricing of Contingent Claims in the One-Factor Term Structure Model*

Farshid Jamshidian
Sakura Global Capital

The concept of the "forward risk-adjusted interest rate process" is introduced and shown to play an important role in the determination of prices in the one factor term structure model. As an application, the Green's function for the square root process and a Gaussian process are derived. This results in closed form solutions for European options on bonds and on bond futures for these interest rate processes. The drift of the Gaussian process can be explicitly defined in such a way that the model reproduces an initially prescribed discount function.

In this paper we prove and apply a general theorem for pricing of contingent claims in the context of the one-factor term structure model. The main idea is the concept of the "forward risk-adjusted interest rate process". In this process, discount bond price volatility plays the role of a market price of risk. While forward rates are biased predictors of future interest rates, they turn out to be the expectation of the forward risk-adjusted interest rate process. The theorem states that prices of contingent claims are discounted expected payoff values with respect to this process. It clarifies the difference between forward and future contracts. It also clarifies the relation between the one-factor term structure model and Merton's option model of 1973 which is essentially in terms of forward prices. The theorem is applied to derive closed-form expressions for the Green's function of the square root process and a Gaussian process.

The drift term of the interest rate process can, in principle, be chosen dependent on time in such a way that the discount function from the model will match an initially prescribed yield curve. Cox, Ingersoll, and Ross (1985) discussed this issue for the square root process and derived an integral equation for the drift. Unfortunately, this equation cannot be solved explicitly.[1] Ho and Lee (1986) have developed a discrete pricing model in which the one-period discount rate moves in such a way as to fit a given term structure. The Gaussian model may be considered as a continuous-time analogue of the Ho–Lee model, with the mean-reverting property. It is quite tractable, with explicit expressions for all quantities of interest and certain interesting properties.

The one-factor model is reviewed in the first section with emphasis on prices as expected discounted values. The main result is presented in the second section and applied to the Green's function of the square root process and a Gaussian process in the next two sections. A final section concludes the paper.

**This article was written whilst working at Trading Analysis Group, Merrill Lynch Capital Markets; last version: July 1987. I wish to thank my colleague Yu Zhu for his very helpful comments on this paper.*

The general framework of the one-factor term structure model

In the one-factor term structure model, it is assumed that the instantaneous interest rate $r(t)$ follows a diffusion process:

$$dr = \mu(r, t)dt + \sigma(r, t)dz \tag{1}$$

An arbitrage argument as in Vasicek (1977) leads to a differential equation for the price $f = f(r, t)$ of an interest rate contingent claim:

$$f_t + \tfrac{1}{2}\sigma^2 f_{rr} + \bar{\mu} f_r - rf + D = 0 \tag{2}$$

where $\bar{\mu} = \mu + \sigma\lambda$. Here, $\lambda = \lambda(r, t)$ is the so called market price of interest rate risk, and $D = D(r, t)$ is the continuous payment flow (payout rate) of the security (for options on discount or coupon bonds $D = 0$, for coupon bonds D is normally assumed constant, and for floaters it is assumed to be dependent on r).

The contractual provision of a European contingent claim is specified by its terminal payout function, g, at expiry, T:

$$f(r, T) = g(r) \tag{3}$$

(For American claims, further constraints are specified before expiry.)

We recognise equation (2) as the (inhomogeneous) Kolmogorov backward equation (with potential term $-r$) not of the actual interest rate process (1), but of the "risk-neutral interest rate process", $\bar{r}(t)$, following

$$d\bar{r} = \bar{\mu}(\bar{r}, t)dt + \sigma(\bar{r}, t)dz \tag{4}$$

In other words, $\bar{r}(t)$ governs prices, not $r(t)$. If there is no risk premium, ie, the local expectation hypothesis holds (see Cox, Ingersoll, and Ross (1981*b*)), then $\lambda = 0$ and $\bar{r}(t) = r(t)$.

Assuming inaccessible boundaries,[2] the solution of the terminal value problem (2), (3) can be represented by the Feynman-Kac functional (see Friedman (1975), Th. 6.5.3). For the price $P = P(r, t; T)$ of the discount bond maturing at time T (corresponding to terminal value of $P(r, t; T) = 1$ and $D = 0$ in equation (2)), one has

$$P(r, t; T) = E_{r,t}\left(e^{-\int_t^T \bar{r}(s)ds}\right) \tag{5}$$

Here, $E_{r,t}$ denotes the expectation operator conditional on $\bar{r}(t) = r$. More generally, when the claim does not collect any payments, ie, when $D = 0$, then

$$f(r, t) = E_{r,t}\left(g[\bar{r}(T)]\, e^{-\int_t^T \bar{r}(s)ds}\right) \tag{6}$$

When the claim collects payments at a known rate $D = D(t)$, then to the right-hand side of equation (6) is added the present value of these payments, namely

$$\int_t^T D(s)\, P(r, t; s)\, ds \tag{7}$$

In the general case where $D = D(r, t)$ (eg, floaters), to the right-hand side of equation (6) is added

$$\int_t^T E_{r,t}\left(D[\bar{r}(s), s]\, e^{-\int_t^s \bar{r}(u)du}\right) ds \tag{8}$$

Note that equation (6) may be interpreted as the expected discounted value of the payoff. But the discount factor is inside the expectation. Our main result in the next section is that we can "decouple" equation (6), ie, pull the discount factor out, and interpret prices as discounted expected values of payoffs, provided we take the latter expectation with respect to a suitably modified interest rate process.

The forward risk-adjusted interest rate process

We now derive an alternative representation for the price of a European contingent claim expiring at T. Recall that $P = P(r, t; T)$ denotes the price of the discount bond maturing at expiry T. Let σ_P denote its volatility, ie,

$$\sigma_P(r, t) = \frac{\sigma P_r}{P} \tag{9}$$

so that $\sigma_P^2 \, dt = VAR_{r,t}[dP/P]$. Define the forward risk-adjusted interest rate process $\tilde{r}(t)$ by

$$d\tilde{r} = \tilde{\mu}(\tilde{r}, t)\, dt + \sigma(\tilde{r}, t)\, dz \tag{10}$$

where

$$\tilde{\mu} = \bar{\mu} + \sigma\sigma_P \tag{11}$$

Observe from (11) that σ_p is playing the role of a market price of risk. We now state the main result of the paper, which is proved in the appendix.

THEOREM

(*a*) The price of the claim, given by equation (6), can be "decoupled" as[3]

$$f(r, t) = P(r, t; T)\, E_{r,t}[g(\tilde{r}(T))] \tag{12}$$

(If the claim collects payments D, then the present value of the payments given by equation (7) or equation (8) is added to the right-hand side of (12).)

(*b*) For the price $f = f(r, t)$ of any contingent claim expiring at $T_1 \geq T$, with no payment flow (ie, with $D = 0$ in equation (2)), we have[4]

$$E_{r,t}[f(\tilde{r}(T), T)] = \frac{f}{P} \tag{13}$$

(*c*) $E_{r,t}[\tilde{r}(T)] = R(r, t; T)$ (14)

where

$$R = R(r, t; T) = \frac{-dP/dT}{P(r, t; T)} \tag{15}$$

denotes the implied forward rate at time t for the instantaneous rate at time T.

Part (*c*) states that the forward rate R is an unbiased estimate of the mean of the forward risk-adjusted process.[5]

Part (*a*) states that the price of a contingent claim is the discounted expected value of its payoff, where discounting is done by the discount bond maturing at expiry, and expectation is taken with respect to the forward risk-adjusted process. This is similar to the risk-neutrality argument in the Black–Scholes model, but we note that the prevalent process here is the forward risk-adjusted process, not the risk-neutral process.

Part (*b*) states that the forward price $F = f/P$ of the claim is precisely the expectation of the price of the claim at expiry T, where the expectation is taken with respect to the forward risk-adjusted process. On the other hand, according to formula (46) of Cox, Ingersoll, and Ross (1981*a*), or alternatively by a direct argument from the definition of a future contract, the price H of a future contract with expiry (delivery date) T on the contingent claim is also the expectation of the price of the claim at time T, but this time the expectation is taken with respect to the risk-neutral process.[6] In short,

$$F = \text{forward price of the claim} = E_{r,t}[f(\bar{r}(T))]$$

$$H = \text{future price of the claim} = E_{r,t}[f(\tilde{r}(T))]$$

(The above representations for forward and future prices are valid even in the presence of a general payment flow $D = D(r, t)$. See note 4.) These characterisations are useful for understanding the relation between forward and future contracts. For example, as previously shown by Cox, Ingersoll, and Ross (1981*a*) in a general distribution-free setting, one obtains the result that $F > H$ if the forward price F and the price of the discount bond P are positively correlated (and vice versa).[7]

The theorem can also be used when the terminal payoff function of the contingent claim is expressed in terms of another contingent claim, as is the case for an option on a contingent claim. For example, consider a call option on a (possibly coupon) bond maturing at $T_1 \geq T$. Say this bond is priced at $P_1 = P_1(r, t)$. Then by part (*a*)

$$C = P\,E_{r,t}[\text{MAX}\{0, P_1(\bar{r}(T), T) - K\}] \tag{16}$$

where K is the strike price. The difference between (16) and the risk-neutrality principle is that in (16) it is "the forward risk-adjusted price" $P_1(\bar{r}(T), T)$ that appears inside the expectation, not "the risk-neutral price" $P_1(\tilde{r}(T), T)$. This is an important distinction, since the mean of the former is normally greater than the mean of the latter. Indeed, as we have already seen, the two means are, respectively, the forward and the future prices on the underlying bond P_1, and the former is normally larger than the latter since forward bond prices are normally positively correlated with spot bond prices. (This is the case for the square root process and the Gaussian process below.)

Formula (16) also resembles Merton's model of 1973. There, the counterpart of $P_1(\bar{r}(T), T)$ is lognormally distributed with a mean given by the forward prices as in our case, but with log variance essentially prescribed. Here, the mean of $P_1(\bar{r}(T), T)$ is again the forward price, but its distribution and variance are determined endogenously.

To see the connection with Merton's model more closely, express the forward price, h, of the claim in terms of the forward price $x = P_1(r, t; T_1)/P$ of the discount bond maturing at T_1, ie, define

$$h(x, t) = \frac{f(r, t)}{P(r, t; T)}$$

Then the equation (17) in the following lemma is a direct counterpart to equation (36) of Merton (1973).

LEMMA 1

$$h_t + \tfrac{1}{2}\sigma_x^2 x^2 h_{xx} = 0 \tag{17}$$

where σ_x denotes the price volatility of the forward price,

$$\sigma_x = \sigma_{P_1} - \sigma_P = \sigma\left(\frac{P_{1r}}{P_1} - \frac{P_r}{P}\right)$$

The proof is given in the appendix. The idea is that (17) is the Kolmogorov backward equation of the process $\bar{x}(t) = x(\bar{r}(t), t)$.

Another way of expressing part (*a*) is in terms of the Green's function, or the fundamental solution, of the pricing differential equation (2). The Green's function

$G(r, t; x, T)$ is defined by the property that the solution of the homogeneous equation (2) subject to terminal condition (3) is given by

$$f(r, t) = \int_{-\infty}^{\infty} g(x)\, G(r, t; x, T)\, dx$$

Calculating the Green's function is useful for obtaining closed-form solutions and for sensitivity analysis. Now, part (*a*) of the theorem states that

$$G(r, t; x, T) = P(r, t; T)\, q(r, t; x, T) \tag{18}$$

where $q(x) = q(r, t; x, T)$ is the probability density of $\tilde{r}(T)$ conditional on $\tilde{r}(t) = r$.

Application to the square root process

Consider the square root process

$$d\bar{r} = (b - a\bar{r})\, dt + \delta\sqrt{\bar{r}}\, dz$$

where $a, b\ \delta \geq 0$ are constants.[8] Discount bond prices, as given by Cox, Ingersoll, and Ross (1985)), are (with a change of notation)

$$P(r, t; T) = A(t, T) \exp[-B(t, T) r] \tag{19}$$

where

$$A(t, T) = (2cw\, e^{(c+a)\tau/2})^{2b/\delta^2}$$

$$B(t, T) = 2w(e^{c\tau} - 1)$$

$$w = [(c + a) e^{c\tau} + c - a]^{-1}$$

$$c = (a^2 + 2\delta^2)^{1/2}$$

$$\tau = T - t$$

For the forward risk-adjusted process $r(t)$ we obtain

$$d\tilde{r} = \{b - [a + \delta^2 B(t, T)]\tilde{r}\} dt + \delta\sqrt{\tilde{r}}\, dz$$

ie, $\tilde{r}(t)$ is also a square root process, but with a certain time-varying drift.

LEMMA 2

The probability distribution function Q of $\tilde{r}(T)$ conditioned on $\tilde{r}(t) = r$ is the non-central chi-square

$$Q(x) = \chi^2(xv; d; hr)$$

with d degrees of freedom and non-centrality parameter hr, where

$$d = 4b/\delta^2$$

$$v = 2/\delta^2 w(e^{c\tau} - 1)$$

$$h = 4c^2 e^{c\tau} v w^2$$

The proof is given in the appendix. The density function of the non-central χ^2 distribution is explicitly available in terms of the modified Bessel's function. Together with (19), we thus have an explicit expression for the Green's function given by (18).

As an application we compute the price $C = C(r, t)$ of a European call option on the future contract on a discount bond.

The terminal payoff function at the option expiration date is

$$g(x) = MAX(0, H(x, T) - K)$$

where K is the exercise price and $H(x, T) = H(x, T; T_1; T_2)$ is the price at time T of a future contract with delivery date T_1 on a discount bond maturing at time T_2, given that the interest rate is x at time T. The explicit expression for $H(x, T)$ as given by Cox, Ingersoll, and Ross (1981*a*, Equation 55) is (aside from a change in notation):

$$H(x, T; T_1; T_2) = A(T_1, T_2) E^{d/2} e^{-xD}$$

where

$$E = \frac{2a}{2a + B(T_1, T_2)\,\delta^2 \left(1 - e^{-a(T_1 - T)}\right)}$$

$$D = B(T_1, T_2)\, E\, e^{-a(T_1 - T)}$$

PROPOSITION

$$C(r,t) = C(r, t; T_1; T_2; K)$$

$$= P(r, t; T)\left[G(r,t)\chi^2\left(\frac{r^*}{z}; d; hvzr\right) - K\chi^2(r^* v; d; hr)\right]$$

where $z = 1/(v + 2D)$ and

$$G(r,t) = G(r, t; T; T_1; T_2) = E_{r,t}\{H[\tilde{r}(T)], T; T_1; T_2\}$$

$$= A(T_1, T_2)(Evz)^{\frac{d}{2}} \exp(-rDhz)$$

$$r^* = \frac{\log\left[A(T_1, T_2)\, E^{\frac{d}{2}}\right] / K}{D}$$

The proof is given in the appendix. Note that $H(r^*, T) = K$. It is also assumed that $K < A(T_1, T_2) E^{d/2}$, so that $r^* > 0$, for otherwise the option value is clearly zero.

The price of a call option on a discount bond is found by simply setting $T = T_1$ in the above formula. The resulting expression then reduces to the formula of Cox, Ingersoll, and Ross (1985, Equation 32).

Interestingly, there are also formulas for options on coupon bonds and on coupon bond futures.

Consider a European call option with strike price K, expiring at time T, on a portfolio consisting of $a_i \geq 0$ issues of discount bonds maturing at T_i. Define r_k to be the solution to

$$\sum_j a_j P(r_k, T; T_j) = K$$

where j ranges over indices for which $T_j > T$ (if K is so large that no solution exists, then the call value is zero). Define

$$K_j = P(r_k, T; T_j)$$

Then the price of the call on the portfolio equals the price of the portfolio of a_j calls with strikes K_j on the jth bond.

The proof is a consequence of the equality of the two terminal payoff functions, namely

$$\mathrm{MAX}\left(0, \sum_j a_j P(r,T;T_j) - K\right) = \sum_j a_j \ \mathrm{MAX}[0, P(r,T;T_j) - K_j]$$

This follows by the fact that discount bond prices are decreasing functions of r. The argument remains valid for an option on a portfolio of bond futures, since bond future prices are all decreasing functions of r. More generally, in the case of an arbitrary interest process, the same argument applies to an option on a portfolio of securities, all of which are decreasing (or increasing) functions of the interest rate.

Application to a Gaussian process

For equilibrium pricing of bonds, the coefficients of the interest rate process are normally assumed time-independent. But for the pricing of contingent claims, eg, options on coupon bonds, it is important that the interest rate process be specified so as to incorporate the relevant information in the market yield curve, specially the price of the underlying bond. This requires sufficient degrees of freedom in the choice of coefficients for the interest rate process. For example, one may choose the drift term time-dependent in such a way as to match a prescribed discount function. In general, an equation relating the two does not exist. However, for the square root process, Cox, Ingersoll, and Ross (1985) give an integral equation which may be solved numerically. Ho and Lee (1986) find an explicit solution in a discrete setting. An examination of their expression for the one-period rate $r_i^n(1)$ (Equation 24) shows that $E_{n,i}[\Delta r^n(1)]$ is time-dependent, but state-independent, and $\mathrm{VAR}_{n,i}[\Delta r^n(1)]$ is constant. In the continuous time limit this corresponds to the following Gaussian process for the interest rate, with a vanishing speed of reversion to mean a,

$$d\bar{r} = (b(t) - a\bar{r})\,dt + \delta\,dz$$

Vasicek (1977) investigated the properties of the term structure for the above interest rate process with b constant. The disadvantage of the Gaussian process is that interest rates, being normally distributed, may become negative. Similarly, discount bond prices are lognormally distributed and hence may exceed unity.[9] However, by choosing a positive speed of reversion to mean a, the variance of $\bar{r}(t)$ will not grow linearly with time; rather, it will be bounded. Hence the probability of $\bar{r}(t)$ becoming negative is mitigated. The advantage of the Gaussian process is that it is quite tractable, as shown below.

Recall the forward risk-adjusted interest rate process $\tilde{r}(t)$ from the previous section. From (23) below, we see that

$$\frac{P_r}{P} = \frac{-1(1 - e^{-a\tau})}{a} \tag{20}$$

From this it follows that $\tilde{r}(t)$ is also Gaussian and

$$\mathrm{VAR}_{r,t}\tilde{r}(T) = \mathrm{VAR}_{r,t}\bar{r}(T) = \frac{\delta^2 (1 - e^{-a\tau})}{2a} \tag{21}$$

where $\tau = T - t$. In particular, the variances of $\tilde{r}(T)$ and $\bar{r}(T)$ are equal and do not depend on the drift $b(t)$. (As shown earlier, the mean of $\tilde{r}(T)$ is less than the mean of $\bar{r}(T)$.) Moreover, by the theorem, the mean of $\tilde{r}(T)$ is the forward rate $R(r,t;T)$, which is observable if the discount function is given. Thus, the Green's function (18) is explicitly known, and the expectation (12) may be calculated. Interestingly, we see that the Green's function for a particular expiry date T depends only on the implied forward rate for time T and on the price of the discount bond maturing at T, not on the whole discount function.

As an example, consider a European call on a discount bond maturing at T_1 and priced at $P_1 = P(r, t; T_1)$. From (20) and (21) the log variance of the forward risk-adjusted price $\tilde{P}_1(T) = P(\tilde{r}(T), T; T_1)$ is

$$\sigma_1^2 = \mathrm{VAR}_{r,t}[\log \tilde{P}_1(T)] = \frac{\delta^2 [1 - e^{-a(T_1 - T)}]^2 (1 - e^{-2a\tau})}{2a^3}$$

In particular, the log variance of $\tilde{P}_1(T)$ does not depend on the choice of the drift term $b(t)$. Moreover, by the theorem, the mean of $\tilde{P}_1(T)$ is just the forward price P_1/P.

We now have all the ingredients that go into the pricing formula (16). We emphasise again that in this formula the option price is the discounted expected value of the payoff, where the forward risk-adjusted price $\tilde{P}_1(T)$ appears inside the expectation, not the risk-neutral price $\bar{P}_1(T) = P(\bar{r}(T), T; T_1)$. Both prices are lognormal with the same log variance, but the mean of the former which is the forward price exceeds the mean of the latter which is the future price. (This is because $P(r, T; T_1)$ is negative exponential in r, and the mean of $\bar{r}(T)$ is greater than the mean of $\tilde{r}(T)$.) Interestingly, we see that the call price depends on only the two prices P_1 and P, and not on the whole discount function. (16) immediately leads to a solution similar to the Black-Scholes formula:

$$C = P_1 N(h) - PKN(h - \sigma_1) \tag{22}$$

where $N(\cdot)$ is the cumulative normal distribution, and

$$h = \left(\frac{\log P_1 / PK}{\sigma_1}\right) + \frac{1}{2}\sigma_1$$

For more complicated cases, such as American options, the pricing differential equation must be solved numerically. For this we need an expression for the drift term $b(t)$ in terms of the prescribed forward rates $R(t, T)$

$$b(T) = e^{-a\tau} \frac{d}{dT}\left[e^{a\tau}\left(R(t;T) + \frac{\delta^2 (1 - e^{-a\tau})^2}{2a^2}\right)\right]$$

Conversely, the forward rate may be expressed in terms of the drift

$$R(r, t; T) = e^{-a\tau} r + \int_t^\tau b(s) e^{-a(T-s)} ds - \frac{\delta^2 (1 - e^{-a\tau})^2}{2a^2} \tag{23}$$

The discount function $P(r, t; T)$ is given by the exponential of the negative of the integral of this expression. For b constant, it simplifies to formula (27) of Vasicek (1977).

Conclusion

The concept of the forward risk-adjusted interest rate process contributes both to the understanding of prices of contingent claims in the one-factor term structure model and to deriving closed-form solutions. For option evaluation, it is important to incorporate relevant information from market yield curves in addition to the short-term rate. The Gaussian model is particularly convenient for this purpose. The square root process is theoretically superior but requires numerical treatment.

Appendix

PROOF OF THE THEOREM

Define the forward price

$$F = F(r,t) = \frac{f(r,t)}{P(r,t;T)} \tag{A1}$$

Set

$$F(s) = F(\tilde{r}(s), s) \tag{A2}$$

and write

$$\frac{d\bar{F}}{\bar{F}} = \bar{\mu}_F dt + \sigma_F dz \tag{A3}$$

Let $\sigma_f = \sigma f_r / f$ denote the price volatility of f. Define σ_P similarly. By Itô's division rule

$$\frac{\sigma F_r}{F} = \sigma_F = \sigma_f - \sigma_P$$

$$\bar{\mu}_F = \sigma_P^2 - \sigma_P \sigma_f = \frac{-\sigma_P \sigma F_r}{F} \tag{A4}$$

On the other hand, by Itô's lemma

$$\bar{\mu}_F = \frac{F_t + \bar{\mu} F_r + \frac{1}{2}\sigma^2 F_{rr}}{F} \tag{A5}$$

Combining (A4) and (A5), we get[10]

$$F_t + (\bar{\mu} + \sigma\sigma_P) F_r + \tfrac{1}{2}\sigma^2 F_{rr} = 0 \tag{A6}$$

By the definition of $\tilde{r}(t)$, this is the Kolmogorov backward equation of F with respect to $\tilde{r}(t)$. Thus subject to the terminal value $g(\cdot)$, we have by the Feynman–Kac functional

$$F(r,t) = E_{r,t}[g(\tilde{r}(T))] \tag{A7}$$

Part (*a*) follows.

Part (*b*) is a direct consequence of part (*a*) and the uniqueness of the terminal value problem. (Apply (*a*) to the terminal condition $g(r) = f(r,T)$ at time T.)

Since for $T_1 \geq T$, $P(r,t;T_1)$ is a solution of the pricing equation (2), it follows from linearity that $f(r,T) = -dP/dT(r,t;T)$ is also a solution of equation (2). Moreover, it is easy to see from equation (5) that its terminal value is $f(r,T) = r$. It thus follows from (A7) that

$$\frac{-(dP/dT)}{P(r,t;T)} = E_{r,t}[\tilde{r}(T)]$$

which proves (*c*).

PROOF OF LEMMA 1

By (A6), h, when expressed in terms of r, satisfies the Kolmogorov backward equation (KBE) of $\tilde{r}(t)$. By the invariance of the KBE under changes of coordinates, it follows that $h(x,t)$ satisfies the KBE of $\tilde{x}(t) = x(\tilde{r}(t), t)$. Now, from (A6) again, but applied to $x = P_1/P$ instead of $F = f/P$, and by Itô's lemma, $d\tilde{x}/\tilde{x} = \sigma_x dz$. Thus (17) is the KBE of $\tilde{x}(t)$ and the lemma is established.[10]

PROOF OF LEMMA 2

Consider the moment-generating function of $\tilde{r}(T)$:

$$f = f(r, t; k) = E_{r,t}[e^{k\tilde{r}(T)}]$$

Then f is the solution of the Kolmogorov backward equation of $\tilde{r}(t)$,

$$f_t + \tfrac{1}{2}\delta^2 r f_{rr} + [b - (a + \delta^2 B(t, T))r]f_r = 0$$

subject to the terminal condition $f(r, T; k) = \exp kr$.

Using a separation of variables suggested by Cox, Ingersoll, and Ross (1981*b*) in a similar context, the solution is found to be

$$f(r, t; k) = (1 - uk)^{-2b/\delta^2} \exp\left(\frac{4c^2w^2e^{c\tau}rk}{1 - uk}\right)$$

where $u = \delta^2 w(e^{c\tau} - 1)$. The lemma follows by comparing this with the moment-generating function of the non-central chi-square distribution with d degrees of freedom and non-centrality parameter g, given by (see Johnson and Kotz (1970), Chapter 28, Equation 11):

$$(1 - 2k)^{-d/2} \exp\left(\frac{gk}{1 - 2k}\right)$$

PROOF OF THE PROPOSITION

From the expression for the Green's function (18) and lemma 2 it is clear that

$$G(r, t) = P(J - K\chi^2(r^* v; d; hr))$$

where $P = P(r, t; T)$ and

$$J = v\int_0^{r^*} H(x, T)\, q(xv; d; hr)\, dx$$

with $q = q(y; d; hr)$ denoting the probability density function of the non-central chi-square distribution with parameters d and hr. From the definition of q as an infinite sum (see Johnson and Kotz (1970), Chapter. 28, Equation 3), for all positive L, b, d, f, x one has

$$e^{-Lx}q(bx; d; f) = c_1 q\left((b + 2L)x; d; \frac{bf}{b + 2L}\right)$$

where c_1 is a certain function of L, b, d, f but not of x. Now, $H(x, T) = c_2 e^{-Dx}$, where c_2 and D are functions of T, T_1, T_2, but not of x. It follows that

$$J = G\chi^2\left(r^*(v + 2D); d; \frac{hvr}{v + 2D}\right)$$

where G is a function of r, t, T_1, T_2, but not of K.

It remains to calculate G. Observe that when $K = 0$, then $J = G$ and, hence, $C(r, t) = PG$. On the other hand, from the theorem we know that in this case $C(r, t) = PE_{r,t}[H(\tilde{r}(T), T)]$. Thus,

$$G = E_{r,t}[H(\tilde{r}(T), T)] = A(T_1, T_2)\, E^{\frac{d}{2}} E_{r,t}[e^{-D\tilde{r}(T)}]$$

We have already computed $E_{r,t}[e^{k\tilde{r}(T)}]$ in the proof of lemma 2 for all k. Substituting from that expression results in the expression $G = G(r, t)$, as appears in the statement of the proposition.

REMARK
The above method can also be used to evaluate the price of a European call option on any security whose terminal function is a simple exponential in r, eg, options on forward discount bond contracts.

1 *The integral equation is a convolution equation which may be solved numerically or inverted symbolically by the inverse Laplace transform. There remains the problem of boundary classification.*

2 *In the case of accessible boundaries there are several alternatives. If a boundary is an exit boundary, then a contractual provision must be specified for the boundary (and the contract terminates when the boundary is reached). In this case, theorem 6.5.2 of Friedman (1975) is applicable. In case of natural boundaries, one must specify the behaviour of the process at the boundaries. In this case, the expectation formulas (5)-(8) are to be taken as the definitions of prices.*

3 *Using the Girsanov formula (see Friedman (1975), Th. 7.3.1), the expectation with respect to* $\bar{r}(t)$ *in (12) may be converted back to a certain expectation with respect to* $\bar{r}(t)$*, resulting in yet a third representation of prices as discounted expected values. However, this representation does not seem particularly useful.*

4 *In general, when* $D \neq 0$*, define* f^+ *to be* f *less the present value of payments between now and expiry (given by (7) or (8)). Clearly,* f^+/P *is the forward price. A simple generalisation of part (b) is that* $E_{r,t}[f(\bar{r}(T), T)] = f^+/P$*. In other words,* $E_{r,t}[f(\bar{r}(T), T)]$ *is the forward price whether or not the claim collects payment. (In particular, this is valid for a coupon bond.)*

5 *In contrast, equation (5) and Jensen's inequality imply that* $R(r, t; T) < E_{r,t}[\bar{r}(T)]$*, at least for* T *near* t.

6 *Let* $f(r, t)$ *denote the price of a contingent claim (eg, a coupon bond) expiring at time* $T_1 \geq T$*. Let* $H(r, t)$ *denote the price of a future contract on this claim, with expiry (delivery date)* T*. It follows from Equation (44) of Cox, Ingersoll, and Ross (1981a) that* H *satisfies the KBE of* $\bar{r}(t)$

$$H_t + \tfrac{1}{2}\sigma^2 H_{rr} + \bar{\mu} H_r = 0 \qquad (*)$$

subject to the terminal condition $H(r, T) = f(r, T)$*. By the Feynman-Kac functional the solution is* $H(r, T) = E_{r,t}[f(\bar{r}(T), T)]$*, as claimed.*

Now, (*) can also be established by the usual arbitrage argument. Indeed, set $H(s) = H(r(s), s)$ *and* $P(s) = P(r(s), s; T)$ *and write* $dH/H = \mu_H dt + \sigma_H dz$ *and* $dP/P = \mu_P dt + \sigma_P dz$*. Invest and rebalance dynamically dollar amount* σ_H *in the bond* P *and short dollar amount* σ_P *of the future contract. Since the future contract is marked to the market, the instantaneous return from the portfolio is* $\sigma_H dP/P - \sigma_P dH/H$*, which equals* $(\sigma_H \mu_P - \sigma_P \mu_H) dt$*. Since this return is certain, it must equal the risk-free return* $\sigma_H r\, dt$ *on the investment. Rearranging, we have* $\mu_H/\sigma_H = (\mu_P - r)/\sigma_P$*. But, by definition, the right-hand side is* $-\lambda$*. (This follows also from equation (2) and Itô's lemma.) Thus,* $\mu_H/\sigma_H = -\lambda$*, and (*) follows from Itô's lemma.*

7 *To see this, set* $K = F - H$*. From (A6) and (*) above it follows that* K *satisfies*

$$K_t + \tfrac{1}{2}\sigma^2 K_{rr} + \bar{\mu} K_r + \sigma\sigma_P f_r = 0$$

Moreover, the terminal value of K *is zero. Thus by the Feynman-Kac functional, the solution is*

$$K = \int_t^T E_{r,t}[(\sigma\sigma_P F_r)(r(s), S)]\, ds$$

Now, $\sigma\sigma_P F_r(r, s)$ *is just* $1/P$ *times the instantaneous covariance of the forward price* $F(s)$ *and the discount bond price* $P(s)$*. So if this covariance is positive for all* s*, then* K *is also positive.*

8 *We assume* $2b \geq \delta^2$*, so that the origin is inaccessible. Otherwise an appropriate boundary behaviour must be specified.*

9 *The problem persists in the discrete case. Indeed the expression for* $r_n^n(1)$ *in Ho and Lee (1986) shows that it may be negative even if* n *and* δ *are time- and state-dependent.*

10 *A laborious direct substitution leads to the same result.*

Bibliography

Black, F., and M. Scholes, 1973, "The Pricing of Options and Corporate Liabilities", *Journal of Political Economy* 8, pp. 637-654; reprinted as Chapter 1 of the present volume.

Cox, J. C., J. E. Ingersoll, and S. A. Ross, 1985, "A Theory of the Term Structure of Interest Rates", *Econometrica* 53, pp. 385–407; reprinted as Chapter 6 of the present volume.

Cox, J. C., J. E. Ingersoll, and S. A. Ross, 1981*a*, "The Relation Between Forward Prices and Future Prices", *Journal of Financial Economics* 9, pp. 321–346.

Cox, J. C., J. E. Ingersoll, and S. A. Ross, 1981*b*, "A Re-examination of Traditional Hypotheses about the Term Structure of Interest Rates", *Journal of Finance* 36, pp. 769–799.

Friedman, A., 1975, *Stochastic Differential Equations and Applications*, Vol. 1, Academic Press.

Ho, T. S., and S. Lee, 1986, "Term Structure Movements and Pricing Interest Rate Contingent Claims", *Journal of Finance* 41, pp. 1011–1028; reprinted as Chapter 13 of the present volume.

Johnson, N. L., and S. Kotz, 1970, Distributions in Statistics: Continuous Univariate Distributions-2, Boston: Houghton Mifflin Company.

Merton, R. C., 1973, "Theory of Rational Option Pricing", *Bell Journal of Economics and Management Science* 4, pp. 141–183.

Vasicek, O. A., 1977, "An Equilibrium Characterization of the Term Structure", *Journal of Financial Economics* 5, pp. 177–188; reprinted as Chapter 4 of the present volume.

8

An Exact Bond Option Formula*

Farshid Jamshidian
Sakura Global Capital

This paper derives a closed-form solution for European options on pure discount bonds, assuming a mean-reverting Gaussian interest rate model as in Vasicek (1977). The formula is extended to European options on discount bond portfolios.

In this paper we derive a closed-form solution for European options on default-free bonds. We assume that the term structure is completely determined by the value of the instantaneous interest rate $r(t)$ and that $r(t)$ follows a mean-reverting Gaussian (normal) process as in Vasicek (1977). The resulting pricing formula resembles the Black–Scholes formula and has a similar interpretation. Moreover, an option on a portfolio of pure discount bonds (in particular, an option on a coupon bond) decomposes into a portfolio of options on the individual discount bonds in the portfolio.

In the Vasicek model it is assumed that $r(t)$ evolves according to the diffusion process:

$$dr = a(r_0 - r)\,dt + \sigma\,dw$$

where σ, a, and r_0 are positive constants and $w(t)$ is a standard Wiener process. The constant r_0 is interpreted as the historical average instantaneous rate and a is interpreted as the speed of reversion to this average. It is assumed that prices of bonds and their derivative securities depend on r as the only state variable. Standard arbitrage arguments as in Dothan (1982) and Vasicek (1977) imply that (i) the price of risk $\lambda(r,t)$ (defined as the expected instantaneous excess return above the riskless rate, divided by the instantaneous standard deviation of return) is the same for all these securities and (ii) the price $U(r,t)$ of a security paying continuously at a rate $h(r,t)$ and yielding a terminal payoff $g(r_T)$ at time T is the solution of

$$U_t + \tfrac{1}{2}\sigma^2 U_{rr} + a(\bar{r} - r)U_r - rU + h = 0 \tag{1}$$

$$U(r, T) = g(r) \tag{2}$$

where $\bar{r} = r_0 + \lambda\sigma/a$. We further assume that λ is a constant.

Let $P(r, t, s)$ denote the price at time t, given that $r(t) = r$, of a pure discount bond maturing at a time s (the solution to (1)–(2) with $T = s$, $g(r) \equiv 1$ and $h \equiv 0$). Let

**This paper was first published in* The Journal of Finance, *Vol. 44 (1989). It is reprinted with the permission of the American Finance Association. At the time of writing the author was Vice-president, Financial Strategies Group, Merrill Lynch Capital Markets. I am grateful to an anonymous referee for numerous helpful comments and to Yu Zhu for useful discussions.*

$$f(r, t, s) = -\frac{\partial}{\partial s} \log P(r, t, s) \tag{3}$$

denote the forward rate at time t and state r, implied for the instantaneous rate at time s. Finally, set

$$v^2(t, s) = \text{var}_{r,t}[r(s)] = \frac{\sigma^2 (1 - e^{-2a(s-t)})}{2a} \tag{4}$$

where the second equality is obtained as in Arnold (1974), Section 8.3.

PROPOSITION:

(a) Under the above assumptions, the solution of (1)-(2) *is given by*

$$U(r,t) = P(r,t,T)E[g(R_{r,t,T})] + \int_t^T P(r,t,s)E[h(R_{r,t,s}, s)]ds \tag{5}$$

where $R_{r,t,s}$ *denotes a normal random variable with mean* $f(r, t, s)$ *and variance* $v^2(t, s)$. *Moreover,*[1]

$$P(r, t, s) = \exp[\tfrac{1}{2}k^2(t, s) - n(r, t, s)] \tag{6}$$

$$f(r, t, s) = m(r, t, s) - q(t, s) \tag{7}$$

where (denoting $\tau = s - t$)

$$m = m(r, t, s) = e^{-a\tau}r + (1 - e^{-a\tau})\bar{r}$$

$$n = n(r,t,s) = \tau\bar{r} + \frac{(r - \bar{r})(1 - e^{-a\tau})}{a}$$

$$k^2 = k^2(t,s) = \frac{\sigma^2(4e^{-a\tau} - e^{-2a\tau} + 2a\tau - 3)}{2a^3}$$

$$q = q(t,s) = \frac{\sigma^2(1 - e^{-a\tau})^2}{2a^2}$$

(b) In particular, Equation (5) *with* $g(r) = P(r, T, s)$ and $h \equiv 0$ *entails that*

$$E[\tilde{P}] = \text{forward price} \equiv \frac{P(r, t, s)}{P(r, t, T)}$$

$$\tilde{P} \equiv P(R_{r,t,T}, T, s)$$

Equation (5) *also entails that the price at time* t, *given that* $r(t) = r$, *of a call option on the* s*-maturity pure discount bond with exercise price* K *and expiration* $T < s$ *is given by*

$$C(r, t, T, s, K) = P(r, t, T)\, E[\max\{0, \tilde{P} - K\}] \tag{8}$$

Moreover, $\tilde{P}$ *is lognormal with*

$$\text{var}[\log \tilde{P}] = \text{var}_{r,t}[\log P(r(T), T, s)] \equiv \sigma_P^2$$

where

$$\sigma_P = \frac{v(t,T)(1-e^{-a(s-T)})}{a}$$

Hence,

$$C(r, t, T, s, K) = P(r, t, s)\, N(h) - K P(r, t, T)\, N(h - \sigma_P) \qquad (9)$$

where

$$h = \frac{\log\left[P(r,t,s)/P(r,t,T)K\right]}{\sigma_P} + \frac{\sigma_P}{2}$$

(c) More generally, Equation (5) entails that the price C_a *at time* t *and state* r *of a European call option with exercise price* K *and expiration* T *on a portfolio consisting of* $a_j > 0$ *issues of* s_j*-maturity discount bonds is given by*

$$C_a = P(r, t, T)\, E\{\max[0, \tilde{P}_a - K]\}$$

where $\tilde{P}_a = \sum a_j P(R_{r,t,T}, T, s_j)$ *and* j *runs over all indices for which* $T < s_j$. *Moreover,*

$$E[\tilde{P}_a] = \frac{\sum a_j P(r,t,s_j)}{P(r,t,T)} \equiv \textit{forward portfolio price}$$

One also has the decomposition

$$\max\{0, \tilde{P}_a - K\} = \sum a_j \max\{0, P(R_{r,t,T}, T, s_j) - K_j\} \qquad (10)$$

where $K_j = P(r^*, T, s_j)$ *and* r^* *is the solution to* $\sum a_j P(r^*, T, s_j) = K$. *Hence,*[2]

$$C_a = \sum a_j C(r, t, T, s_j, K_j)$$

The proof is given in the Appendix. The primary conclusion from the proposition is that the price of the European call option equals the discounted expected value of $\max\{0, X - K\}$ for some random variable X (independent of K) with expectation equal to the forward bond (portfolio) price. It can be shown that a similar statement is valid in *all* one-factor term structure models.[3]

The resemblance between the option pricing formula (9) and the Black-Scholes formula is obvious. In both cases, the random variable X above is lognormal, resulting in similar formulas. The discount factor $P(r, t, T)$ plays the role of $e^{-r(T-t)}$ in the Black-Scholes model, and σ_P^2, which is the variance of the logarithm of the price of the underlying security at option expiration, replaces $\sigma^2(T - t)$ of the Black-Scholes model, which has the same meaning. In other words, with these substitutions the Black-Scholes model and the Vasicek model produce identical option values.

Part (*c*) of the proposition states that an option on a portfolio is equivalent to a portfolio of options with appropriate strike prices. It is clear from the proof that this decomposition extends to other situations where the prices of the portfolio components are all strictly decreasing (or all strictly increasing) functions of the same state variable.

Equation (9) is also similar to the option pricing formula of Cox, Ingersoll, and Ross (1985), equation (32), except for the appearance of the normal distribution instead of the chi-squared distribution. The simpler formula here has the theoretical disadvantage of yielding positive call option prices for arbitrarily large strike prices. However, the magnitude of this deviation is often small, and the computational simplicity of the formula makes it an attractive practical alternative, especially for the evaluation of European options on bond portfolios and coupon bonds.

Appendix

PROOF OF THE PROPOSITION:

(*a*) Let $\tilde{r}(t)$ be the "risk-neutral interest rate process", defined by $d\tilde{r} = a(\bar{r} - \tilde{r})dt + \sigma dw$. Set $Y(t, s) = \int_t^s \tilde{r}(u)du$. Then it follows from Friedman (1975), Theorem 6.5.3, that the solution to (1)–(2) is[4]

$$U(r,t) = E_{r,t}\left(g[\tilde{r}(T)]e^{-Y(t,T)} + \int_t^T h[\tilde{r}(s), s]e^{-Y(t,s)}ds\right)$$

This is equivalent to

$$U(r, t) = \int_{-\infty}^{\infty} G(r, r', t, T)\, g(r')\, dr' + \int_t^T \int_{-\infty}^{\infty} G(r, r', t, s)\, h(r', s)\, dr'\, ds \qquad (11)$$

where

$$G(r, r', t, s) = \int_{-\infty}^{\infty} e^{-y} p(r, t, s, r', y)\, dy \qquad (12)$$

and $p(r, t, s, \cdot, \cdot)$ denotes the joint probability density of $\tilde{r}(s)$, $Y(t, s)$ conditional on $\tilde{r}(t) = r$. To calculate p and G, we note that, by Corollary 8.2.4 in Arnold (1974), $\tilde{r}(s)$ can be expressed as

$$\tilde{r}(s) = a^{-a(s-t)}\tilde{r}(t) + \int_t^s e^{-a(s-u)}[a\bar{r}du + \sigma dw(u)]$$

$$= e^{-a(s-t)}(\tilde{r}(t) - \bar{r}) + \bar{r} + \sigma \int_t^s e^{-a(s-u)} dw(u)$$

and, in particular (as in Arnold (1974), Section 8.3),

$$E_{r,t}[\tilde{r}(s)] = m(r, t, s), \qquad var_{r,t}[\tilde{r}(s)] = v^2(t, s)$$

where m and v^2 are as above.[5] It also follows that $\tilde{r}(s)$ and $Y(t, s)$ are bivariately normally distributed, and $E_{r,t}[Y(t, s)] = n$, $var_{r,t}[Y(t, s)] = k^2$, and $cov_{r,t}[\tilde{r}(s), Y(t, s)] = q$.[6] This uniquely determines p, and (12) can now be integrated to yield

$$G(r, r', t, s) = e^{\left(\frac{1}{2}k^2 - n\right)}\left(2\pi v^2\right)^{-\frac{1}{2}} e^{-\frac{[r' - (m-q)]^2}{2v^2}} \qquad (13)$$

Setting $h \equiv 0$, $g \equiv 1$ and $T = s$ in (11), (13) implies that $P(r, t, s) = \exp(\tfrac{1}{2}k^2 - n)$. Taking the logarithmic derivative gives $f(r, t, s) = m - q$. In view of (11) and (13), Part (*a*) is now established.

(*b*) Applying (5) with $h \equiv 0$ and $g(r) = \max\{0, P(r, T, s) - K\}$ gives (8). The fact that $\tilde{P}$ and $P(r(T), T, s)$ are lognormal follows from (6) and the expression for n, which shows that $P(r, T, s)$ is the exponential of a linear function of r. The coefficient of r in this linear term is $\{1 - \exp[-a(s - I)]\}/a$; thus the expression for σ_p follows. Equation (9) now follows from a well-known calculation involving the lognormal distribution.

(*c*) The first statement follows as in Part (*b*). To prove (10), it suffices to show that

$$\max\{0, \Sigma a_j P(r, T, s_j) - K\} = \Sigma a_j \max\{0, P(r, T, s_j) - K_j\}$$

However, this follows from the fact that all $P(r, T, s_j)$ are decreasing functions of r. Indeed, from the way r^* and K_j are defined, we see that if $r < r^*$, then $\Sigma a_j P(r, T, s_j) > K$ and $P(r, T, s_j) > K_j$, with the reverse inequality holding if $r > r^*$.

1 *Equation (6) can readily be shown to be identical to equation (27) in Vasicek (1977). Also, note that, if* g *is a constant and* h *is a deterministic function of time, equation (5) reduces to the obvious present value expression.*

2 *European put prices follow by put-call parity, namely,*

$$\text{call} - \text{put} = \sum a_j P(r, t, s) - P(r, t, T)K$$

3 *A derivation of this more general result and its application to the square-root process of Cox, Ingersoll, and Ross (1985) and a mean-reverting generalization of the Gaussian continuous-time limit of the Ho and Lee model (1986) is given in Jamshidian (1987).*

4 *Here* $E_{r,t}[\cdot]$ *means* $E[\cdot \mid \tilde{r}(t) = r]$ *– similarly for variance.*

5 *Note that* $\text{var}_{r,t}[\tilde{r}(s)]$ *equals* $\text{var}_{r,t}[r(s)]$ *and does not depend on* r. *A similar statement holds for the other variance and covariance terms.*

6 *These results are obtained by interchanging the order of integration and taking expectation (or covariance). Details of these and other calculations in the paper may be obtained from the author.*

Bibliography

Arnold, L., *Stochastic Differential Equations.* New York: John Wiley & Sons, Inc., 1974.

Cox, J. C, J. E. Ingersoll, and S. A. Ross, 1985, "A Theory of the Term Structure of Interest Rates", *Econometrica* 53, pp. 385–407; reprinted as Chapter 6 of the present volume.

Dothan, L. U., 1982, "On the Term Structure of Interest Rates", *Journal of Financial and Quantitative Analysis* 17, pp. 75–100.

Friedman, A., *Stochastic Differential Equations and Applications,* Vol. 1. New York: Academic Press, 1975.

Ho, T. S. and S. Lee, 1986, "Term Structure Movements and Pricing Interest Rate Contingent Claims", *Journal of Finance* 41, pp. 1011–28; reprinted as Chapter 13 of the present volume.

Jamshidian, F., "Pricing of Contingent Claims in the One Factor Term Structure Model". Chapter 7 of the present volume.

Merton, R. C., 1973, "Theory of Rational Option Pricing", *Bell Journal of Economics and Management Science* 4, pp. 141–83.

Vasicek, O. A., 1977, "An Equilibrium Characterization of the Term Structure", *Journal of Financial Economics* 5, pp. 177–88; reprinted as Chapter 4 of the present volume.

9

Pricing Interest Rate Derivative Securities*

John Hull and Alan White
University of Toronto

This article shows that the one-state-variable interest-rate models of Vasicek (1977) and Cox, Ingersoll, and Ross (1985b) can be extended so that they are consistent with both the current term structure of interest rates and either the current volatilities of all spot interest rates or the current volatilities of all forward interest rates. The extended Vasicek model is shown to be very tractable analytically. The article compares option prices obtained using the extended Vasicek model with those obtained using a number of other models.

In recent years, interest rate contingent claims such as caps, swaptions, bond options, captions and mortgage-backed securities have become increasingly popular. The valuation of these instruments is now a major concern of both practitioners and academics.

Practitioners have tended to use different models for valuing different interest rate derivative securities. For example, when valuing caps, they frequently assume that interest rates are lognormal and use Black's (1976) model for valuing options on commodity futures. When valuing European bond options, practitioners often also use Black's (1976) model. However, in this case, bond prices rather than interest rates are assumed to be lognormal. Using different models in different situations has a number of disadvantages. First, there is no easy way of making the volatility parameters in one model consistent with those in another model. Second, it is difficult to aggregate exposures across different interest rate dependent securities. For example, it is difficult to determine the extent to which the volatility exposure of a swaption can be offset by a position in caps. Finally, it is difficult to value non-standard derivatives.

Several models of the term structure have been proposed in the academic literature. Examples are Brennan and Schwartz (1979, 1982), Courtadon (1982), Cox, Ingersoll, and Ross (1985*b*), Dothan (1978), Langetieg (1980), Longstaff (1989), Richard (1979), and Vasicek (1977). All these models have the advantage that they can be used to value all interest rate contingent claims in a consistent way. Their major disadvantages are that they involve several unobservable parameters and do not provide a perfect fit to the initial term structure of interest rates.

Ho and Lee (1986) pioneered a new approach by showing how an interest rate model can be designed so that it is automatically consistent with any specified initial term structure. Their work has been extended by a number of researchers including Black, Derman and Toy (1990), Dybvig (1988), and Milne and Turnbull (1989). Heath, Jarrow and Morton (1987) present a general multi-factor interest rate model that is

**This paper was first published in the* Review of Financial Studies, *Vol. 3 (1990). It is reprinted with the permission of Oxford University Press.*

consistent with the existing term structure of interest rates and any specified volatility structure. Their model provides important theoretical insights, but in its most general form has the disadvantage of being computationally quite time-consuming.

In this paper, we present two one-state-variable models of the short-term interest rate. Both are consistent with both the current term structure of interest rates and the current volatilities of all interest rates. In addition, the volatility of the short-term interest rate can be a function of time. The user of the models can specify either the current volatilities of spot interest rates (which will be referred to as the term structure of spot rate volatilities) or the current volatilities of forward interest rates (which will be referred to as the term structure of forward rate volatilities). The first model is an extension of Vasicek (1977). The second model is an extension of Cox, Ingersoll, and Ross (1985*b*).

The main contribution of this paper is to show how the process followed by the short-term interest rate in the two models can be deduced from the term structure of interest rates and the term structure of spot or forward interest rate volatilities. The parameters of the process can be determined analytically in the case of the extended Vasicek model and numerically in the case of the extended Cox, Ingersoll, and Ross model. Once the short-term interest rate process has been obtained, either model can be used to value any interest rate contingent claim. European bond options can be valued analytically when the extended Vasicek model is used.

The analytical tractability of the extended Vasicek model makes it very appealing as a practical tool. It is therefore of interest to test whether the option prices given by this model are similar to those given by other models. In this paper we compare the extended Vasicek model with the one-factor Cox-Ingersoll-Ross model and with two different two-factor models. The results are encouraging. They suggest that, if two models are fitted to the same term structure of interest rates and the same term structure of interest rate volatilities, the differences between the option prices produced by the models are small.

The rest of this paper is organised as follows. The first section outlines the properties of the Vasicek and Cox-Ingersoll-Ross models. The second and third sections develop extensions of the two models. The fourth section discusses how market data can be used to estimate the unknown functions in the models whilst the fifth section compares the bond option and cap prices calculated using the extended Vasicek model with their true values when interest rates are assumed to follow the one-factor Cox-Ingersoll-Ross model. The sixth section compares bond option prices calculated using the extended Vasicek model with the true prices when interest rates are assumed to follow two different two-factor models. A general summary appears at the end of this paper.

The Vasicek and Cox–Ingersoll–Ross models

A number of authors have proposed one-state-variable models of the term structure in which the short-term interest rate r follows a mean-reverting process of the form

$$dr = a(b - r)\,dt + \sigma r^{\beta}\,dz \tag{1}$$

where a, b, σ and β are positive constants and dz is a Wiener process. In these models, the interest rate r is pulled towards a level b at rate a. Superimposed upon this "pull" is a random term with variance $\sigma^2 r^{2\beta}$ per unit time.

The situations where $\beta = 0$ and $\beta = 0.5$ are of particular interest because they lead to models that are analytically tractable. The $\beta = 0$ case was first considered by Vasicek (1977), who derived an analytical solution for the price of a discount bond. Jamshidian (1989) showed that, for this value of β, it is also possible to derive relatively simple analytical solutions for the prices of European call and put options on both discount bonds and coupon-bearing bonds. One drawback of assuming $\beta = 0$ is that the short-term interest rate, r, can become negative. Cox, Ingersoll, and Ross consider the alternative $\beta = 0.5$. In this case r can, in some circumstances, become zero, but it can never become negative. Cox, Ingersoll, and Ross derive analytical solutions for the prices of both discount bonds and European call options on discount bonds.

It is reasonable to conjecture that in some situations the market's expectations about future interest rates involve time-dependent parameters. In other words, the drift rate and volatility of r may be functions of time as well as being functions of r and other state variables. The time-dependence can arise from the cyclical nature of the economy, expectations concerning the future impact of monetary policies and expected trends in other macroeconomic variables.

In this paper we extend the model in (1) to reflect this time-dependence. We add a time-dependent drift, $\theta(t)$, to the process for r and allow both the reversion rate a and the volatility factor σ to be functions of time. This leads to the following model for r:

$$dr = [\theta(t) + a(t)(b - r)]\,dt + \sigma(t) r^{\beta} dz \tag{2}$$

This can be regarded as a model in which a drift rate, $\theta(t)$, is imposed on a variable that would otherwise tend to revert to a constant level b. Since (2) can be written

$$dr = a(t)\left(\frac{\theta(t)}{a(t)} + b - r\right) dt + \sigma(t) r^{\beta} dz$$

it can also be regarded as a model in which the reversion level is a function, $\theta(t)/a(t) + b$, of time. We will examine the situations where $\beta = 0$ and $\beta = 0.5$. The $\beta = 0$ case is an extension of Vasicek's model; the $\beta = 0.5$ case is an extension of the Cox-Ingersoll-Ross model. We will show that, when appropriate assumptions are made about the market price of interest rate risk, the model can be fitted to the term structure of interest rates and the term structure of spot or forward rate volatilities.

As shown by Dybvig (1988) and Jamshidian (1988), the continuous-time equivalent of the Ho and Lee (1986) model is

$$dr = \theta(t)\,dt + \sigma\,dz$$

This is the particular case of (2) where $\beta = 0$, $a(t) = 0$ and $\sigma(t)$ is constant. If the market price of interest rate risk is a function of time, $\theta(t)$ can be chosen so that the model fits the initial term structure of interest rates. The model has the disadvantage that it incorporates no mean reversion; the instantaneous standard deviations of all spot and forward rates are the same.

The continuous-time equivalent of the Black, Derman and Toy (1990) model can be shown to be

$$d(\log r) = \left(\theta(t) + \frac{\sigma'(t)}{\sigma(t)} \log r\right) dt + \sigma(t)\,dz$$

In this model $\log r$ is mean reverting. The function $\sigma(t)$ is chosen to make the model consistent with the term structure of spot rate volatilities and may not give reasonable values for the future short rate volatility. The model has the disadvantage that neither bond prices nor European bond option prices can be determined analytically.

The extended Vasicek model

Our proposed extension of Vasicek's model is given by (2) with $\beta = 0$:

$$dr = [\theta(t) + a(t)(b - r)]\,dt + \sigma(t)\,dz \tag{3}$$

We will assume that the market price of interest rate risk is a function, $\lambda(t)$, of time that is bounded in any interval $(0, \tau)$.[1] From Cox, Ingersoll, and Ross (1985*a*), this means that the price, f, of any contingent claim dependent on r must satisfy

$$f_t + [\phi(t) - a(t)r]\, f_r + \tfrac{1}{2}\sigma(t)^2 f_{rr} - rf = 0 \tag{4}$$

where

$$\phi(t) = a(t)b + \theta(t) - \lambda(t)\sigma(t)$$

The price of a discount bond that pays off \$1 at time T is the solution to (4) that satisfies the boundary condition f = 1 when t = T. Consider the function

$$f = A(t, T)\,e^{-B(t,T)r} \tag{5}$$

This satisfies (4) and the boundary condition when

$$A_t - \phi(t)AB + \tfrac{1}{2}\sigma(t)^2 AB^2 = 0 \tag{6}$$

and

$$B_t - a(t)B + 1 = 0 \tag{7}$$

with

$$A(T, T) = 1; \quad B(T, T) = 0 \tag{8}$$

It follows that if (6) and (7) are solved subject to the boundary conditions in (8), then equation (5) provides the price of a discount bond maturing at time T. Solving (6) and (7) for the situation where $a(t)$, $\phi(t)$ and $\sigma(t)$ are constant leads to the Vasicek bond-pricing formula:

$$B(t,T) = \frac{(1 - e^{-a(T-t)})}{a}$$

$$A(t,T) = \exp\left(\frac{(B(t,T) - T + t)\left(a\phi - \sigma^2/2\right)}{a^2} - \frac{\sigma^2 B(t,T)^2}{4a}\right)$$

The function $\sigma(t)$ in the extended model should be chosen to reflect the current and future volatilities of the short-term interest rate, r. As shown below, $A(0, T)$ and $B(0, T)$ are defined by $\sigma(0)$, the current term structure of interest rates, and the current term structure of spot or forward interest rate volatilities. The first step in the analysis is therefore to determine $a(t)$, $\phi(t)$, $A(t, T)$ and $B(t, T)$ in terms of $A(0, T)$, $B(0, T)$ and $\sigma(t)$.

Differentiating (6) and (7) with respect to T, we obtain

$$A_{tT} - \phi(t)[A_T B + AB_T] + \tfrac{1}{2}\sigma(t)^2[A_T B^2 + 2ABB_T] = 0 \tag{9}$$

$$B_{tT} - a(t)B_T = 0 \tag{10}$$

Eliminating $a(t)$ from (7) and (10) gives

$$B_t B_T - BB_{tT} + B_T = 0 \tag{11}$$

Eliminating $\phi(t)$ from (6) and (9) yields

$$ABA_{tT} - BA_t A_T - AA_t B_T + \tfrac{1}{2}\sigma(t)^2 A^2 B^2 B_T = 0 \tag{12}$$

The boundary conditions for (11) and (12) are the known values of $A(0, T)$ and $B(0, T)$, $A(T, T) = 1$ and $B(T, T) = 0$. The solutions to (11) and (12) that satisfy these boundary conditions are

$$B(t,T) = \frac{B(0,T) - B(0,t)}{\partial B(0,t)/\partial t} \tag{13}$$

$$\hat{A}(t,T) = \hat{A}(0,T) - \hat{A}(0,t) - B(t,T)\frac{\partial \hat{A}(0,t)}{\partial t} - \frac{1}{2}\left[B(t,T)\frac{\partial B(0,t)}{\partial t}\right]^2 \int_0^t \left[\frac{\sigma(\tau)}{\partial B(0,\tau)/\partial \tau}\right]^2 d\tau \tag{14}$$

where $\hat{A}(t,T) = \log[A(t,T)]$. Substituting into (6) and (7), we obtain

$$a(t) = -\frac{\partial^2 B(0,t)/\partial t^2}{\partial B(0,t)/\partial t} \tag{15}$$

$$\phi(t) = -a(t)\frac{\partial \hat{A}(0,t)}{\partial t} - \frac{\partial^2 \hat{A}(0,t)}{\partial t^2} + \left(\frac{\partial B(0,t)}{\partial t}\right)^2 \int_0^t \left(\frac{\sigma(\tau)}{\partial B(0,\tau)/\partial \tau}\right)^2 d\tau \tag{16}$$

We now move on to discuss option valuation under the extended Vasicek model. Define $P(r, t_1, t_2)$ as the price at time t_1 of a discount bond maturing at time t_2. From the above analysis,

$$P(r, t_1, t_2) = A(t_1, t_2)\, e^{-B(t_1,t_2)r}$$

Using Itô's lemma, the volatility of $P(r, t_1, t_2)$ is $\sigma(t_1)\, B(t_1, t_2)$. Since this is independent of r, the distribution of a bond price at any given time conditional on its price at an earlier time must be lognormal.

Consider a European call option on a discount bond with exercise price X. Suppose that the current time is t, the option expires at time T, and the bond expires at time $s (s \geq T \geq t)$. The call option can be regarded as an option to exchange X units of a discount bond maturing at time T for one unit of a discount bond maturing at time s. Define $\alpha_1(\tau)$ and $\alpha_2(\tau)$ as the volatilities at time τ of the prices of discount bonds maturing at times T and s, respectively, and $\rho(\tau)$ as the instantaneous correlation between the two bond prices. From the lognormal property mentioned above and the results in Merton (1973), it follows that the option price, C, is given by

$$C = P(r,t,s)\, N(h) - X P(r,t,T)\, N(h - \sigma_P) \tag{17}$$

where

$$h = \frac{1}{\sigma_P}\log\frac{P(r,t,s)}{P(r,t,T)X} + \frac{\sigma_P}{2}$$

$$\sigma_P^2 = \int_t^T \left[\alpha_1(\tau)^2 - 2\rho(\tau)\alpha_1(\tau)\alpha_2(\tau) + \alpha_2(\tau)^2\right] d\tau \tag{18}$$

and $N(\cdot)$ is the cumulative normal distribution function. Since we are using a one-factor model, $\rho = 1$. Furthermore,

$$\alpha_1(\tau) = \sigma(\tau)\, B(\tau, s)$$

$$\alpha_2(\tau) = \sigma(\tau)\, B(\tau, T)$$

Hence,

$$\sigma_P^2 = \int_t^T \sigma(\tau)^2\,[B(\tau,s) - B(\tau,T)]^2\,d\tau$$

From (13) this becomes

$$\sigma_P^2 = [B(0,s) - B(0,T)]^2 \int_t^T \left(\frac{\sigma(\tau)}{\partial B(0,\tau)/\partial\tau}\right)^2 d\tau \tag{19}$$

Equations (17) and (19) provide a simple analytical solution for European call option prices. European put option prices can be obtained using put-call parity. In the case where a and σ are constant,

$$B(\tau,s) = \frac{1 - e^{-a(s-\tau)}}{a}$$

$$B(\tau,T) = \frac{1 - e^{-a(T-\tau)}}{a}$$

and (19) becomes

$$\sigma_P = v(t,T)\,\frac{1 - e^{-a(s-T)}}{a}$$

where

$$v(t,T)^2 = \frac{\sigma^2\left(1 - e^{-2a(T-t)}\right)}{2a}$$

This is the result in Jamshidian (1989). It is interesting to note that Jamshidian's result does not depend on $\theta(t)$ and $\lambda(t)$ being constant.

To value European options on coupon-bearing bonds, we note (similarly to Jamshidian (1989)) that, since all bond prices are decreasing functions of r, an option on a portfolio of discount bonds is equivalent to a portfolio of options on the discount bonds with appropriate exercise prices.[2] Consider a European call option with exercise price X and maturity T on a coupon-bearing bond that pays off c_i at a time $s_i > T (1 \le i \le n)$. The option will be exercised when $r(T) < r^*$, where r^* is the solution to

$$\sum_{i=1}^{n} c_i P(r^*, T, s_i) = X$$

The payoff from the option is

$$\max\left[0, \sum_{i=1}^{n} c_i P(r, T, s_i) - X\right]$$

This is the same as

$$\sum_{i=1}^{n} c_i \max\left[0, P(r, T, s_i) - X_i\right]$$

where

$$X_i = P(r^*, T, s_i)$$

The option on the coupon-bearing bond is therefore the sum of n options on discount bonds with the exercise price of the ith option being X_i.

American bond options and other interest rate contingent claims can be valued by first calculating $a(t)$ and $\phi(t)$ from (15) and (16) and then using numerical procedures to solve the differential equation in (4) subject to the appropriate boundary conditions. One approach that can be used is described in Hull and White (1990).

The extended Cox–Ingersoll–Ross model

Our proposed extension of the Cox-Ingersoll-Ross model is given by (2) with $\beta = 0.5$:

$$dr = [\theta(t) + a(t)(b - r)]dt + \sigma(t)\sqrt{r}dz$$

We assume that the market price of interest rate risk is $\lambda(t)\sqrt{r}\,dz$ for some function λ of time that is bounded in any interval $(0, \tau)$.[3]

The differential equation that must be satisfied by the price, f, of any claim contingent on r is

$$f_t + [\phi(t) - \psi(t)r]f_r + \tfrac{1}{2}\sigma(t)^2 r f_{rr} - rf = 0 \tag{20}$$

where

$$\phi(t) = a(t)b + \theta(t)$$

and

$$\psi(t) = a(t) + \lambda(t)\sigma(t)$$

Again, we consider the function

$$f = A(t, T)\,e^{-B(t,T)r} \tag{21}$$

This satisfies (20) when

$$A_t - \phi(t)AB = 0 \tag{22}$$

and

$$B_t - \psi(t)B - \tfrac{1}{2}\sigma(t)^2 B^2 + 1 = 0 \tag{23}$$

If A and B are the solutions to the ordinary differential equations (22) and (23) subject to the boundary conditions $A(T, T) = 1$ and $B(T, T) = 0$, equation (21) gives the price at time t of a discount bond maturing at time T. Solving (22) and (23) for the situation where $\phi(t)$, $\psi(t)$ and $\sigma(t)$ are constants leads to the Cox-Ingersoll-Ross bond-pricing formula:

$$B(t, T) = \frac{2(e^{\gamma(T-t)} - 1)}{(\gamma + \psi)(e^{\gamma(T-t)} - 1) + 2\gamma} \tag{24}$$

$$A(t, T) = \left[\frac{2\gamma e^{(\gamma+\psi)(T-t)/2}}{(\gamma + \psi)(e^{\gamma(T-t)} - 1) + 2\gamma}\right]^{2\phi/\sigma^2} \tag{25}$$

where

$$\gamma = \sqrt{\psi^2 + 2\sigma^2}$$

The function $\sigma(t)$ in the extended model should be chosen to reflect the current and future volatilities of the short-term interest rate. As in the case of the extended Vasicek model, $A(0, T)$ and $B(0, T)$ can be determined from $\sigma(0)$, the current term structure of interest rates, and the current term structure of interest rate volatilities. These, together with the conditions $A(T, T) = 1$ and $B(T, T) = 0$, are the boundary conditions for determining $A(t, T)$ and $B(t, T)$ from (22) and (23).

Differentiating (23) with respect to T and eliminating $\psi(t)$, we obtain

$$B_t B_T - BB_{tT} + B_T + \tfrac{1}{2}\sigma(t)^2 B^2 B_T = 0 \tag{26}$$

This equation can be solved using finite-difference methods. The function $\Psi(t)$ can then be obtained from (23). The solution to (22) is

$$A(t,T) = A(0,T)\exp\left[\int_0^t \phi(s)B(s,T)\,ds\right] \tag{27}$$

Since $A(T,T) = 1$, $\phi(t)$ can be obtained iteratively from

$$\int_0^T \phi(s)B(s,T)\,ds = -\log A(0,T)$$

It does not appear to be possible to obtain European option prices analytically except when ϕ, ψ and σ are constant. All option prices must therefore be computed using numerical procedures such as those in Hull and White (1990).

Fitting the models to market data

In order to apply the models, it is necessary to estimate the functions $A(0,T)$ and $B(0,T)$. The appendix derives results showing how the $B(0,T)$ function is related to the term structure of spot and forward rate volatilities. Historical data can be used in conjunction with these results to estimate this function. We can calculate $A(0,T)$ from $B(0,T)$ and the current term structure of interest rates using the bond-pricing equation

$$P(r(0), 0, T) = A(0,T)\,e^{-B(0,T)r(0)}$$

where $r(0)$ is the short-term interest rate at time zero.

An alternative approach to using historical data is to imply $A(0,T)$ and $B(0,T)$ from the term structure of interest rates and the prices of options. Caps are actively traded options that are particularly convenient for this purpose. In the case of the extended Vasicek model they allow $B(0,T)$ to be implied directly in a relatively straightforward way.[4]

An interesting question is whether the functions $A(t,T)$ and $B(t,T)$ estimated at some time τ_1 are the same as those estimated at another time $\tau_2(\tau_1, \tau_2 < t < T)$. In other words, does the same model describe the term structure of interest rates and the term structure of interest rate volatilities at two different times? If it is found that the functions $A(t,T)$ and $B(t,T)$ change significantly over time, it would be tempting to dismiss the model as being a "throw-away" of no practical value. However, this would be a mistake. It is important to distinguish between the goal of developing a model that adequately describes term structure movements and the goal of developing a model that adequately values most of the interest rate contingent claims that are encountered in practice. It is quite possible that a two- or three-state-variable model is necessary to achieve the first goal.[5] Later in this paper we will present evidence supporting the argument that the extended Vasicek one-state-variable model achieves the second goal.

In this context it is useful to draw an analogy between the models used to describe stock price behaviour and our proposed model for interest rates. The usual model of stock price behaviour is the one-factor geometric Brownian motion model. This leads to the Black and Scholes (1973) stock option pricing model, which has stood the test of time and appears to be adequate for most purposes. Since stock price volatilities are in practice stochastic, we cannot claim that a one-factor model perfectly represents stock price behaviour. Indeed, practitioners, when they use the Black–Scholes model, frequently adjust the value of the volatility parameter to reflect current market conditions. The justification for the Black–Scholes model is that, when fitted as well as possible to current market data, it gives similar option prices to more complicated two-state-variable models.[6] Our justification of the one-factor models we have presented here will be similar.[7]

Another interesting issue is whether the choice of the $\sigma(t)$ function affects the shape of the current term structure of interest rate volatilities. Suppose that $R(r, t, T)$ is the yield at time t on a discount bond maturing at time T. Itô's lemma shows that the instantaneous standard deviation of R in the general model of equation (2) is $\sigma(t) r^{\beta} \partial R/\partial r$. In the extended Vasicek model ($\beta = 0$), $\partial R/\partial r$ is independent of $\sigma(t)$. The function $\sigma(t)$ therefore affects the instantaneous standard deviations of all discount yields equally and has no effect on the shape of the term structure of instantaneous standard deviations. When $\beta \neq 0$, the shape of the term structure of instantaneous standard deviations is affected by $\sigma(t)$ to the extent that $\partial R/\partial r$ is affected by the path followed by σ between t and T.[8]

Comparisons of one-factor models

Of the two models proposed in this paper, the extended Vasicek model is particularly attractive because of its analytical tractability. A key question is whether it gives similar prices to other models when $A(0, T)$ and $B(0, T)$ are fitted to the initial term structure of interest rates and the initial term structure of interest rate volatilities, and $\sigma(t)$ is chosen to match the expected future instantaneous standard deviation of the short rate. In this section, we compare the bond option prices and cap prices produced by the extended Vasicek model with those produced by the original one-factor Cox-Ingersoll-Ross model. We also calculate volatilities implied by these prices when Black's model is used.

Assume that ϕ, ψ and σ are the parameters of the Cox-Ingersoll-Ross model and that this model describes the true evolution of the term structure. This means that the $A(0, T)$ and $B(0, T)$ functions that would be estimated for the extended Vasicek model from historical data are

$$A(0,T) = \left[\frac{2\gamma e^{(\gamma+\psi)(T/2)}}{(\gamma+\psi)(e^{\gamma T}-1)+2\gamma} \right]^{2\phi/\sigma^2} \tag{28}$$

$$B(0,T) = \frac{2(e^{\gamma T}-1)}{(\gamma+\psi)(e^{\gamma T}-1)+2\gamma} \tag{29}$$

where $\gamma = \sqrt{\psi^2 + 2\sigma^2}$. The complete A and B functions for the extended Vasicek model can be calculated from $A(0, T)$ and $B(0, T)$ using (13) and (14). Equations (17) and (19) can be used to value European options on discount bonds. The analytical results in Cox, Ingersoll, and Ross (1985*b*) can be used to obtain the true European option prices.

The parameter values chosen were $\sigma = 0.06$, $\phi = 0.02$ and $\psi = 0.2$. The initial short-term interest rate was assumed to be 10% per annum. For the extended Vasicek model, $\sigma(t)$ was set equal to the constant $0.06\sqrt{0.1}$. This ensured that the initial short-term interest rate volatility equalled that in the Cox-Ingersoll-Ross model.

(*a*) BOND OPTIONS

Table 1 shows the prices given by the two models for European call options on a five-year bond that has a face value of $100 and pays a coupon of 10% per annum semi-annually.[9] It can be seen that the models give very similar prices for a range of different exercise prices and maturity dates. The biggest percentage differences are for deep-out-of-the-money options. The extended Vasicek model gives higher prices than Cox-Ingersoll-Ross for these options. This is because very low interest rates (and, therefore, very high bond prices) have a greater chance of occurring in the extended Vasicek model.

Table 1. Prices of call options on a five-year bond with a face value of \$100 and a coupon of 10% per annum paid semi-annually

Option maturity (years)	Model	Exercise price 95.0	97.5	100.0	102.5	105.0
0.5	Ext Vas	4.27 (4.50)	2.30 (4.51)	0.94 (4.51)	0.27 (4.52)	0.05 (4.52)
	CIR	4.30 (4.73)	2.32 (4.63)	0.94 (4.52)	0.25 (4.40)	0.04 (4.28)
1.0	Ext Vas	4.28 (4.05)	2.51 (4.05)	1.23 (4.05)	0.50 (4.06)	0.16 (4.06)
	CIR	4.32 (4.27)	2.54 (4.17)	1.24 (4.06)	0.46 (3.94)	0.13 (3.82)
1.5	Ext Vas	4.20 (3.59)	2.54 (3.59)	1.33 (3.60)	0.59 (3.60)	0.22 (3.60)
	CIR	4.25 (3.81)	2.59 (3.71)	1.33 (3.60)	0.55 (3.49)	0.17 (3.37)
2.0	Ext Vas	4.06 (3.13)	2.48 (3.13)	1.31 (3.14)	0.58 (3.14)	0.22 (3.14)
	CIR	4.12 (3.35)	2.52 (3.25)	1.31 (3.14)	0.54 (3.03)	0.17 (2.91)
3.0	Ext Vas	3.68 (2.18)	2.16 (2.19)	1.05 (2.19)	0.40 (2.19)	0.12 (2.19)
	CIR	3.73 (2.39)	2.21 (2.20)	1.05 (2.19)	0.36 (2.08)	0.08 (1.96)
4.0	Ext Vas	3.31 (1.16)	1.74 (1.16)	0.59 (1.16)	0.11 (1.16)	0.01 (1.16)
	CIR	3.32 (1.34)	1.77 (1.26)	0.60 (1.16)	0.08 (1.05)	0.00 (0.89)

The current short-term interest rate is 10% per annum. Interest rates are assumed to follow the original Cox–Ingersoll–Ross model with $\sigma = 0.06$, $\phi = 0.02$ and $\psi = 0.2$. The extended Vasicek (Ext Vas) model is chosen to fit the initial term structure of interest rates and the initial term structure of interest rate volatilities. Numbers in parentheses are the forward bond price volatilities (% per annum) implied from the option prices when Black's model is used.

Since Black's model is frequently used by practitioners to value bond options, it is interesting to compare it with the two models.[10] The numbers in parentheses in Table 1 are the forward bond price volatilities implied by the option prices when Black's model is used. It will be noted that the implied volatilities decline dramatically as the time to expiration of the option increases. In the limit, when the expiration date of the option equals the maturity date of the bond, the implied volatility is zero. For the extended Vasicek model, implied volatilities are roughly constant across different exercise prices. This is because the bond price distributions are approximately lognormal.[11] Under the Cox-Ingersoll-Ross model, the implied volatilities are a decreasing function of the exercise price. If the same volatility is used in Black's model for all bond options with a certain expiration date, there will be a tendency under a Cox-Ingersoll-Ross type economy for in-the-money options to be underpriced and out-of-the-money options to be overpriced.

(*b*) INTEREST RATE CAPS

Consider an option that caps the interest rate on \$1 at R_x between times t_1 and t_2. The payoff from the option at time t_2 is

$$\Delta t \max(R - R_x, 0)$$

where $\Delta t = t_2 - t_1$ and R is the actual interest rate at time t_1 for the time period (t_1, t_2). (Both R and R_x are assumed to be compounded once during the time period.)

The discounted value of this payoff is equivalent to

$$(1+R_x\Delta t)\max\left(\frac{1}{1+R_x\Delta t}-\frac{1}{1+R\Delta t}, 0\right)$$

at time t_1. Since $1/(1 + R\Delta t)$ is the value at time t_1 of a bond maturing at time t_2, this expression shows that the option can be regarded as $1 + R_x\Delta t$ European puts with exercise price $1/(1 + R_x\Delta t)$ and expiration date t_1 on a \$1 face value discount bond maturing at time t_2. More generally, an interest rate cap is a portfolio of European puts on discount bonds.

Table 2 shows the prices given by the two models for caps on the risk-free interest rate when the principal is \$100. Again we see that the prices are very close for a range of different cap rates and maturities. The percentage differences between the prices are greatest for deep-out-of-the-money caps. The Cox-Ingersoll-Ross model gives higher

Table 2. Price of caps on the risk-free interest rate when the principal is $100, interest payments are made every 6 months, and the cap rate is compounded semi-annually

Life of cap (years)	Model	Cap rate (% per annum) 8.0	9.0	10.0	11.0	12.0
1.0	Ext Vas	2.10 (19.68)	1.21 (18.63)	0.41 (17.73)	0.10 (16.94)	0.02 (16.24)
	CIR	2.09 (18.56)	1.20 (18.11)	0.41 (17.72)	0.10 (17.36)	0.03 (17.04)
2.0	Ext Vas	4.05 (18.42)	2.47 (17.59)	1.13 (16.81)	0.45 (16.04)	0.16 (15.27)
	CIR	4.03 (17.30)	2.45 (17.08)	1.13 (16.80)	0.47 (16.46)	0.19 (16.07)
3.0	Ext Vas	5.86 (17.42)	3.70 (16.70)	1.89 (15.99)	0.87 (15.25)	0.37 (14.48)
	CIR	5.82 (16.32)	3.66 (16.20)	1.89 (16.00)	0.91 (15.66)	0.43 (15.26)
4.0	Ext Vas	7.52 (16.57)	4.85 (15.92)	2.62 (15.28)	1.30 (14.56)	0.61 (13.79)
	CIR	7.44 (15.49)	4.79 (15.44)	2.63 (15.28)	1.36 (14.97)	0.69 (14.56)
5.0	Ext Vas	9.03 (15.82)	5.90 (15.24)	3.31 (14.64)	1.72 (13.95)	0.84 (13.19)
	CIR	8.92 (14.76)	5.83 (14.77)	3.32 (14.65)	1.80 (14.36)	0.95 (13.95)

The current short-term interest rate is 10% per annum. Interest rates are assumed to follow the original Cox–Ingersoll–Ross model with $\sigma = 0.06$, $\phi = 0.02$ and $\psi = 0.2$. The extended Vasicek (Ext Vas) model is chosen to fit the initial term structure of interest rates and the initial term structure of interest rate volatilities. The numbers in parentheses are the forward rate volatilities implied by the cap prices when Black's model is used. The same volatility is applied to all forward interest rates for the purpose of the calculations underlying this table.

prices than the extended Vasicek model for these caps. This is because very high interest rates have a greater chance of occurring under the Cox–Ingersoll–Ross model.

Practitioners frequently use Black's (1976) model for valuing caps. The numbers in parentheses in Table 2 show the forward rate volatilities implied by the cap prices when Black's model is used. It can be seen that the implied volatilities decrease as the life of the cap increases for both the extended Vasicek and Cox–Ingersoll–Ross models. This is a reflection of the fact that the mean reversion of interest rates causes the volatility of a forward rate to decrease as the maturity of the forward contract increases. Implied volatilities also decrease as the cap rate increases for both models. This means that, if the same volatility is used for all caps with a certain life, there will be a tendency for Black's model to underprice in-the-money caps and overprice out-of-the-money caps.

Comparison with two-factor models

In this section we test how well the extended Vasicek model can duplicate the bond option prices given by a two-factor model. We consider two different models. The first is a two-factor Vasicek model where the risk-neutral process for r is

$$r = x_1 + x_2, \quad dx_i = (\phi_i - a_i x_i)\,dt + \sigma_i\,dz_i \quad (i = 1, 2) \tag{30}$$

We choose $\phi_2 = a_2 = 0$. This means that σ_2 equals the long-term rate's instantaneous standard deviation. The second model is a two-factor Cox–Ingersoll–Ross model where the risk-neutral process for r is

$$r = x_1 + x_2, \quad dx_i = (\phi_i - \psi_i x_i)\,dt + \sigma_i \sqrt{x_i}\,dz_i \quad (i = 1, 2) \tag{31}$$

These types of models were analysed by Langetieg (1980). In both cases we assume zero correlation between dz_1 and dz_2.

Discount bond prices for both models are given by

$$P(r, t, T) = P_1(x_1, t, T)\,P_2(x_2, t, T)$$

where

$$P_i(x_i, t, T) = A_i(t, T)\,e^{-B_i(t,T)x_i}$$

denotes the price of a bond under the corresponding constant parameter one-factor

Table 3. Values of European call options on a five-year discount bond with a face value of $100

Option maturity (years)	Model	0.96	0.98	Exercise price 1.00	1.02	1.04
1.0	Ext Vas	2.80	1.93	1.24	0.74	0.40
	Two-factor Vas	2.80	1.93	1.24	0.73	0.40
2.0	Ext Vas	2.86	2.00	1.32	0.81	0.46
	Two-factor Vas	2.85	1.99	1.31	0.80	0.46
3.0	Ext Vas	2.69	1.79	1.08	0.59	0.29
	Two-factor Vas	2.69	1.78	1.07	0.58	0.28
4.0	Ext Vas	2.47	1.41	0.63	0.20	0.04
	Two-factor Vas	2.47	1.40	0.62	0.20	0.04

Interest rates are assumed to follow the two-factor Vasicek model described by equation (30). The parameter values are $\phi_1 = 0.005$, $a_1 = 0.1$, $\sigma_1 = 0.01$, $\sigma_2 = 0.01$, $\phi_2 = 0$, $a_2 = 0$, and the initial values of both x_1 and x_2 are 0.05. The extended Vasicek (Ext Vas) model is chosen to fit the initial term structure of interest rates and the initial term structure of interest rate volatilities. The exercise price is expressed as a proportion of the forward bond price.

model when the short-term rate is x_i. When the extended Vasicek model is fitted to the two-factor Vasicek model,

$$\sigma(0) = \sqrt{\sigma_1^2 + \sigma_2^2}$$

and

$$\sigma(0)B(0,T) = \sqrt{\sigma_1^2 B_1(0,T)^2 + \sigma_2^2 B_2(0,T)^2}$$

When it is fitted to the two-factor Cox-Ingersoll-Ross model,

$$\sigma(0) = \sqrt{\sigma_1^2 x_1 + \sigma_2^2 x_2}$$

and

$$\sigma(0)B(0,T) = \sqrt{\sigma_1^2 x_1 B_1(0,T)^2 + \sigma_2^2 x_2 B_2(0,T)^2}$$

In both cases the prices of European call options on discount bonds can be calculated using (17) and (19). We assume that $\sigma(t)$ is constant.

For the two-factor Vasicek model the prices of a European call options on discount bonds are given by (17) with[12]

$$\sigma_P^2 = \left(v_1(t,T)\frac{1-e^{-a_1(s-T)}}{a_1}\right)^2 + \left(v_2(t,T)\frac{1-e^{-a_2(s-T)}}{a_2}\right)^2$$

where

$$v_i(t,T)^2 = \frac{\sigma_i^2\left(1-e^{-2a_i(T-t)}\right)}{2a_i} \quad (i=1,2)$$

To compute option prices under the two-factor Cox-Ingersoll-Ross model, we used Monte Carlo simulation in conjunction with the antithetic variable technique. Each price was based on a total of 40,000 runs and the maximum standard error was 0.0043.

The results are shown in Tables 3 and 4. The extended Vasicek model produces prices that are very close to those of the other models. Other tests similar to those reported here have been carried out. In all cases we find that the extended Vasicek model provides a good analytical approximation to other more complicated models.

Table 4. Values of European call options on a five-year discount bond with a face value of $100

Option maturity (years)	Model	Exercise price 0.96	0.98	1.00	1.02	1.04
1.0	Ext Vas	2.54	1.55	0.81	0.35	0.12
	Two-factor CIR	2.55	1.56	0.81	0.34	0.11
2.0	Ext Vas	2.56	1.60	0.87	0.40	0.15
	Two-factor CIR	2.58	1.61	0.86	0.38	0.13
3.0	Ext Vas	2.49	1.47	0.71	0.27	0.08
	Two-factor CIR	2.51	1.48	0.70	0.24	0.06
4.0	Ext Vas	2.43	1.27	0.41	0.06	0.00
	Two-factor CIR	2.44	1.28	0.40	0.05	0.00

Interest rates are assumed to follow the two-factor Cox–Ingersoll–Ross model described by equation (31). The parameter values are $\phi_1 = 0.05$, $\phi_2 = 0.05$, $\sigma_1 = 0.03$, $\sigma_2 = 0.03$, $\psi_1 = 0.1$, $\psi_2 = 0.001$, and the initial values of both x_1 and x_2 are 0.05. The extended Vasicek (Ext Vas) model is chosen to fit the initial term structure of interest rates and the initial term structure of interest rate volatilities. The exercise price is expressed as a proportion of the forward bond price.

Conclusions

This paper has shown that the Vasicek and Cox-Ingersoll-Ross interest rate models can be extended so that they are consistent with both the current term structure of spot or forward interest rates and the current term structure of interest rate volatilities. In the case of the extension to Vasicek's model, the parameters of the process followed by the short-term interest rate and European bond option prices can be determined analytically. This makes the model very attractive as a practical tool.

The extended Vasicek model can be compared to another interest rate model by fitting it to the initial term structure of interest rates, the initial term structure of interest rate volatilities and the expected future instantaneous standard deviation of short rate volatilities given by the other model, and then testing to see whether the interest rate option prices it gives are significantly different from those of the other model. We have tested it against a variety of different one- and two-factor models in this way. Our conclusion is that it provides a good analytical approximation to the European option prices given by these other models.

Appendix

In this appendix we derive the relationship between $B(t, T)$ and the current term structure of spot rate and forward rate volatilities. As is the usual convention, the term "volatility" will be used to refer to the standard deviation of proportional changes, not actual changes, in the value of a variable.

Define

$P(r, t, T)$: price at time t of a discount bond maturing at time T;

$R(r, t, T)$: continuously compounded interest rate at time t applicable to period (t, T);

$F(r, t, T_1, T_2)$: instantaneous forward rate at time t corresponding to the time period (T_1, T_2);

$\sigma_r(r, t)$: volatility of r at time t;

$\sigma_R(r, t, T)$: volatility of $R(r, t, T)$;

$\sigma_F(r, t, T_1, T_2)$: volatility of $F(r, t, T_1, T_2)$.

In both models, P has the functional form

$$P(r, t, T) = A(t, T)\, e^{-B(t,T)r} \qquad \text{(A1)}$$

Since

$$R(r,t,T) = -\frac{1}{T-t}\ln P(r,t,T)$$

it follows that

$$R(r,t,T) = -\frac{1}{T-t}\left[\ln A(t,T) - rB(t,T)\right]$$

and

$$\frac{\partial R(r,t,T)}{\partial r} = \frac{B(t,T)}{T-t}$$

From Itô's lemma,

$$R(r,t,T)\,\sigma_R(r,t,T) = r\sigma_r(r,t)\frac{\partial R(r,t,T)}{\partial r}$$

Hence,

$$B(t,T) = \frac{R(r,t,T)\,\sigma_R(r,t,T)(T-t)}{r\sigma_r(r,t)} \tag{A2}$$

The forward rate F is related to spot rates by

$$F(r,t,T_1,T_2) = \frac{R(r,t,T_2)(T_2-t) - R(r,t,T_1)(T_1-t)}{T_2-T_1}$$

Since $R(r,t,T_1)$ and $R(r,t,T_2)$ are instantaneously perfectly correlated in a one-state-variable model, it follows from (A2) that

$$F(r,t,T_1,T_2)\,\sigma_F(r,t,T_1,T_2) = \frac{B(t,T_2) - B(t,T_1)}{T_2-T_1}\,r\sigma_r(r,t)$$

or

$$B(t,T_2) - B(t,T_1) = \frac{F(r,t,T_1,T_2)\,\sigma_F(r,t,T_1,T_2)(T_2-T_1)}{r\sigma_r(r,t)} \tag{A3}$$

Equation (A2) enables $B(0,T)$ to be determined for all T from the current term structure of spot rate volatilities. Equation (A3) enables $B(0,T)$ to be determined from the current term structure of forward rate volatilities. $A(0,T)$ can be determined from $B(0,T)$ and the current term structure of interest rates using (A1). Thus, $A(0,T)$ and $B(0,T)$ can be determined for all T from the current term structure of interest rates and the current term structure of spot rate or forward rate volatilities.

1 *This corresponds to the assumption made by Vasicek. In fact, the same final model is obtained if the market price of interest rate risk is set equal to* $\lambda(t)r$ *or even if it is set equal to* $\lambda_1(t) + \lambda_2(t)r$. *If* $\chi(r,t)$ *is the market price of risk, Girsanov's theorem shows that, for no arbitrage, the condition* $E[\exp(\frac{1}{2}\int_0^T \chi^2 ds)] < \infty$ *must hold. Duffie (1988: p. 229) provides a discussion of this. The function* $\chi(r,t) = \lambda_1(t) + \lambda_2(t)r$ *presents no problems as far as this condition is concerned if we assume* $\lambda_1(t)$ *and* $\lambda_2(t)$ *are always bounded in any interval* $(0,\tau)$.

2 *This argument can be used to value options on coupon-bearing bonds in other one-state-variable models. Later in this paper we will use it in conjunction with the Cox-Ingersoll-Ross model.*

3 *This corresponds to the assumption made by the Cox-Ingersoll-Ross model. It is interesting to note that a market price of risk equal to* $\lambda(t)/\sqrt{r}$ *appears to give rise to the same final model as* $\lambda(t)\sqrt{r}$. *However, it violates the no-arbitrage condition referred to in footnote 1.*

4 *As will be explained later, a cap is a portfolio of European put options on discount bonds. A matrix of cap prices can be used in conjunction with equations (17) and (19) and put-call parity to obtain best-fit values for points on the* $B(0, T)$ *function.*

5 *In fact, empirical research in Dybvig (1988) shows that a one-factor Vasicek-type model provides a surprisingly good fit to observed term structure movements.*

6 *See Hull and White (1987) for a comparison of Black-Scholes with a two-factor stock option pricing model that incorporates stochastic volatility.*

7 *When using Black-Scholes, practitioners monitor their exposure to changes in the volatility parameter even though the model assumes that the parameter is constant. Similarly, when using the models suggested here, practitioners should monitor their exposure to (a) all possible shifts in the term structure of interest rates (not just those that are consistent with the model) and (b) all possible shifts in the term structure of volatilities.*

8 *In most circumstances we can expect* $\partial R/\partial r$ *to be relatively insensitive to the path followed by* $\sigma(t)$.

9 *For both models, the bond option was decomposed into discount bond options using the approach described in second section of this paper.*

10 *Black's model assumes that forward bond prices are lognormal. In the case of options on discount bonds, it is equivalent to the extended Vasicek model, but does not provide a framework within which the volatilities of different forward bond prices can be related to each other.*

11 *For a discount bond, the bond price distribution is exactly lognormal. For a coupon-bearing bond, it is the sum of lognormal distributions.*

12 *Note that an option on a coupon-bearing bond cannot be decomposed into a portfolio of options on discount bonds in the case of the two-factor models considered here.*

Bibliography

Black, F., 1976, "The Pricing of Commodity Contracts", *Journal of Financial Economics*, 3, pp. 167-179.

Black, F., E. Derman, and W. Toy, 1990, "A One-Factor Model of Interest Rates and its Application to Treasury Bond Options", *Financial Analysts Journal*, Jan-Feb 1990, pp. 33-39.

Black, F., and M. Scholes, 1973, "The Pricing of Options and Corporate liabilities", *Journal of Political Economy*, 81, pp. 637-659; reprinted as Chapter 1 of the present volume.

Brennan, M. J., and E. S. Schwartz, 1979, "A Continuous Time Approach to the Pricing of Bonds", *Journal of Banking and Finance*, 3, pp. 133-155; reprinted as Chapter 5 of the present volume.

Brennan, M. J., and E. S. Schwartz, 1982, "An Equilibrium Model of Bond Pricing and a Test of Market Efficiency", *Journal of Financial and Quantitative Analysis*, 17, pp. 301-329.

Courtadon, G., 1982, "The Pricing of Options on Default-Free Bonds", *Journal of Financial and Quantitative Analysis*, 17, pp. 75-100.

Cox, J. C., J. E. Ingersoll, and S. A. Ross, 1985*a*, "An Intertemporal General Equilibrium Model of Asset Prices", *Econometrica*, 53, pp. 363-384.

Cox, J. C., J. E. Ingersoll, and S. A. Ross, 1985*b*, "A Theory of the Term Structure of Interest Rates", *Econometrica*, 53, pp. 385-467; reprinted as Chapter 6 of the present volume.

Dothan, L. U., 1978, "On the Term Structure of Interest Rates", *Journal of Financial Economics*, 6, pp. 59-69.

Duffie, D., 1988, Security Markets: Stochastic Models. Boston: Academic Press.

Dybvig, P. H., 1988, "Bond and Bond Option Pricing based on the Current Term Structure", Working Paper, Olin School of Business, University of Washington.

Heath, D., R. Jarrow, and A. Morton, 1992, "Bond Pricing and the Term Structure of Interest Rates: A New Methodology for Contingent Claims Valuation", *Econometrica*, 60, pp. 77-105; reprinted as Chapter 14 of the present volume.

Ho, T. S. Y., and S.-B. Lee, 1986, "Term Structure Movements and Pricing of Interest Rate Claims", *Journal of Finance*, 41, pp. 1011-1029; reprinted as Chapter 13 of the present volume.

Hull, J., and A. White, 1987, "The Pricing of Options on Assets with Stochastic Volatilities", *Journal of Finance*, 42, pp. 281-300.

Hull, J., and A. White, 1990, "Valuing Derivative Securities using the Explicit Finite difference Method", *Journal of Financial and Quantitative Analysis*, 25, pp. 87-100.

Jamshidian, F., 1988, "The One-Factor Gaussian Interest Rate Model: Theory and Implementation", Working Paper, Financial Strategies Group, Merrill Lynch Capital Markets, New York.

Jamshidian, F., 1989, "An Exact Bond Option Formula", *Journal of Finance*, 44, pp. 205-209; reprinted as Chapter 8 of the present volume.

Langetieg, T. C., 1980, "A Multivariate Model of the Term Structure", *Journal of Finance*, 35, pp. 71-97.

Longstaff, F. A., 1989, "A Nonlinear General Equilibrium Model of the Term Structure of Interest Rates", *Journal of Financial Economics*, 23, pp. 195-224.

Merton, R. C., 1973, "Theory of Rational Option Pricing", *Bell Journal of Economics and Management Science*, 4, pp. 141-183.

Milne, F., and S. Turnbull, 1989, "A Simple Approach to Interest Rate Option Pricing", Working Paper, Australian National University.

Richard, S., 1979, "An Arbitrage Model of the Term Structure of Interest Rates", *Journal of Financial Economics*, 6, pp. 33-57.

Vasicek, O. A., 1977, "An Equilibrium Characterization of the Term Structure", *Journal of Financial Economics*, 5, pp. 177-188; reprinted as Chapter 4 of the present volume.

10

A One-Factor Model of Interest Rates and its Application to Treasury Bond Options*

Fischer Black,† Emanuel Derman and William Toy
Goldman Sachs

In one simple and versatile model of interest rates, all security prices and rates depend on only one factor – the short rate. The current structure of long rates and their estimated volatilities are used to construct a tree of possible future short rates. This tree can then be used to value interest-rate-sensitive securities.

For example, a two-year, zero-coupon bond has a known price at the end of the second year, no matter what short rate prevails. Its possible prices after one year can be obtained by discounting the expected two-year price by the possible short rates one year out. An iterative process is used to find the rates that will be consistent with the current market term structure. The price today is then determined by discounting the one-year price (in a binomial tree, the average of the two possible one-year prices) by the current short rate.

Given a market term structure and resulting tree of short rates, the model can be used to value a bond option. First the future prices of a Treasury bond at various points in time are found. These prices are used to determine the option's value at expiration. Given the values of a call or put at expiration, their possible values before expiration can be found by the same discounting procedure used to value the bond. The model can also be used to determine option hedge ratios.

This article describes a model of interest rates that can be used to value any interest-rate-sensitive security. In explaining how it works, we concentrate on valuing options on Treasury bonds.

The model has three key features.

1. Its fundamental variable is the short rate – the annualised one-period interest rate. The short rate is the one factor of the model; its changes drive all security prices.

2. The model takes as inputs an array of long rates (yields on zero-coupon Treasury bonds) for various maturities and an array of yield volatilities for the same bonds. We

**This paper was first published in the* Financial Analysts Journal, *January/February (1990).*
†Fischer Black died in August 1995. Fischer Black, January 11, 1938–August 30, 1995.

call the first array the *yield curve* and the second the *volatility curve*. Together these curves form the *term structure*.

3. The model varies an array of means and an array of volatilities for the future short rate to match the inputs. As the future volatility changes, the future mean reversion changes.

We examine how the model works in an imaginary world in which changes in all bond yields are perfectly correlated; expected returns on all securities over one period are equal; short rates at any time are lognormally distributed; and there are no taxes or trading costs.

Valuing securities

Suppose we own an interest-rate-sensitive security worth S today. We assume that its price can move up to S_u or down to S_d with equal probability over the next time period. Figure 1 shows the possible changes in S for a one-year time step, starting from a state where the short rate is r.

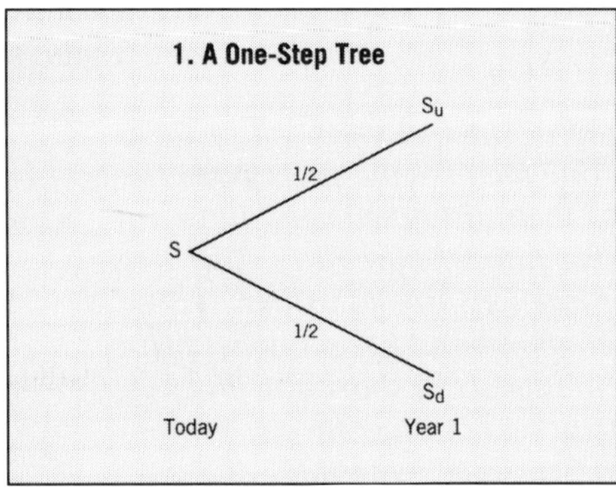

The expected price of S one year from now is $\frac{1}{2}(S_u + S_d)$. The expected return is $\frac{1}{2}(S_u + S_d)/S$. Because we assume that all expected returns are equal, and because we can lend money at r, we deduce:

$$S = \frac{\frac{1}{2}S_u + \frac{1}{2}S_d}{1+r} \tag{1}$$

where r is today's short rate.

Getting today's prices from future prices

We can use the one-step tree to relate today's price to the prices one step away. Similarly, we can derive prices one step in the future from prices two steps in the future. In this way, we can relate today's prices to prices two steps away.

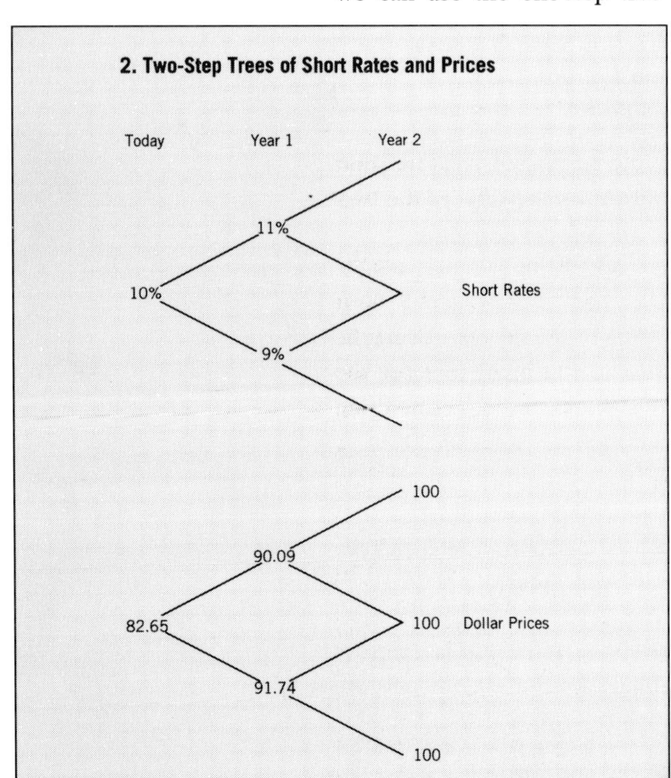

Figure 2 shows two-step trees for rates and prices. The short rate starts out at 10%. We expect it to rise to 11% or drop to 9% with equal probability.

The second tree shows prices for a two-year, zero-coupon Treasury. In two years, the zero's price will be \$100. Its price one year from now may be \$91.74 (\$100 discounted by 9%) or \$90.09 (\$100 discounted by 11%). The expected price one year from now is the average of \$90.09 and \$91.74, or \$90.92. Our valuation formula, Equation (1), finds today's price by discounting this average by 10% to give \$82.65.

We can in this way value a zero of any maturity, provided our tree of future short rates goes out far enough. We simply start with the security's face value at maturity and find the price at each earlier node by discounting future prices using the valuation formula and the short rate at that node. Eventually we work back to the root of the tree and find the price today.

Finding short rates from the term structure

The term structure of interest rates is quoted in yields, rather than prices. Today's annual yield, y, of the N-year zero in terms of its price, S, is given by the y that satisfies:

$$S = \frac{100}{(1+y)^N} \qquad (2)$$

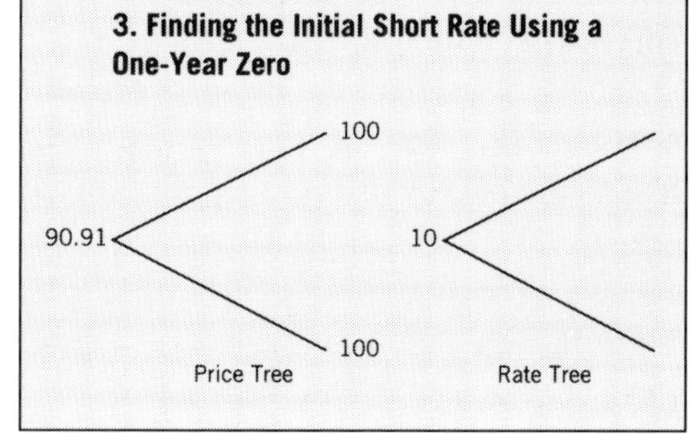

Similarly, the yields y_u and y_d one year from now corresponding to prices S_u and S_d are given by:

$$S_{u,d} = \frac{100}{(1+y_{u,d})^{N-1}} \qquad (3)$$

We want to find the short rates that assure that the model's term structure matches today's market term structure. Table 1 gives the assumed market term structure.

The price of a zero today is the expected price one period in the future discounted to today using the short rate. The short rate, r, is 10%. Using the price tree of Figure 3, we see that $S_u = S_d = 100$, and $S = 90.91$:

$$90.91 = \frac{\frac{1}{2}(100) + \frac{1}{2}(100)}{1+r} = \frac{100}{1+r}$$

Short rates one period in the future

We can now find the short rates one year from now by looking at the yield and volatility for a two-year zero using the term structure of Table 1.

Table 1. A Sample Term Structure

Maturity (years)	Yield (%)	Yield Volatility (%)
1	10	20
2	11	19
3	12	18
4	12.5	17
5	13	16

Look at the two-year short-rate tree in Figure 4. Let's call the unknown future short rates r_u and r_d. We want their values to be such that the price and volatility of the two-year zero match the price and volatility in Table 1.

We know today's short rate is 10%. Suppose we guess that $r_u = 14.32$ and $r_d = 9.79$. Now look at the price and yield trees in Figure 4. A two-year zero has a price of $100 at all nodes at the end of the second period, no matter what short rate prevails. Using the valuation formula - Equation (1) - we can find the one-year prices by discounting the expected two-year price by r_u and r_d; we get prices of $87.47 and $91.08. Using

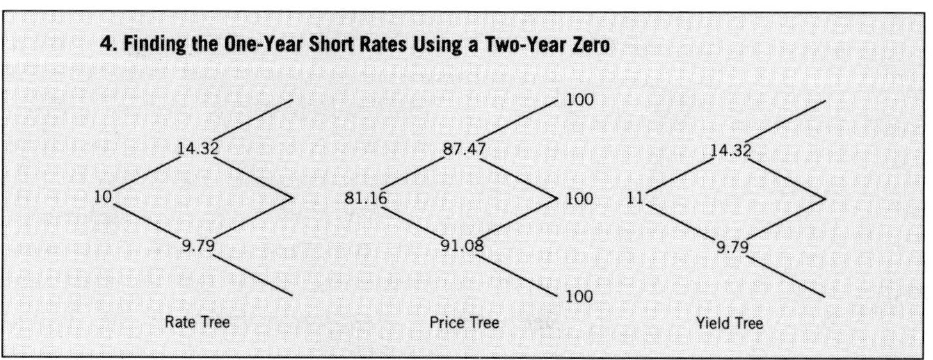

Equation (3), we find that yields of 14.32 and 9.79% correspond to these prices. These are shown on the yield tree in Figure 4.

Now that we have the two-year prices and yields one year out, we can use the valuation formula to get today's price and yield for the two-year zero. Today's price is given by Equation (1) by discounting the expected one-year-out price by today's short rate:

$$\frac{\frac{1}{2}(87.47)+\frac{1}{2}(91.08)}{1.1}=81.16$$

We can get today's yield for the two-year zero, y_2, by using Equation (2) with today's price as S. As the yield tree in Figure 4 shows, y_2 is 11%.

The volatility of this two-year yield is defined as the natural logarithm of the ratio of the one-year yields:

$$\sigma_2=\frac{\ln(14.32/9.79)}{2}=19\%$$

With the one-year short rates we have chosen, the two-year zero's yield and yield volatility match those in the term structure of Table 1. This means that our guesses for r_u and r_d were right. Had they been wrong, we would have found the correct ones by trial and error.

So an initial short rate of 10% followed by equally probable one-year short rates of 14.32 and 9.79% guarantee that our model matches the first two years of the term structure.

More distant short rates

We found today's single short rate by matching the one-year yield. We found the two one-year short rates by matching the two-year yield and volatility. Now we find the short rates two years out.

Figure 5 shows the short rates out to two years. We already know the short out to one year. The three unknown short rates at the end of the second year are r_{uu}, r_{ud} and r_{dd}.

The values for these three short rates should let our model match the yield and yield volatility of a three-year zero. We must therefore match two quantities by guessing at three short rates. This contrasts with finding the one-year short rates, where we had to match two quantities with two short rates. As a rule, matching two quantities with two short rates is unique; there is only one set of values for the short rates that produces the right match. Matching two quantities with three short rates is not unique; many sets of three short rates produce the correct yield and volatility.

Remember, however, that our model assumes that the short rate is lognormal with a volatility (of the log of the short rate) that depends only on time. One year in the future, when the short rate is 14.32%, the volatility is $\frac{1}{2}\ln(r_{uu}/r_{ud})$; when the short rate is 9.79%, the volatility is $\frac{1}{2}\ln(r_{ud}/r_{dd})$. Because these volatilities must be the same, we know that $r_{uu}/r_{ud}=r_{ud}/r_{dd}$, or $r_{ud}^2=r_{uu}r_{dd}$.

So we do not really make three independent guesses for the rates; the middle one, r_{ud}, can be found from the other two. This means we have to match only two short rates - r_{uu} and r_{dd} - with two quantities - the three-year yield and volatility in the model. This typically has a unique solution.

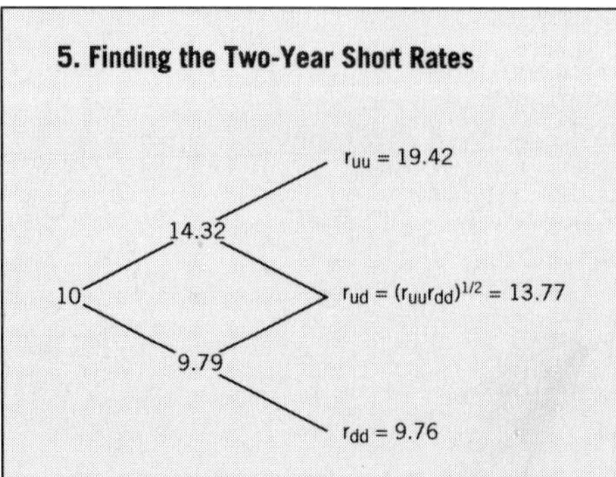

5. Finding the Two-Year Short Rates

In this case, Figure 5 shows that values for r_{uu}, r_{dd} and r_{ud} of 19.42, 9.76 and 13.77%, respectively, produce a three-year yield of 12% and volatility of 18%, as Table 1 calls for.

We now know the short rates for one and two years in the future. Using a similar process, we can find the short rates on tree nodes farther in the future. Figure 6 displays the full tree of short rates at one-year intervals that matches the term structure of Table 1.

Valuing options on Treasury bonds

Given the term structure of Table 1 and the resulting tree of short rates shown in Figure 6, we can use the model to value a bond option.

Coupon bonds as collections of zeroes

Before we can value Treasury bond options, we need to find the future prices of a Treasury bond at various nodes on the tree. Consider a Treasury with a 10% coupon, a face value of $100 and three years left to maturity. For convenience, consider this 10% Treasury as a portfolio of three zero-coupon bonds - a one-year zero with $10 face value; a two-year zero with a $10 face value; and a three-year zero with a $110 face value.

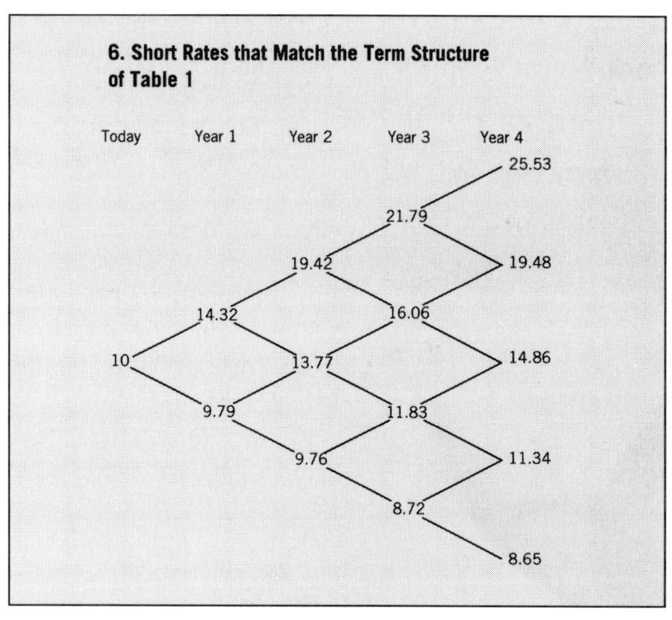

6. Short Rates that Match the Term Structure of Table 1

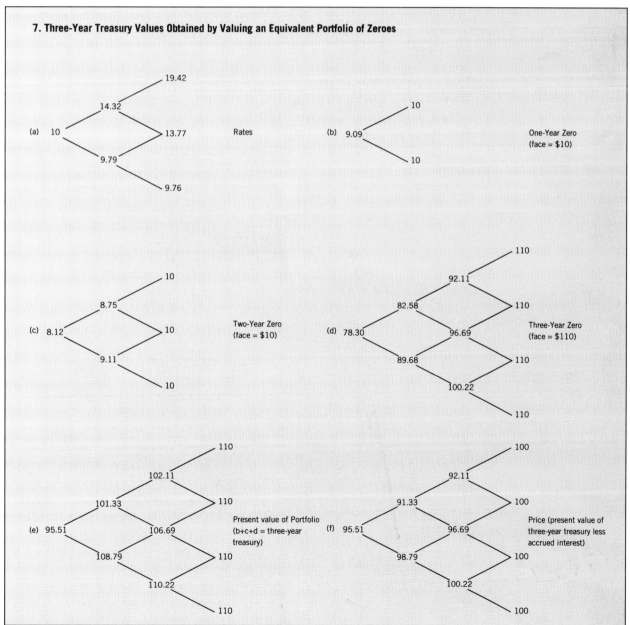

7. Three-Year Treasury Values Obtained by Valuing an Equivalent Portfolio of Zeroes

(a) 10; 14.32, 9.79; 19.42, 13.77, 9.76 — Rates

(b) 9.09; 10, 10 — One-Year Zero (face = $10)

(c) 8.12; 8.75, 9.11; 10, 10, 10 — Two-Year Zero (face = $10)

(d) 78.30; 82.58, 89.68; 92.11, 96.69, 100.22; 110, 110, 110, 110 — Three-Year Zero (face = $110)

(e) 95.51; 101.33, 108.79; 102.11, 106.69, 110.22; 110, 110, 110, 110 — Present value of Portfolio (b+c+d = three-year treasury)

(f) 95.51; 91.33, 98.79; 92.11, 96.69, 100.22; 100, 100, 100, 100 — Price (present value of three-year treasury less accrued interest)

This portfolio has exactly the same annual payoffs as the 10% Treasury with three years to maturity. So the portfolio and the Treasury should have the same value. The tree in Figure 6 was built to value all zeroes according to today's yield curve, hence we can use it to value the three zeroes in the portfolio above.

Panel (*e*) of Figure 7 shows the price of the 10% Treasury as the sum of the present values of the zeroes - $95.51. The tree in panel (*f*) gives the three-year Treasury prices obtained after subtracting $10 of accrued interest on each coupon date.

Puts and calls on Treasuries

We found a price of $95.51 for a three-year, 10% Treasury. The security is below par today; it has a 10% coupon, and yields in today's yield curve are generally higher than 10%.

We want to value options on this security - a two-year European call and a two-year European put, both struck at $95. From Figure 7(*e*) we see that in two years the three-year Treasury bond may have one of three prices - $110.22, $106.69 or $102.11. The corresponding prices without accrued interest are $100.22, $96.69 and $92.11.

At expiration, the $95 call is in the money if the bond is worth either $100.22 or $96.69. The value of the call will be the difference between the bond's price and the strike price. The $95 call will be worth $5.22 if the bond is trading at $100.22 at expiration and $1.69 if the bond is trading at $96.69. The call is out of the money, and therefore worth zero, if the bond is trading at $92.11 at expiration. Figure 8 shows the short-rate tree over two years, as well as possible call values at expiration of the option in two years.

At expiration the put is in the money if the bond is worth $92.11 (without accrued interest). The put's value will be the difference between $92.11 and the $95 strike price - $2.89. The put is worthless if the bond's price is one of the two higher values, $100.22 or $96.69. Figure 8 gives the put values.

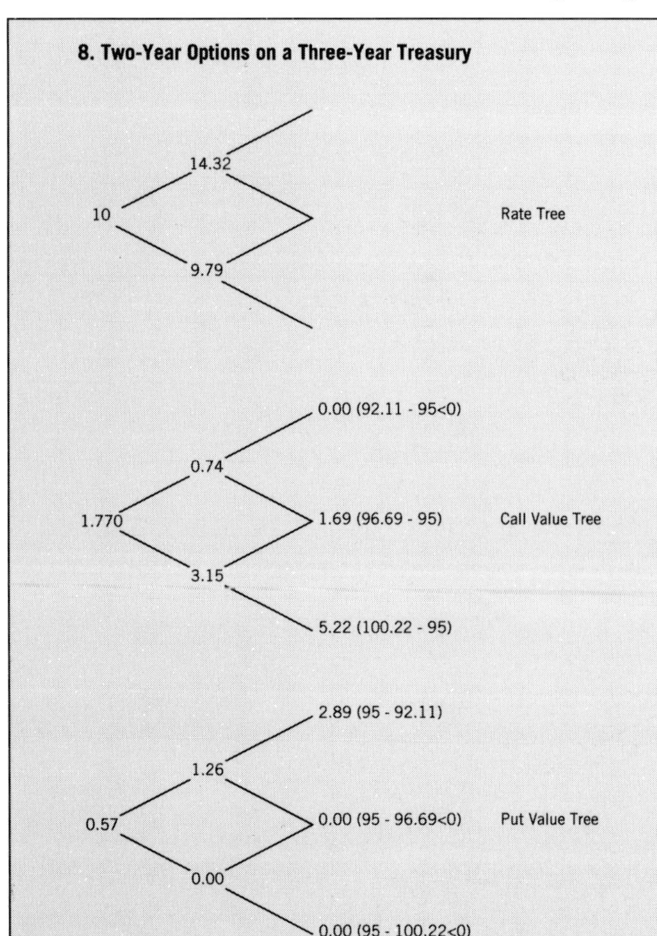

8. Two-Year Options on a Three-Year Treasury

Knowing the call values at expiration we can find the possible values of the call one year before expiration, using the valuation formula given by Equation (1). If the short rate is 14.32% one year from today, the call's value one year before expiration will be:

$$\frac{\frac{1}{2}(0.00)+\frac{1}{2}(1.69)}{1.1432}=0.74$$

If the short rate is 9.79% one year from today, the call's value will be:

$$\frac{\frac{1}{2}(1.69)+\frac{1}{2}(5.22)}{1.0979}=3.15$$

Given the call values one year out, we can find the value of the call today when the short rate is 10%:

$$\frac{\frac{1}{2}(0.74)+\frac{1}{2}(3.15)}{1.1}=1.77$$

Put values are derived in a similar manner. Figure 8 shows the full trees of call and put values.

We have priced European-style options by finding their values at any node as the discounted expected value one step in the future. American-style options can be valued with little extra effort. Because an American option may be exercised at any time, its value at any node is the greater of its value if held or its value if exercised. We obtain its value if held by using the valuation formula to get any node's value in terms of values one step in the future. Its value if exercised is the difference between the bond price at the node and the strike price.

Option hedge ratios

When interest rates change, so do the prices of bonds and bond options. Bond option investors are naturally interested in how much option prices change in response to changes in the price of the underlying bond. We measure this relation by the hedge ratio (or delta).

Figure 9 shows one-step trees for a Treasury, a call and a put. For a call worth C on a Treasury with price T, the hedge ratio is:

$$\Delta_{\text{call}} = \frac{C_u - C_d}{T_u - T_d} \tag{4}$$

where C_u and C_d are the values of the call one period from today in the tree corresponding to possible short rates r_u and r_d. A similar formula holds for a put, P, on a Treasury; we simply replace C with P in Equation (4).

For the two-year put and call on the three-year Treasury considered above, we start by finding the differences between possible prices one year from today. Given the Treasury prices shown in Figure 7 and the option prices from Figure 8:

$$T_u - T_d = 91.33 - 98.79 = -7.46$$

$$C_u - C_d = 0.74 - 3.15 = -2.41$$

$$P_u - P_d = 1.26 = 1.26$$

We can now derive the hedge ratios, using Equation (4):

$$\Delta_{\text{call}} = \frac{-2.41}{-7.46} = 0.32 \tag{5}$$

$$\Delta_{\text{put}} = \frac{1.26}{-7.46} = -0.17 \tag{6}$$

These hedge ratios give us the sensitivity of the option to changes in the underlying Treasury price by describing the change in the option's price per dollar change in the Treasury's price. They therefore tell us how to hedge the Treasury with the option, and vice versa. The call hedge ratio is positive because the call prices increase when the Treasury price increases. In contrast, the put hedge ratio is negative because put prices decrease as the Treasury price increases.

9. Hedge Ratios for a Call and a Put on a Treasury

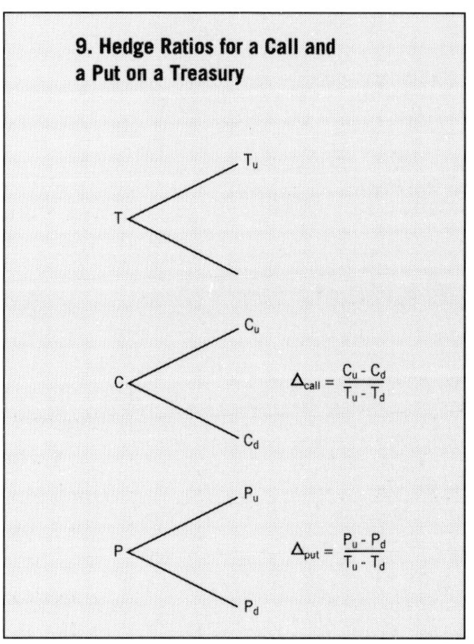

Reducing the interval size

In the examples above, the short-rate tree had coarse one-year steps, Treasuries paid annual coupons and options could only be exercised once a year.

To get accurate solutions for option values, we need a tree with finely spaced steps between today and the option's expiration. Ideally, we would like a tree with one-day steps and a 30-year horizon, so that coupon payments and option exercise dates would always fall exactly on a node. We would also like to have many steps to expiration, even for options on the verge of expiring.

In practice, our computer does not have enough memory to build a 30-year tree with daily steps. And even if it did, it would take us hours to value a security. Instead, we can build a sequence of short-rate trees, each with the same number of steps but compressed into shorter and shorter horizons. Thus each tree has finer spacing than the one before it. For example, we might use today's term structure to build short-rate trees that extend over 30 years, 15 years, $7\frac{1}{2}$ years and so on. In this way, no matter when the option expires, we will always have one tree with enough steps to value the option accurately.

To value an option on any Treasury, we use two trees - a coarse one with enough steps to value the Treasury accurately from its maturity back to today, and a fine one with enough steps to value the option accurately from its expiration until today. We find the Treasury values on the coarse tree by using the model's valuation formula from maturity to today. Then we interpolate these Treasury values onto the fine tree, which may often have as many as 60 periods. Maturity, expiration and coupon dates that fall between nodes are carefully interpolated to the nearest node in time. In this way, the option can be accurately valued.

Interpolating across trees gives us accurate, yet rapid, results. Once model values have been found to match the term structure, we can value options in a few seconds.

Improving the model

We considered more complex models that use more than one factor to describe shifts in the yield curve. Increasing the number of factors improves the model results. But a multifactor model is much harder to think about and work with than a single-factor model. It also takes much more computer time. We therefore think it pays to work with different single-factor models before moving on to a multifactor model.

Along these lines, we examined the effects on our model of letting forward mean reversion and forward short-rate volatility vary independently. (They are tied together in the current model only by the geometry of a tree with equal time spacing throughout.) We found that varying forward mean reversion and varying forward short-rate volatility give very different results. We can use one or the other alone, or a mixture of both, in matching the term structure.

11

Bond and Option Pricing when Short Rates are Lognormal*

Fischer Black† and Piotr Karasinski
Karasinski Consulting Inc.

This article describes a one-factor model for bond and option pricing based on the short-term interest rate and one that allows the target rate, mean-reversion and local volatility to vary deterministically through time. For any horizon, the distribution of possible short rates is lognormal, so the rate neither falls below zero nor reflects off a barrier at zero. This type of model enables one to match the yield curve, the volatility curve and the cap curve.

This article presents a one-factor model of bond prices, bond yields and related options. The single factor that is the source of all uncertainty is the short-term interest rate. We assume no taxes or transaction costs, no default risk and no extra costs for borrowing bonds. We also assume that all security prices are perfectly correlated in continuous time.

We can choose from among a number of models of the local process for the short-term interest rate - a normal process, a lognormal process, a "square-root" process or others.[1] The nominal interest rate cannot fall below zero as long as people can hold cash; it can become stuck at zero for long periods, however, as when prices fall persistently and substantially. None of the models we have to choose from allows for both these features. Lognormal models keep the rate away from zero entirely, while some square-root models make zero into a "reflecting barrier". The lognormal model we use is more general than others, because we allow the local process to change over time. So long as the process for log r is linear in log r at each time, we will have a lognormal distribution for the possible values of the short rate at a given future time. In contrast, the square-root process does not give a square-root distribution at a given future time.

A lognormal model

A lognormal distribution has a mean and a variance. Assuming a different lognormal short-rate distribution for each future time allows both mean and variance to depend on time.

As Hull and White point out, however, a normal (or lognormal) model with mean-reversion can depend on time in three ways, not just two ways.[2] In their notation, the continuous-time limit of the Black-Derman-Toy one-factor model is:[3]

$$d(\log r) = [\theta(t) - \phi(t) \log r]\,dt + \sigma(t)\,dz \tag{1}$$

**This paper was first published in the* Financial Analyst Journal, *July/August (1991).*

†Fischer Black died in August 1995. Fischer Black, January 11, 1938–August 30, 1995.

where r is the local interest rate and $\sigma(t)$ depends on $\phi(t)$.

To create a lognormal model that depends on time in three ways, we can simply drop the time between $\sigma(t)$ and $\theta(t)$. Hull and White do this for a general model.[4] Our model is a special case of theirs.

We make one change in the way Hull and White write their model. We write $\mu(t)$ for the "target interest rate". When $\log r$ is above $\log \mu(t)$, it tends to fall, and when it is below $\log \mu(t)$, it tends to rise. Thus we rewrite Equation (1) as:

$$d(\log r) = \phi(t)\,[\log \mu(t) - \log r]\,dt + \sigma(t)\,dz \tag{2}$$

We take $\mu(t)$ as the target rate, $\phi(t)$ as mean-reversion and $\sigma(t)$ as local volatility in the expression for the local change in $\log r$. We choose these three functions ("inputs") to match three features of the world ("outputs").

For their outputs, Hull and White chose:

- the yields curve;
- the volatility curve; and
- the future local volatilities $\sigma(t)$.

The yield curve gives for each maturity the current yield on a zero-coupon bond. The volatility curve gives for each maturity the current yield volatility on a zero-coupon bond. The future local volatilities output is the same as the corresponding input.

For our outputs, we choose:

- the yield curve;
- the volatility curve; and
- the cap curve.

Our first two outputs are the same as Hull and White's. The cap curve gives, for each maturity, the price of an at-the-money differential cap. A differential cap pays at a rate equal to the difference (if positive) between the short rate and the strike price. For any maturity, an at-the-money cap has a strike equal to the forward rate for that maturity. A full cap is the integral of differential caps over all future horizons up to the full cap's maturity.

An advantage of these outputs over Hull and White's is that all of them are (in principle) observable. They all correspond to market prices.

We do not claim that our inputs imply a reasonable process for the short rate, except as a rough approximation. We choose inputs that give reasonable outputs, though they may be somewhat unreasonable themselves.[5] We are following in the footsteps of Cox, Ross and Rubinstein, who value options by generating a "risk-neutral" distribution of future stock prices.[6] This is not a true distribution, but it nonetheless gives correct option prices.

Input and output volatilities

We were surprised at the relation we found between input and output volatilities. The input volatilities are the local volatilities for the short rate at all horizons. The output volatilities are the current yield volatilities for zero-coupon bonds at all maturities.

Imagine that we hold the local short-rate volatilities fixed out to a certain time, but raise the local volatilities after that time. We hold all other inputs fixed. For our lognormal model, raising the future input volatilities will, if anything, *lower* the output yield volatilities.

One way to raise the output volatilities, then, is to lower the future input volatilities. Another way is to reduce the amount of mean-reversion. To arrive at very high output volatilities, we can even turn to negative mean-reversion.

When all the inputs are constant in a lognormal model the volatility curve will decline. The higher the local short-rate volatility and the greater the mean-reversion, the faster it will decline. A declining volatility curve is a persistent feature of the world. We can model this feature in a lognormal model without using the time-dependence of our inputs.

Building a tree

Black, Derman and Toy show how to build a binomial tree for some lognormal models.[7] They use the location and spacing of the nodes for each future time to vary the inputs. They are able to match two of the outputs (yield curve and volatility curve), but not the third (cap curve). In fact, with their models, choosing a yield curve and volatility curve implies choosing a cap curve. They cannot vary the target rate, local volatility and mean-reversion separately.

Hull and White solve this problem by using a trinomial tree, rather than a binomial tree.[8] From each node of a trinomial tree, you can move to one of three adjacent nodes one period later. What those three nodes are depends on the problem at hand. So do the probabilities associated with the three nodes.

We solve the problem by varying the spacing in the tree. This gives us another degree of freedom, so we can vary all three inputs within a simple binary tree. We can continue to assume that the probabilities of up and down moves are identical and both equal to 0.5. This helps make our use of the tree efficient. We preserve the topology of the simple binary-tree method.

When mean-reversion is positive, this method has a problem of its own - the spacing declines over time. For a reasonable number of nodes, the time separation of the early branches can be so large that we do not have the detail we want for applications such as valuing short-term options on long-term bonds.

We may thus need to prune the tree as we build it. We build it out to a certain point and then chop off half the nodes. When we are working back in the tree, we interpolate and extrapolate when we come to a place where the number of nodes doubles.

Possible outputs

We cannot use our process to match any output curves we might write down. For example, we cannot match a yield curve that implies negative forward rates or a discontinuous volatility curve.

We thus need to use smooth output curves. If we see bumpy curves in the world, we may be seeing swap or arbitrage opportunities, or we may be seeing data errors. In either case, we need to smooth if we hope to match successfully.

A "normal" model that allows negative interest rates may be easier to match. But we prefer our lognormal models because curves we can match only with a "normal" model present profit opportunities.

With known inputs

Suppose we know the functions $\mu(t)$, $\phi(t)$ and $\sigma(t)$ (the target rate, mean-reversion and local volatility). How can we build a tree to fit these functions?

Given the values of $\log r$, the tree will be rectilinear. For a given time, it will have equal spacing, though the time spacing will vary. The spacing for a given time will fit local volatility. The drift of the points from one time to the next will fit the target rate. And the time spacing will fit mean-reversion.

Write τ_n for $t_{n+1} - t_n$, ϕ_n for $\phi(t_n)$ and σ_n for $\sigma(t_n)$. Then the formula for mean-reversion is:

$$\phi_n = \frac{1}{\tau_n}\left(1 - \frac{\sigma_n\sqrt{\tau_n}}{\sigma_{n-1}\sqrt{\tau_{n-1}}}\right) \tag{3}$$

Solving this formula for τ_n, we have:

$$\tau_n = \tau_{n-1}\left(\frac{4\left(\sigma_{n-1}/\sigma_n\right)^2}{\left(1+\sqrt{1+4\phi_n\left(\sigma_{n-1}/\sigma_n\right)^2\tau_{n-1}}\right)^2}\right) \tag{4}$$

We can choose τ_0 as we wish. The smaller it is, the finer the tree and the more accurate the answers. We have σ_0 from $\sigma(0)$, σ_1 from $\sigma(t_0)$ and ϕ_1 from $\phi(t_0)$. We can use Equation (4) to find τ_1 and then repeat. We will gradually build up a full tree. At each time, we will use $\mu(t)$ to help locate the first point.

Suppose, for example, that mean-reversion is constant at 0.1, that local volatility is a constant annual 0.20, and that we divide a 10-year period into N = 160 sub-periods. Table 1 gives the resulting time spacing.

Table 1. Time spacing

n/N	t_n
0	0.0
1/5	4.1
2/5	6.3
3/5	7.9
4/5	9.0
1	10

Recall that t_n represents years until time interval n. Note how the spacing declines over time with positive mean-reversion. The level of mean-reversion in the table is high (0.1) to exaggerate its effect on time spacing.

With known outputs

Suppose we want to choose the inputs ($\mu(t)$, $\phi(t)$ and $\sigma(t)$) to match known outputs (yield curve, volatility curve and cap curve). How can we do it?

We divide time into segments and each segment into many time intervals. We choose μ, ϕ and σ to match the outputs at the end of the first segment. Then we choose μ, ϕ and σ from the start to the end of the second segment to match the output at the end of the second segment, and so on.

We might call the resulting inputs "implied target rate", "implied mean-reversion" and "implied local volatility". We do not say that the short rate follows a process with these features. We do say that securities behave *as if* we lived in a one-factor world and the short rate followed this process.

After a time, we can estimate the model again and get a new process. The implied process changes each time security prices and volatilities change.

We go through similar steps when we figure implied volatility: when the option price changes, the implied volatility changes. When we value the option, we are assuming that its volatility is known and constant. But a minute later, we start using a new volatility. Similarly, we can value fixed income securities by assuming we know the one-factor short-rate process. A minute later, we start using a new process that is not consistent with the old one.

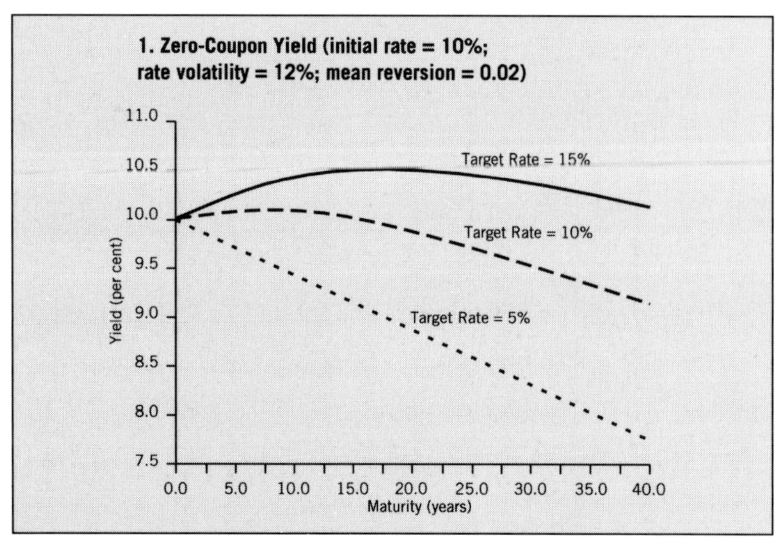

1. Zero-Coupon Yield (initial rate = 10%; rate volatility = 12%; mean reversion = 0.02)

Another approach is to search for an interest-rate process general enough that we can assume it is true and unchanging. It will have many variables and constants. We estimate the constants and hope that when we repeat the estimation, the variables change, but not the constants. While we may reach this goal, we do not know enough to use this approach today. For now, we must continue to re-estimate simple models.

Autocorrelation

Because the distribution of short rates at any horizon is lognormal, we need only a mean and a variance to describe it. Yet we need a target rate, mean-reversion and local volatility to describe the short-rate process in our model. For a given distribution of short rates for every horizon, our model has a whole family of possible processes. How can this be?

It turns out that processes differ in the autocorrelations they imply for future short rates. When mean-reversion is strong, a rise in the short rate above the target will probably be largely reversed before long. When it is weak, we will not see this.

If we have a narrow distribution of possible short rates in the future, we can infer that either mean-reversion is strong or local volatility is low between now and then.

Examples

To see the relation between inputs and outputs, consider what happens when we keep all the inputs (target rate $\mu(t)$, mean-reversion $\phi(t)$ and local volatility $\sigma(t)$) constant.

Figure 1 shows the yield curve for three cases. In each curve, mean-reversion is constant at 0.02, local volatility is constant at 12% and the current short rate is 10%.

For the middle curve, the target rate is the same as the current rate. Note that the curve rises slightly up to about seven years and then falls off. This is a typical pattern when the target rate is constant and equal to the current rate. Note that the curvature eventually reverses from concave down to concave up. This is typical too.

The top curve shows what happens when the current rate is 10% and the target rate 15%. The bottom curve shows a current rate of 10% and a target rate of 5%. Even when the target rate is 15% the yield curve never approaches 15%. In fact, for the case we show, it never goes above 11%. We do not know how to create a model that shows a consistently rising yield curve with reasonable assumptions - even by adding features that our model does not have.

Figure 2 shows the volatility curve for three cases. In each case, the current rate is 10%, the target rate is constant at 10% and mean-reversion is constant at 0.02. The three curves show (from the top down) constant local volatilities of 16, 12 and 8%.

The volatility curve starts at the local volatility and declines. The higher the volatility, the faster it declines. This is also a typical pattern in real-world volatility curves: yield volatilities for shorter-term bonds tend to be higher than yield volatilities for longer-term bonds.

Figure 3 shows that mean-reversion affects the slope of the volatility curve. The higher the mean-reversion, the more negative the slope. But the curve slopes down even when mean-reversion is zero. Actually, the slope of the curve at zero maturity is proportional to the negative of the mean-reversion.

Comparing Figures 2 and 3, we see that we can match both the short end and the long end of the volatility curve even with constant inputs. We choose local volatility to match the short end and mean-reversion to match the long end.

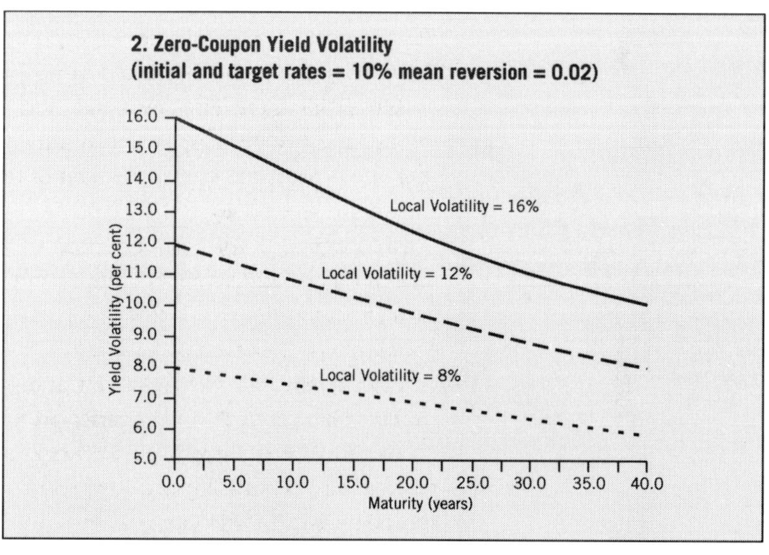

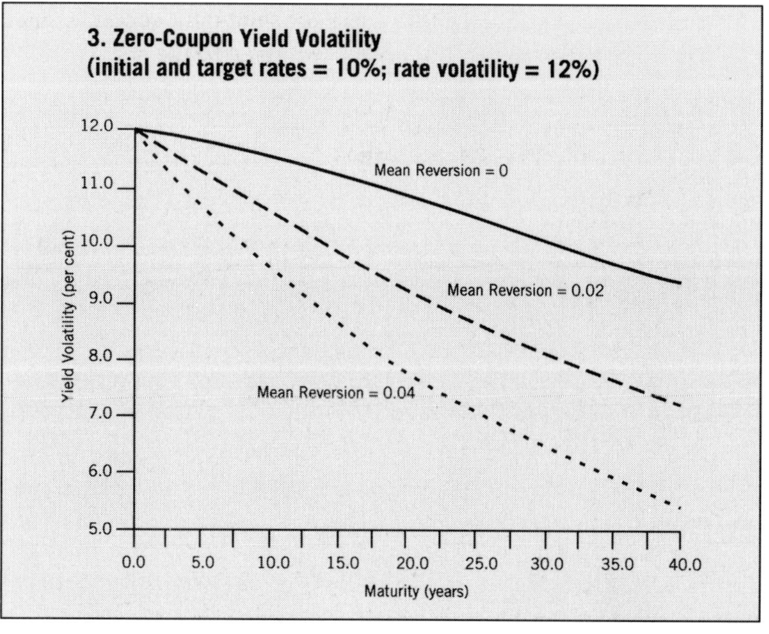

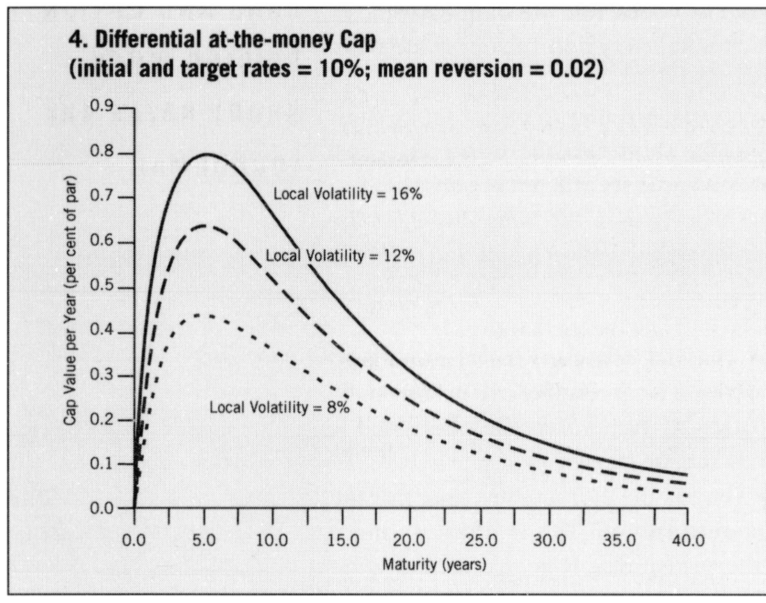

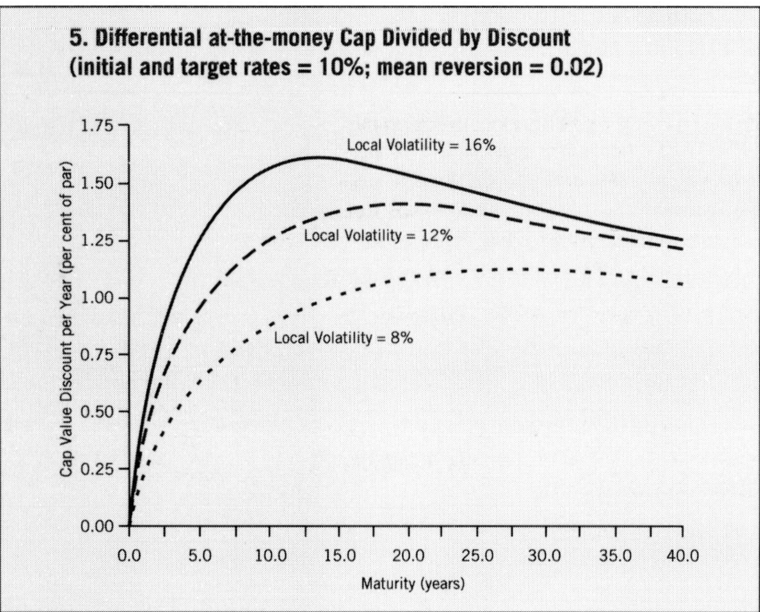

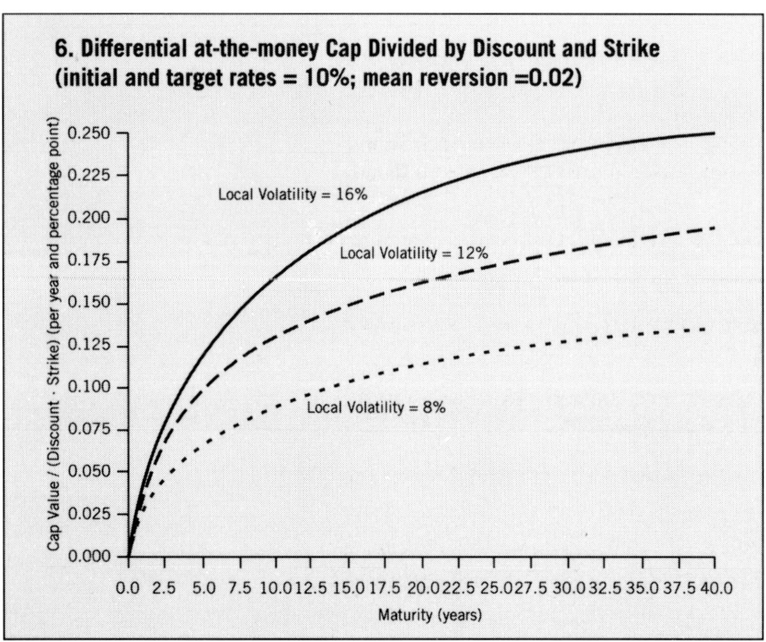

Figure 4 shows the differential cap curves for different levels of local volatility. For each curve, we hold all the inputs fixed and have the current rate equal to the target rate. Note that doubling the local volatility roughly doubles the cap values at every maturity.

For every level of local volatility, the differential cap curve rises sharply to a maximum and then falls sharply. The rise is due to a gain in the effect of volatility as we increase maturity. But two other factors overpower this - an increase in the discount factor and a fall in the forward rate, which is the cap's strike price.

This is analysed in Figures 5 and 6. In Figure 5, we divide the differential cap value by the discount factor (the value of zero-coupon bond with corresponding maturity and unit face value). In Figure 6, we divide by the strike price as well. The resulting curves rise smoothly with maturity, reflecting the impact of volatility.[9]

1 *For a normal process, see Vasicek O., 1977, "An Equilibrium Characterization of the Term Structure",* Journal of Financial Economics *5, pp. 177–188; and Jamshidian F., 1989, "An Exact Bond Option Formula",* Journal of Finance *44, pp. 205–209. For the lognormal process see Dothan U. L., 1978, "On the Term Structure of Interest Rates",* Journal of Financial Economics *6, pp. 56–69. For the square-root process see Cox, J. C., J. E. Ingersoll, Jr. and S. A. Ross, 1985, "A Theory of the Term Structure of Interest Rates",* Econometrica *53, pp. 385–407; Constantinides G. M., 1990, "Theory of the Term Structure of Interest Rates: The Squared Autoregressive Instruments Nominal Term Structure (SAINTS) Model", working paper; Longstaff F., 1990, "The Valuation of Options on Yields",* Journal of Financial Economics *26, pp. 97–123; and Longstaff F., 1993, "The Valuation of Options on Coupon Bonds",* Journal of Banking Finance *17, pp. 27–42. Other processes are given in Ho T. Y., and S-B Lee, 1986, "Term Structure Movements and Pricing Interest Rate Contingent Claims",* Journal of Finance *41, pp. 1011–1029; Heath D., R. Jarrow and A. Morton, 1990, "Bond Pricing and the Term Structure of Interest Rates: A New Methodology for Contingent Claims Valuation",* Econometrica *60, pp. 77–105; Heath D., R. Jarrow and A. Morton, 1990, "Contingent Claim Valuation with a Random Evolution of Interest Rates",* Review of Futures Markets *9, pp. 54–76; Hull J., and A. White, 1990, "New Ways with the Yield Curve",* RISK, *October, pp. 13–17; and Black F., E. Derman and W. Toy, 1990, "A One-Factor Model of Interest Rates and its Application to Treasury Bond Options",* Financial Analysts Journal, *January/February, pp. 33–39. Some of these models of short-rate behaviour are tested in Chan K. C., G. A. Karolyi, F. A. Longstaff and A. B. Sanders, 1990, "Alternative Models of the Term Structure: An Empirical Comparison",* Journal of Finance *47, October, pp. 1209–1227.*

2 *J. Hull and A. White, "Pricing Interest Rate Derivative Securities",* Review of Financial Studies *3 (1990), pp. 573–592 and* Hull-White on Derivatives, *RISK Publications, 1996.*

3 *See Black, Derman and Toy, "A One-Factor Model",* op. cit.

4 *Hull and White, "New Ways with the Yield Curve",* op. cit.

5 *Cox, Ingersoll, and Ross ("A Theory of the Term Structure",* op. cit.) *and Constantinides ("Theory of the Term Structure",* op. cit.) *imagine they are choosing a sensible process for the short rate and look at the resulting outputs, including option prices. Ho and Lee ("Term Structure Movements",* op. cit.), *on the other hand, believe their outputs are reasonable but do not claim that their inputs are reasonable. In fact, their inputs are quite unreasonable, as shown by P. H. Dybvig, "Bond and Bond Option Pricing Based on the Current Term Structure" (Working paper, February 1989).*

6 *J. C. Cox, S. A. Ross and M. Rubinstein, "Option Pricing: A Simplified Approach",* Journal of Financial Economics, *September 1979.*

7 *Black, Derman and Toy, "A One-Factor Model",* op. cit.

8 *Hull and White, "New Ways with the Yield Curve",* op. cit., *and J. Hull and A. White, "One Factor Interest-Rate Models and the Valuation of Interest-Rate Derivative Securities",* Journal of Financial and Quantitative Analysis *28, pp. 235–254, and* Hull-White on Derivatives, *RISK Publications, 1996.*

9 *We thank Emanuel Derman and Francis Longstaff for their helpful comments.*

Bibliography

Black F., E. Derman and W. Toy, 1990, "A One-Factor Model of Interest Rates and its Application to Treasury Bond Options", *Financial Analysts Journal*, January/February, pp. 33–39; reprinted as Chapter 10 of the present volume.

Chan K. C., G. A. Karolyi, F. A. Longstaff and A. B. Sanders, 1990, "Alternative Models of the Term Structure: An Empirical Comparison", *Journal of Finance* 47, October, pp. 1209–1227.

Constantinides G. M., 1990, "Theory of the Term Structure of Interest Rates: The Squared Autoregressive Instruments Nominal Term Structure (SAINTS) Model", Working paper.

Cox, J. C., J. E. Ingersoll, Jr. and S. A. Ross, 1985, "A Theory of the Term Structure of Interest Rates", *Econometrica* 53, pp. 385–407; reprinted as Chapter 6 of the present volume.

Dothan U. L., 1978, "On the Term Structure of Interest Rates", *Journal of Financial Economics* 6, pp. 56–69.

Heath D., R. Jarrow and A. Morton, 1990, "Bond Pricing and the Term Structure of Interest Rates: A New Methodology for Contingent Claims Valuation", *Econometrica* 60, pp.77–105; reprinted as Chapter 14 of the present volume.

Heath D., R. Jarrow and A. Morton, 1990, "Contingent Claim Valuation with a Random Evolution of Interest Rates", *Review of Futures Markets* 9, pp.54–76.

Ho T. Y., and S-B Lee, 1986, "Term Structure Movements and Pricing Interest Rate Contingent Claims", *Journal of Finance* 41, pp. 1011–1029; reprinted as Chapter 13 of the present volume.

Hull J., and A. White, 1990, "New Ways with the Yield Curve", *RISK*, October pp. 13–17.

Jamshidian F., 1989, "An Exact Bond Option Formula", *Journal of Finance* 44, pp. 205–209; reprinted as Chapter 8 of the present volume.

Longstaff F., 1990, "The Valuation of Options on Coupon Bonds", *Journal of Banking Finance* 1, pp. 27–42.

Longstaff F., 1990, "The Valuation of Options on Yields", *Journal of Financial Economics* 26, pp. 97–123.

Vasicek O., 1977, "An Equilibrium Characterization of the Term Structure", *Journal of Financial Economics* 5, pp. 177–188; reprinted as Chapter 4 of the present volume.

12

Bond and Option Evaluation in the Gaussian Interest Rate Model*

Farshid Jamshidian
Sakura Global Capital

Equivalent characterisations of the one-factor Gaussian (and quasi-Gaussian) interest rate model are given, and the model is analysed in detail. Explicit formulas for bond prices, forward rates and Arrow–Debreu state prices are derived, leading to analytical evaluation of American and multiple options in terms of the yield curve. The sub-family of Gaussian models that admit a path-independent binomial discretisation is identified.

The analysis and evaluation of bonds and options simplify considerably in the Gaussian interest rate model. Simply stated, the Gaussian model is a continuous-time model in which interest rates are normally distributed and follow a Gaussian process. The major shortcoming of this assumption is that it implies that interest rates may become negative. Therefore, the Gaussian model is *not* arbitrage-free, but it is "locally" arbitrage-free (in a well-known sense), which is a necessary (though not sufficient) condition for the absence of arbitrage. Despite this shortcoming, special cases of the Gaussian model were among the first interest rate models studied (eg, Merton, 1973; Vasicek, 1977), and more recently it has seen renewed interest and development (eg, Jamshidian, 1987, 1990; Heath, Jarrow and Morton, 1992; Dash, 1988; Hull and White, 1990*a*). This is because the Gaussian model has a simple mathematical structure that makes it analytically tractable and appealing. Furthermore, the probability of negative interest rates is often small, and the insights gained by the Gaussian model can prove useful in the understanding of theoretically more consistent models.

The Gaussian interest rate model is rich in analytical properties and enjoys a high degree of internal symmetry. Many of these properties are scattered among previous studies. However, individually the studies each establish only a few of these properties, mostly as illustrations of more general principals. The results are also largely confined to special cases of the Gaussian model and, in application to analytical evaluation of options, to the European case. Our purpose here is to provide a comprehensive and systemic development of the Gaussian model, not just as an illustration, but as a self-contained theory for its own sake. The uniform treatment here of the general Gaussian model unravels its structure, captures known results and establishes new ones. Among the new results are equivalent characterisations of the Gaussian (and the

**This paper was first published in* Research in Finance *(1991). It is reprinted with the permission of JAI Press Inc.*

"quasi-Gaussian") model and its "volatility and variance structures", the properties of its "Arrow–Debreu state prices", formulas for American and "multiple" bond options, and the introduction of a sub-family of "path-independent" Gaussian models that admit a binomial discretisation.

Two components are basic to all interest rate models: the local no-arbitrage condition and the distributional assumptions of the model. In the Gaussian interest rate model, these two assumptions combine elegantly to yield remarkably simple and intuitive formulas for bond prices, forward prices and the spot rate process, greatly facilitating application to option evaluation.

Classically, the local no-arbitrage condition arose from the observation, originally made by Black and Scholes (1973) for equities, that, in the one-factor case, a portfolio can be constructed from any two securities and continually rebalanced at each time, in such a way that it is instantaneously hedged, in the sense that its instantaneous return is certain and hence must equal the short-term, spot interest rate. This condition has been formalised into a number of useful equivalent statements, some restricting the drifts (instantaneous expectation) of bond (and option) returns, forward rates, or forward prices, others providing means for evaluation of bonds and options, either as solutions of a certain "fundamental" (parabolic) partial differential equation (fundamental pde), or as "risk-neutral" expectations of discounted payoffs, or as discounted "forward-risk-adjusted" expectations of payoff.

The distributional assumptions of a (one-factor) locally arbitrage-free model can be specified either by specifying the spot rate process, as is traditional, or equivalently, as observed in Heath, Jarrow and Morton (1992) (in a general multifactor setting), by specifying the initial yield curve and the volatility structure of the model (ie, the volatilities of forward interest rates or zero-coupon bond returns).

Stated in terms of the spot rate, a Gaussian model is one in which the spot rate follows a Gaussian diffusion process. Stated in terms of the volatility structure, in a Gaussian model the volatility structure is deterministic and assumes an especially simple quasi-Gaussian form that can incorporate an arbitrary initial volatility curve and a spot rate volatility function. Another equivalent definition states that a locally arbitrage-free model is Gaussian if the spot rate is a diffusion process and the volatility structure is deterministic. We will also give several other equivalent characterisations of the Gaussian (and quasi-Gaussian) model in terms of various formulas for bond prices, forward rates and the spot rate drift.

Aside from its volatility structure, the closely related variance structure (ie, the integrals of the squares of the forward-rate and forward price volatility functions) enter and play an important role in the characteristic formulas of the Gaussian model. Our investigation leads to the discovery and equivalent characteristics of a larger family of quasi-Gaussian interest rate models, which in general may have a *stochastic* volatility structure, but otherwise admit formulas for bond prices and the drift of the spot rate that are *identical* in form to those of the Gaussian model.

For our applications to option evaluation, we need an equivalent characterisation of the local no-arbitrage condition stating that forward rates and forward prices are martingales with respect to a certain forward-risk-adjusted measure. This notion, which first appeared in Jamshidian (1987) in a slightly different form, leads to the explicit determination of Arrow–Debreu state prices (ie, prices of "primitive securities" that have a non-zero cashflow at only a single state) in the Gaussian model.

A Black–Scholes type formula for European options on zero-coupon bonds is easily derived in the Gaussian model. In fact, as in Merton (1973), it suffices to assume that the volatility structure is deterministic. However, our main applications are to American and multiple options. Here one needs the full Gaussian assumption, ie, that in addition to a deterministic volatility structure, the spot rate follows a diffusion process, so that bonds and options are functions of the spot rate. This results in a simple formula for American options on coupon bonds in terms of the "optimal exercise boundary", and a (non-linear) integral equation for the latter (which involves the bond and forward rate formulas). Another result gives a formula for the product of several consecutive pure state prices in terms of the initial yield curve and the covariance structure of the spot rate. This result can be applied to the analytical evaluation of options with discrete strike dates, such as multiple or compound options or, say, a European call option on a one-time-only putable bond.

Numerical evaluation of American and multiple options is based on the fundamental pde. Since we express the coefficient of the pde in terms (only) of the volatility structure and the initial yield curve, options are also evaluated in these terms. For the special case of the path-independent Gaussian model, the fundamental pde is transformed to the heat equation, resulting in a simple and efficient binomial algorithm. We also point out its binomial discretisation analogous to (but more general than) the Ho and Lee (1986) model.

The rest of the paper is organised as follows. The next section reviews the literature and serves as an informal introduction to the theory, with the third section providing general notation. The fourth section gives equivalent formulations of the local no-arbitrage condition. The fifth section defines (quasi-) Gaussian volatility structures, and the sixth gives equivalent characterisations of the (quasi-) Gaussian model. The seventh section derives the fundamental pde and the Arrow–Debreu state prices. The eighth section presents the formula for American options, while the ninth section gives the formulas for multiple options on zero-coupon bonds and the tenth generalises them to coupon bonds. The eleventh section discusses implementation issues and the binomial discretisation of the path-independent Gaussian model. The more illustrative proofs are given in the text. The remaining proofs are supplied in an appendix.

All the results of the paper, except (possibly) those in the eighth, ninth and tenth sections, can be generalised to multifactors with little change or extra effort. (Essentially, a summation sign is inserted in each formula.) But, for ease of exposition, we confine the discussion to the single-factor case.

Review of known results

The literature on interest rate models and option evaluation is abundant. Our purpose here is to review only those results which are directly relevant to an understanding of the Gaussian model and contributions of this paper. The informal discussion of this section also serves as a preparation for the formal development in later sections. For simplicity, we confine the discussion to single-factor models driven by a one-dimensional Brownian motion $w = w(t)$.

Let $P^T = P^T(t)$ denote the price of the T-maturity zero-coupon bond, and assume that it follows an Itô process $dP^T/P^T = \mu^T dt - \sigma^T dw$. Thus $\mu^T(t)$ is the instantaneous bond return and $\sigma^T(t)$ is its volatility. The earliest and most widely used formulation of the (one-factor) local no-arbitrage condition states that the excess expected instantaneous return μ^T over the spot rate $r = r(t)$ divided by the bond's return volatility σ^T is independent of the maturity T. This common ratio $(\mu^T - r)/\sigma^T$ is called the market price of risk and is denoted by $\lambda = \lambda(t)$. Thus, $\mu^T = r + \sigma^T\lambda$. A similar statement holds for options.

The classical condition is equivalent to the statement that

$$P^T(t) = \tilde{E}_t \exp\left(-\int_t^T r(s)\,ds\right)$$

where the expectation is with respect to the risk-neutral Wiener measure $d\tilde{w} = dw - \lambda dt$. This is well known (see, eg, Ingersoll (1987), Chapter 18). To show it, following Harrison and Pliska (1981), let $X(t) = P^T(t)\exp(-\int_0^t r(s)\,ds)$ denote the relative price of the bond. Since $dX/X = (\mu^T - r)dt - \sigma^T dw$, it follows that $\mu^T = r + \sigma^T\lambda$ if and only if $dX/X = -\sigma^T d\tilde{w}$. Thus, relative prices are local martingales with respect to the risk-neutral measure. In particular, $X(t) = \tilde{E}_t[X(T)]$. Since $P^T(T) = 1$, it follows that $P^T(t) = \tilde{E}_t \exp(-\int_t^T r(s)\,ds)$. A similar argument applies to prices $C(t)$ of options (away from strike dates) yielding $C(t) = \tilde{E}_t[\exp(-\int_t^T r(s)\,ds)C(T)]$. This result states that the price of an option equals the risk-neutral expectation of its discounted payoff.

BOND AND OPTION EVALUATION IN THE GAUSSIAN INTEREST RATE MODEL

The above representation of prices as expectations of discounted payoffs does not provide an effective tool for the numerical evaluation of complex option structures. However, if one assumes that the spot rate is a diffusion process, then it follows from the classical local no-arbitrage condition that bond and option prices are functions of the spot rate and satisfy a fundamental pde. This approach to evaluation is classical and widely used, eg, as in Vasicek (1977), Dothan (1978), Cox, Ingersoll, and Ross (1979), Brennan and Schwartz (1979), and Courtadon (1982).

The argument runs as follows. Let the spot rate process $r = r(t)$ follow a diffusion process $dr = \mu dt + \sigma dw$, with $\mu = \mu(r, t)$ and $\sigma = \sigma(r, t)$, respectively, denoting its drift and volatility. Apply Itô's formula to the process $P^T(t) = P^T(r(t), t)$ to express the bond return drift μ^T and volatility σ^T in terms of μ, σ and the partial derivatives of the bond price P^T. Substituting into the classical condition $\mu^T = r + \sigma^T\lambda$ gives the fundamental pde $LP^T(r, t) = 0$, with the operator

$$L = \frac{\partial}{\partial t} + \tilde{\mu}\frac{\partial}{\partial r} + \tfrac{1}{2}\sigma^2\frac{\partial^2}{\partial r^2} - r$$

where $\tilde{\mu} = \tilde{\mu}(r, t) = \mu + \sigma\lambda$ is the risk-neutral drift. By a similar argument, prices of options are also solutions of the fundamental pde.

The above discussion implies in particular that a (one-factor) locally arbitrage-free interest rate model is uniquely determined by its spot rate process $r(t)$ and the market price of risk $\lambda(t)$. There is yet another equivalent formulation of the local no-arbitrage condition that expresses forward interest rates in terms of the initial yield curve, the bond return volatility and the market price of risk. This is the "modern approach" advocated in Heath, Jarrow and Morton (1992). It amounts to an equivalent formulation of the local no-arbitrage condition in terms of forward rates $r_T(t) = -(\partial/\partial T)\log P^T(t)$. Indeed, writing $dr_T = \mu_T dt + \sigma_T dw$, it follows from Itô's lemma applied to the logarithm function that $\sigma_T = \partial\sigma^T/\partial T$ and $\mu_T = -\partial\mu^T/\partial T + \sigma_T\sigma^T$. Applying the classical condition $\mu^T = r + \sigma^T\lambda$, it follows that $\mu_T = \sigma_T(\sigma^T - \lambda)$. (In particular, $\lambda(t) = -\mu_t(t)/\sigma(t)$.) Thus $dr_T = \sigma_T[\sigma^T dt + d\tilde{w}]$, and, integrating, we find that

$$r_T(t) = r_T(0) + \int_0^t \sigma_T(s)[\sigma^T(s)ds + d\tilde{w}(s)]$$

determining the whole term structure in terms of the initial forward-rate curve and the volatility structure $\sigma^T(t)$ and $\sigma_T(t)$. The authors extended the result to the multifactor case.

Thus, given the market price of risk $\lambda(t)$, a (one-factor) locally arbitrage-free model is completely determined by specifying either the stochastic process of the spot rate or, equivalently, the initial yield curve and the volatility structure (ie, the forward rate and bond return volatilities σ_T and σ^T).

For analytical evaluation of options, Jamshidian (1987) proposed the forward-risk-adjusted technique, which resulted in an explicit determination of Arrow–Debreu state prices for the Gaussian model and the square-root model of Cox, Ingersoll, and Ross (1979). This technique, also adopted here, is not unlike that of Merton (1973), which changes variables to the forward-price space, but here it takes place within the proper setting of an interest rate model.

For any expiration time T, define the T-maturity forward-risk-adjusted measure $dw^T = dw + (\sigma^T - \lambda)dt$. The local no-arbitrage argument is then equivalent to $dr_T = \sigma_T dw^T$, ie, to forward rates being martingales with respect to dw^T. A similar argument shows that forward bond and option prices $C(t)/P^T(t)$ are also martingales with respect to dw^T. It follows that $C(t) = P^T(t)E_t^T[C(T)]$, where E^T denotes expectation with respect to dw^T.

In particular, if the option price depends on only the spot rate (which is the case in all the principal one-factor models), then evaluation reduces to the determination of the distribution of the spot rate in the forward-risk-adjusted measure. This is already facilitated, since its mean equals the current forward rate. When the volatility structure is deterministic, the distribution is further shown to be normal and its variance is calculated.

Another component of an interest rate model is its distribution assumptions. As discussed above, this is done by specifying either the spot rate process or, equivalently, the initial yield curve and the volatility structure. The first approach is traditional and common. In the most prominent models to date, the risk-neutral spot rate drift $\tilde{\mu} = \mu + \sigma\lambda$ takes the linear mean-reverting form $\tilde{\mu}(r, t) = b(t) - a(t)r$, while a constant-elasticity spot rate volatility of the form $\sigma(r, t) = \sigma(t)r^c$ is assumed $(0 \leq c \leq 1)$. The general Gaussian model of this paper corresponds to $c = 0$, ie, the spot rate volatility $\sigma(r, t) = \sigma(t)$ is deterministic. But let us first briefly compare other popular models, in which $c = 0.5$ and $c = 1$.

The square-root model of Cox, Ingersoll, and Ross (1979) assumes that $c = 0.5$ and that $a(t)$ and $b(t)$ are positive constants. An extended version of the model in Cox, Ingersoll, and Ross (1985) (see also Jamshidian, 1990), allows $b(t)$ to be time-dependent, enabling incorporation of an arbitrary prescribed initial yield curve. These models are attractive because interest rates do not become negative, yet, like the Gaussian model, they admit a simple zero-coupon bond pricing formula, namely, zero-coupon bonds are exponentially linear in the spot rate (and forward rates are linear in the spot rate). For constant $b(t)$, Cox, Ingersoll, and Ross (1985) report a formula for European options, and, using the forward-risk-adjusted technique, Jamshidian (1992) extends the formula to American options on coupon bonds.

The case $c = 1$ is of particular interest to practitioners, primarily because interest rates are positive and the spot rate volatility in these models is expressed as a percentage, which corresponds to the market conversion. Special cases are the Brennan and Schwartz (1979) and Courtadon (1982) models, where $b(t)$, $a(t)$, and $\sigma(t)$ are positive constants. The distribution of the spot rate is not known in such cases. However, when $b(t) = 0$, the spot rate is clearly lognormally distributed (but forward rates are not). Dothan (1978) analysed the simplest case with $a(t)$, $\sigma(t)$ (positive) constants and $b(t) = 0$, deriving a complicated bond pricing formula. Dyer and Jacob (1989) discussed an extension of Dothan's model by allowing $a(t)$ to be time-varying, so an arbitrary prescribed initial yield curve could be incorporated. A binomial version of such a model is currently popular. Black, Derman and Toy (1990) propose the extension $r(t) = u(t) \times \exp[\sigma(t)z(t)]$, ie, the form

$$\frac{dr}{r} = \left(b(t) + \frac{\sigma'(t)}{\sigma(t)}\log(r)\right)dt + \sigma(t)dz$$

allowing the incorporation of an arbitrary prescribed initial volatility curve. No bond pricing formula is known for these models.

Returning to the Gaussian model, Merton (1973) extended the Black–Scholes option formula to stochastic interest rates by assuming a deterministic volatility structure σ^T. He showed that this holds if the spot interest rate follows a (Gaussian) process $dr = \mu dt + \sigma d\tilde{w}$ with a constant volatility σ and a constant drift μ. Indeed, he presented a formula for zero-coupon bond prices that was exponentially linear in r with coefficient $\sigma(T - t)$. Thus $\sigma^T(t) = \sigma(T - t)$ and $\sigma_T(t) = \sigma$ in the Merton volatility structure. Loosely speaking, the yield curve (over short intervals) moves in parallel in this volatility structure.

Vasicek (1977) generalised Merton's model by introducing mean-reversion into the drift of the spot rate. Here, $dr = (b - ar)dt + \sigma d\tilde{w}$ with a, b and σ positive constants. Using the fundamental pde, he obtained a bond pricing formula similar to Merton's, involving the volatility and drift parameters σ, a, b and the market price of risk. The formula indicated the simple exponential form $\sigma_T(t) = \sigma \exp[-a(T - t)]$ for the volatility structure.

More recently, Ho and Lee (1986) developed a discrete-time, locally arbitrage-free binomial model. Significantly, they took an approach that enabled incorporation of the yield curve, which is the most clearly observable market parameter. The future movements of the yield curve were explicitly related to the current yield curve. Moreover, they showed that bond and options can be evaluated by traversing the binomial tree backward in a fashion similar to the Cox-Ross-Rubinstein binomial model for equity options. This meant that options were evaluated in terms of the current yield curve. As such, their current values were independent of the market price of risk.

Ho and Lee (1986) did not discuss the continuous-time version of their model. Jamshidian (1987) noted that the continuous-time analogue of the Ho-Lee model was the extension of Merton's model to a time-varying but deterministic spot rate drift. In particular, it had the same volatility structure as Merton's. Generalising further to include the Vasicek volatility structure, he allowed a constant mean-reversion parameter. Here, $dr = [b(t) - ar]dt + \sigma d\tilde{w}$. It was now possible to invert the bond pricing formula and solve for the drift parameter $b(t)$ in terms of the initial forward rate curve $r_t(0)$. With this substitution for the drift, the fundamental pde contained the current-forward-rate curve, but not risk and drift parameters. Option prices were thus determined in terms of the current yield curve, as in the Ho-Lee model. In particular, this was evident in the formulas presented for the Arrow-Debreu state prices and European option prices. The latter was the same as Merton's specialised to the variance structure of the Vasicek model. For the unextended case, these results also appeared in Jamshidian (1989*a*).

The aforementioned Gaussian models were defined by specifying the stochastic process of the spot interest rate. As discussed above, Heath, Jarrow and Morton (1992) showed that a locally arbitrage-free model can be equivalently specified by the initial yield curve and the volatility structure. Applying this result to the Merton and Vasicek volatility structures, they found a new and more meaningful form for prices of bonds (and forward rates) as a function of the spot rate - one in terms of the volatility parameters (σ and a) and the initial yield curve rather than drift and risk parameters (b and λ). For the extended Vasicek model, they also obtained the formulas for European options and for the spot rate and its drift in terms of the initial forward-rate curve similar to those in Jamshidian (1987), and they generalised the results to multifactors.

Jamshidian (1990) generalised these Gaussian models by allowing time-dependent parameters for all coefficients, ie,

$$dr = [b(t) - a(t)r]dt + \sigma(t)d\tilde{w}$$

Here, $\sigma_T(t) = \sigma(t)\exp[-\int_t^T a(u)du]$.

Using an alternative technique to that presented here, he obtained a bond (and forward-rate) pricing formula in terms of the initial yield curve, similar to the Heath, Jarrow and Morton formulas for the extended Vasicek model. Jamshidian's more general approach highlighted the important role played by the variance structure of the Gaussian model, which (together with the initial yield curve) appeared in the bond pricing and forward-rate formulas, the fundamental pde and the European option pricing formula.

Hull and White (1990*b*) introduced the general Gaussian model independently. Solving the fundamental pde, they derived the bond pricing formula for the general case in the old form, ie, in terms of the drift parameter $b(t)$. But this form, as opposed to the form in terms of the initial yield curve, is complicated and less intuitive (even in the special cases). Applying Merton's option formula, they also obtained the European bond pricing formula.

Jamshidian (1989*b*) has extended the aforementioned results to the general multifactor Gaussian model and introduced a sub-family of path-independent Gaussian models and a simple and efficient binomial computational algorithm for them. Jamshidian (1992) has found a formula for American options on coupon bonds in the Gaussian model. These results are reproduced in the sections "Analytic evaluation of American options" and "Numerical evaluation and the binomial discretisation of path-independent Gaussian models" for the sake of completeness.

The above results are all derived in the present paper in a uniform and systematic fashion for the general Gaussian model. Beyond these, the following contributions are noteworthy. We give a more comprehensive treatment of the local no-arbitrage condition than is usual; the concept of quasi-Gaussian volatility structures is introduced, and equivalent characterisations are found in terms of the variance structure. It is shown that the aforementioned bond pricing and spot rate formulas are in fact equivalent characterisations of quasi-Gaussian models, and further equivalent definitions of the Gaussian model are given. A formula for the product of consecutive Arrow–Debreu prices is given, which is applied to find formulas for multiple options similar to those of Geske and Johnson (1984) for the equity case.[1] It is shown that a multiple option on coupon bonds decomposes into a portfolio of multiple options on zero-coupon bonds. A binomial discretisation of the path-independent Gaussian model similar to the Ho–Lee model is pointed out (this model is independently derived in Pederson, Shiu and Thorlacius (1989) in a binomial setting).

Before beginning our formal development, a word on our philosophy and style of presentation is in order. In an applied study such as this, we are interested in new formulas and the ideas behind them, not in abstract measure spaces or technical regularity and growth conditions. If we now take an integral, interchange the order of differentiation, apply Itô's formula, etc., we presume, without explicitly stating so, that the necessary details are met, trusting that the interested reader can supply the technical details by consulting a standard text. We only attempt interesting applications to bond and option evaluation.

Notation and terminology

We take the discount function and the forward rates as equivalent representatives of the term structure. For $0 \le t \le T$, let $P^T(t)$ (respectively $r_T(t)$) denote the value of time t and the T-maturity zero-coupon bond (respectively, of the T-maturity continuously compounded, instantaneous forward interest rate). They are related by

$$P^T(t) \equiv \exp\left(-\int_t^T r_u(t)\,du\right), \quad r_T(t) \equiv \frac{-\partial[\log P^T(t)]}{\partial T} \tag{1}$$

Note that $P^t(t) = 1$ for all t. The continuously compounded instantaneous interest rate (the spot rate) $r(t)$ is defined by

$$r(t) \equiv r_t(t) = \left.\frac{-\partial P^T(t)}{\partial T}\right|_{T=t} \tag{2}$$

Throughout the paper, we assume that $P^T(0)$ and $r_T(0)$ are deterministic for all $T \ge 0$ and that the term structure is driven by a single factor, represented by a standard Brownian motion $w(t)[w(0) = 0]$. More precisely, for each T, we assume that $P^T(t)$ and $r_T(t)$ $(0 \le t \le T)$ are Itô processes with respect to $w(t)$, and write

$$\frac{dP^T(t)}{P^T(t)} \equiv \mu^T(t)dt - \sigma^T(t)\,dw(t) \tag{3}$$

$$dr_T(t) \equiv \mu_T(t)\,dt + \sigma_T(t)\,dw(t) \tag{4}$$

$$dr(t) \equiv \mu(t)\,dt + \sigma(t)\,dw(t) \tag{5}$$

We refer to the (positive) diffusion coefficients $\sigma^T(t)$, $\sigma_T(t)$, and $\sigma(t)$ collectively as the *volatility structure*. Clearly, for all $0 \le t \le T$, they satisfy

$$\sigma_T(t) = \frac{\partial \sigma^T(t)}{\partial T}, \quad \sigma^T(t) = \int_t^T \sigma_u(t)\,du \tag{6}$$

$$\sigma(t) = \sigma_t(t), \quad \sigma^t(t) = 0 \tag{7}$$

As for the drifts, we have:

LEMMA 1: For all $0 \leq t \leq T$,

$$\mu_T(t) = \frac{-\partial \mu^T(t)}{\partial T} + \sigma^T(t)\sigma_T(t) \tag{8}$$

$$\mu^T(t) = r(t) - \int_t^T \mu_u(t)\,du + \tfrac{1}{2}[\sigma^T(t)]^2 \tag{9}$$

PROOF:

$$\mu_T(t)\,dt = -\left(\frac{\partial}{\partial T}\right) E_t\{d[\log P^T(t)]\}$$

$$= -\left(\frac{\partial}{\partial T}\right)\left\{\mu^T(t) - \tfrac{1}{2}[\sigma^T(t)]^2\right\} dt$$

where the second equality follows from Itô's formula applied to the logarithm function. Equation (8) follows. Integrating (8) with respect to T from t to T, since $\sigma^t(t) = 0$, we get

$$\int_t^T \mu_u(t)\,du = -\mu^T(t) + \mu^t(t) + \tfrac{1}{2}[\sigma^T(t)]^2$$

Thus (9) follows if we show that $r(t) = \mu^t(t)$. But

$$0 = d(1) = d[P^t(t)] = \left.\frac{\partial P^T(t)}{\partial T}\right|_{T=t} dt + \left. dP^T(t)\right|_{T=t} = [-r(t) + \mu^t(t)]dt$$

Q.E.D.

Notation: For any one-factor term structure model set

$$\lambda(t) = -\mu_t(t)/\sigma(t) \tag{10}$$

$$d\tilde{w}(t) = dw(t) - \lambda(t)\,dt \tag{11}$$

$$dw^T(t) = dw(t) + [\sigma^T(t) - \lambda(t)]\,dt, \quad t \leq T \tag{12}$$

As we will see, $\lambda(t)$ is the market price of risk. The process

$$\tilde{w}(t) = w(t) - \int_0^t \lambda(s)\,ds$$

defined in (11) is a Brownian motion with respect to the equivalent Wiener measure given by Girsanov's theorem, which we call the risk-neutral measure. Expectation (and covariance) taken with respect to this measure is termed risk-neutral expectation and denoted by $\tilde{E}[\cdot]$. By Girsanov's theorem, for an Itô process $x(t)$, $T \geq T$,

$$\tilde{E}_t[x(T)] = E_t\left[\exp\left(-\frac{1}{2}\int_t^T \lambda^2(u)\,du + \int_t^T \lambda(u)\,dw(u)\right) x(T)\right]$$

Similarly, $w^T(t)$ in (12) is an equivalent Brownian motion. Expectation with respect to the equivalent measure is termed the T-maturity forward-risk-adjusted expectation and is denoted by $E^T[\cdot]$.

LEMMA 2: For all $t \geq 0$,

$$dr(t) = \left.\frac{\partial r_T(t)}{\partial T}\right|_{T=t} dt + \sigma(t)d\tilde{w}(t)$$

PROOF:

$$dr(t) = dr_t(t) = \left.\frac{\partial r_T(t)}{\partial T}\right|_{T=t} dt + dr_T(t)\Big|_{T=t}$$

The last term equals $\sigma(t)d\tilde{w}(t)$ by (4), (10), and (11). *Q.E.D.*

Locally arbitrage-free, one-factor interest rate models

THEOREM 1: For any one-factor interest rate model, the following conditions are equivalent:

(*a*) For all $0 \leq t \leq T$, $[\mu^T(t) - r(t)]/\sigma^T(t)$ is independent of T. This then implies that the ratio equals $\lambda(t)$, ie,

$$\mu^T(t) = r(t) + \sigma^T(t)\lambda(t) \tag{13}$$

(*b*) For all $0 \leq t \leq T$,

$$\mu_T(t) = \sigma_T(t)[\sigma^T(t) - \lambda(t)] \tag{14}$$

(*c*) For all $0 \leq t_0 \leq t$,

$$r(t) = r_t(t_0) + \int_{t_0}^{t} \sigma_t(s)[\sigma^t(s)ds + d\tilde{w}(s)] \tag{15}$$

(*d*) For $t_0 = 0$, and hence for all $t_0 \geq 0$ and for all $t_0 \leq t \leq T$,

$$r_T(t) = r_T(t_0) + \int_{t_0}^{t} \sigma_T(s)[\sigma^T(s)ds + d\tilde{w}(s)] \tag{16}$$

(*e*) For all $0 \leq t \leq T$,

$$P^T(t) = \tilde{E}_t\left[\exp\left(-\int_t^T r(u)du\right)\right]$$

(*f*) For all $0 \leq t \leq T$, relative prices $X(t) = \exp(-\int_0^t r(s)ds)P^T(t)$ are martingales with respect to the risk-neutral measure.

(*g*) For all $0 \leq t \leq T$, $r_T(t) = E_t^T[r(T)]$. In other words, forward rates $r_T(t)$ are martingales with respect to $dw^T(t)$, ie, $r_T(t) = E_t^T[r_T(s)]$ for all $t \leq s \leq T$.

(*h*) For all $0 \leq t \leq u \leq T$, forward prices $P^T(t)/P^u(t)$ are martingales with respect to $dw^u(t)$.

Moreover, if these conditions hold, then an Itô process $C(t)$, following on an interval of time $dC/C = \mu_C dt - \sigma_C dw$, satisfies $\mu_C(t) = r(t) + \sigma_C(t)\lambda(t)$ (ie, $dC/C = r dt - \sigma_C d\tilde{w}$) if and only if for all $t \leq T$ in that interval it satisfies either of the following two equations:

$$C(t) = \tilde{E}_t\left[\exp\left(-\int_t^T r(u)du\right)C(T)\right]$$

$$C(t) = P^T(t)E_t^T[C(T)] \tag{17}$$

PROOF: *(b)* ⇒ *(d)* ⇒ *(c)* ⇒ *(b)* *(b)* implies *(d)* by substituting from (14) into (4) and integrating from t_0 to t; *(d)* implies *(c)* by setting $T = t$ in (16); and *(c)* implies *(b)* by differentiating (15) with respect to t_0.

(a) ⇔ *(b)* If *(a)* holds, then set $\tilde{\lambda} = (\mu^T - r)/\sigma^T$, so that $\mu^T(t) = r(t) + \sigma^T(t)\tilde{\lambda}(t)$, which, when differentiated with respect to T, gives $\partial\mu^T(t)/\partial T = \sigma_T(t)/\partial T = \sigma_T(t)\tilde{\lambda}(t)$. Applying equation (8) in Lemma 1 gives equation (14) with $\tilde{\lambda}(t)$ replacing $\lambda(t)$. Evaluating this at $T = t$ gives $\tilde{\lambda}(t) = \lambda(t)$, and *(b)* follows. Conversely, if equation (14) holds, then integrating it with respect to T and using equation (9) in Lemma 1 gives (13), which implies *(a)*.

(a) ⇔ *(f)* It follows from the definition of $X(t)$ that

$$\frac{dx}{X} = (\mu^T - r)\,dt - \sigma^T dw = (\mu^T - r - \sigma^T\lambda)\,dt - \sigma^T d\tilde{w}$$

Thus $X(t)$ is a local martingale with respect to $d\tilde{w}$ if and only if $\mu^T = r + \sigma^T\lambda$.

(f) ⇔ *(e)* If *(f)* holds, then

$$X(t) = \tilde{E}_t[X(T)] = \tilde{E}_t\left[\exp\left(-\int_0^T r(s)\right) ds\right]$$

(e) follows by multiplying both sides by $\exp[\int_0^t r(s)\,ds]$. Conversely, if *(e)* holds, then the reverse of this argument gives $X(t) = \tilde{E}_t[X(T)]$, so $X(t)$ is a martingale.

(g) ⇔ *(b)* Since $dr_T = \mu_T dt + \sigma_T dw$, it follows that $dr_T = \sigma_T dw^T$ if and only if (14) holds.

(a) ⇒ *(b)* ⇒ *(g)* Set $F(t) = P^T(t)/P^u(t)$. Itô's lemma easily implies that

$$\frac{dF}{F} = (\mu^T - \mu^u)\,dt - (\sigma^T - \sigma^u)(\sigma^u dt + dw)$$

Thus if *(a)* holds, then $dF/F = -(\sigma^T - \sigma^u)\,dw^u$, and *(b)* follows. If *(b)* holds, then $P^T(t) = P^u(t)E_t^u[P^T(u)]$. Taking the derivative of both sides with respect to T and evaluating at $T = u$ gives $r_T(t) = E_t^T[r(t)]$, and *(g)* follows.

The last two statements follow respectively as in the proofs of *(a)* ⇒ *(f)* and *(a)* ⇒ *(b)*. *Q.E.D.*

DEFINITION 1

A one-factor interest rate model is said to be *locally arbitrage-free* if it satisfies the equivalent of Theorem 1. In this case, $\lambda(t) \equiv -\mu_t(t)/\sigma(t)$ is called its market price of risk. (In our convention a positive $\lambda(t)$ indicates risk aversion.)

Condition *(a)* is the previously mentioned classical local no-arbitrage condition, dating back to Black and Scholes (1973). It states that the excess expected return over the spot rate divided by the bond's return volatility is independent of the bond's maturity. The following intuitive trading strategy is often supplied (eg, as in Vasicek, 1977) to support this principle: At time t, go long $\sigma^T(t)$ dollars in the u-maturity bond and go short $\sigma^u(t)$ dollars in the T-maturity bond. Then, the instantaneous profit on the portfolio is

$$\frac{\sigma^T dP^u}{P^u} - \frac{\sigma^u dP^T}{P^T} = (\sigma^T\mu^u - \sigma^u\mu^T)\,dt$$

Since this return is deterministic (has no dw term), it must equal the profit on a short-term money market investment, ie, $(\sigma^T - \sigma^u)r\,dt$. Thus $(\mu^T - r)/\sigma^T = (\mu^u - r)/\sigma^u$.

Condition *(b)*, due to Heath, Jarrow and Morton (1992), restates the classical condition in terms of the drifts of forward rates. Its significance lies in that it determines the forward-rate drift in terms of only the volatility structure and the market price of risk. (By contrast, in the classical condition $r(t)$ also appears.) Therefore, the evolution of a locally arbitrage-free model is fully and uniquely determined by the volatility structure, the market price of risk and the initial yield curve. Equation (16) makes this explicit by integration. A forward rate in the future equals the forward rate at an (any) earlier time plus a stochastic integral involving the volatility structure. (A similar equation for bond prices also follows.)

As previously mentioned, conditions (*e*) and (*f*), which are in terms of risk-neutral expectations, are also well known. But conditions (*g*) and (*h*), which are in terms of the forward-risk-adjusted expectation, are less well-known, though they previously appeared in a similar form in Jamshidian (1987).

The various formulations of the local no-arbitrage condition in Theorem 1 are *all* useful. There are yet other useful equivalent characterisations, as in Jamshidian (1990), which relate forward bond prices to forward interest rates.

The final statement of the theorem is applicable to options. Indeed, the trading strategy argument discussed above is also applicable (away from exercise dates) to options yielding $\mu_C = r + \sigma C \lambda$. Equation (17) and the one preceding it can be considered as option pricing formulas in terms of expected payoffs. But the one in terms of the risk-neutral expectation does not prove so effective for analytical evaluation. The difficulty is that the expectation of a *product* needs to be calculated. By contrast, (17), which is in terms of the forward-risk-adjusted expectation, effectively "decouples" that product, providing an effective means for analytical evaluation of options.

As an example, when the volatility structure is deterministic, then, in the forward-risk-adjusted measure, a zero-coupon bond price is lognormally distributed with the forward bond price as mean. We find, as in Black and Scholes (1973) and more generally Merton (1973), the following:

COROLLARY 1: In a locally arbitrage-free model with deterministic volatility structure $\sigma^T(t)$, the price $C(t)$ of a European call option on a T-maturity zero-coupon bond with strike price K and expiration t' is given by

$$C(t) = P^T(t) N(h_+) - P^{t'}(t) K N(h_-)$$

where $N(x)$ is the standard normal distribution function and

$$h_\pm = \frac{\log\left(P^T(t)/P^{t'}(t)K\right)}{v^T(t,t')} \pm \tfrac{1}{2} v^T(t,t')$$

where

$$[v^T(t,t')]^2 = \tilde{\text{var}}_t[\log P_T(t')] = \int_t^{t'} [\sigma^T(s) - \sigma^{t'}(s)]^2 \, ds$$

PROOF: By (17) and the definition of the payoff of a call option,

$$C(t) = P^{t'}(t) E_t^T[\max\{0, P^T(t') - K\}]$$

Let $F(t) = P^T(t)/P^{t'}(t)$ be the forward price. By Theorem 1, part (*h*), $dF/F = -\sigma_F dw^{t'}$. By assumption, $\sigma_F = \sigma^T - \sigma^{t'}$ is deterministic. Thus, $F(t') = P^T(t')$ is lognormally distributed in the t'-maturity forward-risk-adjusted measure, with variance of logarithm equal to $v^T(t,t')$ (given above) and mean $F(t)$. (Since $\sigma^T(t)$ is deterministic, the variance of $\log F(t)$ is the same as that taken in the risk-neutral measure.) The desired result now follows by a standard calculation of the expectation. *Q.E.D.*

To evaluate more complex options analytically, we will need the notion of Arrow–Debreu state prices, ie, prices of primitive securities that have a non-zero cashflow only at a single state.

DEFINITION 2: In a one-factor, locally arbitrage-free interest rate model, for fixed r', t', an Itô process $G(t) = G(t; r', t')$, following $dG(t)/G(t) = \mu_G(t) - \sigma_G(t) dw(t)$ $(t \le t')$, is called ***Arrow-Debreu state prices*** if $\mu_G = r + \sigma_G \lambda$ and $G(t') = \delta(r(t') - r')$, where $\delta(x)$ is the Dirac delta function.[2]

The next corollary follows directly from (17).

COROLLARY 2: In a locally arbitrage-free model,

$$G(t; t', r') = P^{t'}(t)\, E_t^{t'}\{\delta[r(t') - r']\}$$

In other words, Arrow–Debreu state prices are the discount factor times the conditional probability density function of the spot rate in the forward-risk-adjusted measure.

Primitive securities are the building blocks of all securities – so are their prices:

PROPOSITION 1: Let $C(t)$ follow an Itô process $dC/C = \mu_C dt - \sigma_C dw$ on an interval of time, satisfying $\mu_C = r + \sigma_C \lambda$. Assume further that there is a function of one variable r', denoted by $C(r', t')$, such that $C(t') = C(r(t'), t')$. Then

$$C(t) = \int G(t; r', t')\, C(r', t')\, dr'$$

PROOF: By (17), $C(t) = P^{t'}(t)\, E_t^{t'}[C(r(t'), t')]$. Now

$$C(r(t'), t') = \int C(r', t')\, \delta(r(t') - r')\, dr'$$

Substituting in the previous equation, pulling the integral out of the expectation and employing Corollary 2 gives the desired result. *Q.E.D.*

Since by the theorem $dr_T = \sigma_T(\sigma^T dt + d\tilde{w}) = \sigma_T dw^T$, it follows that when the volatility structure is deterministic, forward rates are Gaussian processes in both the risk-neutral and the forward-risk-adjusted measures (with the same variance). So the spot rate is normally distributed and Corollary 2 implies:

COROLLARY 3: In a locally arbitrage-free interest rate model with deterministic volatility structure $\sigma_T(t)$,

$$G(t; r', t') = P^{t'}(t)\, \frac{\exp\left(-\frac{1}{2}\left\{\left[r' - r_{t'}(t)\right]/v(t, t')\right\}\right)^2}{\sqrt{2\pi}\, v(t, t')}$$

where

$$v^2(t, t') = \tilde{var}_t[r(t')] = \int_t^{t'} \sigma_{t'}^2(s)\, ds$$

Thus, when the volatility structure is deterministic, Arrow–Debreu state prices are simply the discount factor times the density function of a normal random variable with mean equal to the forward rate and variance equal to that of the spot rate (variance taken either in the risk-neutral or the forward-risk-adjusted measure).

When the volatility structure is deterministic, even though forward rates are Gaussian processes and the spot rate is normally distributed in the risk-neutral and the forward-risk-adjusted measures, it does not necessarily follow that the spot rate is a Gaussian process in these measures. In fact, the spot rate would not even be a diffusion process (Markovian) unless the volatility structure is additionally of a very special and simple form, the quasi-Gaussian form. In this case (the Gaussian model) bond and Arrow–Debreu prices, and hence option prices, are functions of the spot rates and the notion of critical interest rates is well defined for American and multiple options, making their analytical evaluation possible.

(Quasi-) Gaussian volatility structures

Notation: For $0 \le t_0 \le t \le T$, set

$$v(t_0, t) = \left(\int_{t_0}^{t} \sigma_t^2(s)\,ds \right)^{\frac{1}{2}} \tag{18}$$

$$v^T(t_0, t) = \left(\int_{t_0}^{t} [\sigma^T(s) - \sigma^t(s)]^2 ds \right)^{\frac{1}{2}} \tag{19}$$

These important quantities, termed the *variance structure*, are the integrals of the squares of the forward-rate and forward-price volatility functions, respectively. Also set

$$a(T) = -(d/dT)\log \sigma_T(0) \tag{20}$$

THEOREM 2

The following conditions are equivalent.

(*a*) For $t_0 = 0$, and hence for all $t_0 \ge 0$ and all $t_0 \le t \le T$,

$$\sigma_T(t) = \frac{\sigma(t)\sigma_T(t_0)}{\sigma_t(t_0)} \tag{21}$$

(*b*) For all $0 \le t \le T$, $\sigma_T(t)$ is of the form $h(T)g(t)$.[2]

(*c*) For all $0 \le t_0 \le T$, $a(T) = -(\partial/\partial T)\log \sigma_T(t_0)$.

(*d*) There is a function $a(T)$ such that for all $0 \le t \le T$,

$$\sigma_T(t) = \sigma(t)\exp\left(-\int_t^T a(u)\,du\right) \tag{22}$$

In this case then, $a(T)$ is necessarily given by (20).

(*e*) For all $0 \le s \le t \le T$,

$$\sigma^T(s) - \sigma^t(s) = \sigma_t(s)\,\sigma^T(t)/\sigma(t) \tag{23}$$

(*f*) For all $0 \le t_0 \le t \le T$,

$$v^T(t_0, t) = [\sigma^T(t)/\sigma(t)]\,v(t_0, t) \tag{24}$$

(*g*) For all $0 \le t_0 \le t \le T$,

$$\int_{t_0}^{t} \sigma_t(s)\,[\sigma^T(s) - \sigma^t(s)]\,ds = v(t_0, t)\,v^T(t_0, t) \tag{25}$$

PROOF: The equivalence of (*a*), (*b*), (*c*), (*d*), and (*e*) is easy to see. We prove the equivalence of (*e*) with (*f*) and (*g*). Assume (*e*) holds. Then, by (23)

$$\int_{t_0}^{t} [\sigma^T(s) - \sigma^t(s)]^2 ds = \left(\frac{\sigma^T(t)}{\sigma(t)} \right)^2 \int_{t_0}^{t} \sigma_t^2(s)\,ds$$

which is the same as (24). Thus (*f*) follows. Conversely, if (*f*) holds, then the above equation is valid. Differentiating it with respect to t_0 gives (23), and (*e*) follows. Thus (*e*) and (*f*) are equivalent. Next, suppose (*e*) and hence (*f*) hold. Then the integrand of the left-hand side of (25) equals $\sigma_t^2(s)\sigma^T(t)/\sigma(t)$. Thus the left-hand side of (25) equals $v^2(t_0, t)\,\sigma^T(t)/\sigma(t)$, which by (24) equals the right-hand side of (25). Condition (*g*) follows. Finally, the Schwartz inequality states that (25) is always valid as an inequality, with equality holding only if the two factors in the integrand are linearly dependent. Thus, (*g*) implies that $\sigma^T(s) - \sigma^t(s) = \sigma_t(s)\,g(t, T)$ for some function g independent of s. Setting $s = t$ gives $g(t, t) = \sigma^T(t)/\sigma(t)$; hence (*e*) follows. *Q.E.D.*

DEFINITION 3: A volatility structure is said to be *quasi-Gaussian* if the equivalent conditions in Theorem 2 hold. A quasi-Gaussian volatility structure is called *Gaussian* if $\sigma^T(t)$ is deterministic for all $0 \le t \le T$. The function $a(T)$ is called the *mean-reversion parameter*. Together with $\sigma(t)$, they are referred to as the *volatility parameters* of the quasi-Gaussian volatility structure.

By definition (equation (20)), the mean-reversion parameter $a(T)$ and the initial volatility curve $\sigma_T(0)$ are uniquely determined by one another. Moreover, by equations (21) and (22), a quasi-Gaussian volatility structure is uniquely determined by its spot rate volatility function $\sigma(t)$ and either $\sigma_T(0)$ or $a(T)$. Thus, in order to specify an arbitrary quasi-Gaussian volatility structure, it suffices to specify an arbitrary spot rate volatility and either an arbitrary initial volatility curve or a mean-reversion parameter.

To give an example of a Gaussian model, it suffices to exhibit two deterministic functions $\sigma(t)$ and $a(t)$. The simplest example is when $\sigma(t) = \sigma$ is a (positive) constant and $a(t) = 0$. This is the case in the Merton (1973) model and its extended version, which is the Gaussian continuous-time limit of the Ho and Lee (1986) model. In this case,

$$\sigma_T(t) = \sigma$$

$$\sigma^T(t) = \sigma(T-t)$$

$$v(t_0, t) = \sigma\sqrt{t - t_0}$$

$$v^T(t_0, t) = \sigma(T-t)\sqrt{t - t_0}$$

The next simplest case, which is the more general, is when both of $\sigma(t) = \sigma$ and $a(t) = a$ are constants. This is the case in the Vasicek (1977) model and its extended version in Jamshidian (1987) and Heath, Jarrow and Morton (1992). Here,

$$\sigma_T(t) = \sigma \exp[-a(T-t)]$$

and if $a \ne 0$,

$$\sigma^T(t) = \frac{\sigma\{1 - \exp[-a(T-t)]\}}{a}$$

$$v^2(t_0, t) = \frac{\sigma^2\{1 - \exp[-2a(t - t_0)]\}}{2a}$$

Note that if $a \le 0$ $(a > 0)$, then the variance structure is unbounded (bounded).

We now introduce a new family of Gaussian volatility structures.

PROPOSITION 2: The following conditions are equivalent:
(*a*) The volatility structure is Gaussian and, for all $t \ge 0$, $a(t) = -\sigma'(t)/\sigma(t)$.
(*b*) For all $0 \le t_0 \le t$, $\sigma_t(t_0) = \sigma(t)$.
(*c*) For all $0 \le t \le T$, $\sigma^T(t) = \int_t^T \sigma(s)\, ds$.
(*d*) For all $0 \le t_0 \le t$, $v(t_0, t) = \sigma(t)\sqrt{t - t_0}$.

PROOF: The equivalence of (*b*) and (*c*) is obvious, and the equivalence of (*a*) and (*b*) follows by (22). Clearly, (*b*) implies (*d*). Conversely, (*b*) follows from (*d*) by differentiating $v^2(t_0, t)$ with respect to t_0. *Q.E.D.*

DEFINITION 4: A Gaussian volatility structure satisfying the equivalent conditions of Proposition 2 is termed *path-independent*.

Thus a path-independent Gaussian model is uniquely determined by the initial volatility curve $\sigma_T(0)$. Its spot rate volatility function is simply $\sigma(t) = \sigma_t(0)$. Moreover, $\sigma(t)$ is a constant if and only if $a(t) = 0$, reducing to the Merton volatility structure.

One-factor, (quasi-) Gaussian interest rate models

THEOREM 3: In an arbitrary one-factor interest model, the following conditions are equivalent:

(*a*) The model is locally arbitrage-free and the volatility structure is quasi-Gaussian.

(*b*) For all $0 \le t_0 \le t \le T$,

$$P^T(t) = \frac{P^T(t_0)}{P^t(t_0)} \exp\left(-\tfrac{1}{2}\left[v^T(t_0, t)\right]^2 - \left[\frac{\sigma^T(t)}{\sigma(t)}\right]\left[r(t) - r_t(t_0)\right]\right) \tag{26}$$

(*c*) For all $0 \le t_0 \le t \le T$

$$r_T(t) = r_T(t_0) + \left[\frac{\sigma_T(t)}{\sigma(t)}\right][r(t) - r_t(t_0) + v(t_0, t)v^T(t_0, t)] \tag{27}$$

(*d*) There is a function $a(t)$ such that, for all $0 \le t_0 \le t$,

$$dr(t) = \left(\frac{\partial r_t(t_0)}{\partial t} + v^2(t_0, t) + a(t)[r_t(t_0) - r(t)]\right)dt + \sigma(t)d\tilde{w}(t) \tag{28}$$

where $v^2(t_0, t)$ is defined by (18) and (22).

PROOF

(*a*) ⇔ (*c*) Assume (*a*) holds. By (16), and (21), we have

$$r_T(t) = r_T(t_0) + \frac{\sigma_T(t)}{\sigma(t)} \int_{t_0}^{t} \sigma_t(s)[\sigma^T(s)ds + d\tilde{w}(s)]$$

Using (15) to write $\int_{t_0}^{t}\sigma_t(s)d\tilde{w}(s)$ in terms of $r(t)$ gives

$$r_T(t) = r_T(t_0) + \frac{\sigma_T(t)}{\sigma(t)}\left(r(t) - r_t(t_0) + \int_{t_0}^{t} \sigma_t(s)[\sigma^T(s) - \sigma^t(s)]ds\right)$$

Applying (25) to the integral, (*c*) follows. Conversely, if (*c*) holds, then differentiating (27) with respect to t_0 we get

$$dr_T(t_0) = \frac{\sigma_T(t)}{\sigma(t)} \{dr_t(t_0) - d_{t_0}[v(t_0, t)v^T(t_0, t)]\}$$

Setting the stochastic parts (coefficients of $dw(t_0)$) of both sides equal, we get $\sigma_T(t_0) = \sigma_t(t_0)\sigma_T(t)/\sigma(t)$. Therefore, by (21), the volatility structure is quasi-Gaussian. Setting the drift parts equal and applying equation (25), we get

$$\mu_T(t_0) = \frac{\sigma_T(t)}{\sigma(t)} \{\mu_t(t_0) + \sigma_t(t_0)[\sigma^T(t_0) - \sigma^t(t_0)]\}$$

Setting $t = t_0$ gives the no-arbitrage condition (14) and (*a*) follows.

(*b*) ⇔ (*c*) Assume (*b*) holds. Then, differentiating the logarithm of (26) with respect to T, we get

$$r_T(t) = r_T(t_0) + \frac{\sigma_T(t)}{\sigma(t)}[r(t) - r_r(t_0)] + \frac{\tfrac{1}{2}\partial[v^T(t_0, t)]^2}{\partial T}$$

In particular, as in the proof of (*c*) ⇒ (*a*) Assume (*c*) holds. Then, as we showed above, the volatility structure is quasi-Gaussian. Therefore, (24) holds, and the last term in the above equation equals $[\sigma_T(t)/\sigma(t)]v(t_0, t)v^T(t_0, t)$, yielding (27). Similarly, (*b*) follows from (*c*) by integrating (27) with respect to T.

(*c*) ⇒ (*d*) Assume (*c*) holds. Then, as we showed above, the volatility structure is quasi-

Gaussian and hence (24) holds. Differentiating (27) with respect to T thus gives

$$\left.\frac{\partial r_T(t)}{\partial T}\right|_{T=t} = \frac{\partial r_t(t_0)}{\partial t} + v^2(t_0, t) + a(t)[r_t(t_0) - r(t)]$$

Equation (28) now follows from Lemma 2.

(d) ⇒ *(a)* Set

$$x(t) = [r(t) - r_t(t_0)]\exp\left(\int_{t_0}^{t} a(s)\,ds\right)$$

It follows from (28) that

$$dx(t) = \exp\left(\int_{t_0}^{t} a(s)\,ds\right)[v^2(t_0, t)\,dt + \sigma(t)\,d\tilde{w}(t)]$$

Integrating, since $x(t_0) = 0$, we get

$$r(t) - r_t(t_0) = \int_{t_0}^{t} \exp\left(-\int_{s}^{t} a(u)\,du\right)[v^2(t_0, s)\,ds + \sigma(s)\,d\tilde{w}(s)]$$

Now take the differential of both sides with respect to t_0. Setting the stochastic parts equal, we get $\sigma_t(t_0) = \sigma(t_0)\exp[-\int_{t_0}^{t} a(s)\,ds]$, which by (22) implies that the volatility structure is quasi-Gaussian with mean-reversion parameter $a(t)$. Setting the drift parts equal and using the fact that by (18) $d_{t_0} v^2(t_0, s) = -\sigma_s^2(t_0)$ (and that $v(t_0, t_0) = 0$), we find

$$\mu_t(t_0) = \int_{t_0}^{t} \exp\left(-\int_{s}^{t} a(u)\,du\right)\sigma_s^2(t_0)\,ds - \sigma_t(t_0)\lambda(t)$$

Using (21) and (22), the above integral equals $\sigma_t(t_0)\sigma^t(t_0)$. Thus, by (14), the model is locally arbitrage-free. *Q.E.D.*

DEFINITION 5

A one-factor, locally arbitrage-free interest rate model that satisfies the equivalent conditions of Theorem 3 is called a (one-factor) *quasi-Gaussian interest rate model*. If in addition the volatility structure $\sigma_T(t)$ is deterministic, then the model is called a (one-factor) *Gaussian interest rate model*, or a Gaussian model for short. A Gaussian model is called *path-independent* if its volatility structure is so.

Equations (26) and (27) explicitly relate the term structures between *any* two times t and t_0. They appeared in Heath, Jarrow and Morton (1992) for the special case of the Vasicek volatility structure (where $\sigma(t)$ and $a(t)$ are constant). The fact that here the initial trade date t_0 can be arbitrary shows the translation invariance of the Gaussian model, and it establishes (26) and (27) as equivalent characterisations of the Gaussian model. These formulas also appear in Jamshidian (1990), using a different derivation.

Equation (26) can also be viewed as a bond pricing formula in terms of the spot rate. Note that the market price of risk does not enter the equation, but the forward price and forward rate at an (any) earlier time are present. As a bond pricing formula, (26) has a simple form and is easy to interpret. The term $P^T(t_0)/P^t(t_0)$ is the forward bond price at time t_0. The exponential term may thus be interpreted as a "perturbation", measuring for the most part the extent to which the future spot rate deviates from the current forward rate.

Equation (28) relates the drift of the interest rate process to an (any) initial forward rate curve. For the special case of the Vasicek volatility structure, it appeared in similar forms in Jamshidian (1987) and Heath, Jarrow and Morton (1992). In essence, it states that the "initial" forward rate curve has a big say in controlling the trend of future spot rates. It also shows that, aside from the term $v^2(t_0, t)$ and the risk premium, the spot rate process exhibits a reversion towards the forward rate (hence the term "mean-reversion") with "speed of adjustment" equal to $a(t)$.

As Theorem 3 states, formulas (26)–(28) hold for all quasi-Gaussian models, including those in which the spot rate volatility $\sigma(t)$ is not deterministic. But in the latter case, it is easy to see that the spot rate is not a diffusion process and that bond prices and forward rates are not functions of the spot rate. By contrast, in the Gaussian model, (28) with $t_0 = 0$ implies that

$$dr(t) = [b(t) - a(t)r(t)]\,dt + \sigma(t)\,d\tilde{w}(t)$$

where

$$b(t) = dr_t(0)/dt + v^2(0,t) + a(t)r_t(0)$$

is deterministic, ie, the spot rate is a Gaussian diffusion process with respect to $\tilde{w}(t)$ (also with respect to $w(t)$ if $\lambda(t)$ is linear in $r(t)$). The converse is also true:

PROPOSITION 3: For a one-factor, locally arbitrage-free interest rate model, the following conditions are equivalent:
(*a*) The model is Gaussian.
(*b*) The volatility structure is deterministic and the spot rate is a diffusion process with respect to $\tilde{w}(t)$.
(*c*) The spot rate is Gaussian with respect to $\tilde{w}(t)$, ie,

$$dr(t) = [b(t) - a(t)r(t)]\,dt + \sigma(t)\,d\tilde{w}(t)$$

for some deterministic functions $b(t)$, $a(t)$, and $\sigma(t)$. In this case, $a(t)$ is the mean-reversion parameter of the Gaussian model and, for all $0 \le t_0 \le t$,

$$b(t) = \partial r_t(t_0)/\partial t + v^2(t_0,t) + a(t)r_t(t_0) \tag{29}$$

and, for all $0 \le t \le T$,

$$r_T(t) = \left(\frac{\sigma_T(t)}{\sigma(t)}\right) r(t) + \int_t^T \sigma_T(u)\left(-\sigma^T(u) + \frac{b(u)}{\sigma(u)}\right) du \tag{30}$$

Equation (30), when integrated and exponentiated, gives a bond pricing formula in terms of the spot rate and the "drift parameter" $b(t)$. Apart from notational differences, this bond pricing formula is similar to those in Merton (1973), Vasicek (1977), Jamshidian (1987) and Hull and White (1990*a*) mentioned in the second section. The problem with this form is that, unlike (26) and (27), it is not simple or easy to interpret. But, substituting from (29) for the drift parameter $b(u)$ in (30), the formula simplifies remarkably, reducing to (27). The difference between these two forms is that one is in terms of the drift parameter $b(t)$, while the other is in terms of an initial yield curve. The latter form is simpler and more meaningful financially.

PROPOSITION 4: In a Gaussian model the spot rate and all forward rates follow Gaussian diffusion processes with respect to both the risk-neutral measure and the forward-risk-adjusted measure, and zero-coupon bond prices are lognormally distributed. Moreover, for all $0 \le t_0 \le t \le T$ we have

$$\tilde{\mathrm{var}}_{t_0}[r(t)] = v^2(t_0,t) \tag{31}$$

$$\{\tilde{\mathrm{var}}_{t_0}[\log P^T(t)]\}^{\frac{1}{2}} = v^T(t_0,t) = \left(\frac{\sigma^T(t)}{\sigma(t)}\right) v(t_0,t) \tag{32}$$

Equations (31) and (32) also hold if variance is taken with respect to the s-maturity forward-risk-adjusted measure for any $t \le s \le T$.

Arrow–Debreu state prices in the Gaussian model

Equations (26) and (27) express the discount function and forward rates as explicit functions of the spot rate and an initial term structure. For $t_0 = 0$, we denote these functions by $P^T(r,t)$ and $r_T(r,t)$. Thus $P^T(t) = P^T(r(t),t)$ and $r_T(t) = r_T(r(t),t)$.

As in the formula for Arrow-Debreu state prices in Corollary (3), we define

$$G(r,t,r',t') = \frac{P^{t'}(r,t)\exp\left\{-\frac{1}{2}\left[r'-r_{t'}(r,t)/v(t,t')\right]^2\right\}}{\sqrt{2\pi}v(t,t')} \tag{33}$$

Thus $G(t; r', t') = G(r(t), t; r', t')$.

THEOREM 4: Let $C(t)$ follow an Itô process $dC/C = \mu_C dt - \sigma_C dw$ on an interval of time, satisfying $\mu_C = r + \sigma_C\lambda$. Assume further that there is a function of one variable r', denoted by $C(r',t')$, such that $C(t') = C(r(t'),t')$. Then, in the Gaussian model, $C(t) = C(r(t),t)$ for all $t < t'$ in that interval, where $C(r,t)$ is the function of two variables (analytic in r) defined by

$$C(r,t) = \int_{-\infty}^{\infty} G(r,t,r',t')\,C(r',t')\,dr' \tag{34}$$

Moreover, $LC(r,t) = 0$, where L is the differential operator

$$LC(r,t) \equiv \frac{\partial C}{\partial t} + \left(\frac{dr_t(0)}{dt} + v^2(0,t) + a(t)[r_t(0) - r]\right)\frac{\partial C}{\partial r} + \frac{1}{2}\sigma^2(t)\frac{\partial^2 C}{\partial r^2} - rC \tag{35}$$

In particular, for $t < t'$, $LG(r,t,r',t') = 0$. Conversely, if a function $C(r,t)$ satisfies either (34) or (35), then $C(t) = C(r(t),t)$ satisfies $\mu_C = r + \sigma_C\lambda$ in that interval.

PROOF: Equation (34) follows by Proposition 1. Next, apply Itô's lemma to $C(t) = C(r(t),t)$ to write μ_C and σ_C in terms of the partial derivatives of $C(r,t)$, the spot rate volatility $\sigma(t)$ and the drift given in (28). Substituting into $\mu_C = r + \sigma_C\lambda$, (35) follows. Conversely, if (34) is satisfied, then $LC = 0$, since $LG = 0$. And if $LC = 0$, then the above argument applies in reverse, showing that $\mu_C = r + \sigma_C\lambda$. *Q.E.D.*

The pricing formula (34) is our main tool for analytical evaluation. The fundamental pde (35) provides the means for numerical evaluation. Since these equations are in terms of the initial term structure and are independent of risk parameters, so will be option evaluation. Note also that the assumption of the theorem is satisfied for options because their terminal payoffs are defined in terms of bond prices, which by (26) are functions of the spot rate.

In the context of (34) and (35), $G(r,t,r',t')$ is known as the *fundamental solution* or *Green's function* of the differential operator (35). Applying (34) to $C(r,t) = G(r,t,r'',t'')$, it follows that for all $t < t' < t''$ Green's function satisfies the semi-group property

$$G(r,t,r'',t'') = \int_{-\infty}^{\infty} G(r,t,r',t')\,G(r',t',r'',t'')\,dr' \tag{36}$$

We also need the fact that the solution of the inhomogeneous pde, $LC + h = 0$, is expressed by[4]

$$C(r,t) = \int_{-\infty}^{\infty} G(r,t,r^*,t^*)\,C(r^*,t^*)\,dr^* + \int_t^{t^*}\int_{-\infty}^{\infty} G(r,t,r',t')\,h(r',t')\,dr'\,dt' \tag{37}$$

Indeed, by Theorem 4, $LG(r,t,r',t') = 0$ for $t < t'$, while clearly $G(r,t,r',t') = \delta(r - r')$. Applying the operator L to the right-hand side of (37) easily gives $-h$.

The explicit knowledge of Arrow–Debreu state prices also serves to establish comparative statistics of bond and option prices. In particular, we need:

LEMMA 3: Assume $C(r', t')$ is a continuous, piecewise differentiable, positive, non-increasing function of r', and for $t < t'$ define $C(r, t)$ by (34). Then $C(r, t)$ is analytic and strictly decreasing in r, and its range is the entire positive axis.

In particular, for a fixed initial yield curve, prices of call options and callable and/or putable bonds are strictly decreasing functions of the spot interest rate and can reach any positive price. A similar result shows that (positive) convexity is preserved. In particular, prices of call options and putable bonds are convex functions of the spot interest rate.

Analytic evaluation of American options

Let $D(u)$, $t \le u \le T$, represent a (continuous or discrete) coupon stream, and let

$$P_D(t) = P_D(r(t), t) = P^T(t) + \int_t^T D(u)\, P^u(t)\, du$$

represent the price at time t of a bond with coupon stream $D(u)$, maturity T and principal 1. Clearly, $LP_D(r, t) + D(t) = 0$. Next let

$$C(t) = C(r(t), t) = C(t; t^*, K(u), T, D(u))$$

denote the price at time t of an American call option with expiration t^* and strike prices $K(u)$ $(u \le t^*)$ on the T-maturity coupon bond. By definition, $C(t^*) = \max\{0, P_D(t^*) - K(t^*)\}$.

For an American call option, there is a path $r^*(t)$ $(t \le t^*)$, known as the "optimal exercise boundary" or "critical interest rates", below which (price is high and) the option is exercised, ie, for $r(t) \le r^*(t)$, $C(t) = P_D(t) - K(t)$. Above it (price is low and) the option is kept "alive". A similar trading strategy argument as in the section "(Quasi-) Gaussian volatility structures" applies to the live American option, indicating that for $r(t) > r^*(t)$, $\mu_C = r + \sigma_C \lambda$, and hence, as in the previous section, $LC(r, t) = 0$ for $r > r^*(t)$. Moreover, among all possible exercise boundaries, the path $r^*(t)$ maximises the value of the American option. Using an argument similar to Ingersoll (1987, p. 374), this shows that $C(r, t)$ is continuously differentiable at $r^*(t)$.

Noting that $L(P_D(r, t) = K(t)) - D(t) - K'(t)$, it now follows that

$$LC(r, t) + [D(t) + K'(t) - rK(t)]\, H[r^*(t) - r] = 0 \tag{38}$$

where $H(x)$ denotes the Heaviside unit step function, ie, $H(x) = 0$ for $x \le 0$ and $H(x) = 1$ for $x > 0$.[5] Equation (37) now implies that

$$C(r, t) = c(r, t) + \int_t^{t^*} \int_{-\infty}^{r^*(u)} G(r, t, r', u)\, [D(u) + K'(u) - r'K(u)]\, dr'\, du \tag{39}$$

where $c(r, t)$ denotes the price of the European option with the same parameters. Given the explicit expression (33) for the Arrow-Debreu state prices G, the dr'-integral is now easily calculated, yielding:

PROPOSITION 5: In the Gaussian model,

$$C(t) = c(t) + \int_t^{t^*} P^u(t) \left([D(u) + K'(u) - K(u) r_u(t)] N(z^*) + K(u)\, v(t, u) \frac{e^{-z^{*2}/2}}{\sqrt{2\pi}} \right) du \tag{40}$$

where $z^* = [r^*(u) - r_u(t)]/v(t, u)$.

American put options are handled similarly. With the obvious notation for the price of the put, we have

$$P(t)=p(t)+$$

$$\int_t^{t^*} P^u(t)\left([-D(u)-K'(u)+K(u)r_u(t)]N(-z^*)+K(u)v(t,u)\frac{e^{-z^{*2}/2}}{\sqrt{2\pi}}\right)du \tag{41}$$

In the most common application the coupon is discrete, with a constant annual rate D_0 at discrete payment dates T_i, and the "flat" or "quoted" strike price K is also a constant. In this case,

$$D(t) = D_0 \sum (T_i - T_{i-1})\, \delta(t - T_i)$$

and by market convention, $K(t) = K + A(t)$, where $A(t)$ is the accrued interest. From the definition of accrued interest, it is easy to see that $A'(t) = D_0 - D(t)$. Thus (39), (40) and (41) hold with $D(t) + K'(t)$ simply replaced by D_0.

Note that, as a function of r (with $P^u(r, t)$, etc.), the right-hand side of (40) at $r = r^*(t)$ must equal $P_D(r^*(t), t) - K(t)$. This gives a non-linear integral equation for $r^*(t)$, which can be solved numerically. Once $r^*(t)$ is determined, American call (or put) options can be evaluated by numerically integrating (40) (or (41)).[6]

Analytic evaluation of multiple options

Our formulas for multiple options involve the covariance structure. For any $t_0 < t < t'$ set[7]

$$v(t_0, t, t') \equiv \int_{t_0}^{t} \sigma_t(s)\,\sigma_{t'}(s)\,ds \tag{42}$$

$$\rho(t_0, t, t') \equiv \frac{v(t_0, t, t')}{v(t_0, t)\, v(t_0, t')} \tag{43}$$

(For $t' < t$ we set $v(t_0, t, t') \equiv v(t_0, t', t)$; similarly for ρ.) A similar argument as in Proposition 3 shows that, in the Gaussian model, these quantities are, respectively, the conditional covariance and the correlation matrix of the spot rate with respect to the risk-neutral (and the forward-risk-adjusted) measure:

$$v(t_0, t, t') = \tilde{\text{cov}}_{t_0}[r(t), r(t')], \qquad \rho(t_0, t, t') = \tilde{\text{cor}}_{t_0}[r(t), r(t')]$$

Next, for any $n \times n$ positive definite symmetric matrix Q and vector $u = (u_1, \ldots, u_n)$, let $p(x; Q, u)$ denote the multivariate normal density function with covariance matrix Q and mean vector u, ie,

$$p(x;Q,u)=\frac{\exp\left[-\frac{1}{2}(x-u)Q^{-1}(x-u)'\right]}{[(2\pi)^n \det(Q)]^{\frac{1}{2}}} \tag{44}$$

We are now ready to state the main technical result of the paper.

THEOREM 5

For $t < t_1 < \ldots < t_i$, the product of the Arrow–Debreu state prices in the Gaussian model is given by

$$G(r, t, r_1, t_1) \ldots G(r_{i-1}, t_{i-1}, r_i, t_i) = P^{t_i}(r, t)\, p(r_1, \ldots, r_i; Q, u^{(i)}) \tag{45}$$

where Q is the matrix with element (j, k) equal to $v(t, t_j, t_k)$, and $u^{(i)}$ is the vector with kth coordinate

$$u_k^{(i)} = r_{t_k}(r, t) - v(t, t_k)\, v^{t_i}(t, t_k) \tag{46}$$

The theorem states that the product of consecutive pure state prices is the "long" discount factor times the density function of a multivariate normal distribution with covariance matrix of the spot rate and mean related to forward rates. Again, the market price of risk does not appear in it. This result is applicable to the analytical evaluation of options with discrete strike dates, as we now demonstrate. Its practical usefulness is, however, limited to the cases when there are only two or three strike dates, for higher-dimensional multivariate normal distributions are computationally formidable.

A *multiple call option* with call dates $t_1 < \ldots < t_n$ and strike prices $K_1, \ldots, K_n$ $(K_i > 0)$ is an option that gives the holder the right to purchase the bond at any (but only one) of the call dates t_i $(1 \le i \le n)$ at the strike price K_i. A multiple put option is defined similarly. American options are limits of multiple options with a continuum of strike dates.

We first study multiple options on zero-coupon bonds and generalise the results to coupon bonds in the next section. Actually, it is analytically more convenient to analyse bonds with embedded multiple options. Thus let

$$C(t) = C^{(n)}(t) = C^{(n)}(r(t), t) = C^{(n)}(t; K_1, \ldots, K_n, t_1, \ldots, t_n, T)$$

denote the price at time t of a zero-coupon callable bond with n call dates $t_1 < \ldots < t_n$, call prices $K_1, \ldots, K_n$, maturity $T > t_n$ and principal 1. The price of a call option with the same parameters is simply $P^T(t) - C^{(n)}(t)$.

The definition of $C(t) = C^{(n)}(t)$ is as follows. First, for $t_i < t < t_{i+1}$, $1 \le i \le n$, it is postulated that $C(t)$ satisfies $\mu_C = r + \sigma_C \lambda$. At a call date t_i, $C(t_i)$ is defined basically by replacing the "diffused price" by its minimum with the call price K_i. More precisely, for $t_n < t \le T$, define $C(t) = P^T(t)$. At $t = t_n$, define $C(t_n) = \min\{K_n, P^T(t_n)\}$. (Thus the value of the embedded call option at t_n is $P^T(t_n) - \min\{K_n, P^T(t_n)\} = \max\{0, P^T(t_n) - K_n\}$.) Having defined $C(t)$ for $t \ge t_i$, $i \le n$, we define $C(t)$ for $t \ge t_{i-1}$ inductively as follows. For $t_{i-1} < t < t_i$, $C(t)$ is defined by the pricing formula (34), with $t' = t_i$. Next, set

$$C_+(t_{i-1}) = \int_{-\infty}^{\infty} G(t_{i-1}; r_i, t_i)\, C(r_i, t_i)\, dr_i$$

and define $C(t_{i-1}) = \min\{K_{i-1}, C_+(t_{i-1})\}$. For $t < t_1$, $C(t)$ is defined similarly by (34), with $t' = t_1$.

Next, we define the critical interest rates r_i^*. For $i = n$, r_n^* is the unique solution to the equation $P^T(r_n^*, t_n) = K_n$. For $1 \le i \le n-1$, r_i^* is the unique solution to the equation $C_+(r_i^*, t_i) = K_i$, the existence and uniqueness of which is guaranteed by Lemma 3.

Applying the pricing formula (34) for $t < t_1$, we now get

$$\begin{aligned} C(t) &= \int_{-\infty}^{\infty} G(t; r_1, t_1) \min\{K_1, C(r_1, t_1)\}\, dr_1 \\ &= K_1 \int_{-\infty}^{r_1^*} G(t; r_1, t_1)\, dr_1 + \int_{r_1^*}^{\infty} G(t; r_1, t_1)\, C(r_1, t_1)\, dr_1 \end{aligned}$$

By a similar calculation, the term $C(r_1, t_1)$ in the above equation has a similar form. Substituting this expression for $C(r_1, t_1)$ back in the equation and repeating in this manner, we obtain inductively[8]

$$\begin{aligned} C^{(n)}(t) = K_1 &\int_{-\infty}^{r_1^*} G(t; r_1, t_1)\, dr_1 + \\ K_2 &\int_{r_1^*}^{\infty} \int_{-\infty}^{r_2^*} G(t; r_1, t_1)\, G(r_1, t_1, r_2, t_2)\, dr_1\, dr_2 + \ldots \\ + K_n &\int_{r_1^*}^{\infty} \ldots \int_{r_{n-1}^*}^{\infty} \int_{-\infty}^{r_n^*} G(t; r_1, t_1) \ldots G(r_{n-1}, t_{n-1}, r_n, t_n)\, dr_1 \ldots dr_{n-1}\, dr_n + \\ &\int_{r_1^*}^{\infty} \ldots \int_{r_n^*}^{\infty} G(t; r_1, t_1) \ldots G(r_{n-1}, t_{n-1}, r_n, t_n)\, P^T(r_n, t_n)\, dr_1 \ldots dr_n \end{aligned} \tag{47}$$

The product of Arrow–Debreu state prices was calculated in Theorem 5. There now remains the simple step of "completing the square" in the last integral above.[9]

PROPOSITION 6: The value $C^{(n)}(t)$ of a multiple callable zero-coupon bond in the one-factor Gaussian interest rate model is given by

$$C^{(n)}(t) = \sum_{i=1}^{n} P^{t_i}(t) K_i N\left(h_1^{(i)}, \ldots, h_{i-1}^{(i)}, -h_i^{(i)}; \rho^{(i)^-}\right) + P^T(t) N\left(h_1^T, \ldots, h_n^T; \rho^{(n)}\right) \quad (48)$$

where

$$h_k^{(i)} = \frac{r_{t_k}(t) - r_k^*}{v(t, t_k)} - v^{t_i}(t, t_k), \quad 1 \le k \le i \le n \quad (49)$$

$$h_k^{(T)} = h_k^{(n)} - v^T(t, t_n)\, \rho(t, t_k, t_n), \quad 1 \le k \le n \quad (50)$$

$\rho^{(i)}$ is the $i \times i$ correlation matrix with element (k, j) equal to $\rho(t, t_k, t_j)$, and $\rho^{(i)^-}$ denotes the $i \times i$ matrix obtained from the matrix $\rho^{(i)}$ by multiplying its last row and last column by -1, and where for any $i \times i$ correlation matrix ρ, the function $N(h_1, \ldots, h_i; \rho)$ denotes the "standard" multivariate normal distribution function given by the i-dimensional integral $\int_{-\infty}^{h} p(x; \rho, 0)\, dx$.

A number of comments are in order. First, viewing the T-maturity bond as the underlying risky asset, let us express $h_k^{(i)}$ and h_n^T in terms of the critical prices $K_k^* = P^T(r_k^*, t_k)$. (Note that $K_n^* = K_n$.) Substituting from the bond pricing formula (26) into (49) and (50), forward rates cancel and we obtain

$$h_k^{(i)} = h_k^* + \tfrac{1}{2} v^T(t, t_k) - v^{t_i}(t, t_k), \quad 1 \le k \le i \le n \quad (51)$$

where

$$h_k^* = \frac{\log\left(P^{t_k}(t) K_k^* / P^T(t)\right)}{v^T(t, t_k)} \quad 1 \le k \le n$$

Next, putable bonds are defined similarly by replacing "min" in the payoff by "max". This has the effect of reversing the limits of integration in (47), which in turn changes the sign of the arguments in (48). Therefore, the value $P^{(n)}(t)$ of a putable bond is[10]

$$P^{(n)}(t) = \sum_{i=1}^{n} P^{t_i}(t) K_i N\left(-h_1^{(i)}, \ldots, -h_{i-1}^{(i)}, h_i^{(i)}; \rho^{(i)^-}\right) + P^T(t) N\left(-h_1^T, \ldots, -h_n^T; \rho^{(n)}\right) \quad (52)$$

The value of the embedded multiple put option is of course $P^{(n)}(t) - P^T(t)$.

Finally, note that the multiple pricing formula (48) has effectively decomposed the price of the callable bond into the contributions of each of its contingent cashflows (call prices and principal). In a loose sense, the various coefficients $N(\cdot\,;\cdot)$ in (48) can be interpreted as the probabilities that these cashflows occur, ie, the probabilities that the bond will be called at corresponding call dates. A similar observation holds for putable bonds.

Decomposition of a multiple option on a coupon bond into a portfolio of multiple options on zero-coupon bonds

For convenience, we first develop this decomposition for coupon bonds with embedded multiple options. If there are m coupon and principal cashflows, then the decomposition is a sum of m multiple options. A similar decomposition for (embedded) options then follows.[11]

Let $T_1 < \ldots < T_m$ denote the coupon (and principal) cashflow dates (T_m = maturity), and $a_1, \ldots, a_m$ denote the corresponding cashflows. As before, the call dates are denoted by $t_1, \ldots, t_n$ and the call prices by $K_1, \ldots, K_n$.[12] The price of a callable bond with these parameters is denoted by $C^{(n,m)}(t)$. (Its formal definition is similar to the one given for the zero-coupon case of the previous section.) The price of the call option with the same parameters simply equals the price of the non-callable bond (with same maturity and coupon) minus the price of the callable bond, ie, it equals $\sum_{j=1}^{m} a_j P^{T_j}(t) - C^{(n,m)}(t)$.

LEMMA 4: If $f_1(r), \ldots, f_k(r)$ are decreasing functions with range the entire positive axis, then for any $X > 0$ and $b_k > 0$,

$$\min\left[X, \sum b_i f_i(r)\right] = \sum b_i \min[X_i, f_i, (r)]$$

where $X_i = f_i(r^*)$, and r^* is the unique solution of the equation $\sum b_i f_i(r^*) = X$.

PROOF: If $r > r^*$, then $f_i(r) < X_i$, so both sides of the above equation equal $\sum b_i f_i(r)$. Similarly, if $r \le r^*$, then both sides equal X. *Q.E.D.*

PROPOSITION 7:

(*a*) Assume $n = 1$, ie, the option is European, and suppose $t < T_1 < \ldots < T_q \le t_1 < T_{q+1} < \ldots T_m$. Then

$$C^{(1,m)}(t) = \sum_{k=1}^{q} a_k P^{T_k}(t) + \sum_{j=q+1}^{m} a_j C^{(1)}(t; K^j, t_1, T_j)$$

where $K^j = P^{T_j}(r^*, t_1)$ and where r^* is the unique solution of the equation $\sum a_j P^{T_j}(r^*, t_1) = K_1$.

(*b*) A multiple callable bond with n call dates and m coupon cashflows is linearly decomposed into a portfolio of m zero-coupon multiple callable bonds as follows. Break the coupon dates into $n + 1$ (some possibly empty) pieces lying between the call dates:

$$T_1 < \ldots < T_{m_1} \le t_1 < T_{m_1+1} \ldots < T_{m_2} \le t_2 < \ldots \le t_{n-1} < \ldots < T_{m_n} \le t_n < T_{m_n+1} < \ldots < T_m$$

Then

$$C^{(n,m)}(t) = \sum_{j_0=1}^{m_1} a_{j_0} P^{T_{j_0}}(t) + \sum_{j_1=m_1+1}^{m_2} a_{j_1} C^{(1)}(t; K_1^{j_1}, t_1, T_{j_1}) +$$
$$\sum_{j_2=m_2+1}^{m_3} a_{j_2} C^{(2)}(t; K_1^{j_2}, K_2^{j_2}, t_1, t_2, T_{j_2}) + \cdots$$
$$\sum_{j_n=m_n+1}^{m} a_{j_n} C^{(n)}(t; K_1^{j_n}, \ldots, K_n^{j_n}, t_1, \ldots, t_n, T_{j_n})$$

where $K_n^{j_n}$ is uniquely defined jointly with r_n^* by the two relations

$$K_n^{j_n} = P^{T_{j_n}}(r_n^*, t_n), \quad K_n = \sum_{j_n=m_n+1}^{m} a_{j_n} K_n^{j_n}$$

and, for $i \le n-1$, the values $K_i^{j_k}$ $(i \le k \le n)$ are defined inductively as follows: $K_n^{j_k}$ are uniquely defined with r_i^* by the $n + 1 - i$ relations

$$K_i^{j_i} = P^{T_{j_i}}(r_i^*, t_i)$$

$$K_i^{j_{i+1}} = C^{(1)}(r_i^*, t_i; K_{i+1}^{j_{i+1}}, t_{i+1}, T_{j_{i+1}}), \ldots$$

$$K_i^{j_n} = C^{(n-i)}(r_i^*, t_i; K_{i+1}^{j_n}, \ldots, K_n^{j_n}, t_{i+1}, \ldots, t_n, T_{j_n})$$

$$K_i = \sum_{j_i=m_{i+1}}^{m_{i+1}} a_{j_i} K_i^{j_i} + \cdots + \sum_{j_n=m_n+1}^{m} a_{j_n} K_i^{j_n}$$

It follows from the proposition that the call option with the same parameters decomposes similarly into a portfolio consisting of $m-m_1$ multiple-call options, the jth of which ($m_{i+1} \le j \le m$) is on the T_j-maturity zero-coupon bond and has exercise prices $K_1^j, \ldots, K_{i_j}^j$, where i_j is the largest integer for which $t_{i_j} < T_j$. Also, since putable bonds are decreasing functions of the spot rate, an identical decomposition holds for putable bonds. Hence put options are also so decomposed. The decomposition also extends to bonds that are both callable and putable.

Numerical evaluation and the binomial discretisation of path-independent Gaussian models

Options and bonds with embedded options can be evaluated by numerically solving the fundamental pde (35). For example, one may employ an explicit finite-difference technique, which amounts to a "trinomial" algorithm as in Hull and White (1990*b*). Alternatively, one may employ the general binomial discretisation of Heath, Jarrow and Morton (1990), which requires computation along 2^n yield curve paths, where n is the total number of time steps. But, this is computationally prohibitive for n larger than, say, 20. For solving the fundamental pde, it is better first to simplify the differential equation by a change of variable. Set $R = r - r_t(0)$, and define $c(R, t) = P^t(0)\, C(r, t)$. Then one easily verifies that (35) transforms into the equivalent equation

$$\frac{\partial c}{\partial t} + [v^2(0,t) - a(t)R]\,\frac{\partial c}{\partial R} + \tfrac{1}{2}\sigma^2(t)\,\frac{\partial^2 c}{\partial R^2} - Rc = 0$$

This differential equation no longer contains any initial yield curve data. The term structure is incorporated directly into $c(R, t)$. This has the effect of simply replacing all coupon and principal cashflows and strike prices by their discounted present values. In particular, it follows that in the Gaussian model prices of options and callable and/or putable bonds depend only on the discount factors to maturity, coupon and strike dates and are homogeneous of degree one in these discount factors.

Further simplification is possible for path-independent Gaussian models. In this case, the spot rate and hence the entire yield curve depend only on the level (not the prior history) of the Brownian motion. Indeed, in this case $\sigma_t(s) = \sigma(t)$, and an easy calculation using (15) (with $t_0 = 0$) shows that

$$r(t) = r_t(0) + \sigma(t)\left(\int_0^t s\sigma(s)\,ds + \tilde{w}(t)\right)$$

It is therefore not surprising that in a path-independent Gaussian model the differential equation (33) can be transformed to the heat equation. For this purpose, set

$$z = \frac{r - r^t(0)}{\sigma(t)} - t\sigma^t(0)$$

$$p(z, t) = P^t(0)\exp\{-\tfrac{1}{2}t[\sigma^t(0)]^2 - \sigma^t(0)z\}$$

$$c(z, t) = p(z, t)\, C(r, t)$$

A straightforward but lengthy calculation then gives[13]

$$\frac{\partial c}{\partial t} + \frac{1}{2}\frac{\partial^2 c}{\partial z^2} = 0 \qquad (53)$$

Applying the explicit finite-difference technique with $\Delta z = \sqrt{\Delta t}$, one gets

$$c(z, t - \Delta t) = \tfrac{1}{2}[c(z + \Delta z, t) + c(z - \Delta z), t] + O(\Delta t)^2$$

If this algorithm is applied to evaluate the T-maturity zero-coupon bond, it would not exactly yield the current bond price. However, it would if we replace $p(z, t)$ above by

$$\tilde{q}(z, t) = P^t(0)\exp(-\sigma^t(0)z)\left\{\cosh\left[\sigma^t(0)\sqrt{\Delta t}\right]\right\}^{-t/\Delta t} \tag{54}$$

(Details are given in Jamshidian (1989*b*) for the more general multifactor case.) We may now state our algorithm for the evaluation of multiple callable bonds as follows.

Let Δt denote the length of a period. Identify a period n by the time $t = n\Delta t$ and the maturity by period $M = T_m/\Delta t$. (For simplicity we assume that the maturity, coupon and call dates are integer multiples of Δt.) Set $q(j, t) = \tilde{q}(j\sqrt{\Delta t}, t)$.

```
Begin algorithm:
    c(j) ← a_m q(j, T_m),  j = −M, −M + 2, ..., M − 2, M.
    Do N = M − 1 to 0 step −1.
        c(j) ← ½[c(j + 1) + c(j − 1)],  j = −N, −N + 2, ..., N − 2, N.
        If period N = t/Δt is a call date with call price K, then
        c(j) ← Min{c(j), Kq(j, t)},  j = −N, −N + 2, ..., N − 2, N.
        If period N = t/Δt is a coupon date with cashflow a, then
        c(j) ← c(j) + aq(j, t),  j = −N, −N + 2, ..., N − 2, N.
    End Do.
    (Full) price of callable bond = c(0).
End algorithm.
```

Finally, let us mention a binomial discretisation of the path-independent Gaussian model, which reduces to the Ho and Lee model when $\sigma(t)$ is a constant. This binomial model has been derived independently in Pederson, Shiu and Thorlacius (1989), to which we refer the reader for a detailed discussion. Here we just point out how the path-independent Gaussian model obtains as its continuous-time limit.

The binomial model is derived by relaxing the requirement of Ho and Lee (1986) that δ be a constant. Adopting a notation similar to Ho and Lee, the one-period discount factors for period n are given by

$$P_t^{(n)}(1) = \left(\frac{P(n+1)}{P(n)}\right)\delta_n^{n-i}h_0(n)\left(\frac{h_1(n-1)}{h_0(n-1)}\right)\cdots\left(\frac{h_{n-1}(1)}{h_{n-2}(1)}\right)$$

where $h_n(T) = 1/[\pi + (1-\pi)\delta_n \ldots \delta_{n+T-1}]$. If $\delta_j = \delta$ is a constant, then terms cancel and the above equation simplifies to equation (25) of Ho and Lee. One can show that as the length Δt of a period shrinks to zero, then a path-independent Gaussian model would obtain if

$$\pi(1-\pi)(\log\delta_n)^2 = \sigma^2(t)\Delta t^3$$

where $t = n\Delta t$. The fastest convergence occurs for $\pi = \tfrac{1}{2}$. (A Poisson limit obtains if π and $\log\delta_n$ approach zero in the first order in Δt.)

Utilising the above formula for the one-period discount factors, securities can be evaluated by the usual backward-induction technique, ie, by averaging and discounting values. But we notice that the first algorithm above is more efficient, because it does not require the calculation of the various $h_n(T)$.

Conclusion

The primary advantage of the Gaussian model is its simplicity and analytical tractability. In particular, there are simple and intuitive formulas for bond prices, the spot rate process and Arrow-Debreu prices in terms of the initial yield curve. American and multiple options admit simple analysis, the fundamental differential equation can be written (and numerically evaluated) in terms of the initial yield curve independently of the market price of risk, and the sub-family of path-independent Gaussian models admits a binomial discretisation and a simple and efficient evaluation algorithm. The disadvantage of the Gaussian model is that interest rates can become negative.

One of the most interesting results of the paper gives equivalent characterisations of quasi-Gaussian interest rate models. Quasi-Gaussian models can incorporate (in fact are parameterised by) arbitrary initial yield and volatility curves and an arbitrary (in general stochastic) spot rate volatility. In particular, by choosing the spot rate volatility to be a function of (time and) the spot rate that vanishes at the origin, one obtains abundant examples of models with positive interest rates, which yet admit semi-explicit formulas for bond prices and forward rates in terms of the spot rate. Unless the spot rate volatility is deterministic, ie, the model is Gaussian, the spot rate in a quasi-Gaussian model is not a diffusion process, the fundamental pde does not exist and the analysis here of American and multiple options does not apply.

Much of the theory can be extended to multifactor (quasi-) Gaussian models (see Jamshidian, 1989*b*). However, it is an open problem whether or not American and multiple options admit similar formulas in the multifactor case. Another interesting direction is further investigation of quasi-Gaussian models, especially regarding option evaluation.

Appendix

PROOF OF PROPOSITION 3

We have already seen that (*a*) implies both (*b*) and (*c*). It suffices to show that (*b*) ⇒ (*c*) ⇒ (*a*).

(*b*) ⇒ (*c*) Since $r(t)$ is a diffusion process with respect to $w(t)$, it is Markovian. Hence, by Theorem 1, part (*e*), $P^T(t) = P^T(r(t), t)$, where

$$P^T(r,t) = \tilde{E}\left(\exp - \int_t^T r(s)\,ds \middle| r(t) = r\right)$$

Letting $r_T(r, t)$ be the negative of the logarithmic derivative of $P^T(r, t)$, we see that $r_T(t) = r_T(r(t), t)$. By Itô's lemma $\partial r_T/\partial r = \sigma_T(t)/\sigma(t)$, which by assumption is deterministic and hence independent of r. Thus

$$r_T(t) = \left(\frac{\sigma_T(t)}{\sigma(t)}\right) r(t) + B_T(t)$$

for some deterministic function $B_T(t)$, and

$$\mu_T(t) = \left(\frac{\sigma_T(t)}{\sigma(t)}\right)\mu(t) + \left(\frac{\sigma_T}{\sigma}\right)'(t)\,r(t) + B_T'(t)$$

Evaluating at $T = t$, it follows that $\mu(t) - \mu_t(t)$ (which equals $\mu + \sigma\lambda$) is linear in $r(t)$, and (*c*) follows.

(*c*) ⇒ (*a*) Set

$$\tilde{\sigma}_T(t) = \sigma(t)\exp\left(\int_t^T - a(u)\,du\right), \quad \tilde{\sigma}^T(t) = \int_t^T \tilde{\sigma}_u(t)\,du$$

Define the interest rate model $\tilde{r}_T(t)$ by the right-hand side of (30) with $\sigma_T(\sigma^T)$ replaced by $\tilde{\sigma}_T(\tilde{\sigma}^T)$. Clearly, $\tilde{r}(t) \equiv \tilde{r}_t(t) = r(t)$, and $\tilde{r}_T(t)$ has a Gaussian volatility structure with parameters $\sigma(t)$ and $a(t)$. Calculating $d\tilde{r}_T(t)$ using (29), we find that $d\tilde{r}_T(t) = \tilde{\sigma}_T(t)[\tilde{\sigma}^T(t) + d\tilde{w}(t)]$. In particular, setting $T = t$, we find that $\tilde{\lambda}(t) = \lambda(t)$, and so by (16) the model $\tilde{r}_T(t)$ is locally arbitrage-free. Since in addition it has the same spot rate and market price of risk as the original model $r_T(t)$, it follows by Theorem 1, part (*e*), that the two models are identical.[14] *Q.E.D.*

PROOF OF PROPOSITION 4

We have already seen that the spot rate is Gaussian. The remaining statements follow as in the section "(Quasi-) Gaussian Volatility Structures". Note that equation (32) is consistent with (31), (26), and (24). *Q.E.D.*

PROOF OF LEMMA 3

The fact that $C(r, t)$ is analytical in r follows since $G(r, t, r', t')$ is so. Changing variables in the integral (34) to the variable $R' = r' - r_{t'}(r, t)$ followed by differentiation inside the integral sign, and the fact that $\partial r_{t'}(r, t)/\partial r > 0$, show that $C(r, t)/P^{t'}(r, t)$ is a decreasing function of r. The lemma now follows by the fact that $P^{t'}(r, t)$ is a strictly decreasing function of r with range the entire positive axis. *Q.E.D.*

PROOF OF THEOREM 5

Clearly the product of the Arrow–Debreu state prices is the exponential of a polynomial of degree 2 in $r_1, \ldots, r_i$. We claim that the quadratic part is Q. Indeed, since the spot rate is Gaussian in the risk-neutral measure, a similar product of probability transition functions of the spot rate in this measure is a multivariate normal distribution with covariance matrix Q. But each transition function has the same quadratic part as the corresponding Arrow–Debreu price, namely, $v(t_j, t_k)$. Since the quadratic part of the product is determined only by the quadratic part of each term (exponents of products add), the claim follows. It follows that

$$G(r, t, r_1, t_1) \ldots G(r_{i-1}, t_{i-1}, r_i, t_i) = f(r, t)\, p(r_1, \ldots, r_i; Q^{(i)}, v^{(i)}) \qquad (55)$$

for some function $f(r, t)$ and some mean vector $v^{(i)}$. We show that $f(r, t) = P^{t_i}(r, t)$ and $v^{(i)} = u^{(i)}$ by induction. First let $i = 2$. Integrating both sides of (55) over r_1, the left-hand side by the semi-group property (36) becomes $G(r, t, r_2, t_2)$, which by (33) is $P^{t_2}(r, t)$ times a Gaussian (in r_2) with mean $r_{t_2}(r, t)$, while the right-hand side becomes $f(r, t)$ times a Gaussian with mean $v_2^{(2)}$. Thus $f(r, t) = P^{t_2}(r, t)$ and $v_2^{(2)} = r_{t_2}(r, t)$. Next, integrating both sides of (55) over r_2, the right-hand side becomes $P^{t_2}(r, t)$ times a Gaussian with mean $v_1^{(2)}$, while by (36), the left-hand side becomes $A \equiv P^{t_1}(r, t)\, P^{t_2}(r_1, t_1)$ times a Gaussian mean $r_{t_1}(r, t)$. Using (26), $A = P^{t_2}(r, t)$ times a linear exponential in r_1, which, when multiplied by the latter Gaussian and squares completed, produces a Gaussian with mean $u_1^{(2)}$. Thus $v_1^{(2)}$ also equals $u_1^{(2)}$, and the proof for the case $i = 2$ is complete. Now let $i \geq 3$. Integrating both sides of (55) over r_1, the left-hand side by the semi-group property becomes $G(r, t, r_2, t_2) \ldots G(r_{i-1}, t_{i-1}, r_i, t_i)$, which is a product of $i - 1$ terms, and therefore by induction (and an obvious notational shift in the index i) equals $P^{t_i}(r, t)$ times a Gaussian with mean vector $(u_2^{(i)}, \ldots, u_i^{(i)})$. The right-hand side becomes $f(r, t)$ times a Gaussian with mean vector $(v_2^{(i)}, \ldots, v_i^{(i)})$. Thus $f(r, t) = P^{t_i}(r, t)$, and all except possibly the first components of $u^{(i)}$ and $v^{(i)}$ are equal. That the first components are also equal follows by integrating both sides of (55) over r_2 and employing a similar argument. This completes the proof. *Q.E.D.*

PROOF OF PROPOSITION 6

There are basically two steps from equation (47) and Theorem 4 to equation (48). One step involves the appropriate change of variables and change of the limits of integration in (47) to conform to the standard multivariate form. In the ith integral in (47), $i \leq n$, the change of variable that accomplishes this is

$$x_k^{(i)} = \frac{u_k^{(i)} - r_k}{v(t, t_k)} \qquad 1 \le k \le i-1$$

$$x_i^{(i)} = \frac{r_i - u_i^{(i)}}{v(t, t_i)}$$

(Note that the change in the sign of the ith row and column of $\rho^{(i)-}$ is caused by this different treatment of the last component of $x^{(i)}$.) The second step involves the completing of squares in the last (n + 1)st integral in (47). Indeed, in this integral the term $P^T(r_n, t_n)$ and the term $P^{t_n}(r, t)$ coming from the product of the Gs in (47) combine by (26) to give $P^T(r, t)$ times a linear exponential in r_n. The latter combines with the multivariate Gaussian to change its mean vector from $u^{(n)}$ to the vector u^T, where

$$u_k^T = u_k^{(n)} - v(t, t_k)\, \rho(t, t_k, t_n)\, v^T(t, t_n)$$

Here, we have used (24) and the easily verified fact that (with $c \equiv \sigma^T(t_n)/\sigma(t_n)$)

$$p(x_1, \ldots, x_n; Q; u + cQ_n) = \exp[-\tfrac{1}{2}c^2 Q_{nn} + c(x_n - u_n)]\, p(x_1, \ldots, x_n; Q; u)$$

where Q_n denotes the last column vector of Q and c is any constant. One finally performs in the last integral the change of variable

$$x_k^T = \frac{u_k^T - r_k}{v(t, t_k)} \qquad 1 \le k \le n$$

PROOF OF PROPOSITION 7

The terminal function of the European callable bond at t_1 equals $\min\{K_1, \sum a_j P^{T_j}(r, t_1)\}$. By Lemma 4, this equals a linear combination of the terminal functions of European options on zero-coupon bonds with appropriate call prices. Part (*a*) follows. Part (*b*) follows similarly by an induction on the number of call dates n. Indeed, at $t = t_1$, the terminal function of the bond is the minimum of K_1 with the value at time t_1 of the bond that is not callable at t_1 but is otherwise similar. This bond has $n - 1$ call dates, so by induction it is given as a portfolio of zero-coupon callable bonds. Applying Lemma 4, it follows that the terminal condition of the original bond is also a linear combination of prices of zero-coupon callable bonds with the appropriate call prices as given. *Q.E.D.*

Acknowledgements

I am grateful to former colleagues Oren Cheyette, Jan Dash, Michael Driscoll, Michael Fein, Jim Meisner, Alain Nairay, Robert Russell and Yu Zhu for valuable discussions. I also thank Warren Bailey, Darrell Duffie, Jorgen Nielsen and Stanley Pliska for commenting on an earlier version of the paper entitled "Closed-Form Solution for American Options on Coupon Bonds in the General Gaussian Interest Rate Model". This paper was completed while the author was director in the Financial Strategies Group at Merrill Lynch & Co., Inc.

1 *The product formula (Theorem 5) is the main step in the derivation of our multiple-option formula, and it uses more or less the entire theory developed in this paper. By contrast, its counterpart in the equity case is an immediate consequence of the geometric random-walk assumption. For this reason, the derivation here of the multiple-option formula for bonds is considerably more involved than that of Geske and Johnson (1984) for equities.*

2 *The Dirac delta function* $\delta(x)$ *is the distributional limit of the probability density functions of a sequence of normal random variables with mean zero and variance approaching zero. Intuitively, it is a measure concentrated at the origin with* $\delta(x) = 0$ *if* $x \neq 0$ *and* $\delta(0) = \infty$. *It satisfies* $f(x) = \int f(y)\,\delta(y - x)\,dy$ *for all functions* $f(x)$, *or, equivalently, for all random variables* X *the probability density of* X *at* x *equals* $E[\delta(X - x)]$.

3 *I thank Oren Cheyette for pointing out condition* (b).

4 *See Friedman (1975, Chapter 6) for a discussion of these properties of fundamental solutions of parabolic differential equations.*

5 *The second partial derivative of* $C(r,t)$ *in (38) is taken in the sense of distribution (generalised functions). Similarly, if* $K(t)$ *is discontinuous (as is the case for a discrete coupon),* $K'(t)$ *is defined in the sense of distribution. We also point out that in the derivation of (38) we used the fact that a distribution with support at the origin is a linear function of the delta function and its derivative. But these terms do not appear in (38) because* $C(r,t)$ *is continuously differentiable.*

6 *Similar techniques apply to the Black-Scholes framework, yielding similar formulas for American equity options. See Jamshidian (1992) and the references there. In the equity case, Barone-Adesi and Elliot (1989) report an algebraic equation for the optimal boundary. But a comparable result is not known for American bond options in the Gaussian model. We also point out that the results of this section up to equation (39) are valid in any locally arbitrage-free model in which the spot rate follows a diffusion process. Of course, the fundamental pde and the Arrow-Debreu prices change appropriately, but our arguments remain valid (see Jamshidian (1990b) for details).*

7 *A straightforward calculation of (43) gives*

$$\rho^2(t_0,t,t') = \frac{\int_{t_0}^{t} \sigma^2(s)\exp\left(2\int_{t_0}^{s} a(u)\,du\right) ds}{\int_{t_0}^{t'} \sigma^2(s)\exp\left(2\int_{t_0}^{s} a(u)\,du\right) ds}$$

For path-independent Gaussian models this simplifies to $(t-t_0)/(t'-t_0)$, *while in the Vasicek volatility structure it becomes* $(e^{2a(t-t_0)}-1)/(e^{2a(t'-t_0)}-1)$.

8 *Equation (47) in general form and specific application to the equity case appears in Dash (1988), where a systematic application of Green's function and path integral technology to option evaluation is pursued.*

9 *The formulas of Geske and Johnson (1984) for equity multiple options are similar, though the term* $v^{t_i}(t,t_k)$ *in (49) and (51) does not appear in the equity case. See also note 1.*

10 *Of course, the* r_i^* *in (52) are now defined as solutions of appropriate* putable *bond equations.*

11 *This portfolio decomposition (and our proof) is valid in all one-factor models in which callable bond prices are decreasing functions of the spot rate.*

12 *To conform to conventions governing accrued interest,* K_i *here equals the quoted (flat) call price plus accrued interest.*

13 *The significance of this transformation should not be confused with that in Merton (1973, equation (36)). The latter (like the concept of the* T*-maturity forward-risk-adjusted measure) is with respect to a fixed expiration date. By contrast, our transformation is global in time.*

14 *An alternative derivation of (30) follows by explicitly calculating* $P^T(r,t)$, *either by a separation of variables in the fundamental pde, or as* $\tilde{E}[\exp -\int_t^T r(u)\,du \mid r(t)=r]$.

Bibliography

Barone-Adesi, G., and Elliot, R., 1989, "Free Boundary Problems in the Valuation of Securities", Working Paper, University of Alberta.

Black, F., and Scholes, M., 1973, "The Pricing of Options and Corporate Liabilities", *Journal of Political Economy* 81, pp. 637–654; reprinted as Chapter 1 of the present volume.

Black, F., Derman, E., and Toy, W., 1990, "A One-Factor Model of Interest Rates and its Application to Treasury Bond Options", *Financial Analysts Journal* January–February, pp. 33–39; reprinted as Chapter 10 of the present volume.

Brennan, M., and Schwartz, E., 1979, "A Continuous-Time Approach to the Pricing of Bonds", *Journal of Banking and Finance* 3, pp. 133–155; reprinted as Chapter 5 of the present volume.

Courtadon, G., 1982, "The Pricing of Options on Default-Free Bonds", *Journal of Financial and Quantitative Analysis* 17, pp. 75–100.

Cox, J. C., Ingersoll, J. E., and Ross, S. A., 1979, "Duration and the Measurement of Basis Risk", *Journal of Business* 52, pp. 51–61.

Cox, J. C., Ingersoll, J. E., and Ross, S. A., 1985, "A Theory of the Term Structure of Interest Rates", *Econometrica* 53, pp. 385-407; reprinted as Chapter 6 of the present volume.

Dash, J. W., 1988, "Path Integrals and Options - 1", Working paper, Merrill Lynch Capital Markets, New York.

Dothan, L. U., 1978, "On the Term Structure of Interest Rates", *Journal of Financial Economics* 7, pp. 229-264.

Dyer, L. and Jacob, D., 1989, "Guide to Fixed Income Option Pricing Models", pp. 63-109 in *The Handbook of Fixed Income Options* (F. Fabozzi, ed.), Chicago: Probus.

Friedman, A., 1975, *Stochastic Differential Equations and Applications*, Vol. 1, New York Academic Press.

Geske, R., and Johnson, H., 1984, "The American Put Option Valued Analytically", *Journal of Finance* 29, pp. 1551-1524.

Harrison, J. M., and Pliska, S., 1981, "Martingales and Stochastic Integrals in the Theory of Continuous Trading", *Stochastic Processes and their Applications* 11, pp. 215-260.

Heath, D., Jarrow, R, and Morton, A., 1990, "Bond Pricing and the Term Structure of Interest Rates: A Discrete Time Approximation", *Journal of Financial and Quantitative Analysis* 25, pp. 419-440; reprinted as Chapter 14 of the present volume.

Heath, D., Jarrow, R, and Morton, A., 1992, "Bond Pricing and the Term Structure of Interest Rates: A New Methodology for Contingent Claim Valuation", *Econometrica* 60, pp. 77-105.

Ho, T. S., and Lee, S.-B., 1986, "Term Structure Movements and Pricing Interest Rate Contingent Claims", *Journal of Finance* 42(5), pp. 1129-1142; reprinted as Chapter 13 of the present volume.

Hull, J., and White, A., 1990*a*, "Pricing Interest-Rate Derivative Securities", *Review of Financial Studies* 3(4), pp. 573-592.

Hull, J., and White, A., 1990*b*, "Valuing Derivative Securities Using the Explicit Finite Difference Method", *Journal of Financial and Quantitative Analysis* 25, pp. 87-100; reprinted as Chapter 9 of the present volume.

Ingersoll, J., 1987, *Theory of Financial Decision Making*, Rowman & Littlefield.

Jamshidian, F., 1987, "Pricing of Contingent Claims in the One-Factor Term Structure Model", published as Chapter 7 of this volume.

Jamshidian, F., 1989*a*, "An Exact Bond Option Formula", *Journal of Finance* 44, pp. 205-209.

Jamshidian, F., 1989*b*, "The Multifactor Gaussian Interest Rate Model and Implementation", Working paper, Merrill Lynch Capital Markets, New York.

Jamshidian, F., 1990, "The Preference-Free Determination of Bond and Option Prices from the Spot Interest Rate", pp. 51-67 in *Advances in Futures and Options Research*, Vol. 4, Greenwich, CT: JAI Press.

Jamshidian, F., 1992, "An Analysis of American Options", *Review of Futures Markets* 11, pp. 72-80.

Merton, R. C., 1973, "The Theory of Rational Option Pricing", *Bell Journal of Economics and Management Science* 4, pp. 141-183.

Pederson, H, Shiu, E., and Thorlacius, A. E., 1989, "Arbitrage-Free Pricing of Interest-Rate Contingent Claims", *Transactions of the Society of Actuaries* 41, pp. 231-266.

Vasicek, O. A., 1977, "An Equilibrium Characterization of the Term Structure", *Journal of Financial Economics* 5, pp. 177-188; reprinted as Chapter 4 of the present volume.

III

THE HEATH-JARROW-MORTON FAMILY

13

Term Structure Movements and Pricing Interest Rate Contingent Claims*

Thomas S. Y. Ho and Sang-Bin Lee
Global Advanced Technology Corporation; Hanyang University

This article develops a no-arbitrage interest rate movements model that takes the complete term structure as given and derives the subsequent stochastic movement of the term structure such that the movement is arbitrage-free. We then show that the no-arbitrage model can be used to price interest rate contingent claims with regard to the observed complete term structure of interest rates. This article also studies the behaviour and the economics of the model. Our approach can be used to price a broad range of interest rate contingent claims, including bond options and callable bonds.

Interest rate options, callable bonds and floating rate notes are a few examples of interest rate contingent claims. They are characterised by their finite lives and their price behaviour, which crucially depends on the term structure and its stochastic movements. In recent years, with the increase in interest rate volatility and the prevalent use of the contingent claims, the pricing of these securities has become a primary concern in financial research. The purpose of this paper is to present a general methodology to price a broad class of interest rate contingent claims.

The crux of the problem in pricing interest rate contingent claims is to model the term structure movements and to relate the movements to the assets' prices. Much academic literature has been devoted to this problem. One earlier attempt is that of Pye (1966). He assumed that the interest rates move according to a (Markov) transition probabilities matrix, and he then used the expectation hypothesis to price the expected cashflow of the asset - in his case, a callable bond (Pye (1967)). Recently, investigators have focused more on developing equilibrium models.

Cox, Ingersoll, and Ross (1985) assumed that the short rate follows a mean-reverting process. By further assuming that all interest rate contingent claims are priced contingent on only the short rate, using a continuous arbitrage argument they derived an equilibrium pricing model. Brennan and Schwartz (1979) extended the Cox-Ingersoll-Ross model to incorporate both short and long rates and studied the pricing of a broad range

**This paper was first published in the* Journal of Finance, *Vol. 41 (1986). It is reprinted with the permission of American Finance Association. The paper contains results presented in an earlier paper entitled "Term Structure Movements and the Pricing of Corporate Bonds Provisions", May 1985, Salomon Brothers Center, New York University. We would like to thank Michael Brennan, Bill Carleton, Georges Courtadon, Art Djang, Steve Figlewski, Bob Geske, David Jacob, In Joon Kim, and Eduardo Schwartz for their helpful comments on the earlier version of the paper. We would also like to thank, in particular, the referee, Eduardo Schwartz, for many of his helpful comments on this paper. We are responsible for the remaining errors.*

of contingent claims (Brennan and Schwartz 1977, 1982). In these approaches, both the term structure and the contingent claims are derived in an equilibrium context.[1]

This paper proposes an alternative approach to these pricing models. We take the term structure as given and derive the feasible subsequent term structure movements. These movements must satisfy certain constraints to ensure that they are consistent with an equilibrium framework. Specifically, the movements cannot permit arbitrage profit opportunities. We shall call these interest rate movements arbitrage-free rate movements. When the arbitrage-free movements are determined, the interest rate contingent claims are then priced by the arbitrage methodology used in Cox, Ingersoll, and Ross, and Brennan and Schwartz. Therefore, our model is a relative pricing model in the sense that we price our contingent claims relative to the observed term structure; we do not endogenise the term structure as the Cox-Ingersoll-Ross and Brennan-Schwartz models do.

The main advantage of our approach is that it enables us to utilise the full information of the term structure to price contingent claims. To the extent that the shape of the yield curve should affect the contingent-claim value, our approach can be more applicable. Further, when our model is used to price a straight bond (when viewed as a contingent claim to the term structure movements), the theoretical price is assured to be that determined by the observed term structure. In this way, when we analyse a bond with various (interest rate) provisions, for example, the model can properly isolate the provision value from the value of the underlying bond. Indeed, when the provision has negligible value, the model's bond price is guaranteed to be that given by the term structure. Our methodology also provides the important linkage between contingent-claims pricing and the pricing of straight bonds. As a result, it integrates the relative pricing theory of contingent claims with the established literature on estimating the term structure of interest rates.[2]

In this paper, we analyse the arbitrage-free model and show how it is related to other interest rate stochastic processes in previous research. Finally, we present the methodology (using the arbitrage-free model) to price interest rate contingent claims. Since our methodology is general and has direct applications to many financial problems, this paper should contribute significantly to the fixed-income research.

The paper is organised as follows. The first part of this paper presents the basic assumptions of the model and describes the binomial lattice of a term structure movement. Such a movement is shown to determine the stochastic movement of a bond price. The second part derives the arbitrage-free model. The economics of the term structure movement is analysed. The third part studies the behaviour of the arbitrage-free model. The fourth part presents the methodology of using the arbitrage-free model to price interest rate contingent claims. Finally, the fifth part contains the conclusions.

Interest rate movements

This section sets up the analytical framework of a term structure movement. We first list the basic assumptions of the model. We then relate the term structure movements to the bond price stochastic process.

THE BASIC ASSUMPTIONS

(A1) The market is frictionless. There are no taxes and no transaction costs, and all securities are perfectly divisible.

(A2) The market clears at discrete points in time, which are separated in regular intervals. For simplicity, we use each period as a unit of time. We define a discount bond of maturity T to be a bond that pays \$1 at the end of the Tth period, with no other payments to its holder.

(A3) The bond market is complete. There exists a discount bond for each maturity n ($n = 0, 1, 2 \ldots$).

(A4) At each time n, there are a finite number of states of the world. For state i, we denote the equilibrium price of the discount bond of maturity T by $P_i^{(n)}(T)$. Note that

$P_i^{(n)}(\cdot)$ is a function that relates the price of a discount bond to its maturity. This function is called the *discount function*. Within the context of the model, the discount function completely describes the term structure of interest rates of the ith state at time n.

The discount function $P_i^{(n)}(\cdot)$ must satisfy several conditions. It must be positive since the function represents assets' values. Also, we require that

$$P_i^{(n)}(0) = 1 \text{ for all i, n} \tag{1}$$

and

$$\lim_{T\to\infty} P_i^{(n)}(T) = 0 \text{ for all i, n} \tag{2}$$

Equation (1) says that a discount bond maturing instantaneously must be worth $1. Equation (2) says that a discount bond with maturity in the distant future must have a negligible value. Assumptions (A1) through (A4) are the standard perfect capital market assumptions in a discrete state-time framework.

THE BINOMIAL LATTICE

Now we describe the evolution of the term structure. Initially, we observe the discount function $P(\cdot)$. At the initial time, by convention, we have the 0-state. So we have

$$P(\cdot) = P_0^{(0)}(\cdot) \tag{3}$$

At time 1, the discount function may be specified by two possible functions, $P_1^{(1)}(\cdot)$ and $P_0^{(1)}(\cdot)$. (The superscript denotes the time and the subscript denotes the state.) Therefore, there are only two states of the world at time 1. When $P_1^{(1)}(\cdot)$ prevails, we say that the upstate is attained; when $P_0^{(1)}(\cdot)$ prevails, the downstate is attained.

Next, consider the second period from time 1 to time 2. We confine each discount function, in either upstate or downstate, to also attain one of two possible functions. Specifically, conditional on the discount function $P(\cdot)$ attaining $P_1^{(1)}(\cdot)$ at time 1, we require the discount function to be either $P_2^{(2)}(\cdot)$ or $P_1^{(2)}(\cdot)$ at time 2. At this point, we do not specify any particular functional forms for $P_2^{(2)}(\cdot)$ and $P_1^{(2)}(\cdot)$. Similarly, conditional on the discount function $P(\cdot)$ attaining the downstate at time 1, the discount function can then only attain an upstate or a downstate, taking on the function $P_1^{(2)}(\cdot)$ and $P_0^{(2)}(\cdot)$, respectively. Note that the binomial lattice assumption requires the discount function attained by an upstate followed by a downstate to be equal to the discount function reached by a downstate followed by an upstate.

The stochastic process of the discount function in subsequent periods is described analogously. For the (n + 1)th period, from time n to time n + 1, let $P_1^{(n)}(\cdot)$ denote the discount function at time n after i upstate movements and (n – i) downstate movements. We require the discount function to depend only on the number of upstate movements and not on the sequence in which they occur. Thus, the binomial process at time n is specified by

$$P_i^{(n)}(\cdot) \begin{cases} P_{i+1}^{(n+1)}(\cdot) & \text{upstate} \\ P_i^{(n+1)}(\cdot) & \text{downstate} \end{cases} \tag{4}$$

A discount function is defined for each time n and state i. This set of discount functions is said to form a binomial lattice. A vertex of this lattice is specified by (n, i). Notice that, for each time n, there are exactly (n + 1) states (i = 0, ..., n). The term structure can evolve from one vertex to another by different paths, but this will not affect the value of the discount function at the vertex at the end of the path. That is, the discount functions are path-independent.

Often, it is more convenient to represent a term structure by the yield curve as opposed to the discount function. Given the discount function P(T), we define the yield curve to be

$$r(T) = \frac{-\ln P(T)}{T} \tag{5}$$

r(T) is the continuously compounded yield of a discount bond with maturity T.

THE BINOMIAL PROCESS OF BOND PRICES

When the term structure evolves in a binomial lattice, the price of each discount bond must follow a binomial process with time-dependent step size. In particular, consider the discount bond with maturity N. Initially, the bond price is, by definition, P(N).

After the first period, the bond shortens its maturity to (N – 1), and therefore, given the discount functions in the upstate and downstate, we can determine the bond prices; they are $P_1^{(1)}(N-1)$ and $P_0^{(1)}(N-1)$ in an upstate and downstate, respectively. All subsequent prices are determined analogously. In particular, after N periods, the bond values are $P_i^{(N)}(0)$ for all states i (i = 0, ..., N). But by equation (1) the bond value is $1, as one would expect the bond value to be at maturity.

The stochastic price process of a discount bond is depicted in Figure 1. The discount function is depicted in each state and time in a binomial lattice. Figure 1 shows that the discount function always originates from unity. It increases in value in an upstate but drops in value in a downstate. Now consider the three-period bond. Initially, its value is P(3). At time 1, it becomes a two-period bond, and its value can be either $P_1^{(1)}(2)$ or $P_0^{(1)}(2)$. At time 2, this bond becomes a one-period bond, and its value cannot deviate too much from unity in any state of the world and must converge to unity at maturity.

1. The Binomial Lattice of the Term Structure Movement

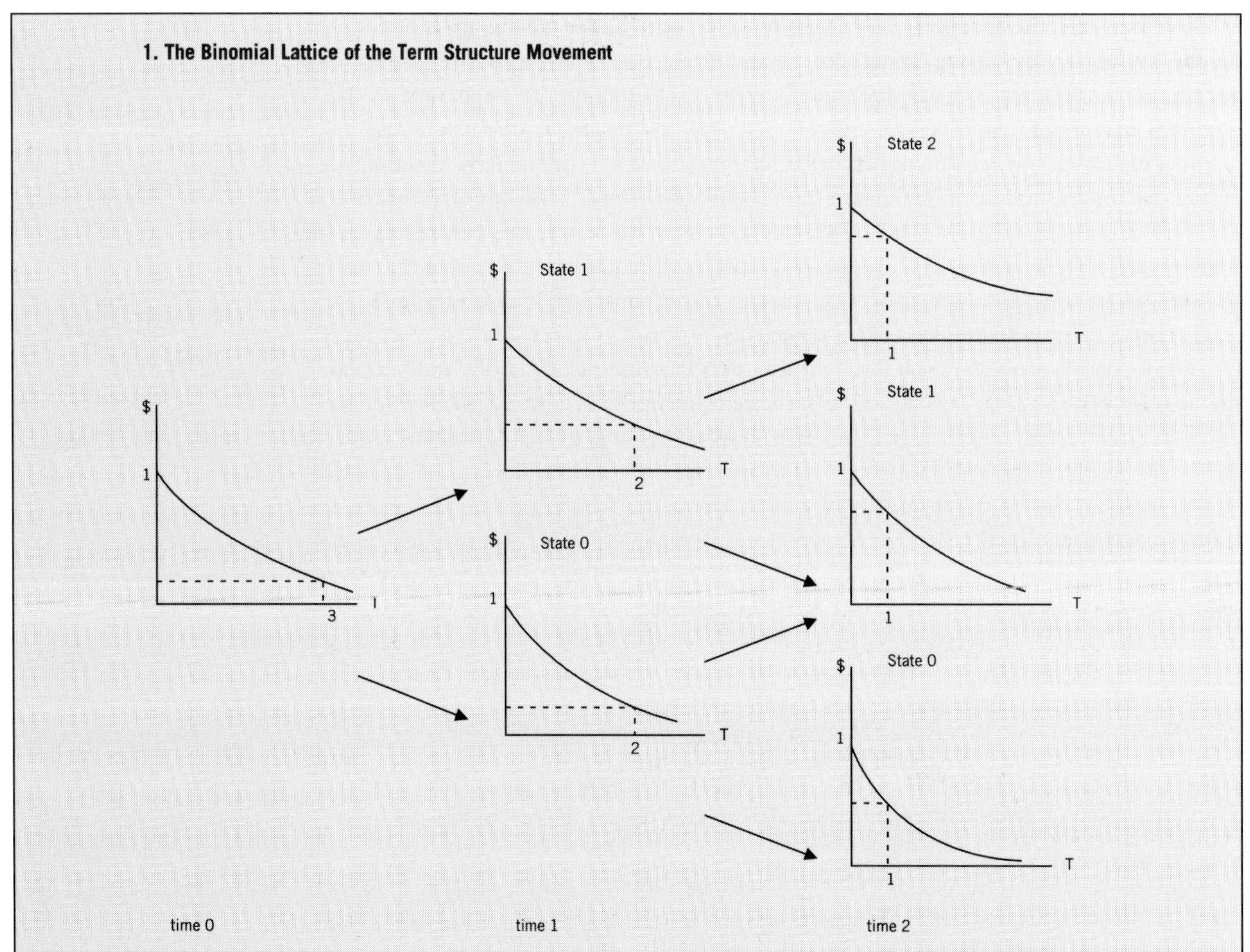

This model of a bond price stochastic process is similar to the binomial process proposed by Cox, Ross and Rubinstein (1979) and Rendleman and Bartter (1979) for stocks. However, there are two main differences. First, when pricing interest rate contingent claims, in most cases we are concerned with how the prices of discount bonds with different maturities move relative to each other. That is why we focus on the binomial lattice of a term structure rather than a binomial process of a particular bond. Second, in our model, the step size is time-dependent to ensure that the bond value converges to unity at maturity.

By taking the binomial lattice approach, we ensure that a bond price stochastic process has the following characteristics. The bond price uncertainty is small at the two extreme time points: for the time horizon in the immediate future and near bond maturity. The price uncertainty is large for time horizons away from these two end-points. We achieve this by isolating the two effects. The first effect is the resolution of uncertainty of the term structure. As the term horizon lengthens, we are more uncertain about the term structure configuration. (There are more variations of the term structure when n is large.) The second effect is that the bond price uncertainty must decrease when the time horizon approaches maturity since the bond price cannot significantly deviate from unity when the maturity is short. Now consider a particular bond. As the time horizon increases, uncertainty of the term structure configuration increases, leading to larger bond price variance. However, at the same time, the bond has shorter maturity in the future, and the latter effect (the maturity effect) prevails. When the time horizon is sufficiently distant in the future, the latter effect may dominate the former, leading to a decrease in bond price uncertainty. We can now compare our model with that of Schaefer and Schwartz (1986). In their approach, they seek to model the stochastic process of a bond price. In their case, they must specify a process such that its variance is time-dependent.[3] Here, we separate the two effects and model them separately.

The arbitrage-free rate movements – the arbitrage-free model

In the previous section, we introduced the binomial lattice of a term structure. This section introduces the necessary constraints on the term structure movement such that the movement is consistent with an arbitrage-free environment. We also introduce some simplifying restrictions so that we can develop a procedure to construct a "desirable" term structure movement.[4]

PERTURBATION FUNCTIONS $h(T)$ AND $h^*(T)$

At any nth period and ith state, we have a discount function $P_i^{(n)}(T)$. If everyone perceives no interest rate risk over the next period, the term structure in the upstate must equal the downstate at time $n + 1$. Furthermore, the discount function must be the implied forward discount function $F_i^{(n)}(T)$ to avoid any arbitrage opportunities. That is,

$$F_i^{(n)}(T) = P_i^{(n+1)}(T) = P_{i+1}^{(n+1)}(T) = \frac{P_i^{(n)}(T+1)}{P_i^{(n)}(1)}, \qquad T = 0,1,... \tag{6}$$

In a certainty world, if the next period discount function differs from $F_i^{(n)}(T)$, then investors can realise arbitrage profits. Therefore, in modelling term structure uncertainty, we are concerned with how the discount function is perturbed from the implied forward function in the following period. For this reason, we define two functions, called *perturbation functions*, $h(T)$ and $h^*(T)$ such that, in the upstate,

$$P_{i+1}^{(n+1)}(T) = \frac{P_i^{(n)}(T+1)}{P_i^{(n)}(1)} h(T) \tag{7}$$

and, in the downstate,

$$P_i^{(n+1)}(T) = \frac{P_i^{(n)}(T+1)}{P_i^{(n)}(1)} h^*(T) \tag{8}$$

The perturbation functions specify the deviations of the discount functions from the implied forward function. Thus, roughly, they specify the difference between the upstate and downstate prices over the next period. When $h(T)$ is significantly greater than unity for all values of T, then all the bond prices will rise substantially in the upstate. Analogously, when $h^*(T)$ is less than unity for all values of T, all the bond prices will fall in the downstate. Equations (1) and (2) impose the following conditions on the functions h and h^*. They must both be positive and, also,

$$h(0) = h^*(0) = 1 \tag{9}$$

Equation (9) follows directly from equations (1), (7) and (8).

The perturbation on the bond price depends on the maturity, and we therefore let h and h^* be functions of T. To construct a binomial lattice of the term structure movement, we need only to specify the set of perturbation functions $h(T)$, $h^*(T)$ and the initial discount function $P(T)$.

THE IMPLIED BINOMIAL PROBABILITY π

Given a binomial lattice of a term structure movement, we also need to ensure that there is no arbitrage profit to be made in forming arbitrary portfolios of the discount bonds. Specifically, if we take any two discount bonds with different maturities and construct a portfolio of these two bonds such that the portfolio realises a risk-free return over the next period, then the risk-free rate must be the return of a one-period discount bond. This arbitrage-free condition imposes a restriction on the perturbation functions at each vertex (n, i). The method to calculate the risk-free hedge is similar to that of Cox, Ross and Rubinstein, and the details of the arguments are given in Appendix A. The result shows that, when the bond price upward movement is significant, the bond price downward movement must also be sizeable such that the weighted average of the movements is the same across all bonds. Specifically, we have

$$\pi h(T) + (1 - \pi) h^*(T) = 1 \quad \text{for } n, i > 0 \tag{10}$$

for some constant π independent of time T and the initial discount function $P(T)$, but possibly dependent on state and time. π will be called the ***implied binomial probability***.

The implied binomial probability can be understood in the Cox, Ross and Rubinstein context of binomial option pricing. Indeed, equation (1) can be rewritten as

$$P_i^{(n)}(T) = \left[\pi P_{i+1}^{(n+1)}(T-1) + (1-\pi) P_i^{(n+1)}(T-1)\right] P_i^{(n)}(1) \tag{11}$$

Equation (11) says that the bond price equals the "expected" bond value at the end of the period discounted by the prevailing one-period bond rate if we interpret π to be a binomial probability. For this reason, the implied binomial probability π is the "risk-neutral" probability of Cox, Ross and Rubinstein within their model's context. To interpret π, it is more useful to rewrite equation (11) as

$$\pi = \frac{(r - d)}{(u - d)}$$

where r is the one-period bond return and u and d are the bond returns for upstate and downstate, respectively.[5] Therefore, π measures the extent of the downstate return as a percentage of the total spread between upstate and downstate returns. For large π, the model says that the price change for the next period is mainly a price decrease. Similarly, when π is small (approximately zero), the price change is dominated by a price rise. Equation (10) shows that, if one cannot arbitrage using the discount bond, then this ratio must be the same for all bonds.

THE PATH-INDEPENDENT CONDITION

In constructing the binomial lattice, we assume a discount function evolving from one state to another depending only on the number of the upward movements and not on the sequence in which they occur. This restriction is equivalent to imposing a constraint on the perturbation functions (h and h^*) and the implied binomial probability (π) such that, at any time n and state i, an upward move followed by a downward move of a bond price equals a downward move followed by an upward move of its price.

To investigate the implication of this constraint, consider the discount function $P_i^{(n)}(T)$ at time n and state i. Using equations (7) and (8), a direct calculation shows that, from an upward move followed by a downward move, we get

$$P_{i+1}^{(n+2)}(T) = \frac{P_i^{(n)}(T+2)}{P_i^{(n)}(2)} \frac{h(T+1)h^*(T)}{h(1)} \tag{12}$$

By a similar calculation, we can analyse the case of a downward movement followed by an upward movement and show that the resulting discount function is

$$P_{i+1}^{(n+2)}(T) = \frac{P_i^{(n)}(T+2)}{P_i^{(n)}(2)} \frac{h^*(T+1)h(T)}{h^*(1)} \tag{13}$$

The path-independent condition implies that

$$h(T+1)\,h^*(T)\,h^*(1) = h^*(T+1)\,h(T)\,h(1) \tag{14}$$

But, by equation (10), we can eliminate h^*, and we obtain

$$h(T+1)[1-\pi h(T)][1-\pi h(1)] = (1-\pi)\,h(1)\,h(T)[1-\pi h(T+1)] \tag{15}$$

We simplify equation (15) and obtain, for $T \geq 1$,

$$\frac{1}{h(T+1)} = \frac{\delta}{h(T)} + \gamma \tag{16}$$

where δ is some constant such that

$$h(1) = \frac{1}{(\pi + (1-\pi)\delta)} \tag{17}$$

and

$$\gamma = \frac{\pi(h(1)-1)}{(1-\pi)h(1)} \tag{18}$$

Equation (16) is a first-order linear difference equation, and its general solution is given by

$$h(T) = \frac{1}{\pi + c\delta^T} \quad \text{for some constant } c$$

But, by equation (9), we require that $h(0) = 1$, and, therefore, the initial condition determines the unique solution

$$h(T) = \frac{1}{\pi + (1-\pi)\delta^T} \quad \text{for } T \geq 0 \tag{19}$$

Note that equation (17) becomes a special case of equation (19).

From equation (10), we get

$$h^*(T) = \frac{\delta^T}{\pi + (1-\pi)\delta^T} \tag{20}$$

For given constraints π and δ, the arbitrage-free model is well defined by equations (7), (8), (19) and (20).

The arbitrage-free model

This section analyses the arbitrage-free model. We compare it with other models of interest rate movements. Equations (19) and (20) show that the arbitrage-free model is uniquely determined by two constants (π and δ). The section on the implied binomial probability has given the intuitive explanation of π. δ determines the spread between the two perturbation functions h and h^*. The larger the spread, the greater the interest rate variability. $h(\cdot)$ is a concave function that increases monotonically, asymptotic to $1/\pi$. $h^*(\cdot)$ is a convex function that decreases monotonically to zero. For this model, at any state-time, consider a bond with maturity T. The bond's upstate price relative to the implied forward price is $h(T)$; therefore, the longer the maturity, the larger the price change. For short-term bonds, the price change is negatively related to δ. For long-term bonds, the price change is quite constant across different maturities and is $(1/\pi)$. δ is a parameter that affects the bond volatility, and it is inversely related to the term structure uncertainty. According to equation (17), we see that $0 \leq \delta \leq 1$. When $\delta = 1$, we reduce to the certainty case.

Vasicek (1977), Dothan (1978), Richard (1978), and Cox, Ingersoll, and Ross (1985) have proposed equilibrium models of the term structure. In these models all the discount bonds are priced relative to the stochastic short rate in such a way that there are no arbitrage opportunities in trading the discount bonds. Since the arbitrage-free model also requires all bonds to be priced relative to a bond, and hence to a specific interest rate, it would provide valuable insight to show how bonds are priced relative to the short rate and how the model may be identified with these single-state-variable models.

The short rate, within the context of our model, is the rate of a one-period discount bond. Now we wish to determine the stochastic process of the short rate. First, we need to express the discount function at any time n and state i in terms of the initial discount function. This can be achieved by applying equations (7) and (8) recursively backwards. This procedure gives the final expression

$$P_i^{(n)}(T) = \frac{P(T+n)}{P(n)} \times \frac{h^*(T+n-1)\,h^*(T+n-2)\cdots h^*(T+i)\,h(T+i-1)\cdots h(T)}{h^*(n-1)\,h^*(n-2)\cdots h^*(i)\,h(i-1)\cdots h(1)} \tag{21}$$

Using equation (20), equation (21) can be simplified to

$$P_i^{(n)}(T) = \frac{P(T+n)h(T+n-1)h(T+n-2)\cdots h(T)\delta^{T(n-1)}}{P(n)h(n-1)h(n-2)\cdots h(1)} \tag{22}$$

Equation (22) gives the explicit expression of the discount function in each state-time. In the special case of a one-period bond ($T = 1$), the bond price is

$$P_i^{(n)}(1) = \frac{P(n+1)\delta^{n-1}}{P(n)(\pi+(1-\pi)\delta^n)} \tag{23}$$

Also, the one-period rate $r_i^{(n)}(1)$, according to equation (5), is

$$\begin{aligned} r_i^{(n)}(1) &= -\ln P_i^{(n)}(1) \\ &= \ln\left(\frac{P(n)}{P(n+1)}\right) + \ln[\pi\delta^{-n} + (1-\pi)] + i\ln\delta \end{aligned} \tag{24}$$

Thus far, we have not assigned any binomial probability to the binomial lattice. If we further assume that the probability is q, it follows directly that, for each n, $r_i^{(n)}(1)$ is a binomial distribution in i, with mean μ given by

$$\mu = \ln\left(\frac{P(n)}{P(n+1)}\right) + \ln[\pi\delta^{-n} + (1-\pi)] + nq\ln\delta \tag{25}$$

By simplifying, we get

$$\mu = \ln\left(\frac{P(n)}{P(n+1)}\right) + \ln(\pi\delta^{-(1-q)n} + (1-\pi)\delta^{qn}) \tag{26}$$

Also, the variance is given by

$$\text{var} = nq(1-q)(\ln\delta)^2 \tag{27}$$

Note that the first term of equation (26) is the implied forward one-period bond rate. Equation (26) says that the expected rate is the implied forward rate plus a bias. The bias would naturally disappear when there is no uncertainty ($\delta = 1$). The variance of the one-period rate depends only on δ. As expected, the variance is negatively related to δ.

This reformulation enables us to compare our model with the single-factor term structure models. Here, our short-rate stochastic process depends on the information of the initial term structure. In this sense, our term structure movements incorporate the full information of the initial term structure. By way of comparison, single-factor models specify the short-rate movements exogenously without using the full information of the initial term structure.

The two approaches differ because they differ in their purposes. The one-factor models seek to endogenise the equilibrium term structure. To do so, they try to determine the short-rate process that can generate a meaningful equilibrium term structure. We take the initial term structure as given and determine the short-rate movement to price the contingent claims. When the discount bonds, viewed as contingent claims, are priced by this term structure movement, they fit the initial discount function. (This assertion will be proved in the following section.) Therefore, our term structure movement is not used to determine the equilibrium term structure. Rather, it is assured to be consistent with the term structure and is used to price other contingent claims.

PROPERTIES OF THE ARBITRAGE-FREE MODEL

To gain insight into the arbitrage-free model, it is useful to view discount function movements in terms of shifts in the yield curve. To this end, we analyse equation (5). At the initial time,

$$r(T) = \frac{-\ln P(T)}{T}$$

In the next period, in the upstate, using equation (7) we have

$$r_1^{(1)}(T) = -\frac{1}{T}\ln\frac{P(T+1)}{P(1)} - \frac{1}{T}\ln[h(T)] \tag{28}$$

Also, in the downstate, using equation (8) we have

$$r_0^{(1)}(T) = -\frac{1}{T}\ln\frac{P(T+1)}{P(1)} - \frac{1}{T}\ln[h^*(T)] \tag{29}$$

Using the behaviour of the functions $h(T)$ and $h^*(T)$, we see that the arbitrage-free model imposes certain restrictions on the yield curve movements. When short rates attain a higher (lower) level, the long rates also attain a higher (lower) level. The movements are made relative to the implied forward yield curve. Since the implied forward yield curve can take on any shape (we do not impose any condition on the initial term structure), the yield curve in subsequent periods, in principle, can take on any shape.

LOCAL EXPECTATIONS HYPOTHESIS AND THE TERM PREMIUM

Following the definition of Cox, Ingersoll, and Ross (1981), the T-*period term premium* is the expected return (holding the bond for one period) of a T-period bond in excess of the one-period bond return. One may expect that the longer-term bonds have higher expected returns, and hence positive term premiums. When all bonds have the same expected return (i.e. no term premiums exist), we say the *local expectations hypothesis* holds. The following proposition determines the term premium and specifies the necessary conditions for the local expectations hypothesis.

Proposition 1: *The* T*-period term premium is given by*

$$\tau(T) = \frac{1}{P(1)}\left[\left(\frac{(1-q)\delta^T + q}{(1-\pi)\delta^T + \pi}\right) - 1\right] \tag{30}$$

and the local expectations hypothesis holds if and only if $q = \pi$, *i.e., if and only if the implied binomial probability* (π) *is the binomial probability* (q).

Proof: Note that the rate of return of the $(T+1)$-period bond over one period is

$$\frac{q\dfrac{P(T+1)}{P(1)}h(T) + (1-q)\dfrac{P(T+1)}{P(1)}h^*(T)}{P(T+1)}$$

Also, the one-period bond rate of return is $1/P(1)$. By taking the difference between these two rates of return, we get the desired result of equation (30). Now, it follows that the premium is zero if and only if $q = \pi$. Q.E.D.

The T-period term premium is the product of two terms. The first term is the one-period risk-free rate of return. The second term is a function of q, π and δ. If the binomial probability q is greater than the implied binomial probability π, we have a positive term premium. Long-term bonds would have higher expected returns. This is intuitively clear. π can be viewed as the risk-neutral probability. If the actual probability q for an upstate is greater than π, then the expected return must be higher than the risk-neutral return - hence, a positive term premium. Otherwise, if q is less than π, then the term premium is negative. More importantly, when π is the binomial probability, the local expectations hypothesis must hold.

PRICE OF INTEREST RATE CONTINGENT CLAIMS

This section presents a procedure to price interest rate contingent claims using an arbitrage-free model. In order to present the pricing procedure clearly, we confine our discussion to pricing only a category of contingent claims. These securities are characterised as follows.

Let C be an interest rate contingent claim. We require that its price $C(n, i)$ be uniquely defined at each vertex (n, i) of the binomial lattice. C has a finite life, and it expires (or matures) at time T, with payoffs given by $\{f(i)\}$, $0 \le i \le T$; we call $\{f(i)\}$ the terminal condition and hence

$$C(T, i) = f(i), \quad 0 \le i \le T \tag{31}$$

The contingent claim is also satisfied by its upper bound $U(n, i)$ and lower bound $L(n, i)$ conditions such that

$$L(n, i) \le C(n, i) \le U(n, i) \tag{32}$$

Equation (32) contains the boundary conditions. Also, the contingent claim pays $X(n, i)$ to its holder at time n and state i, $1 \le n < T$.

There are many examples of contingent claims belonging to this category. Interest rate futures (taking marking-to-market into account), both European and American bond options, callable and sinking fund bonds, and interest rate futures options are some of the examples.[6] These contingent claims differ by the specification of their terminal and boundary conditions and the payoff during their lives.

PRICING OF THE CONTINGENT CLAIMS

The following Lemma is central to our pricing procedure for the above model.

LEMMA (Risk-Neutral Pricing Formula): *Consider any interest rate contingent claim* $C(n, i)$ *that can be bought and sold in a frictionless market environment described by assumptions (A1)–(A5). If no arbitrage profit is to be realised in holding any portfolio of the contingent claim and the discount bonds, the following equation must hold:*

$$C(n, i) = [\pi\{C(n+1, i+1) + X(n+1, i+1)\} + (1-\pi)\{C(n+1, i) + X(n+1, i)\}]\, P_i^{(n)}(1) \tag{33}$$

where $P_i^{(n)}(1)$ *is the one-period discount bond price at state-time* (n, i).

The proof of the Lemma is similar to that of Proposition 1, and, for this reason, we give the details in Appendix B.

The Lemma enables us to price the initial contingent claim by the backward substitution procedure – a method often used in recent finance literature. The terminal condition of equation (31) specifies the asset value in all states at time T. Then, equation (33) enables us to determine the arbitrage-free price of the asset at one period before expiration. Let that price be $C^*(T-1, i)$. But the actual market price must satisfy the boundary conditions of equation (32). That is, the market price must be

$$C(T-1, i) = \max[L(T-1, i), \min(C^*(T-1, i), U(T-1, i))] \tag{34}$$

We now apply this procedure repeatedly, rolling back in time. That is, given the contingent-claim prices at all states at time n, we can always calculate the arbitrage-free contingent-claim prices at time $n-1$ by equation (33). Then, by applying the boundary conditions of equation (32), we can derive the market prices in all states at time $n-1$. After T steps, we reach the asset value at $n = 0$, and that is the initial price.

This recursive procedure has been applied elsewhere – for example, Cox, Ross and Rubinstein (1979) – but there are two interesting features in our case. First, the one-period discount rate, a constant in Cox, Ross and Rubinstein, is state- and time-dependent in our model. It is specified by $P_i^{(n)}(1)$ and is endogenised by the arbitrage-free model. Since we have noted that these one-period rates depend on the initial discount function, we have explicitly shown how the initial term structure affects the contingent-claim pricing.

Second, in the arbitrage-free model, the terminal conditions (equation (31)) and boundary conditions (equation (32)) can in turn be specified by interest rate contingent claims. This is because, at each state and time, the prevailing discount function and its subsequent movement are both specified. Therefore, other interest rate contingent claims can in turn be priced to determine the conditions. For example, for interest rate futures options, the futures can first be priced by the arbitrage-free model, and then the options can be priced by the futures.

When the initial discount function is given by $P(\cdot)$, the price of the discount bond with maturity T is, by definition, $P(T)$. But the discount bond can also be priced by the recursive method described in this section. That is, the discount bond can be viewed as a contingent claim with maturity T, with terminal conditions $f(i) = 1$, and without any lower and upper bounds and interim cashflow.

Hence, the discount bond can be priced by the recursive method described in this section. Appendix C shows that the calculated price is assured to be the observed price $P(T)$. This result is intuitively clear. We use the observed price $P(T)$ to derive an arbitrage-free term structure movement. When we use the arbitrage-free model to price the discount bond, we should find the price to be $P(T)$; otherwise, we would realise arbitrage opportunities.

This result suggests an important implication. Suppose we know the short-rate (the one-period rate) evolution over time. Specifically, at each time n and state i (at each vertex (n, i) of the binomial lattice), we know the one-period bond price $P_i^{(n)}(1)$ and the implied binomial probability π. In this case, we do not need to know the complete term structure at each vertex, and there is no arbitrage-free condition to be checked. Knowing π and $P_i^{(n)}(1)$ only, according to this section, we can always price interest rate contingent claims. This model of asset pricing depends crucially on the stochastic movement of the short rate, and, for this reason, we call such a model a *one-factor model*.

The one-factor model is analogous to the continuous-time model of Cox, Ingersoll, and Ross, with one subtle difference. Their model specifies the actual binomial probability (q) of the short-rate process and the term premium (τ). Here we use the implied binomial probabilities, π, and do not isolate the actual binomial probabilities from the term premium. (Proposition 1 has shown how the implied binomial probability π is related to the actual binomial probability q and the term premium τ in a special case.)

In sum, the arbitrage-free model is a one-factor model in the sense that all the contingent claims are priced by the short-rate movement. But, in the arbitrage-free model, the short-rate movement is subject to some constraint. The short-rate must evolve in such a way that, when the discount bonds (or portfolio of discount bonds) are priced as contingent claims (by the backward substitution methodology described in this section), the solution price is guaranteed to be that given by the initial discount function.[7]

What is important about the arbitrage-free model is its practical implications. Discount bond prices are, in principle, observable, and these prices are fully utilised by the arbitrage-free model to price the bond contingent claims; in this sense, interest rate contingent claims are priced *relative* to the term structure. In contrast, the one-factor model of, for example, Cox, Ingersoll, and Ross, ignores these bond prices in hypothesising the short-rate stochastic process without ensuring that the model prices of the underlying bonds are those observed in the term structure.

ESTIMATING THE ARBITRAGE-FREE MODEL

To price any interest rate contingent claim by our approach, we must first specify the parameters of the arbitrage-free model (π and δ). To estimate π and δ, we take three main steps. First, we need to estimate the discount function at the time of pricing the contingent claims. To this end, we can apply any of the known procedures, including the cubic spline-fitting procedure used by a number of authors – for example, McCulloch (1975) or, more recently, Litzenberger and Rolfo (1984).

Second, by using the properties of the no-arbitrage model, we can develop theoretical pricing models of some contingent claims – for example, interest rate options. Since we have already estimated the initial discount function, the only unspecified inputs to the pricing model are the parameters π and δ. But these two parameters are related to the stochastic movement of the term structure and not to a specific instrument. Therefore, they should be the same for all contingent claims, according to our model.

The third and final step is to use a non-linear estimation procedure to determine π and δ such that the theoretical prices of a sample of contingent claims can best fit their observed prices. The estimates of π and δ are then used in the arbitrage-free model to price other contingent claims.[8]

Our approach is similar to that used to estimate the "implied" volatility of a stock option (see, for example, Whaley (1982)). For a stock option, the stock return volatility is not directly observable, and, therefore, it can be estimated by the observed option price via a pricing model. This estimated volatility (the implied volatility) is then used to price other options on the same stock. In the case of the arbitrage-free model, the parameters of the model are not directly observable from the term structure, but their values are reflected in the interest rate contingent claims. For this reason, we can use the observed prices of the contingent claims to estimate the arbitrage-free parameters via their pricing models derived by the general procedure used for pricing contingent claims.

Conclusions

In this paper we propose an approach to pricing interest rate contingent claims. This approach prices these securities relative to the term structure of interest rates. The crux of the argument hinges on modelling the term structure movement in such a way that the stochastic movement is arbitrage-free. In so doing, security prices are derived consistent with a partial equilibrium framework.

We present an arbitrage-free interest rate movement model (arbitrage-free model). We then show that, if we use the arbitrage-free model to price a discount bond as a contingent claim, the bond price must equal the price determined by the initial discount function. This consistency enables us to fully utilise the information observed in the term structure to price the contingent claims. Also, in this paper we relate the arbitrage-free model to other models proposed in previous literature. We show how the initial discount function is used to specify the interest rate stochastic process, something that alternative models do not consider.

This paper is important to financial research because it provides a direct and tractable procedure for pricing a broad range of securities relative to the discount function. These pricing models should have significant implications on fixed-income analysis and management. On the theoretical side, this paper may be viewed as an initial step to acquire insight into pricing the interest rate contingent claims relative to the term structure. More general arbitrage-free models should be developed to enable us to better understand the "feasible" movements of interest rates. On the empirical side, our paper should enable researchers to test a range of pricing models and the empirical validity of alternative arbitrage-free models.

Appendix A

Proof of Equation (10)

Proof: At any time n and state i, we can construct a portfolio of one discount bond with maturity T and ξ discount bonds with maturity t. To simplify our notations, we will drop all the indices (n, i). Then, the portfolio value is $V = P(T) + \xi P(t)$.

At the end of the period, when an upstate prevails, the portfolio value is, by equation (7),

$$V\,(\text{upstate}) = \frac{P(T)h(T-1)+\xi P(t)h(t-1)}{P(1)} \tag{A1}$$

Similarly, when a downstate prevails, we have

$$V\,(\text{downstate}) = \frac{P(T)h^*(T-1)+\xi P(t)h^*(t-1)}{P(1)} \tag{A2}$$

Choose ξ such that V (upstate) = V (downstate); then, using equation (A1) and (A2), we can show that

$$\xi = \frac{P(T)[h(T-1)-h^*(T-1)]}{P(t)[h^*(t-1)-h(t-1)]} \tag{A3}$$

To avoid arbitrage opportunities, this portfolio should yield a one-period discount bond return, i.e., $1/P(1)$. That is,

$$P(T)h^*(T-1)+\xi P(t)h^*(t-1) = P(T)+\xi P(t) \tag{A4}$$

Substituting equation (A3) in equation (A4), we get

$$\frac{1-h^*(T-1)}{h(T-1)-h^*(T-1)} = \frac{1-h^*(t-1)}{h(t-1)-h^*(t-1)} \quad \text{for all } T \text{ and } t>0 \tag{A5}$$

Equation (A5) can hold for all T and t only if there is a constant π, independent of T and t, such that

$$\frac{1 - h^*(T)}{h(T) - h^*(T)} = \pi \tag{A6}$$

Equation (A6) can be re-expressed as

$$\pi h(T) + (1 - \pi) h^*(T) = 1 \quad \text{for } T = 0, 1, 2, \ldots \tag{A7}$$

This completes the proof. Note that we require that $h^*(0) = h(0) = 1$, but these conditions are consistent with equation (A7). Q.E.D.

Appendix B

Proof of the Lemma

Proof: For expository reasons, we will ignore the payoffs $X(n, i)$ in this derivation. Incorporating these payoffs is a trivial extension. In state i and time n, consider a discount bond with maturity T (some arbitrary T). We form a risk-free portfolio of this bond and asset C by buying one bond and ξC assets. When an upstate prevails, the portfolio value is

$$V(\text{upstate}) = \frac{P_i^{(n)}(T)h(T-1)}{P_i^{(n)} + \xi C(n+1, i+1)} \tag{B1}$$

Similarly, when the downstate prevails, the portfolio value is

$$V(\text{downstate}) = \frac{P_i^{(n)}(T)h^*(T-1)}{P_i^{(n)} + \xi C(n+1, i)} \tag{B2}$$

Since the portfolio is risk-free, we require that

$$V(\text{upstate}) = V(\text{downstate}) \tag{B3}$$

In combining equations (B1), (B2) and (B3) and rearranging, we get

$$\xi = P_i^{(n)}(T)[h^*(T-1) - h(T-1)] \times P_i^{(n)}(1)[C(n+1, i+1) - C(n+1, i)] \tag{B4}$$

Now the initial portfolio value at time n is

$$V = P_i^{(n)}(T) + \xi C(n, i) \tag{B5}$$

By the arbitrage-free argument, we have

$$V = V(\text{downstate})\, P_i^{(n)}(1) \tag{B6}$$

Using equations (B4), (B5) and (B6), and also equation (B2), we get the desired results. Q.E.D.

Appendix C

When the term structure movement is generated by the arbitrage-free model, the recursive procedure in pricing a discount bond gives the price equalling that determined by the initial term structure. Therefore, while the implied binomial probability, π, and the perturbation functions, $h(\cdot)$ and $h^*(\cdot)$, are all used in the recursive procedure, they do not affect the final solution price of a discount bond.

Proof: We prove the theorem by induction on m, the number of periods till maturity of a discount bond. The result clearly holds for m = 1. When there is only one period to maturity at any time scale (n, i), we put C(n + 1, i + 1) = C(n + 1, i) = 1. By equation (33), we have

$$C(n, i) = \{\pi + (1 - \pi)\} P_i^{(n)}(1) = P_i^{(n)}(1)$$

Hence, the value of a one-period bond at time (n, i) is $P_i^{(n)}(1)$, as required.

Now, suppose the theorem holds for all times to maturity (m) less than some number N. Now consider the case when a discount bond has N + 1 periods to maturity at time-state (n, i). In the next period upstate, the bond would have maturity N. By the induction hypothesis, the recursive procedure would yield the contingent-claim price to be $P_{i+1}^{(n+1)}(N)$. Similarly, for the downstate in the next period, the contingent-claim price must be $P_i^{(n+1)}(N)$.

By equation (33), again, we have

$$C(n,i) = \left(\pi P_{i+1}^{(n+1)}(N) + (1-\pi) P_i^{(n+1)}(N)\right) P_i^{(n)}(1) \tag{C1}$$

Using equations (7) and (8) to simplify equation (C1), we can reduce the expression to

$$C(n, i) = P_i^{(n)}(N + 1) \tag{C2}$$

Equation (C2) says that the contingent claim at time-state (n, i) takes the value of the discount bond with maturity N + 1. It, thus, completes the induction proof. Note that this result holds even if the arbitrage-free model is not time- and state-independent, with h^*, h and π being functions of i and n. Q.E.D.

1 *There are many subsequent papers following this approach to pricing various interest rate contingent claims. For example, Courtadon (1982) priced the interest rate options, and Ramaswamy and Sundaresan (1985) analysed the floating rate notes.*

2 *Many papers have dealt with the problem of estimating the term structure (or pricing default-free straight bonds). Examples are McCulloch (1975), Carleton and Cooper (1976), Litzenberger and Rolfo (1984), and Shea (1985).*

3 *For an Itô process to specify a bond price stochastic movement, the instantaneous variance must necessarily be time-dependent. This observation was made in Merton (1973). Schaefer and Schwartz (1986) analyse a particular process where the instantaneous variance is proportional to the underlying bond duration.*

4 *In order to exposit the basic idea of an arbitrage-free rate movement clearly here, we confine ourselves to a special case. We only consider the case when the perturbation functions (see Perturbation Functions above)* h(T) *and* $h^*(T)$ *and the implied binomial probability (see The Implied Binomial Probability above)* π *are independent of state* i *and time* n. *In general,* h^*, h *and* π *can be dependent on* n *and* i, *and a more general class of arbitrage-free models can be determined. (See Ho and Lee (1986).)*

5 *We use the notations* (r, u, d) *here in order to be consistent with those in Cox, Ross and Rubinstein (1979). In our case,* $r = 1/P_i^{(n)}(1)$, $u = P_{i+1}^{(n+1)}(T-1)/P_i^{(N)}(T)$ *and* $d = P_i^{(n+1)}(T-1)/P_i^{(n)}(T)$. *Then, the above expression, derived also in Cox, Ross and Rubinstein, follows in a straightforward manner from equation (11).*

6 *A floating rate note is an example that does not belong to this category. This is because, at a particular time-state* (n, i), *the coupon rate on the note depends on the time path of the term structure movement. Therefore, the floating value is ambiguously defined at each vertex. However, with appropriate adjustments to the pricing procedure, the arbitrage-free model can still be used to price these instruments.*

7 *Ho and Lee (1985) have used this procedure to price callable sinking-fund bonds and have shown that the methodology is quite tractable.*

8 *It would be interesting to investigate how the arbitrage-free model can be extended to a two-factor model where the pricing depends on both the short rate and long rate. But the importance of such extensions will depend partly on the empirical results, and these issues will have to be left for future research.*

Bibliography

Brennan, M. J., and E. S. Schwartz, 1977, "Saving Bonds, Retractable Bonds and Callable Bonds", *Journal of Financial Economics* 5, pp. 67–88.

Brennan, M. J., and E. S. Schwartz, 1979, "A Continuous-Time Approach to the Pricing of Bonds", *Journal of Banking and Finance* 3, pp. 135–55; reprinted as Chapter 5 of the present volume.

Brennan, M. J., and E. S. Schwartz, 1982, "An Equilibrium Model of Bond Pricing and a Test of Market Efficiency", *Journal of Financial and Quantitative Analysis* 17, pp. 303–29.

Carleton, W. T., and I. A. Cooper, 1976, "Estimation and Uses of the Term Structure of Interest Rates", *Journal of Finance* 31, pp. 1067–83.

Courtadon, G., 1982, "The Pricing of Options on Default Free Bonds", *Journal of Financial and Quantitative Analysis* 17, pp. 75–100.

Cox, J. C., J. E. Ingersoll, and S. A. Ross, 1981, "A Re-examination of Traditional Hypotheses about the Term Structure of Interest Rates", *Journal of Finance* 36, pp. 769–99.

Cox, J. C., J. E. Ingersoll, and S. A. Ross, 1985, "A Theory of the Term Structure of Interest Rates", *Econometrica* 53, pp. 385–407; reprinted as Chapter 6 of the present volume.

Cox, J. C., S. A. Ross and M. Rubinstein, 1979, "Option Pricing: A Simplified Approach", *Journal of Financial Economics* 7, pp. 229–63; reprinted as Chapter 2 of the present volume.

Dothan, L. U., 1978, "On the Term Structure of Interest Rates", *Journal of Financial Economics* 6, pp. 59–69.

Ho, T., and S-B. Lee, 1985, "Pricing of Corporate Bond Provisions: An Empirical Evidence", Working Paper, New York University.

Ho, T., and S-B. Lee, 1986, "Term Structure Movements and Interest Rates Contingent Claims Pricing", Salomon Brothers Center Series, New York University.

Litzenberger, R. H., and J. Rolfo., 1984, "An International Study of Tax Effects on Government Bonds", *Journal of Finance* 39, pp. 1–22.

Houston McCulloch, J., 1975, "The Tax Adjusted Yield Curves", *Journal of Finance* 30, pp. 811–30.

Merton, R. C., 1973, "The Theory of Rational Option Pricing", *Bell Journal of Economics and Management Science* 4, pp. 141–83.

Pye, G., 1966, "A Markov Model of the Term Structure", *Quarterly Journal of Economics* 25, pp. 60–72.

Pye, G., 1967, "The Value of a Call Deferment on a Bond: Some Empirical Evidence", *Journal of Finance* 22, pp. 623–37.

Ramaswany, K. and S. Sundaresan, 1985, "The Valuation of Floating Rate Investments: Theory and Evidence", Working Paper, Columbia University.

Rendleman, R., and B. Bartter, 1979, "Two-State Option Pricing", *Journal of Finance* 34, pp. 1093–1110.

Richard, S. F., 1978, "An Arbitrage Model of the Term Structure of Interest Rates", *Journal of Financial Economics* 6, pp. 33–57.

Schaefer, S. M., and E. S. Schwartz, 1986, "Time-Dependent Variance and the Pricing of Bond Options", Working Paper, University of British Columbia.

Shea, G. S., 1985, "Interest Rate Term Structure Estimation with Exponential Splines: A Note", *Journal of Finance* 40, pp. 319–25.

Vasicek, O. A., 1977, "An Equilibrium Characterization of the Term Structure", *Journal of Financial Economics* 5, pp. 177–88; reprinted as Chapter 4 of the present volume.

Whaley, R., 1982, "Valuation of American Call Options on Dividend-Paying Stocks: Empirical Tests", *Journal of Financial Economics* 10, 29–57.

14

Bond Pricing and the Term Structure of Interest Rates: A New Methodology for Contingent Claims Valuation*

David Heath, Robert Jarrow and Andrew Morton
Cornell University; Lehman Brothers

This article presents a unifying theory for valuing contingent claims under a stochastic term structure of interest rates. The methodology, based on the equivalent martingale measure technique, takes as given an initial forward rate curve and a family of potential stochastic processes for its subsequent movements. A no-arbitrage condition restricts this family of processes yielding valuation formulae for interest sensitive contingent claims which do not explicitly depend on the market prices of risk. Examples are provided to illustrate the key results.

In relation to the term structure of interest rates, arbitrage pricing theory has two purposes. The first is to price all zero-coupon (default-free) bonds of varying maturities from a finite number of economic fundamentals, called state variables. The second is to price all interest rate sensitive contingent claims, taking as given the prices of the zero-coupon bonds. This paper presents a general theory and a unifying framework for understanding arbitrage pricing theory in this context, of which all existing arbitrage pricing models are special cases (in particular, Vasicek (1977), Brennan and Schwartz (1979), Langetieg (1980), Ball and Torous (1983), Ho and Lee (1986), Schaefer and Schwartz (1987), and Artzner and Delbaen (1989)). The primary contribution of this paper, however, is a new methodology for solving the second problem, ie, the pricing of interest rate sensitive contingent claims given the prices of all zero-coupon bonds.

The methodology is new because (i) it imposes its stochastic structure directly on the evolution of the forward rate curve, (ii) it does not require an "inversion of the term structure" to eliminate the market prices of risk from contingent claim values, and (iii) it has a stochastic spot rate process with multiple stochastic factors influencing the

**This paper was first published in* Econometrica, *Vol. 60 (1992). As a research paper, it was titled "Bond Pricing and the Term Structure of Interest Rates: A New Methodology". It is reprinted with the permission of The Econometric Society. Helpful comments from P. Artzner, F. Delbaen, L. Hansen, an anonymous referee and workshops at Berkeley, Columbia University, Cornell University, Dartmouth College, Duke University, New York University, Stanford University, U.C.L.A., the University of Illinois at Chicago and Yale University are gratefully acknowledged.*

term structure. The model can be used to consistently price (and hedge) all contingent claims (American or European) on the term structure, and it is derived from necessary and (more importantly) *sufficient* conditions for the absence of arbitrage.

The arbitrage pricing models of Vasicek (1977), Brennan and Schwartz (1979), Langetieg (1980) and Artzner and Delbaen (1989) all require an "inversion of the term structure" to remove the market prices of risk when pricing contingent claims. This inversion is required due to the two-step procedure utilised in these papers to price contingent claims. The first step is to price the zero-coupon bonds from a finite number of state variables. Given these derived prices, the second step is to value contingent claims. It is the first step in this procedure that introduces the explicit dependence on the market prices of risk in the valuation formulae. The equilibrium model of Cox, Ingersoll, and Ross (1985), when used to value contingent claims, also follows this same two-step procedure. To remove this dependence, for parameterised forms of the market prices for risk, it is possible to invert the bond pricing formula after step one to obtain the market prices for risk as functions of the zero-coupon bond prices.

This "inversion of the term structure" removes the market prices for risk from contingent claim values, but it is problematic. First, it is computationally difficult since the bond pricing formulae are highly non-linear. Secondly, as will be shown later, the spot rate and bond price processes parameters are not independent of the market prices for risk. Hence, arbitrarily specifying a parameterised form of the market prices for risk as a function of the state variables can lead to an inconsistent model, ie, one which admits arbitrage opportunities. This possibility was originally noted by Cox, Ingersoll, and Ross (1985, p. 398).

A second class of arbitrage pricing models, illustrated by Ball and Torous (1983) and Schaefer and Schwartz (1987), avoids this two-step procedure by taking a finite number of initial bond prices and bond price processes as exogenously given. Unfortunately, Schaefer and Schwartz's model requires a constant spot rate process, and as shown by Cheng (1991), Ball and Torous' model is inconsistent with stochastic spot rate processes and the absence of arbitrage.

The model of Ho and Lee (1986) also avoids the two-step procedure by taking the initial bond prices and bond price processes as exogenously given. Unlike all the previous models, however, they utilise a discrete trading economy. In this economy, the zero-coupon bond price curve, in contrast to a finite number of bond prices, is assumed to fluctuate randomly over time according to a binomial process. Unfortunately, it is only a single factor model, so bonds of all maturities are perfectly correlated. Furthermore, to implement their model, they estimate the parameters of the discrete time binomial process including the risk-neutral probability. For large step sizes, as shown by Heath, Jarrow and Morton (1990), the parameters are not independent. This makes estimation problematic, as the dependence is not explicitly taken into account. The continuous time version of this model, which is studied below as a special case, is not subject to this same estimation difficulty.

We generalise the Ho and Lee model to a continuous time economy with multiple factors. Unlike the Ho and Lee model, however, we impose the exogenous stochastic structure upon forward rates, and not the zero-coupon bond prices. This change in perspective facilitates the mathematical analysis and it should also facilitate the empirical estimation of the model. Indeed, since zero-coupon bond prices are a fixed amount at maturity, their "volatilities" must change over time. In contrast, constant forward rate volatilities are consistent with a fixed value for a zero-coupon bond at maturity.

The model in this paper takes as given the initial forward rate curve. We then specify a general continuous time stochastic process for its evolution across time. To ensure that the process is consistent with an arbitrage-free economy (and hence with some equilibrium), we use the insights of Harrison and Kreps (1979) to characterise the conditions on the forward rate process such that there exists a unique, equivalent martingale probability measure. Under these conditions, markets are complete and contingent claim valuation is then a straightforward application of the methods in Harrison and

Pliska (1981). We illustrate this approach with several examples.

An outline of this paper is as follows: the first section presents the terminology and notation, leading on to the second section, which presents the forward rate process. The third section characterises arbitrage-free forward rate processes, while the fourth section extends the model to price interest rate-dependent contingent claims, with examples. The final two parts of the paper relate the arbitrage pricing approach to the equilibrium pricing approach, summarise the paper and discuss generalisations.

Terminology and notation

We consider a continuous trading economy with a trading interval $[0, \tau]$ for a fixed $\tau > 0$. The uncertainty in the economy is characterised by the probability space (Ω, F, Q), where Ω is the state space, F is the σ-algebra representing measurable events and Q is a probability measure. Information evolves over the trading interval according to the augmented, right continuous, complete filtration $\{F_t: t \in [0, \tau]\}$ generated by $n \geq 1$ independent Brownian motions $\{W_1(t), W_2(t), \ldots, W_n(t): t \in [0, \tau]\}$ initialised at zero. We let $E(\cdot)$ denote expectation with respect to the probability measure Q.

A continuum of default-free discount bonds trade with differing maturities, one for each trading date $T \in [0, \tau]$. Let $P(t, T)$ denote the time t price of the T maturity bond for all $T \in [0, \tau]$ and $t \in [0, T]$. We require that $P(T, T) = 1$ for all $T \in [0, \tau]$, $P(t, T) > 0$ for all $T \in [0, \tau]$ and $t \in [0, T]$, and that $\partial \log P(t, T)/\partial T$ exists for all $T \in [0, \tau]$ and $t \in [0, T]$. The first condition normalises the bond's payoff to be a certain dollar at maturity. The second condition excludes the trivial arbitrage opportunity where a certain dollar can be obtained for free. The last condition guarantees that forward rates are well defined.

The instantaneous *forward rate* at time t for date $T > t$, $f(t, T)$, is defined by

$$f(t, T) = \frac{-\partial \log P(t, T)}{\partial T} \quad \text{for all } T \in [0, \tau],\ t \in [0, T] \tag{1}$$

It corresponds to the rate that one can contract for at time t on a riskless loan that begins at date T and is returned an instant later. Solving the differential equation of expression (1) yields

$$P(t, T) = \exp\left(-\int_t^T f(t, s)\, ds\right) \quad \text{for all } T \in [0, \tau],\ t \in [0, T] \tag{2}$$

The *spot rate*[1] at time t, $r(t)$, is the instantaneous forward rate at time t for date t, ie,

$$r(t) = f(t, t) \quad \text{for all } t \in [0, \tau] \tag{3}$$

Term structure movements

This section of the paper presents the family of stochastic processes representing forward rate movements, condition (C.1). This condition describes the evolution of forward rates, and thus uniquely specifies the spot rate process and the bond price process. Additional boundedness conditions, (C.2) and (C.3), are required to guarantee that the spot rate and the bond price process are well behaved.

C.1 – A FAMILY OF FORWARD RATE PROCESSES *For fixed, but arbitrary* $T \in [0, \tau]$, $f(t, T)$ *satisfies the following equation:*

$$f(t, T) - f(0, T) = \int_0^t \alpha(v, T, \omega)\, dv + \sum_{i=1}^{n} \int_0^t \sigma_i(v, T, \omega)\, dW_i(v) \quad \text{for all } 0 \leq t \leq T \tag{4}$$

where: (i) $\{f(0, T): T \in [0, \tau]\}$ *is a fixed non-random initial forward rate curve which is measurable as a mapping* $f(0, \cdot): ([0, \tau], B[0, \tau]) \to (R, B)$ *where* $B[0, \tau]$ *is the*

Borel σ-algebra restricted to $[0,\tau]$; *(ii)* α: $\{(t,s): 0 \le t \le s \le T\} \times \Omega \to R$ *is jointly measurable from* $B\{(t,s): 0 \le t \le s \le T\} \times F \to B$, *adapted, with*

$$\int_0^T |\alpha(t,T,\omega)|\,dt < +\infty \quad \text{a.e. } Q$$

and (iii) the volatilities σ_i: $\{(t,s): 0 \le t \le s \le T\} \times \Omega \to R$ *are jointly measurable from* $B\{(t,s): 0 \le t \le s \le T\} \times F \to B$, *adapted, and satisfy*

$$\int_0^T \sigma_i^2(t,T,\omega)\,dt < +\infty \quad \text{a.e. } Q \quad \text{for } i = 1,\ldots,n$$

In this stochastic process n independent Brownian motions determine the stochastic fluctuation of the *entire* forward rate curve starting from a fixed initial curve $\{f(0,T): T \in [0,\tau]\}$. The sensitivity of a particular maturity forward rate's change to each Brownian motion is reflected by differing volatility coefficients. The volatility coefficients $\{\sigma_i(t,T,\omega): T \in [0,\tau]\}$ for $i = 1, \ldots, n$ are left unspecified, except for mild measurability and integrability conditions, and can depend on the entire past of the Brownian motions. Different specifications for these volatility coefficients generate significantly different qualitative characteristics of the forward rate process. The family of drift functions $\{\alpha(\cdot,T): T \in [0,\tau]\}$ is also unrestricted (at this point), except for mild measurability and integrability conditions.

It is important to emphasise that the only substantive economic restrictions imposed on the forward rate processes are that they have continuous sample paths and that they depend on only a finite number of random shocks (across the entire forward rate curve).

Given condition (C.1), we can determine the dynamics of the spot rate process:

$$r(t) = f(0,t) + \int_0^t \alpha(v,t,\omega)\,dv + \sum_{i=1}^n \int_0^t \sigma_i(v,t,\omega)\,dW_i(v) \quad \text{for all } t \in [0,T] \tag{5}$$

The spot rate process is similar to the forward rate process, except that both the time and maturity arguments vary simultaneously.

For the subsequent analysis, it is convenient to define an accumulation factor, $B(t)$, corresponding to the price of a money market account (rolling over at $r(t)$) initialised at time 0 with a dollar investment, ie,

$$B(t) = \exp\left(\int_0^t r(y)\,dy\right) \quad \text{for all } t \in [0,\tau] \tag{6}$$

Given the dynamics of the spot rate process, we need to ensure that the value of the money market account satisfies

$$0 < B(t,\omega) < +\infty \text{ a.e. } Q \quad \text{for all } t \in [0,\tau] \tag{7}$$

This is guaranteed by condition (C.2).

C.2 – REGULARITY OF THE MONEY MARKET ACCOUNT

$$\int_0^\tau |f(0,v)|\,dv < +\infty \quad \text{and} \quad \int_0^\tau \left(\int_0^t |\alpha(v,t,\omega)|\,dv\right) dt < +\infty \quad \text{a.e. } Q$$

Next, we are interested in the dynamics of the bond price process. The following condition imposes sufficient regularity conditions so that the bond price process is well behaved.

C.3 - REGULARITY OF THE BOND PRICE PROCESS

$$\int_0^t \left(\int_v^t \sigma_i(v,y,\omega)\,dy \right)^2 dv < +\infty \quad \text{a.e. Q} \quad \text{for all } t \in [0,\tau] \text{ and } i = 1,\dots,n$$

$$\int_0^t \left(\int_t^T \sigma_i(v,y,\omega)\,dy \right)^2 dv < +\infty \quad \text{a.e. Q} \quad \text{for all } t \in [0,T],\ T \in [0,\tau],\ i = 1,\dots,n$$

and

$$t \to \int_t^T \left(\int_0^t \sigma_i(v,y,\omega)\,dW_i(v) \right) dy \text{ is continuous a.e. Q} \quad \text{for all } T \in [0,\tau] \text{ and } i = 1,\dots,n$$

It is shown in the Appendix that under conditions C.2–C.3 the dynamics of the bond price process (suppressing the notational dependence on ω) are

$$\ln P(t,T) = \ln P(0,T) + \int_0^t [r(v) + b(v,T)]\,dv - \frac{1}{2}\sum_{i=1}^n \int_0^t a_i(v,T)^2\,dv + \sum_{i=1}^n \int_0^t a_i(v,T)\,dW_i(v) \quad \text{a.e. Q} \tag{8}$$

where

$$a_i(t,T,\omega) = -\int_t^T \sigma_i(t,v,\omega)\,dv \quad \text{for } i = 1,\dots,n$$

and

$$b(t,T,\omega) \equiv -\int_t^T \alpha(t,v,\omega)\,dv + \frac{1}{2}\sum_{i=1}^n a_i(t,T,\omega)^2$$

A straightforward application of Itô's lemma to expression (8) yields $P(t,T)$ as the strong solution to the following stochastic differential equation:

$$dP(t,T) = [r(t) + b(t,T))P(t,T]\,dt + \sum_{i=1}^n a_i(t,T)P(t,T)\,dW_i(t) \quad \text{a.e. Q} \tag{9}$$

In general, the bond price process is non-Markov since the drift term $(r(t,\omega) + b(t,T,\omega))$ and the volatility coefficients $a_i(t,T,\omega)$ for $i = 1,\dots,n$ can depend on the history of the Brownian motions. The form of the bond price process as given in expression (9) is similar to, but more general than, that appearing in the existing literature (see, for example, Brennan and Schwartz (1979) or Langetieg (1980)), because it requires fewer regularity assumptions and it need not be Markov.

We define the relative bond price for a T-maturity bond as $Z(t,T) = P(t,T)/B(t)$ for $T \in [0,\tau]$ and $t \in [0,T]$. This is the bond's value expressed in units of the accumulation factor, not dollars. This transformation removes the portion of the bond's drift due to the spot rate process. As such, it is particularly useful for analysis. Applying Itô's lemma to the definition of $Z(t,T)$ yields

$$\ln Z(t,T) = \ln Z(0,T) + \int_0^t b(v,T)\,dv - \frac{1}{2}\sum_{i=1}^n \int_0^t a_i(v,T)^2\,dv + \sum_{i=1}^n \int_0^t a_i(v,T)\,dW_i(v) \quad \text{a.e. Q} \tag{10}$$

Again, the relative bond price at date t may depend on the path of the Brownian motion through the cumulative forward rate drifts and volatilities. In general, it cannot be written as a function of only the current values of the Brownian motions.

Arbitrage-free bond pricing and term structure movements

Given conditions C.1–C.3, this section characterises necessary and sufficient conditions on the forward rate process such that there exists a unique, equivalent martingale probability measure.

C.4 – EXISTENCE OF THE MARKET PRICES FOR RISK *Fix* $S_1, \ldots, S_n \in [0, \tau]$ *such that* $0 < S_1 < S_2 < \ldots < S_n \leq \tau$. *Assume there exist solutions*

$$\gamma_i(\cdot, \cdot; S_1, \ldots, S_n): \Omega \times [0, S_1] \to R \quad \textit{for } i = 1, \ldots, n \quad \text{a.e. } Q \times \lambda$$

to the following system of equations:

$$\begin{bmatrix} b(t, S_1) \\ \vdots \\ b(t, S_n) \end{bmatrix} + \begin{bmatrix} a_1(t, S_1) \ldots a_n(t, S_1) \\ \vdots \\ a_1(t, S_n) \ldots a_n(t, S_n) \end{bmatrix} \begin{bmatrix} \gamma_1(t; S_1, \ldots, S_n) \\ \vdots \\ \gamma_n(t; S_1, \ldots, S_n) \end{bmatrix} = \begin{bmatrix} 0 \\ \vdots \\ 0 \end{bmatrix} \tag{11}$$

which satisfy

$$\int_0^{S_1} \gamma_i(v; S_1, \ldots, S_n)^2 \, dv < +\infty \quad \text{a.e. } Q \text{ for } i = 1, \ldots, n \tag{12a}$$

$$E\left[\exp\left(\sum_{i=1}^{n} \int_0^{S_1} \gamma_i(v; S_1, \ldots, S_n) \, dW_i(v) - \frac{1}{2}\sum_{i=1}^{n} \int_0^{S_1} \gamma_i(v; S_1, \ldots, S_n)^2 \, dv\right)\right] = 1 \tag{12b}$$

$$E\left[\exp\left(\sum_{i=1}^{n} \int_0^{S_1} [a_i(v, y) + \gamma_i(v; S_1, \ldots, S_n)] \, dW_i(v) - \right.\right.$$
$$\left.\left. \frac{1}{2}\sum_{i=1}^{n} \int_0^{S_1} [a_i(v, y) + \gamma_i(v; S_1, \ldots, S_n)]^2 \, dv\right)\right] = 1 \quad \text{for } y \in [S_1, \ldots, S_n] \tag{12c}$$

where λ *is Lebesgue measure.*

The system of equations in expression (11) gives $\gamma_i(t; S_1, \ldots, S_n)$ for $i = 1, \ldots, n$ the interpretation of being the *market prices for risk* associated with the random factors $W_i(t)$ for $i = 1, \ldots, n$, respectively. Indeed, to see this, we can rewrite expression (11) for the T-maturity bond as

$$b(t, T) = \sum_{i=1}^{n} a_i(t, T)\,(-\gamma_1(t; S_1, \ldots, S_n)) \tag{13}$$

The left side of expression (13) is the instantaneous excess expected return on the T-maturity bond *above* the risk-free rate. The right side is the sum of (minus) the "market price of risk for factor i" times the instantaneous covariance between the T-maturity bond's return and the ith random factor for i = 1 to n. It is important to emphasise that the solutions to expression (11) depend, in general, on the vector of bonds $\{S_1, \ldots, S_n\}$ chosen.

The following proposition shows that condition C.4 guarantees the existence of an equivalent martingale probability measure.

PROPOSITION 1 – Existence of an Equivalent Martingale Probability Measure *Fix* $S_1, \dots, S_n \in [0, \tau]$ *such that* $0 < S_1 < S_2 < \dots < S_n \le \tau$. *Given a vector of forward rate drifts* $\{\alpha(\cdot, S_1), \dots, \alpha(\cdot, S_n)\}$ *and volatilities* $\{\sigma_i(\cdot, S_1), \dots, \sigma_i(\cdot, S_n)]$ *for* $i = 1, \dots, n$ *satisfying conditions C.1–C.3, then condition C.4 holds if and only if there exists an equivalent probability measure* $\tilde{Q}_{S_1,\dots,S_n}$ *such that* $(Z(t, S_1), \dots, Z(t, S_n))$ *are martingales with respect to* $\{F_t : t \in [0, S_1]\}$.

PROOF: In the Appendix.

This proposition asserts that under conditions C.1–C.3, condition C.4 is both necessary and sufficient for the existence of an equivalent martingale probability measure $\tilde{Q}_{S_1,\dots,S_n}$. The key arrangement in the proof is Girsanov's Theorem, and it identifies this probability measure as

$$\frac{d\tilde{Q}_{S_1,\dots,S_n}}{dQ} = \exp\left(\sum_{i=1}^{n} \int_0^{S_1} \gamma_i(v; S_1, \dots, S_n)\, dW_i(v) - \frac{1}{2} \sum_{i=1}^{n} \int_0^{S_1} \gamma_i(v; S_1, \dots, S_n)^2\, dv\right) \tag{14}$$

Furthermore, it can also be shown that

$$\tilde{W}_i^{S_1,\dots,S_n}(t) = W_i(t) - \int_0^t \gamma_i(v; S_1, \dots, S_n)\, dv \quad \text{for } i = 1, \dots, n \tag{15}$$

are independent Brownian motions on $\{(\Omega, \tilde{Q}_{S_1,\dots,S_n}, F), \{F_t : t \in [0, S_1]\}$.

Although condition C.4 guarantees the existence of an equivalent martingale probability measure, it does not guarantee that it is unique. To obtain uniqueness, we impose the following condition.

C.5 – UNIQUENESS OF THE EQUIVALENT MARTINGALE PROBABILITY MEASURE *Fix* $S_1, \dots, S_n \in [0, \tau]$ *such that* $0 < S_1 < S_2 < \dots < S_n \le \tau$. *Assume that*

$$\begin{bmatrix} a_1(t, S_1) & \dots & a_n(t, S_1) \\ \vdots & & \vdots \\ a_1(t, S_n) & \dots & a_n(t, S_n) \end{bmatrix} \quad \textit{is non-singular a.e. } Q \times \lambda$$

The following proposition demonstrates that condition C.5 is both necessary and sufficient for the uniqueness of the equivalent martingale measure.[2]

PROPOSITION 2 – Characterisation of Uniqueness of the Equivalent Martingale Probability Measure: *Fix* $S_1, \dots, S_n \in [0, \tau]$ *such that* $0 < S_1 < S_2 < \dots < S_n \le \tau$. *Given a vector of forward rate drifts* $\{\alpha(\cdot, S_1), \dots, \alpha(\cdot, S_n)\}$ *and volatilities* $\{\sigma_i(\cdot, S_1), \dots, \sigma_i(\cdot, S_n)\}$ *for* $i = , \dots, n$ *satisfying conditions C.1–C.4, then condition C.5 holds if and only if the martingale measure is unique.*

PROOF: In the Appendix.

Conditions C.1–C.5, through the functions $\gamma_i(t; S_1, \dots, S_n)$ for $i = 1, \dots, n$ impose restrictions upon the drifts for the forward rate processes $\{\alpha(\cdot, S_1), \dots, \alpha(\cdot, S_n)\}$. It imposes just enough restrictions so that there is a unique equivalent martingale probability measure for the bonds $(Z(t, S_1), \dots, Z(t, S_n))$ with $0 < S_1 < \dots < S_n \le \tau$. Both the market prices for risk and the martingale measure, however, depend on the particular bonds $\{S_1, \dots, S_n\}$ chosen. To guarantee that there exists a unique equivalent martingale measure simultaneously making *all* relative bond prices martingales, we prove the following proposition.

PROPOSITION 3 - Uniqueness of the Martingale Measure Across All Bonds: *Given a family of forward rate drifts* $\{\alpha(\cdot, T): T \in [0, \tau]\}$ *and a family of volatilities* $\{\sigma_i(\cdot, T): T \in [0, \tau]\}$ *for* $i = 1, \ldots, n$ *satisfying conditions C.1–C.5, the following are equivalent:*

$$[\tilde{Q}, \text{ defined by } \tilde{Q} = \tilde{Q}_{S_1,\ldots,S_n} \text{ for any } S_1, \ldots, S_n \in [0, \tau], \text{ is the unique equivalent probability measure such that } Z(t, T) \text{ is a martingale for all } T \in [0, \tau] \text{ and } t \in [0, S_1]] \tag{16}$$

$$[\gamma_i(t; S_1, \ldots, S_n) = \gamma_i(t, T_1, \ldots, T_n) \text{ for } i = 1, \ldots, n \text{ and all } S_1, \ldots, S_n, T_1, \ldots, T_n \in [0, \tau],\ t \in [0, \tau], \text{ such that } 0 \le t < S_1 < \ldots < S_n \le \tau \text{ and } 0 \le t < T_1 < \ldots < T_n \le \tau] \tag{17}$$

$$[\alpha(t, T) = -\textstyle\sum_{i=1}^{n} \sigma_i(t, T)(\phi_i(t) - \int_t^{\tau} \sigma_i(t, v)\,dv) \text{ for all } T \in [0, \tau] \text{ and } t \in [0, T] \text{ where for } i = 1, \ldots, n,\ \phi_i(t) = \gamma_i(t; S_1, \ldots, S_n) \text{ for any } S_1, \ldots, S_n \in [t, \tau] \text{ and } t \in [0, S_1]] \tag{18}$$

PROOF: From Proposition 2, for each vector $(S_1, \ldots, S_n)$ with $S_1 < S_2 < \ldots < S_n \le \tau$, $\tilde{Q}_{S_1,\ldots,S_n}$ is the unique equivalent probability measure making $Z(t, S_i)$ a martingale over $t \le S_1$ for $i = 1, \ldots, n$. These measures are all equal to $\tilde{Q}$ if and only if $\gamma_i(t; S_1, \ldots, S_n) = \gamma_i(t; T_1, \ldots, T_n)$ for $i = 1, \ldots, n$ and all $S_1, \ldots, S_n, T_1, \ldots, T_n \in [0, \tau]$ and $t \in [0, \tau]$ such that $0 \le t < S_1 < \ldots < S_n \le \tau$ and $0 \le t < T_1 < \ldots < T_n \le \tau$. To obtain the third condition, by expression (13) and the fact that $(\phi_1(t), \ldots, \phi_n(t))$ is independent of T, one obtains $b(t, T) = -\sum_{i=1}^{n} a_i(t, T)\phi_i(t)$. Substitution for $b(t, T)$, $a_i(t, T)$ for $i = 1, \ldots, n$ and taking the partial derivative with respect to T gives (18). *Q.E.D.*

This proposition asserts that the existence of a unique equivalent probability measure, $\tilde{Q}$, making relative bond prices martingales (condition (16)) is equivalent to the condition that the market prices for risk are independent of the vector of bonds $\{S_1, \ldots, S_n\}$ chosen (condition (17)). Furthermore, condition (17) is also equivalent to a restriction on the drift of the forward rate process (condition (18)). We discuss each of these conditions in turn.

The martingale condition (16) implies that

$$P(t, T) = B(t) E\left[\left.\frac{\exp\left(\sum_{i=1}^{n}\int_0^T \phi_i(t)\,dW_i(t) - \frac{1}{2}\sum_{i=1}^{n}\int_0^T \phi_i(t)^2\,dt\right)}{B(T)}\right| F_t\right] \tag{19}$$

Expression (19) demonstrates that the bond's price depends on the forward rate drifts $\{\alpha(\cdot, T): T \in [0, \tau]\}$, the initial forward curve $\{f(0, T): T \in [0, \tau]\}$, and the forward rate volatilities $\{\sigma_i(\cdot, T): T \in [0, \tau]\}$ for $i = 1, \ldots, n$. All of these parameters enter into expression (19) implicitly through $\phi_i(t)$ for $i = 1, \ldots, n$, the market prices for risk and $B(T)$, the money market account.

Condition (17) of Proposition 3 is called the *standard finance condition* for arbitrage-free pricing. This is the necessary condition for the absence of arbitrage used in the existing literature to derive the fundamental partial differential equation for pricing contingent claims (see Brennan and Schwartz (1979) or Langetieg (1980)).

Last, for purposes of contingent claim valuation, the final condition contained in expression (18) will be most useful. It is called the *forward rate drift restriction*. It shows the restriction needed on the family of drift processes $\{\alpha(\cdot, T): T \in [0, \tau]\}$ in order to guarantee the existence of a unique equivalent martingale probability measure. As seen below, not all potential forward rate processes satisfy this restriction.

Contingent claim valuation

This section demonstrates how to value contingent claims in the preceding economy. As this analysis is a slight extension of the ideas contained in Harrison and Kreps (1979) and Harrison and Pliska (1981), the presentation will be brief. More importantly, it also provides the unifying framework for categorising the various arbitrage pricing theories in the literature (ie, Vasicek (1977), Brennan and Schwartz (1979), Langetieg (1980), Ball and Torous (1983), Ho and Lee (1986), Schaefer and Schwartz (1987), Artzner and Delbaen (1989)) in relation to our own.

Let conditions C.1–C.5 hold. Fix any vector of bonds $\{S_1, \ldots, S_n\} \in [0, \tau]$ where $0 < S_1 < S_2 < \ldots < S_n \leq \tau$. By Proposition 2, there exists a unique $\tilde{Q}_{S_1,\ldots,S_n}$ making all $Z(t, S_i)$ martingales for $i = 1, \ldots, n$. The uniqueness of $\tilde{Q}_{S_1,\ldots,S_n}$ implies that the market is *complete* (Harrison and Pliska (1981); Corollary 3.36, p. 241)), ie, given any random variable $X: \Omega \to R$ which is non-negative, F_{S_1} measurable with $\tilde{E}_{S_1,\ldots,S_n}(X/B(S_1)) < +\infty$ where $\tilde{E}(\cdot)_{S_1,\ldots,S_n}$ denotes expectation with respect to $\tilde{Q}_{S_1,\ldots,S_n}$, there exists an admissible[3] self-financing trading strategy $\{N_0(t), N_{S_1}(t), \ldots, N_{S_n}(t): t \in [0, S_1]\}$ such that the value of the portfolio satisfies

$$N_0(S_1)B(S_1) + \sum_{i=1}^{n} N_{S_i}(S_1)\, P(S_1, S_i) = X \quad \text{a.e. } Q \tag{20}$$

The random variable X is interpreted as the payout to a *contingent claim* at time S_1. Harrison and Pliska (1981) define an arbitrage opportunity and show, in the absence of arbitrage, that the time t price of the contingent claim to X at time S_1 must be given by

$$\tilde{E}_{S_1,\ldots,S_n}\left(\frac{X}{B(S_1)} \middle| F_t \right) B(t) \tag{21}$$

Substituting expression (20) into (21) yields

$$\tilde{E}_{S_1,\ldots,S_n}\left(N_0(S_1) + \frac{N_{S_1}(S_1)}{B(S_1)} + \sum_{i=2}^{n} N_{S_i}(S_1)\, Z(S_1, S_i) \middle| F_t \right) B(t) \tag{22}$$

To value this contingent claim, expression (22) demonstrates that we need to know the dynamics for $r(t)$ and $Z(t, S_i)$ for $i = 1, \ldots, n$, all under the martingale measure; that is,

$$r(t) = f(0,t) + \int_0^t \alpha(v,t)\,dv + \sum_{i=1}^{n} \int_0^t \sigma_i(v,t)\, d\tilde{W}_i^{S_1,\ldots,S_n}(v) + \sum_{i=1}^{n} \int_0^t \gamma_i(v; S_1,\ldots,S_n)\, \sigma_i(v,t)\,dv \quad \text{a.e. } Q \tag{23}$$

and

$$Z(t,u) = Z(0,u) \times \exp\left(-\frac{1}{2}\sum_{i=1}^{n} \int_0^t a_i(v,u)^2\,dv + \sum_{i=1}^{n} \int_0^t a_i(v,u)\, d\tilde{W}_i^{S_1,\ldots,S_n}(v) \right) \quad \text{a.e. } Q \tag{24}$$

for $u \in \{S_1, \ldots, S_n\}$. Therefore, we need to know $\gamma_i(v; S_1, \ldots, S_n)$ for $i = 1, \ldots, n$, the market prices for risk. These enter through the dynamics of the spot rate process in expression (23). This is true even though the evaluation proceeds in the risk-neutral economy under the martingale measure.

All other bonds of differing maturities $u \in [0, \tau]$ are assumed to have values at time S_1, through expression (8), which are F_{S_1} measurable. Since $\tilde{E}_{S_1,\ldots,S_n}(P(S_1, u)/B(S_1)) < +\infty$ for all $u \in [0, \tau]$ and the market is complete, every other bond can be duplicated with an admissible self-financing trading strategy involving only the n bonds $\{S_1, \ldots, S_n\}$ and the money market account. Thus, one can price *all* the remaining bonds and all contingent claims. These are the two purposes for the arbitrage pricing methodology as stated in the introduction.

As expressions (23) and (24) make clear, the dynamics for the bond price process, spot rate process, and the market prices for risk cannot be chosen independently. Independently specifying these processes will in general lead to inconsistent pricing models. This is the logic underlying the criticism of the arbitrage pricing methodology presented in Cox, Ingersoll, and Ross (1985, p. 398).

The model, as presented above, captures the essence of all the existing arbitrage pricing models. To see this, let us first consider Vasicek (1977), Brennan and Schwartz (1979), Langetieg (1980) and Artzner and Delbaen (1989). Since all four models are similar, we focus upon that of Brennan and Schwartz. The Brennan–Schwartz model has $n = 2$. Instead of specifying the two bond processes for $\{S_1, S_2\}$ directly as in expression (24), they derive these expressions from other assumptions. First, they exogenously specify a long rate process and a spot rate process. Second, they assume that *all* bond prices at time t can be written as twice-continuously differentiable functions of the current values of these long and short rates. In conjunction, these assumptions (by Itô's lemma) imply condition (24). The analysis could then proceed as above, yielding contingent claim values dependent on the market prices for risk.[4,5]

Along with the framework for categorising the various models, an additional contribution of our approach is to extend the above analysis to eliminate the market prices for risk from the valuation formulas. Intuitively speaking, this is done by utilising the remaining information contained in the bond price process to "substitute out" the market prices for risk. For thus purpose, we add the following condition.

C.6 - COMMON EQUIVALENT MARTINGALE MEASURES *Given conditions C.1-C.3, let C.4 and C.5 hold for all bonds* $\{S_1, \ldots, S_n) \in [0, \tau]$ *with* $0 < S_1 < \ldots < S_n \leq \tau$. *Further, let* $\tilde{Q} = \tilde{Q}_{S_1, \ldots, S_n}$ *(on their common domain).*

To remove the market prices for risk from expression (23), we assume condition C.6. Proposition 3, the no-arbitrage condition (expression (18)) gives

$$\int_0^t \alpha(v, t)\, dv = -\sum_{i=1}^n \int_0^t \sigma_i(v, t)\, \phi_i(v)\, dv + \sum_{i=1}^n \sigma_i(v, t) \int_v^t \sigma_i(v, y)\, dy\, dv \tag{25}$$

Substitution of this expression into expression (23) for the spot rate yields

$$r(t) = f(0, t) + \sum_{i=1}^n \int_0^t \sigma_i(v, t) \int_v^t \sigma_i(v, y)\, dy\, dv + \sum_{i=1}^n \int_0^t \sigma_i(v, t)\, d\tilde{W}_i(v) \tag{26}$$

The market prices for risk *drop out* of expression (23) and they are replaced with an expression involving the volatilities across different maturities of the forward rates, ie, a "term structure of volatilities". Thus, contingent claim values can be calculated independently of the market prices for risk. We illustrate this abstract procedure further with concrete examples in the next two sections.

Examples

This section presents two examples to illustrate and to clarify the analysis in the previous section. One example, a continuous time limit of Ho and Lee's (1986) model (see Heath, Jarrow and Morton (1990)), may prove useful in practical applications due to its computational simplicity.[6]

We assume that forward rates satisfy the stochastic process from condition C.1 with a single Brownian motion and the volatility $\sigma_1(t, T, \omega) \equiv \sigma > 0$, a positive constant. We let the initial forward rate curve $\{f(0, T): T \in [0, \tau]\}$ be measurable and absolutely integrable (as in condition C.2). Given a particular, but arbitrary, stochastic process for the market price of risk, $\phi: [0, \tau] \times \Omega \to R$, which is predictable and bounded, we also assume that the forward rate drift condition (18) is satisfied:

$$\alpha(t, T) = \sigma\phi(t) + \sigma^2(T - t) \quad \text{for all } T \in [0, \tau] \text{ and } t \in [0, T] \tag{27}$$

It is easy to verify that conditions C.1–C.6 are satisfied. This implies, therefore, that contingent claim valuation can proceed as in the previous section. Before that, however, we analyse the forward rate, spot rate and bond price processes in more detail.

Under the equivalent martingale measure, and in terms of its Brownian motion (see expression (15)), the stochastic process for the forward rate is

$$f(t, T) = f(0, T) + \sigma^2 t\left(T - \frac{t}{2}\right) + \sigma\tilde{W}(t) \tag{28}$$

Under condition (28), forward rates can be negative with positive probability.

The stochastic spot rate process under the equivalent martingale measure is

$$r(t) = f(0, t) + \sigma\tilde{W}(t) + \frac{\sigma^2 t^2}{2} \tag{29}$$

Spot rates can also be negative with positive probability.

The dynamics of the bond price process over time is given by substituting expression (28) into expression (2):

$$P(t, T) = \frac{P(0, T)}{P(0, t)}\, e^{-(\sigma^2/2)Tt(T-t) - \sigma(T-t)\tilde{W}(t)} \tag{30}$$

Next, consider a European call option on the bond $P(t, T)$ with an exercise price of K and a maturity date t^*, where $0 \le t \le t^* \le T$. Let $C(t)$ denote the value of this call option at time t. The cashflow to the call option at maturity is

$$C(t^*) = \max[P(t^*, T) - K, 0] \tag{31}$$

With reference to the previous section, the time t value of the call is

$$C(t) = \tilde{E}\left(\frac{\max[P(t^*, T) - K, 0]B(t)}{B(t^*)}\,\middle|\, F_t\right) \tag{32}$$

An explicit calculation,[7] using normal random variables, shows that expression (32) simplifies to

$$C(t) = P(t, T)\Phi(h) - KP(t, t^*)\Phi\left(h - \sigma(T - t^*)\sqrt{t^* - t}\right) \tag{33}$$

where

$$h = \frac{\log\left(\dfrac{P(t, T)}{KP(t, t^*)}\right) + \frac{1}{2}\sigma(T - t^*)^2(t^* - t)}{\sigma(T - t^*)\sqrt{t^* - t}} \tag{34}$$

and $\Phi(\cdot)$ is the cumulative normal distribution.

The value of the bond option is given by a modified Black-Scholes formula. The parameter, $\sigma(T - t^*)$, is not equal to the variance of the instantaneous return on the T-maturity bond, but it is equivalent to the variance of the instantaneous return on the forward price (at time t^*) of a T-maturity bond, $(P(t, T)/P(t, t^*))$.

For the second example, assume that forward rates satisfy condition C.1 with the volatilities $\sigma_1(t, T, \omega) \equiv \sigma_1 > 0$ and $\sigma_2(t, T, \omega) \equiv \sigma_2 e^{-(\lambda/2)(T\ \ t)} > 0$, where σ_1, σ_2 and λ are strictly positive constants, ie,

$$df(t,T) = \alpha(t,T)\,dt + \sigma_1\,dW_1(t) + \sigma_2 e^{-(\lambda/2)(T-t)}\,dW_2(t) \tag{35}$$

for all $T \in [0,\tau]$ and $t \in [0,T]$

Here, the instantaneous changes in forward rates are caused by two sources of randomness. The first, $\{W_1(t): t \in [0,\tau)\}$, can be interpreted as a "long-run factor" since it uniformly shifts all maturity forward rates equally. The second, $\{W_2(t): t \in [0,\tau)\}$, affects the short maturity forward rates more than it does long-term rates and can be interpreted as a spread between a "short" and "long-term factor".

The volatility functions are strictly positive and bounded. Furthermore, the matrix

$$\begin{bmatrix} a_1(t,S) & a_2(t,S) \\ a_1(t,T) & a_2(t,T) \end{bmatrix} = \begin{bmatrix} -\sigma_1(S-t) + 2\sigma_2\left(e^{-(\lambda/2)(S-t)} - 1\right)/\lambda \\ -\sigma_1(T-t) + 2\sigma_2\left(e^{-(\lambda/2)(T-t)} - 1\right)/\lambda \end{bmatrix} \tag{36}$$

is non-singular for all $t, S, T \in [0,\tau]$ such that $t \leq S < T$.

We arbitrarily fix two bounded, predictable processes for the market prices of risk, $\phi_i: [0,\tau] \times \Omega \to T$ for $i = 1, 2$. To ensure that the process is arbitrage-free, we set

$$\alpha(t,T) = -\sigma_1\phi_1(t) - \sigma_2 e^{-(\lambda/2)(T-t)}\phi_2(t) + \sigma_1^2(T-t) - 2\left(\frac{\sigma_2^2}{\lambda}\right) e^{-(\lambda/2)(T-t)}\left(e^{-(\lambda/2)(T-t)} - 1\right) \tag{37}$$

The above forward rate process satisfies conditions C.1–C.6. Under the martingale measure $\tilde{Q}$ and its Brownian motions $\{\tilde{W}_1(t), \tilde{W}_2(t): t \in [0,\tau]\}$, the forward rate process is

$$f(t,T) = f(0,T) + \sigma_1^2 t\left(T - \frac{t}{2}\right) - 2\left(\frac{\sigma_2}{\lambda}\right)^2 \left[e^{-\lambda T}\left(e^{\lambda t} - 1\right) - 2e^{-(\lambda/2)T}\left(e^{(\lambda/2)t} - 1\right)\right] + \sigma_1\tilde{W}_1(t) + \sigma_2\int_0^t e^{-(\lambda/2)(T-v)}\,d\tilde{W}_2(v) \tag{38}$$

This expression shows that forward rates can be negative with positive probability. The spot rate follows the simpler process:

$$r(t) = f(0,t) + \frac{\sigma_1^2 t^2}{2} - 2\left(\frac{\sigma_2}{\lambda}\right)^2 \left[\left(1 - e^{-\lambda t}\right) - 2\left(1 - e^{-(\lambda/2)t}\right)\right] + \sigma_1\tilde{W}_1(t) + \sigma_2\int_0^t e^{-(\lambda/2)(t-v)}\,d\tilde{W}_2(v) \tag{39}$$

As before, we can calculate the value of a European call option on the bond $P(t,T)$ with an exercise price of K and a maturity date t^* where $0 \leq t \leq t^* \leq T$. Let $C(t)$ denote the value of this call option at time t. With regard to the previous section, the call's value is

$$C(t) = P(t,T)\,\Phi(h) - KP(t,t^*)\,\Phi(h-q) \tag{40}$$

where

$$h = \frac{\log\left(\dfrac{P(t,T)}{KP(t,t^*)}\right) + \frac{1}{2}q^2}{q}$$

$$q^2 = \sigma_1^2(T-t^*)^2(t^*-t) + \left(\frac{4\sigma_2^2}{\lambda^3}\right)\left(e^{-(\lambda/2)T} - e^{-(\lambda/2)t^*}\right)^2\left(e^{\lambda t^*} - e^{\lambda t}\right) \tag{41}$$

A class of stochastic differential equations

The previous section provides examples of forward rate processes satisfying conditions C.1-C.6. These processes have deterministic volatilities which are independent of the state $\omega \in \Omega$. This section provides a class of processes with the volatilities dependent on $\omega \in \Omega$. This class of processes can be described as the solutions (if they exist) to the following stochastic integral equation with restricted drift:

$$f(t,T)-f(0,T)=\int_0^t \alpha(v,T,\omega)dv+\sum_{i=1}^n\int_0^t \sigma_i(v,T,f(v,T))\,dW_i(v)$$

$$\text{for all } 0 \le t \le T \tag{42}$$

where

$$\alpha(v,T,\omega) \equiv -\sum_{i=1}^n \sigma_i(v,T,f(v,T))\left(\phi_i(v)-\int_v^T \sigma_i(v,y,f(t,y))dy\right)$$

$$\text{for all } T \in [0,\tau]$$

σ_i: $\{(t,S): 0 \le t \le S \le T\} \times R \to R$ is jointly measurable and satisfies

$$\int_0^T \sigma_i(t,T,f(t,T))^2\,dt < +\infty \quad \text{a.e. } Q \text{ for } i=1,\ldots,n$$

and ϕ_i: $\Omega \times [0,\tau] \to R$ is a bounded predictable process for $i = 1, \ldots, n$.

We now study sufficient conditions on the volatility functions such that strong solutions to this class of stochastic differential equations exist. The continuous time analogue of Ho and Lee's (1986) model as given in expression (28) is a special case of this theorem. The example of a proportional volatility function is also provided below to show that additional hypotheses are needed.

A key step in proving the existence theorem is the following lemma, which asserts that the existence of a class of forward rate processes in the initial economy is guaranteed if and only if it can be guaranteed in an "equivalent risk-neutral economy".

LEMMA 1 - Existence in an Equivalent Risk-Neutral Economy

[*The processes* $\{f(t,T): T \in [0,\tau]\}$ *satisfy* (42) *with* $\gamma_i(t; S_1, \ldots, S_n) = \phi_i(t)$ *for all* $0 \le t < S < \ldots S_n \le \tau$ *and* $i = 1, \ldots, n$] (43)

if and only if

[*The process* $\{\tilde{\alpha}(\cdot,T): T \in [0,\tau]\}$ *defined by* $\tilde{\alpha}(t,T) = \sum_{i=1}^n \sigma_i(t,T,f(t,T)) \times \int_t^T \sigma_i(t,v,f(t,v))\,dv$ *for all* $T \in [0,\tau]$ *satisfies* (42) *with* $\tilde{\alpha}(t,T)$ *replacing* $\alpha(t,T)$, $\tilde{W}_i(t)$ *replacing* $W_i(t)$ *where* $\tilde{W}_i(t) \equiv W_i(t) - \int_0^t \phi_i(y)\,dy$ *is a Brownian motion with respect to* $[(\Omega, F, \tilde{Q}), \{F_t: t \in [0,\tau]\}$, *and* $\tilde{Q}$ *replacing* Q *where* $d\tilde{Q}/dQ = \exp\{\sum_{i=1}^n \int_0^T \phi_i(t)\,dW_i(t) - \tfrac{1}{2}\sum_{i=1}^n \int_0^T \phi_i(t)^2 dt\}$] (44)

PROOF: A straightforward application of Girsanov's Theorem. *Q.E.D.*

Combined with this, the next lemma generates our existence theorem given in Proposition 4.

LEMMA 2 - Existence of Forward Rate Processes: *Let* σ_i: $\{(t,s): 0 \le t \le s \le T\} \times R \to R$ *for* $i = 1, \ldots, n$ *be Lipschitz continuous in the last argument, non-negative and bounded. Let* $(\Omega, F, \tilde{Q})$ *be any equivalent probability space with* $\{\tilde{W}_i(t), \ldots, \tilde{W}_n(t)$:

$t \in [0, \tau]\}$ *independent Brownian motions; then, there exists a jointly continuous* $f(\cdot, \cdot)$ *satisfying* (42) *with* $\tilde{W}_i(t)$ *replacing* $W_i(t)$ *and*

$$\tilde{\alpha}(t, T) = \sum_{i=1}^{n} \sigma_i(t, T, f(t, T)) \int_t^T \sigma_i(t, v, f(t, v))\, dv \quad \text{for all } T \in [0, \tau]$$

replacing $\alpha(t, T)$.

The proof of this lemma is contained in Morton (1988). The hypotheses of Lemma 2 differ from the standard hypotheses guaranteeing the existence of strong solutions to stochastic differential equations due to the boundedness condition on the volatility functions.

PROPOSITION 4 – Existence of Arbitrage-Free Forward Rate Drift Processes *Let* $\phi_i: [0, \tau] \times \Omega \to R$ *be bounded predictable processes for* $i = 1, \ldots, n$. *Let* $\sigma_i: \{(t, s): 0 \le t \le s \le T\} \times R \to R$ *for* $i = 1, \ldots, n$ *be Lipschitz continuous in the last argument, non-negative and bounded; then, there exists a jointly continuous forward rate process satisfying condition* (42).

By appending the non-singularity condition C.5, this proposition provides sufficient conditions guaranteeing the existence of a class of forward rate processes satisfying conditions C.1–C.6. This set of sufficient conditions is easily verified in applications.

To show that the boundedness condition in Proposition 4 cannot be substantially weakened, we consider the special case of a single Brownian motion where $\sigma_1(t, T, f(t, T)) \equiv \sigma \times f(t, T)$ for a fixed constant $\sigma > 0$. This volatility function is positive and Lipschitz continuous, but not bounded.

For this volatility function, the no-arbitrage condition of Proposition 4 with $\phi_i(t) \equiv 0$ implies that the forward rate process must satisfy

$$f(t, T) = f(0, T) \exp\left(\int_0^t \int_u^T f(u, v)\, dv\, du \right) \exp\left(-\frac{\sigma^2 t}{2} + \sigma W(t) \right) \tag{45}$$

$$\text{for all } T \in [0, \tau] \text{ and } t \in [0, T]$$

Unfortunately, it can be shown (see Morton (1988)) that there is no finite-valued solution to expression (45). In fact, it can be shown that under (45), in finite time, forward rates explode with positive probability for the martingale measure and, hence, for any equivalent probability measure. Infinite forward rates generate zero bond prices and hence arbitrage opportunities.

The forward rate process given in (45) is in some ways the simplest model consistent with non-negative forward rates. The incompatibility of this process with arbitrage-free bond prices raises the issue as to the general existence of a drift process $\{\alpha(\cdot, T): T \in [0, \tau]\}$ satisfying conditions C.1–C.6, *and* with non-negative forward rates. This existence issue is resolved through an example.

This example can be thought of as a combination of the two previous examples. When forward rates are "small" the process has a proportional volatility, and when forward rates are "large" it has a constant volatility. Intuitively, as shown below, rates cannot fall below zero nor explode. Formally, consider a single Brownian motion process with $\sigma_1(t, T, f(t, T)) = \sigma \min(f(t, T), \lambda)$ for $\sigma, \lambda > 0$ positive constants. This volatility function is positive, Lipschitz continuous and bounded; thus, for an arbitrary initial forward rate curve Proposition 4 guarantees the existence of a jointly continuous $f(t, T)$ which solves

$$df(t, T) = \sigma \min(f(t, T), \lambda) \left(\int_t^T \sigma \min(f(t, s), \lambda)\, ds \right) dt + \sigma \min(f(t, T), \lambda)\, dW(t) \tag{46}$$

The following proposition guarantees that this forward rate process remains positive for any strictly positive initial forward rate curve.

PROPOSITION 5 – A Non-negative Forward Rate Process: *Given that* $f(t,T)$ *solves expression* (46) *and given an arbitrary initial forward rate curve* $f(0,t) = l(t) > 0$ *for all* $t \in [0,\tau]$*, then, with probability one,* $f(t,T) \geq 0$ *for all* $T \in [0,\tau]$ *and* $t \in [0,\tau]$.

PROOF: In the Appendix.

Since the forward rate process is a mixture of the constant volatility and proportional volatility models, it is easy to see (using expression (46)) that the forward rate drifts $\{\sigma(\cdot,T)\colon T \in [0,\tau]\}$ will be dependent upon the path of the Brownian motion. Another forward rate process consistent with non-negative forward rates is provided in the next section.

The equilibrium pricing versus the arbitrage pricing methodology

The crucial difference between our methodology for pricing contingent claims on the term structure of interest rates and that of Cox, Ingersoll, and Ross (1985) is the difference between the arbitrage-free pricing methodology and that of equilibrium pricing, respectively. To clarify the relationship between these approaches, we illustrate how to describe (or model) the equilibrium determined Cox-Ingersoll-Ross square-root model in our framework. The Cox-Ingersoll-Ross model is based on a single state variable, represented by the spot interest rate $r(t)$ for $t \in [0,\tau]$.

The spot rate is assumed to follow a square-root process:

$$dr(t) = K(\theta(t) - r(t))\,dt + \sigma\sqrt{r(t)}\,dW(t) \tag{47}$$

where $r(0)$, K, σ are strictly positive constants, $\theta\colon [0,\tau] \to (0,+\infty)$ is a continuous function of time, $\{W(t)\colon t \in [0,\tau]\}$ is a standard Wiener process initialised at zero, and $2K\theta(t) \geq \sigma^2$ for all $t \in [0,\tau]$.

The condition that $2K\theta(t) \geq \sigma^2$ for all $t \in [0,\tau]$ guarantees that zero is an inaccessible boundary for spot rates. Although this stochastic differential equation has a solution (see Feller (1951)), an explicit representation is unavailable. In equilibrium, Cox, Ingersoll, and Ross show that the equilibrium bond dynamics are:

$$dP(t,T) = r(t)\,[1 - \lambda\bar{B}(t,T)]\,P(t,T)\,dt - \bar{B}(t,T)\,P(t,T)\,\sigma\sqrt{r(t)}\,dW(t) \tag{48}$$

where λ is a constant,

$$\bar{B}(t,T) = \frac{2\left(e^{\gamma(T-t)} - 1\right)}{(\gamma + K + \lambda)\left(e^{\gamma(T-t)} - 1\right) + 2\gamma} \quad \text{and} \quad \gamma = \left[(K+\lambda)^2 + 2\sigma^2\right]^{\frac{1}{2}}$$

The parameter λ is related to the market price of risk $\phi(t) = -\lambda\sqrt{r(t)}/\sigma$. The market price of risk is restricted in equilibrium to be of this particular functional form. Cox, Ingersoll, and Ross solve for the bond price process, and from this one can deduce the forward rate process:

$$f(t,T) = r(t)\left(\frac{\partial\bar{B}(t,T)}{\partial T}\right) + K\int_t^T \theta(s)\left(\frac{\partial\bar{B}(s,T)}{\partial T}\right) ds \tag{49}$$

Given its parameters, the Cox-Ingersoll-Ross model has a predetermined functional form for the forward rate process at time 0 given by expression (49). To match any arbitrary, but given, initial forward rate curve, Cox, Ingersoll, and Ross suggest that one "inverts" expression (49) when $t = 0$ for $\{\theta(t)\colon t \in [0,\tau]\}$ to make the spot rate process's parameters implicitly determined by the initial forward rate curve; see Cox, Ingersoll, and Ross (1985, p. 395).

Cox, Ingersoll, and Ross never prove that such an inversion is possible, ie, that a "solution" $\{\theta(t): t \in [0, \tau]\}$ exists to expression (49) with $t = 0$. In fact, if $\{\partial f(0, T)/\partial T: T \in [0, \tau]\}$ exists and is continuous, then there is a *unique* continuous solution.[8] Using standard procedures, one can show that the solution $\{\theta(s): s \in [0, \tau]\}$ to equation (49) with $t = 0$ can be approximated to any order of accuracy desired (see Taylor and Lay (1980, pp. 196–201)). Nonetheless, the Cox-Ingersoll-Ross model is not consistent with all initial forward rate curves. This is due to the requirement that $2K\theta(t) \geq \sigma^2$ for all $t \in [0, \tau]$. Indeed, consider expression (49) initialised at $t = 0$. Substitution of the inaccessible boundary condition into it, and simplification, yield

$$f(0,T) \geq \frac{r(0)\partial \bar{B}(0,T)}{\partial T} + \frac{\sigma^2 \bar{B}(0,T)}{2} \tag{50}$$

Not all initial forward rate curves will satisfy this expression.

Hence, in our framework we have that the Cox-Ingersoll-Ross term structure model can be written as

$$df(t,T) = r(t)K\left(\frac{\partial^2 \bar{B}(t,T)}{\partial t\, \partial T} - \frac{\partial \bar{B}(t,T)}{\partial T}\right)dt + \left(\frac{\partial \bar{B}(t,T)}{\partial T}\right)\sigma\sqrt{r(t)}\, dW(t) \tag{51}$$

where

$$r(t) = \left[f(t,T) - K\int_t^T \theta(s)\left(\frac{\partial \bar{B}(s,T)}{\partial T}\right)ds\right] \Bigg/ \frac{\partial \bar{B}(t,T)}{\partial T}$$

$\{f(0, T): T \in [0, \tau]\}$ is a continuously differentiable, fixed, initial forward rate curve, and $\theta: [0, \tau] \to (0, \infty)$ is the unique continuous solution to expression (49) with $t = 0$.

To apply our analysis based on expression (51), we need to guarantee that conditions C.1–C.6 are satisfied. Recall that conditions C.1–C.3 guarantee that the bond price process satisfies expression (8). Next, given expression (8), conditions C.4 and C.5 guarantee that for any vector of bonds $\{S_1, \ldots, S_n\}$ an equivalent martingale measure exists and is unique. Finally, condition C.6 ensures that the martingale measure is identical across all vectors of bonds. These conditions are sufficient to price all contingent claims when starting from forward rates.

Alternatively, Cox, Ingersoll, and Ross exogenously specify the spot rate process. Consequently, using different methods, they are able to guarantee that the bond price process satisfies expression (8). Hence, we do not need to check sufficient conditions C.1–C.3, since expression (8) is the starting point of our analysis. Next, given that the bond prices are generated by an equilibrium with a single Brownian motion, conditions C.4, C.5 and C.6 are easily verified. In fact, to check condition C.6 one can easily verify that expression (18) is satisfied.

Given the form of the Cox-Ingersoll-Ross model as in expression (51), we can now proceed to price contingent claims. This analysis will generate the *identical* contingent claim values as in the Cox-Ingersoll-Ross model subject to the determination of $\{\theta(s): s \in [0, \tau]\}$. Note that the forward rate's quadratic variation

$$\langle f(t,T)\rangle_t = \int_0^t \left[\left(\frac{\partial \bar{B}(s,T)}{\partial T}\right)\sigma\sqrt{r(s)}\right]^2 ds$$

depends on the parameters λ, σ, K, $r(0)$ and $\{f(0, T): T \in [0, \tau]\}$. The parameter λ, however, is functionally related to the market price of risk. This makes contingent claim valuation explicitly dependent on this parameter as well (eg, see Cox, Ingersoll, and Ross, expression (32), p. 396).

With this analysis behind us, we can now discuss some differences between the two pricing approaches. First, the Cox-Ingersoll-Ross model fixed a particular market price for risk and endogenously derived the stochastic process for forward rates. In contrast, our approach takes the stochastic process for forward rates as a given (it could be from an equilibrium model) and prices contingent claims from it.

Summary

This paper presents a new methodology for pricing contingent claims on the term structure of interest rates. Given an initial forward rate curve and a mechanism which describes how it fluctuates, we develop an arbitrage pricing model that yields contingent claim valuations which do not explicitly depend on the market prices for risk.

For practical applications, we specialise our abstract economy and study particular examples. For these examples, closed-form solutions are obtained for bond options depending only upon observables and the forward rate volatilities. These models are testable and their empirical verification awaits subsequent research.

The paper can be generalised by embedding our term structure model into the larger economy of Harrison and Pliska (1981), which includes trading in alternative risky assets (eg, stocks) generated by additional (perhaps distinct) independent Brownian models. Our model provides a consistent structure for the interest rate process employed therein. This merging of the two analyses can be found in Amin and Jarrow (1989).

Appendix

PROOF OF EXPRESSION (8) Before proving expression (8), we need to state a generalised form of Fubini's theorem for stochastic integrals. This proof of this theorem follows Ikeda and Watanabe (1981, p. 116) very closely and is available from the authors on request.

LEMMA 0.1: *Let* (Ω, F, Q) *be a probability space. Let* (F_t) *be a reference family satisfying the usual conditions and generated by a Brownian motion* $\{W(t): t \in [0, \tau]\}$.

Let $\{\Phi(t, a, \omega): (t, a) \in [0, \tau] \times [0, \tau]\}$ *be a family of real random variables such that:*

(i) $((t, \omega), a) \in \{([0, \tau] \times \Omega) \times [0, \tau]\} \to \Phi(t, a, \omega)$

is $L \times B[0, \tau]$ *measurable, where* L *is the predictable σ-field;*

(ii) $\int_0^t \Phi^2(s, a, \omega)\, ds < +\infty$ *a.e. for all* $t \in [0, \tau]$;

(iii) $\int_0^t \left(\int_0^\tau \Phi(s, a, \omega)\, da\right)^2 ds < +\infty$ *a.e. for all* $t \in [0, \tau]$;

If $t \to \int_0^T \{\int_0^t \Phi(s, a, \omega)\, dW_s\}\, da$ *is continuous a.e., then*

$$\int_0^t \left(\int_0^\tau \Phi(s, a, \omega)\, da\right) dW_s = \int_0^t \left(\int_0^t \Phi(s, a, \omega)\, dW_s\right) da \quad \textit{for all } t \in [0, \tau]$$

COROLLARY 1: *Let the hypotheses of Lemma* 0.1 *hold. Define*

$$\Phi(s, a, \omega) = \begin{bmatrix} 0 & \text{if } (s, a) \notin [0, t] \times [t, \tau] \\ \sigma(s, a, \omega) & \text{if } (s, a) \in [0, t] \times [t, \tau] \end{bmatrix}$$

Then

$$\int_0^y \left(\int_t^T \sigma(s, a, \omega)\, da\right) dW(s) = \int_t^T \left(\int_0^y \sigma(s, a, \omega)\, dW(s)\right) da \quad \textit{for all } y \in [0, t]$$

COROLLARY 2: *Let the hypotheses of Lemma* 0.1 *hold. Define*

$$\Phi(s,a,\omega)=\begin{bmatrix}0 & \text{if } (s,a)\notin[0,t]\times[0,t]\\ \sigma(s,a,\omega)1_{s\le a} & \text{if } (s,a)\in[0,t]\times[0,t]\end{bmatrix}$$

Then

$$\int_0^y\left(\int_s^t\sigma(s,a,\omega)\,da\right)dW(s)=\int_0^t\left(\int_0^{a\wedge y}\sigma(s,a,\omega)\,dW(s)\right)da \quad \textit{for all } y\in[0,t]$$

Now we can proceed with the proof of expression (8).

$$\ln P(t,T)=-\int_t^T f(0,y)dy-\int_t^T\left(\int_0^T\alpha(v,y)dv\right)dy-\sum_{i=1}^n\int_t^T\left(\int_0^t\sigma_i(v,y)dW_i(v)\right)dy$$

Note that the integrals are well defined by conditions C.1 and C.2.

By condition C.2, we can apply the standard Fubini's theorem. By conditions C.1-C.3 we can apply Corollary 1 with $y = t$ to get

$$\ln P(t,T)=-\int_t^T f(0,y)dy-\int_0^t\left(\int_t^T\alpha(v,y)dv\right)dy-\sum_{i=1}^n\int_0^t\left(\int_t^T\sigma_i(v,y)dy\right)dW_i(v)$$

Adding and subtracting the same terms yields

$$=-\int_0^T f(0,y)dy-\int_0^t\left(\int_v^T\alpha(v,y)dy\right)dv-\sum_{i=1}^n\int_0^t\left(\int_v^T\sigma_i(v,y)dy\right)dW_i(v)+$$

$$\int_0^t f(0,y)dy+\int_0^t\left(\int_v^t\alpha(v,y)dy\right)dv+\sum_{i=1}^n\int_0^t\left(\int_v^t\sigma_i(v,y)dy\right)dW_i(v)$$

But, expression (5) yields with Corollary 2 (by C.1-C.3) for $y = t$:

$$\ln P(t,T)=$$

$$\ln P(0,T)+\int_0^t r(y)dy-\int_0^t\left(\int_v^T\alpha(v,y)dv\right)dy-\sum_{i=1}^n\int_0^t\left(\int_v^T\sigma_i(v,y)\,dy\right)dW_i(v)$$

This completes the proof.

PROOF OF PROPOSITION 1: This proposition is proved through the following two lemmas. The straightforward proofs of these lemmas are omitted.

LEMMA 1.1: *Assume C.1-C.3 hold for fixed* $\{S_1,\dots,S_n\}\in[0,\tau]$ *such that* $0<S_1<\dots<S_n\le\tau$. *Define*

$$X(t,y)=\int_0^t b(v,y)dv+\sum_{i=1}^n\int_0^t a_i(v,y)\,dW_i(v)$$

$$\textit{for all } t\in[0,y] \textit{ and } y\in\{S_1,\dots,S_n\}$$

Then $\gamma_i:\Omega\times[0,\tau]\to R$ *for* $i = 1, \dots, n$ *satisfies:*

(i) $$\begin{bmatrix}b(t,S_1)\\ \vdots\\ b(t,S_n)\end{bmatrix}+\begin{bmatrix}a_1(t,S_1)\dots a_n(t,S_1)\\ \vdots\\ a_1(t,S_n)\dots a_n(t,S_n)\end{bmatrix}\begin{bmatrix}\gamma_1(t)\\ \vdots\\ \gamma_n(t)\end{bmatrix}=\begin{bmatrix}0\\ \vdots\\ 0\end{bmatrix} \quad \text{a.e. } \lambda\times Q$$

(ii) $$\int_0^{S_1}\gamma_i(v)^2\,dv<+\infty \quad \text{a.e. } Q \quad \textit{for } i=1,\dots,n$$

(iii) $E\left[\exp\left(\sum_{i=1}^{n}\int_0^{S_1}\gamma_1(v)\,dW_i(v)-\frac{1}{2}\sum_{i=1}^{n}\int_0^{S_1}\gamma_1(v)^2\,dv\right)\right]=1$

(iv) $E\left[\exp\left(\sum_{i=1}^{n}\int_0^{S_1}\left[a_1(v,y)+\gamma_i(v)\right]dW_i(v)-\frac{1}{2}\sum_{i=1}^{n}\int_0^{S_1}\left[a_1(v,y)+\gamma_i(v)\right]^2 dv\right)\right]=1$

for $y \in S_1, \ldots, S_n$ *if and only if: there exists a probability measure* $\tilde{Q}_{S_1,\ldots,S_n}$ *such that*

(a) $\dfrac{d\tilde{Q}_{S_1,\ldots,S_n}}{dQ}=\exp\left(\sum_{i=1}^{n}\int_0^{S_1}\gamma_i(v)\,dW_i(v)-\frac{1}{2}\sum_{i=1}^{n}\int_0^{S_1}\gamma_i(v)^2\,dv\right)$

(b) $\tilde{W}_i^{S_1,\ldots,S_n}(t)=W_i(t)-\int_0^{S_1}\gamma_i(v)\,dv$ *are Brownian motions on*

$\left\{\left(\Omega, F, \tilde{Q}_{S_1,\ldots,S_n}\right), \left(F_t; t\in[0,S_1]\right)\right\}$ *for* $i = 1, \ldots, n$

(c) $\begin{bmatrix} dX(t,S_1) \\ \vdots \\ dX(t,S_n) \end{bmatrix} = \begin{bmatrix} a_1(t,S_1) \ldots a_n(t,S_1) \\ \vdots \\ a_1(t,S_n) \ldots a_n(t,S_n) \end{bmatrix} \begin{bmatrix} d\tilde{W}_1^{S_1,\ldots,S_n}(t) \\ \vdots \\ d\tilde{W}_n^{S_1,\ldots,S_n}(t) \end{bmatrix}$ *for* $t\in[0,S_1]$

and

(d) $Z(t,S_i)$ *are martingales on* $\{(\Omega, F, \tilde{Q}_{S_1,\ldots,S_n}), \{F_t: t\in[0,S_1]\}\}$ *for* $i = 1, \ldots, n$.

LEMMA 1.2: *Assume that C.1–C.3 hold for fixed* $\{S_1, \ldots, S_n\}\in[0,\tau]$ *such that* $0 < S_1 < \ldots < S_n \le \tau$. *Define*

$$X(t,y)=\int_0^t b(v,y)\,dv+\sum_{i=1}^{n}\int_0^t a_i(v,y)\,dW_i(v)$$

for all $t\in[0,y]$ *and* $y\in\{S_1, \ldots, S_n\}$

There exists a probability measure $\bar{Q}$ *equivalent to* Q *such that* $Z(t,S_i)$ *are martingales on* $\{(\Omega, F, \bar{Q}), \{F_t: t\in[0,S_1]\}\}$ *for all* $i = 1,\ldots,n$ *if and only if there exists* $\gamma_i: \Omega\times[0,\tau]\to R$ *for* $i = 1, \ldots, n$ *and a probability measure* $\tilde{Q}_{S_1,\ldots,S_n}$ *such that (a), (b), (c)* and *(d) of Lemma* 1.1 *hold.*

PROOF OF PROPOSITION 2: The proof of this proposition requires the following two lemmas.

LEMMA 2.1: *Fix* $S < \tau$. *Let* $\beta_i: \Omega\times[0,\tau]\to R$ *for* $i = 1, \ldots, n$ *be such that* $\int_0^S \beta_i^2(v)\,dv < +\infty$ *a.e.* Q. *Define*

$$T_m \equiv \inf\left\{t\in[0,S];\ E\left[\exp\left(\frac{1}{2}\sum_{i=1}^{n}\int_0^t \beta_i(v)^2\,dv\right)\right]\ge m\right\}$$

$$M^m(t) \equiv \exp\left(\sum_{i=1}^{n}\int_0^{\min(T_m,t)}\beta_i(v)\,dW_i(v) - \frac{1}{2}\sum_{i=1}^{n}\int_0^{\min(T_m,t)}\beta_i(v)^2\,dv\right)$$

Then

$$E\left[\exp\left(\sum_{i=1}^{n}\int_0^S \beta_i(v)\,dW_i(v)-\frac{1}{2}\sum_{i=1}^{n}\int_0^S \beta_i(v)^2\,dv\right)\right]=1$$

if and only if $\{M^m(S)\}_{m=1}^{\infty}$ *are uniformly integrable.*

PROOF: Define $\beta_i^m(v)\equiv\beta_i(v)1_{(v\le T_m)}$; then by Elliott (1982, p. 165),

$$M^m(t)=\exp\left(\sum_{i=1}^{n}\int_0^S \beta_i^m(v)\,dW_i(v)-\frac{1}{2}\sum_{i=1}^{n}\int_0^S \beta_i^m(v)^2\,dv\right)$$

is a super-martingale. Since

$$E\left[\exp\left(\frac{1}{2}\sum_{i=1}^{n}\int_0^{T^m} \beta_i(v)^2\,dv\right)\right]=E\left[\exp\left(\frac{1}{2}\sum_{i=1}^{n}\int_0^S \beta_i^m(v)^2\,dv\right)\right]\le m$$

by Elliott (1982, p. 178) $E(M^m(S))=1$. Hence, $M^m(t)$ is a martingale. Note

$$\lim_{m\to\infty}M^m(S)=\exp\left(\sum_{i=1}^{n}\int_0^S \beta_i(v)\,dW_i(v)-\frac{1}{2}\sum_{i=1}^{n}\int_0^S \beta_i^2(v)\,dv\right)$$

with probability one since $T_m\to S$ with probability one. Observe that $\{M^m(S)\}_{m=1}^{\infty}$ is a martingale with respect to $m=1,2,\ldots$ because $\sup E(M^m(S))=1<+\infty$ and $E(M^{m+1}(S)\,|\,F_{\min(S,T_m)})=M^{m+1}(\min(S,T_m))$ by the Optional Stopping Theorem (since $T_m\le S$, see Elliott (1982), p. 17) $=M^m(S)$ by the definition of M^m.

Step 1: Suppose $\{M^m(S)\}_{m=1}^{\infty}$ are uniformly integrable; then

$$\lim_{m\to\infty}M^m(S)=\exp\left(\sum_{i=1}^{n}\int_0^S \beta_i(v)\,dW_i(v)-\frac{1}{2}\sum_{i=1}^{n}\int_0^S \beta_i(v)^2\,dv\right)$$

in L^1 (see Elliott (1982, p. 22)), and thus

$$E\left[\exp\left(\sum_{i=1}^{n}\int_0^S \beta_i(v)\,dW_i(v)-\frac{1}{2}\sum_{i=1}^{n}\int_0^S \beta_i(v)^2\,dv\right)\right]=\lim_{m\to\infty}E[M^m(S)]$$

But, $E(M^m(S))=1$. This completes the proof in one direction.

Step 2: Conversely, suppose that

$$E\left[\exp\left(\sum_{i=1}^{n}\int_0^S \beta_i(v)\,dW_i(v)-\frac{1}{2}\sum_{i=1}^{n}\int_0^S \beta_i(v)^2\,dv\right)\right]=1$$

We know

$$E\left[\exp\left(\sum_{i=1}^{n}\int_0^S \beta_i(v)\,dW_i(v)-\frac{1}{2}\sum_{i=1}^{n}\int_0^S \beta_i(v)^2\,dv\right)\Bigg|F_{T_n}\right]=M^m(S)$$

Hence $M^m(S)$ is uniformly integrable. *Q.E.D.*

LEMMA 2.2: *Assume that conditions C.1–C.3 hold for fixed* $S_1,\ldots,S_n\in[0,\tau]$ *such that* $0<S_1<\ldots<S_n\le\tau$. *Suppose that conditions (i), (ii), (iii) and (iv) of Lemma 1.1 hold; then* $\gamma_i(t)$ *for* $i=1,\ldots,n$ *satisfying (i), (ii), (iii) and (iv) are unique (up to* $\lambda\times Q$ *equivalence) if and only if*

$$A(t) \equiv \begin{bmatrix} a_1(t, S_1) \ldots a_n(t, S_1) \\ \vdots \\ a_1(t, S_n) \ldots a_n(t, S_n) \end{bmatrix}$$

is singular with $(\lambda \times Q)$ *measure zero.*

PROOF: Suppose that $A(t)$ is singular with $(\lambda \times Q)$ measure zero. Then, by condition (i) of Lemma 1.1, $\gamma_i(t)$ for $i = 1, \ldots, n$ are unique (up to $\lambda \times Q$ equivalence).

Conversely, suppose that $\Sigma \equiv \{t \times \omega \in [0, S] \times \Omega: A(t) \text{ is singular}\}$ has $(\lambda \times Q)(\Sigma) > 0$. We want to show that the functions satisfying conditions (i), (ii), (iii) and (iv) are not unique. First, by hypothesis, we are given a vector of functions $(\gamma_1(t), \ldots, \gamma_n(t))$ satisfying (i), (ii), (iii) and (iv).

Step 1: Show that there exists a bounded, adapted, measurable vector of functions $(\delta_1(t), \ldots, \delta_n(t))$ non-zero on Σ such that

$$A(t)\begin{bmatrix} \delta_1(t) \\ \vdots \\ \delta_n(t) \end{bmatrix} = \begin{bmatrix} 0 \\ \vdots \\ 0 \end{bmatrix}$$

and

$$g(t) \equiv \exp\left[\sum_{i=1}^{n} \int_0^t \delta_i(v)\, dW_i(v) - \sum_{i=1}^{n}\left(\int_0^t \delta_i(v)\, \gamma_i(v)\, dv\right) - \frac{1}{2}\sum_{i=1}^{n} \int_0^t \delta_i^2(v)\, dv\right]$$

is bounded a.e. Q. Let $\Sigma_i = \{(t, w): A(t) \text{ has rank } i\}$. Σ_i is a measurable set. Then $\Sigma = \cup_{i=1}^{n-1}\Sigma_i$ and $\Sigma_i \cap \Sigma_j = \varnothing$ for $i \neq j$. Fix $\eta > 0$. On each set Σ_i, set $\delta_i^\eta(t)$ for $i = 1, \ldots, n$ equal to a solution to

$$A(t)\begin{bmatrix} \delta_1^\eta(t) \\ \vdots \\ \delta_n^\eta(t) \end{bmatrix} = \begin{bmatrix} 0 \\ \vdots \\ 0 \end{bmatrix}$$

such that $\delta_i^\eta(t)$ are bounded by $\min(\eta, 1/\gamma_i(t)$ for $i = 1, \ldots, n)$. Finally, let $\delta_i^\eta(t)$ be zero on Σ^c for $i = 1, \ldots, n$. Note that we shall always interpret superscripts on δ as the upper bound on the process and not as an exponent.

By construction, $\delta_i^\eta(t)$ are adapted, measurable, bounded by η, and

$$\left|\sum_{i=1}^{n} \int_0^t \delta_i^\eta(v)\, \gamma_i(v)\, dv + \frac{1}{2}\sum_{i=1}^{n} \int_0^t \delta_i^\eta(v)^2\, dv\right| \le \left[2 + \eta^2\right]\tau \quad \text{a.e. Q}$$

Let $\alpha = \inf\{j \in \{1, 2, 3, \ldots\}: (1/2)^{2j} S < 1\}$. Define inductively the stopping times:

$$\tau_1 = \inf\left(t \in [0, S]: \sum_{i=1}^{n} \int_0^t \delta_i^{(1/2)^\alpha}(v)\, dW_i(v) \ge \frac{1}{2}\right)$$

$$\tau_j = \inf\left(t \in [0, S]: \sum_{i=1}^{n} \int_{\tau_{j-1}}^t \delta_i^{(1/2)^{2j+\alpha}}(v)\, dW_i(v) \ge \left(\frac{1}{2}\right)^j\right) \quad \text{for } j = 2, 3, 4, \ldots$$

We claim that $Q(\lim_{j\to\infty} \tau_j = S) = 1$. Indeed,

$$Q\left(\tau_j < S \,\middle|\, F_{\tau_{j-1}}\right) \le Q\left(\left|\sum_{i=1}^{n} \int_{\tau_{j-1}}^{S} \delta_i^{(1/2)^{2j+\alpha}}(v)\, dW_i(v)\right| \ge \left(\tfrac{1}{2}\right)^j \,\middle|\, F_{\tau_{j-1}}\right)$$

$$\leq \frac{1}{(1/2)^{2j}} \int_{\tau_{j-1}}^{S} \left[\delta_i^{(1/2)^{2j+\alpha}}(v) \right]^2 dv \quad \text{by Chebyshev's inequality}$$

$$\leq \frac{1}{(1/2)^{2j}} \left[\left(\tfrac{1}{2}\right)^{2j+\alpha} \right]^2 S < \left(\tfrac{1}{2}\right)^{2j} \quad \text{by choice of } \alpha$$

Hence $E[Q(\tau_j < S \mid F_{\tau_{j-1}})] = Q(\tau_j < S) < (\frac{1}{2})^{2j}$. Since

$$Q\left(\lim_{j\to\infty} \tau_j = S\right) = 1 - Q\left(\lim_{j\to\infty} \tau_j < S\right) \quad \text{and}$$

$$Q\left(\lim_{j\to\infty} \tau_j < S\right) < Q\left(\bigcap_{j=1}^{\infty} (\tau_j < S)\right) \leq \inf\left[Q(\tau_j < S):\ j = 1, 2, 3\ldots\right] = 0$$

this proves the claim.

Set

$$\delta_i(t) = \sum_{j=0}^{\infty} 1_{[\tau_j, \tau_{j+1}]}^{(t)} \, \delta_i^{(1/2)^{2j+\alpha}}(t) \quad \text{for } i = 1, \ldots, n$$

$\delta_i(t)$ is bounded, adapted and measurable and satisfies

$$A(t) \begin{bmatrix} \delta_1(t) \\ \vdots \\ \delta_n(t) \end{bmatrix} = \begin{bmatrix} 0 \\ \vdots \\ 0 \end{bmatrix} \quad \text{a.e. } \lambda \times Q$$

Note that for all $t \in [0, S]$,

$$\left| \sum_{i=1}^{n} \int_0^t \delta_i(t)\, dW_i(t) \right| \leq \sum_{j=0}^{\infty} \left(\tfrac{1}{2}\right)^j = 2$$

so

$$\exp\left(\sum_{i=1}^{n} \int_0^t \delta_i(t)\, dW_i(t) - \sum_{i=1}^{n} \int_0^t \delta_i(v)\, \gamma_i(v)\, dv - \frac{1}{2} \sum_{i=1}^{n} \int_0^t \delta_i^2(v)\, dv \right)$$

is bounded a.e. $\lambda \times Q$. This completes Step 1.

Step 2: Show that $(\gamma_1(t) + \delta_1(t), \ldots, \gamma_n(t) + \delta_n(t))$ satisfies conditions (i), (ii), (iii) and (iv) of Lemma 1.1. This step will complete the proof.

Conditions (i) and (ii) are obvious. To obtain condition (iii), define

$$T_m = \inf\left\{ t \in [0, T] : E\left[\exp\left(\frac{1}{2} \sum_{i=1}^{n} \int_0^t (\gamma_i(t) + \delta_i(t))^2\, dv \right) \right] \geq m \right\}$$

$$M^m(t) = \exp\left(\sum_{i=1}^{n} \int_0^{\min(T_m, t)} (\gamma_i(v) + \delta_i(v))\, dW_i(v) - \frac{1}{2} \sum_{i=1}^{n} \int_0^{\min(T_m, t)} (\gamma_i(v) + \delta_i(v))^2\, dv \right)$$

By Lemma 2.1, we need to show that $M^m(S)$ is uniformly integrable. But

$$M^m(s) = \exp\left(\sum_{i=1}^{n} \int_0^{\min(S, T_m)} \gamma_i(v)\, dW_i(v) - \frac{1}{2} \sum_{i=1}^{n} \int_0^{\min(S, T_m)} \gamma_i(v)^2\, dv \right) \times$$

$$\exp\left(\sum_{i=1}^{n} \int_0^{\min(S, T_m)} \delta_i(v)\, dW_i(v) - \frac{1}{2} \sum_{i=1}^{n} \int_0^{\min(S, T_m)} (2\gamma_i(v)\, \delta_i(v) + \delta_i(v)^2)\, dv \right)$$

Since

$$\exp\left(\sum_{i=1}^{n}\int_0^{\min(S,T_m)}\delta_i(v)\,dW_i(v) - \frac{1}{2}\sum_{i=1}^{n}\int_0^{\min(S,T_m)}(2\gamma_i(v)\delta_i(v)+\delta_i(v)^2)\,dv\right)$$

is bounded,

$$0 \le M^m(S) \le K\exp\left(\sum_{i=1}^{n}\int_0^{\min(S,T_m)}\gamma_i(v)\,dW_i(v) - \frac{1}{2}\sum_{i=1}^{n}\int_0^{\min(S,T_m)}\gamma_i(v)^2\,dv\right)$$

for some $K > 0$

By Lemma 2.1, since $\gamma_i(t)$ satisfies (iii), the right-hand side is uniformly integrable. By Kopp (1984, p. 29), it can be shown that $M^m(S)$ is uniformly integrable. Finally, an analogous argument used to prove (iii) shows that (iv) holds as well. *Q.E.D.*

PROOF OF PROPOSITION 5: Fix a T_0. Consider

$$\eta(t) \equiv -\sigma\min(f(t,T_0),\lambda)\int_t^{T_0}\frac{\sigma\min(f(t,s),\lambda)\,ds}{\sigma\min(f(t,T_0),\lambda)}$$

$$= -\int_t^{T_0}\sigma\min(f(t,s),\lambda)\,ds$$

Since $\sigma\min(f(t,s),\lambda)$ is bounded, $\eta(t)$ is bounded. Hence,

$$E\left[\exp\left(\frac{1}{2}\int_0^{T_0}\eta(t)^2\,dt\right)\right] < +\infty$$

By Girsanov's theorem, there exists an equivalent probability measure $\bar{Q}$ and a Brownian motion $\bar{W}(t)$ such that $df(t,T_0) = \sigma\min(f(t,T_0),\lambda)\,d\bar{W}(t)$. Define $t_0 = \inf\{t \in [0,T_0]: f(t,T_0) = 0\}$. By Karlin and Taylor (1981, Lemma 15.6.2), zero is an unattainable boundary, ie, $\bar{Q}\{t_0 \le T_0\} = Q\{t_0 \le T_0\} = 0$. Since $f(t,T_0)$ has continuous sample paths, $f(t,T_0) > 0$ a.e. Let $\{T_i: i = 1,2,3,\ldots\}$ be the rationals in $[0,\tau]$:

$$Q\{f(t,T_i) = 0 \text{ for some } T_i \text{ and some } t \in [0,T_i]\}$$

$$= Q\left\{\bigcup_{i=1}^{\infty}\{f(t,T_i) = 0 \text{ for some } t[0,T_i]\}\right\}$$

$$\le \sum_{i=1}^{\infty} Q\{f(t,T_i) = 0 \text{ for some } t \in [0,T_i]\} = 0$$

By the joint continuity of $f(t,T)$, $Q\{f(t,T) \ge 0$ for all $T \in [0,\tau]$ and all $t \in [0,T]\} = 1$.

Q.E.D.

1 *This is equivalent to* $r(t) = \lim_{h\to 0}[1 - P(t,t+h)]/P(t,t+h)h = f(t,t)$.

2 *For the case of a single Brownian motion, condition C.5 simplifies to the statement that* $\sigma_1(t,S_1) > 0$ *a.e.* $Q \times \lambda$.

3 *For the definition of an admissible self-financing trading strategy, see Harrison and Pliska (1981).*

4 *Brennan and Schwartz (1979), however, didn't use this martingale approach. Instead, they priced based on the necessary conditions given by the partial differential equation satisfied by a contingent claim's value under condition (17). Artzner and Delbaen (1989) use the martingale approach.*

5 *Ball and Torous (1983) and Schaefer and Schwartz (1987) exogenously specify two bond price processes* $\{P(t, S_1), P(t, S_2)\}$ *directly. They price contingent claims based on necessary, but not sufficient conditions, for the absence of arbitrage. Unfortunately, both the Ball and Torous model (as shown by Cheng (1991)) and the Schaefer and Schwartz model can be shown to be inconsistent with stochastic spot rate processes and the absence of arbitrage.*

6 *The example in this section is similar to a model independently obtained by Jamshidian (1989).*

7 *This calculation and the one in the next section can be found in Brenner and Jarrow (1992).*

8 *Let* $\{f(0, T): T \in [0, \tau]\}$ *be twice continuously differentiable. Note that* $\bar{B}_T(t, T) \equiv \partial\bar{B}(t, T)/\partial T$ *and* $\bar{B}_{TT}(t, T) \equiv \partial^2\bar{B}_T(t, T)/\partial T$ *are continuous on* $0 \le t \le T \le \tau$ *with* $\bar{B}(t, t) = 0$ and $\bar{B}_T(t, T) = 1$. *Expression (49) with* $t = 0$ *is*

$$f(0, T) = r(0)\bar{B}_T(0, T) + K\int_0^T \theta(s)\,\bar{B}_T(s, T)\,ds$$

Differentiating with respect to T *yields*

$$\frac{[\partial f(0, T)/\partial T] - r(0)\bar{B}_{TT}(0, T)}{K} = \theta(T) + \int_0^T \theta(s)(K\bar{B}_{TT}(s, T))\,ds$$

This is a Volterra integral equation of the second kind with a unique continuous solution $\theta(\cdot)$ *on* $[0, \tau]$*; see Taylor and Lay (1980, p. 200).*

Bibliography

Amin, K., and R. Jarrow, 1989, "Pricing American Options on Risky Assets in a Stochastic Interest Rate Economy"; reprinted as Chapter 15 of the present volume.

Artzner, P., and D. Delbaen, 1989, "Term Structure of Interest Rates: The Martingale Approach", *Advances in Applied Mathematics* 10, pp. 95-129.

Ball, C., and W. Torous, 1983, "Bond Price Dynamics and Options." *Journal of Financial and Quantitative Analysis* 18, pp. 517-531.

Brennan, M. J., and E. S. Schwartz, 1979, "A Continuous-Time Approach to the Pricing of Bonds." *Journal of Banking and Finance* 3, pp. 135-155; reprinted as Chapter 5 of the present volume.

Brenner, R., and R. Jarrow, 1992, "A Simple Formula for Options on Discount Bonds", *Advances in Futures and Options Research* 6.

Cheng, S. T., 1991, "On the Feasibility of Arbitrage-Based Option Pricing when Stochastic Bond Price Processes are Involved", *Journal of Economic Theory* 53, pp. 185-198.

Cox, J. C., J. E. Ingersoll, and S. A. Ross, 1985, "A Theory of the Term Structure of Interest Rates", *Econometrica* 53, pp. 385-407; reprinted as Chapter 6 of the present volume.

Elliott, R. J., 1982, *Stochastic Calculus and Applications*. New York: Springer-Verlag.

Feller, W., 1951, "Two Singular Diffusion Problems." *Annals of Mathematics* 54, pp. 173-182.

Harrison, J. M., and D. M. Kreps, 1979, "Martingales and Arbitrage in Multiperiod Security Markets", *Journal of Economic Theory* 20, pp. 381-408.

Harrison, J. M., and S. Pliska, 1981, "Martingales and Stochastic Integrals in the Theory of Continuous Trading", *Stochastic Processes and Their Applications* 11, pp. 215-260.

Heath, D., R. Jarrow, and A. Morton, 1990, "Bond Pricing and the Term Structure of Interest Rates: A Discrete Time Approximation", *Journal of Financial and Quantitative Analysis* 25, pp. 419-440.

Ho, T. S., and S. Lee, 1986, "Term Structure Movements and Pricing Interest Rate Contingent Claims", *Journal of Finance* 41, pp. 1011-1028; reprinted as Chapter 13 of the present volume.

Ikeda, N., and S. Watanabe, 1981, *Stochastic Differential Equations and Diffusion Processes*. New York: North-Holland.

Jamshidian, F., 1989, "An Exact Bond Option Formula", *Journal of Finance* 1, pp. 205-209; reprinted as Chapter 8 of the present volume.

Karlin, S., and H. Taylor, 1981, *A Second Course in Stochastic Processes*. New York: Academic Press.

Kopp, P. E., 1984, *Martingales and Stochastic Integrals*. New York: Cambridge University Press.

Langetieg, T. C., 1980, "A Multivariate Model of the Term Structure", *Journal of Finance* 35, pp. 71-97.

Morton, A, 1988, "A Class of Stochastic Differential Equations Arising in Models for the Evolution of Bond Prices", Technical Report, School of Operations Research and Industrial Engineering, Cornell University.

Schaefer, S., and E. Schwartz, 1987, "Time-Dependent Variance and the Pricing of Bond Options", *Journal of Finance* 42, pp. 1113-1128.

Taylor, A., and D. Lay, 1980, *Introduction to Functional Analysis*, 2nd Edition. New York: John Wiley and Sons.

Vasicek, O., 1977, "An Equilibrium Characterization of the Term Structure", *Journal of Financial Economics* 5, pp. 177-188; reprinted as Chapter 4 of the present volume.

15

Pricing Options on Risky Assets in a Stochastic Interest Rate Economy*

Kaushik Amin and Robert Jarrow
Lehman Brothers; Cornell University

This paper studies contingent claim valuation of risky assets in a stochastic interest rate economy. The model employed generalises the approach utilised by Heath, Jarrow and Morton (1992) by embedding their stochastic interest rate economy into one containing an arbitrary number of additional risky assets. We derive closed-form formulae for certain types of European options in this context, notably call and put options on risky assets, forward contracts and futures contracts. We also value American contingent claims whose payoffs are permitted to be general functions of both the term structure and asset prices, generalising Bensoussan (1984) and Karatzas (1988) in this regard. Here, we provide an example where an American call's value is well defined, yet there does not exist an optimal trading strategy which attains this value. Furthermore, this example is not pathological as it is a generalisation of Roll's (1977) formula for a call option on a stock that pays discrete dividends.

This paper makes three contributions to the literature on the arbitrage-free pricing of contingent claims. The first contribution is to generalise Heath, Jarrow and Morton's (1992) interest rate option pricing model to include additional risky assets. This extension enables the Heath–Jarrow–Morton methodology to be utilised, for example, to price options on common stocks under stochastic interest rates (generalising Merton 1973) or options on futures (generalising Black (1976) and Jarrow (1987)). To illustrate these procedures, closed-form solutions for European type call and put options on risky assets, forward contracts and futures contracts are provided.

The second contribution of this paper is to extend Heath, Jarrow and Morton (1992) to incorporate American-type options. Consequently, this analysis generalises Bensoussan (1984) and Karatzas (1988) to unbounded interest rate processes and claims whose payoffs are dependent on the term structure of interest rates. Finally, the third contribution of this paper is to provide an example of a discontinuous sample path price process where the American call's value is well defined but where there exists no trading strategy attaining this value. This example highlights the important role that sample path continuity of the price process plays in the existing literature on

**This paper was first published in* Mathematical Finance, *Vol. 2 (1992) and is reprinted with the permission of Blackwell Publishers. It includes the content from earlier papers by K. Amin, "Pricing American Options in a Term Structure Economy", 1989, and R. Jarrow, "Option Valuation of Risky Assets in a Stochastic Interest Rate Economy", 1988. Helpful comments from Robin Brenner, Peter Carr, David Heath and the participants in the Finance Workshop at Cornell University are gratefully acknowledged.*

American claim valuation. This example is also of independent interest as it generalises Roll (1977).

An outline for this paper is as follows. The next section reviews the Heath–Jarrow–Morton economy. The third section extends this economy to include trading in an arbitrary number of risky assets. The fourth section prices American-type contingent claims, the fifth section provides the example demonstrating the non-existence of optimal trading strategies, and the sixth section concludes the paper.

The term structure model

This section briefly reviews the Heath, Jarrow and Morton (1992) setup for pricing interest rate options. Consider a probability space (Ω, F, Q) with an augmented Brownian filtration $\{F_t: t \in [0, \tau]\}$ generated by an n-dimensional Brownian motion $\{W_1(t), \ldots, W_n(t): t \in [0, \tau];\ \tau < \infty\}$ initialised at zero. Let the trading interval be $[0, \tau]$ and define λ as the Lebesgue measure on the Borel subsets of $[0, \tau]$. Define $f(t, T)$, $0 \le t \le T \le \tau$, to be the forward rate contracted at time t for instantaneous borrowing and lending at time T.

ASSUMPTION 2.1: *Given an initial forward rate curve* $\{f(0, T): T \in [0, \tau]\}$, *forward rates satisfy the following stochastic integral equation:*

$$f(t,T) = f(0,T) + \int_0^t \alpha(u,T,\omega)\,du + \sum_{i=1}^{n} \int_0^t \sigma_i(u,T,\omega)\,dW_i(u)$$

$$\text{for all } 0 \le t \le T \text{ and } 0 \le T \le \tau \tag{1}$$

where $\alpha(t, T, \omega)$ *and* $\sigma_i(t, T, \omega)$ *for* $i = 1, \ldots, n$ *are assumed to be adapted with respect to* F_t *and jointly measurable and uniformly bounded on* $\{(t, v): 0 \le t \le v \le T\} \times \Omega$.

Define an accumulation factor (corresponding to a continuously rolled-over money market account) by $B(t) = \exp[\int_0^t r(y)\,dy]$, where $r(y)$ equals the instantaneous spot rate at time y, ie, $r(y) = f(y, y)$.

Next, let $P(t, T)$ be the time t price of a pure discount bond paying \$1 at time $T (T \ge t)$. By definition of the forward rates,

$$P(t,T) = \exp\left(-\int_t^T f(t,v)\,dv\right) \quad \text{for all } T \in [0,\tau],\ t \in [0,T] \tag{2}$$

The discounted value of the T-maturity bond is

$$Z(t,T) = \frac{P(t,T)}{B(t)} \tag{3}$$

Applying Itô's lemma to $Z(t, T)$ (for details see Heath, Jarrow and Morton (1992)),

$$dZ(t,T) = b(t,T)\,Z(t,T)\,dt + \sum_{i=1}^{n} a_i(t,T)\,Z(t,T)\,dW_i(t)$$

$$\text{for all } T \in [0,\tau],\ t \in [0,T] \tag{4}$$

where

$$a_i(t,T) = -\int_t^T \sigma_i(t,u,\omega)\,du \quad \text{for } i = 1, \ldots, n$$

and

$$b(t,T) = -\int_t^T \alpha(t,u)\,du + \frac{1}{2}\sum_{i=1}^{n}\left(\int_t^T \sigma_i[t,u,f(t,u)]\,du\right)^2$$

Given Assumption 2.1, $a_i(t, T)$ for $i = 1, \ldots, n$ and $b(t, T)$ are uniformly bounded on $[0, \tau] \times [0, \tau] \times \Omega$.

This completes the set-up of the term structure component of our economy.

The expanded risky asset economy

This section extends the previous term structure economy to include trading in an arbitrary number of risky assets. We do not restrict our asset set to be finite as in Bensoussan (1984), Karatzas (1988) or Merton (1973). This added level of generality is needed, for example, to price foreign currency options where an infinite number of foreign bonds must be considered (see Amin and Jarrow (1991)). We enlarge the previous economy to include $d - n$ additional independent Brownian motions where $\infty > d > n$. The new probability space is (Ω, G, Q) where $\{G_t: t \in [0, \tau]\}$ is the augmented filtration generated by the d-dimensional standard Brownian motion $\{W_1(t), \ldots, W_d(t): t \in [0, \tau]\}$ initialised at zero.

Let X be the arbitrary index set of asset types in the economy with x and $y \in X$ denoting generic elements. Let $S(t, x, \omega)$ be the price at time t of asset type $x \in X$ under state $\omega \in \Omega$.

ASSUMPTION 3.1: *Trading takes place continuously in time and there are no transaction costs, taxes, restrictions on short selling or "other market imperfections" in the economy.*

ASSUMPTION 3.2: *Risky asset prices satisfy the stochastic integral equation*

$$S(t,x,\omega) = S(0,x)\exp\left\{\int_0^t \left[\mu(v,x,\omega) - s(v,x,\omega) - \left(\frac{1}{2}\sum_{i=1}^d \delta_i^2(v,x,\omega)\right)\right] dv + \sum_{i=1}^d \int_0^t \delta_i(v,x,\omega)\,dW_i(v)\right\} \quad \text{a.e. } Q \tag{5}$$

where $s(t, x, \omega)$, $\mu(t, x, \omega)$ and $\delta_i(t, x, \omega)$ *for* $i = 1, \ldots, d$ *are* G_t*-adapted, jointly measurable in* $(t, \omega) \in [0, \tau] \times \Omega$ *and uniformly bounded in* $(t, x, \omega) \in [0, \tau] \times X \times \Omega$, *and* $E[\int_0^\tau |\mu(t, x, \omega) - s(t, x, \omega)|^2 dt] < \infty$ *for all* $x \in X$.

Given Assumption 3.2, (5) can be written as the solution to

$$dS(t,x,\omega) = [\mu(t,x,\omega) - s(t,x,\omega)]S(t,x,\omega)\,dt + \sum_{i=1}^d \delta_i(t,x,\omega)S(t,x,\omega)\,dW_i(t) \tag{6}$$

Here, $s(t, x, \omega)$ represents the dividend rate at time t for asset x. Its sign is unrestricted. Next, consider an individual who owns the asset and continuously reinvests his dividends $(s(t, x, \omega))$ by purchasing additional units of the asset. Define the stochastic process $Z(t, x)$ to represent the discounted value of these accumulated holdings, ie,

$$Z(t,x) = \frac{S(t,x)}{B(t)}\exp\left(\int_0^t s(v,x)\,dv\right) \tag{7}$$

This stochastic process satisfies

$$dZ(t,x) = Z(t,x)\left(\sum_{i=1}^d \delta_i(t,x)\,dW_i(t) + [\mu(t,x) - r(t)]dt\right) \tag{8}$$

Fix $d - n$ assets indexed by x_j for $j = 1, \ldots, (d - n)$ and consider n bonds of maturities T_i for $i = 1, \ldots, n$, where $0 < T_1 < T_2 < \ldots < T_n \leq \tau$. From a theoretical perspective, however, we could have chosen any d assets (and no bonds). We want to find a probability measure $\tilde{Q}$ (if it exists) which is equivalent to Q such that $Z(t, x_j)$ and $Z(t, T_i)$ are $\tilde{Q}$-martingales for $j = 1, \ldots, (d - n)$ and $i = 1, \ldots, n$.

Define

$$A_1 = \begin{bmatrix} b(t,T_1) \\ \vdots \\ b(t,T_n) \\ [\mu(t,x_1)-r(t)] \\ \vdots \\ [\mu(t,x_{d-n})-r(t)] \end{bmatrix} \tag{9}$$

and

$$A_2 = \begin{bmatrix} a_1(t,T_1) & \cdots & a_n(t,T_1) & 0 & \cdots & 0 \\ \vdots & & \vdots & \vdots & & \vdots \\ a_1(t,T_n) & \cdots & a_n(t,T_n) & 0 & \cdots & 0 \\ \delta_1(t,x_1) & \cdots & \delta_n(t,x_1) & \delta_{n+1}(t,x_1) & \cdots & \delta_d(t,x_1) \\ \vdots & & \vdots & \vdots & & \vdots \\ \delta_1(t,x_{d-n}) & \cdots & \delta_n(t,x_{d-n}) & \delta_{n+1}(t,x_{d-n}) & \cdots & \delta_d(t,x_{d-n}) \end{bmatrix}$$

ASSUMPTION 3.3: A_2 *is non-singular a.e.* $\lambda \times Q$.

Define $\eta(t, T_1, \ldots, T_n; x_1, \ldots, x_{d-n})$, a d-dimensional vector, to be the solution to

$$A_1 + A_2\eta = 0 \tag{10}$$

on the set Ω where it exists, and define it to be zero on the (null measurable) set where it does not. Given Assumption 3.3, the solution to (10) is unique (modulo modifications). Equation (10) implies that

$$\mu(t,x)-r(t) = -\sum_{i=1}^{d}\delta_i(t,x)\eta_i(t) \quad \text{a.e. } Q \tag{11}$$

Hence, the "excess" return on each risky asset is proportional to its variance component, with each η_i the proportionality factor. The components of η are termed the *market prices of risk* corresponding to the sources of randomness in the economy.

Examining the solution to (10) reveals that the first n components $(\eta_1, \ldots, \eta_n)$ of η are identical to those in Heath, Jarrow and Morton (1992). A sufficient condition in Heath, Jarrow and Morton to guarantee the existence of forward rate processes consistent with no arbitrage is that $(\eta_1, \ldots, \eta_n)$ are bounded. As Bensoussan (1984) and Karatzas (1988) also require this assumption, we impose:

ASSUMPTION 3.4: $\eta_i(v, T_1, \ldots, T_n; x_1, \ldots, x_{d-n})$ *for* $i = 1, \ldots, d$ *are uniformly bounded on* $(v, \omega) \in [0, \tau] \times \Omega$.

An immediate consequence is that $(\mu(t, x, \omega) - r(t))$ is uniformly bounded for every $x \in \{x_1, x_2, \ldots, x_{d-n}\}$ on $[0, \tau] \times \Omega$. It is now clear why one cannot assume that μ is bounded as in Karatzas (1988) and Bensoussan (1984). Indeed, as r is unbounded, one must allow μ to be unbounded.

PROPOSITION 3.1: *Under Assumptions* (3.1)-(3.4) *there exists an equivalent probability measure* $\tilde{Q}_{T_1 \ldots, T_n; x_1 \ldots, x_{n-d}}$ *such that* $Z(t, x_j)$ *and* $Z(t, T_i)$ *are martingales with respect to* $\{G_t: 0 \le t \le \tau\}$ *for* $j = 1, \ldots, (d-n)$ *and* $i = 1, \ldots, n$.

PROOF: Let $\tilde{Q} \equiv \tilde{Q}_{T_1 \ldots, T_n; x_1 \ldots, x_{n-d}}$ be a probability measure on (Ω, G) which is equivalent to Q and is defined by

$$\frac{d\tilde{Q}}{dQ} = \exp\left(\sum_{i=1}^{d}\int_0^{T_1}\eta_i(v, T_1,\ldots,T_n; x_1,\ldots,x_{d-n})\,dW_i(v) - \frac{1}{2}\sum_{i=1}^{d}\int_0^{T_1}\eta_i^2(v, T_1,\ldots,T_n; x_1,\ldots,x_{d-n})\,dv\right) \quad (12)$$

Let $\tilde{E}$ be the expectation w.r.t. $\tilde{Q}$. By Girsanov's theorem,

$$\tilde{W}_i(t) = W_i(t) - \int_0^t \eta_i\,dv \quad \text{for } i = 1, \ldots, d \quad (13)$$

is a d-dimensional Brownian motion with respect to $\tilde{Q}$.

Defining $\bar{Z}(t) \equiv [Z(t, T_1), \ldots, Z(t, T_n); Z(t, x_1), \ldots, Z(t, x_{d-n})]'$ and substituting (13) into (4) and (8), we can write the vector equation

$$d\bar{Z} = \bar{Z}[A_1 dt + A_2 dW(t)] \quad (14)$$

$$d\bar{Z} = \bar{Z}[A_2 d\tilde{W}(t)] \quad (15)$$

Since $||A_2||$ is bounded, Novikov's condition implies that $\bar{Z}(t)$ is a $\tilde{Q}$-martingale.

PROPOSITION 3.2: The equivalent martingale measure identified in Proposition 3.1 is unique.

PROOF: If $\bar{Q}$ is another probability measure on (Ω, G), which is equivalent to Q and under which $\bar{Z}(t)$ is a martingale with respect to G_t, then define $\beta = d\bar{Q}/dQ$. By Liptser and Shiryayev (1977, p. 234) there exist G_t-adapted processes $Y_j(t)$ for $j = 1, \ldots, d$ such that $\int_0^\tau (Y_j(t))^2\,dt < \infty$ a.e. $\bar{Q}$ and

$$\beta(t) = \beta(0) + \sum_{j=1}^{d}\int_0^t Y_j(v)\,dW_j(v) \quad \text{for all } 0 < t < \tau$$

where $\beta(t) = E[\beta \mid G_t]$. Now let $\zeta_j(v) = \beta^{-1}(v)\,Y_j(v)$. Using Liptser and Shiryayev (1977, Theorem 6.4, p. 234), $\bar{W}_j(t) = W_j(t) - \int_0^t \zeta_j(v)\,dv$ is a d-dimensional Brownian motion with respect to $\bar{Q}$. Substituting this into (14) and rearranging, we get

$$d\bar{Z} = \bar{Z}[[A_1 + A_2\zeta]\,dt + A_2 d\bar{W}_t] \quad (16)$$

Now, $\bar{Z}$ is a $\bar{Q}$-martingale by hypothesis. This implies that the drift term must be a.s. zero in (20). Therefore, $\zeta = \eta$ a.s. Q because the solution to $A_1 + A_2\zeta = 0$ is a.s. unique. Hence we obtain the equivalent of $\bar{Q}$ and $\tilde{Q}$.

The martingale measure in Proposition 3.2 depends upon the assets $T_1, \ldots, T_n$ and $x_1, \ldots, x_{d-n}$. To obtain a martingale measure independent of the assets selected, we add:

ASSUMPTION 3.5: $\eta_k(t, T_1, \ldots, T_n; x_1 \ldots, x_{d-n})$ *is independent of* $T_1, \ldots, T_n; x_1, \ldots, x_{d-n}$ *for each* $t \in [0, \tau]$ *and* $k = 1, \ldots, d$.

Henceforth, we will denote the market prices of risk by the vector $\phi(t) = (\phi_1(t), \ldots, \phi_d(t))$ and write $\tilde{Q}_{T_1 \ldots, T_n; x_1 \ldots, x_{n-d}} \equiv \tilde{Q}$. Brennan and Schwartz (1979), implicitly, and Heath, Jarrow and Morton (1992), explicitly, require this assumption to obtain their pricing relationships across all maturity bonds.

Using Harrison and Pliska (1981) or the analysis presented in the next section, we can now price European options as the expected value, under $\tilde{Q}$, of the discounted payoffs to the option at maturity. This present value operator is often called the "risk-neutral" operator. To illustrate this procedure, we provide an example.

EXAMPLE: This example corresponds to an extension of the economy analysed by Merton (1973) to include a random evolution of the entire term structure of interest rates. We provide explicit solutions for the values of European call options on a risky asset, a forward contract and a futures contract. The corresponding put option formulae are obtainable by put-call parity.

We consider a case where $n = 1$ and $d = 2$. The forward rate process, satisfying Assumption 2.1, is given by

$$df(t, T) = \alpha(t, T, \omega)\,dt + \sigma(t, T)\,dW_1(t) \tag{17}$$

where $\sigma: \{(u, v): 0 \le u \le v \le \tau\} \to R$ is a bounded, deterministic, strictly non-zero function. The risky asset satisfies

$$dS(t) = \mu S(t)\,dt + \delta_1 S(t)\,dW_1(t) + \delta_2 S(t)\,dW_2(t) \tag{18}$$

where δ_1, δ_2 and $S(0) > 0$ are positive constants and μ satisfies the conditions in Assumption 3.2.

It is easy to see that Assumption 3.2 and 3.3 are satisfied. Define $\eta_1(t)$, $\eta_2(t)$ by

$$\begin{bmatrix} b(t,T) \\ \mu - r(t) \end{bmatrix} + \begin{bmatrix} a(t,T) & 0 \\ \delta_1 & \delta_1 \end{bmatrix} \begin{bmatrix} \eta_1(t) \\ \eta_2(t) \end{bmatrix} = \begin{bmatrix} 0 \\ 0 \end{bmatrix} \tag{19}$$

where

$$a(t,T) \equiv -\int_t^T \sigma(t,v)\,dv \quad \text{and} \quad b(t,T) \equiv -\int_t^T \alpha(t,v)\,dv + \tfrac{1}{2}\left(\int_t^T \sigma(t,v)\,dv\right)^2$$

We assume that the conditions of Assumptions 3.4 and 3.5 hold. By Proposition 3.1, there exists a probability measure $\tilde{Q}$ on $\{(\Omega, G), \{G_t: t \in [0, \tau]\}\}$ making $Z(t, T) = P(t, T)/B(t)$ and $z(t) = S(t)/B(t)$ $\tilde{Q}$-martingales. Note that

$$\begin{bmatrix} dZ(t,T)/Z(t,T) \\ dz(t)/z(t) \end{bmatrix} = \begin{bmatrix} a(t,T) & 0 \\ \delta_1 & \delta_2 \end{bmatrix} \begin{bmatrix} d\tilde{W}_1(t) \\ d\tilde{W}_2(t) \end{bmatrix} \tag{20}$$

where

$$\tilde{W}_i(t) = W_i(t) - \int_0^t \eta_i(v)\,dv \quad \text{for } i = 1, 2 \tag{21}$$

are Brownian motions with respect to $\tilde{Q}$. Our goal is to write out explicit representations of $B(t)$, $S(t)$ and $P(t, T)$ in terms of the parameters of the system. It can be shown that (see Heath, Jarrow and Morton (1992))

$$B(t) = \frac{1}{P(0,t)} \exp\left(\frac{1}{2}\int_0^t a(s,t)^2\,ds - \int_0^t a(s,t)\,d\tilde{W}_1(s)\right) \tag{22}$$

where $\int_0^t a(s, t)\,d\tilde{W}_1(s)$ is normal $(0, \int_0^t a(s, t)^2\,ds)$ under $\tilde{Q}$. Further, tedious algebra yields

$$S(t) = S(0)B(t)\exp\left\{-\tfrac{1}{2}\left[\delta_1^2 + \delta_2^2\right]t + \delta_1\tilde{W}_1(t) + \delta_2 W_2(t)\right\} \tag{23}$$

where $\delta_1\tilde{W}_1(t) + \delta_2\tilde{W}_2(t)$ is normal $(0, [\delta_1^2 + \delta_2^2]t)$ and

$$P(t,T) = \frac{P(0,T)}{P(0,t)} \exp\left[\int_t^T \int_0^t \sigma(y,s)a(y,s)\,dy\,ds - \int_0^t \left(\int_t^T \sigma(y,s)\,ds\right) d\tilde{W}_1(y)\right] \tag{24}$$

where

$$\int_0^t \left(\int_t^T \sigma(y,s)\,ds\right) d\tilde{W}_1(y) \text{ is normal } \left(0, \int_0^t \left[\int_t^T \sigma(y,s)\,ds\right]^2 dy\right) \text{ under } \tilde{Q}$$

Consider a European call option on the risky asset $S(t)$ with an exercise price of K and a maturity date $T < \tau$. The call's value at time 0 is:

$$C(0) = \tilde{E}\left(\frac{\max[S(T) - K, 0]}{B(T)}\right) \quad (25)$$

A calculation yields

$$C(0) = S(0)\,\Phi(h) - KP(0,T)\,\Phi(h - \Psi) \quad (26)$$

where

$$h = \frac{\log\left[S(0)/KP(0,T)\right] + \frac{1}{2}\psi^2}{\psi}$$

$$\psi^2 = (\delta_1^2 + \delta_2^2)T - 2\delta_1 \int_0^T a(t,T)\,dt + \int_0^T a(t,T)^2\,dt$$

and $\Phi(\cdot)$ is the cumulative normal distribution. This is Merton's (1973) call option formula for a bond process given by (24).

Now consider forward and futures contracts on this risky asset. It is easy to show that the forward price, $K(t)$, at time t, corresponding to contract maturity τ, is given by

$$K(t) = \frac{S(t)}{P(t,\tau)} \quad (27)$$

The value of a European call option, with maturity date τ and exercise price $M > 0$, on this forward contract is

$$C_K(0) = \tilde{E}\left(\frac{\max[K(T) - M, 0]}{B(T)}\right)$$

Substituting (27) and the expressions for $S(T)$, $P(T,\tau)$ and $B(T)$ yields

$$C_K(0) = S(0)\frac{P(0,T)}{P(0,\tau)}e^{\xi}\,\Phi(h) - MP(0,T)\,\Phi(h - \eta) \quad (28)$$

where

$$\xi = \delta_1 \int_0^T \left(\int_T^\tau \sigma(y,v)\,dv\right)dy + \frac{1}{2}\int_0^T \left(\int_T^\tau \sigma(y,v)\,dv\right)^2 dy - \int_T^\tau \int_0^T \sigma(y,v)\,a(y,v)\,dy\,dv$$

$$h = \frac{1}{\eta}\left[\log\left(\frac{S(0)e^{\xi}}{P(0,\tau)M}\right) + \frac{1}{2}\eta^2\right]$$

and

$$\eta = \int_0^T \left(\delta_1 + \int_T^\tau \sigma(s,v)\,dv - a(s,t)\right)^2 ds + \delta_2^2 T$$

We now consider a futures contract. Again, a standard argument shows that the futures price, $k(t)$, is a $\tilde{Q}$ martingale. Therefore,

$$k(T) = \tilde{E}\left[S(\tau)\middle|G_T\right] = \frac{S(T)}{P(T,\tau)}\exp\left(-\delta_1 \int_T^\tau a(s,\tau)\,ds + \int_T^\tau a(s,\tau)^2\,ds\right) \quad (29)$$

Given (29) for the futures price, (27) implies that

$$k(t) = K(t)\exp\left(-\delta_1 \int_t^\tau a(s,\tau)\,ds + \int_t^\tau a(s,\tau)^2\,ds\right) \quad (30)$$

The futures price equals the forward price times an adjustment factor. If $\delta_1 > 0$, the futures prices can exceed the forward price as the adjustment factor, $\exp\{-\delta_1 \times \int_t^\tau a(s,t)\,ds + \int_t^\tau a(s,t)^2\,ds\}$ will be greater than 1 since $a(s,t) = -\int_s^t \sigma(s,v)\,dv < 0$.

A European option on the futures contract with a maturity date $T < \tau$ and exercise price M has a terminal payoff equal to $C_k(T) = \max(k(T) - M, 0)$. Thus,

$$C_k(0) = \tilde{E}\left(\frac{\max[k(T) - M, 0]}{B(T)}\right)$$

$$= \tilde{E}\left\{\frac{\max\left[\{S(T)/P(T,\tau)\}\exp\left(-\delta_1\int_T^\tau a(s,\tau)\,ds + \int_T^\tau a(s,\tau)^2\,ds\right) - M, 0\right]}{B(T)}\right\}$$

Substitution of the appropriate expressions yields

$$C_K(0) = S(0)\frac{P(0,T)}{P(0,\tau)}e^{\xi+\lambda}\Phi(h) - MP(0,T)\,\Phi(h-\eta) \tag{31}$$

where

$$\xi = \delta_1\int_0^T\left(\int_T^\tau \sigma(y,v)\,dv\right)dy + \tfrac{1}{2}\int_0^T\left(\int_T^\tau \sigma(y,v)\,dv\right)^2 dy -$$
$$\int_T^\tau\int_0^T \sigma(y,v)\,a(y,v)\,dy\,dv$$

$$\lambda = -\delta_1\int_T^\tau a(s,\tau)\,ds + \int_T^\tau a(s,\tau)^2\,ds$$

$$h = \frac{1}{\eta}\left[\log\left(\frac{S(0)e^{\xi+\lambda}}{P(0,\tau)M}\right) + \tfrac{1}{2}\eta^2\right]$$

and

$$\eta = \int_0^T\left(\delta_1 + \int_T^\tau \sigma(s,v)\,dv - a(s,t)\right)^2 ds + \delta_2^2 T$$

This valuation formula differs from that of a forward option through the parameter λ, which is positive if $\delta_1 > 0$ (since $a(s,t) = -\int_s^t \sigma(s,v)\,dv$), so that $C_K(0) < C_k(0)$. Interest rates being non-stochastic (ie, $\sigma(s,v) \equiv 0$) is a sufficient condition for this formula to collapse to that of the forward option. This completes the example.

Valuing American contingent claims

To extend the previous model to value American contingent claims we need to investigate the concept of a "trading strategy".

DEFINITION 4.1: An *American contingent claim* is a triplet (τ_M, c, Y) consisting of:

(i) An expiration date $\tau_M \in (0, \tau]$.
(ii) A continuous, non-negative, G_t-adapted cashflow $c(t)$ per unit time on $[0, \tau_M]$.
(iii) The selection of an exercise date θ and a continuous, non-negative, G_t-adapted payoff $Y(\theta)$. $Y(\theta)$ is the reward on the exercise date θ.

The exercise date θ is chosen from $\theta \in \tau_{(0,\tau_M]}$, where $\tau_{(0,\tau_M]}$ is the class of all stopping times in $(0, \tau_M]$. As written, an American contingent claim has intermediate cashflows. To simplify the mathematics, we can transform this American contingent claim into one without intermediate cashflows by reinvesting the intermediate cashflows into a *fund* (a money market account) which earns the riskless rate. We will denote the amount of wealth invested in this fund at time t to be $F(t)$. Last, we require that only additions (and no withdrawals) be allowed from this fund as the cashflows are assumed to be non-negative.

The *running discounted payoff* from the contingent claim (τ_M, c, Y) is then the discounted accumulated payoff from the claim if exercised at time t, ie,

$$U(t) = \frac{Y(t)}{B(t)} + \int_0^t \frac{c(v)}{B(v)} dv \tag{32}$$

By construction, $U(t)$ is a continuous, non-negative and G_t-adapted process on $[0, \tau_M]$.

We will price claims which satisfy

$$E\left[\left(\sup_{t \in [0, \tau_M]} U(t)\right)^p\right] < \infty \quad \text{for some } p > 1 \tag{33}$$

It can be shown that the common types of options (calls and puts) satisfy this assumption. This assumption is different from that employed by either Bensoussan (1984) or Karatzas (1988). An equivalent version of this assumption under the martingale measure is needed later. To obtain this version, we require a lemma.

LEMMA 4.1: *Given a non-negative random variable* $R \in G_{\tau_M}$ *with* $E(R^p) < \infty$ *for* $p > 1$, *then* $\tilde{E}(R^q) < \infty$, *where* $q = \sqrt{p} > 1$.

PROOF: By the Radon–Nikodym theorem

$$\tilde{E}(R^q) = E[R^q N(\tau_M)] \tag{34}$$

where

$$N(t) = E\left(\frac{d\tilde{Q}}{dQ} \middle| G_t\right) \tag{35}$$

An application of Itô's lemma confirms that

$$[N(\tau_M)]^h = \exp\left(\sum_{i=1}^{d} \int_0^{\tau_M} h\eta_i(t)\,dW_i(t) - \sum_{i=1}^{d} \int_0^{\tau_M} \tfrac{1}{2} h^2 \eta_i^2(t)\,dt\right) \times \exp\left(\sum_{i=1}^{d} \int_0^{\tau_M} \tfrac{1}{2}(h^2 - h)\eta_i^2(t)\,dt\right) \tag{36}$$

where h satisfies $1/q + 1/h = 1$. Using the boundedness of η_i and Novikov's theorem, $E[N(\tau_M)^h] < \infty$. Since Holder's inequality gives

$$E(R^q N(\tau_M)] \leq [E(R^p)]^{1/q} [E(N(\tau_M)^h)]^{1/h} \tag{37}$$

and the first factor is finite by hypothesis, we are done.

Lemma 4.1 and expression (33) imply

$$\tilde{E}\left(\sup_{t \in [0, \tau_M]} U(t)\right)^q < \infty \quad \text{for some } q > 1 \tag{38}$$

For ease of notation, we will denote the money market account as asset 0, the bonds $T_1, \ldots, T_n$ as assets $1, \ldots, n$ and the risky assets x_j for $j = 1, \ldots, (d - n)$ as assets $(n + 1), \ldots, d$. The prices of these assets will be denoted $S_j(t)$ for $j = 0, \ldots, d$. To be consistent, note that $s_j(t) = 0$ for $j = 0, \ldots, n$ (dividend rates are zero for these assets). Let $\delta_{ij}(t)$ be the variance coefficient of $W_i(t)$ for the jth asset price. Note that by (9), $\delta_{ij}(t) = 0$ for $i = (n+1), \ldots, d$ and $j = 1, \ldots, n$. By the definition of the money market account, $B(t)$, we also have that $\delta_{i0}(t) = 0$ for $i = 1, \ldots, d$. Given the previous framework, the $\delta_{ij}(t)$ are well defined.

We will also restrict our "trading strategies" to include only these d assets. From the subsequent discussion it will become clear that we can replicate the payoffs from any other traded asset in the economy using only these assets.

Let $\pi_j(t)$ be the number of shares owned of asset j at time t for $j = 0, \ldots, d$. A *trading strategy* $\pi(t) = \{\pi_j(t): j = 0, \ldots, d\}$ is a G_t-adapted process which satisfies

$$\sum_{i=1}^{d} \int_0^t \left(\frac{\pi_j(t) S_j(t)}{B(t)} \right)^2 \delta_{ij}(t)\, dt < \infty \text{ a.s. } Q \quad \text{for } i = 1, \ldots, d \tag{39}$$

Expression (39) is an integrability condition that is required to define the stochastic integral in (41). Next, define $V(t)$ to be the corresponding *value process* given by

$$V(t) = \sum_{j=0}^{d} \pi_j(t) S_j(t) \tag{40}$$

DEFINITION 4.2: A trading strategy π is *admissible and self-financing (s.f.t.s.)* if $V(t) \geq 0$ a.e. Q for all $t \in [0, \tau_M]$, and

(i) There exists a non-negative, right-continuous, G_t-adapted process $F(t)$, with $F(0) = 0$, such that

$$V(t) + F(t) = V(0) + \sum_{j=0}^{d} \int_0^t \pi_j(v)\, dS_j(v) + \sum_{j=0}^{d} \int_0^t \pi_j(v) S_j(v) s_j(v)\, dv + \int_0^t F(v) r(v)\, dv \text{ a.s. } Q \quad \text{for all } t \in [0, \tau_M] \tag{41}$$

and

(ii) $F(t)/B(t)$ is a.s. non-decreasing on $[0, \tau_M]$, ie, withdrawals from the fund are not allowed.

Equation (41) is the self-financing constraint where the last term incorporates the investment in a fund, $F(t)$, which earns the spot rate. The purpose of this fund is to allow cash inputs into an otherwise self-financing trading strategy. These cash inputs are needed in the construction of a *synthetic* American contingent claim as we must match any intermediate cashflows received on the American contingent claim (see the discussion following Definition 4.1).

Let us consider an arbitrary self-financing trading strategy (π, F). We define the discounted value process (corresponding to the total payoff) of this trading strategy as

$$V_D(t) \equiv \frac{V(t)}{B(t)} + F_D(t) \quad \text{where} \quad F_D(t) \equiv \frac{F(t)}{B(t)} \tag{42}$$

By a standard argument (see Karatzas (1988)), for any admissible self-financing trading strategy (π, F), $V_D(t)$ is a $\tilde{Q}$-supermartingale with respect to G_t. The optional stopping theorem now yields

$$\tilde{E}(V_D(t)) \leq V(0) \quad \text{for all } t \in [0, \tau_M] \tag{43}$$

This implies that

$$\tilde{E}(F_D(t)) \leq V(0) \quad \text{for all } t \in [0, \tau_M] \tag{44}$$

In other words, the non-negativity requirement that $V(t) \geq 0$ restricts the amount of money that can be put into the fund to be no greater (in expectation) than the initial value of the trading strategy.

DEFINITION 4.3: The *arbitrage-free price* for the claim (τ_M, c, Y) at time $t = 0$ is given by $\sup_{\theta \in \tau(0, \tau_M)} \tilde{E}(U(\theta))$.

This definition can be justified by similar arguments as in Karatzas (1988). In the next proposition we prove that this supremum can be attained by a suitable trading strategy which at all times maintains at least as much wealth in the fund as the cumulative cash-flows generated by the contingent claim. Furthermore, the value process from this trading strategy, if exercised, is always greater than or equal to the payoff of the claim.

PROPOSITION 4.1: *There exists an admissible self-financing trading strategy with a value process* $V(t)$ *which satisfies*

$$\frac{V(t)}{B(t)} = \underset{\theta \in \tau_{[t, \tau_M]}}{\text{ess sup}} \tilde{E}\left[U(\theta) \middle| G_t\right] \quad \text{a.e. } \tilde{Q} \tag{45}$$

and a fund process $F(t)$ *such that* $F(t) \geq \int_0^t c(v) \exp(\int_v^t r(u)\,du)\,dv$.

PROOF: The proof is similar to Karatzas (1988, Theorem 5.4). From Fakeev (1970, Theorem 1), there exists a non-negative supermartingale $X(t)$ with RCLL paths such that

$$\sup_{\theta \in \tau_{[t, \tau_M]}} \tilde{E}[U(\theta)] = \tilde{E}[X(t)] \tag{46}$$

and

$$X(t) = \underset{\theta \in \tau_{[t, \tau_M]}}{\text{ess sup}} \tilde{E}\left[U(\theta) \middle| G_t\right] \quad \text{a.e. } \tilde{Q} \tag{47}$$

By Theorem 4 in Fakeev (1970), the random variable $\theta(t) = \inf\{v: v \geq t; X(v) = U(v)\}$ is optimal for the problem. Given that $\tilde{E}[\sup_{\tau \in [0, \tau_M]} U(t)]^q < \infty$ for some $q > 1$ (note that we have proved this under different conditions), we can write (see Lemma 5.5 in Karatzas 1988),

$$X(t) = X(0) + M(t) - \Lambda(t) \tag{48}$$

where $M(t)$ is a $\tilde{Q}$-martingale with $M(0) = 0$ and $\Lambda(t)$ is a continuous, non-decreasing process of bounded variation with $\Lambda(0) = 0$. Applying a martingale representation theorem (Karatzas and Shreve (1988), p. 184) yields

$$X(t) = X(0) + \sum_{i=1}^{d} \int_0^t g_i(v) d\tilde{W}_i(v) - \Lambda(t) \tag{49}$$

where $g_i(v)$ are adapted processes which satisfy $\int_0^{\tau_M} g_i^2(v)\,dv < \infty$ a.s. $\tilde{Q}$ for $i = 1, \ldots, d$. Define $\tilde{V}(t)$ as the solution to the following equation:

$$\left[\frac{\tilde{V}(t)}{B(t)}\right] + \int_0^t \frac{c(u)}{B(u)} du = X(t) \tag{50}$$

Substituting this equation into (49) and integrating,

$$\left[\frac{\tilde{V}(t)}{B(t)}\right] + \int_0^t \frac{c(u)}{B(u)} du + \int_0^t d\Lambda(u) = X(0) + \sum_{i=1}^{d} \int_0^t g_i(v) d\tilde{W}_i(v) \tag{51}$$

Now define $\tilde{F}_D(t)$ $(= \tilde{F}(t)/B(t))$, $\tilde{A}(t)$ and $\tilde{V}_D(t)$ by

$$\tilde{F}_D(t) = \int_0^t d\Lambda(u) + \int_0^t \frac{c(u)}{B(u)} du \tag{52}$$

$$\frac{\tilde{A}(t)}{B(t)} = \int_0^t d\Lambda(u) \tag{53}$$

$$\tilde{V}_D(t) = \frac{\tilde{V}(t)}{B(t)} + \tilde{F}_D(t) \tag{54}$$

As $\Lambda(t)$ is non-decreasing, (52) implies that $\tilde{F}_D(t) \geq \int_0^t c(v)\exp[\int_0^t r(u)\,du]\,dv$. Noting that $X(0) = \tilde{V}(0)$, (51) can be rewritten as

$$\tilde{V}_D(t) = \left[\frac{\tilde{V}(t)}{B(t)}\right] + \tilde{F}_D(t) = \tilde{V}(0) + \sum_{i=1}^{d} \int_0^t g_i(v)\,d\tilde{W}_i(v) \tag{55}$$

Now define the trading strategy $\pi(t)$ as the solution to

$$g_i(t) = \sum_{j=1}^{d} \frac{\pi_j(t)\exp\left(-\int_0^t s(v)\,dv\right) S_j(t)\delta_{ij}(t)}{B(t)} \quad \text{for } i = 1,\ldots,d \tag{56}$$

and

$$\pi_0(t)B(t) = \tilde{V}(t) - \sum_{j=1}^{d} \pi_j(t)S_j(t) \tag{57}$$

As A_2 is invertible (assumption 3.3), the above system of equations has a unique solution. As $s(v)$ is bounded and $\int_0^{\tau_M} g_i^2(v)\,dv < \infty$ a.s. $\tilde{Q}$, this satisfies the definition of a trading strategy.

Now, substituting (15) and (56) into (55), we get

$$\tilde{V}_D(t) = \tilde{V}(0) + \sum_{j=0}^{d} \int_0^t \pi_j(v)\exp\left(-\int_0^t s(v)\,dv\right) dZ_j(v) \tag{58}$$

An application of Itô's lemma shows that this satisfies (41). To complete the proof that it is both admissible and self-financing, we only need to show that $\tilde{V}(t) \geq 0$. Theorem 2 in Fakeev (1970) gives us the result that $X(t)$ is the smallest, non-negative supermartingale that majorises $U(t)$. This implies that $X(t) \geq U(t)$ and $X(\tau_M) = U(\tau_M)$. Hence, $\tilde{V}(t) \geq Y(t)$ and $\tilde{V}(\tau_M) = Y(\tau_M)$. In particular, $\tilde{V}(t) \geq 0$ because $Y(t) \geq 0$ by assumption.

Proposition 4.1 allows us to value any contingent claim satisfying expression (33). Unfortunately, no general closed-form solutions to (49) are known under stochastic interest rates. Consequently, the standard procedure for determining these values is to resort to numerical approximation techniques.

Example: Non-existence of optimal exercise strategies

In previous sections, given that the accumulated price process (7) is continuous a.e., we have shown both the existence of the American claim's value and an appropriate trading strategy which attains this value. Here we analyse an example where this analysis fails in the presence of a discontinuity. This example generalises Roll's (1977) formula for an American call option on a stock with known discrete dividends on fixed dates. For this example, the value function exists and can be characterised but there does not exist an optimal "early exercise strategy" nor a trading strategy that generates the claim's value. As Roll's formula is widely used in the academic literature, this example is of considerable interest.

Consider the introduction of an additional stock $S^*(t)$ in the economy. Let

$$S^*(t) \equiv S(t, x_d) + d_1 P(t, T^*) 1_{(t<T^*)}$$

ie,

$$S^*(t) = S(0, x_d)\exp\left[\int_0^t \left(\mu(u, x_d) - \tfrac{1}{2}\sum_{i=1}^{d} \delta_i^2(u, x_d)\right) du + \sum_{i=1}^{d}\int_0^t \delta_i(u, x_d)\,dW_i(u)\right] + d_1 P(t, T^*)1_{(t<T^*)} \tag{59}$$

where d_1 is the fixed dividend paid at date T^* and $1(t<T^*)$ is the indicator function equal to one if $t<T^*$ and zero otherwise. Note that the stock price is everywhere right-continuous, but discontinuous from the left at $t = T^*$. The assets S^* can be viewed as a portfolio consisting of the risky asset $S(t, x_d)$, which does not pay any dividends, and d_1 bonds with maturity T^*. With this insight, it will be easier to understand the subsequent manipulations. At this stage we add one additional assumption.

ASSUMPTION 5.1: *Non-negative interest rates and no capital losses on zero coupon bonds:*

(i) $Q(B(t+\varepsilon) \geq B(t)) = 1$ *and*
$Q(B(t+\varepsilon) > B(t)) > 0$ *for all* $\varepsilon > 0$ *and* $t \in [0, \tau]$.
(ii) $Q(P(t+\varepsilon, T) \geq P(t, T)) = 1$ *and*
$Q(P(t+\varepsilon, T) > P(t, T)) > 0$ *for all* $\varepsilon > 0$ *and* $t, T \in [0, \tau]$.

Assumption 5.1 is included to simplify the subsequent analysis. It is the simplest stochastic generalisation possible of a non-negative and deterministic term structure of interest rates. Define $Z^*(t)$ by

$$\begin{aligned} Z^*(t) &\equiv \frac{S(t, x_d)}{B(t)} + \frac{d_1 P(t, T^*)1(t<T^*)}{B(t)} + \frac{d_1}{B(t)}1(t \geq T^*) \\ &\equiv Z(t, x_d) + Z_d(t) \end{aligned} \tag{60}$$

where

$$Z(t, x_d) \equiv \frac{S(t, x_d)}{B(t)}$$

$$Z_d(t) \equiv \frac{d_1}{B(t)}[P(t, T^*)1(t<T^*)] + 1(t \geq T^*)\frac{d_1}{B(T^*)} \tag{61}$$

Thus, the quantity $Z_d(t)$ corresponds to an admissible self-financing trading strategy involving d_1 bonds $P(t, T^*)$ held before T^* and rolled over into the money market account after time T^*. Under the $\tilde{Q}$ defined in the preceding two sections, $Z(t, x_d)$ is a square-integrable $\tilde{Q}$-martingale (Proposition 3.1). Given Assumption 5.1, $Z_d(t)$ is bounded and

$$\tilde{E}[Z_d(t)] = d_1[P(0, T^*)/B(0)] \tag{62}$$

Hence, $Z_d(t)$ is a $\tilde{Q}$-martingale, and correspondingly $Z^*(t)$ is a $\tilde{Q}$-martingale.

Now consider an American call option on this new stock with a strike price K and maturity date τ_M where $T^* \leq \tau_M$. By analogy to the definition given in the preceding section, the *arbitrage-free price at time* t of the American call option, $C(t)$, is defined as

$$\frac{C(t)}{B(t)} = \operatorname*{ess\,sup}_{\theta \in \tau_{[t, \tau_M]}} \tilde{E}\left[\left(\frac{S^*(\theta) - K}{B(\theta)}\right)^+ \middle| G_t\right] \tag{63}$$

Next, we turn to trading strategies which attain this value.

DEFINITION 5.1: An ε-*optimal early exercise strategy* starting at time t is a $\theta_\varepsilon^t \in \tau_{[t, \tau_M]}$ such that for a given $\varepsilon > 0$,

$$\frac{C(t)}{B(t)} \leq \tilde{E}\left[\left(\frac{S^*(\theta_\varepsilon^t) - K}{B(\theta_\varepsilon^t)}\right)^+ \middle| G_t\right] + \varepsilon \quad \text{a.e. } \tilde{Q} \tag{64}$$

The early exercise strategy is said to be *optimal* if it is 0-optimal.

The following lemma shows that ε-optimal strategies exist.

LEMMA 5.1 (Existence of ε-optimal strategies): $(C(t)/B(t): t \in [0, \tau_M])$ *is a right-continuous* $\tilde{Q}$-*supermartingale, and the stopping time*

$$y_\varepsilon^t \equiv \inf\left[s \in (t, \tau_M]: \frac{C(s)}{B(s)} \leq \left(\frac{S^*(s) - K}{B(s)}\right)^+ + \varepsilon\right] \tag{65}$$

is ε-*optimal for* $\varepsilon > 0$.

PROOF: By Theorems 1 and 2 in Fakeev (1970), there exists a right-continuous supermartingale $f(t)$ such that $f(t)$ is the minimal right-continuous supermartingale that majorises $\max[(S^*(t) - K)/B(t), 0]$ and

$$f(t) = \operatorname*{ess\,sup}_{\theta \in [0, \tau_M]} \tilde{E}\left[\left(\frac{S^*(\theta) - K}{B(\theta)}\right)^+ \middle| G_t\right] \quad \text{a.e. } \tilde{Q} \tag{66}$$

The call price $C(t) = f(t)/B(t)$, and so the first part of the lemma is established. To show that Y_ε^t is ε-optimal, it suffices to show

$$\tilde{E}\left[\sup_{t \in [0, \tau_M]}\left(\frac{S^*(t) - K}{B(t)}\right)^+\right] < \infty$$

because we can invoke Theorem 4 of Fakeev (1970). But

$$\tilde{E}\left[\sup_{t \in [0, \tau_M]}\left(\frac{S^*(t) - K}{B(t)}\right)^+\right] \leq \tilde{E}\left[\sup_{t \in [0, \tau_M]}\left(\frac{S^*(t)}{B(t)}\right)\right]$$

$$\leq \tilde{E}\left[1 + \sup_{t \in [0, \tau_M]}\left(\frac{S^*(t)}{B(t)}\right)^2\right] \tag{67}$$

Applying Doob's maximal inequality, (67) is less than or equal to

$$\tilde{E}\left[1 + 4\left(\frac{S^*(\tau_M)}{B(\tau_M)}\right)^2\right] = \tilde{E}\left[1 + 4\left(\frac{S(\tau_M, x_d)}{B(\tau_M)} + \frac{d_1}{B(\tau_M)}\right)^2\right]$$

$$\leq 1 + 8\tilde{E}\left[\left(\frac{S(\tau_M, x_d)}{B(\tau_M)}\right)^2 + \left(\frac{d_1}{B(\tau_M)}\right)^2\right] \tag{68}$$

This is finite from the square integrability of $S(\tau_M, x_d)/B(\tau_M)$.

Define a fictitious American contingent claim $C(t; y_\varepsilon^t)$ to be one which has a payoff = $[S^*(y_\varepsilon^t) - K]^+$ at date y_ε^t. Given Lemma 5.1, the proof to Proposition 4.1 yields that there exists a trading strategy corresponding to this claim which requires a time t investment of

$$\tilde{E}\left[\left(\frac{S^*(y_\varepsilon^t)-K}{B(y_\varepsilon^t)}\right)^+ \middle| G_t\right] B(t) \qquad (69)$$

Hence, if the original American contingent claim traded, its value must be within ε of (69) for all $\varepsilon > 0$. However, for $\varepsilon = 0$, an optimal strategy does not exist, as will be shown in Proposition 5.2.

Using this analysis, (63) can now be given an alternative characterisation.

PROPOSITION 5.1.

$$\frac{C(t)}{B(t)} = \tilde{E}\left(\frac{\max[\bar{C}(T^*), S^*(T^*) + d_1 - K]}{B(T^*)} \middle| G_t\right) \qquad (70)$$

where

$$\bar{C}(T^*) = \tilde{E}\left(\frac{[S^*(\tau_M) - K]^+}{B(\tau_M)} \middle| G_{T^*}\right) B(T^*) \qquad (71)$$

PROOF: The first step is to show that the right side of (68) provides an upper bound for $C(t)/B(t)$. Take any $\theta \in \tau_{[t,\tau_M]}$. Then

$$\tilde{E}\left[\left(\frac{S^*(\theta)-K}{B(\theta)}\right)^+ \middle| G_t\right] = \tilde{E}\left[\left(\frac{S^*(\theta)-K}{B(\theta)}\right) 1_{(\theta<T^*)} 1_{[S(\theta,x_d)>K]} \middle| G_t\right] +$$

$$\tilde{E}\left[\left(\frac{S^*(\theta,x_d)-K}{B(\theta)}\right) 1_{(T^*\le\theta<\tau_M)} 1_{[S(\theta,x_d)>K]} \middle| G_t\right] +$$

$$\tilde{E}\left[\max\left(\frac{S(\tau_M,x_d)-K}{B(\tau_M)}, 0\right) 1_{(\theta=\tau_M)} \middle| G_t\right]$$

But, $B(\theta) \ge B(T^*)$ on $T^* \le \theta < \tau_M$. So using the optional sampling theorem and the law of iterated expectations, the above quantity is less than or equal to

$$\tilde{E}\left[\left(\frac{S(T^*,x_d)+d_1-K}{B(T^*)}\right) 1_{(\theta<T^*)} 1_{[S(\theta,x_d)>K]} \middle| G_t\right] +$$

$$\tilde{E}\left[\left(\frac{S(\tau_M,x_d)-K}{B(\tau_M)}\right) 1_{(T^*\le\theta<\tau_M)} 1_{[S(\theta,x_d)>K]} \middle| G_t\right] +$$

$$\tilde{E}\left[\left(\frac{S(\tau_M,x_d)-K}{B(\tau_M)}\right)^+ 1_{(\theta=\tau_M)} \middle| G_t\right]$$

The sum of the second and third terms is less than or equal to

$$\tilde{E}\left[\left(\frac{S(\tau_M, x_d)-K}{B(\tau_M)}\right)^+ 1_{(T^* \le \theta < \tau_M)} \middle| G_t\right] = \tilde{E}\left[\left(\frac{\bar{C}(T^*)}{B(T^*)}\right) 1_{(T^* \le \theta < \tau_M)} \middle| G_t\right]$$

The first term is less than or equal to

$$\tilde{E}\left[\left(\frac{S(T^*, x_d)+d_1-K}{B(T^*)}\right)^+ 1_{(\theta < T^*)} \middle| G_t\right]$$

Therefore,

$$\frac{C(t)}{B(t)} \le \tilde{E}\left(\frac{\max[\bar{C}(T^*), S^*(T^*)+d_1-K]}{B(T^*)} \middle| G_t\right)$$

The second step is to show that there exists an ε-optimal strategy y_ε^t such that

$$\lim_{\varepsilon \to 0} C(t; y_\varepsilon^t) = \tilde{E}\left(\frac{\max[\bar{C}(T^*), S^*(T^*)+d_1-K]}{B(T^*)} \middle| G_t\right) B(t) \quad \text{a.e.}$$

Consider

$$y_\varepsilon^t \equiv \begin{cases} T^* - \varepsilon & \text{if } S(T^* - \varepsilon, x_d) + d_1 P(T^* - \varepsilon, \varepsilon) - K > \bar{C}(T^* - \varepsilon) \\ \tau_M & \text{otherwise.} \end{cases}$$

A calculation similar to that just completed shows that

$$\frac{C(t; y_\varepsilon^t)}{B(t)} = \tilde{E}\left[\max\left(\frac{S(T^*-\varepsilon, x_d)+d_1 P(T^*-\varepsilon, \varepsilon)-K, \bar{C}(T^*-\varepsilon)}{B(T^*-\varepsilon)}\right) \middle| G_t\right]$$

Letting $\varepsilon \to 0$ and using the sample path continuous of our square-integrable martingales gives the result.

This proposition gives a simple method for calculating the American call's value. First, at date T^*, calculate a European call's value with exercise price K and which matures at time τ_M (ie, $\bar{C}(T^*)$). Second, take the minimum of this value and that obtained by exercising the American call at time T^* (ie, $S^*(T^*) + d_1 - K$). This yields the American call's value at time T^*. Third, discount to any earlier date by using the risk-neutral operator as given in (68).

Now we are in a position to prove the main result of this section.

PROPOSITION 5.2: *Corresponding to the American call option* $C(t)$, *there does not exist an optimal exercise strategy* y *with* $Q(y < \tau_M) > 0$.

PROOF: Suppose there exists an optimal exercise strategy $y \in \tau_{[t, \tau_M]}$ with $Q[y < \tau_M] > 0$. Define

$$y^* = \begin{cases} y + \dfrac{T^* - y}{2} & \text{if } t \le y < T^* \\ y + \dfrac{\tau_M - y}{2} & \text{if } T^* \le y \le \tau_M \end{cases}$$

Then $y^* \in \tau_{[t, \tau_M]}$ and $y^* > y$ if $y < T^*$, whereas $y^* = y$ if $y = T^*$. Further, let

$$V^{y} = \tilde{E}\left[\left(\frac{S^*(y)-K}{B(y)}\right)^{+} \middle| G_t\right] B(t)$$

$$V^{y*} = \tilde{E}\left[\left(\frac{S^*(y^*)-K}{B(y^*)}\right)^{+} \middle| G_t\right] B(t)$$

We will show that $V^{y} < V^{y^*}$, which contradicts the optimality of y.

Now, $S^*(y) = S(y, x_d) + d_1 P(t, T^*) 1_{(y<T^*)}$. Hence,

$$V^{y}(t) = \tilde{E}\left[\left(\frac{S(y, x_d)}{B(y)} + \frac{d_1 P(y, T^*)}{B(y)} 1_{(y<T^*)} - \frac{K}{B(y)}\right) 1_{(S^*(y)>K)} \middle| G_t\right] B(t)$$

Using the optimal stopping theorem, $S(t, x_d)/B(t)$ is a $\tilde{Q}$-martingale. Therefore

$$V^{y}(t) =$$

$$\left\{\tilde{E}\left[\tilde{E}\left(\frac{S(y^*, x_d)}{B(y^*)} + \frac{d_1 P(y, T^*)}{B(y)} 1_{(y<T^*)} - \frac{K}{B(y)}\right) 1_{(S^*(y)>K)} \middle| G_y\right] \middle| G_t\right\} B(t)$$

$$= \tilde{E}\left[\left(\frac{S(y^*, x_d)}{B(y^*)} + \frac{d_1 P(y, T^*)}{B(y)} 1_{(y<T^*)} - \frac{K}{B(y)}\right) 1_{(S^*(y)>K)} \middle| G_t\right] B(t)$$

From the definition of y^*, $1_{(y<T^*)} = 1_{(y^*<T^*)}$. Hence,

$$V^{y}(t) = \tilde{E}\left[\left(\frac{S(y^*, x_d)}{B(y^*)} + \frac{d_1 P(y, T^*)}{B(y)} 1_{(y^*<T^*)} - \frac{K}{B(y)}\right) 1_{(S^*(y)>K)} \middle| G_t\right] B(t)$$

$$= \tilde{E}\left[\left(\frac{S^*(y^*)}{B(y^*)} - \frac{K}{B(y)}\right) 1_{(S^*(y)>K)} \middle| G_t\right] B(t)$$

Noting that $\tilde{Q}(B(y^*) > B(y)) > 0$, $\tilde{Q}(B(y^*) \geq B(y)) = 1$ and $\tilde{Q}(y < T) > 0$, this implies that $\tilde{Q}(y^* > y) > 0$ and $\tilde{Q}(y^* \geq y) = 1$. Hence,

$$V^{y}(t) < \tilde{E}\left[\left(\frac{S^*(y^*)}{B(y^*)} - \frac{K}{B(y^*)}\right) 1_{(S^*(y)>K)} \middle| G_t\right] B(t)$$

But

$$\left(\frac{S^*(y^*)-K}{B(y^*)}\right) 1_{(S^*(y)>K)} \leq \left(\frac{S^*(y^*)}{B(y^*)} - \frac{K}{B(y^*)}\right) 1_{(S^*(y^*)>K)} \quad \text{a.e. } \tilde{Q}$$

This implies that

$$V^{y}(t) < \tilde{E}\left[\left(\frac{S^*(y^*)}{B(y^*)} - \frac{K}{B(y^*)}\right) 1_{(S^*(y)>K)} \middle| G_t\right] B(t)$$

ie, $V^{y}(t) < V^{y^*}(t)$.

This proposition proves that there does not exist an optimal exercise strategy for the American call option. The intuition for this result is straightforward. As it is sub-optimal to exercise early if there are no future dividends, optimal exercise must lie in the time interval before the dividend payment date. If it is optimal to exercise early, one would like to exercise the option as close as possible to the dividend date. But given that the stock price is right-continuous and that there is a discrete jump at the dividend date, the time interval over which one can exercise the option is an open interval whose supremum cannot be attained.

Conclusion

This paper extends Heath, Jarrow and Morton (1992) to include risky assets. Various closed-form solutions for European-type options on risky assets, forward contracts and futures contracts are provided. Secondly, it studies the pricing of American-type contingent claims on risky assets in a stochastic interest rate economy. It generalises the previous works of Heath, Jarrow and Morton (1992), Bensoussan (1984), Karatzas (1988), and Roll (1977) in this regard. The analysis justifies the use of the standard procedures for calculating American contingent claim values in stochastic interest rate economies.

Bibliography

Amin, K., and R. Jarrow, 1991, "Pricing Foreign Currency Options under Stochastic Interest Rates", *Journal of International Money Finance* 10(3), pp. 310-29.

Bensoussan, A., 1984, "On the Theory of Option Pricing", *Acta Applicandae Mathematicae* 2, pp. 139-58; reprinted as Chapter 3 of the present volume.

Black, F., 1976, "The Pricing of Commodity Contracts", *Journal of Financial Economics* 3, pp. 167-79.

Brennan, M. J., and E. S. Schwartz, 1979, "A Continuous Time Approach to the Pricing of Bonds", *Journal of Banking Finance* 3, pp. 133-55; reprinted as Chapter 5 of the present volume.

Cox, J. C., J. E. Ingersoll, and S. A. Ross, 1985, "A Theory of the Term Structure of Interest Rates", *Econometrica* 53, pp. 385-407; reprinted as Chapter 6 of the present volume.

Durrett, R., 1984, *Brownian Motion and Martingales in Analysis*, Belmont, CA: Wadsworth.

Fakeev, A. G., 1970, "Optimal Stopping Rules for a Stochastic Process with Continuous Parameter", *Theory Probab. Appl.*, 15, pp. 324-31.

Harrison, J. M., and D. M. Kreps, 1979, "Martingales and Arbitrage in Multiperiod Security Markets", *Journal of Economic Theory* 20, pp. 381-408.

Harrison, J. M., and S. R. Pliska, 1981, "Martingales and Stochastic Integrals in the Theory of Continuous Trading", *Stochastic Processes Applied* 11, pp. 215-60.

Heath, D. C., R. A. Jarrow, and A. J. Morton, 1992, "Bond Pricing and the Term Structure of Interest Rates: A New Methodology for Contingent Claims Valuation", *Econometrica* 60 (1), pp. 77-105; reprinted as Chapter 14 of the present volume.

Jarrow, R., 1987, "Pricing of Commodity Options with Stochastic Interest rates", *Adv. Futures Options Res.* 2, pp. 19-45.

Karatzas, I., 1988, "On the Pricing of American Options", *Appl. Math. Optim.* 17, pp. 37-60.

Karatzas, I., and S. Shreve, 1988, *Brownian Motions and Stochastic Calculus*, New York: Springer-Verlag.

Liptser, R. S., and A. N. Shiryayev, 1977, *Statistics of Random Processes. I: General Theory*, New York: Springer-Verlag.

Merton, R. C., 1973, "The Theory of Rational Option Pricing", *Bell Journal of Economic Management Science*, 4, pp. 141-83.

Morton, A. J., 1989, "Arbitrage and Martingales", Ph.D. thesis, School of Operations Research, Cornell University.

Roll, R., 1977, "An Analytic Formula for Unprotected American Call Options on Stocks with Known Dividends", *Journal of Financial Economics* 5, pp. 251-58.

16

A Family of Itô Process Models for the Term Structure of Interest Rates*

Simon Babbs
First National Bank of Chicago and the University of Warwick

A family of Itô process models is constructed for the dynamics of the term structure of interest rates on default-free bonds, consistent with whatever term structure is initially observed. The results of Harrison and Kreps (1979) are extended to cover term structure models. It is shown that the family of models constructed in this paper can be supported in general equilibrium; in particular, arbitrage opportunities are absent. A general formula is provided for the valuation of contingent claims. Consideration of sub-families sheds a fresh light, in a generalised setting, on the term structure dynamics under which conventional duration is the correct risk measure for bond portfolios. A number of other models are shown to be special cases.

The prices at which fixed interest obligations[1] are traded in financial markets - and the term structure of interest rates those prices embody[2] - have long been a focus of attention for investors, borrowers, governments and academics, not only as providing, obviously, a schedule of current opportunities for the placement or raising of funds, but also as embodying market participants' anticipations of future opportunities.

Alongside markets in fixed interest obligations, markets have grown up over the last couple of decades in a range of derivative instruments.[3] Some of these securities, such as options on bond or interest rate futures contracts, are derivative twice over, in that they are defined in relation to what are themselves derivative securities.

Interest rate derivatives are important in a number of ways. Firstly some of them (eg, the long gilt futures contract on LIFFE; and some Forward Rate Agreements) provide a superior means of price discovery, in that the bid/offer spread can be tighter than those in the fixed interest obligations themselves; moreover, in the case of exchange traded derivative securities, it is only necessary to obtain the bid/offer prices on the exchange floor, rather than to seek quotations from a number of traders. The former point may be particularly important if, for example, one wishes to know on what terms a forward position can be constructed. Secondly, it may be possible to infer from market prices of certain derivative securities, notably options, via an appropriate model, the degree of uncertainty attaching to market participants' anticipations of future interest rates. Thirdly, the volume of trading in some derivative securities is enormous, and such trading constitutes a significant activity of a large number of financial institutions.

**At the time of writing the author was at Midland Montagu Capital Markets.*

Derivative instruments are used in a wide variety of ways, for both speculative and hedging purposes. For instance, a considerable number of financial institutions use combinations of fixed interest obligations and derivative securities to hedge positions in other derivative securities; thus, for example, government securities, futures on government securities and options on government securities may be used in combination to hedge a portfolio of over-the-counter (OTC) options on government securities. The latter options themselves could be of varying times to expiry and relate to underlying securities of a wide range of maturities.

From the foregoing it is clear that there is a need for models of the dynamics of the term structure, both because of interest in the term structure itself and also to provide a consistent basis for the valuation of a broad range of derivative instruments. In addition, to be of use to practitioners in the derivative instruments markets, the initial state of whatever processes are used to model the term structure must be consistent with the current term structure actually observed, so that, for example, the value of an immediately expiring in-the-money option to purchase a fixed interest obligation will equal the excess of the current price of that obligation over the exercise price of the option.[4]

Until the last few years, the main foci of the substantial academic literature on the term structure were measurement[5] and explanation.

A pivotal paper in the latter field is Cox, Ingersoll, and Ross (1981). In this paper, as its title, "A Re-examination of Traditional Hypotheses about the Term Structure of Interest Rates", suggests, the authors reassess the theories previously advanced. Specifically, they consider the various forms of the "Expectations Hypothesis", the "Hicksian Liquidity Preference" approach, and the "Preferred Habitat Theory" of Modigliani and Sutch, under which last head they effectively subsume the Segmented Market Hypothesis of Culbertson. They also review a number of linear adaptive interest rate forecasting models.

The overall thrust of the paper can perhaps be summed up[6] in two propositions. Firstly, any hypothesis about the term structure not informed by rigorous use of the mathematical tools of stochastic processes might well find itself reduced to palpable absurdity (and this applied to a disturbing fraction of the previous literature). Secondly, any term structure model wishing to hold itself out as consistent with an economic equilibrium requires very careful establishment of its credentials in that regard.

Stochastic process models of the term structure, both earlier (eg, Vasicek (1977), Richard (1978) and Dothan (1978)) and subsequent (eg, Brennan and Schwartz (1982) and Cox, Ingersoll, and Ross (1985)) supposed that the evolution of the term structure could be described in terms of one or two state variables and a process (usually a constant parameter) describing the market price of interest rate risk. These models can be solved to produce theoretical initial term structures, and thus, of course, are generally inconsistent with the term structure actually observed.[7]

The first model of term structure dynamics to incorporate consistency with the initial term structure actually observed as a fundamental feature is that of Ho and Lee (1986*b*).[8] Ho and Lee adopt a discrete-time approach based on the construction of an arbitrage-free binomial lattice to describe the evolution of the entire term structure from its observed initial state. By way of illustration of their binomial framework, they devote much space to an extreme special "state–time independent" case of their framework, characterised in terms of two parameters.

The chief weakness of their work is that a discrete time binomial model of term structure movements is, in itself, unrealistic; its validity can reside only in representing an approximation to something more plausible. The immediate question is that of convergence, namely, as the length of the time-step tends to zero, to what if anything do the distribution of the term structure and the values obtained for derivative instruments converge. Unfortunately, Ho and Lee do not discuss such matters. The issues have, however, been addressed independently by a number of authors.[9]

An obvious idea, building on the contribution of Ho and Lee, is to seek to construct a family of continuous time stochastic processes for the term structure consistent with its observed initial state. This programme has been tackled independently by Babbs (1990) and by Heath, Jarrow and Morton (1989) (HJM).

Both Babbs and HJM model each instantaneous forward interest rate by an Itô process.[10] The constructions used are similar in outline, but take somewhat different courses. The approach of Babbs, to be presented in this paper, clarifies the role played by the various regularity conditions. In addition, Babbs goes on to show that the family of models he has constructed is viable, ie, can be supported in general equilibrium. This is achieved, as we shall see in the "Viability" section of this paper, by adapting and extending the work of Harrison and Kreps (1979) to a term structure context and allowing a rich class of trading strategies. HJM, like Babbs, obtain the key technical result of the existence of a "unique equivalent martingale measure" (EMM), a reassignment of probabilities under which normalised security price processes are martingales; however, HJM do not demonstrate viability and adopt a heavily circumscribed definition of trading strategies. While Babbs and HJM use different numeraire securities in order to obtain their EMMs, their formulae for the value of contingent claims can be shown to be equivalent.

Pursuing a similar programme at a less generalised level, Hull and White (1990) have produced "extended Vasicek" and "extended Cox-Ingersoll-Ross" models to reconcile the models of Vasicek (1977) and Cox, Ingersoll, and Ross (1985) with the observed initial term structure.

The purpose and structure of this paper

The aim of this paper is to provide a general continuous time framework for modelling term structure dynamics for use: in research on the term structure itself; for analysis of bond portfolios; and for the pricing of contingent claims.

The first task is to present the construction of a family of Itô process models, given in Chapter 4 of Babbs (1990). The initial state of each member of the family is consistent with whatever term structure is currently observed and the price of each bond attains par at maturity.

Our construction makes use of an argument found in Vasicek (1977) concerning absence of arbitrage opportunities between bonds of different maturities. The necessity of the restrictions imposed is more apparent than their sufficiency. The second task of this paper is therefore to demonstrate that all arbitrage opportunities have indeed been eliminated. This is achieved as a consequence of establishing the stronger result that the models are "viable" in the sense defined by Harrison and Kreps (1979), ie, that they could be supported in a general equilibrium in an economy populated by rational agents.[11] The key technical concept used in Harrison and Kreps is that of an "equivalent martingale measure" (EMM). Harrison and Kreps established a link between viability and the existence of one or more EMMs, under the restrictive assumption that agents can trade only at a finite number of pre-specified fixed times.[12] We adapt Harrison-Kreps' framework to a term structure context and make use of results in Babbs which link EMMs to viability under a square integrability condition on trading strategies, of the kind widely accepted as a means of eliminating arbitrage (see, eg, Dybvig and Huang (1988)).[13]

A by-product of the second task of the paper is that the equivalent martingale measure is in fact unique. It then follows that all contingent claims are priced by arbitrage.

We go on to discuss a number of sub-families of our models. We shed fresh light on the question of under what term structure dynamics conventional duration is the correct bond portfolio risk measure, generalising the setting used in Cox, Ingersoll, and Ross (1979). We also derive a number of existing models as special cases of our family. In particular, the "extended Vasicek" model of Hull and White (1990) is shown to be a special case; the continuous time limit of the "state-time-independent" model of Ho and Lee (1986*b*) represents a further specialisation. One effect of this is that our results can be applied to show that these models are viable. At the end of the paper we provide some brief concluding remarks.

The construction of Itô processes

A common assumption is that the state of the world at any time can be described by the values of some fixed finite set of state variables. We have no need to impose this restriction, and therefore omit it. Instead, we shall focus directly on the term structure itself. We shall see, however, (see the Section "Properties of sub-families", below) that certain subclasses of our family of Itô processes can be described using state variables.

In setting out to construct stochastic processes for the term structure, one immediate question is whether to base the construction on asset prices – those of pure discount bonds are the natural choice – or with interest rates. Inspection of the stochastic processes of asset prices in existing literature (eg, equation (30) in Section 8 of Merton (1973)) reveals that the instantaneous riskless interest rate can be a prominent element of the "drift" or "trend" component. If, therefore, having eschewed the use of state variables, we base the construction on the prices of pure discount bonds, we may find it difficult to specify their stochastic processes fully without prior analysis of the instantaneous riskless rate, which is itself a function[14] of bond prices. To avoid this kind of vicious circle, we base our construction on interest rates.

To limit the burdens of notation, we will present our results in single-factor form, ie, using only one Brownian motion to drive the dynamics of the term structure. We would emphasise that this is a purely expositional device, since the multi-factor version of our results can be obtained by simply adding additional terms identical in form to those arising from the single-factor case, a procedure whose details we regard as self-evident. We believe that our approach to this issue best serves expositional clarity.

CONSTRUCTION

By means of the proposition and theorem below, we construct a collection of Itô processes, one for each pure discount bond, that is consistent with the initial term structure and which ensures that each bond price converges to par at maturity.

We then proceed to employ an argument, due to Vasicek (1977), to obtain a restriction on the drift terms that is a necessary condition for the absence of arbitrage opportunities. Imposing that restriction enables the stochastic processes for the term structure to be re-expressed in an intuitively appealing way:

$$\frac{dB(M,t)}{B(M,t)} = [r(t,\omega)+\theta(t,\omega)\sigma(M-t,t,\omega)]dt+\sigma(M-t,t,\omega)dZ(t) \qquad (1)$$

where: $B(M, t)$ denotes the price at time t of unit nominal of a pure discount bond maturing at time $M \geq t$; $r(t, \omega)$ denotes the instantaneous spot interest rate; and $Z(\ )$ is a standard Brownian motion.[15]

Equation (1) bears the straightforward interpretation that each pure discount bond has an expected instantaneous rate of return which differs from the instantaneous spot interest rate by an amount proportional to the bond's instantaneous price volatility. The factor of proportionality represents the market price of interest rate risk and is the same across all bonds. The presence, as a functional argument, of the representative element $\omega \in \Omega$ of the set of all possible paths for the evolution of the term structure, indicates that the instantaneous spot rate, the price of risk and the volatility of bond prices are allowed to be state-dependent in a very general fashion, as well as time-dependent.

Unfortunately, (1) is not a satisfactory starting point since, as discussed above, the instantaneous spot rate is itself a function of the prices of pure discount bonds. To avoid this kind of vicious circle, we base our construction upon instantaneous forward interest rates for all dates. An heuristic preview may be helpful.

Having no particular intuitions about the dynamics of instantaneous forward interest rates, we suppose (see the proposition, below) that they follow very general Itô processes, subject only to conditions on the processes of the different rates sufficient to ensure that the prices at all dates of pure discount bonds can be recovered via the appropriate integration (see (7)). It follows from that integration that bond prices attain par at maturity (see (5)) and that future instantaneous spot interest rates are well defined (see (6), (8) and (9)).

To turn the expression (10) for future bond prices (obtained in our proposition) into an Itô process, we must reverse the order of some repeated integrals, one of them involving an Itô stochastic integral. We achieve this in the theorem below, subject to additional regularity conditions upon the instantaneous standard deviations of the forward rate processes.

We then make the final step to reach our conjectured bond price dynamics (ie, (1)), by noting that an argument due to Vasicek (1977), concerning arbitrage between bonds of different maturities, requires a relationship (see equation (14)) between the drifts and instantaneous standard deviations of instantaneous forward rates.

PROPOSITION

Let the initial term structure $B(\cdot, 0) : [0, \infty) \to \Re$ *be strictly positive and differentiable on* $[0, \infty)$.

Let $a, b : [0, T] \times [0, \infty) \times \Omega \to \Re$ *satisfy appropriate*[16] *measurability conditions and the following regularity conditions.*

(i) $\alpha(\cdot, \cdot, \omega) : [0, T] \times [0, \infty) \to \Re$ *is integrable over bounded rectangles almost surely.*

(ii) $E\left[\int_0^t b^2(s, m, \omega)\, ds\right] < \infty; \quad \forall t \le m$

(iii) $\int_0^t b(s, m, \omega)\, dZ(s)$ *is integrable in* $m \ge t$ *over bounded intervals.*

Then we may construct Itô processes, consistent with the initial term structure, for the instantaneous forward interest rate $f(m, \cdot)$ *for each date* $m \ge 0$:

$$f(m, t) = f(m, 0) + \int_0^t a(s, m, \omega)\, ds + \int_0^t b(s, m, \omega)\, dZ(s), \quad t \le m \tag{2}$$

where

$$f(m, 0) = -\frac{d}{dm} \ln B(m, 0) \tag{3}$$

Moreover, we can derive from these processes an expression for the price of any pure discount bond at any future date:

$$\ln B(M, t) = \ln B(M, 0) + \int_0^t f(s, 0)\, ds - \int_t^M \int_0^t a(s, m, \omega)\, ds\, dm - \int_t^M \int_0^t b(s, m, \omega)\, dZ(s)\, dm \tag{4}$$

with

$$B(M, M) = 1 \text{ almost surely}, \ \forall M > 0 \tag{5}$$

Furthermore, the instantaneous spot interest rate $r(t)$ *follows a well-defined process:*

$$r(t) = f(t, 0) + \int_0^t a(s, t, \omega)\, ds + \int_0^t b(s, t, \omega)\, dZ(s) \tag{6}$$

PROOF

By the assumed differentiability of the initial term structure, (3) well defines an initial curve $f(., 0) : [0, \infty) \to \Re$ of instantaneous forward interest rates.

By assumptions (i) and (ii), we may now define a family of Itô processes, indexed by $m \ge 0$, as given by (2).

By assumptions (i) and (iii), each summand on the right-hand side of (2) is integrable in m over bounded intervals. Therefore, we have a well-defined stochastic process:

$$\ln B(M, t) = -\int_t^M f(m, t)\,dm, \quad \forall t \in [0, M] \tag{7}$$

for the price of each pure discount bond.

Equation (5) follows immediately from (7), while substituting (2) and performing elementary manipulations gives (4). Also from (7), we have that

$$\frac{-\ln B(M, t)}{M-t} \to f(t, t) \text{ as } M \downarrow t \tag{8}$$

whence we may well-define the spot instantaneous interest rate, $r(t)$ and establish (6), by setting:

$$r(t) = f(t, t), \quad \forall t \geq 0 \tag{9}$$

and substituting (2) on the right-hand side.

To turn (4) into an Itô process, we need to reverse the order of integration of the repeated integration. This requires some additional regularity conditions which, as we shall see in later sections, are satisfied in a number of significant cases.

THEOREM 1

If the conditions of our proposition hold and, in addition, $b(\ )$ *satisfies the following regularity conditions:*

(iv) $\int_0^t b(s, t, \omega)\,dZ(s)$ *is almost surely pathwise integrable in* t.

(v) $b(s, \cdot, \omega) : \Re \to \Re$ *is integrable over finite intervals* $\forall s$ *almost surely.*

(vi) $E\left[\int_0^t \left(\int_s^M b(s, m, \omega)\,dm\right)^2 ds\right] < \infty, \quad \forall t \leq M$

(vii) $\left[E\left(\int_0^t b^2(s, m, \omega)\,ds\right)\right]^{\frac{1}{2}}$ *is integrable with respect to* m *over finite intervals* $(m \geq t)$.

Then we may construct Itô processes for the price of each pure discount bond, consistent with the initial term structure, with the stochastic differential form:

$$\frac{dB(M, t)}{B(M, t)} = \left[r(t) - \int_t^M a(t, m, \omega)\,dm + \frac{1}{2}\left(\int_t^M b(t, m, \omega)\,dm\right)^2\right] dt - \left(\int_t^M b(t, m, \omega)\,dm\right) dZ(t) \tag{10}$$

where $r(\ )$ *is the spot instantaneous interest rate process given by* (6) *and where each bond price converges to par at maturity, as described by* (5).

PROOF

By assumptions (i) and (iv), equation (6) is almost surely pathwise integrable over finite intervals, giving:

$$\int_0^t r(m)\,dm = \int_0^t f(s, 0)\,ds + \int_0^t \int_0^m a(s, m)\,ds\,dm + \int_0^t \int_0^m b(s, m)\,dZ(s)\,dm \tag{11}$$

in which, being pathwise an ordinary integral, is absolutely continuous (cf., eg, Weir (1973), p. 67) and thus, *a fortiori*, a continuous VF process and a semi-martingale.

Subtracting (11) from (4) and combining the ranges of integration now yields:

$$\ln B(M, t) - \ln B(M, 0) = \int_0^t r(m)\,dm - \int_0^M \int_0^{\min\{m, t\}} a(s, m)\,ds\,dm - \int_0^M \int_0^{\min\{m, t\}} b(s, m)\,dZ(s)\,dm \tag{12}$$

Applying Fubini's theorem to

$$\int_0^M \int_0^{\min\{m,t\}} a(s,m)\,ds\,dm$$

and using assumptions (ii), (v), (vi) and (vii) to enable us to apply a Fubini-type theorem for stochastic integrals[17] to

$$\int_0^M \int_0^{\min\{m,t\}} b(s,m)\,dZ(s)\,dm$$

we may rewrite (12) as:

$$\ln B(M,t) - \ln B(M,0) =$$

$$\int_0^t r(m)\,dm - \int_0^t \int_s^M a(s,m)\,dm\,ds - \int_0^t \int_s^M b(s,m)\,dm\,dZ(s) \tag{13}$$

The final term on the right-hand side of (13) is a continuous martingale by assumption (vi). The preceding terms are absolutely continuous in t and thus VF. Hence, $\ln B(M,\cdot)$ is an Itô process. By Itô's lemma, we deduce that $B(M,\cdot)$ is itself an Itô process, whose differential form is (10) as required.

NECESSARY RESTRICTION FOR THE ABSENCE OF ARBITRAGE OPPORTUNITIES

We may apply an argument identical to that used in the third section of Vasicek (1977), concerning arbitrage between bonds, to deduce from (10) that we require:

$$-\int_t^M a(t,m,\omega)\,dm + \frac{1}{2}\left(\int_t^M b(t,m,\omega)\,dm\right)^2 = -\theta(t,\omega)\int_t^M b(t,m,\omega)\,dm \tag{14}$$

where

$$\theta(t,\omega) = \text{price of interest rate risk at } (t,\omega) \tag{15}$$

If we now define

$$\sigma(M-t,t,\omega) \equiv -\int_t^M b(t,m,\omega)\,dm \tag{16}$$

we may use (15) to re-express (10) in the form of (1), completing the construction.

Viability

While we took steps, in the preceding subsection, to eliminate arbitrage opportunities, we have not established that none remain. A strictly wider question is whether members of our family of models are "viable", ie, capable of being supported in a general equilibrium in an economy populated by rational agents.

To address these matters, we must embed our term structure dynamics in an economy and decide what class of trading strategies is available to economic agents. For simplicity, we will utilise the pure exchange economy employed in Harrison and Kreps; in the interests of brevity, we refer the reader to Sections 1 and 2 of Harrison and Kreps (1979) for details.

We need however to make some various adaptations to accommodate term structure models. In particular, we will suppose that the set of traded securities consists of pure discount bonds;[18] we do not require the collection of available securities to be finite, and we allow for maturing bonds by prescribing that bonds may not be held beyond their maturity dates.

Harrison and Kreps demonstrated a link between viability and equivalent martingale measures (EMMs). An EMM is a reassignment of probabilities under which appropriately normalised security prices are martingales; we give a formal definition below. The first stage of the link was to show that a price system for the traded subset of contingent claims (here understood as state-contingent claims to consumption at the terminal date of the economy) is viable if and only if it can be extended[19] to all claims. The second was to show that each such extension could be used to define an EMM, and vice versa.

The natural numeraire in this economy is the security which has a certain unit payoff at T, ie, the pure discount bond maturing at that date. With this numeraire, Harrison and Kreps's definition of an EMM is modified to become the definition below.

DEFINITION

A probability measure P^* *on* (Ω, F) *is said to be an equivalent martingale measure if and only if the following three conditions hold:*

(i) P^* *and* P *are equivalent, ie, have the same null sets. A necessary and sufficient condition for this is that the Radon-Nikodym derivative* dP^*/dP *be strictly positive;*[20]

(ii) *bond price processes, after normalisation by dividing through by* $B(T,\cdot)$, *are martingales under* P^**;*

$$\text{(iii)}\quad \frac{dP^*}{dP} \in L^2(\Omega, F, P) \tag{17}$$

The second stage of the link demonstrated by Harrison and Kreps was achieved under the assumption that each agent can follow only "simple" trading strategies, involving trading only at a finite set of fixed dates selected at the outset of the economy. As Harrison and Kreps observed, this is undesirably restrictive. At this stage, therefore, we make instead a provisional definition.

PROVISIONAL DEFINITION

A trading strategy is provisionally defined as a non-negative integer n*, a selection of bond maturity dates,* $M_1, \ldots, M_n$*, together with an* n*-dimensional real valued stochastic process* $\Psi : [0, T] \times \Omega \to \Re^n$*, whose* j*th component* Ψ_j *represents time-state-dependent holdings of bond* j*, satisfying:*

(i) *The stochastic integral in* (18) *is well defined;*

(ii) $\Psi_j(t, \omega) = 0$ *if bond* j *matures strictly before* t*;*

(iii) *self-financing:* $\forall t, \omega$:

$$V_\psi(t,\omega) \equiv \sum_{j=1}^{n} \psi_j(t,\omega) B(M_j, t) = V_\psi(0,\omega) + \sum_{j=1}^{n} \int_0^t \psi_j(u,\omega)\, dB(M_j, u) \tag{18}$$

This requirement says that changes in the value of the strategy must be attributable precisely to capital gains on bond holdings, ie, with no net injections or extractions of funds.

(iv) *terminal value in the terminal consumption space:*

$$V_\psi(T,\cdot) \in L^2(\Omega, F, P) \tag{19}$$

We now avail ourselves of a result in Babbs (Chapter 5, pp. 134–9) which extends Harrison and Kreps' work to admit a wider class of trading strategies.

THEOREM 2

Suppose P^* *is an EMM and that we further restrict strategies by requiring that their discounted*[21] *value processes are* P^**-martingales; then the model is viable, with* $\kappa : L^2(\Omega, F, P) \to \Re$ *defined by:*

$$\kappa(x) = B(T, 0)\, E^*[x] \tag{20a}$$

extending the price system to all contingent claims.

Conversely, if we suppose that the model is viable, with κ *extending the price system to all claims, and make the alternative restriction that the discounted price of each traded bond is* P*-square integrable, then there exists an EMM,* P^**, given by:*

$$P^*(A) = \frac{\kappa(1_A)}{B(T,0)} \tag{20b}$$

where 1_A *is the indicator function of* A.

PROOF (See Babbs, *loc. cit.*)

We are now ready to address the viability of the Itô process models of the term structure constructed in the previous section. We begin (Theorem 3) by showing that there is at most one EMM and specifying its Radon-Nikodym derivative with respect to P - a step which lends itself to obtaining sufficient regularity conditions for existence. By imposing these conditions, we establish (Theorem 4) the existence of an EMM and hence viability.

Theorem 3

If the bond price processes are described by (1)*, then the economy just specified has at most one EMM. If this EMM,* P^**, exists, then*[22]

$$\xi(t) \equiv \exp\left(-\int_0^t [\theta(u) - \sigma(T-u,u)]dZ(u) - \frac{1}{2}\int_0^t [\theta(u) - \sigma(T-u,u)]^2 du\right)$$

$$\text{is a P-martingale, with } \xi(T) \in L^2(P) \tag{21}$$

and P^* *has Radon-Nikodym derivative*

$$\frac{dP^*}{dP} = \xi(T) \tag{22}$$

Conversely, if (21) *holds, define a probability measure,* P^**, by* (22)*. Then a sufficient condition for* P^* *to be an EMM is:*

$$\exp\left(\int_0^t [\sigma(M-u,u) - \sigma(T-u,u)]\, dZ^*(u) - \frac{1}{2}\int_0^t [\sigma(M-u,u) - \sigma(T-u,u)]^2 du\right)$$

$$\text{is a } P^* \text{ martingale } \forall M \in [0,T] \tag{23}$$

where $Z^*(\ )$ *is the standard Brownian motion under* P^* *given by* (35).

PROOF

Define the discounted bond price processes:

$$B^*(M,t) \equiv \frac{B(M,t)}{B(T,t)} \quad \forall M, t \tag{24}$$

(The argument which now follows is largely due to Pages (1987).)

Suppose that there exists an EMM, P^*. By the definition of an EMM,

$$\frac{dP^*}{dP} \in L^2(P) \tag{25}$$

Hence $\eta(\ )$, defined by:

$$\eta(t) \equiv E\left(\frac{dP^*}{dP}\middle| F_t\right) \tag{26}$$

is a square-integrable P-martingale with

$$\eta(0) = E\left(\frac{dP^*}{dP}\right) = 1 \tag{27}$$

We can therefore apply martingale representation theory[23] to obtain that[24]

$$\eta(t) = 1 + \int_0^t \alpha(u, \omega)\, dZ(u) \tag{28}$$

for some P-square-integrable process $\alpha(\ )$.

By (1),

$$\frac{dB^*(M,t)}{B^*(M,t)} = [\sigma(M-t,t) - \sigma(T-t,t)]\{[\theta(t) - \sigma(T-t,t)]dt + dZ(t)\} \tag{29}$$

Since P^* is an EMM, $B^*(M,\cdot)$ is a P^*-martingale, implying[25] that $B^*(M,\cdot)\eta(\ )$ is a P-martingale. Applying Itô's lemma,

$$\frac{d[B^*(M,t)\eta(t)]}{B^*(M,t)} =$$

$$[\sigma(M-t,t) - \sigma(T-t,t)]\{\alpha(t) + [\theta(t) - \sigma(T-t,t)]\,\eta(t)\}dt +$$

$$\alpha(t) + [\sigma(M-t,t) - \sigma(T-t,t)]\,\eta(t)\}\, dZ(t) \tag{30}$$

Now an Itô process is a martingale only if[26] it has zero drift. Thus we require

$$\alpha(t) + \{\theta(t) - \sigma(T-t, t)\}\,\eta(t) = 0 \tag{31}$$

Multiplying this through by $dZ(t)$, substituting for $\alpha(t)\,dZ(t)$ by means of (28), and re-arranging:

$$\frac{d\eta(t)}{\eta(t)} = -[\theta(t) - \sigma(T-t,t)]\, dZ(t) \tag{32}$$

whose solution is

$$\eta(t) = \xi(t) \quad \forall t \tag{33}$$

Thus, if P^* is an EMM, then $\xi(\ )$ is a P-martingale with

$$\xi(T) = \eta(T) = \frac{dP^*}{dP} \in L^2(P) \tag{34}$$

Conversely, if the condition (21) in the theorem is fulfilled, then, by the Girsanov Theorem,[27] (22) defines a probability measure P^* equivalent to P under which

$$Z^*(t) \equiv Z(t) + \int_0^t \{\theta(u) - \sigma(T-u, u)\}\, du \tag{35}$$

is a standard Brownian motion, and we may re-express the discounted security price process (29) as

$$\frac{dB^*(M,t)}{B^*(M,t)} = [\sigma(M-t,t) - \sigma(T-t,t)]\, dZ^*(t) \tag{36}$$

whose unique solution is the P^*-supermartingale

$$B^*(M,t) = B^*(M,0)\exp\left(\int_0^t [\sigma(M-u,u) - \sigma(T-u,u)]dZ^*(u) - \right.$$

$$\left. \frac{1}{2}\int_0^t [\sigma(M-u,u) - \sigma(T-u,u)]^2 du\right) \tag{37}$$

If (23) holds, the right-hand side of (37) is, in fact, a P^*-martingale; thus P^* is an EMM as required.

To utilise the above theorem in the most straightforward way, we now impose the following conditions.

REGULARITY CONDITIONS
The conditions (21) *and* (23) *of Theorem 3 are fulfilled.*

REMARK
These regularity conditions are satisfied in a range of interesting cases. For example, by the Novikov condition,[28] (23) will always be fulfilled if $\sigma(\ )$ is globally bounded (eg, when it is deterministic); similarly (21) will be satisfied if $\theta(\ )$ is also globally bounded. We shall see examples of this when we investigate the properties of sub-families.

Since Theorem 3 tells us that there is at most one EMM, and mindful of Theorem 2, we elect to finalise our definition of trading strategies by the following definition.

DEFINITION
Define a trading strategy by the Provisional Definition above, supplemented by the following additional requirement:

(v) $\dfrac{V_\psi(.,.)}{B(T,.)}$ *is a* P^**-martingale*

We can now conclude:

THEOREM 4
Our term structure model is viable, with a unique EMM. In particular, arbitrage opportunities and "suicide" strategies are precluded.

PROOF
The unique EMM follows immediately from the regularity conditions given above and Theorem 3. Viability follows by Theorem 2. Arbitrage and suicide strategies are readily shown to be precluded by requirement (v) on trading strategies.

The Pricing of Contingent Claims

As Harrison and Kreps (1979), (Section 3, Corollary to Theorem 2), pointed out, the existence of a unique EMM implies that there is a unique extension of market prices to all contingent claims. Thus every claim has a unique price consistent with equilibrium; Harrison and Kreps termed this price "determined by arbitrage".

THEOREM 5
Let the conditions of Theorem 4 be fulfilled. Then any $x \in L^2(\Omega, F, P)$ *is priced by arbitrage, at a value:*

$$V^{(x)} = B(T, 0)\, E^*[x] \tag{38}$$

PROOF
Let P^* be the unique EMM. Let κ be the corresponding extension of the price system. Then, by Theorem 2, κ is given by:

$$\kappa(x) = B(T, 0)\, E^*[x] \tag{39}$$

The result follows.

The valuation equation (38) applies across the whole family of models constructed in this paper and is thus inevitably abstract. For particular models, formulae capable of explicit computation can be derived from it.

For example, for a broad class of models within the b( )-state-independent sub-family as discussed below, Babbs has obtained closed-form pricing formulae for a wide range of contingent claims (Babbs, Chapters 6–17, pp. 153–272). These include: European bond options;[29] interest rate caps and floors; futures contracts on bonds[30] and on short-term interest rates; and for options, margined in a manner akin to futures, on those futures contracts such as are traded on the London International Financial Futures Exchange (LIFFE). A computationally efficient binomial approximation scheme, using the general framework of Ho and Lee (1986*b*), extends the coverage (Babbs, Chapters 18–25, pp. 273–370) to include, *inter alia*: American bond options; and non-margined options on futures. We hope to present a number of these results in future papers.

The properties of sub-families

In this section, we consider various sub-families of the models we constructed at the beginning of this paper. In each case we are able to shed light on topics discussed in earlier literature in more restricted settings, or to obtain existing models as special cases. One effect of this is that our results on viability (Theorem 4) and the valuation of contingent claims (Theorem 5) can be applied to a range of models of theoretical and practical interest.

We shall see that in some cases - though not in others - the evolution of the term structure can be described in terms of a finite set of state variables. This vindicates our decision, at the outset of constructing our models, to eschew basing our construction upon state variables. At the same time, the existence of a state variable representation for some classes of our models may be useful to other researchers seeking to incorporate our models in wider endeavours.

b( ) INDEPENDENT OF M

If we write

$$b(t, M, \omega) = b(t, \omega) \tag{40}$$

in (16), we see that the volatility of $B(M, t)$ is

$$\sigma(M-t, t, \omega) = (M-t)\, b(t, \omega) \tag{41}$$

Moreover, from (14) we find that

$$a(s, M, \omega) = b(s, M, \omega)\left(\theta(s, \omega) + \int_s^M b(s, m, \omega)\, dm\right) \quad \forall\, s, M \tag{42}$$

From (41) it is easy to verify[31] that the volatility of the value of any bond portfolio, not just that of a single pure discount bond, is proportional to conventional duration. Thus the sub-family discussed here is significant as the sub-family for which conventional duration is the correct tool for portfolio immunisation.

However, if we substitute (41) and (42) into (2), it is readily shown that

$$f(M_2, t) - f(M_1, t) = f(M_2, 0) - f(M_1, 0) + (M_2 - M_1) \int_0^t b^2(s, \omega)\, ds \tag{43}$$

The interpretation of (43) is that, with probability one, the forward instantaneous rate curve, with respect to forward date, steepens as time elapses. Thus the sub-family for which conventional duration is the correct immunisation tool has implausible properties.

Cox, Ingersoll, and Ross (1979) suggested (p. 55) that the only dynamics for which conventional duration is a valid measure of risk is that which corresponds in our framework to the case b( ) = constant. This stemmed from their restricting their attention to term structure dynamics for which their equation (6) holds. Our findings thus reinforce, from the vantage point of a more general framework, the conclusion of Cox *et al.*

that using conventional duration as a measure of risk is consistent only with implausible term structure dynamics.

Substituting (40) and (42) into (2) also yields:

$$f(m,t) = f(m,0) + m\int_0^t b^2(s,\omega)\,ds - \int_0^t \{s b^2(s,\omega) - \theta\{s,\omega) b(s,\omega)\}\,ds + \int_0^t b(s,\omega)\,dZ(s) \tag{44}$$

Hence

$$\int_0^t b^2(s,\omega)\,ds \tag{45a}$$

and

$$\int_0^t \{s b^2(s,\omega) - \theta(s,\omega) b(s,\omega)\}\,ds - \int_0^t b(s,\omega)\,dZ(s) \tag{45b}$$

constitute the state variables for the entire forward instantaneous rate curve and hence, via (7), of the entire term structure itself.

b( ) CONSTANT

Setting

$$b(t, M, \omega) \equiv b \tag{46}$$

obviously represents an extreme case of the sub-family just considered above, with the proportionality factor between volatility and conventional duration being state- and time-independent. Various authors[32] have shown that the Ho and Lee (1986*b*) state-time-independent model represents a discrete time approximation to precisely this extreme case.

For this sub-family, it is possible to derive a closed-form expression for future term structures, as follows.

Substituting (46) into (41) and (42) and thence both into (6) and (1) yields:

$$r(t) = f(t,0) + b\int_0^t \theta(s,\omega)\,ds + \tfrac{1}{2}b^2t^2 + bZ(t) \tag{47}$$

and

$$\frac{dB(M,t)}{B(M,t)} = [r(t) + \theta(t,\omega)(M-t)b]dt + (M-t)b\,dZ(t) \tag{48}$$

whence straightforward manipulations give

$$B(M,t) = \frac{B(M,0)}{B(t,0)} \exp\left[(M-t)[f(t,0) - r(t)] - \tfrac{1}{2}t(M-t)^2 b^2\right] \tag{49}$$

(Note that if, in (48), we set $\theta(\ ) \equiv 0$ and $b = -g$, we obtain the model described in footnote 43 on p. 163 of Merton (1973).)

It may be seen from (49) that, for this sub-family, the instantaneous interest rate $r(t)$ is a state variable and that no other such variable is required.

b( ) STATE-INDEPENDENT

By removing state-dependence, ie, dependence on ω, from b( ), the volatility of pure discount bond prices becomes state-independent, as can be seen from (16), but may nevertheless be a function of time as well as of term to maturity. Models in this family are readily shown to be viable, if (say) the market price of risk is globally bounded (see Theorem 3 and subsequent Remark).

For this sub-family the impact of the innovations of the Brownian motion Z( ) upon any particular part of the term structure depends on the maturity date in question.[33] In general, therefore, no finite set of state variables for the entire term structure exists for this sub-family.

In pricing contingent claims, Babbs focuses much attention upon a portion[34] of this sub-family in which b( ) has the functional form:

$$b(s, m) = -G'(m)\lambda(s) \tag{50}$$

where $G, \lambda : [0, \infty) \rightarrow [0, \infty)$ with $G(0) = 0$ and where $G'(\;)$ denotes the first derivative of $G(\;)$.

For this portion, it is easy to verify that (2) becomes

$$f(m,t) = f(m,0) + G'(m)\int_0^t [G(m) - G(s)]\lambda^2(s)ds - G'(m)\left(\int_0^t \theta(s,\omega)\lambda(s)ds + \int_0^t \lambda(s)dZ(s)\right) \tag{51}$$

so that

$$Y(t,\omega) \equiv \int_0^t \theta(s,\omega)\lambda(s)\,ds + \int_0^t \lambda(s)\,dZ(s) \tag{52}$$

constitutes the single state variable for the whole term structure.

It is worth exploring the properties of the instantaneous spot rate of interest for this portion of the wider sub-family.

Recalling from (9) that $r(t) = f(t, t);\ \forall t \geq 0$, we put $m = t$ in (51) and use (52) to obtain

$$r(t) = f(t,0) + G'(t)\int_0^t \{G(t) - G(s)\}\lambda^2(s)\,ds - G'(t)\,Y(t) \tag{53}$$

If $G'(\;)$ is differentiable,[35] we may re-express (53) in differential format:

$$dr(t) = \mu'(t)dt - \frac{G''(t)}{G'(t)}[\mu(t) - r(t)]dt - G'(t)dY(t) \tag{54}$$

where $\mu'(t)$ is the derivative of

$$\mu(t) \equiv f(t,0) + G'(t)\int_0^t \{G(t) - G(s)\}\lambda^2(s)\,ds \tag{55}$$

(54) can be interpreted as expressing a mean-reversion process involving a moving mean, $\mu'(t)$, and a generalised innovations process $G'(t)\,dY(t)$. Analysing contingent claims under this model, Babbs has obtained (Chapters 6–25, pp. 153–370) an extensive range of continuous time closed-form results and a binomial approximation scheme (see also the end of the previous section).

Within the b( )-state-independent sub-family, Hull and White (1990) proposed the "extended Vasicek" model,[36] in which the dynamics of the instantaneous spot rate can be written in the form:[37]

$$dr(t) = \{\alpha(t) + \beta(t)\,r(t)\}\,dt - \gamma(t)\,dZ(t) \tag{56}$$

and the market price of risk process is a function of time alone, to be determined from the other parameters and the initial term structure.

Hull and White propose that $\alpha(\;)$, $\beta(\;)$ and $\gamma(\;)$ be chosen so that the model fits: the initial term structure, the initial variabilities of spot interest rates of all maturities, and the prospective variability across time of the instantaneous spot rate.

It is readily shown, by comparing (56) with (54), that any "extended Vasicek" model is a special case of our "b( )-state-independent" sub-family, with:

$$G(t) = \int_0^t \exp\left(\int_0^s \beta(u)\,du\right) ds \tag{57a}$$

$$\lambda(t) = \gamma(t)\exp\left(-\int_0^t \beta(u)\,du\right) \tag{57b}$$

and

$$\theta(t) = -\alpha(t) - \beta(t)f(t,0) + f_1(t,0) + \int_0^t \gamma^2(s)\exp\left(2\int_s^t \beta(u)\,du\right) ds \tag{57c}$$

The significance of this representation is threefold:

Firstly, we can apply the results in this paper to establish that Hull–Whites' "extended Vasicek" model is viable – an issue that Hull and White overlook.

Secondly, Hull and White achieve the "fit" of their model by imposing an artificial structure, (57*c*), on the market price of risk, $\theta(\ )$. By contrast, the greater generality of (54) over that of (56) enables us to achieve the same "fit" while leaving the price of risk, $\theta(\ )$, free to take any form.

Under our approach, all we need to parameterise[38] the model are $G(\ )$ and $\lambda(\ )$. The former, together with $\lambda(0)$, is determined from the initial absolute variabilities of spot rates of all maturities:

$$\sigma_{spot}(M,0)\begin{cases} = \dfrac{G(M)}{M}\lambda(0), & M>0 \\ = G'(0)\lambda(0), & M=0 \end{cases} \tag{58}$$

where, without loss of generality, we set $G'(0) = 1$. We can now determine $\lambda(\ )$ from the anticipated absolute variability of instantaneous spot rates:

$$\sigma_{spot}(0,t) = G'(t)\lambda(t) \tag{59}$$

Thus, not only is our approach more general but also, as comparison of (58) and (59) with Hull and White's equations (15) and (16) reveals, we are able to parameterise our model using substantially simpler – and more computationally tractable – expressions.

Thirdly, in pricing contingent claims, we can apply the results in Babbs (Chapters 6–25, pp. 153–370) referred to at the end of the previous section above.

Conclusions

In this paper we have identified a need for continuous time models of the dynamics of the term structure of interest rates, consistent with the initial term structure actually observed. We have addressed that need by constructing a general family of Itô process models and by extending the work of Harrison and Kreps (1979) in such a way as to enable us to identify modest sufficient conditions under which members of that family are viable, ie, can be supported in general equilibrium. As a by-product of our analysis of viability, we have established that all contingent claims are priced by arbitrage and exhibited a general pricing equation.

We have examined some sub-families of our models. In so doing, we shed fresh light on the implausibility of the term structure dynamics under which conventional duration is the correct measure of bond portfolio risk, extending a critique advanced by Cox, Ingersoll, and Ross (1981). We also pointed out that various existing models, including the continuous time limit of the state- and time-independent model of Ho and Lee (1986*b*) and the "extended Vasicek" model of Hull and White (1990), are special cases of our framework. In particular, we showed that we could generalise the "extended Vasicek" model in such a way as to remove the artificial form of the market price of risk imposed by Hull and White.

Acknowledgement

The author is very grateful to Michael Selby for numerous suggestions for improving the presentation of this paper. The contents are based in part on Chapters 1, 2, 4 and 5 of the author's Ph.D. thesis (Babbs (1990)); the author is grateful for the support and encouragement of his Ph.D. supervisor, Gerry Salkin of Imperial College.

1 *"Fixed interest obligations" refers to any security whose terms comprise the payment of one or more cashflows, known at the outset in respect of both date and amount, by the issuer of the security, the obligor, to the holder of the security. This definition includes both coupon-paying and pure discount bonds. We will assume that all contracts are default-free.*

2 *In the absence of default risk and of certain types of market "frictions", a fixed interest obligation may be valued by summing the values of its component cashflows, ie, by regarding the obligation as a bundle of pure discount bonds (see, eg, the start of Section VI of Merton (1974), or the first section of Cox, Ingersoll, and Ross (1981)). Thus the way the market prices fixed interest obligations at any time can be expressed by a function describing the price per unit nominal, or, equivalently, yield to maturity, of pure discount bonds of arbitrary tenor. This function is called "the term structure of interest rates", or often simply "the term structure". Therefore to model the term structure is precisely to model the dynamics of the prices of fixed interest obligations.*

3 *That is, instruments which are not fixed interest obligations, but which generate cashflows between their counterparties which are functions of the price paths of fixed interest obligations.*

4 *Hull and White (1990) have recently made a similar point.*

5 *Recent papers include Prisman (1990) and Steeley (1989), who also give numerous references to earlier literature.*

6 *Babbs (1990), pp. 61-3, discusses Cox* et al. *in greater depth.*

7 *A recent paper by Dybvig (1989), however, offers hope that it may be possible to "reconcile" a number of existing term structure models with the actual observed term structure, thus making them - for the first time - candidates as models of practical use for the modelling of interest rate derivative instruments.*

8 *The (1986*b) *paper is the published version of the (1986a) paper. The unpublished version describes the general form of the binomial framework more fully, whereas the other devotes more attention to the extreme special case in which the framework is time- and state-independent. At a mathematical level, however, the contents of the two versions are essentially identical.*

9 *See, eg, Babbs (1990), especially Chapter 20, pp. 308-15; Hull and White (1990); and Heath, Jarrow and Morton (1990).*

10 *In an earlier paper, HJM (1987) allowed the process followed by each forward rate to depend on the rate in question; HJM (1989) relaxed this in favour of general dependence on the history of the entire term structure.*

11 *All the results here are contained in Chapter 5, pp. 129-52, of Babbs.*

12 *Harrison and Kreps made no attempt to defend this restriction on economic grounds and pointed out its undesirability, eg, in excluding the option replication strategy in the Black and Scholes (1973) model.*

13 *The results in Babbs are of independent interest and we hope to present them fully elsewhere.*

14 *See equations (8) and (9).*

15 *To be precise,* $Z(\ )$ *denotes a standard Brownian motion starting at zero, defined on some probability space* (Ω, F, P) *equipped with an increasing family of sub-sigma-algebras of* F, $\{F_t : t \in [0, T]\}$ *for some fixed* $T > 0$, *satisfying the "usual conditions" (see, eg, Karatzas and Shreve (1987) 1.2.25 Definition p. 10), and where, without loss of generality,* F_0 *is almost trivial, and* $F_0 = F$.

16 *The measurability conditions are omitted for the sake of brevity. They are simply the kind of conditions customary in stochastic calculus; see, eg, Ikeda and Watanabe(1981).*

17 *The required theorem is an adaptation of Lemma 4.1 on pp. 116-9 of Ikeda and Watanabe (1981) to the special case of martingales based on Brownian motion. See Babbs (Chapter 28, pp. 379-83) for details.*

18 *A far richer setting, involving coupon bonds and other assets, is readily constructed but would obscure the essentials of the exposition.*

19 *By a continuous and strictly positive linear functional.*

20 *Note that since* P, P* *have the same null sets, we may use the term "almost surely" without qualification as to which probability measure is intended.*

21 *That is, normalised by dividing by the price of the numeraire security.*

22 *From this point on, we usually drop notational dependence on* ω *in the interests of brevity.*

23 *See, eg, Liptser and Shiryayev (1977), Theorem 5.5, p. 162 - essentially the Kunita-Watanabe Representation Theorem.*

24 *We have generally not felt the need to make explicit the various measurability conditions involved in the stochastic calculus we have been undertaking. The validity of (28), however, depends on the assumption that the increasing family* $\{F_t : t \in [0, T]\}$ *with which our probability space is equipped is that generated by* $Z(\ )$. *Restrictions of this kind, introduced by Harrison and Kreps (Section 5), and subsequently commonplace, restrict agents' information to the past price history of the traded securities.*

25 *See, eg, Liptser and Shiryayev (1977), Lemma 6.6, p. 226; Pages (1987) cites Dellacherie and Meyer (1982), Lemma VII.48.*

26 *It is well known that this condition is necessary but not sufficient. Its necessity flows from the result that, on a finite interval, a continuous local martingale of finite variation is constant (see, eg, M. U. Dothan (1990), Theorem 10.28, p. 249).*

27 *See, eg, Karatzas and Shreve (1987), Theorem 3.5.1, p. 191.*

28 *See, eg, Karatzas and Shreve (1987), Corollary 3.5.13, p. 199.*

29 *The formula in question yields that of Jamshidian (1989) as a special case, when applied to the Vasicek (1977) term structure model.*

30 *The analysis sets aside the various delivery options often embedded in such contracts.*

31 *Let the promised cashflows from the portfolio be* $c_1, \ldots, c_n$ *at dates* $M_1 < \ldots < M_n$, *respectively, with* M_1 *greater than current time,* t. *Then the value of the portfolio is:*

$$V(t) = \sum_{j=1}^{n} c_j B(M_j, t)$$

Applying Itô's lemma and substituting (1),

$$dV(t) = \sum_{j=1}^{n} c_j B(M_j, t)[r(t) + \theta(t)\sigma(M_j - t, t)]dt + \sum_{j=1}^{n} c_j B(M_j, t)\,\sigma(M_j - t, t)dZ(t)$$

whence

$$\frac{dV(t)}{V(t)} = [r(t) + \theta(t)D(t)]dt + D(t)dZ(t)$$

where

$$D(t) = \left(\sum_{j=1}^{n} c_j B(M_j, t)\sigma(M_j - t, t)\right) \div \left(\sum_{j=1}^{n} c_j B(M_j, t)\right)$$

Thus $D(t)$ *is the volatility of the value of the portfolio and the appropriate measure of risk. Comparison with conventional duration:*

$$C(t) = \left(\sum_{j=1}^{n} c_j B(M_j, t)(M_j - t)\right) \div \left(\sum_{j=1}^{n} c_j B(M_j, t)\right)$$

quickly reveals that volatility will be proportional to conventional duration, for all portfolios, if and only if $\sigma(\ )$ *is of the form given by (41).*

32 *Babbs (Chapter 20, pp. 308-15) and Heath, Jarrow and Morton (1990) provide independent, and indeed quite different, treatments. We are unclear to what extent Carverhill (1989) and Hull and White (1990) are indebted to Heath* et al.

33 *For example, it is easy to verify that, for this sub-family, (2) becomes:*

$$f(m, t) = f(m, 0) + \int_0^t b(s, m)\left(\int_s^m b(s, n)dn - \theta(s, \omega)\right)ds + \int_0^t b(s, m)dZ(s)$$

34 *Babbs shows that, after adjusting the probability assignment to the "equivalent martingale measure", future term structures can be described by a single Gaussian state variable. This facilitates the derivation of concrete valuation techniques - in many cases closed-form expressions - for a very wide range of contingent claims of commercial interest (see the end of the "Pricing of Contingent Claims" section above).*

35 *Assumption (iii) of the proposition in the construction of Itô processes implicitly imposes the requirement that* G′( ) *exist, but it will not necessarily be differentiable.*

36 *Hull and White also put forward an "extended Cox-Ingersoll-Ross" model, building on that in Cox, Ingersoll, and Ross (1985). A similar analysis to that given here for the "extended Vasicek" model can be brought to bear (see Babbs p. 96), but no gain in tractability accrues.*

37 *We have changed the notation, to avoid confusion below when Hull and White's models are compared with ours.*

38 *The "price of risk" process is irrelevant to the pricing of contingent claims and so can be left unspecified.*

Bibliography

Babbs, S. H., 1990, "The Term Structure of Interest Rates: Stochastic Processes and Contingent Claims", PhD Thesis, London University.

Black, F., and M. S. Scholes, 1973, "The Pricing of Options and Corporate Liabilities", *Journal of Political Economy* 81, pp. 637–659; reprinted as Chapter 1 of the present volume.

Brennan, M. J., and E. S. Schwartz, 1982, "An Equilibrium Model of Bond Pricing and a Test of Market Efficiency", *Journal of Financial and Quantitative Analysis* 17, pp. 301–329; reprinted as Chapter 5 of the present volume.

Carverhill, A. P., 1989, "The Ho and Lee Term Structure Theory: A Continuous Time Version", Preprint 88/5, Financial Options Research Centre, University of Warwick.

Cox, J. C., J. E. Ingersoll, and S. A. Ross, 1979, "Duration and the Measurement of Basis Risk", *Journal of Business* 52, pp. 51–61.

Cox, J. C., J. E. Ingersoll, and S. A. Ross, 1981, "A Re-examination of Traditional Hypotheses about the Term Structure of Interest Rates", *Journal of Finance* 36, pp. 769–799.

Cox, J. C., J. E. Ingersoll, and S. A. Ross, 1985, "A Theory of the Term Structure of Interest Rates", *Econometrica* 53, pp. 385–407; reprinted as Chapter 6 of the present volume.

Dellacherie, C., and P. Meyer, 1982, *Probabilities and Potential B: Theory of Martingales*, North-Holland.

Dothan, L. U., 1978, "On the Term Structure of Interest Rates", *Journal of Financial Economics* 6, pp. 59–69.

Dothan, M. U., 1990, *Prices in Financial Markets*, Oxford University Press.

Dybvig, P. H., 1989, "Bond and Bond Option Pricing Based on the Current Term Structure", Washington University in St Louis, Working Paper.

Dybvig, P. H., and C.-f. Huang, 1988, "Non-Negative Wealth, Absence of Arbitrage, and Feasible Consumption Plans", *Review of Financial Studies*, 1, pp. 377–401.

Harrison, J. M., and D. M. Kreps, 1979, "Martingales and Arbitrage in Multiperiod Securities Markets", *Journal of Economic Theory* 20, pp. 381–408.

Heath, D. C., R. A. Jarrow, and A. Morton, 1987, "Bond Pricing and the Term Structure of Interest Rates: A New Methodology", Working paper, Cornell University.

Heath, D. C., R. A. Jarrow, and A. Morton, 1992, "Bond Pricing and the Term Structure of Interest Rates: A New Methodology for Contingent Claims Valuation", *Econometrica* 60, pp. 77–105; reprinted as Chapter 14 of the present volume.

Heath, D. C., R. A. Jarrow and A. Morton, 1990, "Bond Pricing and the Term Structure of Interest Rates: A Discrete Time Approximation", *Journal of Financial and Quantitative Analysis* 25, pp. 419–440.

Ho, T. S. Y., and S.-B. Lee, 1986a, "Term Structure Movements and Interest Rates Contingent Claims Pricing", Working Paper Series 375, Salomon Brothers Center for the Study of Financial Institutions.

Ho, T. S. Y., and S.-B. Lee, 1986b, "Term Structure Movements and Pricing Interest Rate Contingent Claims", *Journal of Finance* 41, pp. 1011–1029; reprinted as Chapter 13 of the present volume.

Hull, J., and A. White, 1990, "Pricing Interest Rate Derivative Securities", *Review of Financial Studies* 3, pp. 573-592; reprinted as Chapter 9 of the present volume.

Ikeda, N., and S. Watanabe, 1981, *Stochastic Differential Equations and Diffusion Processes*, North-Holland Mathematical Library 24, North-Holland/Kodansha.

Jamshidian, F., 1989, "An Exact Bond Option Pricing Formula", *Journal of Finance* 44, pp. 205-209; reprinted as Chapter 8 of the present volume.

Karatzas, I., and S. E. Shreve, 1987, *Brownian Motion and Stochastic Calculus*, Graduate Texts in Mathematics 113, Springer Verlag.

Liptser, R. S., and A. N. Shiryayev, 1977, *Statistics of Random Processes I: General Theory*, Springer-Verlag.

Merton, R. C., 1973, "Theory of Rational Option Pricing", *Bell Journal of Economics and Management Science* 4, pp. 141-183.

Merton, R. C., 1974, "On the Pricing of Corporate Debt: the Risk Structure of Interest Rates", *Journal of Finance* 29, pp. 449-470.

Pages, H. F., 1987, "Optimal Consumption and Portfolio Policies When Markets are Incomplete", Working Paper No. 1883, A P Sloan School of Management, Massachusetts Institute of Technology.

Prisman, E. Z., 1990, "A Unified Approach to Term Structure Estimation: A Methodology for Estimating the Term Structure in a Market with Frictions", *Journal of Financial and Quantitative Analysis* 25, pp. 127-142.

Richard, S. F., 1978, "An Arbitrage Model of the Term Structure of Interest Rates", *Journal of Financial Economics* 6, pp. 33-57.

Steeley, J. M., 1989, "Estimating the Gilt-Edged Term Structure: Basis Splines and Confidence Intervals", Preprint 89/1, Financial Options Research Centre, University of Warwick.

Vasicek, O. A., 1977, "An Equilibrium Characterization of the Term Structure", *Journal of Financial Economics* 5, pp. 177-188; reprinted as Chapter 4 of the present volume.

Weir, A. J., 1973, *Lebesgue Integration and Measure*, Cambridge University Press.

17

State-Space Models of the Term Structure of Interest Rates*

Darrell Duffie
Graduate School of Business, Stanford University

This is a survey of models of the term structure of interest rates, concentrating on models in which the term structure has a Markov state-space representation.

Stochastic models for random fluctuations of the term structure of interest rates are commonly used in the finance industry for at least the following purposes: pricing fixed-income derivative securities, such as options and mortgage-backed securities; analysing the risk of fixed-income portfolio strategies; and managing the interest-rate risk of fixed-income positions.

By "fixed income" we mean assets whose payoffs depend on the term structure itself. In a wide sense, this can include bonds; bond derivatives such as options, swaps, or caps; defaultable bonds; and even foreign bonds or derivatives based in sometimes complicated ways on domestic and foreign interest rates. There are many other reasons for understanding the process by which interest rates are determined and change over time, but our focus will be on models that are particularly useful for the above three purposes.

While various classes of stochastic models are used, the most common language of term-structure modellers in industry and universities is that of continuous-time stochastic calculus, which reached popularity following the impact of the Black and Scholes (1973) option pricing formula and the associated modelling ideas developed by Merton (1973) and others. Even in the early work of Pye (1966), however, one finds discrete-time models that capture much of the mechanics and principles of term-structure models in a Markov state-space setting, where we will focus our efforts. We will review how such models are constructed and applied, with particular emphasis on Markov diffusions, or jump diffusions, that represent the current term structure. Within this class, one can make reasonable trade-offs between economic realism and computational tractability, bearing in mind that no tractable model can fully capture the complexity of unexpected changes in interest rates.

The second section gives the basic definitions and pricing relationship simplified by the absence of arbitrage. The third section introduces Markov models in a one-dimensional diffusion setting, with examples. The fourth section moves to a multi-dimensional diffusion setting, emphasising the tractability offered by a special "affine"

**The first section through to the fifth extend and update work presented at The Royal Society, London, November 10–11, 1993, and published in the* Philosophical Transactions of the Royal Society, *Series A, Volume 347 (1994), pp. 577–586, co-authored with Rui Kan. Permission is granted by Birkhäuser Boston to use "State Space Models of the Term Structure of Interest Rates" from the book* Stochastic Analysis and Related Topics V: The Silivri Workshop 1994, *edited by H. Körezlioğlu, B. Øksendal and A. S. Üstünel.*

class. The fifth section is devoted to derivative pricing and hedging. The sixth and seventh sections introduce jumps and default, respectively. The eighth section describes the Heath–Jarrow–Morton model, while the ninth places Heath–Jarrow–Morton models in a Markov state-space setting. The tenth section considers foreign term-structure derivative valuation in a Heath–Jarrow–Morton framework. The eleventh section adds comments on new research directions.

Set-up

We begin with a probability space (Ω, F, P) and filtration $\{F_t: t = [0, \infty)\}$ of sub-σ-algebras of F satisfying the usual conditions. (For technical details see, for example, Protter (1990) or other standard references.) Given is a progressively measurable "short rate" process r that is integrable, in the sense that $\int_0^T |r_t| \, dt < \infty$ almost surely for all $T > 0$. We may think of r_t as the interest rate at time t on loans of infinitesimal maturity. More properly, a short rate process r implies the ability to invest one unit of account at any time t and, with continual reinvestment, to receive at any time $s \geq t$ the payoff $\exp(\int_t^s r_u du)$.

For our purposes here a financial security is a contract that promises to pay, at some time T, possibly a stopping time, some F_T-measurable random variable Z. Each such *claim* (Z, T) is assigned a price process given by a semimartingale $S^{Z,T}$. An "arbitrage" is, loosely speaking, a strategy for trading various claims, at no initial investment cost, so as to generate only positive (and non-zero) cashflows. According to a formalisation of this conceived by Harrison and Kreps (1979), and subsequently developed by many,[1] under technical conditions there is no arbitrage if and only if there is a probability measure Q, equivalent to P, under which, for any such triple $(Z, T, S^{Z,T})$,

$$S_t^{Z,T} = E\left[\exp\left(-\int_t^T r_s ds\right) Z \,\middle|\, F_t\right] \qquad t \leq T \tag{1}$$

where "E" denotes expectation under Q. We fix such a measure Q throughout.

A simple example of a claim, a zero-coupon bond, is defined by letting T be deterministic and $Z = 1$. For such a claim (1, T), the price $S_t^{Z,T}$ is denoted $p_{t,T}$. The continuously-compounding yield of a zero-coupon bond of maturity $m \in (0, \infty)$ is then defined as

$$y_{t,m} = -\frac{1}{m} \log p_{t,t+m} \qquad (t, m) \in \mathbf{R}_{++}^2 \tag{2}$$

At time t, the "term structure of interest rates" is the function mapping the maturity m to the yield $y_{t,m}$ at that maturity.

For practical applications, the basic issue is how to model the probabilistic behaviour of the short-rate process r under Q. One wants a model for r that is sufficiently rich to capture the essential nature of actual interest rates, while at the same time sufficiently tractable for purposes of econometric estimation and for computation of the prices of contingent claims by (1), for a range of commonly traded claims. There are also many theoretically interesting questions regarding the equilibrium determination of the short rate process r and the equivalent "martingale" measure Q. It is known that, under weak technical conditions, any short rate process r can be supported in a simple and standard model of market equilibrium, with easily specified risk preferences. (See, for example, Heston (1991) and Duffie (1996, Exercise 10.3).)

We will focus here only on practical issues and disregard other aspects of the market equilibrium problem. We will review some basic classes of models for the behaviour of the short rate process r under a given equivalent martingale measure Q. We will concentrate on Markovian state-space models, beginning with "single-factor" models, moving to finite-dimensional multi-factor models, and finally describe infinite-dimensional state-space models, in the framework of Heath, Jarrow and Morton (1992), using the approach of stochastic partial differential equations. Along the way we shall review such applications as the valuation and hedging of derivative securities.

For many applications it would be useful to model the distribution of interest rate processes under the original probability measure P. Conversion from P to Q and back will not be dealt with here, but it is an important issue - particularly from the point of view of statistical fitting of models as well as the measurement of risk.

Single-factor models

The simplest class of models that we consider takes the short rate process r to be the solution of a stochastic differential equation of the form

$$dr_t = \mu(r_t)\,dt + \sigma(r_t)\,dW_t \tag{3}$$

where W is a standard Brownian motion that is a martingale under Q, and where $\mu: \mathbf{R} \to \mathbf{R}$ and $\sigma: \mathbf{R} \to \mathbf{R}$ have enough regularity to ensure the existence of a unique solution to (3). (See, for example, Ikeda and Watanabe (1981).) Since r is a strong Markov process under Q, we have $p_{t,T} = F(r_t, t)$ for some measurable function $F: \mathbf{R} \times [0, T] \to \mathbf{R}$, and we can therefore view the entire yield curve $y_t = \{y_{t,m}: m \geq 0\}$ defined by (2) as measurable with respect to r_t. Hence the label "single-factor model" applies, since a single state variable, in this case the short rate r_t, determines all yields and is a sufficient statistic (under the equivalent martingale measure Q) for all future yield curves.

While simple and, as it turns out, quite tractable, the single-factor class of models given by (3) is (like any theoretical model) at variance with reality. Consequently, on a given day the yield curve associated with the model differs from that observed in the marketplace. If significant, a discrepancy may suggest the development of a new theoretical model. In the finance industry, however, one needs to use some particular model, even if imperfect. In practice, a discrepancy between the actual and theoretical yield curves is eliminated by introducing, at each current time t, time-dependence in the functions μ and σ to arrive at a "calibrated model", $\mu^t: \mathbf{R} \times [0, \infty) \to \mathbf{R}$ and $\sigma^t: \mathbf{R} \times [0, \infty) \to \mathbf{R}$, of the form

$$dr_s = \mu^t(r_s, s)\,ds + \sigma^t(r_s, s)\,dW_s, \quad s \geq t \tag{4}$$

under technical conditions on (μ^t, σ^t). The *calibrated model* (μ^t, σ^t) is computed with numerical algorithms, examples of which are described in Black, Derman and Toy (1990) and Black and Karasinski (1992). With calibration, an exact match can be achieved between the actual and modelled yield curves.

It is common to calibrate not only with the yield curve, but also with certain "volatility-related" information available in the market through the prices of option-related securities such as caps. A cap is a portfolio $\{(Z_i, T_i): i \in \{1, \ldots, N\}\}$ of claims, of which (Z_i, T_i) is the claim defined by letting $T_i - T_{i-1}$ be a constant, say 0.5 years, independent of i, and by letting $Z_i = \max(Y_i - \bar{Y}, 0)$, where $\bar{Y}$ is a constant and Y_i is the simple interest rate that applies at time T_{i-1} for bonds maturing at time T_i, that is, $(1 + Y_i)^{-1} = p_{T_{i-1}, T_i}$. A cap is often purchased as a hedge against a loan whose interest payments are periodically reset to current market rates. A cap is but one example of a term-structure derivative, a claim (or portfolio of claims) derived from the term structure of interest rates. Through the basic pricing relationship (1), one can search for a calibrated model (μ^t, σ^t) within a given class of models that not only matches the term structure of yields observed in the market with those determined by the model, but also matches the market prices of caps with those determined by the model. Other claims, such as swaptions (options to enter into a swap at a fixed rate set in advance), are also used for calibration purposes. (For the definition of a swaption see, for example, Jarrow and Turnbull (1996).)

In general, calibration is designed to capture the pricing implications of certain "benchmark" financial securities, usually those with a high level of trading activity, in order to estimate the prices of less common claims through the basic relationship (1).

Suppose a term-structure model has been calibrated at time t. At the next time period t + 1, given the likely mis-specification of the model, it is common in practice to recalibrate so as to achieve a new model $(\mu^{t+1}, \sigma^{t+1})$ that is once again consistent with market prices of certain benchmark claims. Since the necessity for recalibration was not considered when using the previous version of the model for pricing purposes, this suggests a theoretical inconsistency in the application of the model. The compromise involved seems reasonable under the circumstances.

Most, if not all, of the parametric single-factor models appearing in the literature or in industry practice are of the form

$$dr_t = [\alpha_1(t) + \alpha_2(t)r_t + \alpha_3(t)r_t \log r_t]\,dt + [\beta_1(t) + \beta_2(t)r_t]^{\gamma}\,dW_t \qquad (5)$$

for time-dependent deterministic coefficients $\alpha_1, \alpha_2, \alpha_3, \beta_1$ and β_2 and for some exponent $\gamma \geq 0.5$. (For existence and uniqueness of solutions, additional coefficient restrictions apply.) Table 1 lists the origins[2] of various special cases of this parametric class, indicating by "•" the coefficients that are non-zero (sometimes constant) for each special case and indicating the choice of exponent γ.

Table 1. Parametric single-factor models

$$dr_t = [\alpha_1(t) + \alpha_2(t)r_t + \alpha_3(t)r_t \log r_t]\,dt + [\beta_1(t) + \beta_2(t)r_t]^{\gamma}\,dW_t$$

	α_1	α_2	α_3	β_1	β_2	γ
Cox–Ingersoll–Ross	•	•			•	0.5
Dothan					•	1.0
Brennan–Schwartz	•	•			•	1.0
Merton	•			•		1.0
Vasicek	•	•		•		1.0
Pearson–Sun	•	•		•	•	0.5
Black–Derman–Toy		•	•		•	1.0
Constantinides–Ingersoll					•	1.5

Multi-factor models

While single-factor models offer tractability, there is compelling reason to believe that a single state variable, such as the short rate r_t, is insufficient to capture reasonably well the distribution of future yield-curve changes. The econometric evidence in favour of this view includes the work of Chen and Scott (1992*b*, 1993), Dai and Singleton (1996), Duffie and Singleton (1995), Litterman and Scheinkman (1988), Pearson and Sun (1994) and Stambaugh (1988). (For empirical comparisons of most of the single-factor models considered in Table 1, see Chan, Karolyi, Longstaff and Sanders (1992).)

In principle, of course, the yield curve sits in an infinite-dimensional space of functions, and there is no reason to believe that the direction of its movements will be restricted to some finite-dimensional manifold. An infinite-dimensional state-space model is outlined in the ninth section ("State-space HJM models"). For practical purposes, however, tractability might call for a finite number of state variables, and it is an empirical issue as to how many might be sufficient to offer reasonable empirical properties. Some of the empirical studies mentioned above suggest that two or three state variables might suffice for many practical purposes.

In any case, we will consider a state process X in some open subset D of $\mathbf{R}^n$, defined as the solution of the stochastic differential equation (SDE)

$$dX_t = \mu(X_t)\,dt + \sigma(X_t)\,dW_t \qquad (6)$$

where W is a standard Brownian motion in $\mathbf{R}^n$ under Q and where $\mu: D \to \mathbf{R}^n$ and

$\sigma: D \to \mathbf{R}^{n \times n}$ satisfy sufficient regularity for existence and uniqueness of solutions. In what follows, we could add time-dependence to μ and σ without changing the major ideas.

We also suppose that the short rate process r is given by $r_t = R(X_t)$ for some $R: D^n \to \mathbf{R}$. (Again, time-dependence may be added at little or no computational burden for what follows.) Thus the zero-coupon bond maturing at T has a price at time $t \le T$ given from (1) by

$$F(X_t, t) = E\left[\exp\left(-\int_t^T R(X_s)\,ds\right) \middle| X_t\right] \tag{7}$$

It is frequently convenient to exploit the Markov setting and solve (7) for the market prices of bonds via the "Feynman-Kac" connection between (7) and the associated partial differential equation (PDE) for F. Under technical regularity (see, for example, Friedman (1975)), F satisfies (7) for all t if and only if F solves the PDE

$$F_t + F_x\mu + \tfrac{1}{2}\text{trace}[F_{xx}\sigma\sigma^{T}] + RF = 0 \tag{8}$$

with boundary condition $F(x, T) = 1$, for $x \in D$.

We may wish to exploit special structure in order to obtain numerical and econometric tractability. For example, it turns out to be convenient for some applications to take μ, $\sigma\sigma^{T}$ and R to be affine functions on D into their respective ranges. (An affine function is a constant plus a linear function.) In this case, we say that the primitive model $(\mu, \sigma\sigma^{T}, R)$ is *affine*. Likewise, we say that the term structure is itself *affine* if there are C^1 functions $c: [0, \infty) \to \mathbf{R}$ and $C: [0, \infty) \to \mathbf{R}^n$ such that

$$p_{t,s} = e^{c(s-t) + C(s-t)\cdot X(t)}, \quad t \ge 0, \ s \ge t$$

so that yields are affine in the state variables. Conditions for an affine term structure can be deduced from (8) and the required form of solution

$$F(x, t) = e^{c(T-t) + C(T-t)\cdot x} \tag{9}$$

In order for (9) to apply, we can then see from (8) that the coefficient functions c and C must solve an ordinary differential equation of the Ricatti form

$$C_i'(m) = k_i + K_i \cdot C(m) + C(m)^{T} Q_i C(m), \quad i \in \{1, \ldots, n\} \tag{10}$$

$$c'(m) = k_0 + K_0 \cdot C(m) + C(m)^{T} Q_0 C(m) \tag{11}$$

with boundary conditions

$$c(0) = C_i(0) = 0, \quad i \in \{1, \ldots, n\} \tag{12}$$

where $\{k_0, \ldots, k_n\} \subset \mathbf{R}$, $\{K_0, \ldots, K_n\} \subset \mathbf{R}^n$ and $\{Q_0, \ldots, Q_n\} \subset \mathbf{R}^{n \times n}$ are constant coefficients given in terms of the coefficients defining the affine functions μ, $\sigma\sigma^{T}$ and R. The Ricatti equation (10)-(11)-(12) can easily be solved numerically, for example by a Runge-Kutta method.

Indeed, Duffie and Kan (1996) show that, under technical conditions, the basic model $(\mu, \sigma\sigma^{T}, R)$ is affine if and only if the term structure is affine. This extends the same result for $n = 1$ given by Brown and Schaefer (1993) and earlier hinted at by Cox, Ingersoll, and Ross (1985), whose model allows for explicit solutions of the coefficient functions c and C. If R, μ and $\sigma\sigma^{T}$ are affine with time-dependent coefficients designed for calibration to given data, then the coefficients k_i, K_i and Q_i in (10)-(11)-(12) will have time-dependencies, but the ODE itself remains numerically tractable.

In general, one could imagine that the state vector X_t might include various economic indices that would affect interest rates, such as economic activity, monetary supply variables, central bank policy objectives and so on. In order to facilitate the pricing and hedging of fixed-income derivatives, however, it is convenient to assume that one can find a change of variables under which we may view X_t as yield-related variables. Given the solution (c, C) of (10)-(11)-(12), relation (8) provides an affine change of variables under which the state may be taken to be an n-dimensional "yield-factor" process Y, where for some fixed maturities $\tau(1), \ldots, \tau(n)$, we take

$$Y_{ti} = y_{t,\tau(i)} = -\frac{1}{\tau(i)}\{c[\tau(i)] + C[\tau(i)] \cdot X_t\}, \quad i \in \{1,\ldots,n\}$$

We need only ensure that the "basis maturities" $\tau(1), \ldots, \tau(n)$ are chosen so that the matrix K in $\mathbf{R}^{n \times n}$, defined by $K_{ij} = -C_j(\tau(i))/\tau(i)$, is non-singular. In that case we have $Y_t = k + K, X_t$, where $k_i = -c(\tau(i))/\tau(i)$, and the new state dynamics are given by

$$dY_t = \mu^*(Y_t)\,dt + \sigma^*(Y_t)\,dW_t \tag{13}$$

where

$$\mu^*(y) = k\mu(K^{-1}y - k)$$

$$\sigma^*(y) = K\sigma(K^{-1}y - k)$$

for $y \in D^* = \{Kx + k : x \in D\}$.

If σ is constant, X and Y are Gauss–Markov processes of the Ornstein–Uhlenbeck form. For abstract factors, this Gaussian model was developed by Langetieg (1980) and Jamshidian (1990, 1991). A Gauss–Markov yield-factor model was developed by El Karoui and Lacoste (1992) in the forward-rate setting of Heath, Jarrow and Morton (1992) and, in the current state-space setting, was developed as a special case of stochastic volatility models by Duffie and Kan (1996).

A simple example of an affine model that is not Gaussian (that is, for which σ depends on the state) is the multivariate Cox-Ingersoll-Ross model:

$$dX_{it} = (a_i - b_i X_{it})dt + c_i\sqrt{X_{it}}\,dW_{it}, \quad i \in \{1,\ldots,n\} \tag{14}$$

for positive constants a_i, b_i, c_i, with $R(x) = x_1 + \ldots + x_n$. This model was developed by Cox, Ingersoll, and Ross (1985), exploiting results by Feller (1951), and extended by Richard (1978), Heston (1991), Jamshidian (1995), Longstaff and Schwartz (1992), Pearson and Sun (1994) and Chen and Scott (1992*a*). Restrictions apply: for all i, we want

$$a_i > c_i^2/2 \tag{15}$$

As shown by Ikeda and Watanabe (1981), (15) is necessary and sufficient to ensure that X will remain in the obvious open state space $D = \text{int}(\mathbf{R}^n_+)$. Another special case of an affine model is the three-dimensional state-space model studied by Chen (1994). Duffie and Kan (1996) study the general affine case, under which one can, without significant loss of generality after a linear change of variables, take

$$\mu(x) = ax + b$$

$$\sigma_{ij}(x) = \gamma_{ij}\sqrt{\alpha_{ij} + \beta_{ij} \cdot x} \tag{16}$$

for some $\gamma_{ij} \in \mathbf{R}$, $\alpha_{ij} \in \mathbf{R}$, $\beta_{ij} \in \mathbf{R}^n$, $a \in \mathbf{R}^{n \times n}$ and $b \in \mathbf{R}^n$. In this case, the natural state space is

$$D = \{x \in \mathbf{R}^n : \alpha_{ij} + \beta_{ij} \cdot x > 0, \quad i, j \in \{1, \ldots, n\}\} \tag{17}$$

Restrictions on the coefficients $(a, b, \gamma, \alpha, \beta)$, analogous to (15) but more complicated, are shown by Duffie and Kan (1996) to imply the affine form and to guarantee the existence and uniqueness of solutions to (6) in D for (16) and (17).

Aside from the affine case, multivariate term-structure models appear in Brennan and Schwartz (1979), Beaglehole and Tenney (1991), Chan (1992), Constantinides (1992), Duffie, Ma and Yong (1995), El Karoui, Myneni and Viswanathan (1992) and Jamshidian (1993). Most of these non-affine multifactor models do not allow direct observation of the state from the yield curve.

If one does not observe the state vector directly, one can in principle filter the state variable from yield-curve data (see, for example, Chen and Scott (1993) and Kennedy (1995)). There are debates concerning how much this limited observation property detracts from the practical application of the models. It can be said, for example, that we do not observe the yield curve in any case, but merely the prices of coupon bonds, from which one infers statistically (and with noise) the zero-coupon curve by some curve-fitting method such as splines or non-linear least squares. In any case, it seems to be of at least some value to have state variables that can be observed in terms of the yield curve, as in the affine models described above.

Derivative pricing and hedging

A major application of term-structure models is the pricing of derivative securities. Given a Markov term-structure model, as defined in the previous section, the price of a claim (Z, T) is given at any time $t \le T$ by

$$E\left[\exp\left(-\int_t^T R(X_s)\,ds\right) Z \,\middle|\, \mathcal{F}_t\right]$$

If Z is measurable with respect to the yield curve at time T, as are bond options and other "path-independent" derivatives, we may take $Z = g(X_T)$ for some $g: D \to \mathbf{R}$, since the yield curve y_T is itself X_T-measurable. In this case, the Markov property of X implies that we can write the derivative price as

$$F(X_t, t) = E\left[\exp\left(-\int_t^T R(X_s)\,ds\right) g(X_t) \,\middle|\, X_t\right] \tag{18}$$

for some $F: D \times [0, T] \to \mathbf{R}$. Under technical regularity we also know that F is the unique solution in $C^{2,1}(D \times [0, T))$, under technical growth conditions, to the parabolic partial differential equation (8) with the boundary condition

$$F(x, T) = g(x), \quad x \in D \tag{19}$$

One can then solve for the derivative price function F via a numerical solution of the PDE (8)–(19), say by a finite-difference algorithm. (See, for example, Ames (1977).) Fully worked examples are given by Duffie and Kan (1996) for the case $n = 2$. For large n, say more than 3, currently available algorithms and hardware may not be up to the task and Monte Carlo simulation may be applied. (See, for example, Boyle, Broadie and Glasserman (1995) for a survey, or Duffie and Glynn (1996) and Kloeden and Platen (1992).) For the "path-dependent" case, in which Z depends non-trivially on the path $\{X_t: 0 \le t \le T\}$ of the state process, it may also be advisable to resort to Monte Carlo simulation. There are only rare cases, such as Jamshidian's (1991) solution for bond options in the Gaussian setting, for which one can obtain explicit solutions for derivative prices. (See also El Karoui and Rochet (1989).)

The term *hedging* has different meanings in different contexts. For our narrow purposes here, we will take it to mean the construction of a trading strategy involving certain claims that replicates the value of another "target" claim. By virtue of such a replication, one can offset the risk of the target security completely by selling the replicating strategy. In practice, of course, this is unrealistic for it usually assumes both that the underlying valuation model is correct and that the necessary hedging strategy can be executed precisely and without transaction costs. This replication approach to hedging has nevertheless been shown to be useful in applications.

To take a simple case, consider the single-factor model (3) and suppose that the target claim to be hedged is defined by the payoff $Z = g(r_T)$ at time T, for some $g: \mathbf{R} \to \mathbf{R}$. As asserted earlier, the price process V for this claim is, under technical regularity, given by $V_t = F(r_t, t)$, for some function differentiable F solving the PDE (8) with boundary condition (19).

For hedging purposes, consider another claim, similarly defined, and with a market value at time t given by $U_t = \Phi(r_t, t)$, for some $\Phi \in C^{2,1}(\mathbf{R} \times [0, T))$, also satisfying (8). We wish to deduce a predictable process $\{\theta_t: 0 \le t \le T\}$, defining a strategy for trading the hedging security, so that the gains or losses associated with the hedging security offset those associated with the target security. The number of units held at time t in state ω is $\theta(\omega, t)$. Thinking of θ_t for the moment as a fixed position b, and fixing the short rate at time t at some level x, the total market value $F(x_t, t) + b\Phi(x, t)$ of the hedged position has a derivative (or "sensitivity") with respect to the short rate of $F_x(x, t) + b\Phi_x(x, t)$. Since the only source of risk in this single-factor setting is the short rate r, an intuitive choice for θ_t is one that equates this derivative to zero. If we do so state by state, time by time, we have

$$\theta_t = -\frac{F_x(r_t, t)}{\Phi_x(r_t, t)}, \qquad t \in [0, T] \tag{20}$$

assuming that Φ_x is everywhere non-zero. In order to show that this intuitive position is in fact appropriate, we augment the position θ_t in the hedging claim with deposits of J_t at the short rate at time t. We also require technical conditions for θ and J so that $\int \theta_t dU_t$ and $\int J_t r_t dt$ make sense as stochastic integrals. The total market value process Y would then satisfy

$$dY_t = dV_t + \theta_t dU_t + J_t r_t dt \tag{21}$$

From Itô's Lemma,

$$dY_t = \mathcal{D}F(r_t, t)\,dt + F_x(r_t, t)\,dr_t + \theta_t[\mathcal{D}\Phi(r_t, t)\,dt + \Phi_x(r_t, t)\,dr_t] + J_t r_t dt \tag{22}$$

where $\mathcal{D}$ is the infinitesimal generator associated, as usual, with (μ, σ). From (8), assuming zero dividend rates for simplicity, we have $\mathcal{D}F(x, t) = xF(x, t)$ and $\mathcal{D}\Phi(x, t) = x\Phi(x, t)$ for all x and t. Thus, once one applies the specified hedge position $\theta_t = -F_x(r_t, t)/\Phi_x(r_t, t)$, we have

$$dY_t = r_t[F(r_t, t) + \theta_t \Phi(r_t, t) + J_t]\,dt \tag{23}$$

In order for the market value Y of the hedged position to remain constant, we can therefore let

$$J_t = -F(r_t, t) - \theta_t \Phi(r_t, t) \tag{24}$$

The total initial cost of the hedge is then

$$\theta_0 \Phi(r_0, 0) + Z_0 = -F(r_0, 0) \tag{25}$$

as one would expect from the fact that the trading strategy (θ, J) in the hedging asset and short-term deposits merely replicates $-F(r_T, T)$. The restrictiveness of a single-factor model is apparent from its implication, just shown, that essentially any derivative (or bond) can be used to perfectly hedge any other. With a state space of dimension n, one can see that $n + 1$ positions would typically be both necessary and sufficient to achieve hedging, in the above sense.

Jumps

The models in the third and fourth sections imply continuous sample paths for any bond yield. For realism, one may introduce jumps and keep essentially all of the pricing tractability of the Markov diffusion setting, although perfect hedging, as described in the previous section, becomes problematic. For example, consider an extension of the single-factor model (3) for the short rate r with state space $D \subset \mathbf{R}$ satisfying

$$dr_t = \mu(r_t)\,dt + \sigma(r_t)\,dW_t + dU(t, r_t) \tag{26}$$

where U is a pure jump process with jumps at inaccessible stopping times, with jump arrival intensity process $\{\lambda(r_t): t \geq 0\}$, where $\lambda: D \to \mathbf{R}_+$ is a measurable function, and with jump distribution process $\{v(r_t): t \geq 0\}$, where $v: D \to P(\mathbf{R})$ is a measurable function mapping each interest rate level x to a probability measure $v(x)$. For any nonzero jump time τ, the jump $\Delta U_\tau = U_\tau - U_{\tau-}$ has $F_{\tau-}$-conditional distribution $v(r_{\tau-})$. This is a loose description of a jump-diffusion, a class of processes treated by Gihman and Skorohod (1972) and Protter (1990).

In order to characterise the yield curve in terms of the state variable r, we can once again compute the zero-coupon bond price function F defined by $F(r_t, t) = p_{t,T}$. From Itô's lemma for semimartingales, we can deduce under technical regularity the integro-differential equation for F that extends (8), given by

$$F_t + F_x\mu + \tfrac{1}{2}F_{xx}\sigma^2 + xF + \lambda(x)\left(\int_{-\infty}^{\infty} F(x+u)\,v(x, du) - F(x, t)\right) = 0 \tag{27}$$

with boundary condition $F(x, T) = 1$. One can solve (27) numerically by an extension of a finite-difference algorithm for PDEs. Likewise, in order to calculate the price of a claim of the form $(g(r_T), T)$, a finite-difference method can be used to solve (27) with the boundary condition (19).

For computational tractability, one can deduce restrictions on $(\mu, \sigma^2, v, \lambda)$ that imply the affine yield model (9). For example, we can see from (27) that it is sufficient that (μ, σ^2, λ) is affine and v is a constant distribution (that is, $v(x)$ does not depend on x). Special cases have been explored by Das and Foresi (1996). For the case of $\sigma(x) = C\sqrt{x}$, for $x \geq 0$, we would want the jump distribution to support the non-negative real line only, in order to allow for the existence of solutions to (26).

For an affine jump-diffusion model, in this univariate setting or in the obvious multivariate extension, an ordinary differential equation of the form of (10)–(11)–(12) characterises the term structure.

With jumps, the hedging calculations in the preceding section do not apply, and in general it is impossible to perfectly hedge a given claim with fewer positions in other claims than the cardinality of the support of the jump distribution.

Default

In practice, any contingent claim (Z, T) may default. That is, the individual, corporation or institution responsible for payment of the claim Z at T may not do so. One usually ignores default risk for certain government obligations, but default risk for corporations and some sovereign states cannot be ignored if one is to explain the fact that the prices of identical claims against different issuers have different market prices. For example, the yields of corporate bonds of low credit quality are typically higher than those of government bonds of the same maturity.

A defaultable claim is defined by a pair $[(Z, T), (Z', T')]$ of claims. The first claim, (Z, T), of the pair represents the obligation of the issuer to pay Z at T. The second claim of the pair is the actual payment of Z' in the event that the issuer defaults at some time T' before T. A defaultable claim $[(Z, T), (Z', T')]$ thus defines a claim $(\hat{Z}, \hat{T})$, in the usual sense by

$$\hat{Z} = Z1_{T<T'} + Z'1_{T\geq T'}, \quad \hat{T} = \min(T, T')$$

Two basic approaches have been applied to the modelling of defaultable claims. The first approach, which we call "structural," begins with Black and Scholes (1973) and Merton (1974) and is based on a stochastic model of the values of the assets and liabilities of the issuer. In this framework, a contingent claim (Z, T) issued by a corporation will result in actual payment of Z at T in the event that the market value of the corporation's assets remains larger than that of its liabilities through time T, and otherwise will result in payment of some claim (Z', T'). Typically, with this structural approach, T' is the first time at which the market value of assets is exceeded by the market value of liabilities. Indeed, the Black-Scholes option pricing formula was actually derived, in part, to value the debt of a corporation in this manner. Nielsen and Saá-Requejo (1992) is a recent example of the literature extending this structural approach.

The second approach starts from a "reduced-form" modelling in which the default time T' is a given stopping time that may or may not be directly tied to the solvency of the issuer of the claim (Z, T) in question. This approach was originated by Pye (1974) (in a deterministic setting for yields) and has been developed by Artzner and Delbaen (1992), Duffie and Huang (1996), Duffie, Schroder and Skiadas (1994), Duffie and Singleton (1994), Jarrow and Turnbull (1995), Jarrow, Lando and Turnbull (1993), Lando (1993, 1994), Madan and Unal (1992), and others. The stopping time is usually assumed to have a "default hazard rate" process, a progressively measurable integrable process h defined by the property that $1_{t>T'} = \Gamma_t$, where

$$d\Gamma_t = 1_{t \le T'} h_t dt + dM_t \tag{29}$$

where M is a Q-martingale. In particular, T' is inaccessible, as opposed to the usual case of the structural models described above, for which T' is the accessible stopping time defined as the first time at which the market value of the assets of the issuer, modelled as a diffusion process, is exceeded by the market value of the liabilities of the issuer, also modelled as a diffusion.

In the reduced-form approach, various models have been proposed for the default recovery value Z'. In some cases the recovery value is a fraction of the market value of a default-free version of the same claim - that is, $Z' = Z_f(T')$, where

$$Z_f(t) = f(t) E\left[\exp\left(-\int_t^T r_s ds\right) Z \,\middle|\, F_t\right] \tag{30}$$

where f is a bounded progressively measurable integrable process. (For practical purposes, we may wish to assume that $0 \le f(t) \le 1$ for all t.)

In other reduced-form models, such as Duffie and Singleton (1994), default generates a given fractional loss of value; that is, the price process S of the defaultable claim in question has the property that

$$Z' = S(T') = \varphi(T')\, S(T'-) \tag{31}$$

where φ is a bounded progressively measurable fractional recovery process. (Again, we may wish to assume that $0 \le \varphi(t) \le 1$ for all t.) One can combine the two approaches, as in Duffie and Singleton (1994) and Duffie, Schroder and Skiadas (1994), by allowing the fractional recovery process φ to be determined endogenously, for example by taking $\varphi(\omega, t) = \Phi[\omega, t, S(\omega, t-)]$, for some well-behaved $\Phi: \Omega \times [0, T] \times \mathbf{R} \to \mathbf{R}$. In order to recover (30) as a special case, we would have

$$\Phi(\omega, t, v) = \frac{Z_f(\omega, t)}{v}, \quad v \neq 0 \tag{32}$$

One may also allow the hazard-rate process h to be determined in terms of the price process S itself. That is, we may have $h(\omega, t) = H[\omega, t, S(\omega, t-)]$, where H is defined as was Φ. Ultimately, of course, the price process S of the defaultable claim must satisfy the pricing relationship (1) in terms of the effective claim $(\hat{Z}, \hat{T})$. Allowing h and φ to be determined endogenously through such functions Φ and H, respectively, presents no essential difficulties. Under regularity conditions on (r, Z, T, H, Φ) found in Duffie, Schroder and Skiadas (1994), a price process S for a given defaultable claim is uniquely well defined as the solution of a recursive stochastic integral equation.

Duffie and Huang (1996) provide an extension of the notion of a defaultable claim in which either of two counterparties to the same contract may default. A natural example is a swap or forward contract, for which the underlying claim (Z, T) calls for both positive and negative outcomes of Z. For this case, one allows the default characteristics h and φ to depend on the price process S through functions H and Φ, as above. Indeed, this is essential in order to capture the impact on pricing of differences in credit quality between the two counterparties.

If we take the simple case in which h and φ are given processes, the defaultable valuation model can be simplified dramatically. Duffie and Singleton (1994) show in this case the simple pricing relationship

$$S_t = E\left[\exp\left(-\int_t^T \rho_s \, ds\right) Z \,\middle|\, F_t\right], \quad t < T' \tag{33}$$

where $\rho_t = r_t + h_t(1 - \varphi_t)$. That is, prior to default, we may treat the price of a defaultable claim $[(Z, T), (Z', T')]$ with default characteristics (h, φ) as identical to that of a default-free claim to (Z, T), with the sole exception that the default-free short interest rate process r is replaced in (1) with a default-adjusted short rate process ρ that captures the pricing effect of the probability distribution of the default time T' as well as the effect of the recovered value $Z' = Z_\varphi$ at default.

In applications, one can take advantage of a state-space representation for (r, ρ). For example, Duffie and Singleton (1994) consider cases in which $r_t = a \cdot X_t$ and $\rho_t = A \cdot X_t$, for a Markov process X in $\mathbf{R}^n$ satisfying an SDE of the form (6), and for a and A in $\mathbf{R}^n$. In order to guarantee that $\rho \geq r$, one can impose restrictions under which X is non-negative and take $A \geq a$.

Heath–Jarrow–Morton models

In modelling the term structure, we have so far taken as the primitive a model of the short rate process r of the form $r_t = R(X_t, t)$, where (under some equivalent martingale measure) X solves a given stochastic differential equation. In the one-factor case one usually takes $r_t = X_t$. This approach has the advantage of a finite-dimensional "state space". For example, with this state-space approach one can compute certain derivative prices or hedges by solving PDEs.

An alternative approach is to take the entire yield curve as a state variable. This can be done by exploiting the model of forward rates introduced by Heath, Jarrow and Morton (1992). This section is a summary of the basic elements of the Heath–Jarrow–Morton (HJM) model. The next section moves the HJM model into a state-space setting.

The forward price at time t of a zero-coupon bond for delivery at time $\tau \geq t$ with maturity at time $s \geq \tau$ is given by $p_{t,s}/p_{t,\tau}$, the ratio of zero-coupon bond prices at maturity and delivery, respectively. (For our purposes, one may take this as a definition. In fact, this relationship is a consequence of assuming the absence of arbitrage and of a more basic definition of a forward contract.) The associated *forward rate* is defined by

$$\Phi_{t,\tau,s} \equiv \frac{\log(p_{t,\tau}) - \log(p_{t,s})}{s - \tau} \tag{34}$$

which can be viewed as the continuously compounding yield of the bond bought forward. The *instantaneous forward rate*, when it exists, is defined for each time t and forward delivery date $\tau \geq t$ by

$$f(t, \tau) = \lim_{s \downarrow \tau} \Phi_{t,\tau,s} \tag{35}$$

Thus, the instantaneous forward rate process f exists if and only if, for all t, the mapping $s \mapsto p_{t,s}$ is differentiable.

A convenient fact is that the price at time t of a zero-coupon bond maturing at s can be computed as

$$p_{t,s} = \exp\left(-\int_t^s f(t, u)\, du\right) \tag{36}$$

so the term structure can be recovered from the instantaneous forward rates, and *vice versa*.

Given a stochastic model f of forward rates, we will assume that $r_t = f(t, t)$ defines the short rate process r. This means that we will treat r_t as the limit of bond yields as maturity goes to zero. Justification of this assumption can be given under technical conditions. See, for example, Carverhill (1994).

The *HJM model of forward rates*, for each fixed maturity s, is given by

$$f(t, s) = f(0, s) + \int_0^t \mu(u, s)\, du + \int_0^t \sigma(u, s)\, dW_u, \quad t \leq s \tag{37}$$

where $\{\mu(t, s): 0 \leq t \leq s\}$ and $\{\sigma(t, s): 0 \leq t \leq s\}$ are adapted processes valued in $\mathbf{R}$ and $\mathbf{R}^n$, respectively, such that (37) is well defined. We may think of μ and σ as measurable functions on $\mathcal{T} \times \Omega$, where $\mathcal{T} = \{(t, s) \in \mathbf{R}_+^2 : t \leq s\}$.

It turns out that there is an important consistency relationship between μ and σ implied by (1). Specifically, one can show under purely technical conditions that if (1) is to apply to *every* claim of the form $(1, T)$ – that is, for all bond prices – then it must be the case that

$$\mu(t, s) = \sigma(t, s) \int_t^s \sigma(t, u)^T\, du \tag{38}$$

This basic "drift restriction" is found by an application of Fubini's theorem for stochastic integrals (see Carverhill (1994) for details).

Given (38), we can use the definition $r_t = f(t, t)$ of the short rate to obtain

$$r_t = f(0, t) + \int_0^t \sigma(\upsilon, t) \int_\upsilon^t \sigma(\upsilon, u)^T\, du\, d\upsilon + \int_0^t \sigma(\upsilon, t)\, d\hat{B}_\upsilon \tag{39}$$

Knowledge of the forward-rate "volatility" process σ and the initial forward-rate curve $\{f(0, s), s \geq 0\}$ is therefore enough for the computation of all prices.

From (39), one can evaluate the price any claim from the basic formula (1). Aside from Gaussian or log-Gaussian special cases – for example those described by Jamshidian (1989) and by Miltersen, Sandmann and Sondermann (1994) – most valuation work in the HJM setting is done numerically.

State-space HJM models

Except for rather restrictive special cases (as in Cheyette (1992), El Karoui and Lacoste (1992), Ritchken and Sankarasubramanian (1993)), there is no finite-dimensional state space for the HJM model, so PDE-based (finite-difference) numerical computational methods cannot be used. Instead, one can build an analogous model in a discrete-time, discrete-state setting and compute prices from "first principles". For the discrete model, the expectation analogous to (1) is obtained by constructing all sample paths for r from the discretisation of (39) and by computing the probability (under Q) of each.

For a general state-space representation of HJM models one can take the forward rate curve itself as the state variable. For example, Musiela (1994) has taken the direct approach of allowing the state space D to be the set of C^1 functions on $[0, \infty)$ into $\mathbf{R}$.

The current state $X(t)$ is the function mapping the maturity m to the current forward rate $f(t, t + m)$ of that maturity. With the goal of viewing X as a Markov process solving a stochastic partial differential equation, Musiela has shown that one can use (37) and (38) to derive the relationship

$$dX_t(m) = \frac{\partial}{\partial m}\left(X_t(m) + \frac{1}{2}\left\| \int_0^m \tau(t,u)\,du \right\|^2\right) dt + \tau(t,m)\,dW_t \tag{40}$$

where $\tau(t, m) = \sigma(t, t + m)$. Then, taking $\tau(t, m) = \Psi(X_t, m)$, for some function $\Psi: D \times [0, \infty) \to \mathbf{R}^n$, we can view (40) as a stochastic PDE, in the sense of Da Prato and Zabczyk (1992) or Walsh (1984). General conditions on Ψ for existence and uniqueness of Markovian solutions to (4) are yet to be deduced. Musiela (1994) and Musiela and Sondermann (1994) have illustrated some special cases, for example in which X is a Gaussian process.

It has sometimes been said that with an HJM model one can avoid the compromise between theory and practice that arises with calibration since essentially any initial forward rate curve is consistent with a given HJM model. In fact, the traditional HJM model admits movements in the yield curve generated only by a finite-dimensional Brownian motion and therefore limits the sorts of movements of the yield curve that can be considered without calibration. Recent work by Kennedy (1994, 1995), however, extends the HJM model to allow for an infinite-dimensional Brownian motion (in the framework of stochastic flows). That is, Kennedy (1994, 1995) has extended the basic HJM model (37) to allow the $\mathbf{R}^n$-valued standard Brownian motion W to be replaced by a Brownian sheet for the case of deterministic volatility process σ. At this point, it seems logical and natural also to view the stochastic PDE (39) as one driven by an infinite-dimensional Brownian motion. There are as yet no results in this vein, however, aside from the special Gaussian cases examined by Kennedy. Moreover, there is a need for special cases that are amenable to statistical estimation. Current estimation methods have been brought to bear only on finite-dimensional Markov special cases. See, for example, Ait-Sahalia (1992), Chen and Scott (1992*b*, 1993), Duffie and Singleton (1995), Pearson and Sun (1994) and Gibbons and Ramaswamy (1993).

Foreign term-structure models

Suppose, as a typical application involving the valuation of term-structure securities in an international setting, that one wishes to price a foreign bond option - say an option granting its owner the right, but not the obligation, to buy a given foreign bond at some time τ before its maturity at a pre-agreed price K. The underlying zero-coupon bond pays one unit of foreign currency at some maturity date T and has a domestic (say, "dollar") price process of S. The bond option therefore defines a claim $[(S_\tau - K)^+, \tau]$, in dollars. Our job is to obtain the bond option price process, say C.

The foreign currency price process, say U, is assumed to satisfy

$$dU_t = \alpha_t U_t\,dt + U_t \beta_t\,dW_t \tag{41}$$

where α is a real-valued progressively measurable process, and β, an $\mathbf{R}^n$-valued progressively measurable process, are both bounded.

Suppose that foreign interest rates are given by a forward-rate process F, as in the Heath-Jarrow-Morton setting. That is, the price of the given zero-coupon foreign bond at time t, in units of foreign currency, is $\exp(\int_t^T -F(t, u)\,du)$. It follows that the bond price process, in dollars, is given by

$$S_t = U_t \exp\left(\int_t^T -F(t,u)\,du\right)$$

and that the price of the bond option, in dollars, is

$$C_t = E\left[\exp\left(\int_t^\tau -r_u du\right)(S_\tau - K)^+ \middle| F_t\right] \tag{42}$$

where r is the dollar short rate process, which may be specified in terms of the HJM model (37). It is assumed that the foreign forward rates are also given by an HJM model. That is, for each t and $s \geq t$:

$$F(t, s) = F(0, s) + \int_0^t a(u, s)\,du + \int_0^t b(u, s)\,dW_u$$

where the s-dependent drift process $a(\cdot, s): \Omega \times [0, T] \to \mathbf{R}$ and the s-dependent diffusion process $b(\cdot, s): \Omega \times [0, T] \to \mathbf{R}^n$ are assumed to satisfy sufficient regularity conditions for (42) to apply to foreign bonds of any maturity. Since the probability measure Q was chosen so that (1) applies when all prices and claims are denominated in *dollars*, it is *not* generally true that we have the drift restriction

$$a(t, s) = b(t, s) \cdot \int_t^s b(u, s)\,du$$

Instead, by methods analogous to those used to derive the drift restriction (38) on the dollar forward rate curve, one can show that the drift restriction on the foreign forward rate process is given by

$$a(t, s) = b(t, s) \cdot \left(\int_t^s b(u, s)\,du - \beta_t\right) \tag{43}$$

The basic pricing relationship (1) can now be applied to value the foreign bond option. Explicit solutions are known for deterministic σ, b and β. For applications and a related formulation, see Amin and Bodurtha (1995).

Where next?

A great deal of work remains to be done, particularly on the topic of statistical estimation of term-structure models. In a multi-dimensional state-space setting, econometric models of the term structure have stayed within a relatively narrow framework. Recent work by Pearson and Sun (1994), Chen and Scott (1992*b*, 1993) and Duffie and Singleton (1995) stays extremely close to the multi-factor Cox–Ingersoll–Ross model (14)–(15). In a univariate setting, Ait-Sahalia (1992) has allowed for non-parametric σ for the special case of (43). For the constant-volatility Gauss–Markov (affine) case, Frachot, Janci and Lacoste (1992), together with Frachot and Lesne (1993), have done some empirical work in the HJM setting. Much remains to be done in integrating the use of statistical models within the practical applications of term-structure models mentioned in the introduction.

Judging from the literature on term-structure modelling, much also remains to be done in the development and application of numerical methods, such as finite-difference or finite-element algorithms for solving multi-dimensional Cauchy problems such as (19)–(21), especially for the cases that arise in term-structure models.

1 *See, for example, references cited in Duffie (1996).*

2 *By offering extensions with time-varying coefficients, Ho and Lee (1986) and Hull and White (1990) have popularised the constant coefficients models of Merton (1973) and Vasicek (1977), respectively.*

Bibliography

Ait Sahalia, Y., 1992, "Nonparametric Pricing of Interest Rate Derivative Securities", *Econometrica* 64, pp. 527–560.

Ames, W., 1977, *Numerical Methods For Partial Differential Equations, 2nd edition,* New York: Academic Press.

Amin K., and J. Bodurtha, 1995, "Discrete-Time Valuation of American Options with Stochastic Interest Rates", *Review of Financial Studies* 8, pp. 193–234.

Artzner P., and F. Delbaen, 1992, "Credit Risk and Prepayment Option", *ASTIN Bulletin* 22, pp. 81–96.

Beaglehole D., and M. Tenney, 1991, "General Solutions of Some Interest Rate Contingent Claim Pricing Equations", *Journal of Fixed Income* 1, pp. 69–83.

Black, F., E. Derman and W. Toy, 1990, "A One-Factor Model of Interest Rates and Its Application to Treasury Bond Options", *Financial Analysts Journal,* pp. 33–39; reprinted as Chapter 10 of the present volume.

Black, F., and P. Karasinski, 1992, "Bonds and Option Pricing when Short Rates are Lognormal", *Financial Analysts Journal,* July–August 1991, pp. 52–59; reprinted as Chapter 11 of the present volume.

Black, F., and M. Scholes, 1973, "The Pricing of Options and Corporate Liabilities", *Journal of Political Economy* 81, pp. 637–654; reprinted as Chapter 1 of the present volume.

Boyle, P., M. Broadie and P. Glasserman, 1995, "Monte Carlo Methods for Security Pricing", forthcoming: *The Journal of Economic Dynamics and Control*.

Brennan M., and E. Schwartz, 1979, "A Continuous Time Approach to the Pricing of Bonds", *Journal of Banking and Finance* 3, pp. 133–155; reprinted as Chapter 5 of the present volume..

Brown R., and S. Schaefer, 1993, "Interest Rate Volatility and the Shape of the Term Structure", *Philosophical Transactions of the Royal Society: Physical Sciences and Engineering* 347, pp. 449–598.

Carverhill, A., 1994, "A Simplified Exposition of the Heath, Jarrow, and Morton Model", Department of Finance, Hong Kong University of Science and Technology.

Chan, K.-C., G. Karolyi, F. Longstaff and A. Sanders, 1992, "An Empirical Comparison of Alternative Models of the Short-Term Interest Rate", *Journal of Finance* 47, pp. 1209–1227.

Chan, Y.-K., 1992, "Term Structure as a Second Order Dynamical System and Pricing of Derivative Securities", Bear Stearns and Company.

Chen, L., 1994, "Stochastic Mean and Stochastic Volatility: A Three-Factor Model of the Term Structure of Interest Rates and its Application to the Pricing of Interest Rate Derivatives: Part I", School of Business, Harvard University.

Chen R.-R., and L. Scott, 1992*a*, "Pricing Interest Rate Options in a Two-Factor Cox-Ingersoll-Ross Model of the Term Structure", *Review of Financial Studies* 5, pp. 613–636.

Chen R.-R., and L. Scott, 1992*b*, "Maximum Likelihood Estimation for a Multi-Factor Equilibrium Model of the Term Structure of Interest Rates", Working Paper, Rutgers University and University of Georgia.

Chen R.-R., and L. Scott, 1993, "Multi-Factor Cox-Ingersoll-Ross Models of the Term Structure: Estimates and Tests from a State-Space Model Using a Kalman Filter", Working Paper, Rutgers University and University of Georgia.

Cheyette, O., 1992, "Markov Representation of the Heath-Jarrow-Morton Model", Capital Management Sciences.

Constantinides, G., 1992, "A Theory of the Nominal Structure of Interest Rates", *Review of Financial Studies* 5, pp. 531–552.

Constantinides, G., and J. Ingersoll, 1984, "Optimal Bond Trading with Personal Taxes", *Journal of Financial Economics* 13, pp. 299–335.

Cox, J., J. Ingersoll, and S. Ross, 1985, "A Theory of the Term Structure of Interest Rates", *Econometrica* 53, pp. 385–408; reprinted as Chapter 6 of the present volume.

Da Prato G., and J. Zabczyk, 1992, "Stochastic Equations in Infinite Dimensions", Cambridge University Press.

Dai Q., and K. Singleton, 1996, "Interpreting Term Structure Dynamics within a Linear Multi-Factor Model of Bond Yields", Research Paper, Graduate School of Business, Stanford University.

Das S., and S. Foresi, 1996, "Exact Solutions for Bond and Option Prices with Systematic Jump Risk", *Review of Derivatives Research* 1, pp. 7–24.

Dothan, M., 1978, "On the Term Structure of Interest Rates", *Journal of Financial Economics* 7, pp. 229–264.

Duffie, D., 1996, *Dynamic Asset Pricing Theory, Second Edition*, Princeton University Press.

Duffie, D., and P. Glynn, 1995, "Efficient Monte-Carlo Estimation of Security Prices", *Annals of Applied Probability* 5, pp. 897–905.

Duffie, D., and M. Huang, 1996, "Swap Rates and Credit Quality", *Journal of Finance* 51, pp. 921–949.

Duffie, D., and R. Kan, 1996, "A Yield-Factor Model of Interest Rates", *Mathematical Finance* 6, pp. 379–406.

Duffie, D., J. Ma and J. Yong, 1995, "Black's Console Rate Conjecture", *Annals of Applied Probability* 5, pp. 356–382.

Duffie, D., M. Schroder and C. Skiadas, 1994, "Recursive Valuation of Defaultable Securities and the Timing of Resolution of Uncertainty", Graduate School of Business, Stanford University, Stanford California; forthcoming: *Annals of Applied Probability*.

Duffie, D., and K. Singleton, 1994, "Modeling Term Structures of Defaultable Bonds", Graduate School of Business, Stanford University, Stanford, California.

Duffie, D., and K. Singleton, 1995, "An Econometric Model of the Term Structure of Interest Rate Swap Yields", Graduate School of Business, Stanford University, Stanford, California; forthcoming: *Journal of Finance*.

El Karoui, N., and V. Lacoste, 1992, "Multifactor Models of the Term Structure of Interest Rates", Working Paper, June, University of Paris VI.

El Karoui, N., R. Myneni and R. Viswanathan, 1992, "Arbitrage Pricing and Hedging of Interest Rate Claims with State Variables: I Theory", Working Paper, January, University of Paris VI.

El Karoui, N., and J.-C. Rochet, 1989, "A Pricing Formula for Options on Coupon Bonds", Working Paper, October, University of Paris VI.

Feller, W., 1951, "Two Singular Diffusion Problems", *Annals of Mathematics* 54, pp. 173–182.

Frachot, A., D. Janci and V. Lacoste, 1992, "Factor Analysis of the Term Structure: A Probabilistic Approach", Banque de France.

Frachot, A., and J.-P. Lesne, 1993, "Econometrics of Linear Factor Models of Interest Rates", Banque de France.

Friedman, A., 1975, *Stochastic Differential Equations and Applications, Volume 1*, New York: Academic Press.

Gibbons M., and K. Ramaswamy, 1993, "A Test of the Cox, Ingersoll and Ross Model of the Term Structure", *Review of Financial Studies* 6, pp. 619–658.

Gihman I., and A. Skorohod, 1972, *Stochastic Differential Equations*, Berlin: Springer-Verlag.

Harrison M., and D. Kreps, 1979, "Martingales and Arbitrage in Multiperiod Security Markets", *Journal of Economic Theory* 20, pp. 381–408.

Heath, D., R. Jarrow and A. Morton, 1992, "Bond Pricing and The Term Structure of Interest Rates: A New Methodology for Contingent Claims Valuation", *Econometrica* 60, pp. 77–105; reprinted as Chapter 14 of the present volume.

Heston, S., 1991, "Testing Continuous-Time Models of the Term Structure of Interest Rates", School of Organization and Management, Yale University.

Ho T., and S. Lee, 1986, "Term Structure Movements and Pricing Interest Rate Contingent Claims", *Journal of Finance* 41, pp. 1011–1029; reprinted as Chapter 13 of the present volume.

Huang, C.-F., 1987, "An Intertemporal General Equilibrium Asset Pricing Model: The Case of Diffusion Information", *Econometrica* 55, pp. 117–142.

Hull J., and A. White, 1990, "Pricing Interest Rate Derivative Securities", *Review of Financial Studies* 3, pp. 573–592; reprinted as Chapter 9 of the present volume.

Ikeda N., and S. Watanabe, 1981, *Stochastic Differential Equations and Diffusion Processes*, Amsterdam: North-Holland.

Jamshidian, F., 1990, "The Preference-Free Determination of Bond and Option Prices From the Spot Interest Rate", *Advances in Futures and Options Research* 4, pp. 51–67.

Jamshidian, F., 1991, "Bond and Option Evaluation in the Gaussian Interest Rate Model and Implementation", *Research in Finance* 9, pp. 131–170; reprinted as Chapter 12 of the present volume.

Jamshidian, F., 1993, "Bond, Futures, and Option Evaluation in the Quadratic Interest Rate Model", mimeo, Fuji Bank, London.

Jamshidian, F., 1995, "A Simple Class of Square-Root Interest-Rate Models", *Applied Mathematical Finance* 2, pp. 61–72.

Jarrow, R., D. Lando and S. Turnbull, 1993, "A Markov Model for the Term Structure of Credit Risk Spreads", Johnson School of Management, Cornell University; forthcoming: *Review of Financial Studies*.

Jarrow, R., and S. Turnbull, 1995, "Pricing Options on Financial Securities Subject to Default Risk", *Journal of Finance* 50, pp. 53–86.

Jarrow, R., and S. Turnbull, 1996, *Derivative Securities*, Cincinnati: Southwestern.

Karatzas I., and S. Shreve, 1988, *Brownian Motion and Stochastic Calculus*, Springer-Verlag.

Kennedy, D. P., 1994, "The Term Structure of Interest Rates as a Gaussian Random Field", *Mathematical Finance* 4, pp. 247–258.

Kennedy, D. P., 1995, "Characterizing and Filtering Gaussian Models of the Term Structure of Interest Rates", Statistical Laboratory, Cambridge University.

Kloeden P., and E. Platen, 1992, *Numerical Solution of Stochastic Differential Equations*, Springer-Verlag.

Lando, D., 1993, "A Continuous Time Markov Model of The Term Structure of Credit Spreads", Copenhagen Institute of Statistics.

Lando, D., 1994, "On Cox Processes and Credit Risky Bonds", Copenhagen Institute of Statistics.

Langetieg, T., 1980, "A Multivariate Model of the Term Structure of Interest Rates", *Journal of Finance* 35, pp. 71–97.

Litterman R., and J. Scheinkman, 1988, "Common Factors affecting Bond Returns", Research Paper, Goldman Sachs Financial Strategies Group.

Longstaff F., and E. Schwartz, 1992, "Interest Rate Volatility and the Term Structure: A Two-Factor General Equilibrium Model", *Journal of Finance* 47, pp. 1259–1282.

Madan D., and H. Unal, 1992, "Pricing the Risks of Default", University of Maryland, Dept. of Finance, working paper.

Merton, R., 1973, "Theory of Rational Option Pricing", *Bell Journal of Economics and Management Science* 4, pp. 141–183.

Merton, R., 1974, "On the Pricing of Corporate Debt: The Risk Structure of Interest Rates", *Journal of Finance* 29, pp. 449–470.

Miltersen, K., K. Sandmann and D. Sondermann, 1994, "Closed Form Solutions for Term Structure Derivatives with Log-Normal Interest Rates", Department of Management, Odense University; forthcoming: *Journal of Finance*.

Musiela, M., 1994, "Stochastic PDEs and Term Structure Models", School of Mathematics, University of New South Wales.

Musiela, M., and D. Sondermann, 1994, Different Dynamical Specifications of the Term Structure of Interest Rates and their Implications", School of Mathematics, University of New South Wales.

Nielsen L. T., and J. Saá-Requejo, 1992. "Exchange Rate and Term Structure Dynamics and the Pricing of Derivative Securities", INSEAD working paper.

Pearson N., and T.-S. Sun, 1994, "An Empirical Examination of the Cox, Ingersoll, and Ross Model of the Term Structure of Interest Rates Using the Method of Maximum Likelihood", *Journal of Finance* 54, pp. 929–959.

Protter, P., 1990, *Stochastic Integration and Differential Equations*, New York: Springer-Verlag.

Pye, G., 1966, "A Markov Model of the Term Structure", *Quarterly Journal of Economics* 81, pp. 61–72.

Pye, G., 1974, "Gauging the Default Premium", *Financial Analysts Journal*, January–February, pp. 49–52.

Richard, S., 1978, "An Arbitrage Model of the Term Structure of Interest Rates", *Journal of Financial Economics* 6, pp. 33-57.

Ritchken P., and L. Sankarasubramanian, 1993, "On Finite State Markovian Representations of the Term Structure", Department of Finance, University of Southern California.

Stambaugh, R., 1988, "The Information in Forward Rates: Implications for Models of the Term Structure", *Journal of Financial Economics* 21, pp. 41-70.

Vasicek, O., 1977, "An Equilibrium Characterization of the Term Structure", *Journal of Financial Economics* 5, pp. 177-188; reprinted as Chapter 4 of the present volume.

Walsh, J., 1984, "An Introduction to Stochastic Partial Differential Equations" P. Hennequin, Ecole d'été de Probabilité de Saint Flour XIV, *Lecture Notes in Mathematics*, Number 1180, pp. 265-439, New York: Springer-Verlag.

18

Changes of Numeraire, Changes of Probability Measure and Option Pricing*

Hélyette Geman, Nicole El Karoui and Jean-Charles Rochet
Université Paris Dauphine and ESSEC; Université Paris VI; Université Toulouse I

The use of the risk-neutral probability measure has proved to be very powerful for computing the prices of contingent claims in the context of complete markets (or, more generally, the prices of attainable securities when the assumption of complete markets is relaxed). However, the risk-neutral probability measure does not allow contingent claims to be priced in a framework of stochastic interest rates. We show here that many other probability measures can be defined in the same way to solve different asset-pricing problems, in particular option pricing. Moreover, these probability measure changes have the merit of being associated with numeraire changes; this feature, besides providing a financial interpretation, permits an efficient selection of the numeraire appropriate for the valuation of a given option and also permits exhibition of the hedging portfolio (which is as important as the valuation itself).

The key theorem of general numeraire change is proved and is illustrated by many examples, among which are the extension to a stochastic interest rates framework of the Margrabe formula, Geske formula, etc.

One of the most popular technical tools for computing asset prices is the so-called "risk-adjusted probability measure". Elaborating on an initial idea of Arrow, Ross (1978) and Harrison and Kreps (1979) have shown that the absence of arbitrage opportunities implies the existence of a probability measure, Q, such that the current price of any basic security is equal to the Q-expectation of its discounted future payments. In particular, between two payment dates, the discounted price of any security is a Q-martingale. When markets are complete, ie, when enough non-redundant securities are being traded, Q is unique.

By using a very simple technical argument (Theorem 1 in the second section) we prove that many other probability measures can be defined in a similar way, which reveal themselves to be equally useful in various kinds of option pricing problems and indispensable for the incorporation of stochastic interest rates. More specifically, if $X(t)$

**This paper was first published in the* Journal of Applied Probability, *32 (1995). It is reprinted with the permission of Applied Probability Trust 1995. Helpful comments from Robert Geske on an earlier version of this paper are gratefully acknowledged. All remaining errors are ours.*

is the price process of a non-dividend-paying security (ie, if the dividend is continuously reinvested), our main theorem states the existence of a probability measure Q_x such that the price of any security S relative to the numeraire X is a Q_x-martingale. A very general numeraire change formula (from reference X to reference Y) is then provided and different applications to exchange options and options on options in a stochastic interest rates environment, options on bonds, etc., illustrate the efficiency of the right choice of numeraire. Some of the results in the paper may be found more or less explicitly in our previous research. Our goal is to emphasise the generality and the efficiency of the numeraire change methodology.

The model and the crucial theorem

We consider a stochastic intertemporal economy, where uncertainty is represented by a probability space (Ω, F, P). The only role of the probability P is in fact to define the negligible sets. Most of our applications will be taken in a continuous-time framework, within a bounded time interval $[0, T]$, but our basic argument is also valid for a discrete-time economy.

We will not completely specify the underlying assumptions on the economy. The flow of information accruing to all the agents in the economy is represented by a filtration $(F_t)t \in [0, T]$, satisfying "the usual hypothesis", ie, the filtration $(F_t)_{0 \leq t \leq \infty}$ is right-continuous and F_0 contains all the P-null sets of F.

In the following, the word "asset" represents a general financial instrument. We distinguish a first class of assets, so-called basic securities, which are traded on the markets and are the components of the portfolios defined below. The other class of assets that will be considered is the class of derivative securities, also called contingent claims, for which the key issues are the valuation and hedging. All asset price processes are continuous F_t-semi-martingales. The prices $S_1(t), \ldots, S_n(t)$ of the basic securities are almost surely strictly positive for all t; more generally, unless otherwise specified, the price of any asset is almost surely positive.

The fundamental concept in the pricing or hedging of contingent claims is the self-financing replicating portfolio, and these self-financing portfolios therefore deserve particular attention (buy and hold portfolios are the simplest example of self-financing portfolios since there is no trade). More generally, these portfolios are meant to track the target changes over time with no addition of money.

The financial value V(t) of a portfolio which includes the quantities $w_1(t), \ldots, w_n(t)$ of the assets 1, 2, ..., n is given by

$$V(t) = \sum_{k=1}^{n} w_k(t) S_k(t) \quad \text{and} \quad V(t) \geqq 0 \quad \text{for all } t \tag{1}$$

where the processes $(w_1(t))_{t \geq 0}, \ldots, (w_n(t))_{t \geq 0}$ are adapted, ie, the quantities $w_1(t), \ldots, w_n(t)$ are chosen according to the information available at time t. The vector process $(w_1(t)), \ldots, (w_n(t))_{t \geq 0}$ is called the portfolio strategy.

DEFINITION 1: The portfolio is called self-financing if the stochastic integral $\int_0^T \sum_{k=1}^n w_k(t)\, dS_k(t)$ exists and

$$dV(t) = \sum_{k=1}^{n} w_k(t) dS_k(t) \tag{2}$$

REMARK: To understand the intuition behind Equation (2), let us take the example of a "simple" strategy, ie, a strategy that is only rebalanced at fixed dates $0 = t_0 < t_1 < \ldots < t_n$ and which we suppose to be left-continuous. The self-financing equation can then be written as

$$V(t_j) - V(t_{j-1}) = \sum_{k=1}^{n} w_k(t_{j-1}^{+})[S_k(t_j) - S_k(t_{j-1})]$$

By definition,

$$V(t_j) = \sum_{k=1}^{n} w_k(t_j) S_k(t_j)$$

The self-financing condition is $V(t_j) = V(t_j^+)$ for all j, ie,

$$\sum_{k=1}^{n} w_k(t_j) S_k(t_j) = \sum_{k=1}^{n} w_k(t_j^+) S_k(t_j) \tag{3}$$

Using (3) at time t_{j-1} and remembering that $w_k(t_j) = w_k(t_{j-1}^+)$, the self-financing condition can also be written as

$$V(t_j) - V(t_{j-1}) = \int_{[t_{j-1}, t_j]} \sum_{k=1}^{n} w_k(u) dS_k(u)$$

More generally, the change of the portfolio value between any dates $t < t'$ is

$$V(t') - V(t) = \int_t^{t'} \sum_{k=1}^{n} w_k(u) dS_k(u)$$

For non-elementary strategies, this will be the definition of self-financing strategies. We have not emphasised so far the fact that there was necessarily an implicit numeraire behind the prices $S_1, S_2, \ldots, S_n$; it is the numeraire relevant for domestic transactions at time t and obviously plays a particular role. Our objective is to show that other quantities may be chosen as numeraires and that, for a given problem, there is a "best" numeraire.

DEFINITION 2: A numeraire is a price process $X(t)$ almost surely strictly positive for each $t \in [0, T)$.

PROPOSITION 1: Self-financing portfolios remain self-financing after a numeraire change.

PROOF: This property is straightforward from a financial viewpoint. Mathematically, it is also clear that Equation (3) still holds after a numeraire change. Let X be a new numeraire. From Itô's lemma, we derive

$$d\left(\frac{S_k(t)}{X(t)}\right) = S_k(t) d\left(\frac{1}{X(t)}\right) + \frac{1}{X(t)} dS_k(t) + d\left\langle S_k, \frac{1}{X}\right\rangle_t$$

where $d\langle S_k, 1/X\rangle$ denotes the instantaneous covariance between the semi-martingales S_k and $1/X$. In the same manner

$$d\left(\frac{V(t)}{X(t)}\right) = V(t) d\left(\frac{1}{X(t)}\right) + \frac{1}{X(t)} dV(t) + d\left\langle V, \frac{1}{X}\right\rangle_t$$

The self-financing condition

$$dV(t) = \sum_{k=1}^{n} w_k(t) dS_k(t) \quad \text{for} \quad V(t) = \sum_{k=1}^{n} w_k(t) S_k(t)$$

implies that

$$d\left(\frac{V(t)}{X(t)}\right) = \sum_{k=1}^{n} w_k(t) \left[S_k(t) d\left(\frac{1}{X(t)}\right) + \frac{1}{X(t)} dS_k(1) + d\left\langle S_k, \frac{1}{X}\right\rangle_t \right]$$

$$= \sum_{k=1}^{n} w_k(t) d\left(\frac{S_k(t)}{X(t)}\right)$$

and the portfolio expressed in the new numeraire remains self-financing.

COROLLARY AND DEFINITION 3:
(a) A contingent claim (ie, a random cashflow H paid at time T) is called "attainable" if there exists a self-financing portfolio whose terminal value equals $H(T)$ in all states of the world.
(b) If a contingent claim is attainable in a given numeraire, it is also attainable in any other numeraire and the replicating strategy is the same.

This property is immediately derived from Proposition 1.

The pricing methodology developed in the paper follows the no-arbitrage assumption as defined in Harrison and Kreps (1979) and Harrison and Pliska (1981): for every self-financing portfolio V (belonging to a particular class of portfolios), $V(0) = 0$ and $V(T) \geq 0$ almost surely imply $V(T) = 0$.

If Ω is finite as well as the set of transaction dates, there is no restriction on the class of portfolios and the no-arbitrage assumption is equivalent to the existence of a "risk-neutral probability measure" (see Harrison and Kreps (1979), Harrison and Pliska (1981)). In our setting, as observed by Duffie and Huang (1985), this equivalence does not hold any longer and some requirements have to be put on the portfolios: the "natural" one involves square-integrability conditions of the weights of the portfolio with respect to the instantaneous variance–covariance matrix of the basic assets. Delbaën and Schachermayer (1992) introduce a weaker formulation of the no-arbitrage assumption, the "no free lunch with vanishing risk" (NFLVR), which only requires portfolios bounded below.

The former condition is clearly not invariant in a numeraire change. The latter is if the lower bound is zero; hence the condition $V(t) \geq 0$ for all t that we introduced earlier and which will remain valid throughout the paper unless otherwise specified. More precisely, our no-arbitrage assumption will be expressed in the following manner.

ASSUMPTION 1: There exists a non-dividend-paying asset $n(t)$ and a probability π equivalent to the initial probability P such that for any basic security S_k without intermediate payments the price of S_k relative to n, ie, $S_k(t)/n(t)$, is a local martingale with respect to π.

By convention, we will take $n(0) = 1$.

OBSERVATIONS:
• Portfolios themselves expressed in this numeraire will be, by definition, π-local martingales.
• Moreover, if they are positive for all t, portfolios are supermartingales, ie,

$$\frac{V(t)}{n(t)} \geq E_\pi\left[\frac{V(T)}{n(T)} \middle| F_t\right] \quad \text{a.s.}$$

• If the terminal value $V(T)/n(T)$ is square-integrable, ie, $E_\pi[(V(T)/n(T))^2]$ is finite, then the portfolio value is a π-martingale and

$$\frac{V(t)}{n(t)} = E_\pi\left[\frac{V(T)}{n(T)} \middle| F_t\right]$$

• The consequence is that if a contingent claim H is attainable and its terminal value in the numeraire n is π-square-integrable, then all replicating portfolios have the same value at any intermediate date t. This value is the price at time t of the contingent claim.
• In the general case (relaxing the assumption of square-integrability), all replicating (positive) portfolios do not necessarily have the same value at any date t (see the proof in Dudley (1977) developed in Karatzas and Shreve (1988) for the non-unicity of these portfolios), but all these values are bounded below by $E_\pi[H(T)/n(T) \mid F_t]$.

Moreover, if there exists one replicating portfolio whose value at any time t is equal to this expectation, this value will be called the price of the contingent claim (with respect to (n, π)) and the corresponding portfolio the hedging portfolio. Keeping the same numeraire n, if there exists another probability π' satisfying the same replicability property, then, by no arbitrage,

$$E_{\pi'}\left[\frac{H(T)}{n(T)}\middle| F_t\right] = E_{\pi}\left[\frac{H(T)}{n(T)}\middle| F_t\right]$$

Hence, the fair price does not depend on the choice of the "risk-neutral" probability measure π (as long as this price exists); this remark is very important for what the article is really about - namely the choice of the optimal numeraire when pricing and hedging a given contingent claim.

We are going to give an example of a situation where all contingent claims have a fair price: let us suppose that the prices $S_1(t), S_2(t), \ldots, S_n(t)$ of the basic securities expressed in the numeraire n are stochastic integrals with respect to q Brownian motions $W_1, \ldots, W_q$ and that the filtration F_t is generated by these Brownian motions. Since $S_1, S_2, \ldots, S_n$ are local martingales, their dynamics under π are driven by the stochastic differential equations.

$$\frac{dS_i}{S_i} = \sum_{j=1}^{q} \sigma_{ij} dW_j, \quad i = 1, \ldots, n$$

If we assume that the matrix $\Sigma = [\sigma_{ij}]$ is invertible (which obviously implies $q = n$), then the martingale representation allows us to write any conditional expectation as a stochastic integral with respect to the basic asset prices, hence the portfolio as well.

The same property holds if the number, n, of basic securities is greater than the number of Brownian motions (and rank $\Sigma = q$).

THEOREM 1: Let $X(t)$ be a non-dividend-paying numeraire such that $X(t)$ is a π-martingale. Then there exists a probability measure Q_x defined by its Radon–Nikodym derivative with respect to π

$$\left.\frac{dQ_x}{d\pi}\right| F_t = \frac{X(T)}{X(0)n(T)}$$

such that:

(i) the basic securities prices are Q_x-local martingales;

(ii) if a contingent claim H has a price under (n, π), then it has a price under (X, Q_x) and the hedging portfolio is the same.

PROOF:

(i) If we denote by $\tilde{S} = (S(t)/X(t))$ the relative price of a security S with respect to the numeraire X, the conditional expectations formula gives

$$E_x\left(\frac{dQ_x}{d\pi}\tilde{S}(T)\middle| F_t\right) = E_{Q_x}\left[\tilde{S}(T)\middle| F_t\right] E_x\left(\frac{dQ_x}{d\pi}\middle| F_t\right)$$

By Assumption 1, we have

$$\frac{S(t)}{n(t)X(0)} = E_x\left(\frac{dQ_x}{d\pi}\tilde{S}(T)\middle| F_t\right)$$

and similarly

$$\frac{X(t)}{n(t)X(0)} = E_{\pi}\left(\frac{dQ_x}{d\pi}\middle| F_t\right)$$

This gives the martingale property for any basic security $\tilde{S}(t)$ under Q_x, and consequently for any portfolio.

(ii) If H has a fair price under (n, π), $E_x[H(T)/n(T) | F_t]$ is a self-financing portfolio. Since

$$E_{Q_x}\left[\frac{H(T)}{X(T)}\bigg| F_t\right] = E_\pi\left[\frac{H(T)}{n(T)}\bigg| F_t\right] \Big/ \frac{X(t)}{n(t)}$$

and we observed earlier that the property of being a self-financing portfolio is invariant through a numeraire change, $E_{Q_x}[H(T)/n(T) | F_t]$ is also a self-financing portfolio and Theorem 1 holds.

From now on, we will concentrate on the changes of numeraire techniques.

COROLLARY 2: If X and Y are two arbitrary securities, the general numeraire change formula can be written at any time $t < T$ as

$$X(0)E_{Q_X}\left[Y(T)\Phi | F_t\right] = Y(0)E_{Q_Y}\left[X(T)\Phi | F_t\right]$$

where Φ is any random cashflow F_T-measurable.

PROOF: The formula can be immediately derived from Theorem 1, which entails

$$\left.\frac{dQ_X}{dQ_Y}\right|_{F_t} = \frac{dQ_X}{d\pi}\frac{1}{dQ_Y/d\pi} = \frac{X(T)}{X(0)n(T)} \times \frac{1}{Y(T)/Y(0)n(T)} = \frac{X(T)/Y(T)}{X(0)/Y(0)}$$

We will show later on in the paper how the choice of an appropriate numeraire permits the simplification of pricing and hedging problems.

We start by giving two examples of such numeraire changes already encountered in the literature. We wish to emphasise the fact that in both cases the important message is the financial suitability of the chosen numeraire for a given problem; the probability changes that follow are not only technically useful but they also convey an economic interpretation.

EXAMPLE 1: THE MONEY MARKET ACCOUNT AS A NUMERAIRE. It is natural to take as a first example of numeraire the riskless asset (assuming it exists). More precisely, we define $\beta(t)$ (also called the accumulation factor) as the value at date t of a fund created by investing one dollar at time 0 on the money market and continuously reinvested at the (instantaneously riskless) instantaneous interest rate $r(t)$. The interest rate process is denoted by $(r_t)_{t \geq 0}$. At this point we need a technical assumption.

ASSUMPTION 2: For almost all ω, $t \to r_t(\omega)$ is strictly positive and continuous and r_t is an F_t-measurable process on (Ω, F, P). Under this assumption, it is clear that

$$\beta(t) = \exp\int_0^t r(s)\,ds$$

Then the relative price $\tilde{S}(t)$ of a security with respect to the numeraire β is simply its discounted price:

$$\tilde{S}(t) = \left(\exp - \int_0^t r(s)\,ds\right) S(t)$$

The probability measure Q_β is the usual "risk-neutral" probability measure Q defined by

$$\frac{dQ}{d\pi} = \frac{1}{n(T)} \exp\int_0^T r(s)\,ds$$

Historically (see Harrison and Pliska (1981)), $Q = \pi$ was the first "risk-neutral" probability measure (associated with the numeraire β) expressing that discounted asset prices are Q-martingales.

EXAMPLE 2: ZERO-COUPON BONDS AS NUMERAIRES. A zero-coupon bond imposes itself as the numeraire when one looks at the price at time t of an asset generating a single cashflow at a well-defined future time T. Keeping in mind the general martingale property of Theorem 1, the right numeraire to introduce when interest rates are stochastic is the zero-coupon bond maturing at time T. Let us make explicit the corresponding probability measure change.

The price process of the bond will be denoted either by B(t, T) or by $B_T(t)$,

$$B_T(t) = E_Q\left(\exp - \int_t^T r(s)\,ds \,\middle|\, F_t\right)$$

where Q is the probability defined in Example 1.

Corollary 2 of Theorem 1 gives

$$\frac{dQ_T}{dQ} = \frac{1}{\beta(T)}\frac{\beta(0)}{B(0,T)} = \frac{1}{B(0,T)}\exp - \left(\int_0^T r(s)\,dt\right)$$

The relative price S(t)/B(t, T) is precisely the forward price $F_s(t)$ of the security S, and from Theorem 1 we get

$$F_S(t) = E_{Q_T}\left[\frac{S(T)}{B(T,T)}\,\middle|\, F_t\right]$$

The forward price relative to time T *of a non-dividend-paying security is a martingale under the* T*-forward neutral probability measure.*

The financial intuition of this result can be found in Bick (1988) and Merton (1973); the mathematics were developed in a Gaussian interest rates framework by Jamshidian (1989) and in a more general framework by Geman (1989), who introduced the interpretation of the change of probability measure as a *change of numeraire*. This *numeraire* change reveals itself to be a remarkably powerful tool when evaluating a future random cashflow in a stochastic interest rates environment. Besides its applications to option pricing presented in the next section, it also gives noteworthy results in the pricing of floating-rate notes and of interest rate swaps, as shown in El Karoui and Geman (1991 and 1993), as well as in the evaluation of options embedded in life insurance policies (see Albizzati and Geman (1994)).

Applications to options

We focus in this section on finding interesting expressions for option prices rather than discussing their existence. Consequently, we will suppose that all options considered in what follows are attainable assets. The best example is the classical Black and Scholes framework, where no assumption of completeness is necessary since it is easy to replicate the condition expectation of the terminal payoff by a portfolio of the riskless asset and the risky asset, and hence to derive a fair price for the European call (the Black and Scholes setting is indeed complete).

A GENERAL FORMULA

Let us consider a call written on a security whose price dynamics S(t) does not require any other specification than the fact of being a positive semi-martingale.

THEOREM 2: Under Assumptions 1 and 2, and denoting respectively by T and K its maturity and exercise price, the price at time 0 of the call can be written as

$$\frac{C(0)}{B(0,T)} = E_{Q_T}\left[\left(\frac{S(T)}{B(T,T)} - K\right)^+\right]$$

or

$$C(0) = S(0)\, Q_S(A) - K B(0,T)\, Q_T(A)$$

where $A = \{\omega \mid S(T,\omega) > K B(T,T)\}$.

The first expression for $C(0)$ is immediately derived from Theorem 1 used in the context of Example 2. We will prove the second one.

$$\frac{C(0)}{B(0,T)} = E_{Q_T}\{[S(T)-K]^+\} = E_{Q_T}\left(\frac{S(T)}{B(T,T)}\, 1_A\right) - KQ_T(A)$$

From the general numeraire change formula (Corollary 2 of Theorem 1), we get

$$E_{Q_T}\left(\frac{S(T)}{B(T,T)}\, 1_A\right) = \frac{S(0)}{B(0,T)}\, E_{Q_S}(1_A)$$

We thus obtain the second expression for $C(0)$.

COROLLARY 3: In the same way, the option of exchanging an asset 2 for an asset 1 at time T gives the right to the cashflow $[S_1(T) - KS_2(T)]^+$ with $K = 1$ and its price $C(0)$ at time 0 is such that

$$\frac{C(0)}{S_2(0)} = E_{Q_{S_2}}\left[\left(\frac{S_1(T)}{S_2(T)} - K\right)^+\right]$$

or

$$C(0) = S_1(0)\, Q_{S_2}(A) - KS_2(0)\, Q_{S_1}(A)$$

where $A = \{\omega \in \Omega \mid S_1(T,\omega) \geq KS_2(T,\omega)\}$.

This formula holds even when risky asset volatilities and interest rates are stochastic.

COROLLARY 4: More generally, an option which gives right to the payment at time T of the quantity $(\Sigma_{k=1}^{n} \lambda_k X_k(T))^+$, where $\lambda_1, \ldots, \lambda_n$ are any real numbers, $X_1, \ldots, X_n$ are risky assets (and possibly $X_1(T) = K$ is the usual strike price of the option), has a value at time 0 which can be written as

$$C(0) = \sum_{k=1}^{n} \lambda_k X_k(0) Q_{X_k}(A)$$

Obviously, this is the situation that is encountered with options on bonds.

APPLICATIONS OF THEOREM 2

(*a*) A RE-EXAMINATION OF THE BLACK AND SCHOLES FORMULA: We will make the usual assumptions of the Black and Scholes model, except that we will allow interest rates to be stochastic. Theorem 2 entails the following call price:

$$C(0) = S(0)\, Q_S(A) - K B(0,T)\, Q_T(A)$$

The asset involved in the second term is in fact the forward price of S,

$$F^S(t) = \frac{S(t)}{B(t,T)}$$

which is a positive martingale under Q_T and can therefore be written as a stochastic integral of a Brownian process:

$$\frac{dF^S(t)}{F^S(t)} = \sigma_{F^S}(t)\,dW_t^{F^S}$$

where $(\sigma_{F^S})^2 = (1/dt)\,\mathrm{Var}(dF^S/F^S)$.

Assuming that σ_{F^S} is deterministic, $Q_T(A)$ is equal to $\Pr(u \geqq 0)$, where u is a Gaussian variable with mean $\ln(S(0)/KB(0,T)) - \frac{1}{2}\sigma_{F^S}T$ and variance $\sigma_{F^S}T$. Consequently $Q_T(A) = N(d_2)$, with

$$d_2 = \frac{1}{\sigma_{F^S}\sqrt{T}}\left(\ln\frac{S(0)}{KB(0,T)} - \frac{1}{2}\sigma_{F^S}T\right)$$

As for the first term in the Theorem 2 formula, it involves the asset

$$\frac{B(t,T)}{S(t)} = \frac{1}{F^S(t)} = Z(t)$$

Whether stochastic or not, the volatility of Z under Q_s is the same as the volatility of F^S under Q_T (with possibly different Brownian processes). Assuming these volatilities deterministic,

$$Q_S(A) = Q_S\left(Z(T) \leqq \frac{1}{K}\right) = Q_S\left[Z(0)\exp\left(\sigma_{F^S}W_T - \frac{\sigma_{F^S}}{2}T\right) \leqq \frac{1}{K}\right]$$

$$Q_S(A) = Q_S\left(\sigma_{F^S}W_T - \frac{\sigma_{F^S}}{2}T \leqq \ln\frac{1}{KZ(0)}\right)$$

$$= N\left(\frac{1}{\sigma_{F^S}\sqrt{T}}\ln\frac{S(0)}{KB(0,T)} + \frac{1}{2}\sigma_{F^S}\sqrt{T}\right) = N(d_1)$$

We obtain in fact the Merton formula and, if interest rates are constant, $B(0,T) = e^{-rT}$ and it becomes the Black and Scholes formula.

We have thus shown that these two formulae hold under the sole hypothesis of a deterministic volatility for the forward contract $S(t)/B(t,T)$, without any other specification of deterministic volatilities for the asset price or interest rates.

Obviously, in the Black and Scholes framework interest rates are assumed constant and the hypothesis of a deterministic volatility of the forward contract is equivalent to the hypothesis of a deterministic volatility of the stock price.

(*b*) APPLICATION TO THE EXCHANGE OPTION: Looking at the option of exchanging a stock S_1 for a stock S_2, we choose S_2 as the numeraire. We specify the dynamics of the two asset prices under the risk-neutral probability:

$$\frac{dX_1}{X_1} = r\,dt + \sigma_1 dW_1 \qquad \frac{dX_2}{X_2} = r\,dt + \sigma_2 dW_2$$

where σ_1 and σ_2 are not necessarily deterministic and $\langle dW_1, dW_2\rangle = r\,dt$. Consequently, the volatility of X_1/X_2 is equal to $\sqrt{\sigma_1^2 + \sigma_2^2 - 2\rho\sigma_1\sigma_2}$; it is clear that interest rates play no role and, for the same reasons as earlier, we see that Margrabe's formula (1978) holds under the sole hypothesis of a deterministic volatility for X_1/X_2 without assuming non-stochastic interest rates.

We can observe that the same methodology could be applied to the pricing of equity-linked foreign exchange options, also called quanto options, which were valuated by Reiner (1992) in a deterministic interest rates setting; this valuation was extended to stochastic interest rates by Geman and Souveton (1994).

(*c*) APPLICATION TO HEDGING: From the calculations conducted in (*a*), we see that in the general situation of stochastic interest rates the right way of hedging should not be read in the Black and Scholes formula but in the Merton formula

$$C(0) = S(0)\,N(d_1) - K\,B(0,T)\,N(d_2)$$

From this, we can derive very symmetrically the quantity $N(d_1)$ to invest in the risky asset and the quantity $N(d_2)$ to invest in K zero-coupon bonds maturing at time T.

Practitioners who use these weights to hedge the option with the underlying asset and money market instruments implicitly assume non-stochastic interest rates. Moreover, it is clear that if interest rates are stochastic, what is usually denominated as the "implied volatility" of the asset is in fact the implied volatility of the forward contract.

If interest rates are stochastic and if one wants to hedge the option with the underlying asset and short-term bills, it is necessary (in order to obtain completeness) to assume that the same Brownian motion perturbates the movement of the risky asset and that of the zero-coupon bond maturing at time T - namely that under the risk-neutral probability we have the following dynamics:

$$\frac{dS}{S} = r\,dt + \sigma_1\,dW \qquad \frac{dB^T}{B^T} = r\,dt + \sigma_2\,dW$$

where σ_2 is a deterministic function of time and from which we derive

$$\frac{dB^T}{B^T} = r\left(1 - \frac{\sigma_2}{\sigma_1}\right)dt + \frac{\sigma_2}{\sigma_1}\frac{dS}{S}$$

Consequently, we see that the quantity to hold short in the risky asset in order to hedge the option is not $N(d_1)$ but in fact

$$\frac{\partial C}{\partial S} + \frac{\sigma_2}{\sigma_1}\frac{B(t,T)}{S(t)}\frac{\partial C}{\partial B}$$

ie,

$$N(d_1) - K\frac{\sigma_2}{\sigma_1}\frac{B(t,T)}{S(t)}N(d_2)$$

The number of risky stocks involved in the self-financing portfolio replicating the European call is not $N(d_1)$ but the partial derivative of the Black and Scholes price with respect to the underlying stock and well known as the delta of the call.

The classical "Δ hedging" is correct under stochastic interest rates only if the hedging portfolio involves, besides the risky stock, the zero-coupon bond maturing at time T.

(*d*) APPLICATION TO COMPOUND OPTIONS: We now extend the pricing formula given in Geske (1977) for a compound option to non-deterministic interest rates. Again, it will involve - besides the risky stock - the zero-coupon bond maturing at time T.

Let us denote:

- $C_1(t, S)$ = price at t of a European call option on the stock, with strike price K_1 and exercise date T_1;
- $C_2(t, S)$ = price at t of a European call option on C_1, with strike price K_2 and $T_2 < T_1$;
- $A_1 = \{\omega \in \Omega \mid S(T_1, \omega) \geq K_1\}$ exercise set of option C_1;
- $A_2 = \{\omega \in \Omega \mid S(T_2, \omega) \geq S^*\}$ exercise set of option C_2, where S^* is defined implicitly by $C_1(T_2, S^*) = K_2$.

In the same spirit as earlier, we write

$$C_2(0) = B(0,T_2)\,E_{Q_{T_2}}\{[C_1(T_2, S(T_2)) - K_2]^+\}$$

$$C_2(0) = -K_2 B(0,T_2)\,Q_{T_2}(A_2) + B(0,T_2)\,E_{Q_{T_2}}[C_1(T_2, S(T_2))\,1_{A_2}]$$

Making explicit $C_1(T_2, S(T_2))$, we get

$$B(0,T_2)E_{Q_{T_2}}[C_1(T_2,S(T_2))1_{A_2}]$$

$$= B(0,T_2)E_{Q_{T_2}}\left\{1_{A_2}B(T_2,T_1)E_{Q_{T_1}}\left[(S(T_1)-K_1)^+\right]\middle|F_{T_2}\right\}$$

Taking in Corollary 1 the asset X as the zero-coupon bond maturing at time T_1, Y as the zero-coupon bond maturing at time T_2 and $T = T_2$, we rewrite this expression as

$$B(0,T_1)E_{Q_{T_1}}\left\{1_{A_2}E_{Q_{T_1}}\left[(S(T_1)-K_1)^+\mid F_{T_2}\right]\right\}$$

or

$$B(0,T_1)\,E_{Q_{T_1}}[1_{A_2}S(T_1)1_{A_1}] - K_1B(0,T_1)\,Q_{T_1}(A_1\cap A_2)$$

Using again the change of numeraire formula, we obtain

$$B(0,T_1)\,E_{Q_{T_1}}[S(T_1)1_{A_1\cap A_2}] = S(0)\,Q_S(A_1\cap A_2)$$

Regrouping the different terms, we write the price of the compound option as

$$C_2(0) = S(0)\,Q_S(A_1\cap A_2) - K_1B(0,T_1)\,Q_{T_1}(A_1\cap A_2) - K_2B(0,T_2)\,Q_{T_2}(A_2)$$

This formula does not assume interest rates and stock price volatility to be non-stochastic.

If we make the assumption of a deterministic stock price volatility, we can prove by the same arguments as in the second section that

$$Q_{T_2}(A_2) = N(\delta_2) = N\left(\frac{1}{\sigma\sqrt{T_2}}\ln\frac{S(0)}{S^*B(0,T_2)} - \tfrac{1}{2}\sigma\sqrt{T_2}\right)$$

$$Q_{T_1}(A_1\cap A_2) = N(\delta_1, \delta_2)$$

where

$$\delta_1 = \frac{1}{\sigma\sqrt{T_1}}\ln\frac{S(0)}{K_1B(0,T_1)} - \tfrac{1}{2}\sigma\sqrt{T_1}$$

and $N(\cdot,\cdot)$ is the cumulative function of a centred bivariate Gaussian distribution with covariance matrix

$$\begin{bmatrix} 1 & \sqrt{\dfrac{T_2}{T_1}} \\ \sqrt{\dfrac{T_2}{T_1}} & 1 \end{bmatrix}$$

and

$$Q_S(A_1\cap A_2) = N\left(\delta_1 + \sigma\sqrt{T_1}, \delta_2 + \sigma\sqrt{T_2}\right)$$

Regrouping the different terms, we obtain Geske's formula for stochastic interest rates

$$C_2(0) = S(0)N\left(\delta_1 + \sigma\sqrt{T_1}, \delta_2 + \sigma\sqrt{T_2}\right) -$$

$$K_1B(0,T_1)N(\delta_1,\delta_2) - K_2B(0,T_2)N(\delta_2)$$

Options on bonds

This section is devoted to European calls on default-free bonds.

OPTIONS ON ZERO-COUPON BONDS

Theorem 2 entails the following formula for the price of a call maturing at date T_0 written on a zero-coupon bond maturing at date T_1:

$$C(0) = B(0, T_1)\, Q_{T_1}(A) - K\, B(0, T_0)\, Q_{T_0}(A)$$

where K is the exercise price, A is the exercise set and $T_0 < T_1$.

(*a*) In the same manner as Heath, Jarrow and Morton (1992), we assume the following dynamics for the bond prices under the risk-adjusted probability measure:

$$\frac{dB(t,T)}{B(t,T)} = r(t)\,dt + \sigma(t,T)\,dW_t$$

where $\sigma(t, T)$ is decreasing in t and $\sigma(T, T) = 0$.

Assuming $\sigma(t, T)$ deterministic, the arguments developed in Example 1 in the third section provide a formula of the Black-Scholes type:

$$C(0) = B(0, T_1)\, N(d_1) - K\, B(0, T_0)\, N(d_2)$$

where

$$d_2 = \tfrac{1}{2}\sigma\sqrt{T_0} + \frac{1}{\sigma\sqrt{T_0}} \ln \frac{B(0,T_1)}{KB(0,T_0)}$$

$$d_1 = d_2 - \sigma\sqrt{T_0}$$

and σ is the volatility of the forward price $B(t, T_1) / B(t, T_0)$ of the zero-coupon bond.

(*b*) Another explicit formula was obtained by Cox, Ingersoll, and Ross (1985) in the context of stochastic volatilities, but with a one-state variable description of the term structure of interest rates. The (risk-adjusted) dynamics of the short rate is defined by

$$dr(t) = a(b - r(t))\,dt + \sigma\, dW_t$$

where a, b and σ are positive constants. From that dynamics it follows that the short rate is distributed under Q (respectively, Q_{T_0}, Q_{T_1}) as a non-central chi-square process with parameter of non-centrality q (respectively, q_0, q_1). More precisely, this process can be written (up to a simple deterministic time change) as a Bessel process, as explained in Geman and Yor (1993); these authors also uncovered the fact that the Cox-Ingersoll-Ross process is indeed the square of a Vasicek process. Cox, Ingersoll, and Ross show that the call is exercised if and only if $r(T_0)$ is less than a critical level d_0; they obtain an explicit formula for a call on a zero-coupon bond, which can be written in our notation as

$$C(0) = B(0, T_1)\, \chi^2(d_1, n_1, q_1) - K\, B(0, T_0)\, \chi^2(d_0, n, q_0)$$

where $\chi^2(\cdot, n, q)$ is the non-centred chi-square distribution with n degrees of freedom and parameter of non-centrality q; n, q_0, q_1, d_0 and d_1 are parameters depending on a, b, σ and the characteristics of the call. It is interesting to note that the assumption of a deterministic volatility of interest rates is not necessary to obtain a formula of the Black and Scholes type. The result holds because the spot rate driven by the dynamics

$$dr = a(b - r)dt + \sigma\sqrt{r}dW$$

follows a χ^2 distribution and that under the "forward neutral" probability associated with any date T this is still true (with a sole change in the drift of dr); this is due to the preservation of the Bessel process structure under the new measures Q_{T_0} and Q_{T_1}. Consequently, probabilities of exercise under the different probability measures are expressed in terms of non-centred chi-square distributions.

OPTIONS ON COUPON BONDS

Let us suppose that the underlying asset is a general default-free bond, characterised by the sequence $F_1, F_2, \ldots, F_n$ of fixed payments it generates at times $T_1, \ldots, T_n$. Under the assumptions and notations in the third section, its price at date $t(t < T_1 \ldots < T_n)$ is given by $P(t) = \Sigma_{i=1}^{n} F_i B(t, T_i)$, where

$$B(t, T) = E_Q\left(\exp - \int_t^T r(s)ds / F_t\right)$$

We consider a call written on the bond, with exercise price K and maturity $T_0 < T_1$.

The probability of exercise will involve the distribution of n variables, namely the prices of the n zero-coupon bonds $B(0, T_1), \ldots, B(0, T_n)$. To obtain a formula of the Black and Scholes type, it is necessary that these n prices depend on only one state variable, for instance the spot rate.

In the Gaussian case with one source of randomness (as in the third section, 1(a)), this is equivalent to assuming a Markovian spot rate, or, in other words, a deterministic volatility $\sigma(t, T)$ which has the form

$$\sigma(t, T) = [h(T) - h(t)]\, g(t)$$

Jamshidian (1989) and El Karoui and Rochet (1989) obtain under these hypotheses a quasi-explicit formula for the call price:

$$C(0) = \sum_{i=1}^{n} F_i B(0, T_i)\, N(d_i) - KB(0, T_0)\, N(d_0)$$

where $d_i = d_0 + \mu_i$

$$\mu_i^2 = \int_0^{T_0} [\sigma(s, T_i) - \sigma(s, T_0)]^2 ds$$

and d_0 is defined implicitly by

$$\sum_{i=1}^{n} F_i B(0, T_i) \exp\left(-\tfrac{1}{2}\mu_i^2 + d_0 u_i\right) = KB(0, T_0)$$

Conclusion

The paper has shown that a change of numeraires does not change the self-financing portfolios, and hence does not change the hedging or replicating portfolios either. An important consequence in option pricing is that, depending on whether the option under analysis is written on a stock, on a bond, is an exchange option, a compound option or a quanto option, the choice of the appropriate numeraire will provide the easiest calculations and the relevant hedging portfolio. This technique can also be extended to Asian options; in the case of floating-strike Asian options, the choice of the stock as the numeraire leads to a fairly simple partial differential equation for the call price.

Bibliography

Albizzati, M. O., and H. Geman, 1994, "Interest Rate Risk Management and Valuation of the Surrender Option in Life Insurance Policies", *Journal of Risk and Insurance* December.

Ball, C. A. and W. N. Torous, 1983, "Bond Price Dynamics and Options", *Journal of Financial and Quantitative Analysis* 18(4), pp 517-531.

Bick, A., 1988, "Producing Derivative Assets with Forward Contracts", *Journal of Financial and Quantitative Analysis* 23(2).

Black, F. and M. Scholes, 1973, "The Pricing of Options and Corporate Liabilities", *Journal of Political Economy* 81, pp. 637-654; reprinted as Chapter 1 of the present volume.

Cox, J. C., J. E. Ingersoll, and S. A. Ross, 1985, "A Theory of the Term Structure of Interest Rates", *Econometrica* 53, pp. 385-407; reprinted as Chapter 6 of the present volume.

Cox, J. C., S. Ross and M. Rubinstein, 1979, "Option Pricing: A Simplified Approach", *Journal of Financial Economics* 3, pp. 145-166; reprinted as Chapter 2 of the present volume.

Delbaën, F. and W. Schachermayer, 1992, "A General Version of the Fundamental Theorem of Asset Pricing", *Conference INRIA-NSF on Mathematical Finance*, Paris.

Dudley, R. M., 1977, "Wiener Functionals as Itô Integrals", *Anal. Probability* 5, pp. 140-141.

Duffie, D. and C. F. Huang, 1985, "Implementing Arrow-Debreu Equilibrium by Continuous Trading of Few Long-Lived Securities", *Econometrica* 53, pp. 1337-1356.

El Karoui, N. and J. C. Rochet, 1989, "A Pricing Formula for Options on Coupon-Bonds", Working paper, GREMAQ.

El Karoui, N. and H. Geman, 1991, "A Stochastic Approach to the Pricing of FRNs", *RISK* 4(3).

El Karoui, N. and H. Geman, 1994, "A Probabilistic Approach to the Valuation of Floating Rate Notes with an Application to Interest Rate Swaps", *Adv. Options and Futures Res.* 7, pp. 47-64.

Geman, H., 1989, "The Importance of the Forward Neutral Probability in a Stochastic Approach of Interest Rates", Working paper, ESSEC.

Geman, H., and M. Yor, 1993, "Bessel Processes, Asian Options and Perpetuities", *Mathematical Finance* 3, pp. 349-375.

Geman, H., and R. Souveton, 1994, "No Arbitrage between Economies and Correlation Risk Management", RISK Conference on Correlation, London.

Geske, R., 1979, "The Valuation of Compound-Options", *Journal of Financial Economics* 7, pp. 63-81.

Harrison, J. M, and D. Kreps, 1979, "Martingale and Arbitrage in Multiperiods Securities Markets", *Journal of Economic Theory* 20, pp. 381-408.

Harrison, J. M. and S. R. Pliska, 1981, "Martingales and Stochastic Integrals in the Theory of Continuous Trading", *Stochastic Probability Applied* 11, pp. 215-260.

Heath, D., R. Jarrow and A. Morton, 1992, "Bond Pricing and the Term Structure of Interest Rates: A New Methodology for Contingent Claims Valuation", *Econometrica* 60, pp. 77-105; reprinted as Chapter 14 of the present volume.

Jamshidian, F., 1989, "An Exact Bond Option Formula", *Journal of Finance* 44, pp. 205-209; reprinted as Chapter 8 of the present volume.

Karatzas, I. and S. E. Shreve, 1988, *Brownian Motion and Stochastic Calculus*, Springer-Verlag, Berlin.

Margrabe, W., 1978, "The Value of an Option to Exchange One Asset for Another", *Journal of Finance* 33.

Merton, R. C., 1973, "Theory of Rational Pricing", *Bell Journal of Economic Management Science*, 4, pp. 141-183.

Reiner, E., 1992, "Quanto Mechanics", *RISK* 5(3), pp. 59-63.

Ross., S. A., 1978, "A Simple Approach to the Valuation of Risky streams", *Journal of Business* 51, pp. 453-75.

Stricker, C., 1990, "Arbitrage et Lois de Martingale", *Ann. Inst. H. Poincaré* 26(3).

19

The Market Model of Interest Rate Dynamics*

Alan Brace, Dariusz Gatarek and Marek Musiela
University of New South Wales; Polish Academy of Sciences; University of New South Wales

A class of term structure models with volatility of lognormal type is analysed in the general Heath-Jarrow-Morton framework. The corresponding market forward rates do not explode, are positive and mean-reverting. Pricing of caps and floors is consistent with the Black formulae used in the market. Swaptions are priced with closed formulae that reduce (with an extra assumption) to exactly the Black swaption formulae when yield and volatility are flat. A two-factor version of the model is calibrated to the UK market price of caps and swaptions and to the historically estimated correlation between the forward rates.

In most markets, caps and floors form the largest component of an average swap derivatives book. A cap/floor is a strip of caplets/floorlets each of which is a call/put option on a forward rate. Market practice is to price the option assuming that the underlying forward rate process is lognormally distributed with zero drift. Consequently, the option price is given by the Black futures formula, discounted from the settlement data.

In an arbitrage-free setting forward rates over consecutive time intervals are related to one another and cannot all be lognormal under one arbitrage-free measure. That is probably what led the academic community to a degree of scepticism towards the market practice of pricing caps and sparked vigorous research with the aim of identifying an arbitrage-free term structure model.

The aim of this paper is to show that this market practice can be made consistent with an arbitrage-free term structure model. Consecutive quarterly or semi-annual forward rates can all be lognormal while the model will remain arbitrage-free. This is possible because each rate is lognormal under the forward (to the settlement date) arbitrage-free measure rather than under one (spot) arbitrage-free measure. Lognormality under the appropriate forward and not spot arbitrage-free measure is needed to justify the use of the Black futures formula with discount for caplet pricing.

**The authors would like to thank Citibank; the discipline of doing fundamental research in an exacting commercial atmosphere contributed to this paper. The backing of individual managers - Mike Hawker, Steve Anthony and Colin McKeith - in Citibank was critical, as was Pratap Sondhi's early appreciation of the technical correctness of our approach followed by his unswerving support. Lognormal numbers are due to the ace implementer Karthikeyan M.S.; normal numbers were produced by the experienced desk quantitative analyst, Soetojo Tanudjaja. The authors also benefited from discussions with a number of participants in the financial mathematics seminar at the University of New South Wales. Comments and suggestions made by Dieter Sondermann during his visits to Sydney were of particular value. Ben Goldys not only helped with many mathematical problems but also found the first probabilistic derivation (available on request) of the Miltersen* et al. *(1994) result (Proposition 3.1). Dariusz Gatarek was supported by an Australian Research Council grant.*

The market seems to interpret the concept of probability distribution in an intuitive rather than mathematical sense and does not distinguish between the forward measures at different maturities.

We work with the term structure parameterisation proposed by Musiela (1995) and later use papers by Musiela and Sondermann (1993), Brace and Musiela (1994*a*), Goldys *et al.* (1994) and Musiela (1994). We denote by $r(t, x)$ the continuously compounded forward rate prevailing at time t over the time interval $[t+x, t+x+dx]$. There is an obvious relationship between the Heath, Jarrow and Morton (1992) forward rates $f(t, T)$ and our $r(t, x)$, namely $r(t, x) = f(t, t+x)$. For all $T > 0$ the process

$$P(t,T) = \exp\left(-\int_0^{T-t} r(t,u)\,du\right) \qquad 0 \le t \le T$$

describes price evolution of a zero coupon bond with maturity T. Time evolution of the discount function

$$x \mapsto D(t,x) = P(t,t+x) = \exp\left(-\int_0^{x} r(t,u)\,du\right)$$

is described by the processes $\{D(t, x);\ t \ge 0\}$, $x \ge 0$. We make the usual mathematical assumptions. All processes are defined on the probability space $(\Omega, \{F_t;\ t \ge 0\}, \mathbf{P})$, where the filtration $\{F_t;\ t \ge 0\}$ is the $\mathbf{P}$-augmentation of the natural filtration generated by a d-dimensional Brownian motion $W = \{W(t);\ t \ge 0)\}$. We assume that the process $\{r(t, x);\ t, x \ge 0\}$ satisfies

$$dr(t,x) = \frac{\partial}{\partial x}\left[\left(r(t,x) + \tfrac{1}{2}\left|\sigma(t,x)\right|^2\right)dt + \sigma(t,x)\cdot dW(t)\right] \tag{1}$$

where for all $x \ge 0$ the volatility process $\{\sigma(t, x);\ t \ge 0\}$ is F_t-adapted with values in $\mathbf{R}^d$, while $|\ |$ and $\cdot$ stand for the usual norm and inner product in $\mathbf{R}^d$, respectively. We also assume that the function $x \mapsto \sigma(t, x)$ is absolutely continuous and the derivative $\tau(t, x) = \partial/\partial x\, \sigma(t, x)$ is bounded on $\mathbf{R}_+^2 \times \Omega$. It follows easily that

$$dD(t, x) = D(t, x)\{[r(t, 0) - r(t, x)]\,dt - \sigma(t, x)\cdot dW(t)\}$$

and hence $\sigma(t, x)$ can be interpreted as price volatility. Obviously, we have $\sigma(t, 0) = 0$.

The spot rate process $\{r(t, 0);\ t \ge 0\}$ satisfies

$$dr(t,0) = \left.\frac{\partial}{\partial x} r(t,x)\right|_{x=0} dt + \left.\frac{\partial}{\partial x}\sigma(t,x)\right|_{x=0} \cdot dW(t)$$

and hence is not Markov, in general. The process

$$\beta(t) = \exp\left(\int_0^t r(s,0)\,ds\right) \qquad t \ge 0$$

represents the amount generated at time $t \ge 0$ by continuously reinvesting \$1 in the spot rate $r(s, 0)$, $0 < s \le t$.

It is well known that if for all $T > 0$ the process $\{P(t, T)/\beta(t);\ 0 \le t \le T\}$ is a martingale under P, then there is no arbitrage possible between the zero coupon bonds $P(\cdot, T)$ of all maturities $T > 0$ and the savings account $\beta(\cdot)$. Note that, under (1), we can easily write that

$$\frac{P(t,T)}{\beta(t)} = P(0,T)\exp\left(-\int_0^t \sigma(s,T-s)\cdot dW(s) - \tfrac{1}{2}\int_0^t \left|\sigma(s,T-s)\right|^2 ds\right) \tag{2}$$

where the right-hand side is a martingale.

In the second section the existence of the model is established, cap and swaption formulae are derived in the third section and the calibration is described in the fourth section.

The model

To specify the model or, equivalently, to define the volatility process $\sigma(t, x)$ in equation (1) we fix $\delta > 0$ (for example, $\delta = 0.25$) and assume that for each $x \geq 0$ the Libor rate process $\{L(t, x);\ t \geq 0\}$ defined by

$$1 + \delta L(t, x) = \exp\left(\int_x^{x+\delta} r(t, u)\,du\right) \tag{3}$$

has a lognormal volatility structure, ie,

$$dL(t, x) = \ldots dt + L(t, x)\,\gamma(t, x) \cdot dW(t) \tag{4}$$

where the deterministic function $\gamma\colon \mathbf{R}_+^2 \to \mathbf{R}^d$ is bounded and piecewise continuous. Using the Itô formula and (1) we get

$$\begin{aligned} dL(t, x) &= \delta^{-1} d \exp\left(\int_x^{x+\delta} r(t, u)\,du\right) = \delta^{-1} \exp\left(\int_x^{x+\delta} r(t, u)\,du\right) d\left(\int_x^{x+\delta} r(t, u)\,du\right) + \\ &\quad \delta^{-1} \tfrac{1}{2} \exp\left(\int_x^{x+\delta} r(t, u)\,du\right) \left|\sigma(t, x+\delta) - \sigma(t, x)\right|^2 dt \\ &= \delta^{-1} \exp\left(\int_x^{x+\delta} r(t, u)\,du\right) \left\{\left[r(t, x+\delta) - r(t, x) + \tfrac{1}{2}\left|\sigma(t, x+\delta)\right|^2 - \right.\right. \\ &\quad \left.\left. \tfrac{1}{2}\left|\sigma(t, x)\right|^2\right] dt + \left[\sigma(t, x+\delta) - \sigma(t, x)\right] \cdot dW(t)\right\} + \\ &\quad \delta^{-1} \tfrac{1}{2} \exp\left(\int_x^{x+\delta} r(t, u)\,du\right) \left|\sigma(t, x+\delta) - \sigma(t, x)\right|^2 dt \\ &= \left\{\frac{\partial}{\partial x} L(t, x) + \delta^{-1}\left[1 + \delta L(t, x)\right] \sigma(t, x+\delta) \cdot \left[\sigma(t, x+\delta) - \sigma(t, x)\right]\right\} dt + \\ &\quad \delta^{-1}\left[1 + \delta L(t, x)\right]\left[\sigma(t, x+\delta) - \sigma(t, x)\right] \cdot dW(t) \end{aligned}$$

Consequently (4) holds for all $x \geq 0$ if and only if for all $x \geq 0$

$$\sigma(t, x+\delta) - \sigma(t, x) = \frac{\delta L(t, x)}{1 + \delta L(t, x)}\,\gamma(t, x) \tag{5}$$

Under (5) the equation for $L(t, x)$ becomes

$$dL(t, x) = \left(\frac{\partial}{\partial x} L(t, x) + L(t, x)\,\gamma(t, x) \cdot \sigma(t, x+\delta)\right) dt + L(t, x)\,\gamma(t, x) \cdot dW(t) \tag{6}$$

Recurrence relationship (5) defines the Heath–Jarrow–Morton volatility process $\sigma(t, x)$ for all $x \geq \delta$ provided that $\sigma(t, x)$ is defined on the interval $0 \leq x \leq \delta$. We set $\sigma(t, x) = 0$ for all $0 \leq x < \delta$ and hence, solving (5), we get for $x \geq \delta$

$$\sigma(t, x) = \sum_{k=1}^{[\delta^{-1} x]} \frac{\delta L(t, x - k\delta)}{1 + \delta L(t, x - k\delta)}\,\gamma(t, x - k\delta) \tag{7}$$

Therefore the process $\{L(t, x);\ t, x \geq 0\}$ must satisfy the following equation:

$$\begin{aligned} dL(t, x) &= \left(\frac{\partial}{\partial x} L(t, x) + L(t, x)\,\gamma(t, x) \cdot \sigma(t, x) + \frac{\delta L^2(t, x)}{1 + \delta L(t, x)} \left|\gamma(t, x)\right|^2\right) dt + \\ &\quad + L(t, x)\,\gamma(t, x) \cdot dW(t) \end{aligned} \tag{8}$$

The above approach to the term structure modelling is quite different from the traditional one based on the instantaneous continuously compounded spot or forward rates and therefore, we believe, its motivations and origins are worth mentioning. The change of focus from the instantaneous continuously compounded rates to the instantaneous effective annual rates was first proposed by Sandmann and Sondermann (1993) in response to the impossibility of pricing a Eurodollar futures contract with a lognormal model of the instantaneous continuously compounded spot rate. A Heath-Jarrow-Morton-type model based on the instantaneous effective annual rates was introduced by Goldys *et al.* (1994). A lognormal volatility structure was assumed on the effective annual rate $j(t, x)$, which is related to the instantaneous continuously compounded forward rate $r(t, x)$ via the formula

$$1 + j(t, x) = e^{r(t, x)}$$

The case of nominal annual rates $q(t, x)$ corresponding to $r(t, x)$, ie,

$$[1+\delta q(t, x)]^{\frac{1}{\delta}} = e^{r(t, x)}$$

was studied by Musiela (1994). It turns out that the Heath-Jarrow-Morton volatility process $\sigma(t, x)$ takes the form

$$\sigma(t, x) = \int_0^x \delta^{-1}(1 - e^{-\delta r(t, u)})\,\gamma(t, u)\,du \tag{9}$$

Obviously, for $\delta = 1$ we obtain the Goldys *et al.* (1994) model and for $\delta = 0$ we get

$$\sigma(t, x) = \int_0^x r(t, u)\,\gamma(t, u)\,du$$

and hence the Heath-Jarrow-Morton lognormal model, which is known to explode (for $\delta > 0$ no explosion occurs).

Unfortunately the above models do not give closed-form pricing formulae for options. In order to price a caplet, for example, one would have to use some numerically intensive algorithms. This would not be practical for model calibration, where an iterative procedure is needed to identify the volatility $\gamma(t, x)$ which returns the market prices for a large number of caps and swaptions.

A key piece in the term structure puzzle was found by Miltersen *et al.* (1994). Firstly, attention was shifted from the instantaneous rates $q(t, x)$ to the nominal annual rates $f(t, x, \delta)$ defined by

$$[1+f(t, x, \delta)]^{\delta} = \exp\left(\int_x^{x+\delta} r(t, u)\,du\right) \tag{10}$$

More importantly, however, it was shown that for $\delta = 1$ the model prices a yearly caplet according to the market standard. Unfortunately the volatility $\sigma(t, x)$ was not completely identified, leaving open the question of the model specification for maturities different from $x = i\delta$ and the existence of a solution to equation (1). These problems were only partially addressed by Miltersen *et al.* (1995), where a model based on the effective rates $f(t, T, \delta)$ defined by

$$1+\delta f(t, T, \delta) = \exp\left(\int_{T-t}^{T+\delta-t} r(t, u)\,du\right) \tag{11}$$

was analysed.

As explained before, we assume a lognormal volatility structure to the Libor rate $L(t, x)$, defined by (3), for all $x \geq 0$ and a fixed $\delta > 0$. This leads to the volatility $\sigma(t, x)$ given in (7) and equation (8) for $L(t, x)$. To prove existence and uniqueness of solution to (8) we need the following result.

LEMMA 2.1: *For all* $x \geq 0$ *let* $\{\xi(t, x);\ t \geq 0\}$ *be an adapted bounded stochastic process with values in* $\mathbf{R}^d$, $a(\cdot, x)\colon \mathbf{R}_+ \mapsto \mathbf{R}^d$ *be a deterministic bounded and piecewise continuous function, and let* $M(t, x) = \int_0^t a(s, x)\,dW(s)$. *For all* $x \geq 0$ *the equation*

$$dy(t,x) = y(t,x)a(t,x)\cdot\left[\left(\frac{\delta y(t,x)}{1+\delta y(t,x)}\,a(t,x)+\xi(t,x)\right)dt + dW(t)\right]$$

$$y(0,x) > 0 \tag{12}$$

where $\delta > 0$ *is a constant and has a unique strictly positive solution on* $\mathbf{R}_+$. *Moreover, if for some* $k \in \{0, 1, 2, \ldots\}$, $y(0,\cdot) \in C^k(\mathbf{R}_+)$ *and for all* $t \geq 0$, $a(t,\cdot)$, $M(t,\cdot)$ *and* $\xi(t,\cdot) \in C^k(\mathbf{R}_+)$, *then for all* $t \geq 0$, $y(t,\cdot) \in C^k(\mathbf{R}_+)$.

PROOF: Since the right-hand side in (12) is locally Lipschitz continuous (with respect to y) on $\mathbf{R} - \{-\delta^{-1}\}$ and Lipschitz continuous on $\mathbf{R}_+$, there exists a unique (possibly exploding) strictly positive solution to (12). By the Itô formula

$$y(t,x) = y(0,x)\exp\left[\int_0^t a(s,x)\cdot dW(s) + \right.$$

$$\left.\int_0^t a(s,x)\cdot\left(\frac{\delta y(s,x)}{1+\delta y(s,x)}\,a(s,x)+\xi(s,x)-\tfrac{1}{2}a(s,x)\right)ds\right] \tag{13}$$

for all $t < \tau = \inf\{t\colon y(t,x) = \infty \text{ or } y(t,x) = 0\}$. But if $y(t,x) = 0$ for some $t < \infty$, then $y(s,x) = 0$ for all $s \geq t$ and hence $\tau = \inf\{t\colon y(t,x) = \infty\}$. Moreover, because

$$\int_0^t |a(s,x)|^2\,ds < \infty$$

for all $t < \infty$ we deduce that $\tau = \infty$. Thus (13) is equivalent to the following Volterra-type integral equation for $\ell(t,x) = \log y(t,x)$:

$$\ell(t,x) = \ell(0,x) + \int_0^t a(s,x)\cdot dW(s) +$$

$$\int_0^t a(s,x)\cdot\left(\frac{\delta e^{\ell(s,x)}}{1+\delta e^{\ell(s,x)}}\,a(s,x)+\xi(s,x)-\tfrac{1}{2}a(s,x)\right)ds \tag{14}$$

Because the right-hand side in (14) is globally Lipschitz continuous with respect to ℓ we deduce, using the standard fixed-point arguments, that there exists a unique pathwise solution of the equation (14). Moreover, for any $t \geq 0$, $\ell(t,\cdot) \in C^k(\mathbf{R}_+)$ provided that $\ell(0,\cdot)$, $a(t,\cdot)$, $\xi(t,\cdot) \in C^k(\mathbf{R}_+)$ for $t \geq 0$.

THEOREM 2.1: *Let* $\gamma\colon \mathbf{R}_+^2 \to \mathbf{R}^d$ *be a deterministic bounded and piecewise continuous function,* $\delta > 0$ *be a constant and let* $M(t,x) = \int_0^t \gamma(s, x+t-s)\cdot dW(s)$. *Equation* (8) *admits a unique non-negative solution* $L(t,x)$ *for any* $t \geq 0$ *and any non-negative initial condition* $L(0,\cdot) = L_0$. *If* $L_0 > 0$, *then* $L(t,\cdot) > 0$ *for all* $t > 0$. *If* $L_0 \in C^k(\mathbf{R}_+)$ *and for all* $t \geq 0$, $\gamma(t,\cdot) \in C^k(\mathbf{R}_+)$, $M(t,\cdot) \in C^k(\mathbf{R}_+)$, $\frac{\partial^j}{\partial x^j}\gamma(t,x)\big|_{x=0} = 0$, $j = 0, 1, \ldots, k$, *then for all* $t \geq 0$, $L(t,\cdot) \in C^k(\mathbf{R}_+)$.

PROOF: By the solution to (8) we mean the so-called mild solution (cf. Da Prato and Zabczyk 1992), ie, $L(t,x)$ is a solution if for all $t, x \geq 0$,

$$L(t,x) = L(0,x+t) + \int_0^t L(s,x+t-s)\gamma(s,x+t-s)\cdot\sigma(s,x+t-s)\,ds +$$

$$\int_0^t \frac{\delta L^2(s,x+t-s)}{1+\delta L(s,x+t-s)}\left|\gamma(s,x+t-s)\right|^2 ds +$$

$$\int_0^t L(s,x+t-s)\gamma(s,x+t-s)\cdot dW(s)$$

This holds true for $0 \leq x < \delta$ because the process $L(t, x-t)$, $0 \leq t \leq x$, $x > 0$, is a solution to (12) with $a(t, x) = \gamma(t, (x-t) \vee 0)$ and $\xi(t, x) = 0$. For $\delta \le x < 2\delta$ the process $L(t, x-t)$, $0 \le t \le x$, satisfies (12) with $a(t, x) = \gamma(t, (x-t) \vee 0)$ and

$$\xi(t,x) = \frac{\delta L[t,(x-\delta-t) \vee 0]}{1+\delta L[t,(x-\delta-t) \vee 0]}$$

By induction we prove that equation (8) admits a unique solution for any $x > 0$ and $0 \le t \le x$. Also by induction, using (7), we deduce that the corresponding $a(t, \cdot)$ and $\xi(t, \cdot)$ satisfy the assumptions of regularity in Lemma 2.1 and hence $L(t, \cdot)$ is smooth as well.

COROLLARY 2.1: *If for some* $k \in \mathbf{N}$ *and all* $t \ge 0$, $\gamma(t, \cdot) \in C^k(\mathbf{R}_+)$ *and* $\frac{\partial^j}{\partial x^j}\gamma(t, x)\big|_{x=0} = 0$, $j = 1, \ldots, k$, *then equation* (1) *has a unique solution* $r(t, \cdot) \in C^{k-1}(\mathbf{R}_+)$ *for any positive initial condition* $r(0, \cdot) \in C^{k-1}(\mathbf{R}_+)$.

PROOF: Consider (1) as an equation with fixed volatility processes $\sigma(t, x)$ given by (7) and (8).

REMARK 2.1: Volatility $\sigma(t, x)$ given in (7) is not differentiable with respect to x for some functions γ (for example piecewise constant with respect to x). In such a case the term structure dynamics cannot be analysed in the Heath-Jarrow-Morton framework (1). However, this difficulty is rather technical. Property (2) is sufficient to eliminate arbitrage. By putting $T = t$ in (2) we may also use it to define the numeraire (savings account) in terms of the price volatility σ. It is also easy to see that for all $t \ge 0$

$$P(t,t+\delta) = \beta(t)P(0,t+\delta)\exp\left(-\int_0^t \sigma(s,t+\delta-s)\cdot dW(s) - \frac{1}{2}\int_0^t |\sigma(s,t+\delta-s)|^2 ds\right)$$

$$= \beta(t)P(0,t+\delta)\exp\left(-\int_0^{t+\delta} \sigma(s,t+\delta-s)\cdot dW(s) - \frac{1}{2}\int_0^{t+\delta} |\sigma(s,t+\delta-s)|^2 ds\right) = \frac{\beta(t)}{\beta(t+\delta)}$$

because $\sigma(t, x) = 0$ for $0 \le x \le \delta$. Solving the recurrence relationship

$$\beta(t+\delta) = \beta(t)\, P(t, t+\delta)^{-1} \tag{15}$$

we get

$$\beta(t) = \prod_{k=0}^{[\delta^{-1}t]} P\{[t-(k+1)\delta]^+, t-k\delta\}^{-1} \tag{16}$$

The discounted by $\{\beta(t), t \ge 0\}$ zero coupon bond prices $\{P(t, T);\ 0 \le t \le T\}$ satisfy (2) and hence there is no arbitrage.

REMARK 2.2: Regularity of γ has an important influence on the dynamics of the short rate $r(t, 0)$. If the process $\{r(t, 0);\ t \ge 0\}$ is a semimartingale, then it satisfies

$$dr(t,0) = \frac{\partial}{\partial x} r(t,x)\Big|_{x=0} dt \tag{17}$$

Consequently the short rate is a process of finite variation and therefore it cannot be a strong Markov, except for the deterministic case (cf. E. Çinlar and J. Jacod (1981), Remark 3.41). The Libor process $\{L(t, 0);\ t \ge 0\}$ satisfies (17) as well.

REMARK 2.3: It follows from (13) and Theorem 2.1 that the process $\{L(t, x); t, x \geq 0\}$ satisfies

$$L(t,x)=L(0,x+t)\exp\left[\int_0^t \gamma(s,x+t-s)\cdot dW(s)+\int_0^t \gamma(s,x+t-s)\times \left(\frac{\delta L(s,x+t-s)}{1+\delta L(s,x+t-s)}\gamma(s,x+t-s)+\sigma(s,x+t-s)-\tfrac{1}{2}\gamma(s,x+t-s)\right)ds\right]$$

and

$$|\gamma(s,x+t-s)\cdot\sigma(s,x+t-s)|\leq \sum_{k=1}^{[\delta^{-1}(x+t-s)]} |\gamma(s,x+t-s)||\gamma(s,x+t-s-k\delta)|$$

Therefore

$$L_1(t,x)\leq L(t,x)\leq L_2(t,x)$$

where

$$L_1(t,x)=L(0,x+t)\exp\left[\int_0^t \gamma(s,x+t-s)\cdot dW(s)-\int_0^t \left(\alpha(s,x+t-s)+\tfrac{1}{2}|\gamma(s,x+t-s)|^2\right)ds\right]$$

$$L_2(t,x)=L(0,x+t)\exp\left[\int_0^t \gamma(s,x+t-s)\cdot dW(s)+\int_0^t \left(\alpha(s,x+t-s)+\tfrac{1}{2}|\gamma(s,x+t-s)|^2\right)ds\right]$$

while

$$\alpha(t,x)=\sum_{k=1}^{[\delta^{-1}x]} |\gamma(t,x)||\gamma(t,x-k\delta)|$$

Consequently the Libor rate is bounded from below and above by lognormal processes. The estimate from above can be used to show that the Eurodollar futures price is well defined. The most common Eurodollar futures contract relates to the Libor rate. The futures payoff at time T is equal to $\delta L(T, 0)$ and hence the Eurodollar futures price at time $t \leq T$ is $E(\delta L(T, 0) \mid F_t)$. Because $L(T, 0) \leq L_2(T, 0)$ and

$$EL_2(T,0)=L(0,T)\exp\left[\int_0^T \left(\alpha(s,T-s)+|\gamma(s,T-s)|^2\right)ds\right]<\infty$$

we conclude that the expectation is finite.

REMARK 2.4: For $n = 1, 2, \ldots$ and $t \geq 0$ define

$$y_n(t) = L(t, (n\delta - t)\vee 0),\ \gamma_n(t) = \gamma(t, (n\delta - t)\vee 0)$$

and assume that $\gamma(t, 0) = 0$. It follows easily that the processes $\{y_n(t); t \geq 0\}$, $n = 1, 2, \ldots$, satisfy the following closed system of stochastic equations:

$$dy_n(t)=y_n(t)\gamma_n(t)\cdot\left(\sum_{j=[\delta^{-1}t]+1}^{n}\frac{\delta y_j(t)}{1+\delta y_j(t)}\gamma_j(t)dt+dW(t)\right)$$

We conclude this section with a study which indicates that our model will typically generate mean-reverting behaviour. Interest rates tend to drop when they are too high and tend to rise when they are too low. This property, well supported by empirical evidence, is known as mean-reversion. We assume that $|\gamma(t,x)| \le \beta(x)$, where

$$\sup_{0\le x\le\delta} \sum_{k=0}^{\infty} \beta(x+k\delta) < \infty \tag{A1}$$

$$\int_0^\infty (x+1)\,\beta^2(x)\,dx < \infty \tag{A2}$$

PROPOSITION 2.1: *Assume (A1) and (A2). Then for any* $p \ge 1$ *and any deterministic initial condition* $L(0,\cdot) \in C_b(\mathbf{R}_+)$

$$\sup_{t\ge0}\sup_{x\ge0} EL^p(t,x) < \infty$$

PROOF: Let α and L_2 be as in Remark 2.3. By (A1) and (A2),

$$\sup_{t\ge0}\sup_{x\ge0}\int_0^t \left(\alpha(t,x+t-s)+\tfrac{1}{2}|\gamma(s,x+t-s)|^2\right)ds < \infty$$

and

$$E\left(\int_0^t \gamma(s,x+t-s)\cdot dW(s)\right)^2 \le \int_0^\infty \beta^2(x+s)\,ds \le \int_0^\infty \beta^2(x)\,dx < \infty$$

Since $\log L_2$ is Gaussian

$$\sup_{t\ge0}\sup_{x\ge0} EL_2^p(t,x) < \infty$$

for any $p \ge 1$. Since $L \le L_2$

$$\sup_{t\ge0}\sup_{x\ge0} EL^p(t,x) < \infty$$

Additionally, assume that

$$\gamma(t,x) = \gamma(x) \tag{A3}$$

$$\int_0^\infty x|\gamma'(x)|^2\,dx < \infty \tag{A4}$$

$$\sup_{0\le x\le\delta}\sum_{k=0}^{\infty}|\gamma'(x+k\delta)| < \infty \tag{A5}$$

$$\int_0^\infty |\gamma(x)|\,dx = C < \frac{1}{K} \tag{A6}$$

Assumption (A3) implies that L is a time-homogenous Markov process. Hence we can study the notion of invariant measures. The proof of existence of an invariant measure will follow the standard Krylov-Bogoliubov scheme: Feller property and tightness of family of distributions $\mathbf{L}(L(t))_{t\ge0}$ implies existence of an invariant measure. For details we refer to Da Prato and Zabczyk (1992).

Let $C_0(\mathbf{R}) = \{u \in C(\mathbf{R}): u(x) \to 0 \text{ as } x \to \infty\}$ and let $C^\alpha(\mathbf{R}) = \{u \in C(\mathbf{R}): |u(x)-u(z)| \le C|x-z|^\alpha\}$ for an $0 < \alpha \ge 1$. The Hölder norm in $C^\alpha(\mathbf{R})$ will be denoted by $\|\cdot\|_\alpha$. The following result will be useful.

LEMMA 2.2: *A family of functions* $\Gamma \subset C_0(\mathbf{R}_+)$ *is relatively compact in* $C_0(\mathbf{R}_+)$ *if and only if the following conditions are satisfied:*
(i) *The family* Γ *is equicontinuous on any bounded set.*
(ii) *There exists a function* $R: \mathbf{R}_+ \to \mathbf{R}_+$ *such that* $R(u) \to 0$ as $u \to \infty$ *and* $|f(u)| \leq R(u)$ *for any* $f \in \Gamma$ *and* $u \geq 0$.

THEOREM 2.2: *Assume (A1)–(A5). Let* L *be the solution of* (8) *and let*

$$\sup_{0 \leq x \leq \infty} |\log L(0, x)| < \infty$$

Then

$$\sup_{t \geq 0} E\|\log L(t)\| < \infty$$

If, moreover, (A6) is satisfied, then there exists an invariant measure for the process L *concentrated on the closed set*

$$U = \{u \in C(\mathbf{R}): u > 0 \textit{ and } u(x) \to 1 \textit{ as } x \to \infty\}.$$

PROOF: Consider the process $l(t, x) = \log L(t, x)$, which can be represented as

$$l(x,t) = l_0(x+t) + \int_0^t F[l(t-s)](x+t-s) \cdot \gamma(x+t-s)\,ds - \frac{1}{2}\int_0^t |\gamma(x+t-s)|^2\,ds + M(t,x) \tag{18}$$

for any $t \geq 0$, where M is defined by

$$M(t, x) = \int_0^t \gamma(x + t - s) \cdot dW(s)$$

and

$$F(l)(x) = \sum_{k=0}^{[\delta^{-1}x]} \frac{\delta e^{l(x-k\delta)}}{1+\delta e^{l(x-k\delta)}} \gamma(x-k\delta)$$

for any $l \in C(\mathbf{R})$. By (A1), $\gamma \cdot F: C_0(\mathbf{R}_+) \to C_0(\mathbf{R}_+)$ is a Lipschitz continuous function. By the standard fixed-point method $l(t)$ depends continuously on the initial condition in the space $C_0(\mathbf{R}_+)$. Therefore the process l is a Feller process. Notice that

$$M'_x(t, x) = \int_0^t \gamma'(x + t - s) \cdot dW(s)$$

By the Itô formula

$$E\int_0^\infty M^2(t,x)\,dx \leq \int_0^\infty \int_0^\infty |\gamma(x+s)|^2\,dx\,ds = \sqrt{2}\int_0^\infty x|\gamma(x)|^2\,dx \tag{19}$$

and

$$E\int_0^\infty M'_x(t,x)^2\,dx \leq \int_0^\infty \int_0^\infty |\gamma'(x+s)|^2\,dx\,ds = \sqrt{2}\int_0^\infty x|\gamma'(x)|^2\,dx \tag{20}$$

By (18), for $t > 0$,

$$E\|l(t)\| \leq \|l(0)\| + K\int_0^\infty |\gamma(x)|\,dx + \frac{1}{2}\int_0^\infty |\gamma(x)|^2\,dx + E\sup_{x \geq 0}|M(t,x)|$$

By (19), (20) and the Sobolev imbedding

$$E\sup_{x\geq u}|M(t,x)|^2\leq C_1\left(\int_0^t\int_u^\infty|\gamma(x+s)|^2dxds+\int_0^t\int_u^\infty|\gamma'(x+s)|^2dxds\right)$$

$$\leq R(u)<\infty$$

and for an $\alpha<\frac{1}{2}$

$$E\|M(t)\|_\alpha^2\leq C_1\left(\int_0^t\int_0^\infty|\gamma(x+s)|^2dxds+\int_0^t\int_0^\infty|\gamma'(x+s)|^2dxds\right)$$

$$\leq R<\infty$$

where R and $R(u)$ are independent of t and $R(u)\to 0$ as $u\to\infty$. Thus

$$\sup_{t\geq 0}E\|I(t)\|<\infty$$

Let (*A6*) be also satisfied. Assume from now that $I_0=0$. In order to prove existence of an invariant measure for the process I we will prove that the family of laws $\mathbf{L}(I(t))_{t\geq 0}$ is tight. Again by (18)

$$\sup_{t\geq 0}E\sup_{x\geq u}|I(t,x)|\leq K\int_u^\infty|\gamma(x)|dx+\frac{1}{2}\int_u^\infty|\gamma(x)|^2dx+E\sup_{x\geq u}|M(t,x)|\to 0 \tag{21}$$

as $u\to\infty$. Moreover, for any $\psi\in C(\mathbf{R})$

$$\frac{|F(\psi)(x)-F(\psi)(u)|}{|x-u|^\alpha}\leq C_1+CK\sup_{x,u\geq 0}\frac{|\psi(x)-\psi(u)|}{|x-u|^\alpha} \tag{22}$$

for a certain constant C_1. By (*A2*), (*A4*) and (*A6*)

$$\sup_{t\geq 0}E\|I(t)\|_\alpha\leq C_2+CK\sup_{t\geq 0}E\|I(t)\|_\alpha$$

Since $CK<1$

$$\sup_{t\geq 0}E\|I(t)\|_\alpha\leq\frac{C_2}{1-CK} \tag{23}$$

By (21), (23) and Lemma 2.2, the family $\mathbf{L}(I(t))_{t\geq 0}$ is tight on $C_0(\mathbf{R})$. Since I is a Feller process, by the standard Krylov-Bogoliubov technique there exists an invariant measure for the process I concentrated on $C_0(\mathbf{R})$. Existence of invariant measures for I on $C_0(\mathbf{R})$ is equivalent to existence of invariant measures for L on U.

Derivatives pricing

In this section we derive formulae for caps and swaptions at different compounding frequencies (for example, quarterly and semi-annually). Consider a payer forward swap on principal 1 settled quarterly in arrears at times $T_j=T_0+j\delta$, $j=1,\ldots,n$. The Libor rate received at time T_j is set at time T_{j-1} at the level (cf. (3)):

$$L(T_{j-1},0)=\delta^{-1}(P(T_{j-1},T_j)^{-1}-1)$$

The swap cashflows at times T_j, $j=1,\ldots,n$, are $L(T_{j-1},0)\delta$ and $-\kappa\delta$, and hence the time $t(t\leq T_0)$ value of the swap is (cf. Brace and Musiela (1994*b*))

$$E\left(\sum_{j=1}^n\frac{\beta(t)}{\beta(T_j)}[L(T_{j-1},0)-\kappa]\delta\middle|\mathcal{F}_t\right)=P(t,T_0)-\sum_{j=1}^n C_jP(t,T_j) \tag{24}$$

where $C_j=\kappa\delta$ for $j=1,\ldots,n-1$ and $C_n=1+\kappa\delta$.

The forward swap rate $\omega_{T_0}(t, n)$ at time t for maturity T_0 is that value of the fixed rate κ which makes the value of the forward swap zero, ie,

$$\omega_{T_0}(t,n) = \left(\delta \sum_{j=1}^{n} P(t,T_j)\right)^{-1} [P(t,T_0) - P(t,T_n)] \tag{25}$$

In a forward cap (res. floor) on principal 1 settled in arrears at times T_j, $j = 1, \ldots, n$, the cashflows at times T_j are $(L(T_{j-1}, 0) - \kappa)^+\delta$ (res. $(\kappa - L(T_{j-1}, 0))^+\delta$). The cap price at time $t \le T_0$ is

$$\begin{aligned} \mathrm{Cap}(t) &= \sum_{j=1}^{n} E\left(\frac{\beta(t)}{\beta(T_j)}[L(T_{j-1},0)-\kappa]^+ \delta \,\middle|\, F_t\right) \\ &= \sum_{j=1}^{n} P(t,T_j) E_{T_j}\left([L(T_{j-1},0)-\kappa]^+ \delta \,\middle|\, F_t\right) \end{aligned}$$

where E_T stands for the expectation under the forward measure $\mathbf{P}_T$ defined by (cf. Musiela (1995))

$$\mathbf{P}_T = \exp\left(-\int_0^T \sigma(t,T-t)\cdot dW(t) - \tfrac{1}{2}\int_0^T |\sigma(t,T-t)|^2 dt\right)\mathbf{P} = [P(0,T)\beta(T)]^{-1}\mathbf{P} \tag{26}$$

The process

$$K(t,T) = L(t,T-t) \quad 0 \le t \le T \tag{27}$$

satisfies (cf. (5) and Theorem 2.1)

$$\begin{aligned} dK(t,T) &= \\ K(t,T)\gamma(t,T-t)&\cdot\left[\left(\frac{\delta K(t,T)}{1+\delta K(t,T)}\gamma(t,T-t)+\sigma(t,T-t)\right)dt + dW(t)\right] \\ &= K(t,T)\gamma(t,T-t)\cdot[\sigma(t,T+\delta-t)dt + dW(t)] \end{aligned}$$

Moreover, the process

$$W_T(t) = W(t) + \int_0^t \sigma(s,T-s)\,ds \tag{28}$$

is a Brownian motion under $\mathbf{P}_T$. Consequently

$$dK(t,T) = K(t,T)\,\gamma(t,T-t)\cdot dW_{T+\delta}(t) \tag{29}$$

and hence $K(t, T)$ is lognormally distributed under $\mathbf{P}_{T+\delta}$. It follows that

$$\begin{aligned} E_{T+\delta}\left([L(T,0)-\kappa]^+ \,\middle|\, F_t\right) &= E_{T+\delta}\left([K(T,T)-\kappa]^+ \,\middle|\, F_t\right) \\ &= K(t,T)N[h(t,T)] - \kappa N[h(t,T)-\zeta(t,T)] \end{aligned}$$

where

$$h(t,T) = \frac{\log[K(t,T)/\kappa] + \frac{1}{2}\zeta^2(t,T)}{\zeta(t,T)}$$

$$\zeta^2(t,T) = \int_t^T |\gamma(s,T-s)|^2 ds$$

and hence we have the following result.

PROPOSITION 3.1: *The cap price at time* $t \le T_0$ *is*

$$\mathrm{Cap}(t) = \sum_{j=1}^{n} \delta P(t, T_j)\Big(K(t, T_{j-1})N[h(t, T_{j-1})] - \kappa N[h(t, T_{j-1}) - \zeta(t, T_{j-1})]\Big)$$

REMARK 3.1: The above $\mathrm{Cap}(t)$ formula corresponds to the market Black futures formula with discount from the settlement date. It was originally derived using a different approach and model set-up by Miltersen *et al.* (1994).

A payer swaption at strike κ maturing at time T_0 gives the right to receive at time T_0 the cashflows of the corresponding forward payer swap settled in arrears or, alternatively, discounted from the settlement dates $T_j = T_0 + j\delta$, $j = 1, \ldots, n$, to T_0 value of the cashflows defined by $(\omega_{T_0}(T_0, n) - \kappa)^+\delta$, where $(\omega_{T_0}(T_0, n)$ is given in (25). Hence the time $t \le T_0$ price of the option is

$$E\left[\frac{\beta(t)}{\beta(T_0)} E\left(\sum_{j=1}^{n} \frac{\beta(T_0)}{\beta(T_j)}\left[\omega_{T_0}(T_0, n) - \kappa\right]^+ \delta \,\Big|\, F_{T_0}\right) \Big|\, F_t\right]$$

$$= E\left[\frac{\beta(t)}{\beta(T_0)}\left(1 - \sum_{j=1}^{n} C_j P(T_0, T_j)\right)^+ \Big|\, F_t\right]$$

$$= E\left\{\frac{\beta(t)}{\beta(T_0)}\left[E\left(\sum_{j=1}^{n} \frac{\beta(T_0)}{\beta(T_j)}\left[L(T_{j-1}, 0) - \kappa\right]\delta \,\Big|\, F_{T_0}\right)\right]^+ \Big|\, F_t\right\} \tag{30}$$

where $C_j = \kappa\delta$ for $j = 1, \ldots, n - 1$ and $C_n = 1 + \kappa\delta$ (cf. Brace and Musiela (1994*b*)). Let

$$A = [\omega_{T_0}(T_0, n) \ge \kappa] = \left(\sum_{j=1}^{n} C_j P(T_0, T_j) \le 1\right) \tag{31}$$

be the event that the swaption ends up in the money. The second expression in (30) can be written as follows

$$P(t, T_0)\mathbf{P}_{T_0}(A|F_t) - \sum_{j=1}^{n} C_j E\left[\frac{\beta(t)}{\beta(T_0)} E\left(\frac{\beta(T_0)}{\beta(T_j)} \Big|\, F_{T_0}\right) I_A \Big|\, F_t\right]$$

$$= P(t, T_0)\mathbf{P}_{T_0}(A|F_t) - \sum_{j=1}^{n} C_j P(t, T_j)\,\mathbf{P}_{T_j}(A|F_t) \tag{32}$$

Also, for all $j = 1, \ldots, n$

$$P(t, T_{j-1})\mathbf{P}_{T_{j-1}}(A|F_t) = E\left(\frac{\beta(t)}{\beta(T_{j-1})} I_A \Big|\, F_T\right)$$

$$= E\left(\frac{\beta(t)}{\beta(T_j)} \frac{1}{P(T_{j-1}, T_j)} I_A \Big|\, F_T\right) = E\left(\frac{\beta(t)}{\beta(T_j)}[1 + \delta K(T_{j-1}, T_{j-1})] I_A \Big|\, F_T\right)$$

$$= P(t, T_j)\mathbf{P}_{T_j}(A|F_t) + \delta P(t, T_j)E_{T_j}\left[K(T_{j-1}, T_{j-1})I_A \,\big|\, F_T\right]$$

$$= P(t, T_j)\mathbf{P}_{T_j}(A|F_t) + \delta P(t, T_j)E_{T_j}\left[K(T_0, T_{j-1})I_A \,\big|\, F_T\right] \tag{33}$$

where the last equality holds because the process $\{K(t, T_{j-1});\ 0 \le t \le T_{j-1}\}$ is a martingale under the measure $\mathbf{P}_{T_j}$ and the event A is F_{T_0} measurable (see (27)–(29) and (31)). Consequently we have the following result.

THEOREM 3.1: *The payer swaption price at time* $t \le T_0$ *is*

$$Ps(t) = \delta \sum_{j=1}^{n} P(t, T_j) E_{T_j} \left\{ \left[K(T_0, T_{j-1}) - \kappa \right] I_A \,\middle|\, F_T \right\}$$

To simplify further the above swaption formula we need to analyse first the relationships between the forward measures $\mathbf{P}_{T_j}$, defined in (26), as well as the corresponding forward Brownian motions W_{T_j}, given in (28), for $j = 1, 2, \ldots, n$. We have

$$\begin{aligned} dW_{T_j}(t) &= dW(t) + \sigma(t, T_j - t)dt = dW_{T_{j-1}}(t) + [\sigma(t, T_j - t) - \sigma(t, T_{j-1} - t)]dt \\ &= dW_{T_{j-1}}(t) + \frac{\delta K(t, T_{j-1})}{1 + \delta K(t, T_{j-1})} \gamma(t, T_{j-1} - t)]dt \end{aligned} \tag{34}$$

Also, because the process $\{K(t, T_{j-1});\ 0 \le t \le T_{j-1}\}$ satisfies

$$dK(t, T_{j-1}) = K(t, T_{j-1}) \gamma(t, T_{j-1} - t) \cdot dW_{T_j}(t)$$

we have

$$\begin{aligned} d\frac{\delta K(t, T_{j-1})}{1 + \delta K(t, T_{j-1})} &= \frac{\delta K(t, T_{j-1})}{[1 + \delta K(t, T_{j-1})]^2} \gamma(t, T_{j-1} - t) \cdot dW_{T_j}(t) - \\ &\quad \frac{\delta^2 K^2(t, T_{j-1})}{[1 + \delta K(t, T_{j-1})]^3} \left| \gamma(t, T_{j-1} - t) \right|^2 dt \\ &= \frac{\delta K(t, T_{j-1})}{[1 + \delta K(t, T_{j-1})]^2} \gamma(t, T_{j-1} - t) \cdot dW_{T_{j-1}}(t) \end{aligned} \tag{35}$$

and hence the process $\{(1 + \delta K(t, T_{j-1}))^{-1} \delta K(t, T_{j-1});\ 0 \le t \le T_{j-1}\}$ is a supermartingale under the measure $\mathbf{P}_{T_j}$ and a martingale under the measure $\mathbf{P}_{T_{j-1}}$.

Let, for $t \le T_0$,

$$F_{T_0}(t, T_k) = \frac{P(t, T_k)}{P(t, T_0)} \tag{36}$$

denote the forward price at time t for settlement at time T_0 on a T_k maturity zero coupon bond. Because we have

$$F_{T_0}(t, T_k) = \prod_{i=1}^{k} F_{T_{i-1}}(t, T_i) = \left(\prod_{i=1}^{k} [1 + \delta K(t, T_{i-1})] \right)^{-1}$$

the event A, defined in (31), can be written as follows

$$\begin{aligned} A &= \left[\sum_{k=1}^{n} c_k \left(\prod_{i=1}^{k} [1 + \delta K(T_0, T_{i-1})] \right)^{-1} \le 1 \right] \\ &= \left\{ \sum_{k=1}^{n} c_k \left[\prod_{i=1}^{k} [1 + \delta K(t, T_{i-1})] \exp\left(\int_t^{T_0} \gamma(s, T_{i-1} - s) \cdot dW_{T_i}(s) - \right.\right.\right. \\ &\quad \left.\left.\left. \tfrac{1}{2} \int_t^{T_0} \left| \gamma(s, T_{i-1} - s) \right|^2 ds \right) \right]^{-1} \le 1 \right\} \end{aligned} \tag{37}$$

Moreover, we deduce from (34) that for $t \le T_0$ and i, j = 1, ..., n

$$dW_{T_j}(t) = dW_{T_i}(t) + \sum_{\ell=0}^{i-1} \frac{\delta K(t, T_\ell)}{1+\delta K(t, T_\ell)} \gamma(t, T_\ell - t)dt - \sum_{\ell=0}^{j-1} \frac{\delta K(t, T_\ell)}{1+\delta K(t, T_\ell)} \gamma(t, T_\ell - t)dt \tag{38}$$

Consequently we can write

$$X_i = \int_t^{T_0} \gamma(s, T_{i-1} - s) \cdot dW_{T_i}(s) = \int_t^{T_0} \gamma(s, T_{i-1} - s) \cdot dW_{T_j}(s) + \sum_{\ell=1}^{i} \int_t^{T_0} \frac{\delta K(s, T_{\ell-1})}{1+\delta K(s, T_{\ell-1})} \gamma(s, T_{\ell-1} - s) \cdot \gamma(s, T_{i-1} - s)ds - \sum_{\ell-1}^{j} \int_t^{T_0} \frac{\delta K(s, T_{\ell-1})}{1+\delta K(s, T_{\ell-1})} \gamma(s, T_{\ell-1} - s) \cdot \gamma(s, T_{i-1} - s)ds \tag{39}$$

We will approximate the conditional on F_t distribution of $X_1, \ldots, X_n$ under the measure P_{T_j} (for each j = 1, ..., n) by the distribution of the random vector $X_1^j, \ldots, X_n^j$, where

$$X_i^j = \int_t^{T_0} \gamma(s, T_{i-1} - s) \cdot dW_{T_j}(s) + \sum_{\ell=1}^{i} \frac{\delta K(t, T_{\ell-1})}{1+\delta K(t, T_{\ell-1})} \Delta_{\ell i} - \sum_{\ell=1}^{j} \frac{\delta K(t, T_{\ell-1})}{1+\delta K(t, T_{\ell-1})} \Delta_{\ell i} \tag{40}$$

while

$$\Delta_{\ell i} = \int_t^{T_0} \gamma(s, T_{\ell-1} - s) \cdot \gamma(s, T_{i-1} - s)\, ds \tag{41}$$

In view of (35) the above approximation corresponds to Wiener chaos order 0 approximation of the process

$$\frac{\delta K(s, T_\ell)}{1+\delta K(s, T_\ell)} \qquad s \le T_\ell \tag{42}$$

under the measure $\mathbf{P}_{T_\ell}$. A more accurate approximation involving Wiener chaos of order 0 to 1 may be used as well. We found, however, that the contribution of order 1 Wiener chaos is not very significant; so we can simply replace the process (42) by its value at t in formula (38) or, because of (35), by the conditional expectation under $P_{T_{\ell-1}}$ given F_t.

Obviously the conditional on F_t distribution of $X_1^j, \ldots, X_n^j$ under the measure $\mathbf{P}_{T_j}$ is $N(\mu^j, \Delta)$, where $\Delta_{\ell i}$ is given in (41) and

$$\mu_i^j = \sum_{\ell=1}^{i} \frac{\delta K(t, T_{\ell-1})}{1+\delta K(t, T_{\ell-1})} \Delta_{\ell i} - \sum_{\ell=1}^{j} \frac{\delta K(t, T_{\ell-1})}{1+\delta K(t, T_{\ell-1})} \Delta_{\ell i} \tag{43}$$

In practice the first eigenvalue of the matrix Δ is approximately 50 times larger than the second, and therefore we can assume that Δ is of rank 1, or equivalently that

$$\Delta_{\ell i} = \Gamma_\ell \Gamma_i \tag{44}$$

for some positive constants $\Gamma_1, \ldots \Gamma_n$. Set $d_0 = 0$ and for $i \ge 1$

$$d_i = \sum_{\ell=1}^{i} \frac{\delta K(t, T_{\ell-1})}{1+\delta K(t, T_{\ell-1})} \Gamma_\ell \tag{45}$$

then it follows from (43) and (44) that

$$\mu_i^j = \Gamma_i (d_i - d_j) \tag{46}$$

For all $j = 1, \ldots, n$ the function

$$f_j(x) = 1 - \sum_{k=1}^{n} C_k \left\{ \prod_{i=1}^{k} \left[1 + \delta K(t, T_{i-1}) \exp\left(\Gamma_i (x + d_i - d_j) - \tfrac{1}{2}\Gamma_i^2 \right) \right] \right\}^{-1}$$

satisfies $f_j'(x) > 0$, $f_j(-\infty) = -n\delta\kappa$, $f(\infty) = 1$. Hence there is a unique point s_j such that $f_j(s_j) = 0$. Moreover, if s_0 is the solution with $j = 0$, clearly $s_j = s_0 + d_j$. Also $f_j(x) \geq 0$ for $x \geq s_j$ and therefore, using (37), (40) and (46), we deduce that

$$\mathbf{P}_{T_j}(A \mid F_t) = \mathbf{P}_{T_j}(X_j^j \geq \Gamma_i s_j \mid F_t) = N\left(-s_0 - d_j\right) \tag{47}$$

Moreover, standard arguments yield

$$E_{T_j}\left[K(T_0, T_{j-1}) I_A \mid F_t\right] = E_{T_j}\left[K(t, T_{j-1}) \exp\left(\int_t^{T_0} \gamma(s, T_{j-1} - s) \cdot dW_{T_j}(s) - \right.\right.$$

$$\left.\left. \frac{1}{2}\int_t^{T_0} \left|\gamma(s, T_{j-1} - s)\right|^2 ds \right) I_A \mid F_t \right] = K(t, T_{j-1}) N\left(-s_0 - d_j + \Gamma_j\right) \tag{48}$$

and finally we obtain the following result.

THEOREM 3.2: *The price at time* $t \leq T_0$ *of the payer swaption can be approximated by*

$$Psa(t) = \delta \sum_{j=1}^{n} P(t, T_j)\left[K(t, T_{j-1}) N\left(-s_0 - d_j + \Gamma_j\right) - \kappa N\left(-s_0 - d_j\right)\right]$$

where s_0 *is given by*

$$\sum_{k=1}^{n} C_k \left\{ \prod_{i=1}^{k} \left[1 + \delta K(t, T_{i-1}) \exp\left(\Gamma_i (s_0 + d_i) - \tfrac{1}{2}\Gamma_i^2 \right) \right] \right\}^{-1} = 1$$

$C_k = \kappa\delta$, $k = 1, \ldots, n = 1$ *and* $C_n = 1 + \kappa\delta$, *while* Γ_i *and* d_i *are defined in* (41), (44) *and* (45), *respectively.*

PROOF: Follows from Theorem 3.1 and formulae (47) and (48).

In the US, UK and Japanese markets caps correspond to rates compounded quarterly, while swaptions are semi-annual. In the German market caps are quarterly and swaptions annual. We deal with this problem by assuming lognormal volatility structure on the quarterly rates. The forward swap rate at time $t \leq T_0$ is

$$\omega_{T_0}^{(k)}(t, n) = \left(k\delta \sum_{j=1}^{n} P(t, T_{kj}) \right)^{-1} [P(t, T_0) - P(t, T_{kn})] \tag{49}$$

and hence the time $t \le T_0$ price of a payer swaption at strike κ maturing at time T_0 is

$$\begin{aligned} Ps^{(k)}(t) &= E\left(\sum_{j=1}^{n} \frac{\beta(t)}{\beta(T_{kj})}\left[\omega_{T_0}^{(k)}(T_0,n)-\kappa\right]^{+} k\delta \Big| F_t\right) \\ &= E\left[\frac{\beta(t)}{\beta(T_0)}\left(1-\sum_{j=1}^{n} C_j^{(k)} P(T_0,T_{kj})\right)^{+} \Big| F_t\right] \\ &= P(t,T_0)\mathbf{P}_{T_0}(A|F_t) - \sum_{j=1}^{n} C_j^{(k)} P(t,T_{kj})\mathbf{P}_{T_{kj}}(A|F_t) \end{aligned}$$

where $C_j^{(k)} = k\kappa\delta$ for $j = 1, \ldots, n-1$ and $C_n^{(k)} = 1 + k\kappa\delta$, while

$$A = \left[\omega_{T_0}^{(k)}(T_0,n) \ge \kappa\right] = \left(\sum_{j=1}^{n} C_j^{(k)} P(T_0,T_{kj}) \le 1\right)$$

From (33) it follows that for all j

$$P(t,T_{k(j-1)})\mathbf{P}_{T_{k(j-1)}}(A|F_t) = P(t,T_{kj})\mathbf{P}_{T_{kj}}(A|F_t) + \delta\sum_{i=1}^{k} P(t,T_{k(j-1)+i}) E_{T_{k(j-1)+i}}\left[K(T_0,T_{k(j-1)+i-1}) I_A \Big| F_t\right]$$

Table 1. Accuracy of the formula Psa$^{(1)}$(0)

Option maturity × Swap length	Strike (%)	Simulation price		Psa$^{(1)}$(0)	Spreads
0.25 × 2	6.00	159.71	(0.25)	160.17	4
	7.00	39.62	(0.25)	40.39	2.5
	8.00	4.25	(0.25)	4.61	2
0.25 × 3	6.25	237.79	(0.25)	238.09	5
	7.25	59.33	(0.25)	60.54	3.5
	8.25	6.11	(0.25)	6.75	2
0.25 × 5	6.60	361.24	(0.25)	362.72	10
	7.60	79.49	(0.25)	81.16	6
	8.60	5.84	(0.25)	6.39	3
0.5 × 5	6.70	386.34	(0.25	389.79	11
	7.70	127.34	(0.25)	131.43	8
	8.70	25.99	(0.25)	28.12	4
1 × 2	6.60	187.23	(0.25)	188.56	7
	7.60	92.93	(0.25)	94.76	5
	8.60	40.29	(0.25)	41.99	3
2 × 2	6.75	230.00	(.025)	231.80	10
	7.75	140.17	(0.25)	142.60	7
	8.75	80.54	(0.25)	82.98	6
2 × 5	7.50	359.41	(0.26)	363.60	20
	8.50	189.24	(0.25)	194.47	16
	9.50	91.64	(0.25)	95.79	10
3 × 2	7.00	227.75	(0.25)	230.28	11
	8.00	148.15	(0.25)	151.14	8
	9.00	92.68	(0.25)	95.67	6
3 × 3	7.00	323.71	(0.25)	327.13	16
	8.00	204.93	(0.25)	208.80	12
	9.00	123.43	(0.25)	127.39	9
5 × 5	7.00	502.54	(0.40)	506.34	27
	8.00	331.56	(0.37)	336.90	22
	9.00	209.39	(0.34)	215.33	22
	10.00	127.85	(0.31)	133.44	18

The difference between calculated and simulated prices is well within spreads. All prices are in basis points (1 bp = $100 per $1M face value).

and hence

$$Ps^{(k)}(t) = \delta \sum_{j=1}^{n} \left[\sum_{i=k(j-1)+1}^{kj} P(t, T_i) E_{T_i}\left(K(T_0, T_{i-1}) I_A \middle| F_t\right) - k\kappa P(t, T_{kj}) \mathbf{P}_{T_{kj}}\left(A \middle| F_t\right) \right] \quad (50)$$

Repeating arguments used in the proof of Theorem 3.1 we deduce the following swaption approximation formula.

THEOREM 3.3: *Let* k *and* δ *be such that* $(k\delta)^{-1}$ *is the compounding frequency per year of the swap rate* $\omega_{T_0}^{(k)}(t, n)$ *given in* (49). *The time* $t \le T_0$ *price of a payer swaption can be approximated by*

$$Psa^{(k)}(t) = \delta \sum_{j=1}^{n} \left[\sum_{i=k(j-1)+1}^{kj} P(t, T_i) K(t, T_{i-1}) N\left(-s_0^{(k)} - d_i + \Gamma_i\right) - k\kappa P(t, T_{kj}) N\left(-s_0^{(k)} - d_{kj}\right) \right] \quad (51)$$

where $s_0^{(k)}$ *is given by*

$$\sum_{j=1}^{n} C_j^{(k)} \left\{ \prod_{i=1}^{kj} \left[1 + \delta K(t, T_{i-1}) \exp\left(\Gamma_i (s_0^{(k)} + d_i) - \tfrac{1}{2} \Gamma_i^2 \right) \right] \right\}^{-1} = 1$$

$C_j^{(k)} = k\kappa\delta$ *for* $j = 1, \ldots, n - 1$, $C_n^{(k)} = 1 + k\kappa\delta$, *while* Γ_i *and* d_i *are defined in* (41), (44) *and* (45) *respectively.*

REMARK 3.2: If one chooses $\delta = 0.25$, for example, in a market with quarterly caps and semi-annual swaptions, then formula (51) with $n = 1$ can be used to price a caplet and hence it can also be used to jointly calibrate off-quarterly caps and semi-annual swaptions.

To analyse differences between the exact swaption value, computed by simulation, and an approximation value computed using formula (51) with $k = 1$ and $t = 0$, a one-factor model was fitted to US cap and swaption data on 12 July 1994, generating a typical volatility structure. Simulation prices were generated under the $\mathbf{P}_{T_n}$ forward measure using the exact formula

Table 2. Black versus calculated price

Option maturity × Swap length	Strike (%)	Black price	$Psa^{(1)}(0)$
0.25 × 1	8	183.88	183.88
	10	36.59	36.59
	12	1.35	1.35
1 × 2	8	344.05	344.05
	10	129.36	129.35
	12	34.87	34.87
1 × 5	8	748.02	747.97
	10	281.24	281.14
	12	75.82	75.73
1 × 10	8	1204.52	1204.19
	10	452.88	452.20
	12	122.08	121.60
3 × 3	8	473.29	473.21
	10	262.20	262.09
	12	136.27	136.17

When yield and volatility are flat (10% and 20%, respectively) the Black swaption formula and $Psa^{(1)}(0)$ are almost identical. All prices are in basis points (1 bp = $100 per $1M face value).

$$P(0,T_n)E_{T_n}\left(\sum_{j=0}^{n-1} C_j \prod_{i=j+1}^{n}[1+\delta K(T_0,T_{i-1})]+C_n\right)^{+} \qquad (52)$$

with $C_0 = 1$, $C_j = -\kappa\delta$, $j = 1, \ldots, n-1$, $C_n = -(1+\kappa\delta)$ and

$$K(t,T_{i-1}) =$$

$$K(0,T_{i-1})\exp\left(\int_0^t \gamma(s,T_{i-1}-s)\cdot dW_{T_i}(s) - \tfrac{1}{2}\int_0^t \left|\gamma(s,T_{i-1}-s\right|^2 ds\right)$$

$$W_{T_{i-1}}(t) = W_{T_i}(t) - \int_0^t \frac{\delta K(s,T_{i-1})}{1+\delta K(s,T_{i-1})}\gamma(s,T_{i-1}-s)\,ds$$

Table 3. GBP yield curve for 3 February 1995

Market rates

Tenor	Rate	Tenor	Rate
Cash 1 Month	6.68750%	Future 18 December 1996	90.94
Cash 2 Month	6.75000%	Future 19 March 1997	90.90
Cash 3 Month	6.78125%	Future 18 June 1997	90.88
Cash 6 Month	7.12500%	Future 17 September 1997	90.85
Cash 9 Month	7.50000%	Future 17 December 1997	90.85
Future 15 March 1995	92.94	Swap 2 year	8.265%
Future 21 June 1995	92.26	Swap 3 year	8.550%
Future 20 September 1995	91.83	Swap 4 year	8.655%
Future 20 December 1995	91.52	Swap 5 year	8.770%
Future 20 March 1996	91.31	Swap 7 year	8.910%
Future 19 June 1996	91.15	Swap 10 year	8.920%
Future 18 September 1996	91.04		

Zero coupon discount function (ZCDF)

Tenor: x	ZCDF (x)	Tenor: x	ZCDS (x)	Tenor: x	ZCDF (x)
0.00000000	1.00000000	2.37260274	0.82165363	7.00821918	0.53980408
0.07671233	0.99489605	2.62191781	0.80338660	7.50684932	0.51675532
0.10958904	0.99268989	2.87123288	0.78546824	8.00547945	0.49467915
0.37808219	0.97422289	3.12054795	0.76794952	8.50410959	0.47353468
0.62739726	0.95577923	3.49863014	0.74363839	9.00547945	0.45317677
0.87671233	0.93669956	4.00273973	0.71105063	9.50410959	0.43378439
1.12602740	0.91730596	4.49863014	0.67976222	10.00821918	0.41501669
1.37534247	0.89785353	5.00273973	0.64895804	10.50821918	0.39720417
1.62465753	0.87847062	5.50136986	0.62032221	11.00821918	0.38015617
1.87397260	0.85927558	6.01095890	0.59213852	11.50821918	0.36383986
2.12328767	0.84029504	6.50136986	0.56589374		

The zero-coupon discount function is calculated from the market rates at various tenors. Intermediate rates can be found by splining.

Table 4. Forward rate correlations for GBP

	0	0.25	0.5	1	1.5	2	2.5	3	4	5	7	9
0	1.0000	0.6853	0.5320	0.3125	0.3156	0.2781	0.1835	0.0617	0.1974	0.1021	0.1029	0.0598
0.25	0.6853	1.0000	0.8415	0.6246	0.6231	0.5330	0.4278	0.3274	0.4463	0.2439	0.3326	0.2625
0.5	0.5320	0.8415	1.0000	0.7903	0.7844	0.7320	0.6346	0.4521	0.5812	0.3439	0.4533	0.3661
1	0.3125	0.6246	0.7903	1.0000	0.9967	0.8108	0.7239	0.5429	0.6121	0.4426	0.5189	0.4251
1.5	0.3156	0.6231	0.7844	0.9967	1.0000	0.8149	0.7286	0.5384	0.6169	0.4464	0.5233	0.4299
2	0.2781	0.5330	0.7320	0.8108	0.8149	1.0000	0.9756	0.5676	0.6860	0.4969	0.5734	0.4771
2.5	0.1835	0.4278	0.6346	0.7239	0.7286	0.9756	1.0000	0.5457	0.6583	0.4921	0.5510	0.4581
3	0.0617	0.3274	0.4521	0.5429	0.5384	0.5676	0.5457	1.0000	0.5942	0.6078	0.6751	0.6017
4	0.1974	0.4463	0.5812	0.6121	0.6169	0.6860	0.6583	0.5942	1.0000	0.4845	0.6452	0.5673
5	0.1021	0.2439	0.3439	0.4426	0.4464	0.4969	0.4921	0.6078	0.4845	1.0000	0.6015	0.5200
7	0.1029	0.3326	0.4533	0.5189	0.5233	0.5734	0.5510	0.6751	0.6452	0.6015	1.0000	0.9889
9	0.0598	0.2625	0.3661	0.4251	0.4299	0.4771	0.4581	0.6017	0.5673	0.5200	0.9889	1.0000

Forward rates were assumed constant on the intervals between the given terms. One year of data (1994) were used to calculate the table.

The above equations permit the recursive calculation of the Brownian motions $W_{T_0}(t), \ldots, W_{T_{n-1}}(t)$ for $0 \le t \le T_0$. For each simulation of $W_{T_n}(t)$ on $[0, T_0]$ that gives values of $K(T_0, T_{i-1})$, $i = 1, \ldots, n$; substitution in (52) gives the corresponding value of the swaption. The simulation procedure, which involves Riemann and stochastic integration steps, was checked by back-calculating the cap prices used in parameterisation. The simulation prices coincided with the closed-form prices calculated using the Cap (0) formula of Proposition 3.1. Table 1 gives the swaption prices for a range of strikes, option maturities and swap lengths. Two standard deviation errors of simulated prices are in brackets. Bid and ask spreads, estimated by professional dealers at Citibank, London, are in the last column.

We also compared formula (51) with the market formula for pricing swaptions, based on assuming that the underlying swap rate is lognormal and given by

$$\delta \sum_{j=1}^{n} P(0, T_j)\left[\omega_{T_0}(0,n)N(h) - \kappa N\left(h - \gamma\sqrt{T_0}\right)\right] \tag{53}$$

where

$$h = \frac{\log\left(\omega_{T_0}(0,n)/\kappa\right) + \frac{1}{2}\gamma^2 T_0}{\gamma\sqrt{T_0}}$$

Table 5. Lognormal Heath–Jarrow–Morton fit for 3 February 1995

Currency: GBP Contract	 Length	At-the-money strike (%)	Black volume (%)	Market price (bp)	Average error (%): 0.64 Error (bp)	 Error (%)
Cap	1	7.88	15.50	27	−0.0	−0.0
Cap	2	8.39	17.75	100	2.5	2.5
Cap	3	8.64	18.00	185	0.8	0.4
Cap	4	8.69	17.75	267	0.3	0.1
Cap	5	8.79	17.75	360	−7.4	−2.1
Cap	7	8.90	16.50	511	2.5	0.5
Cap	10	8.89	15.50	703	−0.0	−0.0
	Option maturity × Swap length					
Swaption	0.25 × 2	8.57	16.75	50	−0.6	−1.2
Swaption	0.25 × 3	8.75	16.50	73	−0.1	−0.1
Swaption	1 × 4	9.10	15.50	172	−0.4	−0.2
Swaption	0.25 × 5	8.90	15.00	103	0.1	0.1
Swaption	0.25 × 7	9.00	13.75	123	1.6	1.3
Swaption	0.25 × 10	8.99	13.25	151	−0.1	−0.1
Swaption	1 × 9	9.12	13.25	271	−1.7	−0.6
Swaption	2 × 8	9.16	12.75	312	1.2	0.4

Contracts to be fitted are on the left with their at-the-money strikes and market-quoted Black volatilities. Prices and the fit, obtained with the volatility functions below, are on the right. Average error in fitting is 0.64%, while the biggest single error is 2.5%. Note: 1 bp = $100 per $1M face value.

Tenor: x, t	$\gamma_1(x)$	$\gamma_2(x)$	f(t)
0.25	0.09481393	0.12146092	1.00000000
0.50	0.08498925	0.05117321	1.00000000
1.00	0.22939966	0.09100802	0.99168448
1.50	0.19166872	0.02876211	1.00388389
2.00	0.08232925	0.01172934	1.00388389
2.50	0.18548202	0.00047705	1.07602593
3.00	0.13817885	−0.01160086	1.07602593
4.00	0.08562258	−0.04673283	1.04727642
5.00	0.14547123	−0.04181446	1.02727799
7.00	0.08869328	−0.05459175	0.96660430
9.00	0.04121240	−0.03631021	0.93012459
11.00	0.15206796	−0.16626765	0.81425256

Piecewise constant on each interval.

Note that because

$$E\sum_{j=1}^{n}\frac{1}{\beta(T_j)}\left[\omega_{T_0}(T_0,n)-\kappa\right]^+\delta = \delta\sum_{j=1}^{n}P(0,T_j)E_{T_j}\left[\omega_{T_0}(T_0,n)-\kappa\right]^+$$

the market seems to identify the forward measures $\mathbf{P}_{T_j}$, $j = 1, \ldots, n$, with the forward measure $\mathbf{P}_{T_0}$ and assumes lognormality of the swap rate process $\omega_{T_0}(t, n)$, $0 \leq t \leq T_0$ under the measure $\mathbf{P}_{T_0}$. In fact formula (51) reduces to (53) if $d_i = 0$, $\Gamma_i = \Delta_{ii}^{1/2} = \gamma\sqrt{T_0}$ and $K(0, T_i) = K$. We assumed constant 10% yield (compounded quarterly) and 20% volatility in formulae (51) and (53). Table 2 gives the swaption prices.

Model calibration

To calibrate the model we used data from the UK market for Friday 3 February 1995. Market cash, futures and swap rates are given in Table 3, together with the corresponding zero coupon discount function (ZCDF). Cap and swaption volatilities, given in Table 5 (or 6), together with the historically estimated correlation between the forward rates, given in Table 4, were used to compute the model volatilities. We assumed a two-factor model with a piecewise constant volatility structure $\gamma(t, x) = f(t)\gamma(x)$, where $\gamma(x) = (\gamma_1(x), \gamma_2(x))$ and $f\colon \mathbf{R}_+ \to \mathbf{R}$. If $f \equiv 1$ the volatility is time-homogeneous, so f represents the term structure of volatility. Because in the UK market caps are quarterly while swaptions are semi-annual, we used the cap formula from Proposition 3.1 with $\delta = 0.25$ and the swaption formula from Theorem 3.3 with $k = 2$. Computed volatility functions for 3 February 1995 are given in Table 5.

Table 6. Normal Heath–Jarrow–Morton fit for 3 February 1995

Currency: GBP Contract	Length	At-the-money strike (%)	Black volume (%)	Market price (bp)	Average error (%): 0.55 Error (bp)	Error (%)
Cap	1	7.88	15.50	27	0.00	0.00
Cap	2	8.39	17.75	100	2.4	2.4
Cap	3	8.64	18.00	185	−0.8	−0.5
Cap	4	8.69	17.75	267	−0.2	−0.1
Cap	5	8.79	17.75	360	−8.9	−2.5
Cap	7	8.90	16.50	511	−5.6	−1.1
Cap	10	8.89	15.50	703	1.7	0.2
	Option maturity × Swap length					
Swaption	0.25 × 2	8.57	16.75	50	−0.0	−0.1
Swaption	0.25 × 3	8.75	16.50	73	0.3	0.5
Swaption	1 × 4	9.10	15.50	172	0.0	0.0
Swaption	0.25 × 5	8.90	15.00	103	−0.0	−0.0
Swaption	0.25 × 7	9.00	13.75	123	−0.2	−0.1
Swaption	0.25 × 10	8.99	13.25	151	0.1	0.1
Swaption	1 × 9	9.12	13.25	271	−1.3	−0.5
Swaption	2 × 8	9.16	12.75	312	−0.2	−0.1

Contracts to be fitted are on the left with their at-the-money strikes and market-quoted Black volatilities. Prices and the fit, obtained with the volatility function below, are on the right. Average error in fitting is 0.55%, while the biggest single error is −2.5%. Note: 1 bp = \$100 per \$1M face value.

Normal Heath–Jarrow–Morton volatility

Tenor: x	σ(x)/x
0.25	0.01236511
0.50	0.01212989
1.00	0.01207662
1.50	0.01692911
2.00	0.01359211
3.00	0.01385645
4.00	0.01384691
5.00	0.01270641
7.00	0.01154330
11.00	0.01093066

Piecewise constant on each interval.

As a comparison a one-factor normal Heath-Jarrow-Morton model was fitted to the same set of data. Normal volatilities for 3 February 1995 are given in Table 6 (formulae 3.2 and 6.1 from Brace and Musiela (1994*a*) were used in the process of model calibration). Lognormal and normal Heath-Jarrow-Morton model fits, expressed in terms of the market cap and swaption prices, are given in Tables 5 and 6, respectively.

Discount functions and volatilities for other days of the week 30 January to 3 February 1995 are available in spreadsheet format on request. The inhomogeneous component $f(t)$ varies over the first 5 years from 0.934 at 0.5 year on 2 February 1995 to 1.133 at 2 years on 1 February 1995. For maturities beyond 5 years the homogeneous component drops to 0.718 at 9 and 11 years on 31 January 1995. The quality of fit can be defined as follows:

	Fit error (%)		
	Tolerable	**Satisfactory**	**Good**
Average error	<2%	<2%	<1%
Individual error	<8%	<5%	<3%

The normal Heath-Jarrow-Morton model can almost always be fitted to the UK and US caps and swaptions data with a one-factor homogeneous volatility; fitting the correlation with a second factor improves the overall fit. The lognormal Heath-Jarrow-Morton model frequently cannot fit with a strictly homogenous volatility, giving errors greater than 3%. That indicates a term structure of volatility in the lognormal case and may also indicate that the price volatility of the normal Heath-Jarrow-Morton model is more stable over time than the yield volatility of the lognormal Heath-Jarrow-Morton model. The implied Black volatilities of caps and swaptions (Table 7) for both models are quite similar, the lognormal volatilities being 1% to 1.5% greater than the normal at longer swaption maturities. That probably reflects the differing impact of correlation on the two models.

Table 7. Implied Black volatility of caps and swaptions for 3 February 1995

Cap/Swap length	Cap	Swaption maturity 0.25	0.5	1.0	2.0	3.0	4.0	5.0
Lognormal								
1	15.50	19.12	19.86	20.42	18.05	17.34	16.31	15.79
2	18.29	16.54	16.99	17.77	16.29	15.75	15.27	14.69
3	18.09	16.48	16.44	16.42	15.24	15.05	14.56	14.02
4	17.77	15.00	15.18	15.47	14.75	14.49	14.03	13.38
5	17.35	15.02	15.08	15.12	14.30	14.03	13.46	13.04
6	16.99	14.38	14.45	14.48	13.72	13.37	13.07	
7	16.59	13.93	13.94	13.87	13.06	13.03		
8	16.21	13.18	13.20	13.14	12.80			
9	15.81	12.60	12.82	13.17				
10	15.50	13.24	13.48					
Normal								
1	15.50	17.72	19.38	19.35	16.39	16.75	15.27	14.37
2	18.25	16.74	16.51	16.45	15.70	15.24	14.09	13.22
3	17.91	16.58	16.49	16.46	15.21	14.46	13.39	12.93
4	17.74	16.25	15.95	15.50	14.27	13.54	12.88	12.51
5	17.27	14.99	14.78	14.48	13.43	13.01	12.49	12.20
6	16.79	14.24	14.06	13.79	13.05	12.72	12.29	
7	16.30	13.73	13.62	13.49	12.85	12.57		
8	16.01	13.54	13.44	13.32	12.74			
9	15.76	13.38	13.30	13.19				
10	15.54	13.26	13.18					

With the determined parameterisations the Black volatilities for at-the-money contracts change smoothly from maturity to maturity and between different underlying swap lengths. That property is important because many dealers presently value swaptions by building similar matrices (by various means) and then using the Black formulae.

Bibliography

Brace, A., and M. Musiela, 1994*a*, "A Multifactor Gauss-Markov Implementation of Heath, Jarrow and Morton", *Mathematical Finance* 2, pp. 259-83.

Brace, A., and M. Musiela, 1994*b*, "Swap Derivatives in a Gaussian HJM Framework", The University of NSW (preprint).

Çinlar, E., and J. Jacod, 1981, "Representation of Semimartingale Markov Processes in terms of Wiener Processes and Poisson Random Measures", Seminar on Stochastic Processes, Ed. Çinlar, E, K. L. Chung and R. K. Getoor, Birkhäuser, pp. 159-242.

Da Prato, G., and J. Zabczyk, 1992, "Stochastic Equations in Infinite Dimensions", Cambridge University Press.

Goldys, B., M. Musiela and D. Sondermann, 1994, "Lognormality of Rates and Term Structure Models", The University of NSW (preprint).

Heath, D., R. Jarrow and A. Morton, 1992, "Bond Pricing and the Term Structure of Interest Rates: A New Methodology", *Econometrica* 60, pp. 77-105; reprinted as Chapter 14 of the present volume.

Miltersen, K., K. Sandmann and S. Sondermann, 1994, "Closed Form Term Structure Derivatives in a Heath-Jarrow-Morton Model with Log-normal Annually Compounded Interest Rates", University of Bonn (preprint).

Miltersen, K., K. Sandmann and D. Sondermann, 1995, "Closed Form Solutions for Term Structure Derivatives with Log-normal Interest Rates", University of Bonn (preprint).

Musiela, M., 1994, "Nominal Annual Rates and Lognormal Volatility Structure", The University of NSW (preprint).

Musiela, M., 1995, "General Framework for Pricing Derivative Securities", *Stochastic Process Applied* 55, pp. 227-51.

Musiela, M., and D. Sondermann, 1993, "Different Dynamical Specifications of the Term Structure of Interest Rates and their Implications", University of Bonn (preprint)

Sandmann, K., and D. Sondermann, 1993, "On the Stability of Lognormal Interest Rate Models", University of Bonn (preprint).

20

Fitting Potential Models to Interest Rate and Foreign Exchange Data*

Chris Rogers and Omar Zane
University of Bath

We fit two two-factor potential models to yield-curve data in the US and the UK and to the exchange rates between them. We analyse the fitting of the model to the data both allowing the parameters to move freely each day and constraining the parameters to only small changes. The filtering approach, used in the latter case, allows us to give confidence intervals for the yields.

Most term structure models to date fall into one of two classes: either one models the spot-rate process $(r_t, t \geq 0)$, as in Vasicek (1977), Cox, Ingersoll and Ross (1985), Longstaff and Schwartz (1991); or alternatively one models the process of forward rates, as in Ho and Lee (1986), Heath, Jarrow and Morton (1992), Babbs (1990). However, as a recent paper of Rogers (1995) shows, there are considerable advantages to a third approach, called the *potential approach*. The idea here is that the fundamental is the state-price density $(\zeta_t, t \geq 0)$, a positive supermartingale, in terms of which the bond prices have the simple expression

$$P(t,T) = \frac{\tilde{E}_t(\zeta_T)}{\zeta_t} \tag{1}$$

where $0 \leq t \leq T$, and $P(t, T)$ denotes the price at time t of a zero-coupon bond which pays out 1 at time T, and $\tilde{P}$ is a reference measure. This approach was also advocated by Constantinides (1992), though this paper did not develop one of the most exciting consequences, namely the simplicity with which exchange rates can be modelled. As Rogers (1995) shows, if at time t one unit of country j's currency is worth Y_t^{ij} units of country i's currency, then under certain assumptions (satisfied in the complete markets case)

$$Y_t^{ij} = \frac{Y_0^{ij}\zeta_t^j}{\zeta_t^i} \tag{2}$$

This important observation was also made by Saa-Requejo (1993). To obtain a wide family of models, then, one needs to have a way of generating positive supermartingales and Rogers (1995) showed how one could make use of classical Markov process theory to generate such examples. By taking a Markov process $(X_t, t \geq 0)$ with resolvent $(R_\lambda)_{\lambda>0}$, the recipe

$$\zeta_t \equiv e^{-\alpha t} R_\alpha g(X_t) \tag{3}$$

**Supported by EPSRC grant GR/J97281.*

defines a positive supermartingale whenever the function g is positive and suitably integrable. Different choices of g and α give a wide range of possible potentials, even within the context of a fixed Markov process. Using this framework, the bond prices can be compactly expressed as

$$P(0,t) = \frac{\tilde{E}^x[e^{-\alpha t} R_\alpha g(X_t)]}{R_\alpha g(X_0)} \tag{4}$$

where $\tilde{P}^x$ denotes the law of the process started at x. Further simple formulae for other derivative prices can be obtained. One even has that the spot-rate process can be given as

$$r_t = \frac{g(X_t)}{R_\alpha g(X_t)} \tag{5}$$

The objective of this paper is to examine the fit of a few such models to data. Throughout, we shall take the underlying Markov process to be a two-dimensional (Gaussian) diffusion X solving

$$dX_t = dW_t - BX_t dt \tag{6}$$

where B is a 2×2 matrix and W is a Brownian motion in two dimensions. It should be noted that what we are attempting here, namely to explain *simultaneously* the yield curves in two countries and the exchange rates between them using a model with *only two underlying sources of noise*, is ambitious; other models would introduce at least one source of noise for each country and one for each exchange rate.

The data we used to fit the model were daily yield-curve data for the US dollar (USD) and the British pound (GBP), along with daily data for the exchange rate between the two currencies. We give more details on the data in the next section.

The reason for restricting attention to this particular Markov process is that the bond price (and the prices of other derivatives more generally) is expressed as an expectation of a function of the process X at some later time, and such expectations are comparatively simple in this case. Indeed, we have that under $\tilde{P}^x$

$$X_t \sim N(e^{-tB}x, V_t), \quad V_t \equiv \int_0^t e^{-sB}(e^{-sB})^T ds \tag{7}$$

as is easily shown. Thus the calculation of prices can commonly be reduced to an integration with respect to a Gaussian density; often, the bond prices can be given in closed form, as examples in Rogers (1995) demonstrate. Nevertheless, it is important to emphasise that the method is not restricted to this one diffusion, nor even to *any* diffusion; it may well turn out in practice that we should take as the underlying process a finite Markov chain, in which case the computations would inevitably be numerical.

Having chosen the underlying Markov process, we now have to pick the function $g \geq 0$, or, more conveniently, $f \equiv R_\alpha g$. Familiar properties of the resolvent then allow us to recover g from $g = (\alpha - G)f$, and Rogers (1995) gave numerous examples. In this paper we shall fit the models where, for some two-vector c, some 2×2 positive-definite symmetric matrix Q and real positive γ chosen suitably, f takes one of the forms:

(*A*) $f(x) = \exp(\frac{1}{2}(x - c) \cdot Q(x - c))$

(*B*) $f(x) = \gamma + \frac{1}{2}(x - c) \cdot Q(x - c)$

Before getting into the details of these models, which we shall attend to in the next section but one, we describe the general methodology used in the fitting procedure. In all cases we are dealing with a family of models parameterised by some vector θ. Some of the components of θ will be parameters relating to the movement of the underlying Markov process X (so, in our example, the entries of the matrix B or, more usefully, the eigenvalues and unit eigenvectors of B); the remainder will be components relating to the functions used in the potential description. On each day we will have the market values of some K observables; let us denote the market value of the jth observable on day n by y_n^j, and let us denote the model price of the jth asset by $y^j(x, \theta)$, a function of the state x of the Markov process, and the parameter vector θ. If we simply want to fit day-to-day, allowing different values of the parameters each day, then on day n we can minimise $F_n(\theta, X)$ defined by

$$F_n(\theta, X) \equiv \frac{1}{2}\sum_{j=1}^{K} \varepsilon_j (y_n^j - y^j(x, \theta))^2$$

where the ε_j are positive weights which are at our disposal. The observables y_n^j do not have to be prices; they could be implied volatilities, log-prices, historical volatilities or any other observable whose value can be computed within the model and which we care to use for the calibration. The results of the day-by-day fits to the data are discussed in a later section.

Allowing the parameters to change each day is a violation of the model assumptions; we should insist that they are the same for all time. Nevertheless, it is not reasonable to imagine that the parameters in a model for interest rates remain absolutely unchanged over very long periods, so for a more sophisticated analysis we will allow the parameters to shift gradually with time; as is to be expected, the more we force the parameters to remain stable, the poorer the fit to the data. If we abbreviate $(x^T, \theta^T) \equiv z^T$, then what we shall do is to minimise each day the function $\tilde{F}_n(z)$ defined by

$$\tilde{F}_n(z) \equiv \frac{1}{2}\sum_{j=1}^{K} \varepsilon_j (y_n^j - y^j(z))^2 + \tfrac{1}{2}(z - \mu_n)^T \tilde{V}_n^{-1}(z - \tilde{\mu}_n)$$

where the vectors $\tilde{\mu}_n$ and the matrices $\tilde{V}_n$ are defined recursively, as is explained in detail in the section "Approximate Kalman filtering". The final section discusses the results of this fitting procedure.

The data

The US yield-curve data (Figure 1) and the GBP/USD exchange rate (Figure 3) were obtained from the World Wide Web site of the Federal Reserve Bank of Chicago.[1] The data that have been used cover the period January 1991 to November 1991. For each day we have nine values corresponding to different maturities for the bonds. The maturities are 3 and 6 months and 1, 2, 3, 5, 7, 10 and 30 years. The UK yield-curve data (Figure 2) were obtained from S. Babbs and they cover the same period of time and have the same maturities.[2]

Let us define some notation for the data that will be used later on. Let M = [0.25, 0.5, 1, 2, 3, 5, 7, 10, 30] be the vector that represents the maturities of the bonds under consideration; let y_{ni}^{US} (resp. y_{ni}^{UK}) be the value of the yield on the nth day for the US (resp. UK) bond with maturity M(i), and y_n^{FX} the logarithm of the foreign exchange rate on the nth day divided by the foreign exchange rate on the (n − 1)th day.

The models

QUADRATIC

Let us consider the case (see Rogers (1995)) in which the function $f: R^d \to R$ is given by

$$f(x) = \gamma + \tfrac{1}{2}(x - c)^T Q(x - c) \qquad (8)$$

and the d-dimensional diffusion $(X_t, t \geq 0)$ is the solution of the linear stochastic differential equation

$$dX_t = -BX_t dt + dW_t, \quad X_0 = x_0 \qquad (9)$$

1. US data

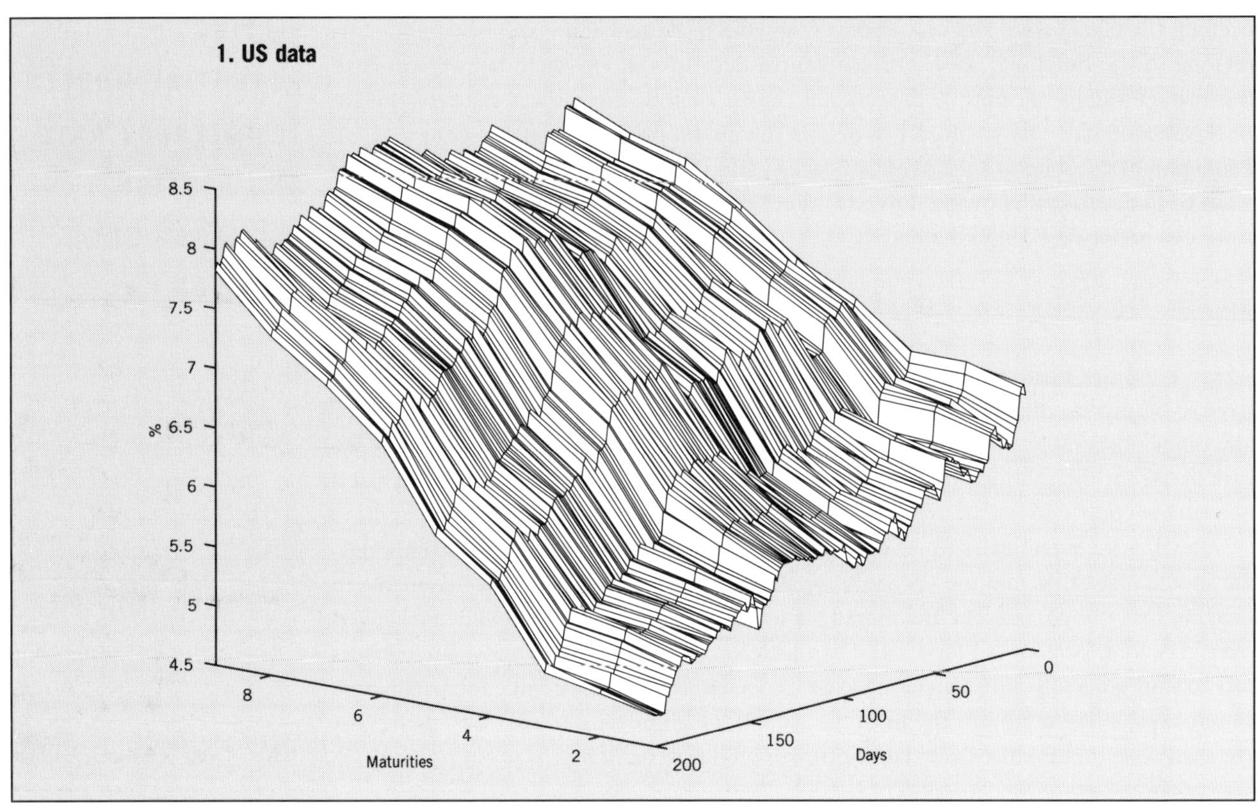

where Q and B are constant $d \times d$ matrices with Q symmetric and positive definite and c is a constant d-dimensional vector.

If we denote by G the infinitesimal generator of the diffusion, the function $g = (\alpha - G)f$ is then given by

$$g(x) = \alpha\gamma - \tfrac{1}{2}\operatorname{tr} Q + \tfrac{1}{2}\alpha c^T Q c + \tfrac{1}{2}(x - v)^T S(x - v) - \tfrac{1}{2} v^T S v \tag{10}$$

where

$$S = \alpha Q + B^T Q + QB \tag{11}$$

and

$$v = S^{-1}(\alpha Q c + B^T Q c) \tag{12}$$

If we choose γ so that

$$\gamma = \frac{\operatorname{tr} Q + v^T S v}{2\alpha} - \tfrac{1}{2} c^T Q c \tag{13}$$

then the spot-rate process is given by

$$r(X_t) = \frac{g(X_t)}{f(X_t)} = \frac{(X_t - v)^T S(X_t - v)}{2\gamma + (X_t - c)^T Q(X_t - c)} \tag{14}$$

the zero-coupon bond prices are given by

$$P(0,t) = \frac{\exp\{-\alpha t\}}{f(x_0)}\left\{\gamma + \tfrac{1}{2}\left[\operatorname{tr}(QV_t) + \mu_t^T Q \mu_t\right]\right\} \tag{15}$$

where

$$\mu_t = \exp\{-tB\} x_0 - c \tag{16}$$

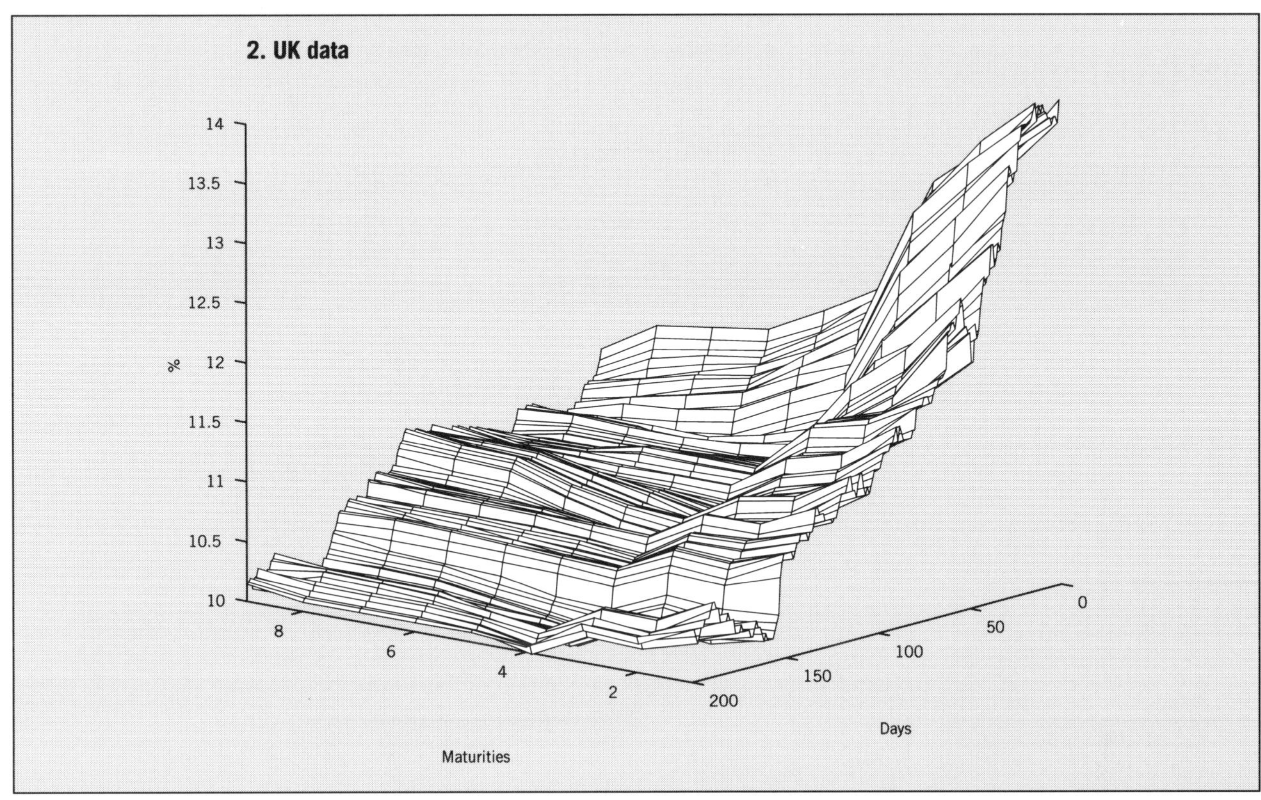

$$V_t = \int_0^t \exp\{-sB\}(\exp\{-sB\})^T ds \tag{17}$$

and the state-price density is given by

$$\zeta_{0,t} = \exp\{-\alpha t\}\frac{\gamma + \frac{1}{2}(X_t - c)^T Q(X_t - c)}{\gamma + \frac{1}{2}(X_0 - c)^T Q(X_0 - c)} \tag{18}$$

EXPONENTIAL QUADRATIC

Let us consider a different model (see example 2 in Rogers (1995)); the function $f: R^d \to R$ is defined by

$$f(x) = \exp\left[\tfrac{1}{2}(x - c)^T Q(x - c)\right] \tag{19}$$

and the diffusion $(X_t, t \geq 0)$ is the solution of the linear stochastic differential equation (9).

In this case the function $g = (\alpha - G)f$ is given by

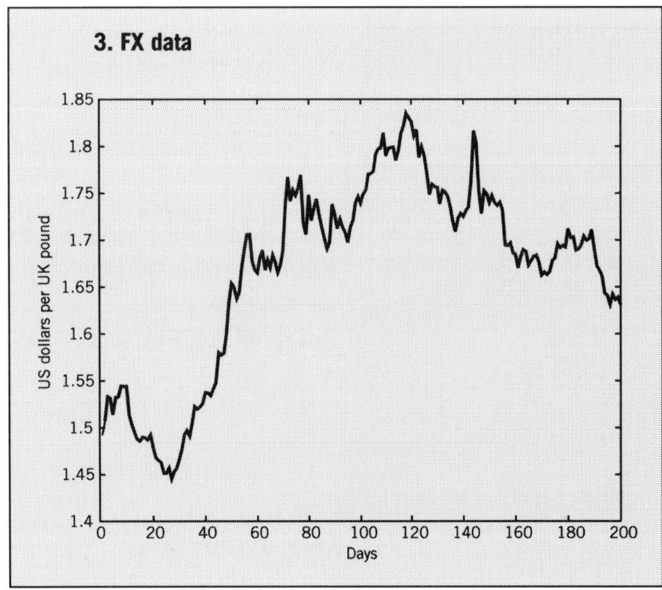

$$g(x) = f(x)\left[\tfrac{1}{2}(x - S^{-1}v)^T S(x - S^{-1}v)\right] \tag{20}$$

where

$$S = B^T Q + QB - Q^2, \quad v = (B^T - Q)Qc \tag{21}$$

and the parameter α has been chosen to be

$$\alpha = \tfrac{1}{2}(\mathrm{tr}(Q) + |Qc|^2 + v^T S^{-1} v) \tag{22}$$

These choices give a squared-Gaussian spot-rate process

$$r_t = \tfrac{1}{2}(X_t - S^{-1}v)^T S(X_t - S^{-1}v) \tag{23}$$

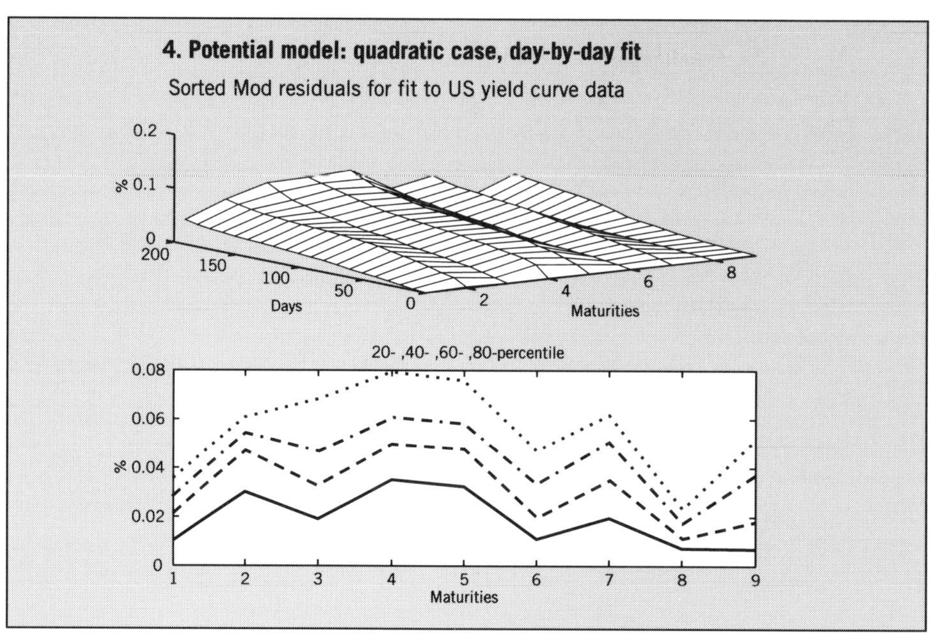

and explicit formulas for the computation of the T-forward measure (see Rogers (1995)) and of the zero-coupon bond prices that for a maturity t are given by

$$P(0,t) = \exp\{-\alpha t\}\det(I - QV_t)^{-\frac{1}{2}} \exp\left(\tfrac{1}{2}\mu_t^T(I - QV_t)^{-1}Q\mu_t - \tfrac{1}{2}\mu_0^T Q\mu_0\right) \tag{24}$$

where

$$\mu_t = \exp\{-tB\}x_0 - c \tag{25}$$

$$V_t = \int_0^t \exp\{-sB\}(\exp\{-sB\})^T ds \tag{26}$$

and I denotes the identity matrix. Moreover, if we consider several countries at once and we assume the same diffusion and the same values for the entries of the matrix Q for all of the countries, then we get that the exchange rates between two countries i and j are log-Brownian processes

$$Y_t^{ij} = Y_0^{ij}\frac{\zeta_t^j}{\zeta_t^i} = Y_0^{ij}\exp[(\alpha^i - \alpha^j)t + (c^i - c^j)Q(X_t - X_0)] \tag{27}$$

Day-by-day fits

QUADRATIC

We are interested in modelling the interest rate of the two countries (US and UK) and the exchange rate of the currencies. We assume that there is only one two-dimensional diffusion driving the evolution of the three processes (same B and X, $d = 2$) and that Q is diagonal and the same for both countries.

The exchange rate process is obtained as the quotient of the state-price densities in the single countries (see earlier section, "The data").

We have 12 parameters $\theta = [\lambda_1, \lambda_2, \beta_1, \beta_2, q_1, q_2, c_1^{US}, c_2^{US}, c_1^{UK}, c_2^{UK}, \alpha^{US}, \alpha^{UK}]'$ and a two-dimensional diffusion X. The first six parameters characterise the two matrices B and Q: q_1 and q_2 are the diagonal elements of Q; λ_1 and λ_2 are the eigenvalues of B, and β_1 and β_2 are angles such that if we define

$$R = \begin{bmatrix} \cos\beta_1 & \cos\beta_2 \\ \sin\beta_1 & \sin\beta_2 \end{bmatrix} \tag{28}$$

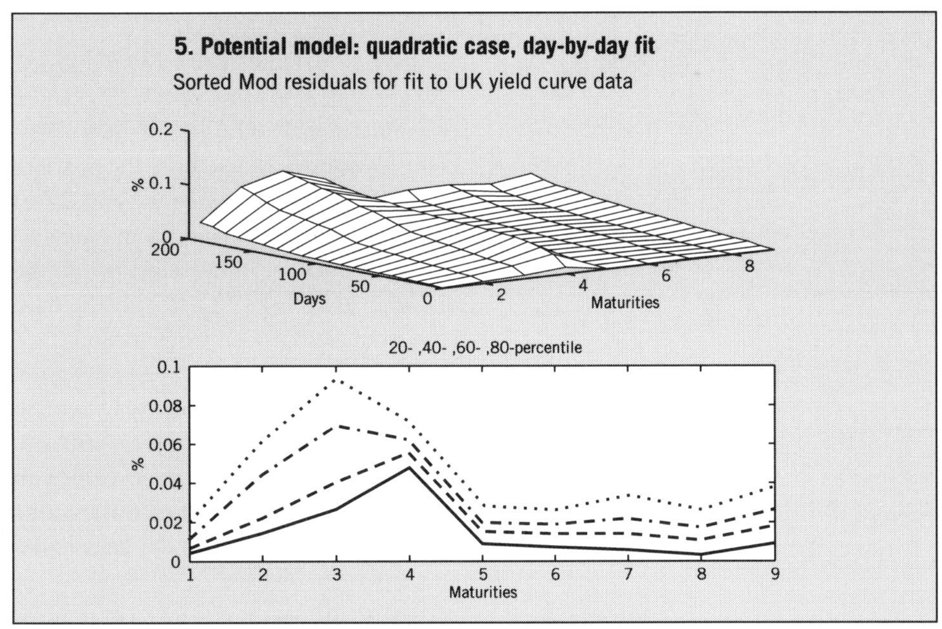

then

$$B = R \begin{bmatrix} \lambda_1 & 0 \\ 0 & \lambda_2 \end{bmatrix} R^{-1} \tag{29}$$

Let us denote by $y_{ni}^{US}(\theta, X)$ and $y_{ni}^{UK}(\theta, X)$ the model value of the yield at the ith maturity in the nth day for the US and the UK, respectively, and by $y_n^{FX}(\theta, X)$ the logarithm of the ratio of the state-price densities in the two countries

$$y_n^{FX}(\theta, X) = \log\left\{\frac{\zeta^{UK}_{t_{n-1}, t_n}}{\zeta^{US}_{t_{n-1}, t_n}}\right\} \tag{30}$$

The fitting is obtained by a minimisation of the function

$$F_n(\theta, X) = \sum_{i=1}^{9} w_i^{US}\left[y_{ni}^{US} - y_{ni}^{US}(\theta, X)\right]^2 + \sum_{i=1}^{9} w_i^{UK}\left[y_{ni}^{UK} - y_{ni}^{UK}(\theta, X)\right]^2 +$$

$$+ w^{FX}\left[y_n^{FX} - y_n^{FX}(\theta, X)\right]^2 \tag{31}$$

with respect to (θ, X) using the NAG routine E04JAF, repeated for the 200 days under consideration (i.e., $n = 1, \ldots, 200$), where the weights are chosen to be $w_i^{US} = w_j^{UK} = 15{,}000$, $(i, j = 1, \ldots, 9)$, and $w^{FX} = 450{,}000$.

Figures 4 and 5 show the modulus of the fitting residuals for every maturity in the 200 days for the two countries; the mod-residuals are sorted by order of magnitude to give a clearer idea of the errors. Figure 6 shows the observed data and the fitting curve for the FX rate (there are two curves in the top picture). The model fitted is completely non-rigid; different parameters are fitted each day. If we follow the procedure described in the introductory section of the paper, we must expect the quality of the fit to deteriorate.

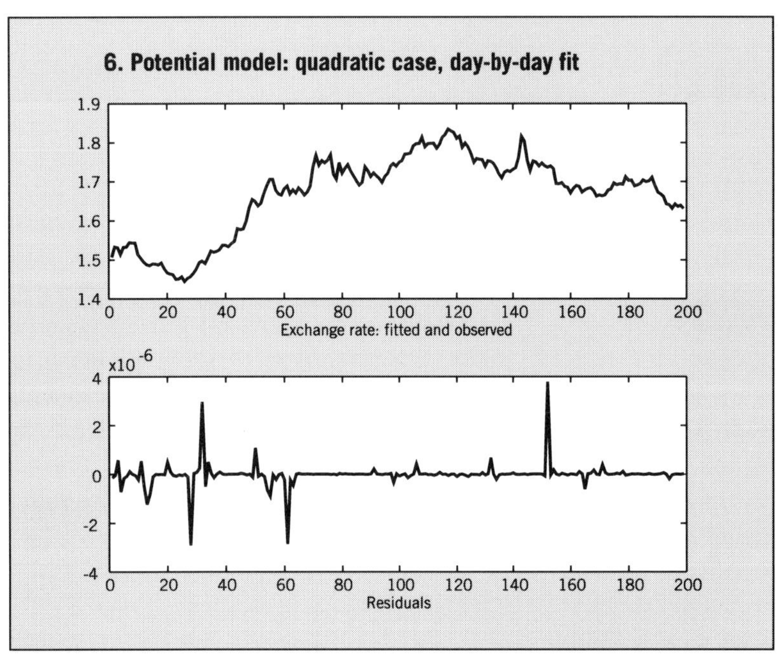

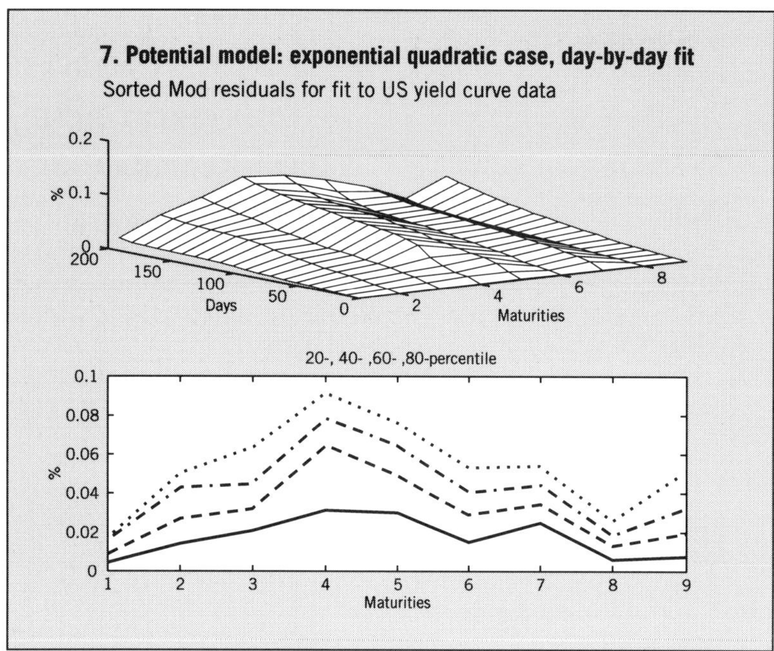

7. Potential model: exponential quadratic case, day-by-day fit

Sorted Mod residuals for fit to US yield curve data

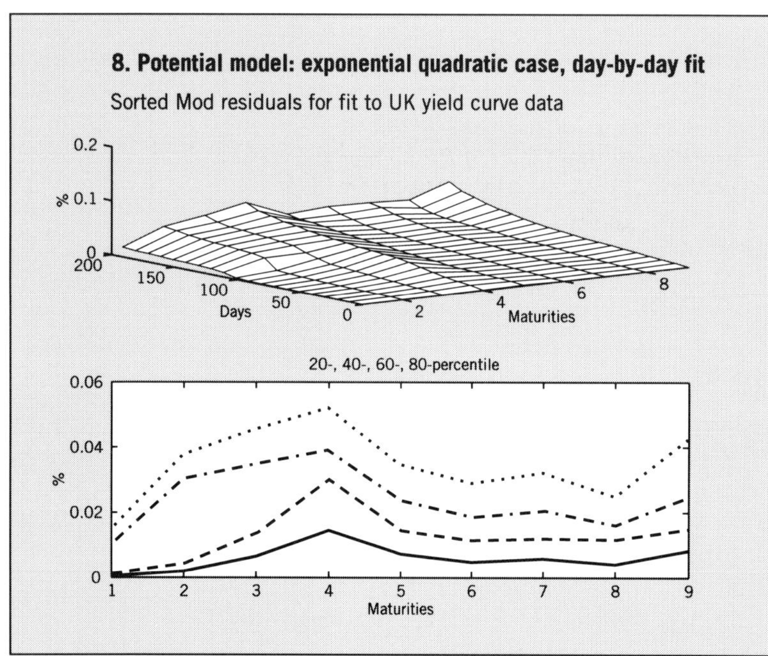

8. Potential model: exponential quadratic case, day-by-day fit

Sorted Mod residuals for fit to UK yield curve data

EXPONENTIAL QUADRATIC

We have 12 parameters $\theta = [\lambda_1, \lambda_2, \beta_1, \beta_2, q_1^{US}, q_1^{US}, q_1^{UK}, q_2^{UK}, c_1^{US}, c_2^{US}, c_1^{UK}, c_2^{UK}]'$ and a two-dimensional diffusion X. The first eight parameters characterise the matrices B, Q^{US} and Q^{UK}: we assume Q^{US} and Q^{UK} to be diagonal matrices and let $q_1^{(\cdot)}$ and $q_2^{(\cdot)}$ be the values of the elements on the diagonal of $Q^{(\cdot)}$; λ_1, λ_2, β_1 and β_2 have been defined in the previous section.

The functions y are defined (using the current model) as in the previous section and the day-by-day fitting is obtained by a minimisation of function (31) with respect to (θ, X) using the NAG routine E04JAF, repeated for the 200 days under consideration, where the weights are chosen to be $w_i^{US} = w_j^{UK} = 30{,}000$, $(i, j = 1, \ldots, 9)$, and $w^{FX} = 9400$.

Figures 7 and 8 show the ordered mod-residuals of the fitting for every maturity in the 200 days for the two countries; Figure 9 shows the observed data and the fitting curve for the foreign exchange rate.

Approximate Kalman filtering

Although it may look appealing to perform the fitting procedure as illustrated at the end of the previous section, it is nevertheless inconsistent with the theoretical model. We are in fact allowing the parameters to move from day to day, while the model was requiring constant parameters. We need therefore to constrain the parameters in the minimisation by adding a penalty for fluctuations of their values.

We do this by using the approximate Kalman filtering approach that we outline in what follows.

(i) If

$$\begin{pmatrix} Z \\ Y \end{pmatrix} \sim N\left\{ \begin{pmatrix} \mu \\ \nu \end{pmatrix}, \begin{bmatrix} A & B \\ B^T & D \end{bmatrix} \right\} \tag{32}$$

is a multivariate Gaussian vector, then it is well known that

$$E(Z \mid Y) = \mu + BD^{-1}(Y - \nu) \tag{33}$$

and

$$\operatorname{var}(Z \mid Y) = A - BD^{-1}B^T \tag{34}$$

(ii) It is an easy exercise to prove that the minimisation problem

$$\min_x \phi(x, y) \tag{35}$$

where

$$\phi(x, y) \equiv \frac{1}{2}\begin{pmatrix} x-\mu \\ y-\nu \end{pmatrix}^{T} \begin{bmatrix} A & B \\ B^{T} & D \end{bmatrix}^{-1} \begin{pmatrix} x-\mu \\ y-\nu \end{pmatrix} \tag{36}$$

is solved by

$$x^* = \mu + BD^{-1}(y - \nu) \tag{37}$$

and that the Hessian of ϕ with respect to x at the minimising value x^* (and, indeed, everywhere) is

$$(A - BD^{-1}B^{T})^{-1} \tag{38}$$

(iii) Thus the conditional distribution of Z given Y can also be obtained by solving the minimisation of the quadratic loss.

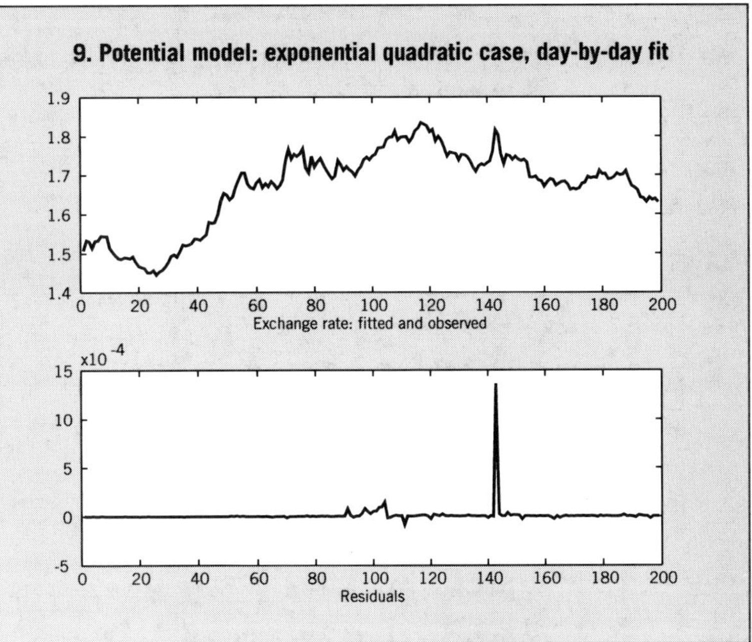

9. Potential model: exponential quadratic case, day-by-day fit

(iv) Suppose that we know $Z_{(n-1)\delta} \sim N(\mu_{n-1}, V_{n-1})$ and that Z solves the SDE

$$dZ_t = b(Z_t)\,dt + \sigma\,dW_t \tag{39}$$

where b is a smooth function and σ is constant. (The constancy of σ is not critical to the argument, but we make this assumption because it is all we shall need and it simplifies the development.) If $\delta > 0$ is small, we have (ignoring second-order terms in $\xi = Z_{n\delta-\delta} - \mu_{n-1}$)

$$\begin{aligned} Z_{n\delta} &= Z_{n\delta-\delta} + \delta b(Z_{n\delta-\delta}) + \sigma(W_{n\delta} - W_{n\delta-\delta}) + o(\delta^{3/2}) \\ &= \mu_{n-1} + \delta b(\mu_{n-1}) + (I + \delta Db(\mu_{n-1}))\xi + \sigma(W_{n\delta} - W_{n\delta-\delta}) + o(\delta^{3/2}) \end{aligned} \tag{40}$$

so that now we have approximately

$$Z_{n\delta} \sim N(\tilde{\mu}_n, \tilde{V}_n) \tag{41}$$

where

$$\tilde{\mu}_n \equiv \mu_{n-1} + \delta b(\mu_{n-1}) \tag{42}$$

$$\tilde{V}_n \equiv (I + \delta Db(\mu_{n-1}))\,V_{n-1}(I + \delta Db(\mu_{n-1}))^{T} + \delta\sigma\sigma^{T} \tag{43}$$

(v) If we now observe

$$Y_n = a + KZ_{n\delta} + \varepsilon \tag{44}$$

where ε is some independent zero-mean Gaussian noise with covariance V_ε, we would find the maximum likelihood estimate of Z by finding

$$\min_{x} \tfrac{1}{2}(Y_n - a - Kx)^{T} V_\varepsilon^{-1}(Y_n - a - Kx) + \tfrac{1}{2}(x - \tilde{\mu}_n)^{T}\,\tilde{V}_n^{-1}(x - \tilde{\mu}_n) \tag{45}$$

The minimising value μ_n will be the conditional mean of Z_n, and the Hessian evaluated at μ_n will be V_n^{-1}.

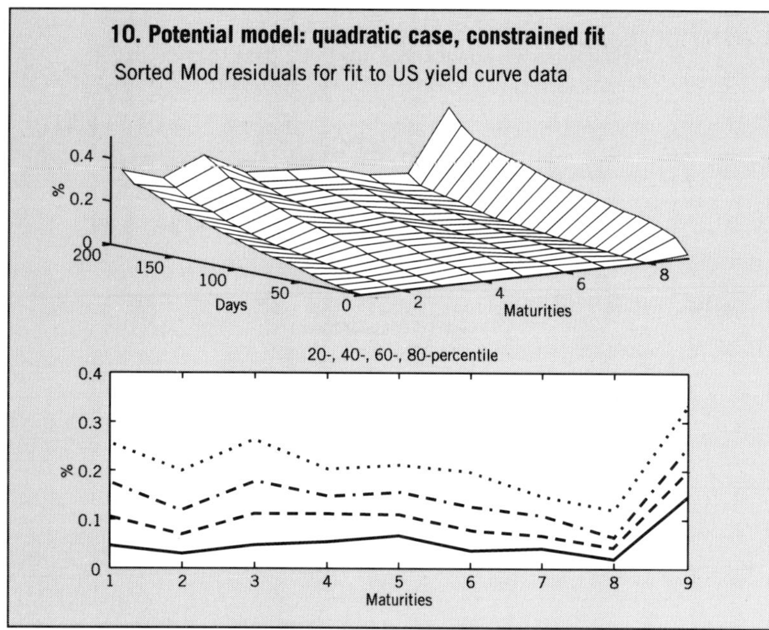

10. Potential model: quadratic case, constrained fit

Sorted Mod residuals for fit to US yield curve data

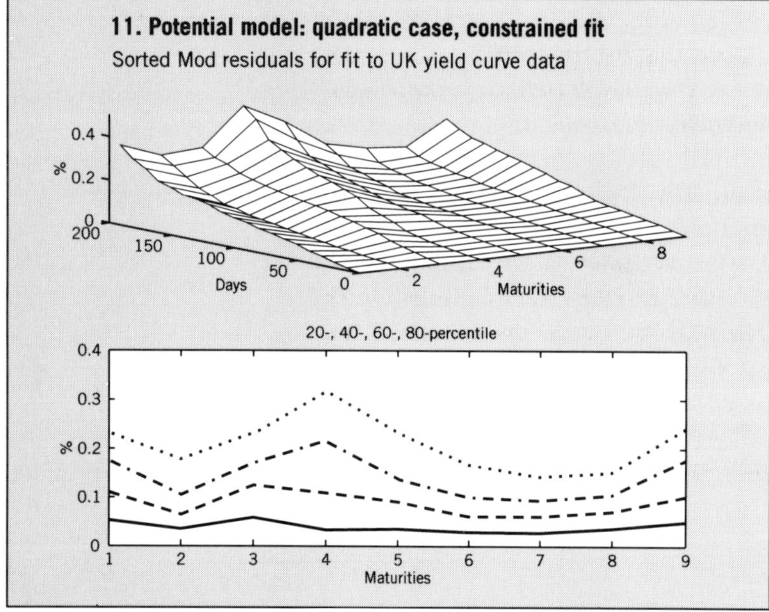

11. Potential model: quadratic case, constrained fit

Sorted Mod residuals for fit to UK yield curve data

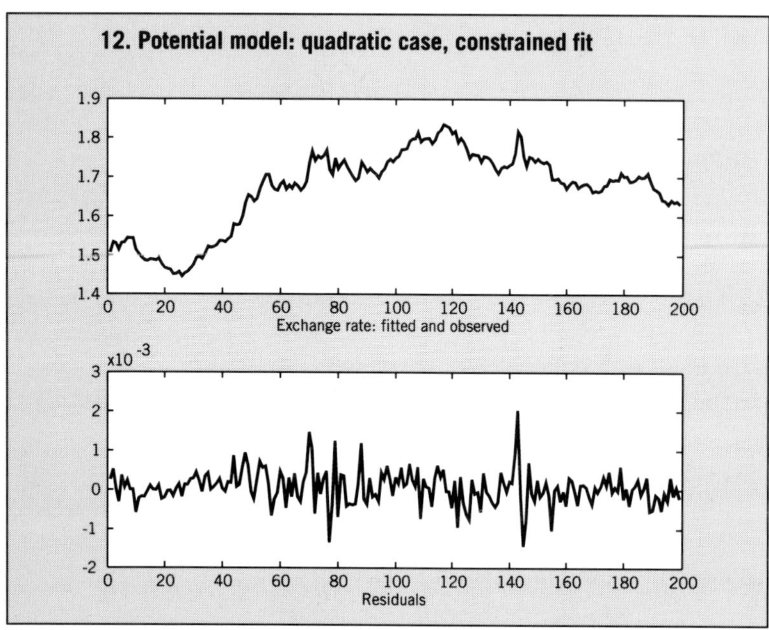

12. Potential model: quadratic case, constrained fit

(vi) If we observe

$$Y_n = f(Z_{n\delta}) + \varepsilon \tag{46}$$

where f is no longer necessarily linear, we assume that the analogue of step (v) may be used; we find

$$\min_{x} \tfrac{1}{2}(Y_n - f(x))^T V_\varepsilon^{-1}(Y_n - f(x)) + \tfrac{1}{2}(x - \tilde{\mu}_n)^T \tilde{V}_n^{-1}(x - \tilde{\mu}_n) \tag{47}$$

and set μ_n to be the minimising value and V_n^{-1} to be the Hessian at μ_n.

Fits of constrained models

QUADRATIC CASE

In this section we apply the approach described in the previous section to the models that are considered in this paper. We suppose that the observations on the prices are not exact and that the values of the components of θ are slowly moving. We therefore have a 14-dimensional random process $(Z_t = (\theta_t, X_t), t \geq 0)$ whose dynamics are given by (compare with equation 39)

$$\begin{cases} d\theta_t = \bar{\sigma}\, d\overline{W}_t \\ dX_t = -BX_t dt + dW_t \end{cases} \tag{48}$$

and a 19-dimensional random process $(Y_t, t \geq 0)$ that models the price observations as actual price plus Gaussian noise given by $\varepsilon \sim N(0, V_\varepsilon)$ (compare with equation 46).

Note that, in order to apply this method, we must assume some values for $\bar{\sigma}$ and V_ε. The choice that we make influences the outcome of the procedure: there is indeed a trade-off between accuracy of the fitting and stability of the parameters (the latter is, after all, one of the reasons for introducing this approach).

We apply the procedure to the quadratic model assuming V_ε and $\bar{\sigma}$ diagonal with $(\text{diag}(V_\varepsilon))_i = (15{,}000)^{-1}$, $(i = 1, \ldots, 18)$; $(\text{diag}(V_\varepsilon))_{19} = (500{,}000)^{-1}$, $\text{diag}(\bar{\sigma})_i = 200^{-1}$, $(i = 1, \ldots, 10)$, and $\text{diag}(\bar{\sigma})_i = 10^{-1}$, $(i = 11, 12)$.

Figures 10, 11 and 12 show the results of the fitting for the constrained quadratic case and Figure 13 shows the values of the parameters in the period that has been considered.

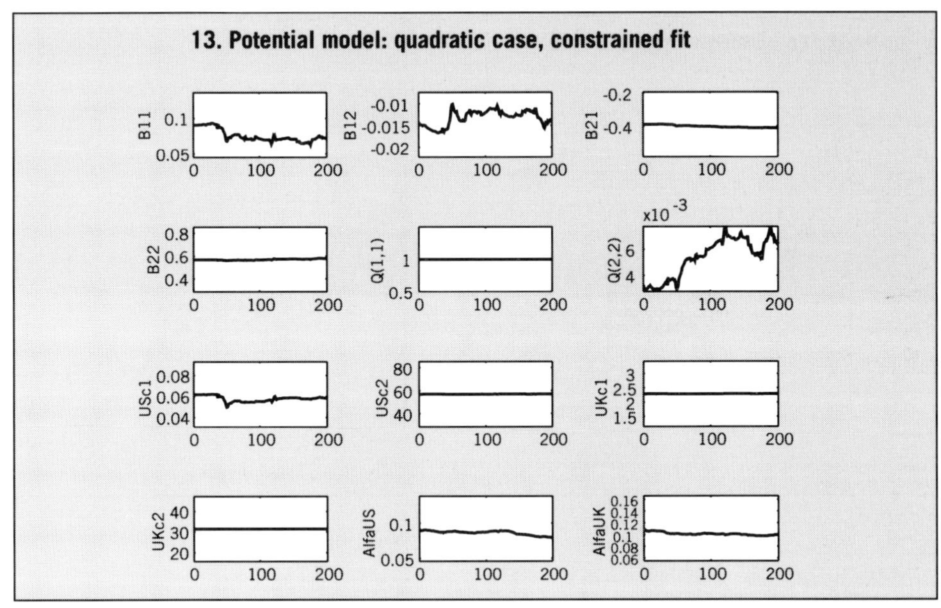

As a by-product of this approach we also obtain confidence intervals for each yield. Using a first-order Taylor expansion we see that an observable $f(z)$ is approximately a normal random variable with mean $f(\mu_n)$ and variance $(\nabla f(\mu_n))^T V_n (\nabla f(\mu_n))$ where the conditional mean μ_n and the conditional covariance V_n are obtained through the minimisation as illustrated in the previous section. We can therefore compute

$$\{[\nabla f(\mu_n)]^T V_n [\nabla f(\mu_n)]\}^{1/2} \tag{49}$$

and obtain the half-length of the one standard deviation confidence interval. Figures 14 and 15 show the data, the fitting curves and the curves and the confidence intervals for the bonds with 3 months and 1, 3 and 10 years maturities in the two countries. The dashed line is the point estimate of the yield, the middle solid line is the actual yield and the outer solid lines are the ends of the confidence intervals.

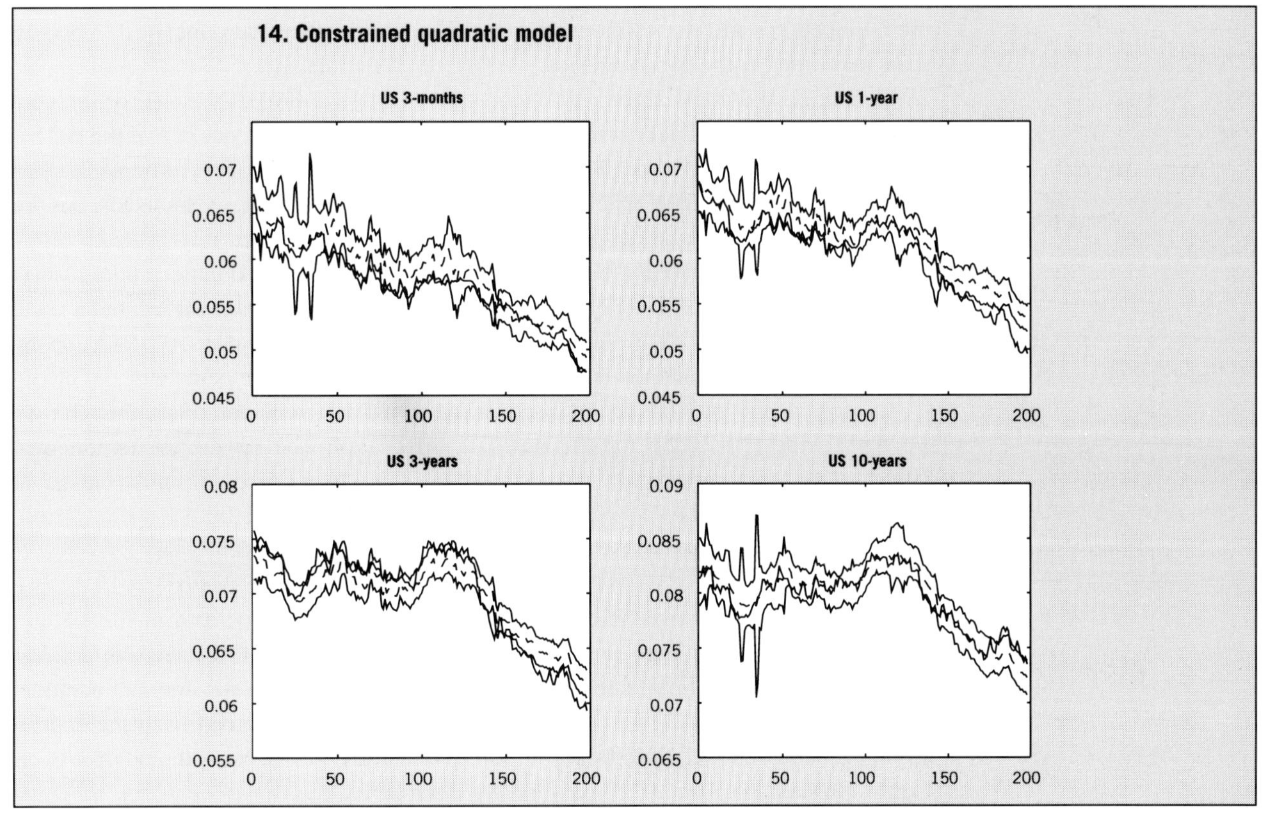

15. Constrained quadratic model

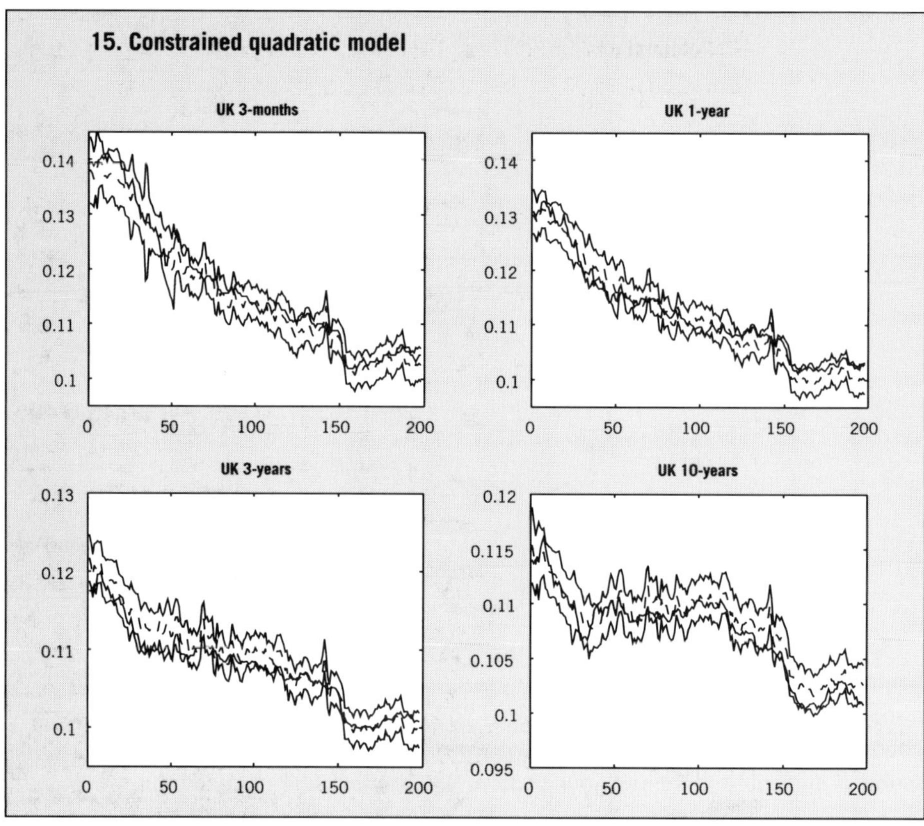

EXPONENTIAL QUADRATIC CASE

We now apply the approximate Kalman filtering method described above to the exponential quadratic model assuming V_ε and $\bar{\sigma}$ diagonal with $(\mathrm{diag}(V_\varepsilon))_i = (30{,}000)^{-1}$, $i = 1, \ldots, 18$; $(\mathrm{diag}(V_\varepsilon))_{19} = (120{,}000)^{-1}$; $(\mathrm{diag}(\bar{\sigma}))_i = 150^{-1}$, $i = 1, \ldots, 12$.

Figures 16, 17 and 18 show the results of the fitting for the constrained exponential quadratic case and Figure 19 shows the values of the parameters.

We can again find confidence intervals using (49). Figures 20 and 21 show the data, the fitting curves and the confidence intervals for the 3 months and for the 1, 3 and 10 years maturities in the two countries.

Comparing the constrained and unconstrained fits, we find that the fit of the constrained model to the yield curves is 3–4 times as bad. Four times out of five the day-by-day fits get within 6 bp in the US and 4 bp in the UK. There appears to be no marked preference for quadratic as against exponential quadratic in the fit of the yields, but the quadratic seems to do a bit better on exchange rates.

As for parameter stability, most of the parameters of the quadratic model display remarkable stability; only $B(1, 2)$ and q_2 seem a bit unsteady, but this can be understood when we notice that both are quite small ($q_2 \simeq 10^{-2} q_1$, $|B(1, 2)| \simeq 2 \times 10^{-2} B(2, 2)$). By contrast, the exponential quadratic model displays less impressive parameter stability.

The confidence intervals generally cover the actual data very effectively, though they are quite wide (30–70 bp for the quadratic model, 60–120 bp for the exponential model). This is a confirmation of the integrity of the procedure, though a tighter fit would be desirable.

Conclusions

We have fitted simple two-factor potential models to yield-curve data in the US and the UK and to the exchange rates between them. The fit is not, of course, perfect, but it is similar to what one obtains when fitting a time-homogeneous one factor model to one country's yield curves. A perfect fit can only be guaranteed by using a time-inhomogeneous model and fitting it afresh each day; the consistency of this is highly questionable, but is conventionally ignored by those who practice it. Time-

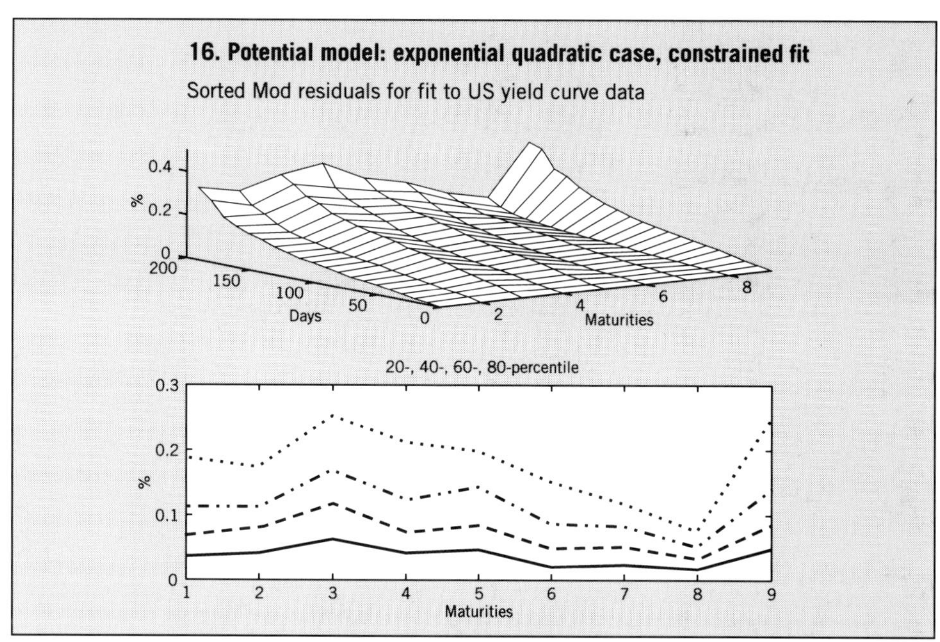
16. Potential model: exponential quadratic case, constrained fit
Sorted Mod residuals for fit to US yield curve data
%
Days
Maturities
20-, 40-, 60-, 80-percentile
%
Maturities

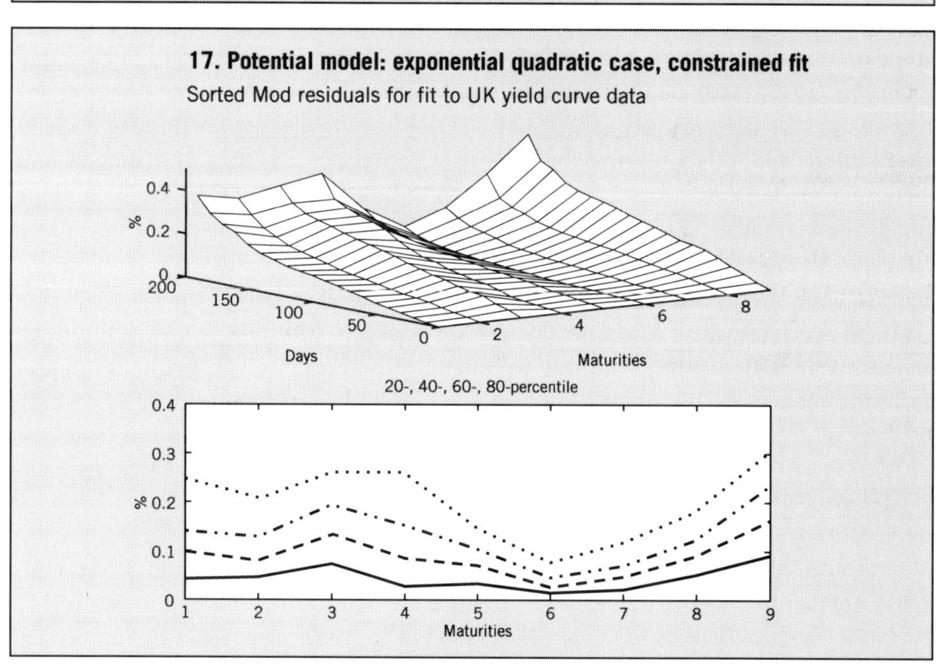
17. Potential model: exponential quadratic case, constrained fit
Sorted Mod residuals for fit to UK yield curve data
%
Days
Maturities
20-, 40-, 60-, 80-percentile
%
Maturities

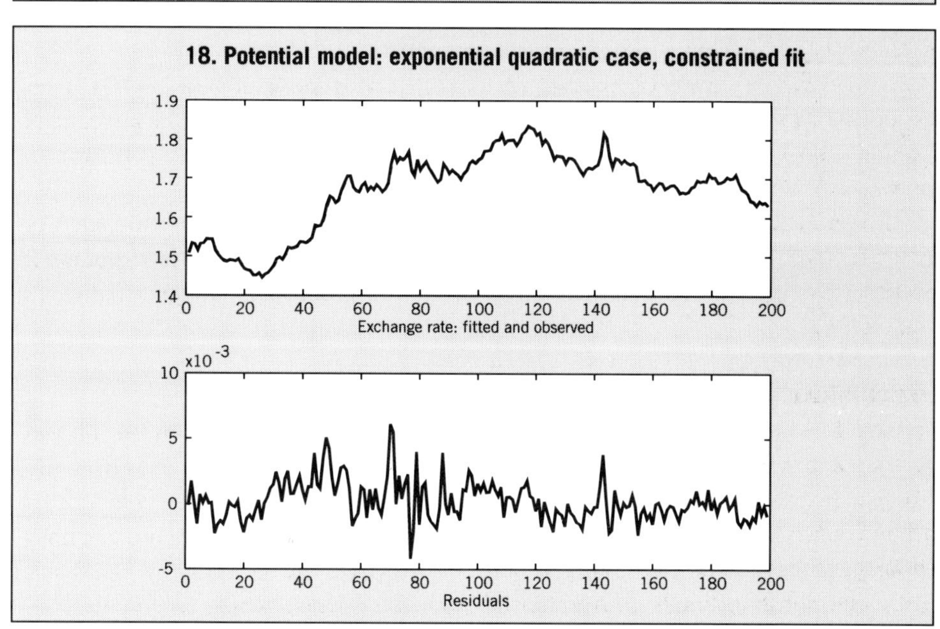
18. Potential model: exponential quadratic case, constrained fit
Exchange rate: fitted and observed
x10 -3
Residuals

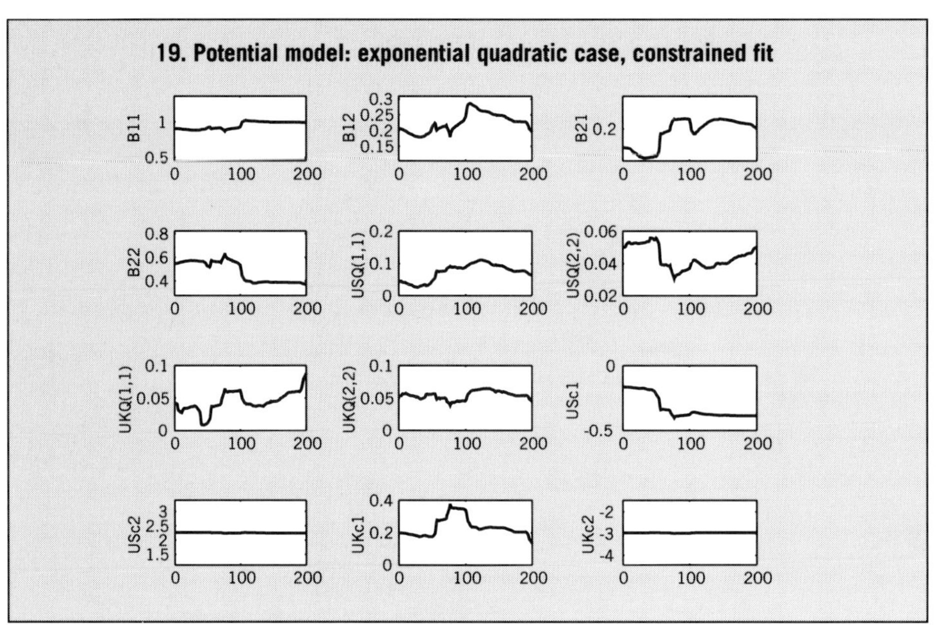
19. Potential model: exponential quadratic case, constrained fit

inhomogeneous versions of potential models can be devised; for example, Flesaker and Hughston (1996) study (amongst others) a class of models which can be described by writing the state-price density as $\zeta_t = a(t) + b(t)M_t$, where a and b are positive decreasing functions and M is a positive log-Brownian martingale. It is probably preferable to think of a pricing routine as a package which outputs a *range* of prices (ie, a confidence interval) rather than a single price. After all, we only have estimates, never true values, and a procedure which fits exactly to input data and pretends there is no error is liable to be severely misleading.

There are three clear directions for further research. The first is to use the fitted models to price derivatives, and this we intend to do once we can get hold of clean derivative price data. The second is to extend to more than two factors; the fit we have

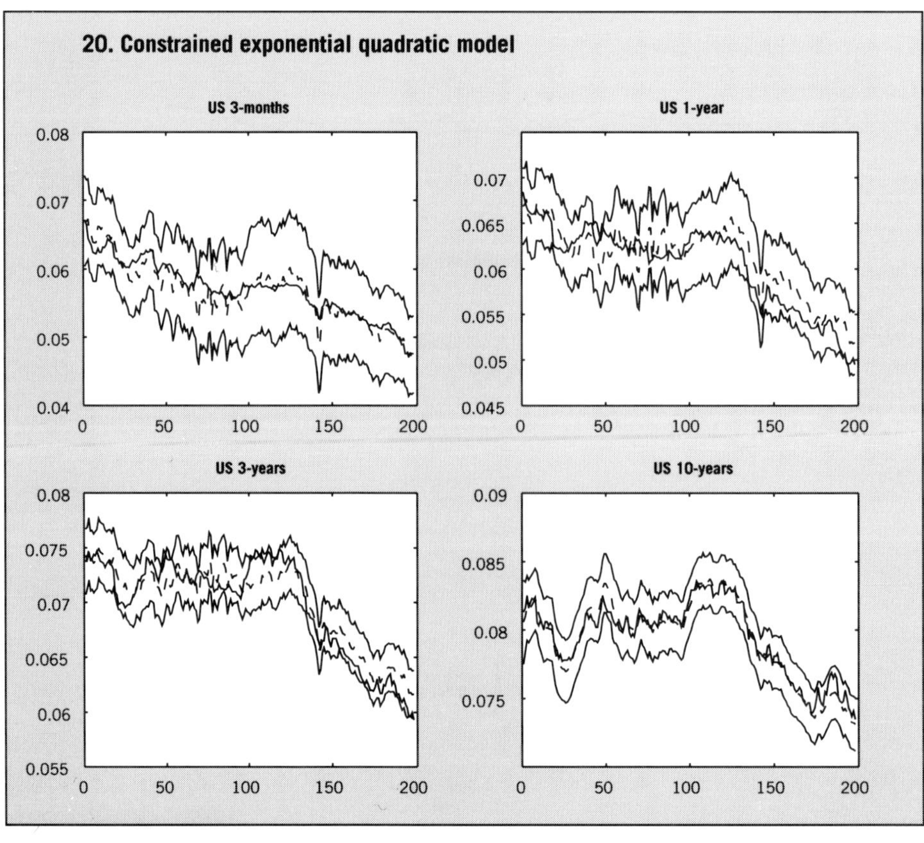
20. Constrained exponential quadratic model

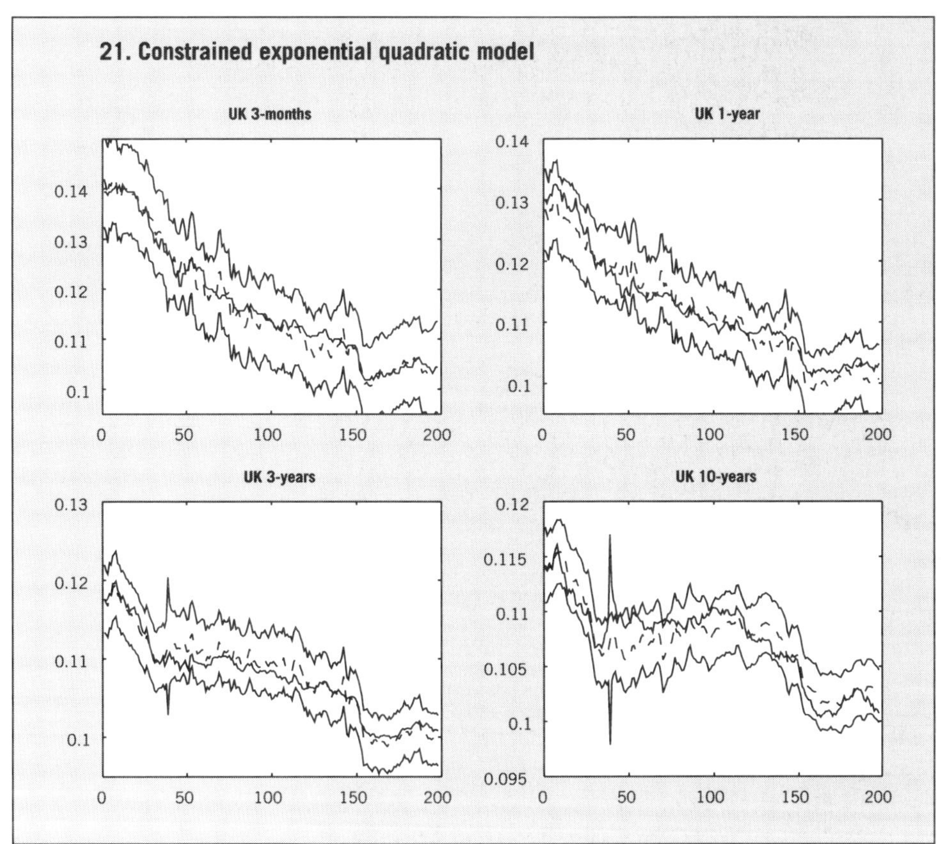

obtained with two factors is reasonable but not marvellous, and we can hope for better with a more flexible model. The third direction is to involve more countries in the model, and this must be the eventual test of the usefulness of the approach. Even with more factors we do not necessarily expect a miraculous fit because of the nature of the data, but if such models can adequately explain the systematic part of the data, we may then address the actual data as a *perturbation* of an underlying time-homogeneous model, and this is structurally more satisfactory than day-by-day fitting.

1 *http://gopher-great-lakes.net:2200/1/partners/ChicagoFed/finance.*

2 *For simplicity the dates not in common have been eliminated from both countries.*

Bibliography

Babbs, S., 1990, "A Family of Itô Process Models for the Term Structure of Interest Rates"; published as Chapter 16 of the present volume.

Cox, J. C., J. E. Ingersoll and S. A. Ross, 1985, "A Theory of the Term Structure of Interest Rates", *Econometrica* 53, pp. 385–407; reprinted as Chapter 6 of the present volume.

Constantinides, G. M., 1992, "A Theory of the Nominal Term Structure of Interest Rates", *Review of Financial Studies* 5, pp. 531–552.

Flesaker, B. and L. P. Hughston, 1996, "Positive Interest", *RISK* 9, pp. 46–49; reprinted as Chapter 21 of the present volume.

Heath, D., R. Jarrow and A. Morton, 1992, "Bond Pricing and the Term Structure of Interest Rates: A New Methodology for Contingent Claims Valuation", *Econometrica* 60, pp. 77–105; reprinted as Chapter 14 of the present volume.

Ho, T. S. Y., and S.-B. Lee, 1986, "Term Structure Movements and Pricing Interest Rate Contingent Claims", *Journal of Finance* 41, pp. 1011–1029; reprinted as Chapter 13 of the present volume.

Longstaff, F. A., and E. S. Schwartz, 1991, "Interest-Rate Volatility and the Term Structure: A Two Factor General Equilibrium Model", *Journal of Finance* 47, pp. 1259–1282.

Rogers, L. C. G., 1995, "The Potential Approach to the Term Structure of Interest Rates and Foreign Exchange Rates", Preprint.

Saa-Requejo, J., 1993, "The Dynamics and the Term Structure of Risk Premia in Foreign Exchange Markets", Preprint.

Vasicek, O. A., 1977, "An Equilibrium Characterization of the Term Structure", *Journal of Financial Economics* 5, pp. 177–188; reprinted as Chapter 4 of the present volume.

21

Positive Interest*

Bjorn Flesaker and Lane Hughston
Bear Stearns; Merrill Lynch

A new framework for valuing interest rate derivatives is introduced that combines a high degree of tractability with a complete absence of negative interest rates.

A drawback of Heath, Jarrow and Morton's interest rate theory (1992) is that it contains no mechanism for ensuring that interest rates remain positive. Special cases of the Heath-Jarrow-Morton (HJM) framework exist in which interest rates are guaranteed to be positive, but these are usually either very specialised, such as the Cox, Ingersoll, and Ross model (1985), or highly artificial, such as the examples based on truncated forward rate volatilities studied by Heath, Jarrow and Morton and, more recently, Miltersen (1994). But none of these approaches is natural or general in character.

Arguments in favour of models allowing negative interest rates have appeared both in the form of economic justifications (Black, 1995), as well as suggestions that the likelihood of negative rates is small and the consequences negligible. Rogers (1996), on the other hand, attacks the viability of Gaussian models on the grounds that under certain circumstances large negative interest rates can arise, thus distorting the pricing of derivatives.

Here we present a new theory of interest rates that builds in positivity in a natural way. Our approach is consistent with the economic arguments of Heath, Jarrow and Morton, in particular their methodology for contingent claims valuation, and thus can be regarded as a precise identification and characterisation of the subclass of HJM models for which rates are positive.

However, there are significant and material differences between the HJM approach and ours. In particular, the HJM theory is a dynamic model for instantaneous forward rates, according to which interest rate derivatives are priced in the risk-neutral measure. Our theory, on the other hand, directly specifies the discount bond price processes, and derivatives are priced from them using a new pricing measure, which we call the terminal measure. Our arguments will demonstrate the economy of thought that can be gained by using the new framework and, in particular, the direct link that can consequently be achieved between theory and practice.

Moreover, in the positive interest framework, the processes for the short rate, the instantaneous forward rates and the money market account are not needed for the foundation or implementation of the theory (Hughston, 1994, and Flesaker and Hughston, 1997).

Along with the initial discount function, the HJM model requires specification of the volatility structure of the instantaneous forward rates. It is often said that one of the main virtues of that model is the way the volatility structure can be freely specified.

**This article first appeared in* RISK Magazine, *Vol. 9, No. 1, pp. 46–49, January 1996.*

The problem is that to ensure positive interest rates the volatility structure itself must depend in a complicated way on the instantaneous forward rates.

But the prescription for achieving this is far from obvious, given the path-dependent structures involved. Even in the simplest examples one is led to complicated non-linear stochastic equations, for which exact solutions are generally out of the question. The situation is further exacerbated by the problem of explosions, ie, that the interest rates determined by the resulting stochastic differential equations (SDEs) can, in certain circumstances (not readily discriminated), shoot up to infinite values, driving discount bond prices to zero.

Our approach, however, is to incorporate the interest rate positivity property into the discount bond process in its very construction, so it does not need to be checked at a later stage. In doing so, we also eliminate the need for systems of SDEs for interest rate processes, and thus avoid the explosion problem by ensuring that bond prices remain positive. Our interest rates are guaranteed to be 100% non-explosive.

To begin, we sketch out a derivation of the main structural equations of the positive interest rate framework. Our procedure will be first to derive these relations where the contingent claims valuation is carried out using a discount bond of fixed maturity T as numeraire (pricing unit). In that case the associated pricing measure is called the T-measure. Then we take the limit as the maturity of the numeraire bond goes to infinity. The limiting measure is also a pricing measure, though not based on the choice of any particular asset as numeraire. We are thus left with a more flexible pricing methodology since it is not tied to one particular asset. The benefit is the ease with which the problem of positive interest rates can be approached: we are led to an entirely novel characterisation of the general price processes for discount bonds, in terms of which the positivity property for the various associated rate processes becomes evident at a glance.

Discount bonds

We assume that interest rate uncertainty is generated by a finite-dimensional Brownian motion. Let $t = 0$ denote the present. We shall write P_{ab} for the value of a discount bond at time a that matures at time b. We can think of P_{ab} as a one-parameter family of random processes indexed by b, and for convenience we assume that P_{ab} is differentiable in b. We shall avoid discussing technicalities and tacitly assume appropriate levels of measurability, differentiability and continuity for the terms under consideration. This is not to say that the technicalities are unimportant, merely that the substantive issues being addressed are of a broader character.

The pricing of interest rate contingent claims is a two-step problem. First, we need a characterisation of the random bond price processes, satisfying the complete markets and no-arbitrage conditions. Then we need a formula for the valuation of contingent claims based on these processes. Suppose we fix a terminal date T and consider the family of bond price processes P_{ab} for which $0 \le a \le b \le T$. For any bond price P_{ab} in this family, we can consider the ratio P_{ab}/P_{aT}, where P_{aT} is the the T-maturity bond. Since the system of bond price processes is, by assumption, complete and arbitrage-free, it follows from Harrison and Pliska (1981) that there is a unique pricing measure (the T-measure) with respect to which the ratio P_{ab}/P_{aT} is a martingale for any bond in the given family. Denoting this martingale by N_{ab}, we have

$$\frac{P_{ab}}{P_{aT}} = N_{ab} \tag{1}$$

Then, by use of $P_{aa} = 1$, we can invert (1) to obtain

$$P_{ab} = \frac{N_{ab}}{N_{aa}} \tag{2}$$

Note that $N_{aT} = 1$ as a consequence of (1). Now let c be such that $0 \le a \le b \le c \le T$.

Then, by (2), we have

$$\frac{P_{ac}}{P_{ab}} = \frac{N_{ac}}{N_{ab}} \tag{3}$$

The positive interest rate property is the requirement that $P_{ac}/P_{ab} < 1$ for $b < c$. This says that, at any time a in the future, the implied forward rates calculated at that time will be positive. From (3) it follows that, under the same condition, we must have $N_{ac}/N_{ab} < 1$, which implies that the derivative $\partial_b N_{ab}$ with respect to the maturity index is negative: $\partial_b N_{ab} < 0$. However, if N_{ab} satisfies the martingale condition, then so does $\partial_b N_{ab}$.

Therefore, there exists a family of positive martingales M_{ab}, subject to the unit initialisation $M_{0b} = 1$, such that $\partial_b N_{ab} = \partial_b N_{0b} M_{ab}$. The solution of this differential equation, subject to the boundary condition $N_{aT} = 1$ and the initial condition $N_{0b} = P_{0b}/P_{0T}$, is given by

$$N_{ab} = 1 - (P_{0T})^{-1} \int_b^T \partial_s P_{0s} M_{as} \, ds \tag{4}$$

By insertion of (4) in (2) we obtain the following striking formula:

$$P_{ab} = \frac{P_{0T} - \int_b^T \partial_s P_{0s} M_{as} \, ds}{P_{0T} - \int_a^T \partial_s P_{0s} M_{as} \, ds} \tag{5}$$

which represents the general bond price process for which interest rates remain positive, valid over the range $0 \le a \le b \le T$. Our approach in what follows will be first to price contingent claims based on such processes, and then take the limit as T approaches infinity, so as to capture the effects of all bond maturities.

For contingent claims pricing in the T-measure let H_a denote the random payout of an interest derivative at time a. Thus H_a can be any suitably measurable function of discount bond prices (of any maturity less than T) over the interval [0, a]. Since the conditional expectation $E_t[H_a/P_{aT}]$ is a martingale for $t \le a$, the present value H_0 of the derivative is

$$H_0 = P_{0T} E\left(\frac{H_a}{P_{aT}}\right) \tag{6}$$

However, by setting $b = T$ in (5) it follows that (6) can be represented directly as

$$H_0 = E\left[\left(P_{0T} - \int_a^T \partial_s P_{0s} M_{as} \, ds\right) H_a\right] \tag{7}$$

So far, the analysis has been based on the choice of a particular discount bond as numeraire such that other bond prices are martingales when expressed in units of it. But the choice of T is arbitrary, so for the greatest generality we want to take the limit as T goes to infinity. It is a remarkable fact, therefore, that both expression (5) for the bond price process and formula (7) for contingent claims evaluation have natural limiting expressions for large T. For the bond price process we obtain

$$P_{ab} = \frac{\int_b^\infty \partial_s P_{0s} M_{as} \, ds}{\int_a^\infty \partial_s P_{0s} M_{as} \, ds} \tag{8}$$

and for the contingent claims valuation formula we get

$$H_0 = E\left[\left(-\int_a^\infty \partial_s P_{0s} M_{as} \, ds\right) H_a\right] \tag{9}$$

These are the main structural equations of the positive interest rate framework.

Relation to Heath, Jarrow and Morton

To specify the bond price process (8) there are two required ingredients. The first is the initial discount function P_{0b}. We have $P_{00} = 1$, and we suppose that $0 < P_{0b} \leq 1$ for all $b \geq 0$. Furthermore, we suppose that the derivative $\partial_b P_{0b}$ exists for $b \geq 0$, and is negative. These conditions imply that initially all rates exist and are positive. The second ingredient is the fundamental family of positive martingales M_{as}. These function as the engine of the model, embodying the random behaviour of interest rates. We require that the process M_{as} should be a positive martingale for $0 \leq a \leq s$, normalised initially and asymptotically to unity. That is, for $0 \leq a \leq b \leq s$ we require: $M_{as} = E_a[M_{bs}]$, $M_{as} > 0$, $M_{0s} = 1$ and that $M_{as} = 1$ in the limit as s goes to infinity.

Since the initial derivative $\partial_s P_{0s}$ is assumed to be negative and the martingale M_{as} is assumed to be positive, it follows from (8) that P_{ab} lies in the desired range $0 < P_{ab} \leq 1$. Likewise we see that $P_{ac}/P_{ab} < 1$ holds for $b < c$, ensuring positive forward rates.

In the HJM framework, emphasis is placed on the processes for the instantaneous forward rates f_{ab} defined by $f_{ab} = -\partial_b \ln P_{ab}$. In the present framework these processes are given by

$$f_{ab} = \frac{\partial_b P_{0b} M_{ab}}{\int_b^\infty \partial_s P_{0s} M_{as} \, ds} \tag{10}$$

Since the numerator and denominator of this expression are both negative by construction, the instantaneous forward rates are manifestly positive. The short rate $r_a = f_{aa}$, also positive, is then given by

$$r_a = \frac{\partial_a P_{0a} M_{aa}}{\int_a^\infty \partial_s P_{0s} M_{as} \, ds} \tag{11}$$

Bond volatilities and correlations

With expression (11) to hand, we can calculate the drift and volatility vector processes for the discount bonds. By the martingale representation theorem we know that the fundamental family of martingales M_{as} satisfies $dM_{as} = M_{as}\sigma_{as} dW_a$ for a suitable family of adapted vector volatility processes σ_{as}. Here W_a is the n-dimensional Wiener process that defines the economic information space, and there is an implied dot product between the vector process σ_{as} and the vector differential dW_a. Then if we set

$$V_{ab} = \frac{\int_b^\infty \partial_s P_{0s} M_{as} \sigma_{as} \, ds}{\int_b^\infty \partial_s P_{0s} M_{as} \, ds} \tag{12}$$

we find, after a calculation making use of the Itô identity:

$$d\left(\frac{X}{Y}\right) = \frac{dX}{Y} - \frac{XdY}{Y^2} + \frac{XdY^2}{Y^3} - \frac{dX\,dY}{Y^2} \tag{13}$$

that the bond price process satisfies the following stochastic equation:

$$\frac{dP_{ab}}{P_{ab}} = r_a da + \Omega_{ab}(dW_a - V_a da) \tag{14}$$

where $V_a = V_{aa}$ and Ω_{ab} is the discount bond vector volatility process, defined by $\Omega_{ab} = V_{ab} - V_a$. The length of Ω_{ab} for a given maturity date is the local discount bond volatility for that maturity. The correlation between movements of bonds of differing maturities is the cosine of the angle between the corresponding vectors.

Risk-neutral measure

The significance of the vector process V_a appearing in (14) is that it can be used to construct the appropriate change of measure density martingale to move from the terminal measure to the risk-neutral measure. The risk-neutral measure is the most commonly applied pricing measure in the valuation of derivatives. In this measure the money market account is given a special status, in the sense that the ratio of the value of any non-dividend paying asset to the value of the money market account is a martingale.

In the risk-neutral measure we want the process W^0_a, defined by $dW^0_a = dW_a - V_a da$, to be a Brownian motion to ensure that in that measure the drift of the discount bond process is the short rate. The density martingale for this transformation is given by

$$\rho_a = \exp\left(\int_{s=0}^{a} V_s dW_s - \tfrac{1}{2}\int_{s=0}^{a} V_s^2 ds\right) \tag{15}$$

That is to say, the risk-neutral expectation, $E^0[X]$, of a random variable X adapted to the filtration up to time a is given by $E^0[X] = E[\rho_a X]$.

By use of (15) we are led to a useful formula for the money market account, which will now be presented. The unit initialised money market process B_t is the value of an ideal bank account that starts at time zero with one unit of currency and accumulates interest at the short rate on a continuous basis. In the present framework, we find

$$B_a = \frac{\rho_a}{-\int_a^\infty \partial_s P_{0s} M_{as}\, ds} \tag{16}$$

with ρ_a given as in (15). One can verify, by use of (13), that $dB_a = r_a B_a da$. An advantage of the use of (16) is that it puts the money market account on an equal footing with other assets in our model by expressing it as the ratio of a martingale and the discount factor Δ_a defined by

$$\Delta_a = -\int_a^\infty \partial_s P_{0s} M_{as}\, ds \tag{17}$$

We can view the process $P_a = 1/\Delta_a$ as defining an absolute numeraire, in terms of which the money market account can be written $B_a = \rho_a P_a$. The vector V_a can then be identified as the volatility vector for the process P_a, for which the relevant stochastic equation is given by

$$\frac{dP_a}{P_a} = \left(r_a + V_a^2\right)da - V_a dW_a \tag{18}$$

Valuation of derivatives

The payouts of interest rate derivatives are often given in terms of various rate processes rather than directly in terms of discount bonds. For example, the basic per-period Libor rate L_{ab} at time a referring to the time interval $[a, b]$ is $L_{ab} = (P_{ab})^{-1} - 1$, and the corresponding annualised rate is $(b - a)^{-1} L_{ab}$. Other examples of rate processes on which claims can be based include zero-coupon rates, swap rates and bond yields, all ultimately defined in terms of discount bond processes. For the specification of derivative payouts it is immaterial whether we work with rate processes or directly with discount bond processes, and for convenience we shall often work with the latter. Now suppose we define the defective discount function Δ_{ab} by

$$\Delta_{ab} = -\int_b^\infty \partial_s P_{0s} M_{as}\, ds \tag{19}$$

for $0 \le a \le b$, so $\Delta_a = \Delta_{aa}$. Alternatively, by using the martingale property we can write $\Delta_{ab} = E_a \Delta_b$. By the normalisation condition $M_{0s} = 1$ we have $\Delta_{0b} = P_{0b}$, and in particular

$E[\Delta_{ab}] = P_{0b}$ and $E[\Delta_b] = P_{0b}$. The contingent claims valuation formula (9) for a random payout H_a at time a can then be expressed as

$$H_0 = E[\Delta_a H_a] \tag{20}$$

More generally, the value H_a at time a of a contingent claim that pays H_b at time b is given by

$$\Delta_a H_a = E_a[\Delta_b H_b] \tag{21}$$

By the appropriate application of (20) and (21) we can now proceed to value interest rate derivatives. As an exercise, we consider the valuation of various fixed and floating-rate payments and standard note structures; we already know what answers to expect in these cases, but it will be instructive to verify that our contingent claims methodology is consistent with these results.

DISCOUNT BONDS. If the payout at time b is $H_b = 1$, a unit of currency, then its value at time a is the random discount function P_{ab}. By use of (21) this shows that $P_{ab} = \Delta_{ab}/\Delta_a$, a compact way of expressing formula (8).

FIXED PAYMENTS. From $E[\Delta_a] = P_{0a}$ and (20) it follows that the present value of a contract that pays one unit of currency at time a is P_{0a}. Formula (20) will thus correctly value any set of fixed payments.

FUTURE DELIVERY OF A DISCOUNT BOND OF GIVEN MATURITY. Suppose a contract pays at time a the value P_{ab} of a discount bond that matures at time b. Then $H_a = P_{ab}$, and if we substitute $P_{ab} = \Delta_{ab}/\Delta_a$ into (20) and use $E[\Delta_{ab}] = P_{0b}$ we get $H_0 = P_{0b}$.

LIBOR RATES, PAID IN ARREARS. Suppose the contract pays at time b the per-period Libor rate L_{ab} set at time a. This is equivalent to a cashflow of $1 - P_{ab}$ at time a, which, as we have seen, has present value $P_{0a} - P_{0b}$.

FLOATING RATE NOTES. Consider the present value of a note with coupon dates a_1, $a_2, a_3, \ldots, a_n$ and principal date a_n, such that on each coupon date a Libor payment is made according to the per-period rate set on the previous coupon date for the period between the two coupon dates. The payment on date a_1 is based on the initial Libor rate L_{0a_1} and the principal payment on date a_n is one unit. It follows from the previous arguments that the present value of such a note is unity. Standard swap contracts can be priced by a similar argument.

MONEY MARKET ACCOUNTS. The value of a unit-initialised money market account at time b is $B_b = \rho_b/\Delta_b$ in accordance with (16), where Δ_b is the absolute discount function and ρ_b is the exponential martingale (15). As a consequence of the martingale property $\rho_a = E_a[\rho_b]$, it follows from (21) that the random value at time a of a contract that pays out, at some later time b, the contents of a unit initialised money market account is simply the value of the money market account at time a.

The examples above indicate the ease with which various non-optional structures can be handled within the positive interest rate framework. They also point the way to the calculations involved when there is a non-trivial optional component, concerning which we make the following general observations.

CAPS AND FLOORS. A typical caplet will note the value of the per-period Libor rate L_{ab} at time a and pay out a fixed multiple of $(L_{ab} - k)_+$ at time b. Here $(x)_+ = \max(x, 0)$. If we discount the payment back to time a, we have a contingent claim with payout function

$H_a = P_{ab}(L_{ab} - k)_+$ at time a, which by use of $L_{ab} = (P_{ab})^{-1} - 1$ can be written in the form $H_a = [1 - (1 + k)P_{ab}]_+$. This is evidently equivalent to $1 + k$ units of a put on the discount bond P_{ab}, struck at $(1 + k)^{-1}$. Similarly a Libor floorlet is equivalent to a call option on a discount bond. It suffices to consider options on discount bonds, so we move to the next example.

OPTIONS ON DISCOUNT BONDS. In the case of a call option we have the payout $H_a = (P_{ab} - K)_+$. By use of the structural equations $H_0 = E[\Delta_a H_a]$ and $P_{ab} = \Delta_{ab}/\Delta_a$ we get $H_0 = E[(\Delta_{ab} - K\Delta_a)_+]$.

Now, suppose we consider the case of a one-factor model for which $\Delta_{ab} = A_b + B_b M_a$, where A_b and B_b are decreasing positive deterministic functions such that $A_b + B_b = P_{0b}$, M_a is a unit-initialised (possibly time-changed) geometric Brownian motion, and B_b/P_{0b} goes to zero for large b. Remarkably, we can solve for the value H_0 of the call option exactly and the result can be expressed in the form of a Black-Scholes formula.

We are thus led to a model with a combination of properties that until now had generally been thought to be impossible: an arbitrage-free interest rate model with positive interest rates (ie, with quasi-lognormal behaviour) and Black-Scholes caplet prices. Astonishingly, the model also prices swaptions analytically. We shall call this the *rational lognormal model*, since discount bonds are given by rational functions of a lognormal martingale. In fact, we have $P_{ab} = (A_b + B_b M_a)/(A_a + B_a M_a)$. An outstanding feature of the rational lognormal model is that the discount function is bounded both above and below, the bounds being determined by the deterministic processes $A_{ab} = A_b/A_a$ and $B_{ab} = B_b/B_a$ obtained for small and large limiting values of the basic martingale.

SWAPTIONS. We consider an option to enter at time a into a swap agreement where we receive a floating rate and pay a fixed rate, struck at the rate K. The option is in the money if at maturity the swap rate is greater than K. Let $a_1, a_2, a_3, \ldots, a_n$ be the series of swap payment dates, not necessarily equally spaced. Then we define the random swap rate at time a associated with these dates by

$$S_a = \frac{P_{a,a_0} - P_{a,a_n}}{\beta_a(a_0, a_1, a_2, a_3, \ldots, a_n)} \tag{22}$$

where a_0 is the first set date and $a \le a_0$. Here β_a is the present value factor associated with this string of payments, defined by

$$\beta_a(a_0, a_1, a_2, a_3, \ldots, a_n) = \sum_{i=1}^{n} F_{i-1,i} P_{a,a_i} \tag{23}$$

where $F_{i-1,i}$ is the daycount fraction between a_{i-1} and a_i for the convention relevant to our currency. The swaption is structured so that we effectively receive the rate $(S_a - K)_+$ on each of the coupon dates. If we discount each coupon payment back to time a, then the effective cashflow at time a is given by

$$H_a = \left[P_{a,a_0} - P_{a,a_n} - K\beta_a(a_0, a_1, a_2, a_3, \ldots, a_n)\right]_+ \tag{24}$$

which, by use of the structural equations, gives

$$H_0 = E\left[\left(\Delta_{a,a_0} - \Delta_{a,a_n} - K\sum_{i=1}^{n} F_{i-1,i}\Delta_{a,a_i}\right)_+\right] \tag{25}$$

for the present value of the swaption. Note that in the case of the rational lognormal model swaption prices also reduce directly to a Black-Scholes formula. This is significant as it opens the door to the possibility of an efficient analytical calibration methodology for interest rate derivatives based on cap and swaption price data.

All considerations here have been confined to a single currency. But the corresponding analysis in the multi-currency case is straightforward, and this will be described at length elsewhere (Flesaker and Hughston, 1996). One remarkable fact that emerges, however, is that a family of fundamental martingales is associated with each currency which defines the term structure of interest rates for that currency and ensures the positivity of these rates. The same measure is used for each currency and the resulting system of martingale families is sufficiently rich to embody both exchange rate risk and interest rate risk. In practical terms, this means that we now have the scope to design a universal risk management technology that treats all currencies on a highly symmetrical basis.

Acknowledgements

The authors wish to thank R. Brenner, M. Gorrod, S. Gregornik, R. Jarrow, O. Jonsson, D. Madan, N. Rabeau, L. Sankarasubramanian and J. Tigg for stimulating discussions.

Bibliography

Black, F., 1995, "Interest Rates as Options", *Journal of Finance* 50 (7), pp. 1371-1376.

Cox, J. C., J. E. Ingersoll, and S. A. Ross, 1985, "A Theory of the Term Structure of Interest Rates", *Econometrica* 53 (2), pp. 385-407; reprinted as Chapter 6 of the present volume.

Flesaker, B., and L. P. Hughston, 1996, "Positive Interest: Foreign Exchange"; Chapter 22 of the present volume.

Flesaker, B., and L. P. Hughston, 1997, "Exotic Interest Rate Options", in *Exotic Options: The State of the Art*, L. Clewlow and C. Strickland, eds.

Harrison, J. M., and S. R. Pliska, 1981, "Martingales and Stochastic Integrals in the Theory of Continuous Trading", *Stochastic Processes and their Applications* 11, pp. 215-260.

Heath, D., R. Jarrow and A. Morton, 1992, "Bond Pricing and the Term Structure of Interest Rates: A New Methodology for Contingent Claims Valuation", *Econometrica* 60 (1), pp. 77-105; reprinted as Chapter 14 of the present volume..

Hughston, L. P., 1994, "Financial Observables", *International Derivative Review* December 1994, pp. 11-14.

Miltersen, K., 1994, "An Arbitrage Theory of the Term Structure of Interest Rates", *Annals of Applied Probability* 4, pp. 953-967.

Rogers, L. C. G., 1996, "Gaussian Errors", *RISK* January 1996, pp. 42-45.

22

Positive Interest: Foreign Exchange

Bjorn Flesaker and Lane Hughston
Bear Stearns; Merrill Lynch

We present a general methodology for the valuation of interest rate and foreign exchange derivatives in which interest rates in all currencies, both domestic and foreign, are guaranteed to be positive. The new model represents the entire class of Amin-Jarrow international economies for which this property holds and for which the associated interest rate and foreign exchange markets are arbitrage-free.

In recent work (Flesaker and Hughston, 1996) we have derived a complete characterisation of arbitrage-free single-currency interest rate processes that respect the initial term structure and guarantee positive interest rates. Here we develop a model of a multi-currency economy that embeds the positive interest rate feature in each currency and which prescribes consistent dynamics for the foreign exchange rates.

Central to our argument is the introduction of a new equivalent martingale measure, which serves as the measure under which key processes are martingales regardless of which currency is chosen as the base. The inherent symmetry of the multi-currency economy is thus represented more naturally than in the usual approach.

From a practical perspective, the framework presented herein is potentially superior to existing frameworks in terms of developing useful models for the pricing and risk management of derivative products in a multi-currency context. The main benefit is the facility to construct fairly simple models where future exchange rates and whole yield curves depend, in a prespecified functional manner, on the smallest possible number of state variables.

For example, it turns out to be a simple exercise to reduce the framework described here to a two-currency economy with positive interest rates, locally lognormal exchange rates, and quite flexible volatility and correlation structure, yet fully described by three Gaussian state variables. Such a model has applications to long-dated foreign exchange options, with or without American or barrier features, as well as to important popular products such as differential swaps and quanto swaps and options.

The paper starts with a review of the single-currency analysis, which will serve to establish notation and to relate our framework to the HJM model (Heath, Jarrow and Morton, 1992). In the single-currency case the main structural equations are given by the expression for the bond price process (1) and the interest rate contingent claims valuation formula (6). In subsequent sections we progress to develop the multi-currency extension of our framework and indicate its relation to the standard multi-currency generalisation of the HJM model due to Amin and Jarrow (1991, 1992).

The main structural equations of the positive interest foreign exchange framework are given by equation (61) for the multi-currency discount bond price processes and by equation (62) for the foreign exchange cross-rate processes. Contingent claims valuation, in the international setting, for multi-currency interest rate and foreign exchange derivatives is given by formula (65).

Domestic interest rates

First we review the basic positive interest rate model for a single currency, which for convenience we call the "domestic" currency. We assume that the domestic interest rate market is arbitrage-free, default-free, and complete. Later we shall drop the assumption of strict market completeness for domestic interest rates and assume completeness only at the "international" level, when the entire system of international interest rates and foreign exchange is taken into account. Interest rate uncertainty is represented by the structure of a probability space endowed with the augmented filtration of a standard multi-dimensional Brownian motion. Much of what we have to say here applies in a more general setting, but for simplicity and definiteness we shall confine the discussion here to the case of a Brownian filtration. As usual we write P_{ab} for the value of a discount bond at time a that matures to pay one unit of domestic currency at time b. It is useful to think of P_{ab} as a one-parameter family of random price processes, parameterised by the maturity index b, and we denote the derivative of P_{ab} with respect to the maturity parameter b by $\partial_b P_{ab}$.

The traditional approaches to interest rate modelling and contingent claims pricing usually start with either (*a*) a stochastic equation to be satisfied by the short rate r_a, or else (*b*) a system of stochastic equations to be satisfied by the instantaneous forward rates defined by $f_{ab} = -\partial_b \ln P_{ab}$. The two approaches are in fact equivalent to one another: that is, barring pathologies, any consistent (ie, market-complete, arbitrage-free) theory of the short rate based on a Brownian filtration can be recast unambiguously as a "whole yield-curve model"; and, conversely, any consistent evolution for the instantaneous forward rates can be characterised entirely in terms of the process for the short rate. See for example Carverhill (1995), and Flesaker and Hughston (1997*a*, 1997*b*).

When a given consistent interest rate theory is expressed in terms of the instantaneous forward rate evolution we say that it is in "HJM form". According to this point of view, the HJM theory is not a "model" as such, but rather an overall framework, with which any consistent interest rate model (based on the given probability space) must ultimately be compatible.

On the other hand, there is no compelling reason to suppose that the HJM theory, taken at face value in its usual presentation, is optimal for practical interest rate derivatives pricing (although of course it is certainly useful for this purpose), and it is valid to ask whether one can do better. The model to be outlined below can thus be viewed as a reformulation of the HJM theory that takes it a significant step further and enables one to characterise in a very natural way certain model subclasses with desirable features, eg, interest rate positivity.

In our approach we model the discount bond price processes directly rather than the underlying short rate or instantaneous forward rates. This policy offers a number of conceptual as well as practical advantages, since interest rate contingent claims payoffs are typically expressed in terms of systems of one or more "finite" rates - eg, Libor or swap rates - the definitions of which involve nothing more than simple algebraic functions of various associated discount bonds.

The single-currency positive interest rate framework is based on the existence of a unique probability measure $\mathbf{P}$, with associated expectation $\mathbf{E}[-]$, called the "terminal measure", with respect to which the discount bond price process P_{ab} can be expressed in the following simple form:

$$P_{ab} = \frac{\int_b^\infty \partial_s P_{0s} M_{as} \, ds}{\int_a^\infty \partial_s P_{0s} M_{as} \, ds} \tag{1}$$

Here M_{as} denotes an essentially arbitrary one-parameter family of unit-initialised positive martingales with respect to $\mathbf{E}[-]$, satisfying the following conditions:

$$M_{0s} = 1 \quad \text{for } s \geq 0 \tag{2}$$

$$\lim_{s \to \infty} M_{as} = 1 \quad \text{for } a \geq 0 \tag{3}$$

$$M_{as} > 0 \quad \text{for } 0 \leq a \leq s \tag{4}$$

$$M_{as} = \mathbf{E}_a[M_{bs}] \quad \text{for } 0 \leq a \leq b \leq s \tag{5}$$

In equation (5) the operator $\mathbf{E}_a$ denotes as usual the conditional expectation under the probability measure $\mathbf{P}$, with respect to the given filtration, given information up to time a. We assume that initially interest rates are positive, which means that the initial discount function satisfies $0 < P_{0s} < 1$ and $\partial_s P_{0s} < 0$. Since $\partial_s P_{0s}$ is assumed to be negative and M_{as} is assumed to be positive, it follows from (1) at a glance that P_{ab} necessarily lies in the desired range $0 < P_{ab} < 1$ for $a < b$, and that $\partial_b P_{ab} < 0$. By the same line of argument we can see immediately that the relation $P_{ac}/P_{ac} < 1$ holds for $b < c$, ensuring that forward rates are always positive. Formula (1) represents the general discount bond price process within the HJM framework for which interest rates remain finite and positive. We note that the model is fully evolutionary in the sense that it admits an essentially arbitrary suitable specification for the initial discount function P_{0s}. This is important for practical applications since interest rate derivative prices are in general extremely sensitive to the given initial configuration of the yield curve.

The significant structural features of the model are captured in the specification of the one-parameter family of positive martingales M_{as}, which encapsulates the full information of the volatility and correlation relationships for discount bonds of all maturities. The other principal ingredient to the model is the contingent claims valuation formula. This is given as follows. Suppose we have a random adapted cashflow H_a at time a, the payoff function of a derivative security. More generally, we can let H_a signify the value at time a of a derivative security adapted to the underlying filtration at time a. Then the present value (ie, the value at time 0) of the contingent claim is given by:

$$H_0 = \mathbf{E}\left[\left(-\int_a^{\infty} \partial_s P_{0s} M_{as}\, ds\right) H_a\right] \tag{6}$$

Note that the expression appearing in the denominator of (1) reappears as the appropriate discount factor in the contingent claims valuation formula (6). It is straightforward to verify that for a variety of simple choices of H_a (such as $H_a = 1$ or $H_a = P_{ab}$) formula (6) immediately leads to the correct valuation.

The terminal numeraire process

Some further conceptual advances can be achieved if we introduce a special process which we call the "terminal numeraire" P_a, defined by

$$P_a = \left(-\int_a^{\infty} \partial_s P_{0s} M_{as}\, ds\right)^{-1} \tag{7}$$

The process P_a is characterised by the property that the ratio of the price of any "pure" asset (ie, non-dividend paying, non-interest paying asset) to P_a is a martingale with respect to the terminal measure $\mathbf{E}[-]$:

$$\frac{H_a}{P_a} = \mathbf{E}_a\left(\frac{H_b}{P_b}\right) \tag{8}$$

for $b \geq a$. In particular, if $H_b = 1$, corresponding to an asset whose value is guaranteed to be one unit of domestic currency at time b (ie, a discount bond with maturity b), then its value at time a must be $H_a = P_{ab}$, and we are led to the following expression:

$$P_{ab} = P_a \mathbf{E}_a\left(\frac{1}{P_b}\right) \tag{9}$$

Formula (9) is easily seen to be equivalent to (1) on account of the martingale property $M_{as} = \mathbf{E}_a[M_{bs}]$, which implies the relation

$$\mathbf{E}_a\left(\frac{1}{P_b}\right) = -\int_b^\infty \partial_s P_{0s} M_{as}\, ds \tag{10}$$

The terminal numeraire process can be usefully interpreted in two distinct ways. First we note that P_a can be obtained as the infinite maturity limit of the ratio of the discount bond process P_{ab} to its initial value P_{0b}. In fact, we have

$$P_a = \lim_{b\to\infty}\left(\frac{P_{ab}}{P_{0b}}\right) \tag{11}$$

which follows, as a consequence of the asymptotic normalisation (3), by an elementary application of l'Hopital's rule. It is worth bearing in mind that P_a is not therefore a price process in the strict sense, because it is given by the limit of the *ratio* of two prices.

The terminal measure $\mathbf{E}[-]$ can thus be thought of as the limiting member of a certain natural family of measures—viz., the one-parameter family of "forward adjusted risk measures", each of which is naturally associated with a discount bond of some given finite maturity. We recall, in particular, that in the forward adjusted risk measure, corresponding to the choice of a discount bond of maturity T as numeraire, the general bond price process can be represented in the form

$$P_{ab} = \frac{P_{0T} - \int_b^T \partial_s P_{0s} M_{as}^T\, ds}{P_{0T} - \int_a^T \partial_s P_{0s} M_{as}^T\, ds} \tag{12}$$

which then reduces to (1) in the limit as T goes to infinity (Flesaker and Hughston, 1996). Here M_{as}^T denotes a one-parameter family of positive processes that satisfy the martingale condition with respect to the T-maturity forward adjusted risk measure $\mathbf{E}^T$. In this measure we have

$$H_0 = P_{0T}\mathbf{E}^T\left(\frac{H_a}{P_{aT}}\right) \tag{13}$$

for the relevant contingent claims valuation formula, which by use of (12) can easily be seen to reduce to (6) in the limit of large T. In particular, for the terminal measure we have

$$\mathbf{E} = \lim_{T\to\infty} \mathbf{E}^T \tag{14}$$

and for the associated one-parameter family of martingales we have

$$M_{as} = \lim_{T\to\infty} M_{as}^T \tag{15}$$

Alternatively, we can define a discount function $\Delta_a = 1/P_a$ in terms of P_a, with respect to which the contingent claims valuation formula (6) is given by $H_0 = \mathbf{E}[\Delta_a H_a]$ or, more generally

$$\Delta_a H_a = \mathbf{E}_a[\Delta_b H_b] \tag{16}$$

In this interpretation Δ_a assigns the correct weighting (discounting) to place on each possible random value of H_a to obtain the present value H_0 of the given contingent claim cashflow.

The discounting approach is very useful in practical applications of our model, and this is explored at greater length in Flesaker and Hughston (1996).

Relation to the Heath–Jarrow–Morton framework

Now we are in a position to indicate in more explicit terms the connection between the positive interest rate framework, as encapsulated in the bond price process formula (1) and the contingent claims valuation formula (6), and the HJM theory. To this end let us calculate an expression for the instantaneous forward rates f_{ab}, defined as above by

$$f_{ab} = -\partial_b \ln P_{ab} \tag{17}$$

It follows by insertion of (1) into (17) that the instantaneous forward rates are given by:

$$f_{ab} = \frac{\partial_b P_{0b} M_{ab}}{\int_b^\infty \partial_s P_{0s} M_{as}\, ds} = f_{0b} \frac{-P_{0b} M_{ab}}{\int_b^\infty \partial_s P_{0s} M_{as}\, ds} \tag{18}$$

Since the numerators and denominators of these expressions are both by construction negative, we verify that the instantaneous forward rates are indeed positive. In the second equality we have a useful product representation of the instantaneous forward rates in terms of their initial values and a random term. It follows from (18) that the short term interest rate $r_a = f_{aa}$ is given by

$$r_a = \frac{\partial_a P_{0a} M_{aa}}{\int_a^\infty \partial_s P_{0s} M_{as}\, ds} = f_{0a} \frac{-P_{0a} M_{aa}}{\int_a^\infty \partial_s P_{0s} M_{as}\, ds} \tag{19}$$

which is also necessarily positive. We note, conversely, that given the process P_{ab} it is straightforward to recover the underlying martingale family M_{ab}, since by virtue of (18) and (19) we have, for example

$$\frac{f_{ab} P_{ab}}{r_a} = \frac{\partial_b P_{0b} M_{ab}}{\partial_a P_{0a} M_{aa}} \tag{20}$$

The ratio process M_{ab}/M_{aa} only determines M_{ab} up to an overall random change of scale $M_{ab} \rightarrow \lambda_a M_{ab}$, but λ_a is fixed by the asymptotic normalisation condition (3).

Given (19), we can calculate the drift and volatility processes for discount bonds and obtain a stochastic equation for their price process. This is achieved as follows. By the martingale representation theorem the martingale family M_{as} satisfies

$$dM_{as} = M_{as} \sigma_{as} dW_a \tag{21}$$

for a suitable family of adapted vector volatility processes σ_{us}. Here we meet W_a, the basic n-dimensional vector Wiener process that defines the underlying economic uncertainty, and there is an implied scalar product between the vector process σ_{us} and the vector differential dW_a. Then, if we define the vector process V_{ab} by

$$V_{ab} = \frac{\int_b^\infty \partial_s P_{0s} M_{as} \sigma_{as}\, ds}{\int_b^\infty \partial_s P_{0s} M_{as}\, ds} \tag{22}$$

it follows by use of the Itô identity

$$d\left(\frac{X}{Y}\right) = \frac{dX}{Y} - \frac{XdY}{Y^2} + \frac{XdY^2}{Y^3} - \frac{dX\,dY}{Y^2} \tag{23}$$

when applied to the quotient (1) that the bond price process P_{ab} satisfies

$$\frac{dP_{ab}}{P_{ab}} = r_a da + \Omega_{ab}(dW_a - V_a da) \tag{24}$$

Here r_a is the short rate, given as in (19) above and Ω_{ab} is the discount bond vector volatility process, given by

$$\Omega_{ab} = V_{ab} - V_a \tag{25}$$

where $V_a \triangleq V_{aa}$. The length of the vector Ω_{ab}, for a given maturity date b, is the local (instantaneous) volatility for a discount bond of that maturity. The correlation between movements of bonds of differing maturities is given by the cosine of the angle between the corresponding vectors; see, for example, Hughston (1994); Flesaker and Hughston (1997*a*, *b*).

Note that the instantaneous drift of the bond price process in (24) is composed of two components, viz., the short rate r_a and a correction term $\Omega_{ab}V_a$ given by the inner product of the discount bond volatility Ω_{ab} and the vector process V_a.

It follows as a consequence of equation (24) that the vector V_a can be identified as the volatility for the terminal numeraire process P_a, for which the relevant stochastic equation is given by

$$\frac{dP_a}{P_a} = (r_a + V_a^2)da - V_a dW_a \tag{26}$$

where V_a^2 denotes the squared length of the vector V_a. To see that (26) indeed holds one proceeds as follows. We note first that σ_{as} must go to zero in the limit as s goes to infinity. This follows as a consequence of condition (3), which implies that the local volatility of the fundamental martingale family must turn off in the limit as the maturity parameter gets very large. It then follows from (22), by use of l'Hopital's rule, that V_{ab} must vanish in the limit as b goes to infinity. This shows that the limiting value of Ω_{ab} as b goes to infinity is indeed $-V_a$. Furthermore, we note that on account of (11) the limiting value of the ratio dP_{ab}/P_{ab} as b goes to infinity is just dP_a/P_a. Armed with these observations, we can then see directly that the stochastic equation (24) for the bond price process implies the corresponding process (26) for the terminal numeraire.

The structure of the drift term in (24) suggests that it is natural to consider a certain change of measure $\mathbf{E} \to \mathbf{E}^0$ such that the process W_a^0, defined by

$$dW_a^0 = dW_a - V_a dt \tag{27}$$

is a Brownian motion with respect to the new measure $\mathbf{E}^0$. In terms of the process W_a^0 the stochastic equation for the bond price can be written

$$\frac{dP_{ab}}{P_{ab}} = r_a da + \Omega_{ab} dW_a^0 \tag{28}$$

Since the drift is now given for bonds of all maturities by the short rate, it follows that the new measure $\mathbf{E}^0$ must in fact be the ***risk-neutral*** expectation. The risk-neutral measure is defined to be the measure with respect to which the expected instantaneous rate of return of any "pure" (non-dividend paying) asset is the short rate. Equivalently, it is the measure for which the ratio of any "pure" asset price process to the money market account process is a martingale.

The domestic money market account

Since the transformation between the risk-neutral measure and the terminal measure is a matter of some interest, and it is essential to a critical understanding of the relationship between the HJM theory and the positive interest rate framework, it will be worth developing the relevant arguments here in a little more detail. This will in turn lead us to a natural expression for the domestic money market account process.

By way of general background we first note that on a filtered probability space $(\Omega, \mathbf{P}, \{F_t\})$ a continuous semimartingale X_t has a unique differential decomposition of the form

$$dX_t = dX_t^m + dX_t^f \tag{29}$$

where X_t^m is a martingale with respect to the given measure $\mathbf{P}$, and X_t^f is a process of finite variation.

The well-known theorem of Girsanov then amounts to the observation that under a change of measure $\mathbf{P} \to \tilde{\mathbf{P}}$ the decomposition of X_t into martingale and finite variation components undergoes a well-defined shift. Under the new measure $\tilde{\mathbf{P}}$ we obtain

$$dX_t^{m,\tilde{P}} = dX_t^{m,P} - dX_t d(\ln \rho_t) \tag{30}$$

for the martingale part of process X_t, and

$$dX_t^{f,\tilde{P}} = dX_t^{f,P} + dX_t d(\ln \rho_t) \tag{31}$$

for the drift (see, eg, Norris, 1992). Here ρ_t is the density martingale characterising the absolutely continuous transformation $\mathbf{P} \to \tilde{\mathbf{P}}$. That is to say, the $\tilde{\mathbf{P}}$-expectation, $\mathbf{E}^{\tilde{P}}[X]$, of a random variable X-adapted to the filtration up to time t is given by the formula

$$\mathbf{E}^{\tilde{P}}[X] = \mathbf{E}^{P}[\rho_t X] \tag{32}$$

In our case we consider a transformation from the terminal measure with expectation $\mathbf{E}$ to the risk-neutral measure with expectation $\mathbf{E}^0$.

In the risk-neutral measure we want the process W_t^0 defined by (27) to be a Brownian motion to ensure, as above, that with respect to the measure $\mathbf{E}^0$ the drift on the discount bond process P_{ab} is the short rate. The density martingale for this transformation is given by

$$\rho_a = \exp\left(\int_{s=0}^{a} V_s dW_s - \frac{1}{2}\int_{s=0}^{a} V_s^2 ds\right) \tag{33}$$

In other words, the risk-neutral expectation, $\mathbf{E}^0[X]$, of a random variable X adapted to the Brownian filtration up to time a is given by $\mathbf{E}^0[X] = \mathbf{E}[\rho_a X]$, where $\mathbf{E}$ is the expectation in the terminal measure.

The unit-initialised domestic money market account ("bank account") process B_a is the process that starts at time zero with one unit of domestic currency and accumulates interest at the short rate on a continuously compounded basis, ie,

$$B_a = \exp\left(\int_{s=0}^{a} r_s ds\right) \tag{34}$$

However, since the money market account is itself an asset price process, it follows that its ratio to the absolute numeraire must be a positive martingale.

It turns out, interestingly enough, that the relevant positive martingale is in fact the density martingale ρ_a as given in (33) above, and we have

$$B_a = \frac{\rho_a}{-\int_a^{\infty} \partial_s P_{0s} M_{as}\, ds} \tag{35}$$

Indeed, it is not difficult to check directly that (35) implies

$$dB_a = r_a B_a da \tag{36}$$

by use of the Itô quotient identity (23) above, which shows that (35) is indeed equivalent to (34). The advantage of the use of (35) is that it puts the money market account on an equal footing with other classes of assets in our model by expressing it as the product of a positive martingale and the terminal numeraire process:

$$B_a = \rho_a P_a \tag{37}$$

Alternatively, this result can be obtained directly, simply by integrating the stochastic equation (26) for P_a. The relation between the risk-neutral measure $\mathbf{E}^0$ and the absolute terminal measure $\mathbf{E}$ can be summarised by the formula

$$\mathbf{E}^0[X] = \mathbf{E}\left[\frac{B_a X}{P_a}\right] \tag{38}$$

for any random variable adapted to the filtration up to time a. In particular, if we set $X = H_a/B_a$, where H_a is a random cashflow at time a, then for the relationship between contingent claims valuation in the two measures we have

$$\mathbf{E}^0\left[\frac{H_a}{B_a}\right] = \mathbf{E}\left[\frac{H_a}{P_a}\right] \tag{39}$$

As a further application of relation (37) one can integrate the stochastic equation (24) for the bond price process to obtain

$$P_{ab} = P_{0b} P_a \exp\left(\int_{s=0}^{a} V_{sb}\, dW_s - \tfrac{1}{2}\int_{s=0}^{a} V_{sb}^2\, ds\right) \tag{40}$$

with V_{sb} as in (22). In this representation the bond price process is expressed as a product of its initial value P_{0b}, times the absolute numeraire, times an exponential martingale. Analogous expressions for foreign discount bonds are given in the final section.

Note that since V_{sb} goes to zero as b goes to infinity, we are able to recover formula (11) swiftly from (40) by inspection. On the other hand, if we set b equal to a in (40), we obtain the following alternative representation for the terminal numeraire process:

$$P_a = (P_{0a})^{-1} \exp\left(-\int_{s=0}^{a} V_{sa}\, dW_s + \tfrac{1}{2}\int_{s=0}^{a} V_{sa}^2\, ds\right) \tag{41}$$

Equations (40) and (41) can be compared with the corresponding expressions for the bond price process and the money market account process in the risk-neutral measure (cf. Flesaker and Hughston, 1997*a*, *b*). In that case we have

$$P_{ab} = P_{0b} B_a \exp\left(\int_{s=0}^{a} \Omega_{sb}\, dW_s^0 - \tfrac{1}{2}\int_{s=0}^{a} \Omega_{sb}^2\, ds\right) \tag{42}$$

and

$$B_a = (P_{0a})^{-1} \exp\left(-\int_{s=0}^{a} \Omega_{sa}\, dW_s^0 + \tfrac{1}{2}\int_{s=0}^{a} \Omega_{sa}^2\, ds\right) \tag{43}$$

Equations (42) and (43) follow directly from (40) and (41) by use of (25), (33) and (37).

Foreign interest rates

All considerations here so far have been confined to the case of a single currency. The corresponding analysis in the multi-currency situation is necessarily rather more intricate but, nevertheless, is straightforward enough, and this will now be described. We shall demonstrate how the terminal measure, initially constructed with respect to a given "domestic" currency, can be extended to an international context. The resulting "international" measure, while still linked in a natural way with the given base currency, has the remarkable property that it allows for the identification of a natural one-parameter family of positive martingales for each currency that defines the term structure of interest rates for that currency and ensures the positivity of these rates. The resulting system of martingale families is sufficiently rich to embody both exchange rate risk and interest rate risk.

In practical terms this means that we have the scope for designing a realistic "universal" derivatives pricing methodology that treats currencies on a broadly equal footing, making use of the inherent symmetries in the foreign exchange markets. In that respect our approach may have advantages over other recent attempts at developing workable interest rate and foreign exchange models, such as in Amin and Jarrow (1991, 1992), Babbs (1993), Flesaker and Hughston (1997*a*), Jamshidian (1993) and Turnbull (1994).

Before treating foreign interest rates and foreign exchange in the positive interest rate model, we shall say a few words about the extension of the HJM framework in general to the international setting (Amin and Jarrow, 1991, 1992). This is a very beautiful and natural theory in its own right, and is not perhaps as well known as it ought to be. First we touch on a few points of terminology. We shall work in an international setting now, with a domestic currency and N foreign currencies, which will be labelled by the index $i = 1, \ldots, N$. When convenient we shall label the domestic currency by $i = 0$. The entire international economy is driven by an underlying multiple Brownian motion of dimension n, and generally speaking we shall require $n \geq 2N + 1$ to allow at least one independent degree of freedom for each interest rate system and each exchange rate.

Rather than developing the theory in "HJM form" - as do Amin and Jarrow (1991, 1992), emphasising the role of the instantaneous forward rates - we shall take advantage of hindsight and express the theory directly in terms of exchange rates and discount bonds (the treatment here follows very closely that given in Flesaker and Hughston, 1997*b*). This will then serve to build up the relevant notation and generally set the scene for an appropriate terminal measure representation for these processes.

For convenience we shall carry over the notation already developed for the domestic economy. Thus, P_{ab} stands for the random value at time a of a b-maturity domestic zero coupon bond and B_a denotes the random value of the unit-initialised domestic money market account at time a. Alternatively, we can view P_{ab} as representing the price at time a for the "advance purchase" of one unit of domestic currency, to be delivered at time b. This is simply another way of stating what is meant by a discount bond, but phrased in this way the concept naturally generalises to other categories of assets, including foreign currencies, shares, commodities, etc.

We shall denote the price process for foreign currency i, as valued in the domestic currency, by $S_t^i (i = 1, \ldots, N)$. By P_{ab}^i we signify the foreign zero coupon bond price as valued in foreign currency i. For our purposes, however, we also need the value of the foreign zero coupon bond in units of the domestic currency. Thus we write

$$S_{ab}^i = S_a^i P_{ab}^i \tag{44}$$

for the domestic value of a b-maturity foreign zero coupon bond. This is, of course, simply the product of the value of the foreign zero coupon bond in the foreign currency times the prevailing exchange rate.

If we take the advance purchase price S_{ab}^i as the more basic process, then we can define the exchange rate process S_a^i by the "at-maturity" relation

$$S_a^i = S_{aa}^i \tag{45}$$

Thus we can refer to $S_a^i = S_{aa}^i$ as the "at-maturity process" associated with S_{ab}^i. Then the foreign-priced foreign discount bond P_{ab}^i is given by the ratio

$$P_{ab}^i = \frac{S_{ab}^i}{S_{aa}^i} \tag{46}$$

It should be apparent that S^i_a and P^i_{ab} can be regarded as subsidiary processes, and we can, if it is desired, concentrate on an appropriate characterisation of the advance purchase currency process S^i_{ab}.

In particular, setting $a = 0$ we see that S^i_{0b} is the advance purchase price today (in domestic units) for delivery of one foreign unit at time b. We can think of the curve S^i_{0b} as representing "initial data" for the process S^i_{ab}. To get the forward price of the foreign currency we divide S^i_{0b} by the domestic discount function P_{0b}. The forward price is, as usual, by definition, the price contracted today to be paid at time b for delivery of one unit of foreign currency at time b. One of the advantages of working with the process S^i_{ab} is that it represents the (domestic) value of a non-dividend, non-interest paying asset. The asset in question is simply a note that promises to pay one unit of foreign currency at the specified future date b.

Now suppose we work in the risk-neutral measure, for which the domestic money market account is the numeraire. Since S^i_{ab} is the price of a non-dividend paying asset, it follows by general principles of no-arbitrage pricing that the value of its ratio to the domestic money market process B_a has to be a martingale, which we can take to be an exponential martingale since S^i_{ab} is always positive. The advance purchase currency process S^i_{ab} is thus necessarily of the general form

$$S^i_{ab} = S^i_{0b} B_a \exp\left(m^i_{ab} - \tfrac{1}{2} Q^i_{ab}\right) \tag{47}$$

where for each foreign currency m^i_{ab} represents a one-parameter family of square-integrable continuous martingales, null at time 0, and Q^i_{ab} is the associated one-parameter family of quadratic variation processes.

A very interesting insight is gained if we write out m^i_{ab} in the form of a one-parameter family of stochastic integrals as follows:

$$m^i_{ab} = \int_0^a \Psi^i_{sb}\, dW_s \tag{48}$$

Then we can split the integrand process Ψ^i_{sb} into an "at-maturity" part and an "off-maturity" part with respect to its index pair by writing

$$\Psi^i_{sb} = \Psi^i_s + \Omega^i_{sb} \tag{49}$$

where

$$\Psi^i_s \triangleq \Psi^i_{ss} \tag{50}$$

and

$$\Omega^i_{sb} \triangleq \Psi^i_{sb} - \Psi^i_s \tag{51}$$

Accordingly, for the basic martingales m^i_{ab} we have:

$$m^i_{ab} = \int_0^a (\Psi^i_s + \Omega^i_{sb})\, dW_s \tag{52}$$

by insertion of (49) into (48). Note that Ω^i_{sb} is defined in such a way that $\Omega^i_{ss} = 0$ automatically. The off-maturity process Ω^i_{sb} is, as the notation suggests, the vector volatility of the foreign term structure of interest rates, and the at-maturity process Ψ^i_s is the local vector volatility of the foreign exchange rate process.

It follows from the foregoing discussion that the domestic value of the advance purchase foreign currency process can be represented in the form

$$S^i_{ab} = S^i_{0b} B_a \exp\left(\int_0^a (\Psi^i_s + \Omega^i_{sb})\, dW_s - \tfrac{1}{2}\int_0^a (\Psi^i_s + \Omega^i_{sb})^2\, ds\right) \tag{53}$$

From this we deduce directly (*a*) that the exchange rate process $S^i_a = S^i_{aa}$ is given by

$$S^i_a = S^i_{0a} B_a \exp\left(\int_0^a (\Psi^i_s + \Omega^i_{sa}) dW_s - \frac{1}{2} \int_0^a (\Psi^i_s + \Omega^i_{sa})^2 \, ds \right) \tag{54}$$

and (*b*) that the foreign currency-denominated foreign zero coupon bond processes, defined by (46), are given by

$$P^i_{ab} = \tilde{P}^i_{ab} \exp\left[\int_{s=0}^a (\Omega^i_{sb} - \Omega^i_{sa})(dW_s - \Psi^i_s \, ds) - \frac{1}{2} \int_{s=0}^a \left({\Omega^i_{sb}}^2 - {\Omega^i_{sa}}^2 \right) ds \right] \tag{55}$$

Equations (54) and (55) constitute the basis of the Amin–Jarrow theory in our formulation. These processes represent the general system of interest rates and foreign exchange rates, subject to the principles of no arbitrage and market completeness, and by virtue of the various cross terms appearing in these expressions one can appreciate in a very general manner the origin of so-called "quanto" effects. We have taken the trouble to illustrate these formulae in fairly explicit terms since they represent the status quo as regards general interest rate and foreign exchange derivatives modelling.

Global models for interest rate and foreign exchange

Now we are in a position to put forward our general theory of interest rates and foreign exchange in an international setting. The resulting model can be viewed as essentially the subclass of Amin–Jarrow economies for which all interest rates, both domestic and foreign, are positive.

However, like the relationship of the basic single-currency positive interest rate model to the original HJM theory, the resulting framework has such a different character from the Amin–Jarrow theory that for practical purposes it is perhaps better to think of it as representing an altogether new approach.

The new framework can be summarised as follows. We have a domestic currency and N foreign currencies. There is a pricing measure $\mathbf{E}[-]$, which is the international extension of the terminal measure associated with the domestic currency. With respect to this measure we define a set of $N + 1$ martingale families, given by a family of "domestic" martingales denoted M_{as}, and a set of N families of "foreign" martingales denoted M^i_{as}.

The domestic martingales are required to satisfy conditions (2), (3), (4) and (5), and the foreign martingales are required to satisfy

$$M^i_{0s} = 1 \quad \text{for } s \geq 0 \tag{56}$$

$$M^i_{as} > 0 \quad \text{for } 0 \leq a \leq s \tag{57}$$

$$M^i_{as} = \mathbf{E}_a[M^i_{bs}] \quad \text{for } 0 \leq a \leq b \leq s \tag{58}$$

The key point here is that all the martingales are defined with respect to the same "universal" measure $\mathbf{E}[-]$, which then introduces a strong element of symmetry in the description of the international economy. The domestic currency remains distinguished by the fact that its martingale family satisfies the limiting normalisation condition (3).

Now we proceed to characterise the various key price processes for the international economy under consideration. Our approach will be first to write down the relevant formulae, and to make various observations about these processes, and then to indicate the derivation that leads to the formulae in the first place.

We recall from the previous section the definition of the price process S^i_{ab}, which is the (advance purchase) price at time a, in units of the domestic currency, for the delivery at time b of one unit of foreign currency i.

As data at time zero we take $P^i_{0s} (i = 0, 1, \ldots, N)$ for the initial discount function for currency i and $\partial_s P^i_{0s}$ for its derivative. For the initial exchange rate (price of foreign currency i in units of the domestic currency) we have S^i_0. Then for the advance purchase price process we have:

$$S^i_{ab} = S^i_0 \frac{\int_b^\infty \partial_s P^i_{0s} M^i_{as}\, ds}{\int_a^\infty \partial_s P_{0s} M_{as}\, ds} \tag{59}$$

Note that (59) is very similar to (1), the only difference being that in the numerator we use the foreign martingale family M^i_{as} and the foreign initial discount function P^i_{0s}. The foreign exchange rate S^i_a for currency i is given by the "at-maturity" value $S^i_a = S^i_{aa}$. Thus we have

$$S^i_a = S^i_0 \frac{\int_a^\infty \partial_s P^i_{0s} M^i_{as}\, ds}{\int_a^\infty \partial_s P_{0s} M_{as}\, ds} \tag{60}$$

For the foreign discount bonds, as valued in the respective foreign currency, we have $P^i_{ab} = S^i_{ab}/S^i_{aa}$, which, by use of (59) and (60), is easily seen to be

$$P^i_{ab} = \frac{\int_b^\infty \partial_s P^i_{0s} M^i_{as}\, ds}{\int_a^\infty \partial_s P^i_{0s} M^i_{as}\, ds} \tag{61}$$

In fact, this expression takes essentially the same overall form as the domestic discount bond process, which illustrates the principle that all currencies are treated here with a high degree of symmetry and that for practical purposes the representation of foreign discount bonds is not very different at all from that of domestic discount bonds. This point is further emphasised if we note the expression for the foreign exchange cross-rate process $S^{ij}_a = S^i_a/S^j_a$ (price of currency i in units of currency j for $i, j = 0, 1, \ldots, N$) which is given by

$$S^{ij}_a = S^{ij}_0 \frac{\int_a^\infty \partial_s P^i_{0s} M^i_{as}\, ds}{\int_a^\infty \partial_s P^j_{0s} M^j_{as}\, ds} \tag{62}$$

where S^{ij}_0 is the initial cross rate.

It is worth pointing out that all the various processes considered above can be subsumed conveniently in the specification of the advance purchase foreign exchange cross-rate process S^{ij}_{ab}. This is the price at time a, in units of currency j, for delivery of one unit of currency i at time b. The relevant expression is

$$S^{ij}_{ab} = S^{ij}_0 \frac{\int_b^\infty \partial_s P^i_{0s} M^i_{as}\, ds}{\int_a^\infty \partial_s P^j_{0s} M^j_{as}\, ds} \tag{63}$$

With these formulae at our disposal, let us turn to consider contingent claims valuation in the international context. We observe that if H_a is a random adapted flow of domestic cash at time a corresponding to the value of a contingent claim at that time, then its present value, in units of the domestic currency, is given by

$$H_0 = \mathbf{E}\left[\left(-\int_a^\infty \partial_s P_{0s} M_{as}\, ds\right) H_a\right] \tag{64}$$

which is superficially identical to (6). However, here the random cashflow H_a can depend on foreign interest rates and exchange rates as well, eg, as in the case of an exotic derivative in which the payment is "quantoed" back into the domestic currency. We remark, more generally, that if H^i_a denotes a random payment in currency i at time a, then its present value, in units of currency i, is given by

$$H_0^i = \mathbf{E}\left[\left(-\int_a^\infty \partial_s P_{0s}^i M_{as}^i \, ds\right) H_a^i\right] \qquad (65)$$

which is, mutatis mutandis, identical in structure to (64).

International volatility structures

Now let us see in more detail how we arrive at the basic formulae above. First we consider the advance purchase process S^i_{ab}. This is the price process for a "pure" asset, and therefore has the property that its ratio to the numeraire process has to be a positive martingale with respect to the equivalent martingale measure associated with the given choice of numeraire.

Suppose we have a complete and arbitrage-free international economy of interest rates and foreign exchange and, as numeraire, we choose the terminal numeraire process associated with the domestic discount bonds. As in the purely domestic situation, this process is defined by forming the ratio of a discount bond price to its initial value and taking the limit as the maturity date goes to infinity, as in (11).

Since the markets are complete and arbitrage-free, there exists a unique equivalent martingale measure such that the ratio of any other asset price to the given absolute numeraire is a martingale. The measure thereby defined is the unique "international" extension of the domestic terminal measure to the entire economy.

With respect to this choice of measure the advance purchase process S^i_{ab} has to be of the form $S^i_{ab} = S^i_0 P_a N^i_{ab}$, where S^i_0 is the initial exchange rate, P_a is the terminal numeraire process associated with the domestic currency, and N^i_{ab} is a family of positive martingales. If we then form the foreign discount bond processes P^i_{ab} by taking the ratio $P^i_{ab} = S^i_{ab}/S^i_{aa}$, it follows that $P^i_{ab} = N^i_{ab}/N^i_{aa}$. Interest rate positivity for each of the foreign sectors then implies that the derivative $\partial_b N^i_{ab}$ is negative and, therefore, the existence of a set of positive martingale families M^i_{ab} subject to the conditions (56) to (58) such that the foreign discount bonds are as given by formula (61), where N^i_{ab} is equal to minus the numerator of this expression.

Substituting this result back into the formula $P^i_{ab} = S^i_{ab}/S^i_{aa}$, we immediately deduce that the exchange rate process $S^i_a = S^i_{aa}$ is of the desired form (60) and that the cross rates are of the form (62). The advance purchase cross-rate process (63) is obtained by formation of the quotient $S^{ij}_{ab} = S^i_{ab}/S^j_a$. The contingent claims valuation formula (64) follows at once by virtue of our original choice of the domestic numeraire process, but if the cashflow of the derivative is in another currency, then we can convert it instantaneously at the spot rate by use of (60) to get an equivalent domestic cashflow, and that leads at once to the general multi-currency valuation formula (65). That establishes the main structural equations of the international framework outlined in the previous section.

It can be illuminating to study the stochastic equations associated with the various basic price processes. Suppose by analogy with equation (22) we define the vector process V^i_{ab} by the ratio

$$V^i_{ab} = \frac{\int_b^\infty \partial_s P_{0s} M^i_{as} \sigma^i_{as} \, ds}{\int_b^\infty \partial_s P_{0s} M^i_{as} \, ds} \qquad (66)$$

and set $V^i_a \triangleq V^i_{aa}$. Here σ^i_{as} is defined by $dM^i_{as} = M^i_{as}\sigma^i_{as} dW_a$. Then it is a straightforward exercise to check that for the advance purchase process S^i_{ab} we have the following dynamics:

$$\frac{dS^i_{ab}}{S^i_{ab}} = r_a da + (V^i_{ab} - V_a)(dW_a - V_a da) \qquad (67)$$

where $V_a \triangleq V_{aa}$. This can be deduced by application of the Itô quotient identity (23).

Note that (as in the purely domestic case) the instantaneous expected rate of return on any "pure" asset price process in the terminal measure associated with the domestic currency is $\mu_a = r_a + V_a^2$. For the exchange rate process a calculation shows that

$$\frac{dS_a^i}{S_a^i} = (r_a - r_a^i)\,da + (V_a^i - V_a)(dW_a - V_a\,da) \tag{68}$$

We are therefore able in the present framework to identify the local vector volatility of the foreign exchange rate process Ψ_s^i, introduced in the last section but one, as being given by

$$\Psi_s^i = V_a^i - V_a \tag{69}$$

It should be observed that if we transform to the risk-neutral measure associated with the use of the domestic money market account process as numeraire, via equation (27), then the instantaneous drift of the exchange rate process is given, as one would expect, by $r_a - r_a^i$, the difference between the domestic and foreign short rates. More generally, for the cross rates (price of currency i in units of currency j) we obtain

$$\frac{dS_a^{ij}}{S_a^{ij}} = (r_a^j - r_a^i)\,da + (V_a^i - V_a^j)(dW_a - V_a^j\,da) \tag{70}$$

and for Ψ_s^{ij}, the local vector volatilities of these cross rates, we can write

$$\Psi_s^{ij} = V_a^i - V_a^j \tag{71}$$

For the foreign discount bond price processes we find

$$\frac{dP_{ab}^i}{P_{ab}^i} = r_a^i\,da + \Omega_{ab}^i(dW_a - V_a^i\,da) \tag{72}$$

where the foreign vector volatility structure Ω_{ab}^i is defined by

$$\Omega_{ab}^i = V_{ab}^i - V_a^i \tag{73}$$

Finally, in the case of the advance purchase cross rates we have

$$\frac{dS_{ab}^{ij}}{S_{ab}^{ij}} = r_a^j\,da + (V_{ab}^i - V_a^j)(dW_a - V_a^j\,da) \tag{74}$$

By use of (69), (71) and (73), appropriate vector inner-product expressions can be formed in our framework for all the various foreign exchange and interest rate volatilities and cross correlations.

Representations in terms of exponential martingales

It is not difficult to appreciate the highly symmetrical relation of the various processes described above to one another, and it is gratifying that the resulting formulae are memorable. In particular we note that the foreign discount bond price process (72) is formally identical in structure to that of its domestic counterpart, equation (24).

Some further insight into the structure of the system under consideration can be gained if we construct the general analogue of the exponential martingale representation (40).

First we consider the advance purchase process S_{ab}^i, the advance purchase price at time a, in domestic currency, for delivery of one unit of currency i at time b. This is given by

$$S_{ab}^i = \frac{S_0^i P_{0b}^i}{P_{0a}} \frac{\exp\left(\int_{s=0}^{a} V_{sb}^i\,dW_s - \frac{1}{2}\int_{s=0}^{a} {V_{sb}^i}^2\,ds\right)}{\exp\left(\int_{s=0}^{a} V_{sa}\,dW_s - \frac{1}{2}\int_{s=0}^{a} V_{sa}^2\,ds\right)} \tag{75}$$

which can easily be seen to reduce to (40) in a purely domestic situation. Instead of (75), we can equivalently write

$$S^i_{ab} = S^i_0 P^i_{0b} \exp\left(\int_{s=0}^{a} V^i_{sb}\, dW_s - \tfrac{1}{2}\int_{s=0}^{a} {V^i_{sb}}^2\, ds \right) P_a \tag{76}$$

which shows S^i_{ab} as the product of its initial value, a unit-initialised exponential martingale, and the terminal numeraire process (41) associated with the domestic currency. It follows that the exchange rate process can be written as a quotient, in the form

$$S^i_a = S^i_0 \frac{P_a}{P^i_a} \tag{77}$$

where

$$P^i_a = (P^i_{0a})^{-1} \exp\left(-\int_{s=0}^{a} V^i_{sa}\, dW_s + \tfrac{1}{2}\int_{s=0}^{a} {V^i_{sa}}^2\, ds \right) \tag{78}$$

For the discount bond price process $P^i_{ab} = S^i_{ab}/S^i_a$ in currency i we then obtain the following formula:

$$P^i_{ab} = \frac{P^i_{0b}}{P^i_{0a}} \frac{\exp\left(\int_{s=0}^{a} V^i_{sb}\, dW_s - \tfrac{1}{2}\int_{s=0}^{a} {V^i_{sb}}^2\, ds \right)}{\exp\left(\int_{s=0}^{a} V^i_{sa}\, dW_s - \tfrac{1}{2}\int_{s=0}^{a} {V^i_{sa}}^2\, ds \right)} \tag{79}$$

or equivalently,

$$P^i_{ab} = P^i_{0b} \exp\left(\int_{s=0}^{a} V^i_{sb}\, dW_s - \tfrac{1}{2}\int_{s=0}^{a} {V^i_{sb}}^2\, ds \right) P^i_a \tag{80}$$

A similar expression can be found for the value in currency i of a unit-initialised money market account in that currency. This is given by

$$B^i_a = \exp\left(\int_{s=0}^{a} V^i_s\, dW_s - \tfrac{1}{2}\int_{s=0}^{a} {V^i_s}^2\, ds \right) P^i_a \tag{81}$$

With these expressions at hand, we can now address the interesting question of the appropriate change of measure if we want to move from the terminal measure associated with the domestic currency to the analogous measure associated with some other currency, say currency i.

We shall demonstrate that the relevant density martingale is in fact given by the exponential martingale constructed from the *asymptotic maturity component* of the vector process V^i_{sb}. This can be seen as follows. We know that, unlike the corresponding "domestic" martingales, the "foreign" martingales M^i_{as} do not generally satisfy an asymptotic condition of the form (3). As a consequence the vector process V^i_{sb} does not necessarily tend to zero as b goes to infinity. Therefore, suppose we define

$$\zeta^i_s \triangleq \lim_{b\to\infty} V^i_{sb} \tag{82}$$

and set

$$\hat{V}^i_{sb} \triangleq \hat{V}^i_{sb} - \zeta^i_s \tag{83}$$

Then clearly

$$\lim_{b\to\infty} \hat{V}^i_{sb} = 0 \tag{84}$$

and a short calculation shows that the foreign discount bond price process can be expressed in terms of the "new" vector process $\hat{V}^i_{sb}$ according to the scheme:

$$P^i_{ab} = \frac{P^i_{0b}}{P^i_{0a}} \frac{\exp\left(\int_{s=0}^{a} \hat{V}^i_{sb}\,(dW_s - \zeta^i_s ds) - \frac{1}{2}\int_{s=0}^{a} \hat{V}^{i\,2}_{sb} ds\right)}{\exp\left(\int_{s=0}^{a} \hat{V}^i_{sa}\,(dW_s - \zeta^i_s ds) - \frac{1}{2}\int_{s=0}^{a} \hat{V}^{i\,2}_{sa} ds\right)} \tag{85}$$

Formula (85) is obtained by substituting (83) into (79) and cancelling certain terms that appear in both the numerator and denominator. It follows by use of arguments indicated in the section on the domestic money market account that a change of measure $\mathbf{E} \to \mathbf{E}^i$ defined by $\mathbf{E}^i[X] = \mathbf{E}[\xi^i_t X]$ with density martingale

$$\xi^i_t = \exp\left(\int_{s=0}^{t} \zeta^i_{ss} dW_s - \frac{1}{2}\int_{s=0}^{t} \zeta^{i\,2}_s ds\right) \tag{86}$$

gives us the terminal measure $\mathbf{E}^i$ associated with currency i. In this representation the discount bond price process for currency i assumes the form

$$P^i_{ab} = \frac{P^i_{0b}}{P^i_{0a}} \frac{\exp\left(\int_{s=0}^{a} \hat{V}^i_{sb} d\hat{W}_s - \frac{1}{2}\int_{s=0}^{a} \hat{V}^{i\,2}_{sb} ds\right)}{\exp\left(\int_{s=0}^{a} \hat{V}^i_{sa} d\hat{W}_s - \frac{1}{2}\int_{s=0}^{a} \hat{V}^{i\,2}_{sa} ds\right)} \tag{87}$$

analogous to (40), where $\hat{V}^i_{sb}$ satisfies (84) and where $\hat{W}_s$ is a Brownian motion with respect to the new measure $\mathbf{E}^i$. We note, incidentally, that the foreign discount bond volatility structure $\Omega^i_{ab} = V^i_{ab} - V^i_a$ is invariant under the transformation $V^i_{ab} \to \hat{V}^i_{sb}$.

Transformation to the natural measure

An interesting conclusion that we can draw from this is that after a further change of measure one can revert to the "natural" economic measure, ie, the measure with respect to which risk premiums are fully expressed, and one can represent the various key price processes in terms of martingale families defined with respect to that measure.

In other words, with respect to the natural measure we can find a set of martingale families Θ^i_{as}, where $i = 0, 1, \ldots, N$, labelling both the domestic and foreign currencies, such that for the bond price processes we have

$$P^i_{ab} = \frac{\int_b^\infty \partial_s P^i_{0s}\, \Theta^i_{as}\, ds}{\int_a^\infty \partial_s P^i_{0s}\, \Theta^i_{as}\, ds} \tag{88}$$

and for the foreign exchange cross rates we have

$$S^{ij}_a = S^{ij}_0 \frac{\int_a^\infty \partial_s P^i_{0s}\, \Theta^i_{as}\, ds}{\int_a^\infty \partial_s P^j_{0s}\, \Theta^j_{as}\, ds} \tag{89}$$

In this way we are able in effect to introduce a nice probabilistic representation of an important economic concept, viz., the market risk premium, by embedding it in the structure of a fundamental class of martingales. This means that our framework may even have some application beyond mere derivatives pricing, in circumstances where market premiums are of more direct concern, eg, simulation and risk management.

Indeed, having established the basic positive interest framework in a multi-currency setting, it is possible to pursue a variety of further extensions. Of immediate practical interest is the specification of testable and implementable models suitable for pricing and hedging derivatives. A particularly appealing subclass, on the grounds of tractability, is one where the fundamental martingales M^i_{ab} are specified as lognormal processes evolving in a-time, scaled by functions of b-time. The empirical implications of such a formulation are under investigation.

Furthermore, there is also scope for generalising the framework to incorporate other asset classes, such as equities and commodities, as well as bonds subject to default risk or linked to the rate of inflation. Such extensions, as well as the consideration of currency and fixed income markets subject to significant "event risk", will naturally lead to questions of how best to incorporate jump processes into this framework. Interesting mathematical and empirical challenges are likely to be discovered down this road.

Acknowledgements

The authors express their gratitude to R. Brenner, A. Hüffmann, S. Gregornik, R. Jarrow, O. Jonsson, D. Madan, N. Rabeau, L. Sankarasubramanian and J. Tigg for stimulating discussions.

Bibliography

Amin, K. I., and J. N. Bodurtha Jr., 1995, "Discrete-Time Valuation of American Options with Stochastic Interest Rates", *Review of Financial Studies* 8, pp. 193-234.

Amin, K. I., and R. Jarrow, 1991, "Pricing Foreign Currency Options under Stochastic Interest Rates", *Journal of International Money and Finance* 10, pp. 310-329; reprinted as Chapter 15 of the present volume.

Amin, K. I., and R. Jarrow, 1992, "Pricing Options on Risky Assets in a Stochastic Interest Rate Economy", *Mathematical Finance* 2, pp. 217-237.

Babbs, S., 1993, "The Valuation of Cross-Currency Interest-Sensitive Claims, with Applications to Diff-Swaps", working paper, First Bank of Chicago, London.

Carverhill, A., 1995, "A Simplified Exposition of the Heath, Jarrow, and Morton Model", *Stochastics and Stochastics Reports* 53, pp. 227-240.

Flesaker, B., and L. P. Hughston, 1996, "Positive Interest", *RISK Magazine* Vol. 9, No. 1, pp. 46-49, January 1996; reprinted as Chapter 21 of the present volume.

Flesaker, B., and L. P. Hughston, 1997*a*, "Dynamic Models of Yield Curve Evolution"; in *Mathematics of Derivative Securities*, M. Dempster and S. Pliska, eds., Cambridge University Press.

Flesaker, B., and L. P. Hughston, 1997*b*, "Exotic interest rate options"; in *Exotic Options: The State of the Art*, L. Clewlow and C. Strickland, eds., Chapman and Hall.

Harrison, J. M., and S. R. Pliska, 1981, "Martingales and Stochastic Integrals in the Theory of Continuous Trading", *Stochastic Processes and their Applications* 11, pp 215-260.

Heath, D., R. Jarrow and A. Morton, 1992, "Bond Pricing and the Term Structure of Interest Rates: A New Methodology for Contingent Claims Valuation", *Econometrica* 60, pp 77-105; reprinted as Chapter 14 of the present volume.

Hughston, L. P., 1994, "Financial Observables", *International Derivative Review, SunGard Capital Markets* December 1994, pp 11-14.

Jamshidian, F., 1993, "Price Differentials", *RISK Magazine* Vol. 6, No. 7, pp. 48-51.

Norris, J. R., 1992, "A Complete Differential Formalism for Stochastic Calculus on Manifolds", Séminaire de Probabilités XXVI, LNM 1526. Springer.

Turnbull, S. M., 1994, "Pricing and Hedging Diff-Swaps", *Journal of Financial Engineering* 2, pp. 297-333.

INDEX